3 copies for library
30/9/93

S.C.Ward
May93   19.95

D1647405

PROJECT MANAGEMENT

Wiley Series in Production/Operations Management

Jack R. Meredith, Advisory Editor

Project Management: A Managerial Approach, 2nd edition

Jack R. Meredith/Samuel J. Mantel, Jr.

The Management of Operations, 3rd edition

Jack R. Meredith

Decision Systems For Inventory Management and Production Planning, 2nd edition

Edward A. Silver

Modern Production and Operations Management, 8th edition

Elwood S. Buffa/Rakesh Sarin

Production Systems: Planning, Analysis, and Control, 4th edition

James L. Riggs

PROJECT MANAGEMENT

A Managerial Approach
Second Edition

Jack R. Meredith
Samuel J. Mantel, Jr.
University of Cincinnati

John Wiley & Sons

New York   Chichester   Brisbane   Toronto   Singapore

To Brandon
J.R.M.

To my three brothers: Tom, Dick, and Jerry
S.J.M.,Jr.

Copyright © 1985, 1989, by John Wiley & Sons, Inc.

All rights reserved. Published simultaneously in Canada.

Reproduction or translation of any part of
this work beyond that permitted by Sections
107 and 108 of the 1976 United States Copyright
Act without the permission of the copyright
owner is unlawful. Requests for permission
or further information should be addressed to
the Permissions Department, John Wiley & Sons.

ISBN 0-471-50534-X   WIE

Printed in Singapore

10 9 8 7 6 5

Preface

The use of projects and project management continues to grow in our society and its organizations. We are able to achieve goals through project organization that could be achieved only with the greatest of difficulty if organized in traditional ways. Though project management has been with us since before the days of the great pyramids, it has enjoyed a surge of popularity beginning in the 1960s. Project Head Start made a major contribution to education. The Polaris project contributed to our national security. A project put Neil Armstrong on the moon. A series of projects build our interstate highway system. A project developed the Cabbage Patch® doll. The use of project management to accomplish the many and diverse aims of our society's varied organizations continues to grow.

Project management is regularly used in business to accomplish unique outcomes with limited resources under critical time constraints. In the service sector of the economy, the use of project management to achieve an organization's goals is even more common. Advertising campaigns, voter registration drives, Girl Scout cookie sales, political campaigns, a family's annual summer vacation, and even seminars on the subject of project management are organized as projects.

Yet, there have been relatively few books devoted to this new way of managing, and there have been even fewer textbooks for teaching project management. Of the books that are available, most fall into two categories. In the first category are engineering-oriented works that describe in detail how to respond to a government Request for Proposal, how to set up the project office, what paper forms should be used for what purposes, and where they should be filed. These are "cookbooks," and we would not denigrate their value. They are of great importance to a new project manager who is working in an organization that has never operated projects before. The project manager and firm are both starting from scratch. But this is not a common condition, and it is becoming less common daily. Most firms have operated projects, have already developed report forms, and the new project manager will almost certainly be trained by an old project manager. In any case, we have not found this set of books particularly helpful in teaching *managers* about the science, and art, of project management. These books seem to identify the details of *how*, but do not address the larger questions of *why*. They tend to ignore the organizational and behavioral aspects of project management, which are both the strength and the weakness of the project management concept.

In the second category are the math/network books. These books describe PERT, CPM, and allied network techniques, extremely useful tools for project scheduling. These books, however, deal with project management as if good management depended primarily on scheduling. We believe that this is misleading because scheduling is only one of several serious problems that the project manager must solve.

What we believe is needed in the field is a book that addresses project management from a *management* perspective rather than an engineering or mathematical perspective. Such a book should address the basic nature of managing projects, and the advantages and disadvantages of this unique way of getting things done. It should deal with the problems of selecting projects, initiating them, and operating and controlling them. It should discuss the demands made on the project manager and the nature of the manager's interaction with the rest of the parent organization. The book should even cover the issues associated with terminating a project.

This managerial perspective is the view we have taken here. Chapter 1 discusses the role and importance of projects in our society. Following this introduction, *Part I: Project Initiation* describes how projects are selected for implementation. It also covers the role of the project manager and the various ways that projects can be organized. This is followed by a description of the project planning process and some tools used in project planning. *Part I* concludes with a topic of major importance to the project manager: negotiation. Project budgeting, scheduling, monitoring/information systems, and controlling are then discussed in *Part II: Project Implementation*. Finally, *Part III: Project Termination* concludes the discussion with a description of final project evaluation and termination, and the future for project management. We do not ignore Requests for Proposal (RFPs), engineering aspects, and network techniques, but they are not the primary focus of the book. Management is our focus.

We have adopted the life cycle approach in this book because we find it a comfortable framework for the reader. We have made one exception to this approach—from the almost unanimous suggestion of some remarkably thoughtful reviewers: We have relegated discussions of idea generation and creativity to Appendix A, and a review of technological forecasting to Appendix B. Our reviewers argued, quite correctly, that few project managers engage in either of these tasks, being appointed to project managership after these activities have taken place. We believe, strongly, that a knowledge of these subjects will make the project manager more effective. Thus we have included them. The reader or instructor may ignore these subjects or include either or both at any point that seems sensible.

This book is primarily intended to be a college textbook for teaching project management at the advanced undergraduate or master's level. We have included numerous pedagogical aids to foster this purpose, such as chapter summaries, review questions, problems, chapter glossaries, incidents for discussion, readings, cases, and bibliographies. Conceptual discussion questions are also included to broaden the students' perspectives and to force them to think beyond the chapter material to its implications. We have also prepared an instructor's manual to accompany the book. It addresses this pedagogical material and includes some additonal materials to aid an instructor teaching the project management course.

In this second edition of the book we have updated a number of topics and added some new material. Paticularly important, is the monitoring/information systems chapter, which was updated to reflect the tremendous growth of microcomputer project management software packages. Some guidance in selecting one of these packages is included. To illustrate the possible use of spreadsheets in project management, a few such applications were added in the appropriate chapters. In addition, we have added a chapter (6) to the text that discusses the critical skill of personal negotiation. This new chapter does not cover the "how to" of negotiation, a topic that goes far beyond the scope of this book, but does discuss the roles negotiation plays in managing projects. As an aid to the student, we have also added chapter glossaries, additional problems, additional cases, and project team assignments to the end-of-chapter pedagogical materials. Finally, almost all the readings have been updated with newer, more contemporary selections.

Our book is also intended for current and prospective project managers who wish to share our insights and ideas about the field. We have drawn freely on our personal experiences working with project managers and on the experiences of friends who have spent much of their working lives serving as project managers in what they like to call "the real world." (These professional readers should feel free to skip the pedagogical necessities of questions, incidents, and readings.)

We have made some assumptions about both student and professional readers. We assume that all readers have taken an elementary course in management or have had equivalent experience. Also, the reader with a background in management theory or practice will note that many of the principles of good project management are also principles of good, general administrative management. Project management and administrative management are not entirely distinct. Furthermore, we assume that readers are familiar with some fundmental principles of accounting, finance, and statistics. Familiarity with mathematical techniques such as linear programming is helpful, but not necessary.

Many of the examples and anecdotes we have cited throughout the book are drawn from large or medium-size projects, say, $500,000 and greater. We do not mean to ignore small projects or to imply that they are not important. Large projects simply provide a richer set of problems, most of which also occur on small projects, but some only rarely. Thus, larger projects are often more useful for teaching purposes.

This book has been a long time in the making, and we owe a debt of gratitude to all those who helped form it. We thank first the managers and students who helped us solidify our ideas about proper methods for managing projects and proper ways of teaching the subject. Next, we thank the project teams who have helped us compile parts of the first edition of this book, and particularly the project managers: Rich Beckert, Jose Abirached, Steve Lucas, Julie Reese, Sonia Nankani, S.J. Mantel III, Sue Miller, Anita Zot, Phil Goelz, and Art Plate.

Special thanks are due to Desmond Cook (Ohio State University) Gerhard Rosegger (Case Western Reserve University); Jeffrey Pinto (University of Maine); James Evans, John McKinney, and William Meyers (University of Cincinnati); Robert Riley (private consultant); and the Staff of the Project Management Institute—all of whom have influenced the way we think about many of the subjects we cover or have supplied materials to help us write this book. And we owe a massive debt of gratitude to Nicholas Aquilano (University of Arizona), Edward Davis (University of Virginia), Herbert Spirer (University of Connecticut), Jerome Weist (University of Utah), for reviewing and commenting on the first edition of this book and to Burton Dean (San Jose State University) and Sam Taylor (University of Wyoming) for their thorough and helpful comments on the second edition.

Cincinnati, Ohio   **Jack R. Meredith**
December, 1988   **Samuel J. Mantel, Jr.**

Contents

PART III PROJECT TERMINATION   479

Chapter 12   Project Evaluation and Auditing   481

Chapter 13   Project Termination   521

CHAPTER 1
Projects in Contemporary Organizations

In the past several decades, project management has made a significant contribution to the practice of management. Project management provides an organization with powerful tools that improve the organization's ability to plan, organize, implement, and control its activities and the ways it uses its people and resources. Much of the credit for this development belongs to the military, which faced a series of major tasks that simply were not achievable by traditional organizations operating in traditional ways. The United States Navy's Polaris program, NASA's Apollo space program, and more recently, the space shuttle and the strategic defense initiative ("star wars") programs are instances of the successful application of these specially developed management approaches to extraordinarily complex projects. Following such examples, nonmilitary government sectors, private industry, public service agencies, and volunteer organizations have all used project management to increase their effectiveness.

Project management emerged because a number of forces in our society required new methods of management. Of the many forces involved, two are paramount: (1) the growing demand for complex, sophisticated, customized goods and services, and (2) the exponential expansion of human knowledge.

The potential complexity and customization of a desired product depends on the integration of product design with production/distribution, whereas the expansion of knowledge *allows* an increasing number of academic disciplines to contribute to the development of goods and services. Both call for high levels of coordination and cooperation between groups of people not particularly used to such interaction. Largely geared to the mass production of simpler goods, traditional organizational structures and management systems were simply not adequate to the task.

Another important societal force is the intense competition among institutions, both profit and not-for-profit, fostered by our economic system. This puts extreme pressure on organizations to make their complex, customized outputs available as quickly as possible. Responses must come faster, decisions must be made sooner, and results must occur more quickly. Imagine the communications problems alone. Information and knowledge are growing explosively, but the allowable time to locate and use the appropriate knowledge is decreasing.

In addition, these forces operate in a society that assumes that technology can do anything. The fact is, this assumption is reasonably true, within the bounds of nature's fundamental laws. The problem lies not in this assumption so much as in a concomitant assumption that allows society to ignore both the economic and noneconomic costs associated with technological progress until some dramatic event forces our attention on the costs. At times, our faith in technology is disturbed by difficulties and threats arising from its careless implementation, as in the case of nuclear power generation, but on the whole we seem remarkably tolerant of technological change. For a case in point, consider California farm workers who waited more than twenty years to challenge a University of California research program devoted to the development of labor-saving farm machinery [34]. The acceptance of technological advancement is so strong it took more than two decades to muster the legal attack.

Finally, the projects we undertake are large and getting larger. The modern machine tool company, for example, advances from a numerically controlled milling machine to a *machining center* to a *flexible manufacturing system.* As each new capability extends our grasp, it serves as the base for new demands that force us to extend our reach even farther. Projects increase in size and complexity because the more we can do, the more we try to do. The path from earth orbit to lunar landing to interplanetary flight is clear—indeed, inevitable.

The projects that command the most public attention tend to be large, complex, multidisciplinary endeavors. Often, such endeavors are both similar to and different from previous projects with which we may be more or less familiar. Similarities with the past provide a base from which to start, but the differences imbue every project with considerable risk. The complexities and multidisciplinary aspects of projects require that the many parts be put together so that the prime objectives—performance, time (or schedule), and cost—are met.

There is a tendency to think of a project solely in terms of its outcome—that is, its performance. But the time at which the outcome is available is itself a part of the outcome, as is the cost entailed in achieving the outcome. The completion of a building on time and on budget is quite a different outcome from the completion of the same physical structure a year late or 20 percent over budget, or both.

The prime objectives of project management are shown in Figure 1-1, with the three specified project objectives on each of the axes. This illustration implies that there is some "function" (not shown in the figure) that relates them, one to another. And so there is. Although the functions vary from project to project, and from time to time for a given project, we will be constantly referring to these relationships, or *trade-offs,* throughout the rest of this book. The primary task of the project manager is to manage these trade-offs.

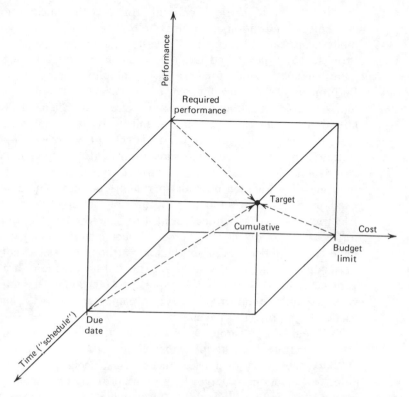

Figure 1-1 Performance, cost, time project targets.

It is in this context that the project manager is expected to integrate all aspects of the project, ensure that the proper knowledge and resources are available when and where needed, and above all, ensure that the expected results are produced in a timely, cost-effective manner. For these reasons, we often refer to the project manager as a *supermanager*.

This book identifies the work facing this supermanager. We investigate the nature of the projects for which the project manager is responsible, the skills that must be used to manage projects, and the means by which the manager can bring the project to a successful conclusion in terms of the three primary criteria: performance, time, and cost. Before delving into the details of this analysis, however, we clarify the nature of *a project* and determine how it differs from the other activities that are conducted in organizations. We also note a few of the major advantages, disadvantages, strengths, and limitations of project management. At the end of the chapter we describe the approach followed in the remainder of this book.

1.1 THE DEFINITION OF A "PROJECT"

There is a rich variety of projects to be found in our society. Although some may argue that the construction of the Tower of Babel or the Egyptian pyramids was the first "project," and it is certainly true that the construction of Boulder Dam and Edison's invention of the light bulb were projects by any sensible definition, modern project management is usually said to have begun with the Manhattan Project, which developed the atomic bomb. In its early days, project management was used mainly for very large, complex research and development (R & D) projects like the development of the ICBM and similar military weapon systems. Massive construction programs were also organized as projects—the construction of dams, ships, refineries, and freeways, among others.

As the techniques of project management were developed, mostly by the military, the use of project organization began to spread. Private construction firms found that project organization was helpful on smaller projects, such as the building of a warehouse or an apartment complex. The automotive companies used project organization to develop new automobile models. Both General Electric and Pratt & Whitney used it to develop new jet aircraft engines for the airlines as well as the Air Force. Project management has even been used to develop new models of shoes and ships (though possibly not sealing wax). Advertising campaigns, mergers, and capital acquisitions are often handled as projects, and the methods have spread to the nonprofit sector. Teas, weddings, Scout-o-ramas, fund drives, election campaigns, parties, and recitals have all made use of project management.

In discussions of project management, it is sometimes useful to make a distinction between such terms as *project, program, task,* and *work packages.* The military, the source of most of these terms, generally uses the term *program* to refer to exceptionally large, long-range projects or a group of similar projects. Projects are further divided into *tasks,* which are, in turn, split into *work packages* that are themselves composed of *work units.* But exceptions to this hierarchical nomenclature abound. The Manhattan Project was a huge "program," but a "task force" was created to investigate the many potential futures of a large steel company.

In the broadest sense, a project is a specific, finite task to be accomplished. Whether large- or small-scale or whether long- or short-run is not particularly relevant. What is relevant is that the project be seen as a unit. There are, however, some attributes that characterize projects.

Purpose

A project is usually a one-time activity with a well-defined set of desired end results. It can be divided into subtasks that must be accomplished in order to achieve the project goals. The project is complex enough that the subtasks require careful coordination and control in terms of timing, precedence, cost, and performance. The project itself must often be coordinated with other projects being carried out by the same parent organization.

Life Cycle

Like organic entities, projects have life cycles. From a slow beginning they progress to a buildup of size, then peak, begin a decline, and finally must be terminated. (Also like other organic entities, they often resist termination.) Some projects end by being phased into the normal, ongoing operations of the parent organization. The life cycle is further discussed in Section 1.3.

Interdependencies

Projects often interact with other projects being carried out simultaneously by their parent organization; but projects *always* interact with the parent's standard, ongoing operations. Although the functional departments of an organization (marketing, finance, manufacturing, and the like) interact with one another in regular, patterned ways, the patterns of interaction between projects and these departments tend to be changing. Marketing may be involved at the beginning and end of a project, but not in the middle. Manufacturing may have major involvement throughout. Finance is often involved at the beginning and accounting (the controller) at the end, as well as at periodic reporting times. The project manager must keep all these interactions clear and maintain the appropriate interrelationships with all external groups.

Uniqueness

Every project has some elements that are unique. No two construction or R & D projects are precisely alike. Though it is clear that construction projects are usually more routine than research and development projects, some degree of customization is a characteristic of projects. In addition to the presence of risk, as noted earlier, this characteristic means that projects, by their nature, cannot be completely reduced to routine. The project manager's importance is emphasized because, as a devotee of *management by exception,* the manager will find there are a great many exceptions to manage by.

Conflict

More than most managers, the project manager lives in a world characterized by conflict. Projects compete with functional departments for resources and personnel. The members of the project team are in almost constant conflict for the project's resources and for leadership roles in solving project problems. The client wants changes, and the parent organization wants profits, which may be reduced if those changes are made. Individuals working on projects are often responsible to two bosses at the same time, bosses with different priorities and objectives. Project management is no place for the timid.

1.2 WHY PROJECT MANAGEMENT?

The basic purpose for initiating a project is to accomplish some goals. The reason for organizing the task as a project is to focus the responsibility and authority for the attainment of the goals on an individual or small group.

In spite of the fact that the project manager often lacks authority at a level consistent with his or her responsibility, the manager is expected to coordinate and integrate all activities needed to reach the project's goals. In particular, the project form of organization allows the manager to be responsive to the client and to the environment, to identify and correct problems at an early date, to make timely decisions about trade-offs between conflicting project goals, and to ensure that managers of the separate tasks that comprise the project do not optimize the performance of their individual tasks at the expense of the total project—that is, that they do not *suboptimize*.

Actual experience [11] with project management indicates that the majority of organizations using it experience better control and better customer relations. A significant proportion of users also report shorter development times, lower costs, higher quality and reliability, and higher profit margins. Other reported advantages include a sharper orientation toward results, better interdepartmental coordination, and higher worker morale.

On the negative side, most organizations report that project management results in greater organizational complexity. Many also report that project organization increases the likelihood that organizational policy will be violated—not a surprising outcome, considering the degree of autonomy required for the project manager. A few firms reported higher costs, more management difficulties, and low personnel utilization.

As we will see in Chapter 4, the disadvantages of project management stem from exactly the same sources as do its advantages. The disadvantages seem to be the price one pays for the advantages. On the whole, the balance weighs in favor of project organization if the work to be done is appropriate for a project.

There are real limitations on project management. For example, the mere creation of a project may be an admission that the parent organization and its managers cannot accomplish the desired outcomes through the functional organization. Further, conflict seems to be a necessary side effect. As we noted, the project manager often lacks authority that is coequal with the assigned level of responsibility. Therefore, the project manager must depend on the goodwill of managers in the parent organization for some of the necessary resources. Of course, if the goodwill is not forthcoming, the project manager may ask senior officials in the parent organization for their assistance, but to use such power often reflects poorly on the skills of the project manager and rarely gets the desired cooperation.

We return to the subject of the advantages, disadvantages, and limitations of the project form of organization later. For the moment, it is sufficient to point out that project management is difficult even when everything goes well. When things go badly, project managers have been known to turn gray and take to hard drink. The trouble is that project organization is the only feasible way to accomplish certain goals. It is literally not possible to design and build a major weapon system, for example, in a *timely and economically acceptable manner,* except by project organization. Tough as it may be, it is all we have—and it works.

1.3 THE PROJECT LIFE CYCLE

Most projects go through similar stages on the path from origin to completion. We define these stages, shown in Figure 1-2, as the project's *life cycle*. The project is born (its start-up phase) and a manager is selected, the project team and initial resources are assembled, and the work program is organized. Then work gets under way and momentum quickly builds. Progress is made. This continues until the end is in sight. But completing the final tasks seems to take an inordinate amount of time, partly because there are often a number of parts that must come together and partly because team members "drag their feet" for various reasons and avoid the final steps.

The pattern of slow–rapid–slow progress toward the project goal is common. Anyone who has watched the construction of a home or building has observed this phenomenon. For the most part, it is a result of the changing levels of resources used during the successive stages of the life cycle. Figure 1-3 shows project effort, usually in terms of person-hours or resources expended per unit of time (or number of people working on the project) plotted against time, where time is broken up into the several phases of project life. Minimal effort is required at the beginning, when the project concept is being developed and is being subjected to project selection processes. (Later, we will argue that increasing effort in the early stages of the life cycle will improve the chance of project success.)

If this hurdle is passed, activity increases as planning is done, and the real

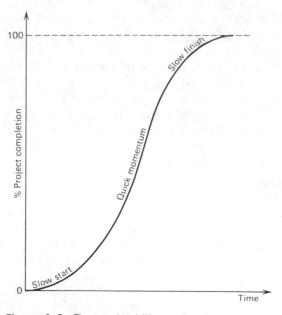

Figure 1-2 The project life cycle.

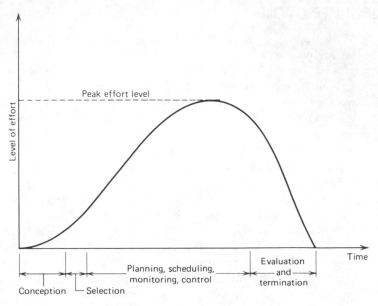

Figure 1-3 Time distribution of project effort.

work of the project gets under way. This rises to a peak and then begins to taper off as the project nears completion, finally ceasing when evaluation is complete and the project is terminated. In some cases, the effort may never fall to zero because the project team, or at least a cadre group, may be maintained for the next appropriate project that comes along. The new project will then rise, phoenix-like, from the ashes of the old.

The ever-present goals of meeting performance, time and cost are the major considerations throughout the project's life cycle. It was generally thought that performance took precedence early in the project's life cycle. This is the time when planners focus on finding the specific methods required to meet the project's performance goals. We refer to these methods as the project's *technology* because they require the application of a science or art.

When the major "how" problems are solved, project workers sometimes become preoccupied with improving performance, often beyond the levels required by the original specifications. This search for better performance delays the schedule and pushes up the costs.

At the same time that the technology of the project is defined, the project schedule is designed and project costs are estimated. Just as it was thought that performance took precedence over schedule and cost early in the life cycle, cost was thought to be of prime importance during the periods of high activity, and then schedule became paramount during the final stages, when the client is demanding delivery. This conventional wisdom turns out to be untrue. Recent research indicates that performance and schedule are more important than cost during *all* stages. The reality of time/cost/performance trade-offs will be discussed in greater detail in Chapter 3.

It would be a great source of comfort if one could predict with certainty, at the start of a project, how the performance, time, and cost goals would be met. In a few cases, routine construction projects, for instance, we can generate reasonably accurate predictions, but often we cannot. There may be considerable uncertainty about our ability to meet project goals. The crosshatched portion of Figure 1-4 illustrates that uncertainty.

Figure 1-4 shows the uncertainty as seen at the beginning of the project. Figure 1-5 shows how the uncertainty decreases as the project moves toward completion. From project start time, t_0, the band of uncertainty grows until it is quite wide by the estimated end of the project. As the project actually develops, the degree of uncertainty about the final outcome is reduced. (See the estimate made at t_1, for example.) A later forecast, made at t_2, reduces the uncertainty still more. It is common to make new forecasts about project performance, time, and cost either at fixed intervals in the life of the project or when specific technological milestones are reached. In any event, the more progress made on the project, the less uncertainty there is about the final goal achievement.

Note that the focus in Figures 1-4 and 1-5 is on the uncertainty associated with project cost—more precisely, the uncertainty of project cost at specific points in time. Without significantly altering the shapes of the curves, we could exchange titles on the axes. The figures would then show the uncertainty associated with estimates of the project schedule, given specific levels of expenditure. The relationship between time and cost (and performance) is emphasized throughout this book. Dealing with the uncertainty surrounding this relationship is a major responsibility of the project manager.

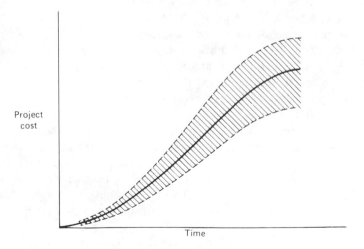

Figure 1-4 Estimate of project cost: Estimate made at project start.

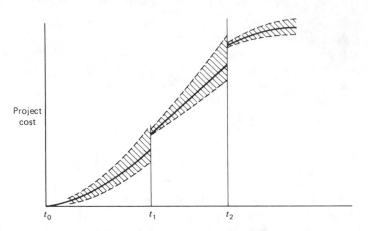

Figure 1-5   Estimates of project cost: estimates made at times t_0, t_1, and t_2.

1.4   THE STRUCTURE OF THIS TEXT

This book, a project in itself, has been organized to follow the life cycle of all projects. It begins with the creative idea that launches most projects and ends with termination of the project (followed by a short discussion of the future of project management). This approach is consistent with our belief that it is helpful to understand the entire process of project management in order to understand and manage its parts. In addition, although this book is intended primarily for the student who wants to study project management, we feel it may also be of value to the prospective or acting project manager, and to senior managers who initiate projects and select, work with, or manage project managers. Therefore, our interests go beyond the issues of primary concern to the beginning student in this field.

Most projects will not be of the size and complexity addressed in many of our discussions. Though our point was not to confine our remarks only to large engineering-oriented projects, these are typically the most complex and place the greatest demands on project management. Smaller, simpler projects may therefore not require the depth of tools and techniques we will present, but the student or manager should be aware that such tools exist.

Project management actually begins with the initial concept for the project. We feel that this aspect of project management is so important, yet so universally ignored in books on project management, that we have included two appendices covering this area. In Appendix A we discuss the concepts of creativity and idea generation, and in Appendix B we describe the techniques of technological forecasting. We realize that these topics may be of more direct interest to the senior manager than the project manager. Though a project manager may prefer to skip this material, since what is past is past, we believe that history holds lessons for the future and wise project managers will wish to know the reasons for, and the history behind, the initiation of their project.

Following this introductory chapter, the material in Part 1 focuses on *project initiation* beginning with selection of the project. Chapter 2 describes the problems of evaluating and selecting projects, including descriptions of the major models used to select projects for funding in government as well as in industry. For those desiring additional depth, special models for evaluating R & D projects are included. In addition, this chapter also covers some of the technical details of proposals. The next step is selecting the project manager. Chapter 3, "The Project Manager," concerns the project manager's roles and responsibilities and some personal characteristics the project manager should possess. Next, Chapter 4 concentrates on establishing the project organization. Different organizational forms are described, together with their respective advantages and disadvantages. The staffing of the project team is also discussed. Chapter 5 deals with project planning where tools found to be useful in organizing and staffing the various project tasks are presented. Concluding this part of the book, Chapter 6 covers a subject of critical importance to the project manager that is almost universally ignored in project management texts, the art of negotiating for resources.

In Part II we consider *project implementation*. This section of the text treats the essentials of ongoing project management. Because of its importance, budgeting is addressed first, in Chapter 7. Scheduling, a crucial aspect of project planning, is then described in Chapter 8, along with the most common scheduling models such as PERT, CPM, and precedence diagramming. Resource allocation is covered in Chapter 9. For single projects, the resource allocation problem concerns resource *leveling* to minimize the cost of the resources; but for multiple projects, the issue is how to allocate limited resources among several projects in order to achieve the objectives of each.

Chapter 10 discusses the information requirements of a project and the need for monitoring critical activities. Included in this chapter is a description of some common Project Management Information Systems (PMIS). Concluding the implementation phase, Chapter 11 describes the control process in project management. The chapter discusses standards for comparison and tools to aid the manager in maintaining control.

The final section of the book, Part III, concerns *project termination*. Chapter 12 deals with methods for both ongoing and terminal evaluations of a project, as well as identifying factors associated with project success and failure.

Chapter 13 describes the different forms of project termination, such as outright shutdown, integration into the regular organization, or extension into a new project. Each of these forms presents unique problems for the project manager to solve. Finally, the future of project management is briefly discussed in Chapter 14.

With this introduction, let us begin our study, a project in itself, and, we hope, an interesting and pleasant one.

1.5 SUMMARY

This chapter introduced the subject of project management and discussed its importance in our society. It defined what we mean by a "project," discussed the need for project management, and described the project life cycle. The final section explained the structure of this text and gave an overview of the material to be described in coming chapters.

The following specific points were made in the chapter.

- Project management, initiated by the military, provides managers with powerful planning and control tools.
- The two primary forces behind project management are (1) the growing demand for complex, customized goods and services and (2) the exponential expansion of human knowledge.
- The three prime objectives of project management are to meet specified performance within cost and on schedule.
- Our terminology follows in this order: program, project, task, work package, work unit.
- Projects are characterized by a singleness of purpose, a definite life cycle, complex interdependencies, some or all unique elements, and an environment of conflict.
- Project management, though not problem-free, is the best way to accomplish certain goals.
- Projects start slowly, build up speed while using considerable resources, and then slow down as completion nears.
- This text is organized along the project life cycle concept, starting with *project initiation* in Chapters 2 to 6, where selection of the project and project manager occurs and project organization and planning begin. *Project implementation,* Chapters 7 to 11, is concerned with budgeting, scheduling, resource allocation, and activity monitoring and control. *Project termination,* concerning final evaluation and completion, is covered in Chapters 12 and 13. Chapter 14 concludes the text with a discussion of the future of project management.

We thus begin our discussion, in Chapter 2, with the topic of selecting the project. We might note, however, that this is not really where project management starts; the important preliminary work is creativity (Appendix A) and technological forecasting (Appendix B).

1.6 GLOSSARY

INTERDEPENDENCIES—Relations between organizational functions where one function or task is dependent on others.

LIFE CYCLE—A standard concept of a product or project wherein it goes through a start-up phase, a building phase, a maturing phase, and a termination phase.

PROGRAM—Often not distinguished from a project, but frequently meant to encompass a group of similar projects.

PROJECT MANAGEMENT—The means, techniques, and concepts used to run a project and achieve its objectives.

RISK—The chance that outcomes will not turn out as planned.

SUBOPTIMIZE—Doing the best within a function or area but at a cost to the larger whole.

SUPERMANAGER—A person who successfully meets the requirements of a project and achieves the desired goals.

TASK—One of the work elements in a project.

TECHNOLOGY—The means for accomplishing difficult tasks.

TRADE-OFF—Taking less on one measure, such as performance, in order to do better on another, such as schedule or cost.

UNCERTAINTY—Having only partial information about the situation or outcomes.

WORK PACKAGE—A subelement of a task that needs to be accomplished in order to achieve the objectives of the task.

1.7 PROJECT TEAM ASSIGNMENT

Every chapter in this text will include assignments for project class teams to complete. The teams will be organized by your class instructor and will work on either individual projects or one large class project. The final project report or term paper will be assigned and discussed by your instructor, too. For now, your task is to form into a team and, if so charged by the instructor, consider potential team projects.

The purpose of this activity is to demonstrate in real terms the project management activities that we describe throughout this book. We hope that the tools, techniques, and concepts we discuss and illustrate will be helpful to you and your project team as you undertake and work to complete your project. Good luck!

1.8 MATERIAL REVIEW QUESTIONS

1. Name and briefly describe the societal forces that have contributed to the need for project management.
2. Why is the project manager often called a supermanager?
3. Describe the life cycle of a project in terms of the degree of project completion; in terms of required effort.
4. Describe the limitations of project management.
5. List the five main characteristics of a project and briefly describe the important features of each.
6. Name and briefly describe the three primary goals of a project.
7. Discuss the advantages and disadvantages of project management.

1.9 CONCEPTUAL DISCUSSION QUESTIONS

1. Give several examples of projects found in our society, avoiding those discussed in the chapter.

2. Describe some situations in which project management would probably not be effective.
3. How does the rate-of-project-progress chart (Fig. 1-2) help a manager make decisions?
4. Expound on the adage, "Projects proceed smoothly until 90 percent complete, and then remain at 90 percent forever."
5. Discuss the duties and responsibilities of the project manager. How critical is the project manager to the success of the project?
6. Would you like to be a project manager? Why, or why not?

1.10   CHAPTER EXERCISE

Select a recent major project you were extensively involved in, such as the selection of a college, the preparation of a resumé, an auto repair, home remodeling, or landscaping. Review the tasks and the time it took to complete them. Construct a rate-of-progress chart and a distribution-of-effort chart similar to those in Figures 1-2 and 1-3. Also recall the initial estimates of either cost or performance and time to completion, and the variability of these estimates, to construct a chart similar to Figure 1-4. Plot the final actual values on the chart and describe the reason for the variance.

How accurate are these charts, in general? Do they picture adequately the concepts they are meant to describe? Archibald [2] portrays the target cost and time (Fig. 1-4) as an ellipse, rather than a band, that continually shrinks as the project nears completion. Is this a better portrayal? How would performance variability then be handled?

1.11   INCIDENTS FOR DISCUSSION

T.T.S Candle Company

Sue Miller, president of T.T.S. Candle Company, has just completed a two-day seminar on project management and is anxious to use the new techniques on a recurring problem faced by her company. About 60 percent of T.T.S.'s gross revenues result from the pre-Christmas sale of the firm's major product, XMAS-PAK. XMAS-PAK consists of twelve candles, all of one color and size. There are six different colors available in three different lengths. XMAS-PAK was introduced eight years ago, and sales have been increasing by approximately 20 percent per year.

Because of the seasonal nature of the product, all orders unfilled on December 16 are lost. Ms. Miller estimated that XMAS-PAK sales would have been about 10 percent higher last year were it not for lost orders. It was a frustrating problem because the loss was not due to a shortage of capacity. Sales forecasts were not very accurate, and her manufacturing managers had strict instructions to minimize investment in finished goods inventories. Miller was sure that project management could somehow help solve the problem without appreciably increasing inventories.

On her return from the seminar, she assigned Sam Joseph, marketing manager, and Kenneth Knight, vice-president of manufacturing, as project managers for this problem. She reviewed the problem with them and gave them eight years of historical sales data, broken down by line item and geographical region. These were the data that she herself had used during her initial investigation. The project objective was to reduce lost sales to 0.5 percent within five years.

Question: Discuss Mrs. Miller's organization of the problem.

Maladroit Machine Tool Company

The plant manager of the Maladroit Machine Tool Company must replace several of his milling machines that have become obsolete. He is about to take delivery of six machines at a total cost of $4 million. These machines must be installed and fully tested in time to be used on a new production line scheduled to begin operation in six months. Because this project is important, the plant manager would like to devote as much time as possible to the job, but he is currently handling several other projects. He thinks he has three basic choices: (1) He can handle the project informally out of his office; (2) he can assign the project to a member of his staff; or (3) the company that manufactures the machines is willing to handle the installation project for a fee close to what the installation would cost Maladroit.

Question: Which of the three choices do you recommend, and why? If the project was one small machine at a total cost of $4,000, would your answer be different?

1.12 BIBLIOGRAPHY

1. Adams, J. R., S. E. Barndt, and M. D. Martin. *Managing by Project Management.* Universal Technology, Dayton, OH, 1979.
2. Archibald, R. D. *Managing High Technology Programs and Projects.* Wiley, New York, 1976.
3. Avots, I. "Why Does Project Management Fail?" *California Management Review,* Fall 1969.
4. Awani, A. O. *Project Management Techniques.* Petrocelli, Princeton, NJ, 1983.
5. Baumgartner, J. *Project Management.* Irwin, Homewood, IL, 1963.
6. Bobrowski, T. M. "A Basic Philosophy of Project Management." *Journal of Systems Management,* May–June 1974.
7. Benningson, L. "The Strategy of Running Temporary Projects." *Innovation,* Sept. 1971.
8. Cleland, D. I. "Why Project Management." *Business Horizons,* Winter 1974.
9. Cleland, D. I., and W. R. King. *Systems Analysis and Project Management,* 3rd ed. McGraw-Hill, New York, 1983.
10. Cleland, D. I., and W. R. King, eds. *Project Management Handbook.* Van Nostrand Reinhold, New York, 1983.

11. Davis, E. W. "CPM Use in Top 400 Construction Firms." *Journal of the Construction Division,* American Society of Civil Engineers, 1974.

12. Davis, E. W. *Project Management: Techniques, Applications, and Managerial Issues,* 2nd ed. AIIE Monograph, 1983.

13. Dean, B. V. *Project Management: Methods and Studies.* Elsevier, New York, 1985.

14. Goodman, L. J. *Project Planning and Management.* Pergamon Press, Elmsford, NY, 1980.

15. Graham, R. J. *Project Management: Combining Technical and Behavioral Approaches for Effective Implementation.* Van Nostrand Reinhold, New York, 1985.

16. Grod, M. C., et al. *Project Management in Progress.* Elsevier, New York, 1986.

17. Harrison, F. L. *Advanced Project Management.* Gower Publishing, Hants, Eng., 1981.

18. Hockney, J. W. *Control and Management of Capital Projects.* Wiley, New York, 1965.

19. Hodgetts, R. M. *An Interindustry Analysis of Certain Aspects of Project Management.* Ph.D. dissertation, University of Oklahoma, 1968.

20. Jacobs, R. A. "Project Management—A New Style for Success." *S.A.M. Advanced Management Journal,* Autumn 1976.

21. Kerzner, H. *Project Management,* Litton Educational Publishing, New York, 1979.

22. Kerzner, H. *Project Management for Executives.* Van Nostrand Reinhold, New York, 1982.

23. Kerzner, H. *Project Management: A Systems Approach to Planning, Scheduling, and Controlling,* 2nd ed. Van Nostrand Reinhold, New York, 1984.

24. Kerzner, H., and H. Thamhain. *Project Management for Small and Medium Sized Businesses.* Van Nostrand Reinhold, New York, 1983.

25. Lock, D. *Project Management,* 3rd ed. St. Martin's Press, New York, 1984.

26. Martin, C. C. *Project Management: How to Make It Work.* AMACOM, New York, 1976.

27. Martino, R. L. *Project Management.* MDI Publications, Management Development Institute, 1968.

28. Roman, D. D. *Managing Projects: A Systems Approach.* Elsevier, New York, 1985.

29. Rosenau, M. D., Jr. *Successful Project Management.* Van Nostrand Reinhold, New York, 1981.

30. Silverman, M. *Project Management: A Short Course for Professionals.* Wiley, New York, 1976.

31. Spirer, H. F. "The Basic Principles of Project Management." *Operations Management Review,* Fall 1982.

32. Stewart, J. M. "Making Project Management Work." *Business Horizons,* Fall 1965.

33. Stuckenbruck, L.D., ed. *The Implementation of Project Management: The Professional's Handbook.* Addison-Wesley, Reading, MA, 1981.

34. Sun, M. "Weighing the Social Costs of Innovation." *Science,* March 30, 1984.

35. Taylor, W. J., and T. F. Watling. *Successful Project Management.* Business Books, London, 1970.

36. Toellner, J. D. "Project Management: A Formula for Success." *Computerworld,* Dec. 1978.

1.13 READING

This article presents an overview of the complexities of managing projects. Initially, it describes the details of organizing a project and their unique characteristics in terms of scope, unfamiliarity, complexity, and stake. Then the special nature of project management is discussed, followed by a description of the special sources of trouble to which projects often give rise. These sources are categorized into three areas: organizational uncertainties, unusual decision pressures, and vulnerability to top-management mistakes.

Next, the actions required of executives, particularly top management, are described as guidelines. The first guideline is to define properly the project objective in terms of management's intent and the scope and desired end results of the project. The second guideline relates to the establishment of the project organization, including both the project manager and the project team. The third guideline is to be sure that good project controls have been established, particularly for monitoring time, cost, and quality of performance. Finally, the author gives some advice concerning the management of human beings in a project setting.

Making Project Management Work
John M. Stewart

Late last year, with a good deal of local fanfare, a leading food producer opened a new plant in a small midwestern town. For the community it was a festive day. For top management, however, the celebration was somewhat dampened by the fact that the plant had missed its original target date by six months and had overrun estimated costs by a cool $5 million.

A material-handling equipment maker's latest automatic lift truck was an immediate market success. But a few more successes of the same kind would spell disaster for the company. An actual introduction cost of $2.6 million, compared to planned expenses of $1.2 million, cut the company's profits by fully 10 percent last year.

A new high-speed, four-color press installed by a leading eastern printing concern has enabled a major consumer magazine to sharply increase its color pages and offer advertisers unprecedented schedule convenience. The printer will not be making money on the press for years, however. Developing and installing it took twice as long and cost nearly three times as much as management had expected.

Fiascos such as these are as old as business itself—as old, indeed, as organized human effort. The unfortunate Egyptian overseer who was obliged, 5,000 years ago, to report to King Cheops that construction work on the Great Pyramid at

Copyright © 1965 by the Foundation for the School of Business at the Indiana University. Reprinted by permission from *Business Horizons* (Fall 1965).

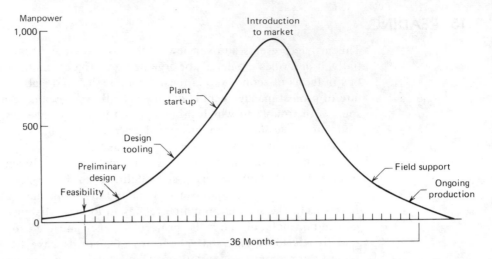

Figure 1 Manpower commitment to a new-product introduction project.

Giza had fallen a year behind schedule had much in common with the vice-president who recoils in dismay as he and the chief executive discover that their new plant will be months late in delivering the production on which a major customer's contract depends. The common thread: poor management of a large, complex, one-time "project" undertaking.

But unlike the Egyptian overseer, today's businessman has available to him a set of new and powerful management tools with the demonstrated capacity to avert time and cost overruns on massive, complex projects. These tools, developed only recently, are not yet in common use outside the construction and aerospace industries, where such projects are a way of life. But there is already solid evidence that they can be successfully applied to a host of important, nonroutine business undertakings where conventional planning and control techniques fail—undertakings ranging from a new product introduction or the launching of a national advertising campaign to the installation of an EDP system or a merger of two major corporations (Figures 1 and 2).

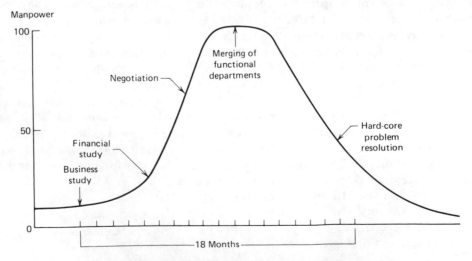

Figure 2 Manpower commitment to a merger project.

PROJECT MANAGEMENT ORGANIZATION

Commercial project management is usually a compromise between two basic forms of organization—pure project management and the more standard functional alignment. In the aerospace and construction companies (Figure 3), complete responsibility for the task, as well as all the resources needed for its accomplishment, is usually assigned to one project manager. In very large projects, the organization he heads, which will be dissolved at the conclusion of the project, resembles a regular division, relatively independent of any other division or staff group. Outside the aerospace and construction industries, however, the project manager is usually not assigned complete responsibility for resources (Figure 4). Instead, he shares them with the rest of the organization. He may have a project organization consisting of a handful of men on temporary assignment from the regular functional organization. The functional managers, however, retain their direct line authority, monitor their staffs' contributions to the project, and continue to make all major personnel decisions.

Reluctance to adopt new tools is typical in any industry; thus, one should not expect the tools of project management to gain instant acceptance. Outside the aerospace industry, few business executives appreciate their value and versatility. Fewer still are able to recognize the need for project management in specific situations, nor do they know how to use the powerful control techniques it offers. Meanwhile, the few companies that have grasped the significance of the new management concepts and learned to apply them enjoy an extraordinary, if temporary, advantage. They are bringing new products to market faster than their competitors, completing major expansions on schedule, and meeting crucial commitments more reliably than ever before.

Project management, however, is far from being a cure-all for the embarrassments, expenses, and delays that plague even the best-managed companies. First, project management requires tem-

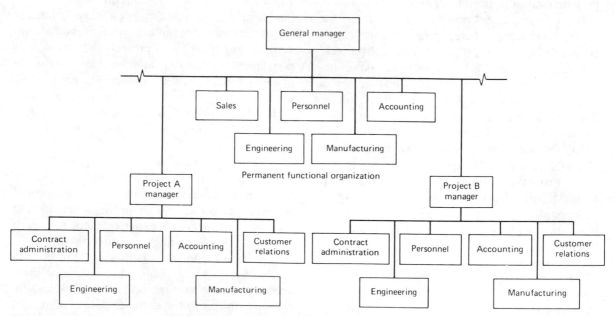

Figure 3   Typical project organization in the aerospace and construction industries.

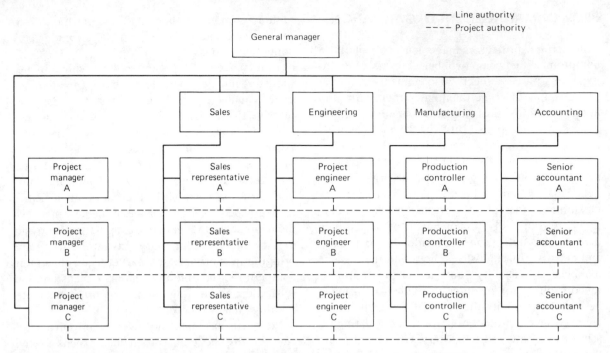

Figure 4 Project organization in general industry.

porary shifts of responsibilities and reporting relationships that may disturb the smooth functioning of the regular organization. Second, it requires unusually disciplined executive effort.

Basic to successful project management is the ability to recognize where it is needed and where it is not. When, in short, is a project a project? Where, in the broad spectrum of undertakings between a minor procedural modification and a major organizational upheaval, should the line be drawn? At what point do a multitude of minor departures from routine add up to the "critical mass" that makes project management operationally and economically desirable? Senior executives must have methods to identify those undertakings, corporate or divisional, that cannot be successfully managed by the regular functional organization working with routine planning and control methods. Although there are no simple rules of thumb, management can determine whether a given undertaking possesses this critical mass by applying four yardsticks: scope, unfamiliarity, complexity, and stake.

Scope

Project management can be profitably applied, as a rule, to a one-time undertaking that is (1) definable in terms of a single, specific end result, and (2) bigger than the organization has previously undertaken successfully. A project must, by definition, end at an objective point in time: the date the new plant achieves full production, the date the parent company takes over operating management of the new acquisition, or the date the new product goes on sale in supermarkets across the nation, to name a few.

The question of size is less easily pinned down. But where substantially more people, more dollars, more organizational units, and more time will be involved than on any other infrequent undertaking in the organization's experience, the test result is clearly positive. Such an undertaking, even though its component parts may be familiar, can easily overwhelm a divisional or corporate management. Project management forces a logical approach to the project, speeds decision making, and cuts management's job to a reasonable level. For example, a large service company, with years of experience in renovating district offices, established a project organization to renovate its 400 district offices over a two-year period. Even though each task was relatively simple, the total undertaking would have swamped the administrative organization had it been managed routinely.

In terms of the number of people and the organizational effort it involves, a project could typically be charted over time as a wave-like curve, rising gradually to a crest and dropping off abruptly with the accomplishment of the end result. Consider, for example, the introduction of a new consumer product. The project begins with a few people studying the desirability of adding a product to the line. After some early decisions to proceed, perhaps a few dozen engineers are employed to design the product. Their work passes to scores of process planners, toolmakers, and other manufacturing engineers, and finally involves entire manufacturing plants or divisions as the first month's production gains momentum. This momentum carries into the field as salesmen increase their effort to introduce the product successfully. Finally, the project effort ebbs as the new product is integrated into routine production and marketing operation.

Again, a merger typically shows a similar "growth and decay" project pattern. Initially, a few senior executives from each company may be involved in discussing the merger possibility. As interest grows, financial and legal advisors are engaged by both sides. Key inside executives are added to the task force to assist in planning. Then, as the deal moves toward completion, widening circles of executives, technical people, and analysts become involved in identifying the changes required after merger. Once the merger has been approved by the directors and stockholders of the two companies, the process of meshing the philosophies, structures, policies, and procedures of the two organizations must begin, possibly requiring the active participation of hundreds or even thousands of people. Eventually, as most of the changes are accomplished, employees return to their normal duties, and the corporation resumes its orderly march toward the end of the fiscal year. The merger project is at an end.

Unfamiliarity

An undertaking is not a project, in our sense of the term, unless it is a unique, or infrequent, effort by the existing management group. Lack of familiarity or lack of precedent usually leads to disagreement or uncertainty as to how the undertaking should be managed. In such a situation, people at the lower management levels need to be told more precisely what they are to do, while senior executives are justifiably troubled by a greater than usual sense of uncertainty about the realism of initial cost estimates, time commitments, or both.

Thus, though a single engineering change to one part of a product would not qualify for project management by this criterion, the complete redesign of a product line that had been basically unchanged for a decade would in most cases call for project management treatment. Individual managers could accomplish the first change easily, drawing on their own past experience, but each would have to feel his way by trial and error through the second.

Complexity

Frequently the decisive criterion of a project is the degree of interdependence among tasks. If a given task depends on the completion of other assignments in other functional areas, and if it will, in turn, affect the cost or timing of subsequent tasks, project management is probably called for. Consider the introduction of a hypothetical new product. Sales promotion plans cannot be completed until introduction dates are known; introduction dates depend on product availability; and availability depends on tooling, which depends in turn on the outcome of a disagreement between engineering and product planning over performance specifications. There are many comparable interdependencies among marketing, engineering, manufacturing, and finance. If, as seems likely in this situation, no one person can produce a properly detailed plan on which all those concerned can agree; if estimates repeatedly fail to withstand scrutiny; or if plans submitted by different departments prove difficult to reconcile or coordinate, the critical mass of a project has probably been reached.

Stake

A final criterion that may tip the scales in favor of project management is the company's stake in the outcome of the undertaking. Would failure to complete the job on schedule or within the budget entail serious penalties for the company? If so, the case for project management is strong.

The corporate stake in the outcome of a project is commonly financial; that is, the failure of a $50,000 engineering project might jeopardize $12 million in annual sales. But it may also involve costs of a different kind. As more than one World's Fair exhibitor can attest, failure to meet a well-publicized project schedule can sometimes do real harm to a company's reputation. Again, failure to meet time and cost objectives may seriously disrupt corporate plans, as in the case of an equipment manufacturer who was obliged to abandon a promising new product line when a poorly managed merger soaked up earnings that had been earmarked for R & D on the new line. In all such cases, the powerful controls of project management offer a much firmer prospect of meeting the time, cost, and quality objectives of the major one-time undertaking.

The specific advantages of project management for ventures that meet the criteria just discussed are easily summarized. Project management provides the concentrated management attention that a complex and unfamiliar undertaking is likely to demand. It greatly improves, at very small cost, the chances of on-time, on-budget completion. And it permits the rest of the organization to proceed normally with routine business while the project is underway. But these benefits are available only if top management clearly understands the unique features of project management, the problems it entails, and the steps required to make it work.

THE NATURE OF PROJECT MANAGEMENT

With respect to organization, project managements calls for the appointment of one man, the project manager, who has responsibility for the detailed planning, coordination, and ultimate outcome of the project. Usually appointed from the middle management ranks, the project manager is supplied with a team, often numbering no more than half a dozen men for a $10 million project.

Team members, drawn from the various functional departments involved in the project, report directly to the project manager. For the duration of the project, he has the authority to insist on thorough planning, the freedom to challenge functional departments' assumptions and targets, and the responsibility to monitor every effort bearing on the successful completion of the project.

Within the limits of the project, the project manager's responsibility and authority are interfunctional, like that of top management for the company as a whole. Despite this similarity, however, his function cannot safely be superimposed on a top executive's normal workload. Every company I know that has tried giving operating responsibility for the management of a complex project to a division manager has found that he is soon swamped in a tidal wave of detail. Most projects call for more and faster decisions than does routine work, and clear precedents are usually lacking. Thus, a general manager who tries to run one of his own projects seldom has any guidelines for making reliable cost and time estimates, establishing cost control at commitment points, or setting adequately detailed targets for each department. Lacking precedents, he is obliged to invent them. This procedure may drain off far more of his time than the division can afford, without really providing the project with the concentrated attention it needs. He may well find that he is spending better than half his working time trying to manage a project representing less than a tenth of his division's annual budget, while divisional performance as a whole is slipping alarmingly. For these reasons, few projects are ever successfully managed on a part-time basis.

The essence of project management is that it cuts across, and in a sense conflicts with, the normal organization structure. Throughout the project, personnel at various levels in many functions of the business contribute to it. Because a project usually requires decisions and actions from a number of functional areas at once, the main flow of information and the main interdependencies in a project are not vertical but lateral. Up-and-down information flow is relatively light in a well-run project; indeed, any attempt to consistently send needed information from one functional area up to a common authority and down to another area through conventional channels is apt to cripple the project and wreck the time schedule.

Projects are also characterized by exceptionally strong lateral working relationships, requiring closely related activity and decisions by many individuals in different functional departments. During a major product development, for example, a design engineer will work more closely with the process engineering manager and the product manager from marketing than with the senior members of his own department. He will need common sense and tolerance to succeed in the scramble for available resources, such as test-cell time or the help of metallurgical specialists, without hurting relationships of considerable importance to his future career.

Necessarily though, a project possesses a vertical as well as a horizontal dimension, since those who are involved in it at various stages, particularly those who make the technical decisions that determine costs, must often go to their superiors for guidance. Moreover, frequent project changes underline the necessity of keeping senior executives informed of the project's current status.

SPECIAL SOURCES OF TROUBLE

Understandably, project managers face some unusual problems in trying to direct and harmonize the diverse forces at work in the project situation. Their main difficulties, observation suggests, arise from three sources: organizational uncertainties, unusual decision pressures, and vulnerability to top-management mistakes.

Organizational Uncertainties

Many newly appointed project managers find that their working relationships with functional department heads have not been clearly defined by management. Who assigns work to the financial analyst? Who decides when to order critical material before the product design is firm? Who decides to delay design release to reduce unit cost? Who determines the quantity and priority of spares? All these decisions vitally concern the project manager, and he must often forge his own guidelines for dealing with them. Unless he does so skillfully, the questions are apt to be resolved in the interest of individual departments, at the expense of the project as a whole.

Because of the number of decisions or approvals that may arise in the course of a large project, and the number of departments that have an interest in each, innumerable possibilities always exist for interdepartmental conflicts. Besides coping with these conflicts, the project manager must juggle the internal schedules of each department with the project schedule, avoid political problems that could create bottlenecks, expedite one department to compensate for another's failure to meet its schedule, and hold the project within a predetermined cost. Moreover, he must do all this single-handedly, with little or none of the experienced top-management guidance that the line manager enjoys.

Unusual Decision Pressures

The severe penalties of delay often compel the project manager to base his decisions on relatively few data, analyzed in haste. On a large project where a day's delay may cost $10,000 in salaries alone, he can hardly hold everything up for a week to perform an analysis that could save the company

$5,000. He must move fast, even if it means an intuitive decision that might expose him to charges of rashness and irresponsibility from functional executives. Decisions to sacrifice time for cost, cost for quality, or quality for time, are common in most projects, and the project manager must be able to make them without panicking. Clearly, therefore, he has a special need for intelligent support from higher management.

Vulnerability to Top-Management Mistakes

Though senior executives can seldom give the project manager as much guidance and support as his line counterpart enjoys, they can easily jeopardize the project's success by lack of awareness, ill-advised intervention, or personal whim. The damage that a senior executive's ignorance of a project situation can create is well illustrated by the following example. A project manager, battling to meet a schedule that had been rendered nearly impossible by the general manager's initial delay in approving the proposal, found functional cooperation more and more difficult to obtain. The functional heads, he discovered, had become convinced—rightly, as it turned out—that he lacked the general manager's full confidence. Unknown to the project manager, two department heads whom he had pressured to expedite their departments had complained to the general manager, who had readily sympathized. The project manager, meanwhile, had been too busy getting the job done to protect himself with top management. As a result, project performance was seriously hampered.

EXECUTIVE ACTION REQUIRED

Because of the great diversity of projects and the lack of common terminology for the relatively new techniques of project management, useful specific rules for project management are virtually impossible to formulate. From the experience of the aerospace and construction industries and of a handful of companies in other industries, however, it is possible to distill some general guidelines.

Guideline 1: Define the Objective

Performing unfamiliar activities at a rapid pace, those involved in the project can easily get off the right track or fall short of meeting their commitments, with the result that many steps of the project may have to be retraced. To minimize this risk, management must clarify the objective of the project well in advance by (1) defining management's intent in undertaking the project, (2) outlining the scope of the project, that is, identifying the departments, companies, functions, and staffs involved, and the approximate degree of their involvement, and (3) describing the end results of the project and its permanent effects, if any, on the company or division.

Defining Management's Intent What are the business reasons for the project? What is top management's motive in undertaking it?

A clear common understanding of the answers to these questions is desirable for three reasons. *First,* it enables the project manager to capitalize on opportunities to improve the outcome of the project. By knowing top management's rationale for building the new plant, for example, he will be able to weigh the one-time cost of plant start-up against the continuing advantage of lower production costs, or the competitive edge that might be gained by an earlier product introduction. *Second,* a clear definition of intent helps avert damaging oversights that would otherwise appear unimportant to lower-level managers and might not be obvious to the senior executive. One company failed to get any repeat orders for a unique product because the project team, unaware of the president's intent, saw their job only in terms of meeting their schedule and cost commitments and neglected to cultivate the market. *Third,* a definition of the intent of the project helps to avoid imbalance of effort at the middle-management level, such as pushing desperately to meet a schedule but missing cost-reduction opportunities on the way.

Outlining the Scope of the Project Which organizational units of the company will be involved in the project, and to what degree? Which sensitive customer relationships, private or governmental, should the project manager cautiously skirt? By crystallizing the answers and communicating them to the organization, the responsible senior executive will make it far easier for the project manager to work with the functional departments and to get the information he needs.

Describing the End Results Top managers who have spent hours discussing a proposed project can easily overlook the fact that middle managers charged with its execution lack their perspective on the project. An explicit description of how a new plant will operate when it is in full production, how a sales reorganization will actually change customer relationships, or how major staff activities will be coordinated after a merger, gives middle managers a much clearer view of what the project will involve and what is expected of them.

Guideline 2: Establish a Project Organization

For a functionally organized company, successful project management means establishing, for the duration of the project, a workable compromise between two quite different organizational concepts. The basic ingredients of such a compromise are (1) appointment of one experienced manager to run the project full-time, (2) organization of the project management function in terms of responsibilities, (3) assignment of a limited number of staff to the project team, and (4) maintenance of a balance of power between the functional heads and the project manager. In taking these steps, some generally accepted management rules may have to be broken, and some organizational friction will almost inevitably occur. But the results in terms of successful project completion should far outweigh these drawbacks and difficulties.

Assigning an Experienced Manager Though the project manager's previous experience is apt to

have been confined to a single functional area of the business, he must be able to function on the project as a kind of general manager in miniature. He must not only keep track of what is happening but also play the crucial role of advocate for the project. Even for a seasoned manager, this task is not likely to be easy. Hence, it is important to assign an individual whose administrative abilities and skill in personal relations have been convincingly demonstrated under fire.

Organizing the Project Manager's Responsibilities While some organizational change is essential, management should try to preserve, wherever possible, the established relationships that facilitate rapid progress under pressure. Experience indicates that it is desirable for senior management to delegate to the project manager some of its responsibilities for planning the project, for resolving arguments among functional departments, for providing problem-solving assistance to functional heads, and for monitoring progress. A full-time project manager can better handle these responsibilities; moreover, the fact that they are normally part of the executive job helps to establish his stature. A general manager, however, should not delegate certain responsibilities, such as monitoring milestone accomplishments, resolving project-related disputes between senior managers, or evaluating the project performance of functional department managers. The last responsibility mentioned strikes too close to the careers of the individuals concerned to be delegated to one of their peers.

For the duration of the project, the project manager should also hold some responsibilities normally borne by functional department heads. These include responsibility for reviewing progress against schedule; organizing for, formulating, and approving a project plan; monitoring project cost performance; and, in place of the department heads normally involved, trading off time and cost. Also, the senior executive must encourage the project manager to direct the day-to-day activities of all functional personnel who are involved full-time in the project. Functional department heads, however, should retain responsibility for the quality of their subordinates' technical performance, as well as for matters affecting their careers.

Limiting the Project Team   Functional department heads may view the project manager as a potential competitor. By limiting the number of staff on the project team, the problem is alleviated and the project manager's involvement in intrafunctional matters is reduced. Moreover, men transferred out of their own functional departments are apt to lose their inside sources of information and find it increasingly difficult to get things done rapidly and informally.

Maintaining the Balance of Power   Because the project manager is concerned with change, while the department head must efficiently manage routine procedures, the two are often in active conflict. Though they should be encouraged to resolve these disputes without constant appeals to higher authority, their common superior must occasional-

ly act as mediator. Otherwise, resentments and frustrations will impair the project's progress and leave a long-lasting legacy of bitterness. Short-term conflicts can often be resolved in favor of the project manager and long-term conflicts in favor of the functional managers. This compromise helps to reduce friction, to get the job accomplished, and to prepare for the eventual phasing out of the project.

Guideline 3: Install Project Controls

Though they use the same raw data as routine reports, special project controls over time, cost, and quality are very different in their accuracy, timing, and use. They are normally superimposed upon the existing report structure for the duration of the project and then discontinued. The crucial relationship between project time control and cost control is shown graphically in Figure 5.

The project in question had to be completed in twenty months instead of the twenty and a half months scheduled by a preliminary network cal-

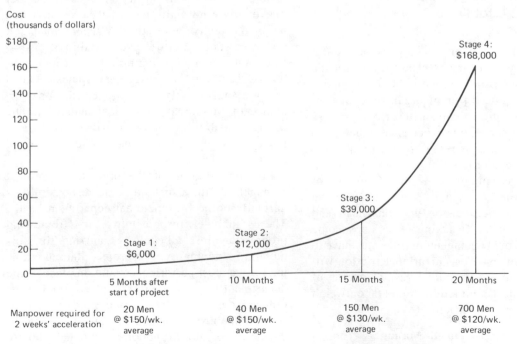

Figure 5 Cost of two weeks' acceleration at various project stages.

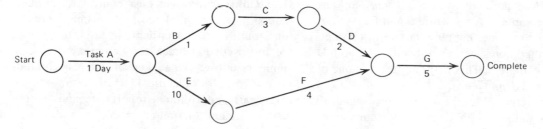

Figure 6 A simple critical path network.

culation. The project manager, who was under strict initial manpower limitations, calculated the cost of the two weeks' acceleration at various stages of the project. Confronted by the evidence of the costs it could save, top management approved the project manager's request for early acceleration. The project was completed two working days before its twenty-month deadline, at a cost only $6,000 over the original estimate. Without controls that clearly relate time to cost, companies too often crash the project in its final stages, at enormous and entirely unnecessary cost.

Time Control Almost invariably, some form of network scheduling provides the best time control of a project. A means of graphically planning a complex undertaking so that it can be scheduled for analysis and control, network scheduling begins with the construction of a diagram that reflects the interdependencies and time requirements of the individual tasks that go to make up a project. It calls for work plans prepared in advance of the project in painstaking detail, scheduling each element of the plan, and using controls to ensure that commitments are met.

At the outset, each department manager involved in the project should draw up a list of all the tasks required of his department to accomplish the project. Then the project manager should discuss each of these lists in detail with the respective departmental supervisors in order to establish the sequence in the project in relation to other departments. Next, each manager and supervisor should list the information he will need from other departments, indicating which data, if any, are habitually

late. This listing gives the project manager not only a clue to the thoroughness of planning in the other departments but also a means of uncovering and forestalling most of the inconsistencies, missed activities, or inadequate planning that would otherwise occur.

Next, having planned its own role in the project, each department should be asked to commit itself to an estimate of the time required for each of its project activities, assuming the required information is supplied on time. After this, the complete network is constructed, adjusted where necessary with the agreement of the department heads concerned, and reviewed for logic.

Once the overall schedule is established, weekly or fortnightly review meetings should be held to check progress against schedule. Control must be rigorous, especially at the start, when the tone of the entire project is invariably set. Thus, the very first few missed commitments call for immediate corrective action.

In critical path scheduling, one of the major network techniques, the diagram is similar in principle to that of Figure 6 for a very simple hypothetical project.

In the diagram, each arrow represents a defined task, with a clear beginning, end, and time requirement, that can be delegated to a single manager or supervisor. Each circle, or node (except the "start" node), represents the completion of a task. Task A, for example, might be "Define the technical objective of the project." The numeral one indicates that the allotted time for its completion is one day.

The arrangement of the arrows is significant. As drawn here, B depends upon A; that is, it may not start until A is complete. Similarly, C may not start until B is complete. Also, while B and E may start at different times, neither may start until A is complete. Further along, G may not start until both D and F are complete. This diagram, then, is one of *sequence* and *dependency.*

The time required for the project corresponds to the longest path through the network from Start to Complete in terms of the time requirement associated with each task. In the diagram above, A-E-F-G is the critical path. To meet the over-all schedule, each of these tasks must begin as soon as its predecessor is completed and must end within its allotted time. To shorten the schedule, one or more of the tasks on the critical path must be accelerated.

There are other more complex varieties of network scheduling. Critical path method calculates both normal and crash schedules (and costs) for a project. Program evaluation and review techniques (PERT) allows the use of multiple time estimates for each activity. PERT/Cost adds cost estimates, as the name implies. RAMPS (resource allocation and multiproject scheduling) adds the further refinement of a tool for allocating limited resources to competing activities in one or more projects. All, however, rest on the basic network concept outlined above.

Cost Control Project cost control techniques, though not yet formalized to the same degree as time controls, are no harder to install if these steps are followed: (1) break the comprehensive cost summary into work packages, (2) devise commitment reports for "technical" decision makers, (3) act on early, approximate report data, and (4) concentrate talent on major problems and opportunities.

Managing a fast-moving $15 million project can be difficult for even the most experienced top manager. For a first-line supervisor the job of running a $500,000 project can be equally difficult. Neither manager can make sound decisions unless cost dimensions of the job are broken down into pieces of comprehensible size. Figure 7, which gives an example of such a breakdown, shows how major costs can be logically reduced to understandable and controllable work packages (usually worth $15,000 to $25,000 apiece on a major project), each of which can reasonably be assigned to a first-line manager.

Cost commitments on a project are made when engineering, manufacturing, marketing, or other functional personnel make technical decisions to take some kind of action. In new-product development, for example, costs are committed or created in many ways—when marketing decides to add a

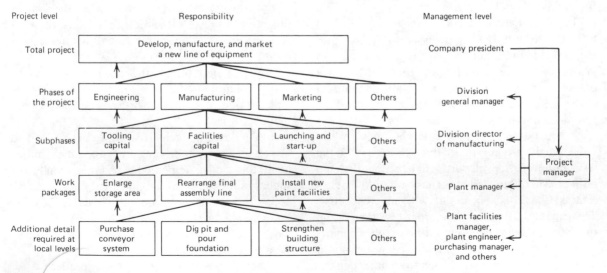

Figure 7 Breakdown of project cost responsibility by management level.

product feature to its product; when engineering decides to insert a new part; when a process engineer adds an extra operation to a routine; when physical distribution managers choose to increase inventory, and so on. Conventional accounting reports, however, do not show the cost effects of these decisions until it is too late to reconsider. To enable the project manager to judge when costs are getting out of control and to decisively take the needed corrective action, he must be able to assess the approximate cost effect of each technical decision. In other words, he must have cost commitment reports at each decision stage.

Almost without exception, experience shows, 20 percent of the project effort accounts for at least 80 percent of the cost to which the company is committed. With the aid of a detailed cost breakdown and current information on cost commitment, the project manager is able, even after the project is underway, to take people off less important activities in order to concentrate more effort where it will do the most good in reducing costs. One company cut its product introduction costs by over $1 million in this way between the dates when the first print was released and the first machine assembled.

Quality Control   Experience with a wide variety of projects—new-product introductions, mergers, plant constructions, introduction of organizational changes, to name a few—indicates that effective quality control of results is a crucial dimension of project success. Quality control comprises three elements: defining performance criteria, expressing the project objective in terms of quality standards, and monitoring progress toward these standards.

The need to define performance criteria, though universally acknowledged, is generally ignored in practice. Such quality criteria can, however, be defined rather easily, that is, simply in terms of senior executives' expectations with respect to average sales per salesman, market penetration of a product line, ratio of accounts to production workers, processing time for customer inquiries, and the like. If possible, these expectations should

be expressed quantitatively. For example, the senior executive might expect the project to reduce emergency transportation costs from 15 percent to 5 percent of total shipping costs. Or he might expect a 30 percent reduction in inventory costs following installation of a mechanized control system.

Since achievement of these quality goals is a gradual process, the project manager should review progress toward them with the general manager monthly or quarterly, depending on the length of the project. Sometimes there will be little noticeable change; in other cases major departures from expectations will be apparent. Here, as in the case of time and cost controls, the importance of prompt action to assure that the objectives will be met cannot be overemphasized.

MANAGING THE HUMAN EQUATION

The typical manager in a commercial business who is handed his first project management assignment finds adjustment to his anomalous new role painful, confusing, and even demoralizing. Lacking real line authority, he must constantly lead, persuade, or coerce his peers through a trying period of change.

Too often, in these difficult early weeks, he receives little support from senior management. Instead, he is criticized for not moving faster and producing more visible results. He may be blamed for flaws in a plan that, through the fault of top management, had to be rushed to completion mere days before the project began. Senior managers need to recognize that naming and needling the project manager is not enough. By giving him needed support at the start, by bringing a broad business perspective to bear on the overall project plan, and by giving the project manager freedom in the details of the doing, the senior executive can greatly enhance the prospects of success.

Another critical point comes at the conclusion of the project, when its results are turned over to the regular organization and the project manager and his team must be returned to their permanent assignments. By virtue of the interfunctional experience gained under pressure, the project manager often matures in the course of a project, becoming a more valuable manager. But he may have trouble slowing down to a normal organizational pace. His routine job is likely to seem less attractive in terms of scope, authority, and opportunity to contribute to the business. Even the best project manager, moreover, can hardly accomplish his project objectives without antagonizing some members of management, quite possibly the very executives who will decide his future. In one instance, a project manager who had brought a major project from the brink of chaos to unqualified success was let go at the end of the project because, in accomplishing the feat, he had been unable to avoid antagonizing one division manager. Such difficulties and dissatisfactions often lead a retired project manager to look for a better job at this time, in or out of the company.

To retain and profit by the superior management material developed on the fertile training ground of the project, senior executives need to be aware of these human problems. By recognizing the growth of the project manager, helping him readjust to the slower pace of the normal organization, and finding ways to put his added experience and his matured judgment to good use, the company can reap a significant side benefit from every successfully managed project.

PART I
Project Initiation

This part of the text begins our formal analysis of project management. Chapter 2 takes the first step in project initiation, evaluating and selecting projects for implementation. That chapter also includes a short discussion of project proposals and their preparation. What is certainly a critically important task in the management of projects, the selection of a project manager, is treated in Chapter 3. The significance and nature of the project manager's role, responsibilities, and desirable personal characteristics are described in detail. Chapter 4 continues with a discussion of the advantages and disadvantages of several different forms of project organization. The nature and formation of the project staff are also briefly covered.

Chapter 5 opens the subject of project planning. Preparation of the fundamental planning document is covered, and some of the tools needed to organize and staff the numerous project tasks are described and illustrated through examples. Finally, Chapter 6 treats the most often used and least-discussed skill of an effective project manager, negotiation.

CHAPTER 2
Project Evaluation and Selection

Project evaluation and selection is the process of evaluating individual projects or groups of projects, and then choosing to implement some set of them so that the objectives of the parent organization will be achieved. This same systematic process can be applied to any area of the organization's business in which choices must be made between competing alternatives. For example, a manufacturing firm can use evaluation–selection techniques to choose which machine to adopt in a part-fabrication process; a trucking firm can use these methods to decide which of several tractors to purchase; a construction firm can select the best subset of a large group of potential projects on which to bid; a hospital can find the best mix of psychiatric, orthopedic, obstetric, pediatric, and other beds for a new wing; or a research lab can choose the set of R & D projects that holds the best promise of reaching a technological goal.

In this chapter we look at the procedures firms use to decide which creative idea to support, which new technology to develop, which repair to authorize. Each project will have different costs, benefits, and risks. Rarely are these known with certainty. In the face of such differences, the selection of one project out of a set is a difficult task. Choosing a number of different projects, a *portfolio,* is even more complex.

This chapter, like Appendixes A and B, may cover a subject not customarily covered in books on project management. Though the project manager often enters the picture at the stage of the project life cycle following selection, in many situations the project manager is the person who has worked and lobbied for the selection of this specific project, particularly if an RFP (Request For Proposal) was involved. Moreover, though project evaluation and selection is usually a task for senior management, this is an important part of the project life cycle because project success is judged by the degree to which the project meets its goals. Since project selection is based on a direct statement of those goals, the project manager needs to know them in order to perform effectively.

In this chapter we discuss several techniques that can be used to help decision makers select projects. Project selection is only one of many decisions associated with project management. To deal with all of these problems, we adopt the use of *decision-aiding models*. We need such models because they abstract the relevant issues about a problem from the welter of detail in which the problem is embedded.

Realists cannot solve problems, only idealists can do that. Reality is far too complex to deal with in its entirety. The reality of this page, for instance, includes the weight of ink imprinted on it as well as the number of atoms in the period at the end of this sentence. Those aspects of reality are not relevant to a decision about the proper width of the left margin or the precise position of the page number. An "idealist" is needed to strip away almost all the reality from a problem, leaving only the aspects of the "real" situation with which he or she wishes to deal. This process of carving away the unwanted reality from the bones of a problem is called *modeling the problem*. The idealized version of the problem that results is called a *model*.

The model represents the problem's *structure*, its form. Every problem has a form, though often we may not understand a problem well enough to describe its structure. Several different types of models are available to make the job of modeling the problem easier. *Iconic* models are physical representations of systems. The category includes everything from teddy bears to the dowel rod and styrofoam model of an atom hanging from the ceiling of a high school chemistry lab. *Analogue* models are similar to reality in some respects and different in others. Traditionally, every student of elementary physics was exposed to the hydraulic analogy to explain electricity. This model emphasized the similarities between water pressure and voltage, between the flow of water and the flow of electrical current, between the reservoir and the capacitor. *Verbal* models use words to describe systems—George Orwell's novel *Animal Farm,* for example. *Diagrammatic* models may be used to explain the hierarchical command structure of an army battalion or a business firm, just as *graphic* models may be used to illustrate the equilibrium solution to problems of supply and demand. We will use all these models in this book, as well as *flow graph* and *network* models to help solve scheduling problems, *matrix* models to aid in project evaluation, and *symbolic* (mathematical) models for a number of purposes.

This wide variety of models allows the decision maker considerable choice. Most problems can be modeled in several different ways, and it is often not difficult to transform a problem from one model to another—the transformation from matrix, to network, to mathematical models, for instance, is usually straightforward. The decision maker usually has some leeway in selecting the model form.

Models may be quite simple to understand, or they may be extremely complex. In general, introducing more reality into a model tends to make the model more difficult to manipulate. If the input data for a model are not known precisely, we often use probabalistic information; that is, the model is said to be *stochastic* rather than *deterministic*. Again, in general, stochastic models are more difficult to manipulate. (Readers who are not familiar with the fundamentals of decision making might find a book such as *The New Science of Management Decisions* [44] useful.) A few of the models we discuss employ mathematical programming techniques for solution. These procedures are rarely used, but they illustrate a logic that can be useful; and it is not necessary to understand mathematical programming to profit from the discussion.

This chapter relies heavily on the use of models for project evaluation and selection. First, we examine fundamental types of project selection models and the characteristics that make any model more or less acceptable. We also discuss the related topics of formal project proposals and contracts. Next, we consider the limitations, strengths, and weaknesses of project selection models, and then hazard a guess about the future of such models.

2.1 CRITERIA FOR PROJECT SELECTION MODELS

We live in the midst of what has been called the "knowledge explosion." We frequently hear such comments as "90 percent of all we know about physics has been discovered since Albert Einstein published his original work on special relativity"; and "80 percent of what we know about the human body has been discovered in the past fifty years." In addition, evidence is cited to show that knowledge is growing exponentially. Such statements emphasize the importance of the *management of change*. To survive, firms must develop strategies for reassessing the use of their resources. Every allocation of resources is an investment in the future. Because of the complex nature of most strategies, many of these investments are in projects.

The proper choice of investment projects is crucial to the long-run survival of every firm. Daily we witness the results of both good and bad investment choices. On the front pages of our newspapers we read about the success or failure of past decisions made by Ashland Oil regarding the maintenance of its fuel storage tanks, by IBM concerning the timing of introducing its PS/2 line of computers, and by General Motors about building and marketing the Cadillac Allante. But can such important choices be made sensibly? Once made, do they ever change, and if so, how? These questions reflect the need for effective selection models.

Within the limits of their capabilities, such models can be used to increase profits, to select investments for limited capital resources, or to improve the competitive position of the organization. They can be used for ongoing evaluation as well as initial selection, and thus are a key to the allocation and reallocation of the organization's scarce resources.

When a firm chooses a project selection model, the following criteria, based on Souder [47], are most important.

1. *Realism*   The model should reflect the reality of the manager's decision situation, including the multiple objectives of both the firm and its managers. Without a common measurement system, direct comparison of different projects is impossible. For example, Project A may strengthen a firm's market share by extending

its facilities, and Project B might improve its competitive position by strengthening its technical staff. Other things being equal, which is better? The model should take into account the realities of the firm's limitations on facilities, capital, personnel, etc. The model should also include factors for risk—both the technical risks of performance, cost, and time and the market risk of customer rejection.

2. *Capability* The model should be sophisticated enough to deal with multiple time periods, simulate various situations both internal and external to the project (e.g., strikes, interest rate changes, etc.), and *optimize* the decision. An optimizing model will make the comparisons that management deems important, consider major risks and constraints on the projects, and then select the best overall project or set of projects.

3. *Flexibility* The model should give valid results within the range of conditions that the firm might experience. It should have the ability to be easily modified, or to be self-adjusting in response to changes in the firm's environment; for example, tax laws change, new technological advancements alter risk levels, and, above all, the organization's goals change.

4. *Ease of Use* *The model should be reasonably convenient, not take a long time to execute, and be easy to use and understand. It should not require special interpretation, data that are hard to acquire, excessive personnel, or unavailable equipment. The model's variables should also relate one to one with those real-world parameters the managers believe significant to the project. Finally, it should be easy to simulate the expected outcomes associated with investments in different project portfolios.*

5. *Cost* Data-gathering and modeling costs should be low relative to the cost of the project and must surely be less than the potential benefits of the project. All costs should be considered, including the costs of data management and of running the model.

2.2 THE NATURE OF THE PROJECT SELECTION MODELS

There are two basic types of project selection models, numeric and nonnumeric. Both are widely used. Many organizations use both at the same time, or they use models that are combinations of the two. Nonnumeric models, as the name implies, do not use numbers as inputs. Numeric models do, but the criteria being measured may be either objective or subjective. It is important to remember that the *qualities* of a project may be represented by numbers, and that *subjective* measures are not necessarily less useful or reliable than so-called *objective* measures. (We will discuss these matters in more detail in Section 2.5.)

Before examining specific kinds of models within the two basic types, let us consider just what we wish the model to do for us, never forgetting two critically important, but often overlooked, facts.

- Models do not make decisions; people do. The manager, not the model, bears responsibility for the decision. The manager may "delegate" the task of making the decision to a model, but the responsibility cannot be abdicated.

- All models, however sophisticated, are only partial representations of the reality they arc meant to reflect. Reality is far too complex for us to capture more than a small fraction of it in any model. Therefore, no model can yield an optimal decision except within its own, possibly inadequate, framework.

We seek a model to assist us in making project selection decisions. This model should possess the characteristics discussed previously: ease of use, flexibility, low cost. Above all, it must evaluate potential projects by the degree to which they will meet the firm's objectives. (In general, we will not differentiate between such terms as *goals, objectives, aims,* etc.) To construct a selection/evaluation model, therefore, it is necessary to develop a list of the firm's objectives.

Such a list should be generated by the organization's top management. It is a direct expression of organizational philosophy and policy. The list should go beyond the typical clichés about "survival" and "maximizing profits," which are certainly real goals but are just as certainly not the only goals of the firm. Others might include maintenance of share of specific markets, development of an improved image with specific clients or competitors, expansion into a new line of business, decrease in sensitivity to business cycles, maintenance of employment for specific categories of workers, and maintenance of system loading at or above some percent of capacity, just to mention a few.

A model of some sort is implied by any conscious decision. The choice between two or more alternative courses of action requires reference to some objective(s), and the choice is thus made in accord with some, possibly subjective, "model."

In the past two or three decades, largely since the development of computers and the establishment of operations research as an academic subject area, the use of formal, numeric models to assist in decision making has expanded. A large majority of such models use financial measures of the "goodness" of a decision. Project selection decisions are no exception, being based primarily on the degree to which the financial goals of the organization are met [25]. As we will see later, this stress on financial goals, largely to the exclusion of other criteria, raises some serious problems for the firm, irrespective of whether the firm is for-profit or not-for-profit.

When the list of objectives has been developed, an additional refinement is recommended. The elements in the list should be weighted. Each item is added to the list because it represents a contribution to the success of the organization, but each item does not make an equal contribution. The weights reflect the different degree of contribution of each element in the set of goals.

Once the list of goals has been developed, one more task remains. A project is selected or rejected because it is predicted to have certain outcomes if implemented. These outcomes are expected to contribute to goal achievement. If the estimated level of goal achievement is sufficiently large, the project is selected. If not, it is rejected. The relationship between the project's expected results and the organization's goals must be understood. In general, the kinds of information required to evaluate a project can be listed under production, marketing, financial, personnel, administrative, and other such categories.

The following is a list of factors that contribute, positively or negatively, to these categories. In order to give focus to this list, we assume that the projects in question involve the possible substitution of a new production process for an existing one. The list is meant to be illustrative. It certainly is not exhaustive.

Production Factors
1. Time until ready to install.
2. Length of disruption during installation.
3. Degree of disruption during installation.
4. Learning curve—time until operating as desired.
5. Effects on waste and rejects.
6. Energy requirements.
7. Facility and other equipment requirements.
8. Safety of process.
9. Other applications of technology.
10. Consistency with current technological knowhow.
11. Change in cost to produce a unit output.
12. Change in time to produce a unit output.
13. Change in raw material usage.
14. Availability of raw materials.
15. Required development time and cost.
16. Impact on current suppliers.
17. Change in quality of output.
18. Change in quality control procedures.

Marketing Factors
1. Size of potential market for output.
2. Probable market share of output.
3. Time until market share is acquired.
4. Impact on current product line.
5. Ability to control quality.
6. Consumer acceptance.
7. Impact on consumer safety.
8. Estimated life of output.
9. Shape of output life cycle curve.
10. Spin-off project possibilities.

Financial Factors
1. Profitability, net present value of the investment.
2. Impact on cash flows.
3. Payout period.
4. Cash requirements.
5. Time until break-even.
6. Size of investment required.
7. Impact on seasonal and cyclical fluctuations.
8. Cost of getting system up to speed.
9. Level of financial risk.

Personnel Factors
1. Training requirements.
2. Labor skill requirements.
3. Availability of required labor skills.
4. Level of resistance from current work force.
5. Other worker reactions.
6. Change in size of labor force.
7. Change in sex, age, or racial distribution of labor force.
8. Inter and intra group communication requirements.
9. Support manpower requirements.
10. Impact on working conditions.

Administrative and Miscellaneous Factors
1. Meet government safety standards.
2. Meet government environmental standards.
3. Impact on information system.
4. Impact on computer usage.
5. Need for consulting help, inside and outside.
6. Reaction of stockholders.
7. Patent and trade secret protection.
8. Impact on image with customers, suppliers, and competitors.
9. Cost of maintaining skill in new technology.
10. Vulnerability to single supplier.
11. Degree to which we understand new technology.
12. Elegance of new process.
13. Degree to which new process differs from current process.
14. Managerial capacity to direct and control new process.

Some factors in this list have a one-time impact and some recur. Some are difficult to estimate and may be subject to considerable error. For these, it is helpful to identify a *range of uncertainty.* In addition, the factors may occur at different times. And some factors may have *thresholds,* critical values above or below which we might wish to reject the project.

Clearly, no single project decision need include all these factors. Not only is the list incomplete, but it contains redundant items. Perhaps more important, the factors are not at the same level of generality: *profitability* and *impact on organizational image* both affect the overall organization, but *impact on working conditions* is more oriented to the production system. Nor are all elements of equal importance. *Change in production cost* is usually considered more important than *impact on computer usage.* Later in this chapter we will deal with the problem of generating an acceptable list of factors and measuring their relative importance.

Although the process of evaluating a potential project is time-consuming and difficult, its importance cannot be overstated. A major consulting firm has argued [27] that the primary cause for the failure of R & D projects is insufficient care in evaluating the proposal before the expenditure of funds. What is true of R & D projects also appears to be true for other kinds of projects. Careful analysis of a potential project is a sine qua non for profitability in the construction business. There are many horror stories [33] about firms that undertook projects for the installation of a computer information system without sufficient analysis of the time, cost, and disruption involved.

Later in this chapter we will consider the problem of conducting an evaluation under conditions of uncertainty about the outcomes associated with a project. Before dealing with this problem, however, it helps to examine several different evaluation–selection models and consider their strengths and weaknesses.

2.3 TYPES OF PROJECT SELECTION MODELS

Of the two basic types of selection models, numeric and nonnumeric, nonnumeric models are older and simpler and have only a few subtypes to consider. We examine them first.

Nonnumeric Models

The Sacred Cow The project is suggested by a senior and powerful official in the organization. Often the project is initiated with a simple comment such as, "If you have the chance, why don't you look into...," and there follows an undeveloped idea for a new product, for the development of a new market, for the installation of a new decision support system, for the adoption of Material Requirements Planning, or for some other project requiring an investment of the firm's resources. The immediate result of this bland statement is the creation of a "project" to investigate whatever the boss has suggested. The project is "sacred" in the sense that it will be maintained until successfully concluded, or until the boss, personally, recognizes the idea as a failure and terminates it.

The Operating Necessity If a flood is threatening the plant, a project to build a protective dike does not require much formal evaluation. Republic Steel Corporation (now a part of LTV Corp.) has used this criterion (and the following criterion also) in evaluating potential projects. If the project is required in order to keep the system operating, the primary question becomes: Is the system worth saving at the estimated cost of the project? If the answer is yes, project costs will be examined to make sure they are kept as low as is consistent with project success, but the project will be funded.

The Competitive Necessity Using this criterion, Republic Steel undertook a major plant rebuilding project in the late 1960s in its steel-bar-manufacturing facilities near Chicago. It had become apparent to Republic's management that the company's bar mill needed modernization if the firm was to maintain its competitive position in the Chicago market area. Although the planning process for the project was quite sophisticated, the decision to undertake the project was based on a desire to maintain the company's competitive position in that market.

Investment in an *operating necessity* project takes precedence over a *competitive necessity* project, but both types of projects may bypass the more careful numeric analysis used for projects deemed to be less urgent or less important to the survival of the firm, or both.

The Product Line Extension A project to develop and distribute new products would be judged on the degree to which it fits the firm's existing product line, fills a gap, strengthens a weak link, or extends the line in a new, desirable direction. Sometimes careful calculations of profitability are not required. Decision makers can act on their beliefs about what will be the likely impact on the total system performance if the new product is added to the line.

Comparative Benefit Model Assume that the firm has many projects to consider, perhaps one or two dozen. Of the several techniques for ordering the projects, the *Q-Sort* [20] is one of the most straightforward. First, the projects are divided into three groups—*good, fair,* and *poor*—according to their relative merits. If any group has more than eight members, it is subdivided into two categories, such as *fair-plus* and *fair-minus*. When all categories have eight or fewer members, the projects within each category are ordered from best to worst. Again, the order is determined on the basis of relative merit. The rater may use specific criteria to rank each project, or may simply use general overall judgment. See Figure 2-1 for an example of a Q-Sort.

Steps	Results at Each Step
1. For each participant in the exercise, assemble a deck of cards, with the name and description of one project on each card. 2. Instruct each participant to divide the deck into two piles, one representing a high priority, the other a low-priority level. (The piles need not be equal.) 3. Instruct each participant to select cards from each pile to form a third pile representing the medium-priority level. 4. Instruct each participant to select cards from the high-level pile to yield another pile representing the very high level of priority; select cards from the low-level pile representing the very low level of priority. 5. Finally, instruct each participant to survey the selections and shift any cards that seem out of place until the classifications are satisfactory.	

Figure 2-1 The Q-sort method.
(Source: Souder, W.E. "Project Evaluation and Selection," in D.I. Cleland, and W.R. King, eds., *Project Management Handbook.* Van Nostrand Reinhold, New York, 1983.)

The process described may be carried out by one person who is responsible for evaluation and selection, or it may be performed by a committee charged with the responsibility. If a committee handles the task, the individual rankings can be developed anonymously, and the set of anonymous rankings can be examined by the committee itself for consensus. It is common for such rankings to differ somewhat from rater to rater, but they do not often vary strikingly because the individuals chosen for such committees rarely differ widely on what they feel to be appropriate for the parent organization. Projects can then be selected in the order of preference, though they are usually evaluated financially before final selection.

The concept of comparative benefits, if not a formal model, is widely adopted for selection decisions on all sorts of projects. Most United Way organizations use the concept to make decisions about which of several social programs to fund. The comparative benefit concept is also commonly used when making funding decisions on fundamental research projects. Organizations such as the National Science Foundation, the Office of Naval Research, and a great many other governmental, private, and university funders of research usually send project proposals to outside experts in the relevant areas who serve as "referees," a process known as *peer review*. The proposal is evaluated according to the referee's technical criteria, and a recommendation is submitted. Senior management of the funding organization then examines all projects with positive recommendations and attempts to construct a portfolio that best fits the organization's aims and its budget.

There are other, similar nonnumeric models for accepting or rejecting projects. Although it is easy to dismiss such models as unscientific, they should not be discounted casually. These models are clearly goal-oriented and directly reflect the primary concerns of the organization. The sacred cow model, in particular, has an added feature; sacred cow projects are visibly supported by "the powers that be." Full support by top management is certainly an important contributor to project success [33]. Without such support, the probability of project success is sharply lowered.

Numeric Models—Profit–Profitability

As noted earlier, a large majority of all firms using project evaluation and selection models use profit–profitability as the sole measure of acceptability. We will consider these models first, and then discuss models that go well beyond the profit test for acceptance.

Payback Period The payback period for a project is the initial fixed investment in the project divided by the estimated annual cash inflows from the project. The ratio of these quantities is the number of years required for the project to repay its initial fixed investment. For example, assume a project costs $100,000 to implement and has annual cash inflows of $25,000. Then

$$\text{Payback period} = \$100,000/\$25,000 = 4 \text{ years}$$

This method assumes that the cash inflows will persist at least long enough to pay back the investment, and it ignores any cash inflows beyond the payback period. The method also serves as an inadequate proxy for risk. The faster the investment is recovered, the less the risk to which it is exposed.

Average Rate of Return Often mistakenly taken to be the reciprocal of the payback period, the average rate of return is the ratio of the average annual profit (either before or after taxes) to the initial or average investment in the project. Because average annual profits are not equivalent to net cash inflows, the average rate of return does not equal the reciprocal of the payback period. Assume, in the example just given, that the average annual profits are $15,000:

$$\text{Average rate of return} = \$15,000/\$100,000 = 0.15$$

Neither of these evaluation methods is recommended for project selection, though payback period is widely used and does have a legitimate value for cash budgeting decisions. The major advantage of these models is their simplicity, but neither takes into account the time value of money. Unless interest rates are extremely low and the rate of inflation is nil, the failure to reduce future cash flows or profits to their present value will result in serious evaluation errors.

Discounted Cash Flow Also referred to as the present value method, the discounted cash flow method determines the net present value of all cash flows by discounting them by the required rate of return (also known as the *hurdle rate, cutoff rate,* and similar terms) as follows,

$$\text{NPV (project)} = A_0 + \sum_{t=1}^{n} \frac{F_t}{(1 + k)^t}$$

where F_t = the net cash flow in period t,
  k = the required rate of return, and
  A_0 = initial cash investment (because this is an outflow, it will be negative).

To include the impact of inflation (or deflation) where p_t is the predicted rate of inflation during period t, we have

$$\text{NPV (project)} = A_0 + \sum_{t=1}^{n} \frac{F_t}{(1 + k + p_t)^t}$$

Early in the life of a project, net cash flow is likely to be negative, the major outflow being the initial investment in the project A_0. If the project is successful, however, cash flows will become positive. The project is *acceptable* if the sum of the net present values of all estimated cash flows over the life of the project is positive. A simple example will suffice. Using our $100,000 investment with a net cash inflow of $25,000 per year for a period of eight years, a required rate of return of 15 percent, and an inflation rate of 3 percent per year, we have

$$\text{NPV (project)} = -\$100,000 + \sum_{t=1}^{8} \frac{\$25,000}{(1 + 0.15 + 0.03)^t}$$
$$= \$101,939$$

Because the present value of the inflows is greater than the present value of the outflow—that is, the net present value is positive—the project is deemed acceptable.

Internal Rate of Return If we have a set of expected cash inflows and cash outflows, the internal rate of return is the discount rate that equates the present values of the two sets of flows. If A_t is an expected cash outflow in the period t and R_t is the expected inflow for the period t, the internal rate of return is the value of k that satisfies the following equation (note that the A_0 will be positive in this formulation of the problem):

$$A_0 + A_1/(1 + k) + A_2/(1 + k)^2 + \cdots + A_n/(1 + k)^n = R_1(1 + k) + R_2(1 + k)^2 + \cdots + R_n(1 + k)^n \quad t = 1,2,3,\cdots,n$$

The value of k is found by trial and error.

Profitability Index Also known as the benefit–cost ratio, the profitability index is the net present value of all future expected cash flows divided by the initial cash investment. If this ratio is greater than 1.0, the project may be accepted.

Other Profitability Models There are a great many variations of the models just described. These variations fall into three general categories: (1) those that subdivide net cash flow into the elements that comprise the net flow, (2) those that include specific terms to introduce risk (or uncertainty, which is treated as risk) into the evaluation, and (3) those that extend the analysis to consider effects that the project might have on other projects or activities in the organization. Two product line extension models, taken from Dean [11], will illustrate these methods.

Pacifico's Method PI is the profitability index of acceptability where

PI $= rdpc \; SP\sqrt{L/C}$,

$r =$ probability of research success,

$d =$ probability of development success, given research success,

$p =$ probability of process success, given development success, and

$c =$ probability of commercial success, given process success.

The investment, C, is the estimated total cost of the R & D effort for the project. Risk is incorporated in the *rdpc* term.

The cash flow is $SP\sqrt{L}$ where

S = estimated average annual sales volume in units of product,

P = estimated average annual profit per unit, and

L = estimated life of the product extension in years. (Note that although the profits are not formally discounted, they are "devalued" over time by multiplying them by $\sqrt{L}$ rather than by L.)

Dean's Profitability Method   Dean's model contains a term that subtracts the unit manufacturing cost and the unit selling and administrative costs from the unit price, multiplies the remainder by the expected number of units sold per year, and then subtracts tooling and development costs (a project risk factor is also included). All costs and revenues are time-indexed and discounted to the present. Dean modifies his model to deal with three distinct cases: (1) where the product extension has no significant impact on the existing system, (2) where the product extension may affect the profitability or the sales of existing products, or both, and (3) where the product extension is a replacement for an existing product.

Several comments are in order about all the profit–profitability numeric models. First, let us consider their advantages.

1. The undiscounted models are simple to use and understand.
2. All use readily available accounting data to determine the cash flows.
3. Model output is in terms familiar to business decision makers.
4. With a few exceptions, model output is on an "absolute" profit–profitability scale and allows "absolute" go/no-go decisions.
5. Some profit models account for project risk.
6. Dean's model incorporates the impact of the project on the rest of the organization.

The disadvantages of these models are the following.

1. These models ignore all nonmonetary factors except risk.
2. Models that do not include discounting ignore the timing of the cash flows and the time value of money.
3. Models that reduce cash flows to their present value are strongly biased toward the short run.
4. Payback-type models ignore cash flows beyond the payback period.
5. All are sensitive to errors in the input data for the early years of the project.
6. All discounting models are nonlinear, and the effects of changes (or errors) in the variables or parameters are generally not obvious to most decision makers.
7. Those models incorporating the risks of research and/or development and/or process (the commercial success risk factor is excluded from this comment) mislead the decision maker. It is not so much that the research–development–process success is risky as it is that the time and cost required to ensure project success is uncertain. The application of these risk terms applies mainly to R & D projects.
8. Some models, Dean's and Pacifico's, for example, are oriented only toward evaluation of projects that result in new products.
9. All these models depend for input on a determination of cash flows, but it is not

clear exactly how the concept of cash flow is properly defined for the purpose of evaluating projects. (This problem is discussed later in this chapter.)

A complete discussion of profit–profitability models can be found in any standard work on financial management—see [54], for example. In general, the net present value models are preferred to the internal rate of return models. They rest on a more sensible and conservative assumption: namely, that earnings from the project can be reinvested at whatever rate of interest is used to discount the cash flows. Internal rate of return models assume that project earnings can be reinvested at whatever rate equates the present values of inflows with outflows.

Numeric Models—Scoring

In an attempt to overcome some of the disadvantages of profitability models, particularly their focus on a single decision criterion, a number of evaluation–selection models that use multiple criteria to evaluate a project have been developed. Such models vary widely in their complexity and information requirements. The examples discussed illustrate some of the different types.

Unweighted 0–1 Factor Model A set of relevant factors is selected by management. These are usually listed in a preprinted form, and one or more raters score the project on each factor depending on whether or not it qualifies for that individual criterion. The raters are chosen by senior management, for the most part from the rolls of senior management. The criteria for choice are a clear understanding of organizational goals and a good knowledge of the firm's potential project *portfolio*. Figure 2-2 shows an example of the rating sheet for an unweighted, 0–1 factor model.

The columns of Figure 2-2 are summed and those projects with a sufficient number of qualifying factors may be selected. The main advantage of such a model is that it uses several criteria in the decision process. The major disadvantages are that it assumes all criteria are of equal importance and it allows for no gradation of the degree to which a specific project meets the various criteria.

Unweighted Factor Scoring Model The second disadvantage of the 0–1 factor model can be dealt with by constructing a simple linear measure of the degree to which the project being evaluated meets each of the criteria contained in the list. The *x* marks in Figure 2-2 would be replaced by numbers. Often a five-point scale is used, where 5 is very good, 4 is good, 3 is fair, 2 is poor, 1 is very poor. (Three-, seven-, and ten-point scales are also common.) The second column of Figure 2-2 would not be needed. The column of scores is summed, and those projects with a total score exceeding some critical value are selected. A variant of this selection process might select the highest-scoring projects (still assuming they are all above some critical score) until the estimated costs of the set of projects equaled the resource limit. The criticism that the criteria are all assumed to be of equal importance still holds.

The use of a discrete numeric scale to represent the degree to which a criterion is satisfied is widely accepted. To construct such measures for project evalua-

Project _____

Rater _____ Date _____

	Qualifies	Does Not Qualify
No increase in energy requirements	x	
Potential market size, dollars	x	
Potential market share, percent	x	
No new facility required	x	
No new technical expertise required		x
No decrease in quality of final product	x	
Ability to manage project with current personnel		x
No requirement for reorganization	x	
Impact on work force safety	x	
Impact on environmental standards	x	
Profitability		
Rate of return more than 15% after tax	x	
Estimated annual profits more than $100,000	x	
Time to break-even less than 3 years	x	
Need for external consultants		x
Consistency with current lines of business		x
Impact on company image		
With customers	x	
With our industry		x
Totals	12	5

Figure 2-2 Sample project evaluation form.

tion, we proceed in the following manner. Select a criterion, say, "estimated annual profits in dollars." For this criterion, determine five ranges of performance so that a typical project, chosen at random, would have a roughly equal chance of being in any one of the five performance ranges. (Another way of describing this condition is: Take a large number of projects that were selected for support in the past, regardless of whether they were actually successful or not, and create five levels of predicted performance so that about one-fifth of the projects fall into each level.) This procedure will usually create unequal ranges, which may offend our sense of symmetry but need not concern us otherwise. It ensures that each criterion performance measure utilizes the full scale of possible values, a desirable characteristic for performance measures.

Consider the following two simple examples. Using the criterion just mentioned, "estimated annual profits in dollars," we might construct the following scale:

Score	Performance Level
5	Above $1,100,000
4	$750,001 to $1,100,000
3	$500,001 to $750,000
2	$200,000 to $500,000
1	Less than $200,000

As suggested, these ranges might have been chosen so that about 20 percent of the projects considered for funding would fall into each of the five ranges.

The criterion "no decrease in quality of the final product" would have to be restated to be scored on a five-point scale, perhaps as follows:

Score	Performance Level
	The quality of the final product is
5	significantly and visibly improved
4	significantly improved, but not visible to buyer
3	not significantly changed
2	significantly lowered, but not visible to buyer
1	significantly and visibly lowered

This scale is an example of scoring cells that represent opinion rather than objective (even if "estimated") fact, as was the case in the profit scale.

Weighted Factor Scoring Model When numeric weights reflecting the relative importance of each individual factor are added, we have a weighted factor scoring model. In general, it takes the form

$$S_i = \sum_{j=1}^{n} s_{ij} w_j \qquad j = 1,2,3,...,n$$

where S_i = the total score of the ith project,
s_{ij} = the score of the ith project on the jth criterion, and
w_j = the weight of the jth criterion.

The weights w_j may be generated by any technique that is acceptable to the organization's policy makers. (The Delphi technique is both effective and acceptable.) When numeric weights have been generated, it is helpful (but not necessary) to scale the weights so that

$$0 \leq w_j \leq 1 \qquad j = 1,2,3,...,n$$

$$\sum_{j=1}^{n} w_j = 1$$

The weight of each criterion can be interpreted as the "percent of the total weight accorded to that particular criterion."

A special caveat is in order. It is quite possible with this type of model to include a large number of criteria. It is not particularly difficult to develop scoring scales and weights, and the ease of gathering and processing the required information makes it tempting to include marginally relevant criteria along with the obviously important items. Resist this temptation! After the important factors have been weighted, there usually is little residual weight to be distributed among the remaining elements. The result is that the evaluation is simply insensitive to major differences in the scores on trivial criteria. A good rule of thumb is to discard elements with weights less than 0.02 or 0.03. (If elements are discarded, and if you wish $\sum w_j = 1$, the weights must be rescaled to 1.0.) Figure 2-3 shows an example of an elaborate weighted scoring model. It has so many parts that the final value rating of a project is not very sensitive to most of the individual elements in the model. (Figure 2-3 shows only a portion of the model.)

It is useful to note that if one uses a weighted scoring model to aid in project selection, the model can also serve as an aid to project improvement. For any given criterion, the difference between a project's score and the highest possible score on that criterion, multiplied by the weight of the criterion, is a measure of the potential improvement in the project score that would result were the project's performance on that criterion sufficiently improved. It may be that such improvement is not feasible, or is more costly than the improvement warrants. On the other hand, such an analysis of each project yields a valuable statement of the comparative benefits of project improvements. In Chapter 13 we will use this kind of analysis to help decide whether or not to terminate a project.

Viewing a project in this way is a type of *sensitivity analysis*. We examine the degree to which a project's score is sensitive to attempts to improve it—usually by adding resources. We will use sensitivity analysis several times in this book. It is a powerful managerial technique.

Constrained Weighted Factor Scoring Model   The temptation to include marginal criteria can be partially overcome by allowing additional criteria to enter the model as constraints rather than weighted factors. These constraints represent project characteristics that *must* be present or absent in order for the project to be acceptable. In the example concerning the quality of the final product, we might have specified that we would not undertake any project that would significantly lower the quality of the final product (visible to the buyer or not).

We would amend the weighted scoring model to take the form:

$$S_i = \sum_{j=1}^{n} s_{ij} w_j \prod_{k=1}^{l} c_{ik}$$

where $c_{ik} = 1$ if the ith project satisfies the kth constraint, and 0 if it does not. Other elements in the model are as defined earlier.

Although this model is analytically tidy, in practice we would not bother to evaluate projects that are so unsuitable in some ways that we would not consider supporting them regardless of their expected performance against other criteria. For example, except under extraordinary circumstances, Procter & Gamble would not consider a project for adding a new consumer product or product line

- that cannot be marketed nationally,
- that cannot be distributed through mass outlets (grocery stores, drugstores),
- that will not generate gross revenues in excess of $ _____ million,
- for which Procter & Gamble's potential market share is not at least 50 percent,
- that does not utilize Procter & Gamble's scientific expertise, manufacturing expertise, advertising expertise, or packaging and distribution expertise.

PROGRAM EVALUATION

FACTOR A DEVELOPMENT EFFORT CONSIDERATIONS							
	0	1	2	3	ASSIGNED VALUES	WEIGHTING FACTOR	WEIGHTED VALUE
(1) TOTAL EXPECTED DEV. FUNDING TO	< 200K	200 - 800K	800K - 2M	> 2M		8	
(2) EXPECTED AVERAGE ANNUAL FUNDING	< 50K	50 - 150K	150 - 500K	> 500K		10	
(3) TIME TO REACH PRODUCTION STAGE	> 8 YRS	5 - 8 YRS	2 - 5 YRS	< 2 YRS		5	
(4) PRE-CONTRACT COST, FROM THIS DATE *	> 20%	10 - 20%	5 - 10%	< 5%		3	
(5) POST-CONTRACT G & A RELATED COST (ANNUAL) *	> 5%	2 - 5%	0 - 2%	0		3	
(6) CAPITAL EQUIPMENT FOR DEVELOPMENT (ONE TIME) *	> 10%	5 - 10%	0 - 5%	0		3	
(7) PROBABILITY OF SOLE SOURCE CONTRACT	0%	< 25%	25 - 75%	> 75%		2	
(8) PROBABILITY OF BEING SOLE DEVELOPER	0%	< 25%	25 - 75%	> 75%		1	
(9) CONTRACT % OF NORMAL ANNUAL FUNDING IN AREA	> 100%	~100%	< 50%	< 20%		1	
(10) RISK OF OVERRUN	EXCELLENT	GOOD	FAIR	POOR		1	

* OF EXPECTED AVERAGE ANNUAL FUNDING . . . . (2)

AVERAGE (TOTAL ÷ 37) ____

PROBABILITY OF SUCCESSFUL DEVELOPMENT, I.E., ACTUALLY ACHIEVING THE PRODUCTION STAGE, MODIFY AVERAGE BY APPROPRIATE MULTIPLYING FACTOR FROM A'

FACTOR WEIGHT 0.3

FACTOR VALUE ____

FACTOR A' PROBABILITY OF SUCCESSFUL DEVELOPMENT							
	0	1	2	3	ASSIGNED VALUES	WEIGHTING FACTOR	WEIGHTED VALUE
(1) POTENTIAL PERFORMANCE OF TRW DEVICE	MARGINAL	FAIR	GOOD	OUTSTANDING		1	
(2) PERFORMANCE FLEXIBILITY	LIMITED	FAIR	GOOD	WIDE		1	
(3) RELIABILITY (AS SEEN BY CUSTOMER)	LOW	FAIR	GOOD	EXCELLENT		5	
(4) SAFETY OF ULTIMATE DEVICE (AS SEEN BY CUSTOMER)	LOW	FAIR	GOOD	EXCELLENT		3	
(5) COMPLEXITY (AS SEEN BY CUSTOMER)	VERY HIGH	HIGH	MEDIUM	LOW		5	
(6) DEVELOPMENT EASE	VERY DIFFICULT	DIFFICULT	MEDIUM	EASY		1	
(7) UNKNOWNS	MANY	SOME	FEW	NONE		3	
(8) SOUNDNESS OF TECHNICAL APPROACH	POOR	FAIR	GOOD	EXCELLENT		3	
(9) TECHNOLOGY ADVANCES AMONG COMPETITORS	POOR	FAIR	GOOD	EXCELLENT		1	
(10) OPEN LITERATURE PUBLICATIONS AVAILABLE	POOR	FAIR	GOOD	EXCELLENT		1	
(11) POSSIBILITY OF BREAK THROUGHS	POOR	FAIR	GOOD	EXCELLENT		1	
(12) NECESSITY OF BREAK THROUGH TO ACHIEVE SUCCESS	HIGH	MEDIUM	LOW	NONE		3	
(13) SEVERITY OF MATERIALS PROBLEM	HIGH	MEDIUM	LOW	NONE		1	
(14) DEPENDENCE ON COMPONENTS SUPPLIED BY VENDORS	HIGH	MEDIUM	LOW	NONE		1	
(15) HAZARDOUS TESTING REQUIRED	CONSIDERABLE	SOME	LITTLE	NONE		1	
(16) TECHNICAL PERFORMANCE ON SIMILAR CONTRACTS	POOR	FAIR	GOOD	EXCELLENT		1	

AVERAGE (TOTAL ÷ 32) ____

FACTOR A' VALUE (AVERAGE ÷ 2) ____

Figure 2-3

IV

FACTOR C
GROWTH CONSIDERATIONS

		0	1	2	3	ASSIGNED VALUES	WEIGHTING FACTOR	WEIGHTED VALUE
(1)	DEGREE WHICH WORK RELATES TO OTHER PROG.	POOR	FAIR	GOOD	EXCELLENT		1	
(2)	POSSIBILITIES OF ACHIEVING TECH. BREAKTHROUGH (I.E., ADVANCE STATE-OF-THE-ART)	POOR	FAIR	GOOD	EXCELLENT		1	
(3)	COMMERCIAL POSSIBILITIES	POOR	FAIR	GOOD	EXCELLENT		2	
(4)	PROBABILITY OF EXPANSION OF PROGRAM (FOLLOW ON CONTRACTS)	POOR	FAIR	GOOD	EXCELLENT		1	
(5)	PROBABILITY OF LEADING TO OTHER CONTRACTS (FOR SIMILAR CONCEPT OR DEVICE)	POOR	FAIR	GOOD	EXCELLENT		1	
(6)	PROBABILITY OF LEADING TO RESEARCH CONTRACTS	POOR	FAIR	GOOD	EXCELLENT		1	

AVERAGE (TOTAL ÷ 7) _____

FACTOR WEIGHT   0.1

FACTOR VALUE _____

V

FACTOR D
CUSTOMER CONSIDERATIONS

		0	1	2	3	ASSIGNED VALUES	WEIGHTING FACTOR	WEIGHTED VALUE
(1)	WRITTEN OR ORAL PROPOSAL REQUEST	NONE	MORE THAN 1 YR AWAY	WITHIN 1 YR	DEFINITE		10	
(2)	CUSTOMER'S PRIORITY FOR DEVICE	LOW	AVERAGE	HIGH	VERY HIGH		3	
(3)	OUR KNOWLEDGE OF CUSTOMER	NONE	FAIR	GOOD	EXCELLENT		1	
(4)	OUR RAPPORT WITH CUSTOMER	NONE-POOR	FAIR	GOOD	EXCELLENT		3	
(5)	EFFECTS ON OTHER CUSTOMERS	POOR	FAIR	GOOD	EXCELLENT		1	
(6)	PROMOTIONAL HELP AVAILABLE FROM OTHER CUSTOMERS (GOVERNMENT)	NONE	FAIR	GOOD	EXCELLENT		1	
(7)	REPUTATION IN THIS AREA	NONE-POOR	FAIR	GOOD	EXCELLENT		3	
(8)	CURRENT CONTRACTS WITH SAME CUSTOMER	MORE THAN OUR SHARE	NONE	EQUAL TO OUR SHARE	LESS THAN OUR SHARE		3	
(9)	CUSTOMER PERSONALITY BIASES	UN-FAVOR-ABLE	NONE	FAVOR-ABLE	VERY FAVOR-ABLE		2	

AVERAGE (TOTAL ÷ 27) _____

FACTOR WEIGHT   0.1

FACTOR VALUE _____

VI

FACTOR E
INTERNAL CONSIDERATIONS

		0	1	2	3	ASSIGNED VALUES	WEIGHTING FACTOR	WEIGHTED VALUE
(1)	PRESENT MANAGEMENT INTEREST IN AREA	NONE	FAIR	GOOD	EXCELLENT		2	
(2)	PRESENT PENETRATION IN AREA	NONE	FAIR	GOOD	EXCELLENT		2	
(3)	G 2 CAPABILITY IN THIS AREA	NONE	FAIR	GOOD	EXCELLENT		1	
(4)	RELATION OF WORK TO PRESENT CAPABILITY	POOR	FAIR	GOOD	EXCELLENT		2	
(5)	AVAILABILITY OF SUITABLE PERSONNEL	POOR	FAIR	GOOD	EXCELLENT		1	
(6)	PERSONNEL STAFFING PROBLEMS	GREAT	SOME	LITTLE	NONE		1	
(7)	PATENT POSSIBILITIES	NONE	FAIR	GOOD	EXCELLENT		1	
(8)	DEGREE COMPETITION ALSO CUSTOMERS	HIGH	SIGNIFI-CANT	LITTLE	NONE		1	
(9)	NUMBER OF COMPETING COMPANIES	> 4	3 - 4	1 - 2	NONE		1	
(10)	CAPIBILITY OF COMPETITION	EXCELLENT	GOOD	FAIR	POOR		1	
(11)	% OF DEVELOPMENT TO BE DONE BY	40%	60%	80%	100%		1	

AVERAGE (TOTAL ÷ 14) _____

FACTOR WEIGHT   0.1

FACTOR VALUE _____

MERIT VALUE _____	MERIT VALUE _____	MERIT VALUE _____	MERIT VALUE _____
ASSOC. G & A _____	ASSOC. G & A _____	ASSOC. G & A _____	ASSOC. G & A _____
MERIT VALUE _____	MERIT VALUE _____	MERIT VALUE _____	MERIT VALUE _____
ASSOC. G & A _____	ASSOC. G & A _____	ASSOC. G & A _____	ASSOC. G & A _____

Figure 2-3   (Continued)

DATE

P₁ — PROBABILITY THAT A PROGRAM WILL BE FUNDED

BOX	VALUE	FACTOR	0%	10	20	30	40	50	60	70	80	90	100	ASSIGNED VALUE	WEIGHTING FACTOR	WEIGHTED VALUE
I		(1) STATUS OF THE CUSTOMER'S REQUIREMENT FOR THE END PRODUCT	WE HAVE A CONCEPT CUSTOMER NOT YET READY		FEAS. REP ISSUED, OR, NONE REC'D NEED FOR DEV. OBVIOUS	FEASIBILITY STUDY UNDERWAY		FEAS STUDY COMPLETED RESULTS FAVORABLE			HARDWARE REP IN PREPARATION		DEV. HARD WARE REP ISSUED		0.4	
III		(2) STATUS OF DEMON-STRATION OF FEASIBILITY	NONE ACCOMPLISHED		ACCOMPLISHED TO SOME EXTENT			SATISFIED - CUSTOMER IS NOT					CUSTOMER IS COMPLETELY SATISFIED		0.2	
IV		(3) AVAILABILITY OF CUSTOMER FUNDS	FUNDS ARE NEITHER AVAILABLE NOR FORESEEN		CUSTOMER SEEKING FUNDS OR PROBABILITY GOOD		CONCLUSIVELY ALLOCATED FOR A FEAS STUDY	FEAS STUDY FUNDS BEING SPENT NOW					CONCLUSIVELY ALLOCATED FOR A HARD. DEV. PROG.		0.2	

TOTAL _____

P₂ — PROBABILITY THAT WE WILL BEAT THE COMPETITION

BOX	VALUE	FACTOR	0%	10	20	30	40	50	60	70	80	90	100	ASSIGNED VALUE	WEIGHTING FACTOR	WEIGHTED VALUE
V		(4) COMPE-TITION	FOUR OR MORE, ALL OF TOP QUALITY	WIRING APPARENT	TWO OR THREE OF TOP QUALITY		ONE OF TOP QUALITY		NONE OF OUR CALIBER				NONE		0.3	
VI		(5) TECHNICAL CONCEPT AND ASSOCIATED BACKGROUND	INADEQUATE		MARGINAL TO US		ADEQUATE TO US BUT NOT TO CUSTOMER		ADEQUATE IN EYES OF CUSTOMER		GOOD IN EYES OF CUSTOMER		OUTSTANDING IN EYES OF CUSTOMER		0.4	
VALUE		(6) PROMOTION	POOR RAPPORT WITH CUSTOMER		MARGINAL RAPPORT WITH CUSTOMER			CUSTOMER NOT KNOWN WELL, NO KNOWN OBSTACLES		GOOD RAPPORT WITH CUSTOMER			EXCELLENT RAPPORT WITH CUSTOMER		0.1	
		(7) CUSTOMER BIASES	HIGHLY UNFAVORABLE		MARGINALLY UNFAVORABLE			NEUTRAL		FAVORABLE			HIGHLY FAVORABLE		0.1	

TOTAL _____

(P₁) EFFECT OF G & A DOLLARS ON WIN PROBABILITY

G & A	$ OK	K	K	K	K	K	PROPOSED ASSIGNED VALUE	WEIGHTING FACTOR	WEIGHTED VALUE
FACTOR 1								0.4	
FACTOR 2								0.2	
FACTOR 3								0.2	

(P₁) FOR PROPOSED G & A EXPENDITURE OF ____ K - _____

(P₁) AT PRESENT - "O"K _____

(P₂) EFFECT OF G & A DOLLARS ON WIN PROBABILITY

								WEIGHTING FACTOR	
FACTOR 4								0.3	
FACTOR 5								0.4	
FACTOR 6								0.1	
FACTOR 7								0.1	

(P₂) FOR PROPOSED G & A EXPENDITURE OF ____ K - _____

(P₂) AT PRESENT - "O"K _____

WIN PROBABILITY (AT PRESENT TIME)

$P_1 \times P_2 = ($ _____ $)($ _____ $) = $ [_____]

WIN PROBABILITY (WITH G & A = ____ K)

$P_1 \times P_2 = ($ _____ $)($ _____ $) = $ [_____]

G & A DOLLARS

WIN PROBABILITY

Figure 2-3 (Continued)

Again, a caveat is in order. Exercise care when adopting constraints. It may seem obvious that we should not consider any project if it has no reasonable assurance of long-run profitability. But such a constraint can force us to overlook a project that, though unprofitable itself, might have a strong, positive impact on the profitability of other projects in which we are interested.

Dean and Nishry's Model Beginning with the weighted factor scoring model, Dean and Nishry [11] cast the project selection decision in the form of an integer programming problem. In the problem

$$S_t = \sum_{j=1}^{n} w_j s_{ij}$$

$$\max x_i \left\{ \sum_{i=1}^{n} x_i S_i \right\}$$

are given so that

$$x_i = 0 \text{ or } 1$$

and

$$\sum_{i=1}^{n} x_i m_i \leq M$$

where m_i is the resource (manpower, capital, etc.) requirement for the ith project, and M is the total amount of the resource available for use. The value of $x_i = 0$ or 1 depends on whether or not the ith project is selected.

In essence, the Dean and Nishry approach selects the highest-scoring project candidates from the scoring model, and selects them one after another until the available resources have been depleted. If there are several scarce resources, the selection problem can be recast and solved by dynamic programming methods. There are several other R & D project evaluation–selection models described in this excellent work [11]. Many are adaptable to a wide variety of project types.

Goal Programming with Multiple Objectives Goal programming is a variation of the general linear programming method that can optimize an objective function with multiple objectives. In order to apply this method to project selection, we adopt a linear, 0–1 goal program.

First, establish a set of objectives such as "maximize equipment utilization," "minimize idle labor crews," "maximize profits," and "satisfy investment budget constraints." Alternative sets of projects are adopted or rejected based on their impact on goal achievement. A detailed discussion of goal programming is beyond the scope of this book. The interested reader should consult any modern text on management science, for example, [51].

Because most real-world problems are too large for analytic solutions, heuristic solutions are necessary. Ignizio [23, pp. 202–206] has developed a heuristic approach that is easily applied to project selection.

As was the case with profitability models, scoring models have their own characteristic advantages and disadvantages. These are the advantages.

1. These models allow multiple criteria to be used for evaluation and decision. They can include profit–profitability models and both tangible and intangible criteria.
2. They are structurally simple and therefore easy to understand and use.
3. They are a direct reflection of managerial policy.
4. They are easily altered to accommodate changes in the environment or managerial policy.
5. Weighted scoring models allow for the fact that some criteria are more important than others.
6. These models allow easy sensitivity analysis. The trade-offs between the several criteria are readily observable.

The disadvantages are the following.

1. The output of a scoring model is strictly a relative measure. Project scores do not represent the value or "utility" associated with a project and thus do not directly indicate whether or not the project should be supported.
2. In general, scoring models are linear in form and the elements of such models are assumed to be independent.
3. The ease of use of these models is conducive to the inclusion of a large number of criteria, most of which have such small weights that they have little impact on the total project score.
4. Unweighted scoring models assume all criteria are of equal importance, which is almost certainly contrary to fact.
5. To the extent that profit–profitability is included as an element in the scoring model, this element has the advantages and disadvantages noted earlier for the profitability models themselves.

The type of model picked to aid the evaluation–selection process depends on the philosophy and wishes of management. Liberatore and Titus [25] conducted a survey of 40 high-level staff persons from 29 Fortune 500 firms. Eighty percent of their respondents report the use of one or more financial models for R & D project decision making. Although their sample is small and nonrandom, their findings are quite consistent with the present authors' experience. None of the respondent firms used mathematical programming techniques for project selection or resource allocation.

We favor scoring models for three fundamental reasons. First, they allow the multiple objectives of all organizations to be reflected in the important decision about which projects will be supported and which will be rejected. Second, scoring models are easily adapted to changes in managerial philosophy or changes in the environment. Third, they do not suffer from the bias toward the short run that is inherent in profitability models that discount future cash flows. This is not a prejudice against discounting per se, but rather an argument against the exclusion of nonfinancial factors that may require a longer-run view of the costs and benefits of a project. For a powerful statement of this point, see [19].

It is also interesting to note that Liberatore and Titus found that firms with a significant amount of contract research funded from outside the organization used scoring models for project screening much more frequently than firms with negligible levels of outside funding. It was also found that firms with significant levels of outside funding were much less likely to use a payback period [25, p. 969].

2.4 ANALYSIS UNDER HIGH UNCERTAINTY

At times an organization may wish to evaluate a project about which there is little information. Research and development projects sometimes fall into this general class. But even in the comparative mysteries of research and development activities, the level of uncertainty about the outcomes of R & D is not beyond analysis. As we noted when discussing Dean's profitability model, there is actually not much uncertainty about whether a product, process, or service can be developed, but there can be considerable uncertainty about *when* it will be developed and at what cost.

As they are with R & D projects, time and cost are also often uncertain in other types of projects. When the organization undertakes projects in which it has little or no recent experience—for example, the installation of a new computer, investment in an unfamiliar business, engaging in international trade, and a myriad of other projects common enough to organizations in general but uncommon to any single organization—there are three distinct areas of uncertainty. First, there is uncertainty about the timing of the project and the cash flows it is expected to generate. Second, though not as common as generally believed, there may be uncertainty about the direct outcomes of the project—that is, what it will accomplish. Third, there is uncertainty about the side effects of the project, its unforeseen consequences.

Typically, we try to reduce such uncertainty by the preparation of *pro forma* documents. *Pro forma* profit and loss statements and break-even charts are examples of such documents. The results, however, are not very satisfactory unless the amount of uncertainty is reflected in the data that go into the documents. When relationships between inputs and outputs in the projects are complex, Monte Carlo simulation can handle such uncertainty by exposing the many possible consequences of embarking on a project. *Risk analysis* is a method based on such a procedure.

Risk Analysis

The term risk analysis is generally credited to David Hertz in his classic *Harvard Business Review* article, "Risk Analysis in Capital Investment" [21]. The principal contribution of this procedure is to focus the decision maker's attention on understanding the nature and extent of the uncertainty associated with some variables used in a decision-making process. Although the method can be used with almost any kind of variable and decision problem, risk analysis is usually understood to use financial measures in determining the desirability of an investment project.

Hertz [22] differentiates risk analysis from both traditional financial analysis and more general decision analysis with the diagrams in Figure 2-4.

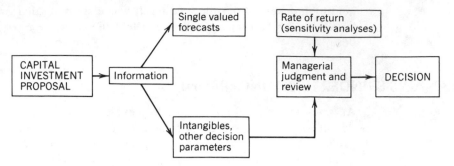

Figure 2-4a

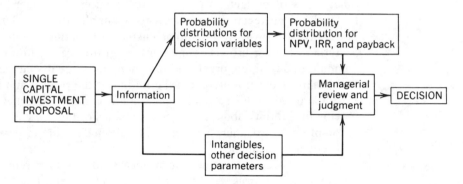

Figure 2-4b

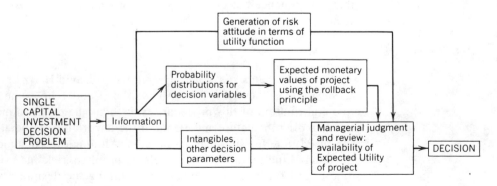

Figure 2-4c

(*Source:* Hertz, D. B., and H. Thomas, *Risk Analysis and Its Applications,* Wiley, New York, 1983.)

Figure 2-4a illustrates traditional financial analysis, Figure 2-4b risk analysis. The primary difference is that risk analysis incorporates uncertainty in the decision input data. Instead of point estimates of the variables, probability distributions are determined or subjectively estimated for each of the "uncertain" variables. With such inputs, the probability distribution for the rate of return (or NPV) is then usually found by simulation. The decision maker not only has probabilistic information about the rate of return and future cash flows but also gains knowledge about the *variability* of such estimates as measured by the standard deviation of the financial returns. Both the expectation and its variability are important decision criteria in the evaluation of the project.

When most managers refer to risk analysis, they are usually speaking of what Hertz and Thomas call "decision analysis." As Figure 2-4c shows, for decision analysis the manager's "utility function" for money must be determined. If the decision maker is seeking a decision that achieves several different objectives simultaneously, this method (utilizing a weighted factor scoring model, for example, rather than simulation) would be appropriate.

This approach is useful for a wide range of project-related decisions. For example, simulation risk analysis was used to select the best method of moving a computer to a new facility [50]. The major task elements and their required sequences were identified. Cost and time distributions were then programmed for analysis and a computer run of 2,000 trials was made, simulating various failures and variations in cost and time for each of three methods of moving the computer. A cost–probability distribution was constructed (see Figure 2-5) to help identify the lowest-cost alternative and also the alternative with the lowest risk

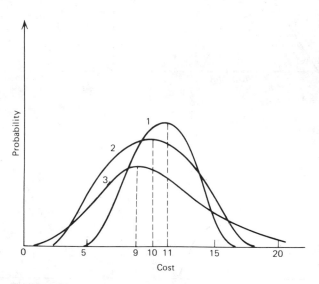

Figure 2-5 Probability density for three alternatives. *Note:* Alternative 3 has the lowest mean, but alternative 1 has a smaller variance.

of a high cost, alternatives that are often not the same. As seen in the illustration, alternative 3 has the lowest expected cost (of 9) but also has the highest likelihood for a cost of 18 or more.

A public utility faced with deciding between several R & D projects [15] used four separate cost-related distributions in a risk analysis simulation (Figure 2-6). (Total wage costs required two separate distributions, as shown in the figure.) The distributions were then combined to generate the distribution of a cost over-run for each potential project. In addition, sensitivity analysis was conducted to determine the effect of court rulings and specific task failures on project costs. High-risk projects were identified in this way, and tasks that posed high risk could then be monitored with tight managerial controls. Following the cost analysis, project schedules were analyzed in the same way. Finally, time and cost analyses were combined to determine interactions and overall project effects.

General Simulation Analysis

Simulation combined with sensitivity analysis is also useful for evaluating R & D projects while they are still in the conceptual stage. Using the net present

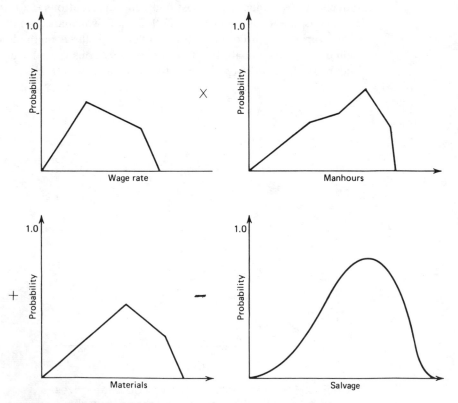

Figure 2-6 Probability distributions for elements of project cost for a utility.

value approach, for example, we would support an R & D project if the net present value of the cash flows (including the initial cash investment) is positive and represents the best available alternative use of the funds. When these flows are estimated for purposes of the analyses, it is well to avoid the *full-cost* philosophy that is usually adopted. The full-cost approach to estimating cash flows forces the inclusion of arbitrarily determined overheads in the calculation—overheads which, by definition, are not affected by the change in product or process and thus are not relevant to the decision. The only relevant costs are those that will be changed by the implementation of the new process or product.

The determination of such costs is not simple. If the concept being considered involves a new process, it is necessary to go to the detailed *route sheet,* or *operations sequence sheet,* describing the operation in which the new process would be used. Proceeding systematically through the operating sequence step by step, one asks whether the present time and cost required for this step are likely to be altered if the new process concept is installed. If and only if the answer is yes, three estimates (optimistic, most likely, and pessimistic) are made of the size of the expected change. These individual estimated changes in the production cost and time, together with upstream or downstream time and cost changes that might also result (e.g., a production method change on a part might also alter the cost of inspecting the final product), are used to generate the required cash flow information—presuming that the time savings have been properly costed. This estimation process will be explained in detail in Chapter 8.

The analysis gives a picture of the proposed change in terms of the costs and times that will be affected. The uncertainty associated with each individual element of the process is included. Simulation runs will then indicate the likelihood of achieving various levels of savings. Note also that investigation of the simulation model will expose the major sources of uncertainty in the final cost distributions. If the project itself is near the margin of acceptability, the uncertainty may be reduced by doing some preliminary research aimed at reducing uncertainty in the areas of project cost estimation where it was highest. This preliminary research can be subjected to a cost–benefit analysis when the benefit is reduced uncertainty. For an example of such an approach, see [31].

2.5 COMMENTS ON THE INFORMATION BASE FOR EVALUATION-SELECTION

The proper input data for the project evaluation-selection decision are whatever is required by the model chosen for use. A number of potentially useful criteria were listed earlier. Many of the information needs can be satisfied by the accounting system. The accounting system is carefully designed to prepare data on a consistent basis, to keep them for reasonable periods of time, and to make them available when needed. But accounting data may not be what they appear, and careful interpretation of such data is required.

The remainder of this section deals with three special problems affecting the data used in project selection models.

Comments on Accounting Data

Whether managers are familiar with accounting systems or not, they can find it useful to reflect on the methods and assumptions used in the preparation of accounting data. Among the more crucial are the following.

1. Accountants live in a linear world. With few exceptions, cost and revenue data are assumed to vary linearly with associated changes in inputs and outputs.
2. The accounting system often provides cost–revenue information that is derived from standard cost analyses and equally standardized assumptions regarding revenues. These standards may or may not be accurate representations of the cost–revenue structure of the physical system they purport to represent.
3. As noted in the previous section, the data furnished by the accounting system may or may not include overhead costs. In most cases, the decision maker is concerned solely with cost–revenue elements that will be changed as a result of the project under consideration. Incremental analysis is called for, and great care must be exercised when using *pro forma* data in decision problems. Remember that the assignment of overhead cost is always arbitrary. The accounting system is the richest source of information in the organization, and it should be used—but with great care and understanding.

Comment on Measurements

It is common for those who oppose a project, for whatever reason, to complain that information supporting the project is "subjective." This epithet appears to mean that the data are false, biased, and have as their source the unbridled imagination of the supplier of the data.

To use the scoring methods discussed, we need to represent expected project performance against all criteria in numeric form. If a performance characteristic cannot be measured directly as a number, it may be useful to characterize performance verbally and then, through a word/number equivalency scale, use the numeric equivalents of verbal characterizations as model inputs.

Subjective versus Objective The distinction between subjective and objective is generally misunderstood. All too often the word *objective* is held to be synonymous with *fact* and *subjective* is taken to be a synonym for *opinion*—where fact = true and opinion = false. The distinction in measurement theory is quite different, referring to the location of the standard for measurement. A measurement taken by reference to an external standard is said to be "objective." Reference to a standard that is internal to the system is said to be "subjective." A yardstick, incorrectly divided into 100 divisions and labeled "meter," would be an objective but inaccurate measure. The eye of an experienced judge is a subjective measure that may be accurate.

Quantitative versus Qualitative The distinction between quantitative and qualitative is also misunderstood. It is not the same as numeric and nonnumeric. Both quantity and quality may be measured numerically. The number of words on this page is a quantity. The color of a red rose is a quality, but it is also a wavelength that can be measured numerically, in terms of microns. The true distinction is that one may apply the law of addition to quantities but not to qualities [53]. Water, for example, has a volumetric measure and a density measure. The former is quantitative and the latter qualitative. Two one-gallon containers of water poured into one container give us 2 gallons, but the density of the water, before and after joining the 2 gallons, is still 1.0.

Reliable versus Unreliable A data source is said to be reliable if repetitions of a measurement produce results that vary from one another by less than a prespecified amount. The distinction is important when we consider the use of statistical data in our selection models.

Valid versus Invalid Validity measures the extent to which a piece of information means what we believe it to mean. A measure may be reliable but not valid. Consider our mismarked yardstick 36 inches long but pretending to be a meter. It performs consistently, so it is reliable. It does not, however, match up well with other meter rules, so it would not be judged valid.

To be satisfactory when used in an evaluation-selection model, the measures may be either subjective or objective, quantitative or qualitative, but they must be numeric, reliable, and valid. Avoiding information merely because it is subjective or qualitative is an error and weakens our decisions. On the other hand, including information of questionable reliability or validity in selection models, even though it may be numeric, is dangerous. It is doubly dangerous if decision makers in the organization are comfortable dealing with the selection model but are unaware of the doubtful character of some input data. A condition a colleague has referred to as GIGO—garbage in, gospel out—may prevail.

Comment on Technological Shock

If the parent organization is not experienced in the type of project being considered for selection, performance measures such as time to installation, time to operation at 80 percent efficiency, cost to install, and the like are often underestimated. It is interesting to observe that an almost certain, immediate result of installing a new, cost-saving technology is that costs rise. Sometimes we blame the cost increases on resistance to change, but a more sensible explanation is that when we alter a system, we disturb it and it reacts in ways we did not predict. A steelmaker recalling the installation of the then new technology for manufacturing tinplate by electrolysis remarked: "We discovered and installed the world's first electrolytic method for making scrap. It took a year before we had that line running the way it was designed."

Of course, if the organization is experienced, underestimation is not likely to be a serious problem. The Reliance Electric Company, now a subsidiary of Exxon Corp., undertook several "18-month" plant construction projects that they predicted, accurately, would require 36 months to build from decision to the point when the plant was capable of operating at or above three-fourths capacity.

To the extent possible, past knowledge of system actions and reactions should be built into estimates of future project performance.

2.6 PROJECT PROPOSALS

Now that evaluation–selection methods have been discussed, it is appropriate to consider what documentation is needed to evaluate a project that is being considered. The set of documents submitted for evaluation is called the project proposal, whether it is brief (a page or two) or extensive, and regardless of the formality with which it is presented.

Several issues face firms preparing proposals, particularly firms in the aerospace, construction, defense, and consulting industries.

1. Which projects should be bid on?
2. How much should be spent on preparing proposals for bids?
3. How should the bid prices be set? What is the bidding strategy?

Generally, these decisions are made on the basis of their overall expected values, perhaps as reflected in a scoring model.

In-house proposals submitted by a firm's personnel to that firm's top management do not usually require the extensive treatment given to proposals submitted to outside clients or such agencies as the Department of Defense. For the Department of Defense, a proposal must be precisely structured, meeting the requirements contained in the official RFP (Request for Proposal) or, more specifically, in the TPR (Technical Proposal Requirements) that is part of the RFP. The construction and preparation of a proposal to be submitted to the government or other outside funder is beyond the scope of this book. The interested reader is referred to [18] or [42].

Four distinct issues should be covered by any proposal: (1) the nature of the technical problem and how it is to be approached; (2) the plan for implementing the project once it has been accepted; (3) the plan for logistic support and administration of the project; and (4) a description of the group proposing to do the work, plus its past experience in similar work.

The Technical Approach

The proposal begins with a general description of the problem to be attacked or project to be undertaken. If the problem is complex, the major subsystems of the problem or project are noted, together with the organization's approach to each. The presentation is in sufficient detail that a knowledgeable reader can understand what the proposer intends to do. The general method of resolving critical problems is outlined. If there are several subsystems, the proposed methods for interfacing them are covered.

In addition, any special client requirements are listed along with proposed ways of meeting them. All test and inspection procedures to assure performance, quality, reliability, and compliance with specifications are noted.

The Implementation Plan

The implementation plan for the project contains estimates of the time required, the cost, and the materials used. Each major subsystem of the project is listed along with estimates of its cost. These costs are aggregated for the whole project, and totals are shown for each cost category. Hours of work and quantities of material used are shown (along with the wage rates and unit material costs). A list of all equipment costs is added, as is a list of all overhead and administrative costs.

Depending on the wishes of the parent organization and the needs of the project, time charts, PERT–CPM, or Gantt charts are given for each subsystem and for the system as a whole. Personnel, equipment, and resource usages are estimated on a period-by-period basis in order to ensure that resource constraints are not violated. Major milestones are indicated on the time charts. Contingency plans are specifically noted. For any facility that might be critical, load charts are prepared to make sure that the facility will be available when needed.

The Plan for Logistic Support and Administration

The proposal includes a description of the ability of the proposer to supply the routine facilities, equipment, and skills needed now and then during any project. Having the means to furnish artist's renderings, special signs, meeting rooms, stenographic assistance, reproduction of oversized documents, computer graphics, word processing, conference telephone calls, and many other occasionally required capabilities provides a "touch of class." But indeed their unavailability can be irritating. Attention to detail in all aspects of project planning increases the probability of success for the project—and impresses the potential funder.

It is important that the proposal contain a section explaining how the project will be administered. The nature and timing of all progress reports, budgetary reports, audits, and evaluations are covered, together with a description of the final documentation to be prepared for users. Termination procedures are described, clearly indicating the disposition of project personnel, materials, and equipment at project end.

Past Experience

All proposals are strengthened by including a section that describes the past experience of the proposing group. It contains a list of key project personnel together with their titles and qualifications. For outside clients, a full résumé for each principal should be attached to the proposal. When preparing this and the other sections of a proposal, the proposing group should remember that the basic purpose of the document is to convince a potential funder that the group and the project are worthy of support. The proposal should be written accordingly.

2.7 THE PAST AND FUTURE OF PROJECT EVALUATION/SELECTION MODELS

In 1964, Baker and Pound [5] surveyed the state of the art of evaluating and selecting R & D projects. Although their investigation focused solely on R & D projects, their findings, and the subsequent findings of Baker and Freeland [3, 4] lead to some tentative conclusions about the past, present, and future use of project selection methods.

The use of formal, numeric procedures for the evaluation and selection of projects is a recent phenomenon, largely post-World War II. At first, payback period (and the related "average annual rate of return") was widely used. It is still used by those who feel that the uncertainties surrounding project selection are so great that a higher level of sophistication is unwarranted.

The use of formal models slowly increased during the 1950s and 1960s, and a large majority of the models employed were strictly profit–profitability models. As might be expected, the emphasis on profitability models tended to shorten the time horizon of project investment decisions. This effect and the results of several studies on the use of project selection models are reported in Mansfield [29, App. A]; also see [30, pp. 15–16].

A similar effect on non-R & D projects is easily observed by noting the sharp decline of investment in long-term projects. The increasing interest rates seen during the 1970s forced cutoff ("hurdle") rates of return higher, which cut back investment in projects for which the time gap between investment and return was more than a very few years. For example, neither new steelmaking capacity nor copper-refining capacity was expanded nearly as rapidly as long-run growth in the demand for steel and copper seemed to justify during this period. Producers tended to blame the lack of investment on foreign competition, but given the aging capacity in the United States, it may well be that the level of foreign competition is as much a result of the lack of growth (that is, our failure to invest in newer technology) as it is a cause. Again, the reader is referred to Hayes and Abernathy [19].

A decade later, Baker [3] and Souder [47] reassessed R & D project selection. In this decade there was a considerable growth in the use of formal models, again with great emphasis on profitability models. But Baker reports a significant growth in the literature on models that use multiple criteria for decision making. He observed a trend away from decision models per se, and toward the use of decision information systems. Among other reasons for this change, he notes [3] that "the decision problem is characterized by multiple criteria, many of which are not easily quantified, and the typical approaches to quantifying subjective preferences are far from satisfactory." He also notes the development of interactive decision systems that allow users to examine the effects of different mixes of possible projects.

More than a decade has passed since Baker's 1974 study. Considerable progress has been made in the development of processes for measuring preferences that yield suitable input data for sophisticated scoring models, models which serve, in turn, as data for goal programming and other resource allocation models. Because it is easy to enter all the parts (data base, decision model, and list of potential projects) in a computer, it is feasible to simulate many solutions to the project selection problem. The decision maker can easily change the criteria being used, as well as the criteria weights. Decision makers can even investigate the sensitivity of their decisions to changes in the estimates of subjective input data, thus directly examining the potential impact of errors in their opinions. In spite of all these capabilities, Liberatore and Titus [25] have found that mathematical programming models are not used for project selection or resource allocation, at least in the firms they interviewed. They did find, however, that scoring models were used for selection—particularly when the firm dealt with outside funding agencies.

We believe that use of these techniques will be extended in the future. As we become more familiar with the construction and use of decision support and expert systems (see [51]), the simulation of project selection decisions will grow in popularity. It seems to us that two concurrent events will support this trend. First is the rapid growth in the ownership and use of microcomputers by organizational executives. The operation of a computer is no longer seen as restricted to computer specialists. Second is the growing realization that profitability alone is not a sufficient test for the quality of an investment.

Almost everyone who has studied project selection in recent years has noted the need for selection processes using multiple criteria. The writings of Michael Porter [37, 38] and others have emphasized the role of innovation in the maintenance or improvement of a competitive position. Indeed, it is now clear that the firm's portfolio of projects is a key element in its competitive strategy. Suresh and Meredith [48] have added a "strategic approach" to the problem of selecting process technologies for implementation. In sum, the methodology and technology for multiple-criteria project selection not only exist but are widely available. Perhaps more important, we are beginning to understand the necessity for using them.

2.8 SUMMARY

This chapter initiated our discussion of the project management process by describing procedures for evaluating and selecting projects. It first outlined some criteria for project selection models and then discussed the general nature of these models. From this basic overview, the chapter then described the types of models in use and their advantages and disadvantages. Considering the degree of uncertainty associated with many projects, a section was devoted to selection models concerned with risk and uncertainty. Concluding the discussion, some general comments were made about data requirements and the use of these models. Finally, two sections discussed the documentation of the evaluation-selection process via project proposals and the general trend of selection models in the past and for the probable future.

The following specific points were made in the chapter.

• Primary model selection criteria are realism, capability, flexibility, ease of use, and cost.

- Preparatory steps in using a model include identifying the firm's objectives, weighting them relative to each other, and determining the probable impacts of the project on the firm's competitive abilities.
- Project selection models can generally be classified as either numeric or non-numeric; numeric models are further subdivided into profitability and scoring categories.
- Nonnumeric models include the sacred cow, the operating necessity, the competitive necessity, and comparative benefit.
- Profitability models include such standard forms as payback period, rate of return, discounted cash flow, and profitability index.
- Scoring models, the authors' preference, include the unweighted 0–1 factor model, the unweighted factor scoring model, the weighted factor scoring model, the constrained weighted factor scoring model, Dean and Nishry's model, and goal programming with multiple objectives.
- For handling uncertainty, *pro forma* documents, risk analysis, and simulation with sensitivity analyses are all helpful.
- Special care should be taken with the data used in project selection models. Of concern are data taken from an accounting data base, how data are measured and conceived, and the effect of technological shock.
- Project proposals generally consist of a number of sections: the technical approach, the implementation plan, the plan for logistic support and administration, and past experience.
- The history of project selection models has shown an increase in the use of formal models, particularly profitability models. We feel the future will extend the use of multiple criteria and simulation models, especially with the wide use of the microcomputer.

In the next chapter we consider the selection of the appropriate manager for a project and what characteristics are most helpful for such a position. We also address the issue of the project manager's special role, and the demands and responsibilities of this critical position.

2.9 GLOSSARY

DECISION SUPPORT SYSTEM—A computer package and data base to aid managers in making decisions. It may include simulation programs, mathematical programming routines, and decision rules.

DELPHI—A formalized method of group decision making that facilitates drawing on the knowledge of experts in the group (described in Appendix B of this book).

DETERMINISTIC—Predetermined, with no possibility of an alternate outcome. Compare with stochastic.

EXPERT SYSTEM—A computer package that captures the knowledge of recognized experts in an area and can make inferences about a problem based on decision rules and data input to the package.

MATRIX—A table of numbers or other items with each row and column having a particular definition.

MODEL—A way of looking at reality, usually for the purpose of abstracting and simplifying it to make it understandable in a particular context.

NETWORK—A group of items connected by some common mechanism.

PORTFOLIO—A group or set of items with varying characteristics.

PRO FORMA—Projected or anticipated, usually applied to financial data such as balance sheets and income statements.

PROGRAMMING—An algorithmic methodology for solving a particular type of complex problem, usually conducted on a compute..

SENSITIVITY ANALYSIS—Investigation of the effect on the outcome of changing some parameters in the procedure or model.

SIMULATION—A technique for emulating a process, usually conducted a considerable number of times to understand the process better and measure its outcomes under different policies.

STOCHASTIC—Probabilistic, or not deterministic.

2.10 PROJECT TEAM ASSIGNMENT

For this topic, the project team is to develop a project proposal, as described in the chapter. *Pro forma* documents should be included, as well as a justification of the project. The team should endeavor to apply as many of the project selection-justification methods as may be applicable, including both numeric and non-numeric models. Both profitability and scoring models should certainly be included.

2.11 MATERIAL REVIEW QUESTIONS

1. What are the four parts of a technical proposal?
2. By what criteria do you think managers judge selection models? What criteria *should* they use?
3. Contrast the competitive necessity model with the operating necessity model. What are the advantages and disadvantages of each?
4. What is a sacred cow? Give some examples.
5. Give an example of a Q-Sort process for project selection.
6. What are some of the limitations of project selection models?
7. What is the distinction between a qualitative and a quantitative measure?

2.12 CONCEPTUAL DISCUSSION QUESTIONS

1. Explain why goal programming is classified as a scoring model. What is the real difference between profitability and scoring models? Describe a model that could fit both categories.
2. Can risk analysis be used for nonproject business decision making? Explain how.

3. Discuss how the following project selection models are used in real-world applications.
   (a) Capital investment with discounted cash flow.
   (b) Goal programming models.
   (c) Simulation models.
4. Why do you think managers underutilize project selection models?
5. Would uncertainty models be classified as profitability models, scoring models, or some other type of model?
6. Contrast validity with reliability. What aspects, if any, are the same?
7. Contrast subjective and objective measures. Give examples of the proper use of each type of measure when evaluating competing projects.

2.13 CHAPTER EXERCISE

Consider the purchase of a used car. Develop a profitability model to compare alternative automobiles. Include depreciation, expenses, repairs, insurance, initial costs, and so on.

Next, devise a scoring model to evaluate the alternative purchases. How should you weight the various factors, and how do you decide?

Last, how would a risk analysis be used to make a decision? What factors would require distributions, and how might these be obtained? Which data are subjective and which objective? Which are qualitative and which are quantitative?

2.14 INCIDENTS FOR DISCUSSION

Multiplex Company

Multiplex Company is in its third year of using a rather complex and comprehensive strategic planning process. Bill Chase, CEO of Multiplex, is very pleased with the output of the planning process. Plans are logical, organized, and pertinent to the firm's business environment. However, implementation of the plans leaves something to be desired. Bill is convinced that his managers do a poor job of estimating the amount of resources and time required to complete the strategic projects associated with the plan.

This fiscal year, eleven new strategic projects were identified. There were six major types of projects: new products, modifications of existing products, research and development, new applications studies, manufacturing process improvements, and reorganization of the sales department. Each project is sponsored by one of the functional department managers, who is required to prepare a simple cost–benefit analysis and a Gantt chart (see Chapter 8, Section 8.3) showing the aggregate time required to finish a project. This sponsor usually, but not always, winds up being assigned as the project manager.

Tomorrow is the final day of the current year's strategic planning session. Mr. Chase plans to make a strong pitch to his managers to prioritize the strategic projects to ensure that those most important to the company get done. In the past it seemed as though all the projects lagged behind when resource problems arose. In the future he wants a consensus from his managers about which projects will go on the back burner and which are to proceed on schedule when problems are encountered.

Question: Mr. Chase is not sure how to go about ranking the projects. Should they use the cost–benefit analysis done by the project sponsor? Perhaps the planning group could use their collective experience to rank the projects subjectively. What method would you recommend to Mr. Chase? Support your recommendation.

L & M Power

In the next two years a large municipal gas and electric company must begin construction on a new electric generating plant to accommodate the increased demand for electricity and to replace one of the existing plants that is fast becoming obsolete. The vice-president in charge of the new project believes he has two options. One is a new coal-fired plant and the other is a new nuclear plant. The vice-president has developed a project selection model and will use it in his presentation of the project to the president. For the models he has gathered the following information:

Generating Initial Cost	Cost/KW	Expected Life	Salvage Value
Steam plant	$10,000,000.00	420 yr	10%
Nuclear plant	25,000,000.00	215 yr	5%

Since the vice-president's background is in finance, he believes the best model to use is a financial one, net present value analysis.

Question: Would you use this model? Why or why not? Base your answer on the five criteria developed by Souder.

Billboard Publications

Billboard's top management, located in New York, has recently authorized a large number of data processing projects. However, when under pressure, they ask Bruce Johnson, manager of data processing, to reassign programmers to the latest "squeaky wheel." This situation was causing such turmoil that it was becoming impossible to manage the various projects, and staff morale was deteriorating rapidly.

Johnson's immediate project manager in Cincinnati agreed with him that this situation needed to be resolved, so a project evaluation and selection meeting was arranged. The meeting was held off-site to get away from the immediate pressures of business. It was attended by vice-presidents and department managers who had outstanding requests for data processing services or personnel assigned to such projects. In preparation for the meeting, Johnson gathered a portfolio of all project requests for data processing services with their labor and equipment requirements.

The meeting was held all day Monday and Tuesday. After the two long days and many discussions, all the projects had been evaluated and ranked. However, no one was truly pleased; there were not enough resources to go around, and no one received what he or she really wanted. But they had been heard and all agreed that, given the demands and the resources available, they would abide by the decisions of the group.

Johnson was exhausted after the meetings, but he returned to the office Wednesday and went right to work implementing the plans agreed to the day before. He held meetings with the project managers, programmers, and project personnel from user departments, explaining the "new" priorities. Much patience and persuasion was required, as some projects were placed on hold, staffing reduced on some and increased on others, and entirely new projects formed. The big selling point was that the working environment should be much more stable and professional because these assignments represented the consensus of management on projects to be pursued for the next several months.

Thursday morning, Johnson was looking forward to a calm, peaceful day in which to tackle the pile on his desk and contribute his individual expertise to some of the projects to which he was personally assigned. Before Johnson had made much progress, a call came from Bill Evans, vice-president of finance in New York, the functional manager to whom Johnson reported. Several managers had complained to Evans about the ranking of their pet projects and he had agreed to call Johnson and "discuss" how they could be "fit in." Johnson reminded Evans of the priorities that they had begun to implement only yesterday, and of the two-day meeting earlier that week that Evans had attended and chaired. All to no avail.

Johnson was now not only faced with reassigning personnel to deal with Evans's latest "squeaky wheels," but knew that it would most likely have to be done again tomorrow and then again on Monday. He asked himself, "Had anything really been accomplished?"

Question: What project evaluation and selection methods do you think were used during the meeting? What should Johnson do? Do you think that hiring more personnel would help?

2.15 BIBLIOGRAPHY

1. Archibald, R. D. *Managing High Technology Programs and Projects.* Wiley, New York, 1976.
2. Atkinson, A. C., and A. H. Bobis. "A Mathematical Basis for the Selection of Research Projects." *IEEE Transactions on Engineering Management,* Jan. 1969.
3. Baker, N. R. "R & D Project Selection Models: An Assessment." *IEEE Transactions on Engineering Management,* Nov. 1974.
4. Baker, N. R., and J. Freeland. "Recent Advances in R & D Benefit Measurement and Project Selection Models." *Management Science,* June 1975.
5. Baker, N. R., and W. H. Pound. "R & D Project Selection: Where We Stand." *IEEE Transactions on Engineering Management,* Dec. 1964.
6. Becker, R. H. "Project Selection for Research, Product Development and Process Development." *Research Management,* Sept. 1980.

7. Clark, P. "A Profitability Project Selection Method." *Research Management,* Nov. 1977.

8. Clayton, R. "A Convergent Approach to R & D Planning and Project Selection." *Research Management,* Sept. 1971.

9. Clifton, D. S., Jr., and D. E. Fyffe. *Project Feasibility Analysis: A Guide to Profitable Ventures.* Wiley, New York, 1977.

10. Cochran, M., E. B. Pyle, III, L. C. Greene, H. A. Clymer, and A. D. Bender. "Investment Model for R & D Project Evaluation and Selection." *IEEE Transactions on Engineering Management,* Aug. 1971.

11. Dean, B. V. *Evaluating, Selecting, and Controlling R & D Projects.* American Management Association, New York, 1968.

12. Dean, B. V., and L. A. Roepcke. "Cost Effectiveness in R & D Organizational Resource Allocation." *IEEE Transactions on Engineering Management,* Nov. 1969.

13. Enrick, N. L. "Value Analysis for Priority Setting and Resource Allocation." *Industrial Management,* Sept.–Oct. 1980.

14. European Industrial Research Management Association. "Top-Down and Bottom-Up Approaches to Project Selection." *Research Management,* March 1978.

15. Garcia, A. and W. Cowdrey. "Information Systems: A Long Way from Wall-Carvings to CRTs." *Industrial Engineering,* April 1978.

16. Gee, R. E. "A Survey of Current Project Selection Practices." *Research Management,* Sept. 1971.

17. Golabi, K., G. W. Kirkwood, and A. Sicherman. "Selecting a Portfolio of Solar Energy Projects Using Multi-Attribute Preference Theory." *Management Science,* Feb. 1981.

18. Hajek, V. G. *Management of Engineering Projects.* McGraw-Hill, New York, 1977.

19. Hayes, R., and W. J. Abernathy, "Managing Our Way to Economic Decline." *Harvard Business Review,* July–Aug. 1980.

20. Helin, A. F., and W. E. Souder. "Experimental Test of a Q-Sort Procedure for Prioritizing R & D Projects." *IEEE Transactions on Engineering Management,* Nov. 1974.

21. Hertz, D. B. "Risk Analysis in Capital Investment." *Harvard Business Review,* Sept.–Oct. 1979.

22. Hertz, D. B., and H. Thomas. *Risk Analysis and Its Applications.* Wiley, New York, 1983.

23. Ignizio, J. P. *Goal Programming and Extensions.* Lexington Books, Lexington, MA, 1976.

24. Johnston, R. D. "Project Selection and Evaluating." *Long Range Planning,* Sept. 1972.

25. Liberatore, M. J., and G. J. Titus. "The Practice of Management Science in R & D Project Management." *Management Science,* Aug. 1983.

26. Maher, P. M., and A. H. Rubenstein. "Factors Affecting Adoption of a Quantitative Method for R & D Project Selection." *Management Science,* Oct. 1974.

27. *Management of New Products,* Booz, Allen, and Hamilton, Inc., New York, 1966.

28. Mann, G. A. "VERT: A Risk Analysis Tool for Program Management." *Defense Management,* May–June 1979.

29. Mansfield, E. *Industrial Research and Technological Innovation.* Norton, New York, 1968.

30. Mansfield, E., J. Rapoport, J. Schnee, S. Wagner, and M. Hamburger. *Research and Innovation in the Modern Corporation.* Norton, New York, 1971.

31. Mantel, S. J., Jr., J. R. Evans, and V. A. Tipnis. "Decision Analysis for New Process Technology," in B. V. Dean, ed., *Project Management: Methods and Studies,* North-Holland, Amsterdam, 1985.

32. Mason, B. M., W. E. Souder, and E. P. Winkofsky. "R & D Budgeting and Project Selection: A Review of Practices and Models" *ISMS,* 1980.

33. Meredith, J. "The Implementation of Computer Based Systems." *Journal of Operations Management,* Oct. 1981.

34. Merrifield, D. B. "How to Select Successful R & D Projects." *Management Review,* Dec. 1978.

35. Moore, J. R., Jr., and N. R. Baker. "Computational Analysis of Scoring Models for R & D Project Selection." *Management Science,* Dec. 1969.

36. Paolini, A., Jr., and M. A. Glaser. "Project Selection Methods That Pick Winners." *Research Management,* May 1977.

37. Porter, M. E. *Competitive Strategy.* Free Press, New York, 1980.

38. Porter, M. E. *Competitive Advantage.* Free Press, New York, 1985.

39. Ramsey, J. E. "Selecting R & D Projects for Development." *Long Range Planning,* Feb. 1981.

40. Reynard, E. L. "A Method for Relating Research Spending to Net Profit." *Research Management,* Dec. 1979.

41. Robinson, B., and C. Lakhani. "Dynamic Models for New Product Planning." *Management Science,* June 1975.

42. Rosenau, M. D., Jr. *Successful Project Management.* Lifetime Learning Publications, Belmont, CA, 1981.

43. Schwartz, S. L., and I. Vertinsky. "Multi-Attribute Investment Decisions: A Study of R & D Project Selection." *Management Science,* Nov. 1977.

44. Simon, H. *The New Science of Management Decisions,* rev. ed. Prentice-Hall, Englewood Cliffs, NJ, 1977.

45. Souder, W. E. "Comparative Analysis of R & D Investment Models." *AIIE Transactions,* April 1972.

46. Souder, W. E. "Analytical Effectiveness of Mathematical Models for R & D Project Selection." *Management Science,* April 1973.

47. Souder, W. E. "Utility and Perceived Acceptability of R & D Project Selection Models." *Management Science,* Aug. 1973.

48. Suresh, N. C., and J. R. Meredith. "Justifying Multimachine Systems: An Integrated Strategic Approach." *Journal of Manufacturing Systems,* Nov. 1985.

49. Thompson, G. E. *Management Science: An Introduction to Modern Quantitative Analysis and Decision Making.* McGraw-Hill, New York, 1976.

50. Townsend, H. W. R., and G. E. Whitehouse. "We Used Risk Analysis to Move Our Computer." *Industrial Engineering,* May 1977.

51. Turban, E., and J. R. Meredith, *Fundamentals of Management Science*, 4th ed. Business Publications, Plano, TX, 1988.
52. U.S. Bureau of the Census. *Statistical Abstracts of the United States: 1980,* 101st ed. Washington, D.C., 1980.
53. Van Gigch, J. P. *Applied General Systems Theory,* 2nd ed. Harper & Row, New York, 1978.
54. Van Horne, J. C. *Fundamentals of Financial Management.* Prentice-Hall, Englewood Cliffs, NJ, 1971.
55. Whaley, W. M., and R. A. Williams. "A Profits-Oriented Approach to Project Selection." *Research Management,* Sept. 1971.
56. Williams, D. J. "A Study of a Decision Model for R & D Project Selection." *Operational Research Quarterly,* Sept. 1969.
57. Zaloon, V. A. "Project Selection Methods." *Journal of Systems Management,* Aug. 1973.

2.16 READING

Based on a wide variety of empirical industrial studies, this article suggests a number of improvements concerning the way managers evaluate new technology. The author's thesis is that technological innovation is much more difficult and complex than managers generally believe and unless more attention is paid to this issue, industry will fall behind worldwide competition in this crucial area.

First, the paper describes a variety of shortcomings found in the way firms evaluate technological innovations and some ways of improving them. Then, weaknesses in the typical manner of soliciting proposals for technological innovation are identified and corrections are suggested. Finally, the errors made in evaluating the results of technological changes are pointed out, and again recommendations are made for improvement.

Strengthening Managerial Approaches to Improving Technological Capabilities

BELA GOLD

Director, Research Program in Industrial Economics, Case Western Reserve University, Cleveland, Ohio, U.S.A.

Regaining and maintaining technological competitiveness is essential to strengthening competitiveness in the market place. Even inspired marketing and creative financing cannot ensure long term survival for products which cost more to produce and which are less attractive to customers than those offered by rivals.

However, more than 25 years of analysing the problems of improving productivity as well as other sectors of industrial performance[1] have convinced me that implementing major advances in technology represents a far more difficult and far-reaching challenge to management than is generally appreciated. The key reason for this is the failure to recognize that basic technologies are built not only into the production machinery, but also into:

1. the expertise of the technical personnel

2. the structure and operation of the production system
3. the economically feasible range of changes in product designs and product-mix
4. the skills and organization of labour
5. and even the very criteria used to evaluate new capital goods proposals.

Each of these represents powerful and mutually reinforcing commitments to preserving existing production and organizational arrangements ex-

[1]For a partial listing, see the References which include studies covering a variety of technological innovations and related productivity cost and other effects in a variety of industries in the United States and abroad. For a perceptive earlier review of allocation processes, see Bower (1970).

©1983 by John Wiley & Sons, Ltd. Reprinted by permission from *Strategic Management Journal* (1983).

cept for small, gradual and localized changes. The influence of such deep-rooted commitments was perceptively captured by the poetic lines:

> *With their eyes firmly fixed upon the past,*
> *They backed reluctantly into the future.*

It would, of course, be undiplomatic in modern industry to voice immediate opposition to proposals for major innovations, but such resistance can be exerted quite effectively through unencouraging evaluations of proposals by the very specialists on whom management depends for expert judgments, as well as by highlighting the uncertainties and difficulties likely to be encountered in applying and using new technologies.

Moreover, even when the need for improvement has come to be accepted, the targets set are often much too low to regain competitiveness. For example, recent efforts by the U.S. steel industry to begin catching up with the higher productivity levels of leading Japanese competitors (Gold, 1978) have generated a variety of company programmes seeking to increase output per man-hour by a long-unattained 5 percent annually. However, the most recently completed integrated mill in Japan, Ohgishima, which had set a target for 1977 of 1000 tons of finished product per wage-earner (more than double the best U.S level at that time), raised its actual output per man to 1800 in 1980, almost three times the best record in a U.S. integrated mill *(Wall Street Journal,* April 7, 1981).

The development of programmes to achieve major advances in technological competitiveness is likely to require basic changes in traditional approaches:

1. to evaluating proposals for adopting technological innovations
2. to generating promising proposals
3. to evaluating the effectiveness with which resulting potentials have been harnessed.

Accordingly, the following discussion will review the limitations of widespread practices in each of these areas before offering suggestions for revising them on the basis of our field studies in a variety of industries in the United States and abroad.

APPROACHES TO EVALUATING PROSPECTIVE TECHNOLOGICAL INNOVATIONS

Revising Common Evaluation Criteria

Prevailing approaches to evaluating proposals to adopt technological innovations commonly involve estimating their prospective contributions to cost savings and revenue increases as compared with current operations and then comparing the resulting gain in profits with the additional investment required (Gold, 1977), but such an essentially static perception leads to reliance on the wrong criteria.

The basic objective in adopting substantial technological innovations must be to safeguard or improve the firm's competitiveness over an extended future period. Instead of comparisons with current operating performance, therefore, relevant evaluation criteria should be developed by estimating needed improvement targets over at least the next 5–10 years. This would require serious efforts to appraise recent and prospective trends, in the availability and prices of needed inputs and possible substitutes, in required product capabilities and in product-mix, in the technologies likely to be employed by competitors, in new sources of competition, and in any relevant governmental policies—thus adding major additional analytical responsibilities to those which currently dominate many corporate planning groups. If significant changes from the present seem likely in any of these determinants of future competitiveness, decisions about prospective innovations might be quite different from those which would be counselled by comparisons only with current operating performance. Such evaluations of needed future improvements might also urge consideration of innovations other than those currently being proposed.

In addition, it is important to recognize the serious negative bias involved in evaluating major technological innovations on the basis of the purportedly sophisticated criterion of the "net present value" of expected future returns. If such returns are discounted at 15–20 percent annually, major projects which take even 3 or 4 years to build, "debug" and bring to high levels of use would invite rejection in comparison with recent high, virtually riskless money market yields, but such a criterion is dangerously myopic because of its failure to consider the effects on long-term competitiveness and profitability of resulting rejections of successive technological advances (Gold and Boylan, 1975). Hence, it would seem necessary to shift such capital budgeting evaluations from maximizing net present value to what I have called a "continuing horizons" approach. This involves recognition that most major innovations achieve only gradually increasing use and benefits, experience an extended period of reasonable competitiveness and attractive contributions, only to succumb in time to yielding progressively declining returns. In order to maximize average returns on a continuing basis, therefore, it is necessary to plan for the periodic introduction of new sources of improved competitiveness, recognizing that they will not yield attractive short term returns, and despite the tendency to underestimate the net present value of their eventual contributions engendered by discounting them at high interest rates. Accordingly, one would seek to choose an array of capital projects such that, when the overlapping time paths of expected net returns from each are aggregated, and the "net present value" is calculated as of *successive* three year intervals, the results promise to safeguard acceptable longer-term as well as short-term rates of profit (Gold, 1975: 24).

Common Errors in Estimating the Prospective Benefits

Our field research suggests that the substantial differences which are commonly found between pre-adoption estimates of the results of major innovations and actual outcomes can be attributed to two different sources: errors in estimating prospective gains in productive efficiency; and errors in estimating resulting cost and profit benefits.

Errors in Estimating Gains in Productive Efficiency One of the important sources of such errors is the tendency to underestimate the time needed to achieve effective functioning of the innovation, often by a considerable margin. Common reasons include inadequate recognition of the delays and extended shortcomings likely to be caused by such factors as: needed modifications in the hardware and controls to adapt to the particular characteristics of the given plant; identification of the detailed operating requirements, capabilities and limitations of the innovation as the basis for developing guidelines for operating practices; inadequate engineering experience in ensuring rapid and effective adaptation of the innovation to changing production requirements; and development of appropriate maintenance procedures. For example, our study of a large flexible manufacturing system revealed that effective functioning was not achieved for more than two years, with substantial additional realization of its capabilities spread over several more years (Gold, 1981c). The utilization rates of continuous slab casters in a number of leading American steel mills have continued to fall far short of those attained in Japanese steel mills even five years after installation (Rosegger, 1980).

A second source of errors in estimating the prospective benefits of major innovations is the tendency to overestimate the average rate of use in calculating expected returns. In part, this often reflects a wilful ignoring of the realities of past fluctuations in total product demand levels and of the limitations on using particular operations due to the uneven effects of shifts in product-mix. Interesting examples of such effects are provided in Skeddle's study of early float glass installations in this country (Skeddle, 1980).

In addition, expected gains in productive efficiency are likely to be exaggerated because of reliance on an overly narrow evaluative framework which ignores the need to develop adaptive adjustments in preceding as well as subsequent operations in order to reintegrate the production process effectively. This may involve the reallocation of some operating tasks, possible changes in prior quality specifications (possibly reaching all the way back to procurement), alterations in production rates and work-in-process inventories, changes in inspection arrangements, and adjustments in machine capabilities and labour inputs. Extensive installations of robotics and of computer-aided manufacturing systems are among the more recent illustrations of the wider ranging impacts of major technological innovations (Gold, 1981c, 1982).

A fourth common source of erroneous estimates of net benefits derives from the associated tendency to concentrate on the prospective operating inputs and outputs of the innovative hardware, while giving inadequate consideration to the often substantial requirements for additional inputs by staff personnel. These may include production planning, quality control, systems engineering, maintenance specialists and even product designers— all of them seeking not only to facilitate integration of the innovation into the larger manufacturing and control system, but also to harness any further potential benefits to the system as a whole made possible by the emerging capabilities of the innovation. In tightly integrated plants, not only must each of these supporting specialties participate in adapting past arrangements to accommodate the new capabilities and requirements, but they must also reintegrate their respective modifications through reiterated system revisions. Our study of American experience with computerization in the steel industry illustrates the difficulties of trying to introduce such innovations on a piecemeal basis and from the bottom-up (Gold, 1978).

A fifth possible source of such erroneous estimates is rooted in the assumptions made concerning the problems of gaining labour acceptance of major innovations. The issues which seem to be encountered most frequently centre around: changes (usually reductions) in employment levels; changes (usually increases) in output quotas; shifts in job classifications (commonly affecting skill levels, seniority and associated relative pay rates); and adjustments in overall wage rates and fringe benefits (usually increases) to gain needed co-operation. Such problems tend to be much less serious than expected by managements during the early stages of innovation, when applications are few, limited in scope, and affect so few employees as to enable managements to ease any associated difficulties readily. It is only when early experiences have finally achieved technical success and substantial economic promise that the labour problems are likely to be generated by wider applications of innovative technologies. Hence, robotics and computer-aided manufacturing have not yet generated the labour difficulties that were associated with the introduction of many earlier advances in mechanization.

Errors in Estimating the Cost and Profit Benefits The most common and most readily remediable among these involves ignoring the probable effects of resource-saving innovations on the price of the inputs affected. For example, increases in output per man-hour tend to engender largely or wholly offsetting increases in wage rates, whether through piece rates, incentives or trade union pressure. Similarly, reductions in unit material requirements often involve changes in qualitative specification, which entail higher prices. A second source of erroneous cost estimates involves overlooking the costs of underusing older facilities used for similar purposes in order to maximize use of the new.

Perhaps the most astonishing source of common errors is the assumption that resulting reductions in unit costs can be fully converted into profits. But this ignores the likelihood that efforts to gain such rewards through lowering prices, and thereby increasing sales, would be matched by competitors determined to retain market share, even if they have not achieved comparable cost-savings. Alternatively, seeking to achieve profit benefits by keeping prices unchanged is not likely to prove tenable for long because the diffusion of cost-saving innovations tends to trigger price reductions by competitors seeking to capitalize on their belated adoptions by regaining or increasing market shares (Gold, 1979: Chapter 14).

Another critical point relating to estimating the benefits of prospective innovations is that the more deviate they are from the expertise and past experience of the staff, the more vulnerable such pre-decision evaluations are likely to be.[2] This is true even of estimates of the effects of prospective major increases in the scale of facilities (Gold, 1981b: 14, 23).

Improving Estimates of the Prospective Effects of Technological Innovations

Our field research has uncovered very little evidence of serious efforts to improve the accuracy of pre-decision estimates of prospective innovational effects on the basis of empirical evaluations of their shortcomings. The reason given most in answer to our enquiries is that each major innovation is regarded as unique along with the factors determining its prospective effects. A second common answer is that such estimates about the performance of hitherto unused innovations under uncertain future conditions are unavoidably subject to wide margins of error. In view of the large stakes involved, however—including future profitability and even survival—systematic efforts to identify the shortcomings of past pre-decision estimates as well as efforts to improve them would seem very much in order.

One of the important sources of such errors, and perhaps the most remediable, is to recognize and try to minimize the biases that have been built into the evaluations generated by different groups within the firm. Engineering development

[2]For example, see the discussion of deviations between traditional expectations and those more likely to result from application of computer-aided systems in manufacturing (Gold, 1981c: 10–16).

personnel who are under pressure to justify their efforts are understandably tempted to offer generous estimates of the advances which they have achieved. Manufacturing supervisors seeking to minimize disruptions to smoothly functioning production operations tend to underestimate the net benefits of proposed major innovations. Marketing executives tend to be more enthusiastic about advanced offering improvements in product capabilities than those affecting production operations alone. And finance officials often have ample cause, on the basis of past experience, to regard estimates of the benefits accompanying such proposals with scepticism expressed in the form of reducing probable revenues and increasing probable investment requirements and operating costs. Such motivational cross-currents can obviously serve as a source of creative tension within a firm. However, results are likely to be far more valuable if efforts are made to modify traditional biases on the basis of more realistic perspectives.

One means of doing so would involve a thorough analysis of the actual results of several past innovations for comparison with *ex ante* expectations in order to identify the component estimates involving the largest errors and then probing for the causes of such misperceptions as a guide to remedial adjustments. The array of common sources of such errors which has been presented offers a starting point for such enquiries and also implies means of improving the various estimates. A second approach to improving pre-decision estimates would involve comprehensive efforts to probe the experiences of earlier adopters of the contemplated innovations. If domestic adopters are competitors who are unwilling to share such learning, it may be fruitful to explore the possible co-operativeness of foreign producers in sharing such experience. Additional means obviously include reviewing the expected advantages, limitations and problems of using the prospective innovation with competing vendors and with specialized consultants.

The points being emphasized are that there are common as well as uncommon elements in appraising the prospective effects of even quite dissimilar innovations; that greater efforts are warranted to use costly past experiences as a means of improving future evaluational efforts; and that resulting insights may yield valuable improvements in such estimates even if they continue to encompass substantial sectors of uncertainty.

GENERATING PROPOSALS FOR TECHNOLOGICAL INNOVATIONS

Weaknesses of Traditional Approaches

In most firms, proposals for technological innovations are expected to emerge from or at least to be approved by, the operating sectors most likely to be affected by them. This process derives from the assumption that the managerial and technical personnel in each sector are the most knowledgeable about its performance requirements and shortcomings, and are also best qualified to evaluate any prospective innovational improvements. Although there is considerable merit in these beliefs, they are less likely to be true in respect to major innovational possibilities. One reason is that the more unfamiliar the technologies to be considered, the less qualified the current operating staff would be to evaluate it. It should also be recognized that such personnel may feel that unfamiliar innovations threaten both the adequacy of their expertise and the security of their organizational status—thereby encouraging underestimates of the innovation's prospective benefits. In the cases of robotics and, to an even greater extent, computer-aided manufacturing, most operating staffs lack sufficient expertise to evaluate either prospective applications or the alternative systems which are available for adoption. Moreover, the readiness of current operating executives and engineers to add personnel with such specialized capabilities may be inhibited by the prospect that increasing reliance on such new technologies would tend to increase the newcomers' opportunities for advancement at the expense of those lacking their expertise.

Managements also frequently act as though the most promising innovational proposals are bound to keep flowing because of an unrestrainable urge of managers and technical specialists to maximize improvements. In fact, however, analysis suggests that both the volume and the magnitude of innovational proposals are closely responsive to the attitudes of top managements, as reflected not by their exhortations but by their decisions about the proposals which have been submitted. Thus, a high proportion of rejections of new kinds of innovational proposals is bound to discourage additional submissions; and evidences that management favours only modest scale or quick repayment proposals tend to evoke conforming adjustments in the characteristics of the proposals which are submitted. It may be of interest in this connection to contrast the steady and impressive progress of computerization in the integrated steel industry of Japan, with its top-down guiding strategy, as against the intermittent and more limited gains resulting from reliance on the earlier but essentially bottom-up efforts in the American integrated mills (Gold, 1978).

Means of Intensifying Technological Improvement Efforts

In order to intensify technological improvement efforts, the most important requirements are for senior management to recognize that ensuring technological competitiveness is absolutely necessary to profitable survival and to commit itself to achieve and maintain such capabilities.

Among the means for demonstrating such a commitment, consideration might be given to a variety of measures. To begin with, it would prove valuable to arrange for a thorough, objective and expert evaluation of the advantages and disadvantages of its current technologies, facilities and products in all major operations and product lines relative to its competitors. Although virtually all companies in our studies professed to be fully informed about such matters, few could offer any persuasive evidence in support of these claims. Yet it is obviously difficult to maximize the benefits of invariably limited investment resources without first identifying the sectors of most urgent needs and the magnitude of the lags to be overcome. Such a mapping of current advantages and disadvantages should then be supplemented by a comparably thorough exploration of prospective changes over the next five years or longer in the capabilities of foreign as well as domestic competitors, in input and output markets, and in any relevant governmental regulations—a second major source of guidance which is seldom subjected to comprehensive analysis. The results of these two surveys would then provide a reasonably solid base for defining a set of improvement targets for technological capabilities and productive efficiency.

In order to ensure progress towards such improvement goals, top management might well consider an array of interconnected measures. Instead of the all-too-common expedient of exhorting everyone to surpass past performance, it might be more useful to begin by establishing a special group, closely tied to top management, to undertake the current and longer-term evaluations suggested above, to build on the findings as a basis for proposing preliminary improvement targets, and to draw on all kinds of internal and external expertise to evaluate alternative innovations capable of furthering progress towards such goals. Key questions might include: which advances should be licensed or bought from the outside and which should we seek to develop internally? How much of needed advances could be achieved through modifying or upgrading existing facilities and products as against the additional gains available only through shifts to new facilities and products in the next two or three years, and over the next five years? Issues like these require consideration of the proportion of current and prospective capital outlays which should be allocated to "strategic investments," meaning those to be evaluated on the basis of expected contributions to longer-term competitiveness and profitability rather than to "net present value."

Decisions about such matters are often rooted in basic philosophical commitments rather than in specified analytical procedures. For example,

during the course of one of our field studies, we heard the director of manufacturing technology support a proposal for the acquisition of major new facilities and equipment with a comprehensive array of estimates of investment requirements, operating costs and revenues over the next six years, only to have them abruptly dismissed by the capital allocations official as "nothing more than unreliable guesses which could not justify the large investments involved." "But," the latter then added, "tell me why the company needs to make such an investment in order to safeguard its future competitiveness." In response to our query about the basis for taking such an unusual position, he told us that, in order to maintain its outstanding position in the industry, this company consistently allocates 15–20 percent of its capital expenditures to projects which are too new to permit persuasive analyses of prospective returns, but which seem of such great future promise as to warrant undertaking significant investments in pioneering their exploration and development.[3]

Progress towards such technological improvement goals also requires development of well-informed and responsive managers, technical per-

---

[3] A somewhat similar approach was reflected by the position of a senior research officer in a major European corporation in justifying his opposition to the detailed economic evaluation of research proposals and similar innovative activities. His management regards such efforts to reach beyond accumulated experiences as "similar to an underground stream which wanders unseen for longer or for shorter distances to emerge eventually at some unexpected spot. 'We do not know where it will emerge, and we do not know when it will emerge, but we want to be there when it does!' In extending his argument, he explained that the company would expect to be first every so often. But even when it was not, its research people would be so familiar with the surrounding technological terrain, and with the paths which had been found unfruitful as well as those which had not yet been explored, that it could in most cases duplicate the achievements of the successful pioneers, or develop a reasonable equivalent, in comparatively short order. And, in his view, it is this combination of insurance against catastrophic lags in whatever quarter the competition manages to leap ahead, plus the chance that it will itself achieve leadership with reasonable frequency, that constitutes the soundest justification of the research investments undertaken under such a cloud of uncertainties." Quoted from Gold (1973: 136).

sonnel and workmen. Towards that end, it would be helpful to initiate educational efforts followed by specialized training programmes to achieve general understanding of the need for major advances, of their implications for future operations, and of the particular stresses likely to be confronted in the course of absorbing various kinds of innovations. At the same time, careful attention must be given to possible needs for changing existing organizational structures so as to facilitate the effective use of major innovations. For example, the introduction of computerized manufacturing systems requires more effective and continuous integration between computer-aided design and computer-aided manufacturing than is likely to be achieved when each represents a separate organizational unit, leaving the critical point of interaction between them at the periphery of each unit's responsbilities (Gold, 1981c: 31). Such organizational adjustments should also provide for detailed periodic monitoring of progress towards technological improvement goals, including evaluation of the causes of any shortcomings as well as consideration of possible shifts in targets in response to changing pressures and opportunities.

EVALUATING THE RESULTS OF INSTALLED TECHNOLOGICAL INNOVATIONS

In contrast to the voluminous literature on pre-decision evaluations of innovational effects, few publications offer serious evaluations of the actual effects of the innovations which have been adopted. The explanation seems to be that the relevant methods and interpretations are considered to be so obvious as to offer no analytical challenges. Our research suggests, however, that such efforts are confronted by significant difficulties concerning the appropriate criteria for evaluation; the timing of such appraisals; who should make them; and how the results should be used.

Criteria of Evaluation

Most efforts to evaluate the results of major technological innovations tend to concentrate on financial measures, especially on comparisons of outlays and costs with original expectations. But such findings tend to be inadequate, and may even be misleading, unless account is also taken of all other changes engendered by the innovation. These may include one or more of the following: changes in the quality as well as in the quantities of inputs and outputs; shifts in operating tasks among production stages; alterations in product-mix and in the length of production runs; adjustments in reject rates; and increases or decreases in equipment downtime.

Moreover, effective appraisal also requires uncovering the causes of observed deviations from expected results. In particular, management needs to know the extent to which such changes were attributable to equipment characteristics; or to engineering modifications of production methods; or to maladjustments in input and work flows; or to changes in labour capabilities and efforts. In the absence of such analytical determinations, there seems to be a tendency to ascribe any observed deficiencies to external or to unpredictable factors—thereby ignoring internal remedial potentials. It should also be recognized that early experiences in introducing and using major innovations often alter original estimates of what tasks can be performed most effectively as well as prospective results. Hence, comparisons with later perceptions may be more meaningful than with the less informed original expectations.

In evaluating the cost effects of technological innovations, results may be heavily affected by decisions concerning whether the following are treated as increases in the investment charged to the innovation or as additions to operating costs; the cost of interruptions to production innovation, including attendant costs of equipment modifications, "debugging," operator training, and trial runs; additional outlays in order to improve the capabilities of the new facilities; and the costs and investments involved in readjusting preceding and subsequent operations in order to improve the capabilities and integration of the encompassing production process. In general, there seems to be a widespread tendency to charge such additional outlays to early operating costs, in respect to which overruns are likely to be regarded sympathetically as virtually inevitable, thereby holding down the investment base to be used in calculating future rates of return.

The Timing of Evaluations

Such firms as undertake "post-audits" or "make good" evaluations of installed innovations tend to rely on a single appraisal, usually within 6–12 months after project completion. These early appraisals often yield overly optimistic findings, however, because generous allowances are made to offset actual shortcomings on the assumption that these are attributable to temporary problems—such as excessive maintenance, inadequate labour experience, or underuse due to incomplete integration with adjacent operations.

If such appraisals are to be more effective, they would have to be made repeatedly over 3–6 month intervals for at least the two to three years which the complete absorption of major technological innovations seems to take (Gold, 1979: Chapter 10). Successive evaluations would reveal trends in various performance measures, demonstrate which shortcomings are transitory and which are not, and identify additional sources of improvement through progressively more thorough integration with the larger manufacturing and control systems.[4]

Responsibility for Evaluations

One of the critical problems faced in evaluating major innovations is the pressure for biased findings. In the case of very large projects, favourable biases tend to be encouraged by fears that negative

findings might reflect on the senior officials who made the basic decisions and be resented by them. Biases may also be generated by assigning evaluations to those who recommended the adoption decision, on the grounds that they alone have the requisite technological competence. Still another source of biases may be the desire of designated evaluators to maintain future co-operative relationships with the project officials involved. As a result of experiences with such problems, some firms have abandoned *ex post* evaluations entirely (Gold et al., 1980: 313) whereas many others seem to have relegated them to relatively routine financial reporting exercises.

However, such carelessness, passivity or defeatism has already helped to undermine awareness of the shortcomings of past efforts to improve technological competitiveness. In addition, such attitudes have also helped to delay recognition of the need to organize more formal, comprehensive, knowledgeable and regularized evaluations of the effects of the large investments in major technological innovations which may be major determinants of future profitability. Provision of the needed objectivity and range of relevant expertise may require that such evaluations be the responsibility of some senior official who is concerned not only with exacting appraisals of performance, but also with uncovering any possible means of improving results and with identifying the sources of errors in pre-decision appraisals and in the processes of introducing innovations so as to develop more effective guides to such efforts in the future. Such an executive could then secure the contributions of various relevant specialists, and surmount the common self-protective devices of lower-level supervisors and technicians, in seeking to uncover the sources and causes of shortcomings in performance as well as of remediable errors in pre-decision appraisals.

Formalizing responsibility for the comprehensive evaluation of major technological innovations might yield two additional benefits. First, by providing top management with systematic assessments from an influential official of the poten-

[4]For example, in one computer-aided manufacturing system, it was found that successive minor modifications in operating methods and control yielded a progressive increase in capacity of approximately 40 percent over a five year period. But such increments were so gradual that management failed to alter production planning and output targets accordingly—leaving the additional capability unused until its belated discovery as the result of a strike.

tials, accomplishments and shortcomings of projects which have absorbed major capital allocations, such periodic reports may help to engender greater sensitivity to the importance of technological improvement efforts throughout the firm. Second, the very seriousness and scope of such efforts may help to overcome the present widespread failure to make any constructive use of even such post-adoption appraisals as are made, either in re-examining means of improving the current results of relatively recent innovations, or in strengthening the bases for evaluating future proposals.

It is also worth noting the seemingly universal avoidance in post-installation evaluations of estimates of resulting contributions to profitability. Estimates are often made of reductions in the direct operating costs of the specific operation affected by the innovation and of attendant savings in labour or materials inputs. But very seldom indeed are such appraisals extended to the point of estimating resulting changes in profits. This implies recognition of the complexities of tracing the effects of the innovation-induced adjustments within its sector of operations through subsequent interactions with other sectors, and through concurrent changes in the level, composition and prices of all other inputs as well as outputs, to determine its distinctive effects on net returns. However, if reasonably persuasive determinations of such contributions are so difficult to make, even on the basis of detailed actual performance data (Gold, 1955: 181), one cannot help wondering about the practical usefulness of continuing to base decisions to adopt or reject major innovations on the estimates of prospective profitability derived on the basis of the far more inadequate and vulnerable information likely to be available at that stage (Gold, 1977).

CONCLUDING OBSERVATIONS

1. There has been a dangerously prolonged underemphasis in a wide array of industries on supporting vigorous development of their technological capabilities. Resulting serious lags behind continuously advancing technological frontiers have been a major source of declining competitiveness.

2. Overcoming such lags is likely to prove far more difficult than is widely recognized. The major reason is that such recovery efforts require not only heavy investments in new facilities and equipment, but also substantial changes in managerial priorities and policies, in staff capabilities and in organizational arrangements. An additional reason is that during the extended period needed to overcome built-in resistances, to effectuate required adjustments and to build momentum towards catching-up, leading competitors may be expected to keep pushing further ahead.

3. Effective efforts to regain technological competitiveness require:

    (a) top management commitment to this objective

    (b) development of an array of improvement targets based on objective, competent and comprehensive evaluations of the current and prospective technological advantages and disadvantages of each sector of production as well as each major component of the firm's product-mix

    (c) establishing organizational arrangements:

        (i) to continue monitoring relative competitiveness and its determinants

        (ii) to evaluate alternative technological innovations proposed as means of progressing towards established targets

        (iii) to appraise the performance of adopted innovations periodically as the basis for uncovering developing shortcomings or additional potentials

        (iv) to ensure effective integration of various technological improvement efforts so as to maximize mutual reinforcement and to minimize maladjustments.

4. In order to encourage needed management commitment to, and support for, such recognizedly long-term programmes, whose major benefits may not be realized for some years, it would seem necessary to alter the incentives and rewards which in recent years have motivated an emphasis on maximizing short-term profitability (Gold, 1979: Chapter 17).

REFERENCES

Bower, J. *Managing the Resource Allocation Process.* Graduate School of Business Administration, Harvard University Press, Cambridge, MA, 1970.

Eilon, S., B. Gold and J. Soesan. *Applied Productivity Analysis for Industry.* Pergamon Press, Oxford, 1976. Russian translation—Ekonomist, Moscow, 1980; Chinese translation—The Technical Economy and Modernization of Management Institute, Beijing, 1982.

Gold, B. *Foundations of Productivity Analysis.* University of Pittsburgh Press, Pittsburgh, PA, 1955.

Gold, B. *Explorations in Managerial Economics: Productivity, Costs. Technology and Growth.* Macmillan, London, 1971: Basic Books, New York, 1971. Japanese translation—Chikura Shobo, Tokyo, 1977.

Gold, B. "What is the place of research and technological innovations in business planning?" *Research Policy* (London), No. 2, Summer 1973.

Gold, B. (ed. and co-author). *Technological Change: Economics, Management and Environment.* Pergamon Press, Oxford, 1975.

Gold, B. "On the shaky foundations of capital budgeting." *California Management Review.* Winter (March) 1977, pp. 51–60.

Gold, B. "Steel technologies and costs in the U.S. and Japan." *Iron and Steel Engineer,* April 1978, pp. 32–37. Japanese translation—Jōhō Shūho (Tokyo), July 1978.

Gold, B. "Factors stimulating technological progress in Japanese industries: The Case of Computerization in Steel." *Quarterly Review of Economics and Business,* Winter (December) 1978, pp. 7–21. Spanish translation in *Cienca y Desarrolo* (Conejo National De Cienca Y Tecnologia, Mexico D.F.), November–December 1979.

Gold, B. (ed. and co-author) *Appraising and Stimulating Technological Advances in Industry.* Special Issue of *Omega: The International Journal of Management Science,* October 1980.

Gold, B. "Approaches to strengthening the Swedish steel industry: A case study of industrial policy issues" in *The Future of the Steel Industry in an International Setting.* Royal Academy of Engineering Sciences, Stockholm, 1981a.

Gold, B. "Changing perspectives on size, scale and returns: an interpretive survey." *Journal of Economic Literature,* March 1981b, pp. 5–33.

Gold, B. *Improving Managerial Evaluations of Computer-Aided Manufacturing.* National Academy of Science Press, Washington, D.C., December 1981c.

Gold, B. *Productivity, Technology and Capital: Economic Analysis. Managerial Strategies and Governmental Policies.* D.C. Heath–Lexington Books, Lexington, MA, 1979, 1982.

Gold, B. "Robotics, programmable automation and increasing competitiveness" in *Exploratory Workshop on the Social Impacts of Robotics.* U.S. Congress Office of Technology Assessment, Washington, D.C., 1982.

Gold, B. and M. G. Boylan. "Capital budgeting, industrial capacity and imports." *Quarterly Review of Economics and Business,* Fall 1975, pp. 17–32.

Gold, B., G. Rosegger and M. G. Boylan. *Evaluating Technological Innovations: Methods, Expectations and Findings.* D.C. Heath–Lexington Books, Lexington, MA, 1980.

Rosegger, G. "Continuous casting: physical and economic performance" in Gold, B., G. Rosegger and M. G. Boylan, *Evaluating Technological Innovations: Methods, Expectations and Findings.* D.C. Heath–Lexington Books, Lexington, MA, 1980.

Skeddle, R. W. "Expected and emerging actual results of a major technological innovation—float glass" in Special Issue of *Omega,* October 1980, pp. 553–567.

CHAPTER 3
The Project Manager

In the last chapter we described how projects are evaluated and selected for development. Before more progress can be made, a project manager (PM) must usually be appointed. This person will take responsibility for implementing and completing the project, beginning with the job of getting things started.

The PM can be chosen and installed as soon as the project is selected for funding or at any earlier point that seems desirable to senior management. If the PM is appointed prior to project selection or if the PM originated the project, several of the usual start-up tasks are simplified. On occasion, a PM is chosen late in the project life cycle, usually to replace another PM who is leaving the project for other work. For example, a large agricultural products firm regularly uses a senior scientist as PM until the project's technical problems are solved and the product has been tested. Then it replaces the scientist with a middle manager from the marketing side of the firm as marketing becomes the focal point of the project. (The transition is difficult and, according to firm spokespeople, the results are sometimes unsatisfactory.)

Usually, a senior manager briefs the PM on the project so that the PM can understand where it fits in the general scheme of things in the parent organization, and its priority relative to other projects in the system and to the routine work of the organization. The PM's first set of tasks is typically to prepare a preliminary budget and schedule, to help select people to serve on the project team, to get to know the client, to make sure that the proper facilities are available, to ensure that any supplies required early in the project life are available when needed, and to take care of the routine details necessary to get the project moving.

As people are added to the project, plans and schedules are refined. The details of managing the project through its entire life cycle are spelled out, even to the point of planning for project termination when the work is finally completed.

Mechanisms are developed to facilitate communication between the PM and top management, the functional areas, and the client. As plans develop still further, the PM holds meetings and briefings to ensure that all those who will affect or be affected by the project are prepared in advance for the demands they will have to meet as the project is implemented.

In this chapter we discuss the unique nature of project management and some of the ways project management differs from *functional* management. Our emphasis is on the role and responsibilities of the PM. We concentrate on the demands placed on the PM, particularly on those unique to project management. Based on our discussions of the nature of the PM's job, we complete the chapter by considering how to identify the skills and characteristics required of this supermanager.

It is best to describe the PM's job relative to some assumptions about the nature of projects and the organization within which the project must function. We assume that the parent firm is functionally organized and is conducting several projects simultaneously with its ongoing, routine operations. We also assume a fairly large firm, a project that has some technical components, with an output to be delivered to an "arms-length" customer. Clearly, not all, and possibly even not *most,* projects operate under these circumstances, but these are the most demanding and we address the most difficult problems a PM might have to face. Smaller, simpler projects may not require the tools we will present here, but the PM for these projects should be aware that such tools exist. The term *technical components* as we apply it includes more than hardware. Any firm with a well-defined methodology of carrying out its mission has a technical component, as we use the phrase.

In this chapter two conditions receive special attention. Both have a profound effect on the outcome of the project, and neither is under the complete control of the PM—though the PM can greatly influence both by dealing with the conditions early in the project life. The first of these concerns the degree to which the project has the support of top management. If that support is strong and reasonably unqualified, the project has a much better chance of success.

The second condition concerns the general orientation of the project team members. If they are highly oriented toward their individual, functional disciplines, as opposed to the project itself, project success is threatened. If, on the other hand, they tend to be oriented toward the project (that is, problem-oriented rather than discipline-oriented), the likelihood of success is much greater. The PM cannot actually control these conditions, but there is often much that can be done to influence them.

3.1 THE PROJECT MANAGER'S ROLE AND RESPONSIBILITIES

The Functional Manager

The best way to explain the unique role of the PM is to contrast it with that of a *functional* manager in charge of one of a firm's functional departments such as marketing, engineering, or finance (see Figure 3-1). Such department heads are usually specialists in the areas they manage. Being specialists, they are analyti-

Figure 3-1 Functional management organization chart:
Marketing department of an insurance company.

cally oriented and they know something of the details of each operation for which they are responsible. When a technically difficult task is required of their departments, they know how to analyze and attack it. As functional managers they are administratively responsible for deciding how something will be done, who will do it, and what resources will be devoted to accomplish the task.

A PM, by contrast, is usually a generalist with a wide background of experience and knowledge. A PM must oversee many functional areas, each with its own specialists (see Figure 3-2). Therefore, what is required is an ability to put many pieces of a task together to form a coherent whole. That is, the project manager must be more skilled at synthesis, whereas the functional manager must be more skilled at analysis. The functional manager uses the *analytic approach* and the PM uses the *systems approach*.

This comparison between the PM and the functional manager reveals another crucial difference between the two. The functional manager is a direct, technical supervisor. The PM is a facilitator. Knowing the technology, the functional manager has the basic technical knowledge required to oversee and advise subordinates on the best ways to handle their work and solve problems met in the normal course of that work. The PM may have detailed technical knowledge in one or two specific areas, but he or she rarely has knowledge in depth beyond these few areas. The PM, therefore, cannot apply knowledge directly, but instead must facilitate cooperation between those who have the various kinds of specialized knowledge and those who need it. This distinction between facilitator and specialist is a key element in the decision to use generalists as PMs rather than specialists.

Three major questions face the PM in this task of synthesis: What needs to be done, when must it be done (if the project is not to be late), and how are the resources required to do the job to be obtained. In spite of the fact that the PM is respon-

Figure 3-2 Project management organization showing typical responsibilities of a project manager.

sible for the project, and depending on how the project is organized, the functional managers may make some of the fundamental and critical project decisions. For example, they may select the people who will actually do the work required to carry out the project. They may also develop the technological design detailing how the project will be accomplished. They frequently influence the precise deployment of the project's resources. Once again, depending on how the project is organized, the functional managers may bear little or no direct responsibility for the results. As we will see later (and in Chapter 4, "Project Organization"), this separation of powers between functional and project managers, which may aid in the successful completion of the project, is also a source of considerable "discomfort" for both.

Note here that the PM is responsible for organizing, staffing, budgeting, directing, planning, and controlling the project. In other words, the PM "manages" it, but the functional managers may affect the choice of technology to be used by the project and the specific individuals who will do the work. Arguments about the logic or illogic of such an arrangement will fall on deaf ears. The PM cannot allow the functional manager to usurp control of the project. If this happens, work on the project is likely to become secondary to the work of the functional group and the project will suffer. But the functional manager cannot allow the PM to take over authority for technical decisions in the functional area or to control the assignment of functional area personnel.

Project Responsibilities

The PM's responsibilities are broad and fall primarily into three separate areas: responsibility to the parent organization, responsibility to the project, and responsibility to the members of the project team. Responsibilities to the firm itself include proper conservation of resources, timely and accurate project communications, and the careful, competent management of the project. Many formal aspects of the communications role will be covered in Chapter 9 when the Project Management Information System is discussed, but one matter must be emphasized here. It is very important to keep senior management of the parent organization fully informed about the project's status, cost, timing, and prospects. Senior managers should be warned about likely future problems. The PM should note the chances of running over budget or being late, as well as methods available to reduce the likelihood of these dread events. Reports must be accurate and timely if the PM is to maintain credibility, protect the parent firm from high risk, and allow senior management to intercede where needed.

The PM's responsibility to the project is met by ensuring that the integrity of the project is preserved in spite of the conflicting demands made by the many parties who have legitimate interests in the project. The manager must deal with the engineering department when it resists a change advised by marketing which is responding to a suggestion that emanated from the client. In the meantime, contract administration (or our attorney) says the client has no right to request changes without the submission of a formal Request for Change order. Manufacturing says that the argument is irrelevant because marketing's suggestion cannot be incorporated into the project without a complete redesign.

The PM is in the middle of this turmoil. The PM must sort out understanding from misunderstanding, soothe ruffled feathers, balance petty rivalries, and cater to the demands of the client. One must, of course, remember that none of these strenuous activities relieves the PM of the responsibility of keeping the project on time, within budget, and up to specifications.

The project manager's responsibilities to members of the project team are dictated by the finite nature of the project itself and the specialized nature of the team. Because the project is, by definition, a temporary entity and must come to an end, the PM must be concerned with the future of the people who serve on the team. If the PM does not get involved in helping project workers with the transition back to their functional homes or to new projects, then as the project nears completion, project workers will pay more and more attention to protecting their own future careers and less to completing the project on time. These matters are discussed in more detail in Chapter 13, "Project Termination."

When some members of project teams are highly educated researchers, it has frequently been suggested that such specialists require a "special type" of managing. Often referred to as "tweed coat management," the implication is that Ph.D.s, scientific researchers, and academically oriented experts need careful shepherding. Articles describing the management of research seem to assume that the higher the level of formal education, the lower the level of "street smarts." To the best of our knowledge, there is no evidence supporting this odd assumption. Like most people, scientists seem to respond positively to a caring, supportive managerial style.

PM Career Paths

Some firms have many different types and sizes of projects in progress simultaneously—and not all these projects are large enough to require a full-time manager. Our observations of several firms seem to indicate that placing these small projects under various functional managers is probably unwise. Too often they are treated as unwanted stepchildren. It seems more effective to group them into related sets and put each set under the direction of an individual project manager. The PM selected to manage several small projects is likely to discover that an important criterion for success is to avoid the appearance of favoring one above the others.

These smaller projects, when managed by an experienced PM, serve a purpose beyond the projects themselves. They provide an excellent training ground for new project managers who often begin their preparation for project management by involvement in some major aspect of a small project. Most would-be PMs seek the self-satisfaction that accomplishing a challenging task can give. PMs have the opportunity to "run their own show." The skills and experiences gained from managing a project are a scaled-down version of what it is like to run a full-sized organization. Thus, projects provide an excellent growth environment for future executives and for developing managerial skills.

The career path of a PM often starts with participation in small projects, and later in larger projects, until the person is given command over small and then larger projects. For example, the path could be tooling manager for small Project U, project engineer for larger Project V, manufacturing manager for large Project

W, deputy project manager for large Project X, project manager for small Project Y, and project manager for large Project Z. If energy, luck, and ambition remain, the PM may progress to corporate plant operations manager, vice-president of manufacturing, president, and chairman of the board.

3.2 SPECIAL DEMANDS ON THE PROJECT MANAGER

A number of demands are unique to the management of projects, and the success of the PM depends to a large extent on how capably they are handled. These special demands can be categorized under the seven following headings.

Acquiring Adequate Resources

It was noted earlier that the resources initially budgeted for a project are frequently insufficient to the task. In part, this is due to the natural optimism of the project proposers about how much can be accomplished with relatively few resources; but it is also caused by the great uncertainty associated with a project. Many details of resource purchase and usage are deferred until the project manager knows specifically what resources will be required and when. For instance, there is no point in purchasing a centrifuge now if in nine months we will know exactly what type of centrifuge will be most useful.

The good PM knows there are resource trade-offs that need to be taken into consideration. A skilled machinist can make do with unsophisticated machinery to construct needed parts, but a beginning machinist cannot. Subcontracting can make up for insufficient plant capacity or supply unavailable skills, but subcontracting will cost more and may cause delays. Crises occur that require special resources not usually provided to the project manager. All these problems produce glitches in the otherwise smooth progress of the project. To deal with these glitches, the PM must scramble, elicit aid, work late, wheedle, threaten, or do whatever seems necessary to keep the project on schedule. On occasion, the additional required resources simply alter the project's cost–benefit ratio to the point that the project is no longer cost-effective. Obviously, the PM attempts to avoid these situations, but some of what happens is beyond the PM's control. This issue will be dealt with in detail in Chapter 13.

The problems of time and budget are aggravated in the presence of a phenomenon that has been long suspected but only recently demonstrated [6,7]. The individual who has the responsibility for performing a task sometimes overestimates the time and cost required to do it. That individual's immediate supervisor often discounts the worker's pessimism but, in so doing, may underestimate the time and cost. Moving up the management hierarchy, each successive level frequently lowers the time and cost estimates again, becoming more optimistic about the ability of those working for them to do with less—or, perhaps, more forgetful about what things were like when they worked at such jobs. The authors have informally observed—and listened to complaints about—such doings in a variety of organizations. We suspect they reflect the superior's natural tendency to provide challenging work for subordinates and the desire to have it completed efficiently. The mere recognition of this phenomenon does not prevent it. Complaints to upper-level managers are usually met with a hearty laugh, a pat on the back, and a verbal comment such as, "I know you can do it. You're my best project manager, and you can...."

Another issue may complicate the problem of resource acquisition for the PM. Project and functional managers alike perceive the availability of resources to be strictly limited and thus a strict "win–lose" proposition. Under these conditions, the "winners" may be those managers who have solid political connections with top management. Often, there are times in the life of any project when success or survival may depend on the PM's "friendship" with a champion high in the parent organization.

Acquiring and Motivating Personnel

A major problem for the PM is the fact that most of the people needed for a project must be "borrowed." With few exceptions, they are borrowed from the functional departments. The PM must negotiate with the functional department managers for the desired personnel, and then, if successful, negotiate with the people themselves to convince them to take on these challenging temporary project assignments.

Most functional managers cooperate when the PM comes seeking good people for the project, but the cooperative spirit has its limits. The PM will be asking for the services of the two types of people most needed and prized by the functional manager: first, individuals with scarce but necessary skills and, second, top producers. Both the PM and functional manager are fully aware that the PM does not want a "has-been," a "never-was," or a "never-will-be." Perceptions about the capabilities of individuals may differ, but the PM is usually trying to borrow precisely those people the functional manager would most like to keep.

A second issue may reduce the willingness of the functional manager to cooperate with the PM's quest for quality people. At times, the functional manager may perceive the project as more glamorous than his or her function and hence a potent source of managerial glory. The functional manager may thus be a bit jealous or suspicious of the PM, a person who may have little interest in the routine work of the functional area even if it is the bread and butter of the organization.

On its surface, the task of motivating good people to join the project does not appear to be difficult, because the kind of people who are most desired as members of a project team are those naturally attracted by the challenge and variety inherent in project work. Indeed, it would not be difficult except for the fact that the functional manager is trying to keep the same people that the PM is trying to attract. The subordinate who is being seduced to leave the steady life of the functional area for the glamour of a project can be gently reminded that the functional manager retains control of personnel evaluation, salary, and promotion for those people lent out to projects. (A few exceptions to these general rules will be discussed in Chapter 4.) There may even be comments about how easy it is to lose favor or be forgotten when one is "out of sight."

Unless the PM can hire outsiders with proven ability, it is not easy to gather competent people; but having gathered them, they must be motivated to work. Because the functional manager controls pay and promotion, the PM cannot promise much beyond the challenge of the work itself. Fortunately, as Herzberg has argued [14], that is often sufficient [also see 25]. Many of the project personnel are professionals and experts in their respective specialities. Given this, and the voluntary nature of their commitment to the project, there is the assumption that they must be managed "delicately."

It has long been assumed that in order to ensure creativity, professionals require minimal supervision, maximum freedom, and little control. As a matter of fact, William Souder has shown [28] that the output of R & D laboratories is actually not correlated with the level of freedom in the lab. This finding is significant. The most likely explanation is that individual scientists have unique requirements for freedom and control. Some want considerable direction in their work, whereas others find that a lack of freedom inhibits creativity. Those who need freedom thus tend to work in organizations where they are allowed considerable latitude, and those who desire direction gravitate to organizations that provide it.

Motivation problems are often less severe for routine, repeated projects such as those in construction, or for projects carried out as the sole activity of an organization (even if it is part of a larger organization). In such cases, the PM probably has considerable de facto influence over salary and promotion. Frequently, the cadre of these projects see themselves as engaged in similar projects for the long term. If the project is perceived as temporary, risky, and important, about all the PM can offer people is the chance to work on a challenging, high-visibility assignment, to be "needed," and to operate in a supportive climate. For most, this is sufficient incentive to join the project.

A story has it that when asked "How do you motivate astronauts?" a representative of NASA responded, "We don't motivate them, but, boy, are we careful about whom we select." The issue of motivating people to join and work creatively for a project is closely related to the kind of people who are invited to join. The most effective team members have some common characteristics. A list of the most important of these follows, but only the first is typically considered during the usual selection process.

1.   *High-quality technical skills*   Team members must be able to solve most of the technical problems for a project without recourse to outside assistance. Although the major technical problems faced by a project are generally solved by the functional departments, the exact way in which such solutions are applied invariably requires some adaptation. In addition, a great many minor technical difficulties occur, always at inconvenient times, and need to be handled rapidly. In such cases, project schedules will suffer if these difficulties must be referred back to the functional departments where they will have to stand in line for a solution along with (or behind) the department's own problems.

2.   *Political sensitivity*   It is obvious that the PM requires political skills of a high order. Although it is less obvious, senior project members also need to be politically skilled and sensitive to organizational politics. As we have noted several times, project success is dependent on support from senior management in the parent organization. This support depends on the preservation of a delicate balance of power between projects and functional units, and between the projects themselves. The balance can be upset by individuals who are politically inept.

3. *Strong problem orientation* Research conducted by Juri Pill [24] has shown that the chances for successful completion of a multidisciplinary project are greatly increased if project team members are *problem-oriented* rather than *discipline-oriented*. Pill indicates that problem-oriented people tend to learn and adopt whatever problem-solving techniques appear helpful, but discipline-oriented individuals tend to view the problem through the eyes of their discipline, ignoring aspects of the problem that do not lie in the narrow confines of their educational expertise.

4. *Strong goal orientation* Projects do not provide a comfortable work environment for individuals whose focus is on activity rather than on results. Work flow is rarely even, and for the professionals a 60-hour week is common, as are periods when there seems to be little to do. "Clock watchers" will not be successful team members.

5. *High self-esteem* A prime law for projects (and one that applies equally well to the entire organization) is *never surprise the boss*. Projects can rapidly get into deep trouble if team members hide their failures, or even a significant risk of failure, from the PM. Individuals on the team should have sufficient self-esteem that they are not threatened by acknowledgment of their own errors, or by pointing out possible problems caused by the work of others. Egos must be strong enough that all can freely share credit and blame. We trust that the PM is aware that "shooting the messenger who brings bad news" will immediately stop the flow of any negative information from below—though negative surprises from above will probably be more frequent.

Dealing with Obstacles

One characteristic of any project is its uniqueness, and this characteristic means that the PM will have to face and overcome a series of crises. From the beginning of the project to its termination, crises appear without warning. The better the planning, the fewer the crises, but no amount of planning can take account of the myriad of changes that can and do occur in the project's environment. The successful PM is a fire fighter by avocation.

At the inception of the project, the "fires" tend to be associated with resources. The technical plans to accomplish the project have been translated into a budget and schedule and forwarded up the managerial hierarchy or sent to the client for approval. In an earlier section we noted that some of the budget and schedule is pared away at each successive step up the hierarchy. Each time this happens, the budget and schedule cuts must be translated into changes in the technical plans. Test procedures may be shortened, suppliers' lead times may be cut. The required cost and schedule adjustments are made, a nip here and a tuck there. To the people affected, these may well be crises.

The PM learns by experience; the wise PM learns from the experiences of others. Every project on which the PM has worked, whether as the project manager or not, is a source of learning. The war stories and horror tales of other PMs are vicarious experiences to be integrated with direct personal experience into a body of lore that will provide early-warning signals of trouble on the way. The lore will also serve as a bank of pretested remedies for trouble already at hand.

To be useful, experience must be generalized and organized. Managing a project is much like managing a business. Business firms often develop special routines for dealing with various types of fires. Expediters, order entry clerks, purchasing agents, dispatchers, shippers, and similar individuals keep the physical work of the system moving along from order to shipment. Human resource departments help put out "people fires" just as engineering helps deal with "mechanical fires." Fire fighting, to be optimally effective, should be organized so that fires are detected and recognized as early as possible. This allows the fires to be assigned to project team members who specialize in dealing with specific types of fires. Although this procedure does not eliminate crises, it does reduce the pain of dealing with them.

As the project nears completion, obstacles tend to be clustered around two issues: first, last-minute schedule and technical changes, and second, a series of problems that have as their source the uncertainty surrounding what happens to members of the project team when the project is completed [see 26, Chapter 18]. These two types of problems are very different from one another, as well as from the problems that faced the PM earlier in the life cycle of the project. The way to deal with last-minute schedule and technical changes is "the best you can." Beyond knowing that such changes will occur and will be disruptive to the project, there is little the PM can do except be prepared to "scramble."

Coping with the uncertainty surrounding what happens at the end of a project is a different matter. The issue will be covered at greater length in Chapter 13, but it deserves mention here because it is certainly an obstacle that the PM must overcome. The key to solving such problems is communication. The PM must make open communications between the PM and team members first priority. The notion of "open communications" requires that emotions, feelings, worries, and anxieties be communicated, as well as factual messages.

Making Project Goal Trade-offs

The PM must make trade-offs between the project goals of cost, time, and performance. The PM must also make trade-offs between project progress and process—that is, between the technical and managerial functions. The first set of trade-offs is required by the need to preserve some balance between the project time, cost, and performance goals. Conventional wisdom had it that the precise nature of the trade-offs varied depending on the stage of the project life cycle. At the beginning of the life cycle, when the project is being planned, performance was felt to be the most important of the goals, with cost and schedule sacrificed to the technical requirements of the project. Following the design phase, the project builds momentum, grows, and operates at peak levels. Because it accumulates costs at the maximum rate during this period, cost was felt to take precedence over performance and schedule. Finally, as the project nears completion, schedule becomes the high-priority goal, and cost (and perhaps performance) suffers. Recent research [17] has shown that these assumptions, sensible as they seem, are not true.

During the design or formation stage of the project life cycle, there is no significant difference in the importance project managers place on the three goals. It appears that the logic of this finding is based on the assumption that the project must be designed in such a way that it meets all the goals set by the client. If compromises must be made, each of the objectives is vulnerable. At times, however, a higher level of technical performance may be possible that, in the client's eyes, merits some softening of the cost or schedule goals. For example, a computer software project required that an information system be able to answer queries within 3 seconds 95 percent of the time. The firm designed such a system by ensuring that it would respond within 1.5 seconds 50 percent of the time. By meeting this additional standard, more stringent than that imposed by the client, it was able to meet the specified standard.

Schedule is the dominant goal during the buildup stage, being significantly more important than performance, which is in turn significantly more important than cost. Kloppenborg conjectures [17, p. 127] that this is so because scheduling commitments are made during the buildup stage. Scheduling and performance are approximately tied for primacy during the main stage of the life cycle when both are significantly more important than cost, though the importance of cost increases sharply between the buildup and main stages. During the final stage, phaseout, performance is significantly more important than schedule, which is significantly more important than cost. Table 3-1 shows the relative importance of each objective for each stage of the project life cycle.

The second trade-off concerns sacrificing smoothness of running the project team for technical progress. Near the end of the project it may be necessary to insist that various team members work on aspects of the project for which they are not well trained or which they do not enjoy, such as copying or collating the final report. The PM can get a fairly good reading on team morale by paying attention to the response to such requests. This is, of course, another reason why the PM should select team members who have a strong problem orientation. Discipline-oriented people want to stick to the tasks for which they have been prepared and to which they have been assigned. Problem-oriented people have little hesitation in helping to do whatever is necessary to bring the project in on time, to "spec," and within budget.

The PM also has responsibility for other types of trade-offs, ones rarely discussed in the literature of project management. If the PM directs more than one project, he or she must make trade-offs between the several projects. As noted earlier, it is critical to avoid the appearance of favoritism in such cases. Thus, we strongly recommend that when a project manager is directing two or more projects, care should be taken to ensure that the life cycles of the projects are sufficiently different that the projects will not demand the same constrained

Table 3-1 Relative Importance of Project Objectives During Different Stages of the Project Life Cycle

Life Cycle Stage	Cost	Schedule	Performance
Formation	1	1	1
Buildup	3	1	2
Main	3	1	1
Phaseout	3	2	1

Note: 1=most important.
Source: Kloppenborg, T. J. *Tradeoffs of Objectives Over Project Life Cycles.* Ph.D. dissertation, University of Cincinnati, 1987. Adapted from p. 78.

resources at the same time, thereby avoiding forced choices between projects.

In addition to the trade-offs between the goals of a project, and in addition to trade-offs between projects, the PM will also be involved in making choices that require balancing the goals of the project with the goals of the firm. Such choices are common. Indeed, the necessity for such choices is inherent in the nature of project management. The PM's enthusiasm about a project—a prime requirement for successful project management—can easily lead him or her to overstate the benefits of a project, to understate the probable costs of project completion, to ignore technical difficulties in achieving the required level of performance, and to make trade-off decisions that are clearly biased in favor of the project and antithetical to the goals of the parent organization. Similarly, this enthusiasm can lead the PM to take risks not justified by the likely outcomes.

Finally, the PM must make trade-off decisions between the project, the firm, and his or her own career goals. Depending on the PM's attitudes toward risk, career considerations might lead the PM to take inappropriate risks or avoid appropriate ones.

Failure and the Risk and Fear of Failure

In Chapter 13, we will consider some research on characteristics that seem to be associated with project success or failure, but sometimes it is difficult to distinguish between project failure, partial failure, and success. Indeed, what appears to be a failure at one point in the life of a project may look like success at another. If we divide all projects into two general categories according to the degree to which the project is understood, we find some interesting differences in the nature and timing of perceived difficulties in carrying out a project. These perceptions have a considerable effect on the PM.

Assume that Type 1 projects are generally well-understood, routine construction projects. Type 2 projects are at the opposite pole; they are not well understood, and there may be considerable uncertainty about specifically what must be done. When they are begun, Type 1 projects appear simple. As they progress, however, the natural flow of events will introduce problems. Mother Nature seems habitually hostile. The later in the life cycle of the project these problems appear, the more difficult it is to keep the project on its time and cost schedule. Contingency allowances for the time and cost to overcome such problems are often built into the budgets and schedules for Type 1 projects, but unless the project has considerable slack in both budget and schedule, an unlikely condition, little can be done about the problems that occur late in the project life cycle. As everyone from engineers to interior decorators knows, change orders are always received *after* the final design is set in concrete. Type 1 projects rarely fail because the project cannot meet specifications, but rather because they come in late, over budget, or both.

Type 2 projects exhibit a different pattern of problems. There are many difficulties early in the life of the project, most of which concern how to accomplish the objectives of the project. As these problems are (apparently) solved, the project is staffed, scheduled, and budgeted. The seeds of future problems are sown at this stage of the life cycle. The basic solution to the major technical problem of how to accomplish the project, after it has been discovered, often seems to be reasonably simple and straightforward—at least, it appears that way to outsiders. But unforeseen technical barriers can suddenly crop up, necessitating technical detours that may wreck the budget and schedule.

Perhaps more serious are the psychic consequences of such technical snags. The occurrence and solution of technical problems tend to cause waves of pessimism and optimism to sweep over the project staff. There is little doubt that these swings of mood have a destructive effect on performance. The PM must cope with these alternating periods of elation and despair, and the task is not simple. Performance will be strongest when project team members are "turned on," but not so much that they blandly assume that "everything will turn out all right in the end," no matter what. Despair is even worse because the project is permeated with an attitude that says, "Why try when we are destined to fail?"

Maintaining a balanced, positive outlook among team members is a delicate job. Setting budgets and schedules with sufficient slack to allow for Murphy's law, but not sufficient to arouse suspicion in cost and time-conscious senior management, is also a delicate job. But who said the PM's job would be easy?

Breadth of Communication

As is the case with any manager, most of the PM's time is spent communicating with the many groups interested in the project [21]. Running a project requires constant selling, reselling, and explaining the project to outsiders, top management, functional departments, clients, and a number of other such parties-at-interest to the project, as well as to members of the project team itself. The PM is the project's liaison with the outside world, but the manager must also be available for problem solving in the lab, for crises in the field, for threatening or cajoling subcontractors, and for reducing interpersonal conflict between project team members. And all these demands may occur within the span of one day—a typical day, cynics would say.

To some extent, every manager must deal with these special demands; but for a PM such demands are far more frequent and critical. As if this were not enough, there are also certain fundamental issues that the manager must understand and deal with so that the demands noted can be handled successfully. First, the PM must know *why* the project exists; that is, the PM must fully understand the project's intent. The PM must have a clear definition of how *success* or *failure* is to be determined. When making trade-offs, it is easy to get off the track and strive to meet goals that were really never intended by top management.

Second, any PM with extensive experience has managed projects that failed. As is true in every area of business we know, competent managers are rarely ruined by a single failure, but repeated failure is usually interpreted as a sign of incompetence. On occasion a PM is asked to take over an ongoing project that appears to be heading for failure. Whether or not the PM will be able to decline such a doubtful honor depends on a great many things unique to each situation, such as the PM's relationship with the Program Manager, the degree of organizational desperation about the project, the PM's seniority and track record in dealing with projects like the one in question, and other matters, not excluding the PM's ability to be engaged elsewhere when the "opportunity" arises. Managing successful projects is difficult enough that the PM is, in general, well advised not to volunteer for undertakings with a high probability of failure.

Third, it is critical to have the support of top management. If support is weak, the future of the project is clouded with uncertainty. If the support is not broadly based in top management, some areas in the firm may not be willing to help the project manager when help is needed. Suppose, for example, that the marketing vice-president is not fully in support of the basic project concept. Even after all the engineering and manufacturing work has been completed, sales may not go all out to push the product. In such a case, only the chief executive officer (CEO) can force the issue, and it is very risky for a PM to seek the CEO's assistance to override a lukewarm vice-president. If the VP acquiesces and the product fails (and what are the chances for success in such a case?), the project manager looks like a fool. If the CEO does not force the issue, then the VP has won and the project manager may be out of a job. As noted earlier, political sensitivity and acumen are mandatory attributes for the project manager. The job description for a PM should include the "construction and maintenance of alliances with the leaders of functional areas."

Fourth, the PM should build and maintain a solid information network. It is critical to know what is happening both inside the project and outside it. The PM must be aware of customer complaints and department head criticism, who is favorably inclined toward the project, when vendors are planning to change prices, or if a strike is looming in a supplier industry. Inadequate information can blind the PM to an incipient crisis just as excessive information can desensitize the PM to early warnings of trouble.

Finally, the PM must be flexible, flexible in many ways, with as many people, and about as many activities as possible throughout the entire life of the project. The PM's primary mode of operation is to trade off resources and criteria accomplishment against one another. Every decision the PM makes limits the scope of future decisions, but failure to decide can stop the project in its tracks. Even here, we have a trade-off. In the end, regardless of the pressures, the PM needs the support of the noninvolved middle and upper-middle management.

Negotiation

In order to meet the demands of the job of project manager—acquiring adequate resources, acquiring and motivating personnel, dealing with obstacles, making project goal trade-offs, handling failure and the fear of failure, and maintaining the appropriate patterns of communication—the project manager must be a highly skilled negotiator. There is almost no aspect of the PM's job that does not depend directly on this skill. We have noted the need for negotiation at several points in the previous pages, and we will note the need again and again in the pages that follow. The subject is so important that Chapter 6 is devoted to a discussion of the matter.

3.3 SELECTING THE PROJECT MANAGER

Selection of the project manager is one of the two or three most important decisions concerning the project. In this section, we note a few of the many skills the PM should possess in order to have a reasonable chance of success.

The following is a list of some of the more popular attributes, skills, and qualities that have been sought when selecting project managers:

- A strong technical background.
- A hard-nosed manager.
- A mature individual.
- Someone who is currently available.
- Someone on good terms with senior executives.
- A person who can keep the project team happy.
- One who has worked in several different departments.
- A person who can walk on (or part) the waters.

These reasons for choosing a PM are not so much wrong as they are "not right." They miss the key criterion. Above all, the best PM is the one who can get the job done! As any senior manager knows, hard workers are easy to find. What is rare is the individual whose focus is on the completion of a difficult job. Of all the characteristics desirable in a PM, this *drive to complete the task* is the most important.

If we consider the earlier sections of this chapter, we can conclude that there are three major categories of skills that are required of the PM and serve as the key criteria for selection, given that the candidate has a powerful bias toward task completion. Moreover, it is not sufficient for the PM simply to possess these skills; they must also be perceived by others. The fact and the perception are equally important.

Credibility

The PM needs two kinds of credibility. First is *technical credibility*. The PM must be perceived by the client, senior executives, the functional departments, and the project team as possessing sufficient technical knowledge to direct the project. The PM does not have to have a high level of expertise, know more than any individual team members (or all of them), or be able to stand toe-to-toe and intellectually slug it out with experts in the various functional areas. Quite simply, the PM has to have a reasonable understanding of the base technologies on which the project rests, must be able to explain project technology to senior management, and must be able to interpret the technical needs and wants of the client (and senior management) to the project team.

Second, the PM must be *administratively credible*. The PM has several key administrative responsibilities that must be performed with apparently effortless skill. One of these responsibilities is to the client and senior management—to keep the project on schedule and within cost and to make sure that project reports are accurate and timely. Another responsibility is to the project team—to make sure that material, equipment, and manpower are available when needed. Still another responsibility is to represent the interests of all parties to the project (team, management, functional departments, and client) to one another. The PM is truly the "person in the middle." Finally, the PM is responsible for making the tough trade-off decisions for the project, and must be perceived as a person who has the mature judgment and courage to do so consistently.

Sensitivity

The preceding pages contain many references to the PM's need for political sensitivity. There is no point in belaboring the issue further. In addition to a good, working set of political antennae, the PM needs to sense interpersonal conflict on the project team or between team members and outsiders. Successful PMs are not conflict avoiders. Quite the opposite, they sense conflict very early and confront it before it escalates into interdepartmental and intradepartmental warfare.

The PM must keep project team members "cool." This is not easy. As with any group of humans, rivalries, jealousies, friendships, and hostilities are sure to exist. The PM must persuade people to cooperate irrespective of personal feelings, to set aside personal likes and dislikes, and to focus on achieving project goals.

Finally, the PM needs a sensitive set of technical sensors. It is common, unfortunately, for otherwise competent and honest team members to try to hide their failures. Individuals who cannot work under stress would be well advised to avoid project organizations. In the pressure-cooker life of the project, failure is particularly threatening. Remember that we staffed the team with people who are task-oriented. Team members with this orientation may not be able to tolerate their own failures (though they are rarely as intolerant of failure in others), and will hide failure rather than admit to it. The PM must be able to sense when things are being "swept under the rug" and are not progressing properly.

Leadership

Leadership has been defined [29] as "interpersonal influence, exercised in situations and directed through the communication process, toward the attainment of a specified goal or goals." But how is interpersonal influence generated? To all the skills and attributes we have mentioned, add enthusiasm, optimism, energy, tenacity, courage, and personal maturity. It is difficult to explain leadership. We tend to recognize it after the fact, rather than before. We define it anecdotally by saying that this person or that one acted like a leader. The PM must capitalize on people's strengths, cover their weaknesses, know when to take over and when to "give the team its head," know when to punish and when to reward, know when to communicate and when to remain silent. Above all, the PM must know how to get others to share commitment to the project. In a word, the PM must be a leader.

3.4 SUMMARY

This chapter addressed the subject of the PM, a *supermanager*. The PM's role in the organization and responsibilities to both the organization and the project team were discussed first. Common PM career paths were also described. Next, the unique demands typically placed on project managers were detailed. Finally, the task of selecting the PM was addressed.

The following specific points were made in the chapter.

Two factors crucial to the success of the project are its support by top management and the existence of a problem orientation, rather than discipline orientation, within the team members.

Compared to a functional manger, a PM is a generalist rather than a specialist, a synthesizer rather than an analyst, and a facilitator rather than a supervisor.

The PM has responsibilities to the parent organization, the project itself, and the project team.

The unique demands on a PM concern seven areas:
—acquiring adequate physical resources
—acquiring and motivating personnel
—dealing with obstacles
—making goal trade-offs
—maintaining a balanced outlook in the team
—communicating with all parties
—negotiating

The most common characteristics of effective project team members are
—high-quality technical skills
—political sensitivity
—strong problem orientation
—high self-esteem

To handle the variety of project demands effectively, the PM must understand the basic goals of the project, have the support of top management, build and maintain a solid information network, and remain flexible about as many project aspects as possible.

The best person to select as PM is the one who will get the job done.

Valuable skills for the PM are technical and administrative credibility, political sensitivity, and an ability to get others to commit to the project, a skill otherwise known as leadership.

In the next chapter we move to the first task of the PM, organizing the project. We deal there not only with various organizational forms, such as functional, project, and matrix, but also with the organization of the *project office*. This task includes setting up the project team and managing the human element of the project.

3.5 GLOSSARY

ANALYTIC APPROACH—Breaking problems into their constituent parts to understand the parts better and thereby solve the problem.

BENEFIT–COST—A ratio to evaluate a proposed course of action.

CHAMPION—A person who spearheads an idea or action and "sells" it throughout the organization.

CONTINGENCY PLAN—An alternative for action if the expected result fails to materialize.

DISCIPLINE—An area of expertise.

FACILITATOR—A person who helps people overcome problems, either with technical issues or with other people.

FUNCTIONAL—One of the standard organization disciplines such as finance, marketing, accounting or operations.

SYSTEMS APPROACH—A wide-ranging, synthesizing method for addressing problems that considers multiple and interacting relationships. Commonly contrasted with the analytic approach.

TECHNOLOGICAL—Having to do with the methods and techniques for doing something.

TRADE-OFF—Allowing one aspect to get worse in return for another aspect getting better.

TWEED COAT MANAGEMENT—The concept that highly educated people such as engineers require a special type of management.

3.6 PROJECT TEAM ASSIGNMENT

The project team now needs to select its project manager. It should detail the various factors important in the selection of a PM and evaluate each member on each of the factors. A weighted scoring model might be appropriate here, with the heaviest weight on ability to get the job done. It is also important that the PM have the support of top management (the instructor) and be a talented facilitator rather than a knowledgeable supervisor.

Following selection of the PM, the team should proceed to evaluate the team members in terms of their effectiveness on the project. Pay particular attention to having a problem orientation rather than a discipline orientation.

3.7 MATERIAL REVIEW QUESTIONS

1. How does the project act as a stepping-stone for the project manager's career?
2. What are the main responsibilities of the project manager to his or her firm?
3. Name the categories of skills that should be considered in the selection of a project manager.
4. Why must the project manager be a generalist rather than a specialist?
5. Discuss the PM's responsibilities toward the project team members.
6. What are the major differences between function managers and project managers?
7. What are some of the essential characteristics of effective project team members?
8. What is the most important characteristic of a project manager?
9. What project goals are most important during the project life cycle stages?

3.8 CONCEPTUAL DISCUSSION QUESTIONS

1. Elaborate on "...it is not sufficient for the PM simply to possess these skills; they must also be perceived by others."
2. Can you think of several ways to assure "breadth of communication" in a project? Do you think "socialization" off the job helps or hinders?
3. Contrast the prime law for projects, "Never surprise the boss," with the corporate adage "Bad news never travels up."
4. "The successful PM is a fire fighter by avocation." How much do you think fire fighting is a result of the PM's style? Can some project managers anticipate problems better than others? Do some PMs create their own fires, perhaps out of a love for fire fighting?
5. Discuss why the project manager must be an overachiever.
6. How does a project manager, in some cases, work like a politician?

3.9 CHAPTER EXERCISE

Assume that your class is faced with the task of producing an answer manual for this book within the next month. Assume that all pedagogical material has to have answers—all the questions, the exercises, the incidents, the problems, the cases. List the characteristics you would look for in choosing a classmate to lead this project. Then compare your list with the advice given in this chapter. What are the differences? Why do they exist? Would your list of characteristics differ if this project constituted 15 percent of your grade as compared to 85 percent? How would the list vary if you were the instructor and were attempting to choose a PM?

3.10 INCIDENTS FOR DISCUSSION

Smithson Company

Eric Smithson is the CEO of the Smithson Company, a privately owned, medium-size manufacturing company. The company is twenty years old and, until recently, had experienced rapid growth. Mr. Smithson believes that the company's recent problems are closely related to the depressed U.S. economy.

John Smatters was hired as the director of corporate planning at Smithson six months ago. After reviewing the performance and financial statements of Smithson for the last few years, Mr. Smatters has come to the conclusion that the economic conditions are not the real problem, but rather exacerbate the real problems. He believes that Smithson Company products are becoming obsolete and that the company has done a bad job of reacting to market threats and opportunities. He also believes that the strong functional organization impedes the kinds of action required to remedy the situation. Accordingly, he has recommended that Mr. Smithson create a new position, manager of special operations, to promote and use project management techniques. The new manager would handle several critical projects himself in the role of a project manager.

Mr. Smithson is cool to the idea. He believes that his functional departments are managed by capable professional people. Why can't these high-level managers work together more efficiently? Perhaps a good approach would be for him (Smithson) to give the group some direction (what to do, when to do it, who should do it) and then put the functional manager most closely related to the problems in charge of the group. He assumes that the little push from him (Smithson) as just described would be enough to "get the project rolling."

Question: After this session Mr. Smatters is more convinced than ever that a separate, nonfunctional project manager is required. Is he right? If you were Smatters, how would you sell Mr. Smithson on the idea?

Ohio Hospital

A 500-bed hospital in Ohio is in the planning and design stage of a new ambulatory service building and is scheduled to begin construction in two months. The engineering department is normally responsible for assigning a project manager for all projects within the hospital. Currently, the engineering department has no one with experience in the construction of an entire building. As a result, the president is considering using the architectural firm that is currently designing the building to do the project management as well. The engineering division head believes his senior project engineer can handle the job for three reasons: He has a good technical background, he pays meticulous attention to detail, and he is currently available.

Question: If you were the president, what would your choice be? Why? What additional information would you try to obtain before making a decision?

BIBLIOGRAPHY

1. Archibald, R. D. *Managing High Technology Programs and Projects.* Wiley, New York, 1976.
2. Atkins, W. "Selecting a Project Manager." *Journal of Systems Management,* Oct. 1980.
3. Avots, I. "Making Project Management Work: The Right Tools for the Wrong Project Manager." *S.A.M. Advanced Management Journal,* Autumn 1975.
4. Friend, F. L. "Be a more Effective Program Manager." *Journal of Systems Management,* Feb. 1976
5. Gaddis, P. O. "The Project Manager." *Harvard Business Review,* May–June 1959.
6. Gagnon, R. J. *An Exploratory Analysis of the Relevant Cost Structure of Internal and External Engineering Consulting.* Ph.D. dissertation, University of Cincinnati, 1982.
7. Gagnon, R. J., and S. J. Mantel, Jr. "Strategies and Performance Improvement for Computer-Assisted Design." *IEEE Transactions on Engineering Management,* Nov. 1987.
8. Gemmill, G. R., and H. J. Thamhain. "The Power Styles of Project Managers: Some Efficiency Correlates." 20th Annual JEMC, *Managing for Improved Engineering Effectiveness,* Oct. 1972.
9. Gemmill, G. R., and H. J. Thamhain. "Project Performance as a Function of The Leadership Styles of Project Managers: Results of a Field Study." *Convention Digest.* 4th Annual Meeting of the Project Management Institute, Philadelphia, Oct. 1972.
10. Gemmill, G. R., and H. J. Thamhain. "The Effectiveness of Different Power Styles of Project Managers in Gaining Project Support." *IEEE Transactions on Engineering Management,* May 1973.
11. Gemmill, G. R., and H. J. Thamhain. "Influence Styles of Project Managers: Some Project Performance Correlates." *Academy of Management Journal,* June 1974.
12. Gemmill, G. R., and D. L. Wilemon. "The Product Manager as an Influence Agent," *Journal of Marketing,* Jan. 1976.
13. Goodman, R. A. "Ambiguous Authority Definitions in Project Management." *Academy of Management Journal,* Dec. 1967.
14. Herzberg, F. H. "One More Time: How Do You Motivate Employees?" *Harvard Business Review,* Jan.–Feb. 1968.

15. Hogetts, R. M., "Leadership Techniques in the Project Organization." *Academy of Management Journal,* June 1968.

16. Kierchner, E. "The Project Manager." *Space Aeronautics,* Feb. 1965.

17. Kloppenborg, T. J. *Tradeoffs of Objectives Over Project Life Cycles.* Ph.D. dissertation, University of Cincinnati, Nov. 1987.

18. Lawrence, P. R., and J. W. Lorsch. "New Management Job: The Integrator." *Harvard Business Review,* Nov.–Dec. 1967.

19. Maieli, V. "Management by Hindsight: Diary of A Project Manager." *Management Review,* June 1971.

20. Melchner, A. J., and T. A. Kayser. "Leadership Without Formal Authority: The Project Department." *California Management Review,* Winter 1970.

21. Mintzberg, H. *The Nature of Managerial Work.* Harper & Row, New York, 1973.

22. Morton, D. H. "The Project Manager, Catalyst to Constant Change: A Behavioral Analysis." *Project Management Quarterly.* March 1975.

23. O'Brien, J. B. "The Project Manager: Not Just A Firefighter." *S.A.M. Advanced Management Journal,* Jan. 1974.

24. Pill, J. *Technical Management and Control of Large Scale Urban Studies: A Comparative Analysis of Two Cases.* Ph.D. dissertation, Case Western Reserve University, 1971.

25. Roche, W. J., and N. L. MacKinnon. "Motivating People with Meaningful Work." *Harvard Business Review,* May–June 1970.

26. Rosenau, M. D., Jr. *Successful Project Management.* Lifetime Learning Publications, Belmont, CA, 1981.

27. Rubin, I. M., and W. Seilig. "Experience as a Factor in the Selection and Performance of Project Managers," *IEEE Transactions on Engineering Management,* Sept. 1967.

28. Souder, W. E. "Autonomy, Gratification, and R & D Output: A Small-Sample Field Study." *Management Science,* April 1974.

29. Tannenbaum, R., and F. Massarick. "Leadership: A Frame of Reference." *Management Science,* Oct. 1957.

30. Wilemon, D. L., and J. P. Cicero. "The Project Manager; Anomalies and Ambiguities." *Academy of Management Journal,* Sept. 1970.

3.12 READING

This article integrates two views about the requirements for good project managers. One view concerns the personal and managerial characteristics of PMs and their ability to lead a team, regardless of the project. The other view considers the critical problems in the project in question and the PM's talents relative to these problems.

A survey is first described and then the critical problems that projects face are identified from the survey responses. Next, the skills required of project managers, as indicated by the survey respondents, are detailed. Last, the skills are related back to the critical project problems for an integrated view of the requirements for a successful project manager.

What It Takes to Be a Good Project Manager

Barry Z. Posner

Santa Clara University

Selecting a good project manager is not a simple task. Being an effective project manager is an on-going challenge. The complex nature and multi-faceted range of activities involved in managing projects precludes easily identifying managerial talent and continually stretches the capabilities of talented project managers. Two seemingly con-tradictory viewpoints have been advanced about what is required to be a good project manager.

One perspective prescribes a set of *personal characteristics* necessary to manage a project [1]. Such personal attributes include aggressiveness, confidence, poise, decisiveness, resolution, entre-preneurship, toughness, integrity, versatility, mul-tidisciplinary, and quick thinking.

However, Daniel Roman [2], maintains that it would take an extraordinary individual to have all of these critical personal characteristics. A more practical solution, he suggests, would be to deter-mine the *critical problems* faced by project managers and to select a person who can handle such difficulties. The shortcoming with this second perspective, argue those like Michael Badaway [3], is that the primary problems of project managers are really not technical ones. The reason managers fail at managing projects, he con-tends, is because they lack critical organization and management skills.

Scholars like Roman and Badaway—as well as practitioners—may actually be raising different issues. On the one hand, good project managers understand the critical problems which face them and are prepared to deal with them. On the other hand, managing projects well requires a set of par-ticular attributes and skills. But, are these two viewpoints really at odds with one another? In this study they were discovered to be two sides of the *same* coin!

STUDY OF PROJECT MANAGER PROBLEMS AND SKILLS

Questionnaires were completed by project man-agers during a nationwide series of project management seminars. Project managers attend-ing these seminars came from a variety of tech-nology-oriented organizations. Responses to the survey instrument were both voluntary and con-fidential.

Information about the respondents and the na-ture of their projects was collected. The typical project manager was a 37-year-old male, had nine people reporting to him, and was responsible for a small to moderate size project within a matrix or-ganization structure. More specifically, there were 189 men and 98 women in the sample ($N = 287$) and their ages ranged from 22 to 60 years of age ($X = 37.4$, S.D. $= 8.3$). Fifty-six percent indicated that they were the formal manager of the project. The size of their immediate project group ranged from 2 to over 100 people (median $= 8.9$). Fifty-nine percent reported that they worked primarily on small projects (involving few people or functions, with a short time horizon) as compared to large projects (involving many people or functions, with a long time horizon). More than 63 percent indi-cated they were working within a matrix organiza-tion structure. No information was collected about the specific nature (e.g., new product develop-ment, R & D, MIS) of their projects.

Two open-ended questions were asked (their order was randomized). The first asked about the skills necessary to be a successful project

©1987 by The Project Management Institute. Reprinted by permission from *Project Management Journal* (March 1987).

manager. The second question investigated the most likely problems encountered in managing projects. Responses to these questions were content analyzed. Content analysis is a systematic approach to data analysis, resulting in both qualitative assessments and quantitative information. Each respondent comment was first coded and then recoded several times as patterns of responses became apparent. The two questions were:

1. What factors or variables are *most* likely to cause you problems in managing a project?
2. What *personal* characteristics, traits, or skills make for "above average" project managers? What specific behaviors, techniques, or strategies do "above average" project managers use (or use better than their peers)?

PROBLEMS IN MANAGING PROJECTS

There were nearly 900 statements about what factors or variables created "problems" in managing a project. Most of these statements could be clustered into eight categories as shown in Table 1.

Inadequate resources was the issue most frequently mentioned as causing problems in managing a project. "No matter what the type or scope of your project," wrote one engineering manager, "if insufficient resources are allocated to the project, you have to be a magician to be successful." Not having the necessary budget or personnel for the

Table 1
Project Management Problems

1. Resources inadequate (69)
2. Meeting ("unrealistic") deadlines (67)
3. Unclear goals/direction (63)
4. Team members uncommitted (59)
5. Insufficient planning (56)
6. Breakdowns in communications (54)
7. Changes in goals and resources (42)
8. Conflicts between departments or functions (35)

Note: Numbers in parentheses represent percentage of Project Managers whose response was included in this cluster.

project was a frequent complaint. However, the specific resource of *time*—and generally the lack thereof—was mentioned just about as often as the general inadequate resource lament. Typically, the problem of time was expressed as "having to meet unrealistic deadlines."

That resources are inadequate is caused by many factors, not the least of which being that resources are generally limited and costly. Before this hue is dismissed by veteran project managers as just so much bellyaching—"after all, there are never enough resources to go around"—it is important to examine the cause(s) of this problem. Respondents pointed out that resource allocation problems were usually created by senior management's failure to be clear about project objectives, which in turn, resulted in poor planning efforts. These two problems—lack of clear goals and effective planning—were specifically mentioned by more than 60 percent of the respondents. It is painfully obvious that vague goals and insufficient planning lead to mistakes in allocating the resources needed by project managers.

The three most significant problems reported by first-line research, development, and engineering supervisors in Lauren Hitchcock's [4] study parallels those identified by project managers. He found "insufficient definition of policy from top downward, how to define the goal of a problem, and budgeting and manpower assignments" to be the major problems confronting supervisors. It remains true that senior management needs to articulate clearly where the project should be going, why, and what it expects from project personnel.

When project goals are not clear, it is difficult (if not impossible) to efficiently plan the project. The lack of planning contributes directly to unrealistic resource allocations and schedules. People assigned to the project are unlikely, therefore, to energetically commit to the endeavor. The lack of commitment (and poor motivation) among project personnel was reported as emerging more from the problems already mentioned than from issues associated with the project's technology or organizational structure (e.g., matrix form).

The communication breakdowns (problems)

Table 2
Project Management Skills

1. Communication Skills (84) • Listening • Persuading	4. Leadership Skills (68) • Sets Example • Energetic • Vision (big picture) • Delegates • Positive
2. Organizational Skills (75) • Planning • Goal-setting • Analyzing	5. Coping Skills (59) • Flexibility • Creativity • Patience • Persistence
3. Team Building Skills (72) • Empathy • Motivation • Esprit de Corps	6. Technological Skills (46) • Experience • Project Knowledge

Note: Numbers in parenthesis represent the percentage of project managers whose response was included in this cluster.

which occur during the life of a project were often referred to as "inevitable." These breakdowns occur as a result of the ambiguity surrounding the project, but also result from difficulties in coordinating and integrating diverse perspectives and personalities. The project manager's challenge is to handle communication breakdowns as they arise rather than being able to predict (and control) communication problems before they happen.

How the problems confronting project managers were interrelated is exemplified by how frequently problems of communication and dealing with conflicts were linked by respondents. The linkage between these two issues was demonstrated in statements like: "My problem is being able to effectively communicate with people when we disagree over priorities." "Conflicts between departments end up as major communication hassles." Conflicts between departments were also linked to earlier problems of poor goal-setting and planning.

Managing changes (e.g., in goals, specifications, resources, etc.) contributed substantially to project management headaches. This was often mentioned as "Murphy's Law," highlighting the context or environment in which project management occurs. Planning cannot accurately account for future possibilities (or better yet, unknowns). Interestingly, less than one in ten project managers mentioned directly a "technological" factor or variable as significantly causing them problems in managing a project.

PROJECT MANAGER SKILLS

The second issue investigated was what project manager skills—traits, characteristics, attributes, behaviors, techniques—make a difference in successfully managing projects. Most respondents easily generated four-to-five items which they believed made the difference between average and superior project performance. The result was nearly 1400 statements. These statements were summarized into six skill areas as shown in Table 2. Several factors within each are highlighted.

Eighty-four percent of the respondents mentioned "being a good communicator" as an essential project manager skill. Being persuasive or being able to sell one's ideas was frequently mentioned as a characteristic of a good communicator within the project management context. Many people also cited the importance of receiving information, or good listening skills. As one systems engineer exclaimed: "The good project managers manage not by the seat of their pants but by the soles of their feet!"

Organizational skills represented a second major set of competencies. Characteristics included in this category were planning and goal-setting abilities, along with the ability to be analytical. The ability to prioritize, captured in the phrases "stays on track" and "keeps the project goals in perspective," was also identified as significant.

While successful project managers were viewed as good problem solvers, what really differentiated them from their so-so counterparts was their problem *finding* ability. Because of their exceptional communication skills, goal clarity and planning, effective project managers were aware of issues *before* they became problems. Problem finding gave them greater degrees of freedom, enabling them to avoid being seriously sidetracked by problems caused by unforeseen events.

The important team building skills involved developing emphatic relationships with other members of the project team. Being sensitive to the needs of others, motivating people, and building a strong sense of team spirit were identified as essential for effectively managing a project. "The best project managers use a lot of *'we'* statements in describing the project," wrote one computer programmer. Being clear about the project's objectives and subsequently breaking down the project into its component parts (e.g., schedules) helped project participants to understand their interdependencies and the need for teamwork.

Several different attributes and behaviors were catalogued under leadership skills. These included setting a good example, seeing the big picture, being enthusiastic, having a positive outlook, taking initiative, and trusting people. Having a vision is closely related to goal clarity (which was included as an organizational skill). The leader-

ship component of this competency was best expressed by one financial analyst as "the ability to see the forest through the trees."

Since, as is often lamented, the only constant in managing a project is change, successful project managers require coping or stress-management skills. Respondents indicated that both flexibility and creativity were involved in effectively dealing (or coping) with change, as were patience and persistence. What project managers experience are generally high levels of stress. How well they handle stress ("grace under pressure") significantly affects their eventual success or failure.

The final cluster of skills was labeled technological. Successful project managers were seen as having relevant experience or knowledge about the technology required by the project. Seldom, however, were effective project managers seen as technological "experts." Indeed, expertise was often felt to be detrimental because it decreased flexibility and the willingness to consider alternative perspectives. Project managers do need to be sufficiently well versed in the technology to be able to ask the right questions. Because, as one senior military officer pointed out, "you've got to be able to know when people are blowing smoke at you."

SKILLS AND PROBLEMS: FUNDAMENTALLY INTERCONNECTED

It has been argued in the literature that project managers require certain skills in order to be effective. It has also been argued that project managers need to be able to handle certain problems in order to be effective. The results of this study suggest that these two perspectives are not contradictory but are fundamentally compatible. When the set of required skills is considered side-by-side with the set of critical problems project managers face, the complementary nature of these two perspectives is evident. This is illustrated in Table 3.

Without arguing which comes first, it is clear that either (a) project managers require certain skills in order to deal effectively with the factors

Table 3

SKILLS ↔ PROBLEMS:
Interconnected In Projected Management

Communication	Breakdowns in Communications
Organizational	Insufficient Planning
	Resources Inadequate
Team Building	Team Members Uncommitted
	Weak Inter-Unit Integration
Leadership	Unclear Goals/Direction
	Interpersonal Conflicts
Coping	Handling Changes
Technological	Meeting ("unrealistic") Deadlines

most likely to create problems for them in managing the project, or (b) because certain problems are most likely to confront project managers, they require particular skills in order to handle them.

While this one-on-one matching in Table 3 obviously oversimplifies the dynamic nature of project management, it does have an inherent logical appeal. Since communication breakdowns are likely to create project management problems, effective project managers need to cultivate their communications (persuading and listening) skills. Project managers with good organizational skills are likely to be more effective at planning and subsequently allocating resources. Unless project managers are able to build strong project teams they are likely to be plagued by problems caused by poorly committed team members and interdepartmental conflict. Project goals are likely to be more easily understood when the project manager's leadership is consistent. Interpersonal conflicts will likely diminish when project managers set clear standards of performance and demonstrate their trust in, and respect for, others. The inevitable changes which accompany any project will be less problematic when not only

coped with calmly, but also when handled with flexibility and creativity. Finally, problems created when deadlines and schedules are unrealistic may be minimized through a project manager's problem finding ability and experience in getting things back on track.

What was found underscores the claim that the primary problems of project managers are not technical, but human. Improving project managers' technological capabilities will be helpful only to the extent that this improves their ability to communicate, be organized, build teams, provide leadership, and deal comfortably with change. The challenge for *technical* managers, or for those moving from technical into managerial positions, is to recognize the need for, and to develop where necessary, their interpersonal skills.

REFERENCES

1. Archibald, R. D. *Managing High-Technology Programs and Projects.* New York: John Wiley & Sons, 1976; Kernzer, H. *Project Management for Executives.* New York: Van Nostrand Reinhold, 1982; Stuckenbruck, L., Ten Attributes of the Proficient Project Manager. *Proceedings of the Project Management Institute,* Montreal, 1976, 40–47; and Thamhain, H. and Wilemon, D., Skill Requirements of Engineering Project Managers. *Twenty-Sixth IEEE Joint Engineerng Management Conference,* 1978.

2. Roman, D. D. *Managing Projects: A Systems Perspective.* New York: Elsevier Science Publishing, 1985.

3. Badaway, M. *Developing Managerial Skills in Scientists and Engineers.* New York: Van Nostrand Reinhold, 1982.

4. Hitchcock, L., Problems of First-Line Supervisors. *Research Management,* 1967, *Vol 10 (6),* 385–397.

CHAPTER 4
Project Organization

A firm, if successful, usually tends to grow, adding resources and people, developing an organizational structure. Commonly, the focus of the structure is specialization of the human elements of the group. As long as its organizational structure is sufficient to the tasks imposed on it, the structure tends to persist. When the structure begins to inhibit the work of the firm, pressures arise to reorganize along some other line. The underlying principle will still be specialization, but the specific nature of the specialization will be changed [see 13].

Any elementary management textbook covers the common bases of specialization [see 34, for example]. In addition to the ever-popular functional division, firms organize by product line, by geographic location, by production process, by type of customer, by subsidiary organization, by time, and by the elements of vertical or horizontal integration. Indeed, large firms frequently organize by several of these methods at different levels. For example, a firm may organize by major subsidiaries at the top level; the subsidiaries organize by product groups; and the product groups organize into customer divisions. These, in turn, may be split into functional departments that are further broken down into production process sections, which are set up as three-shift operating units.

When projects are initiated, two issues immediately arise. First, a decision must be made about how to tie the project to the parent firm. Second, a decision must be made about how to organize the project itself.

In the previous chapter we discussed the selection of the project manager (PM) and described the difficulties and responsibilities inherent in the PM's role. This chapter focuses directly on how to organize the project. First we look at the three major organizational forms commonly used to house projects and see just how each of them fits into the parent organization. We examine the advantages and disadvantages of each form, and discuss some of the critical factors that might lead us to choose one form over the others. We then consider some combinations of the fundamental forms and briefly examine the implications of using combination structures. Finally, we discuss some of the details of organizing the project team, describing the various roles of the project staff. We also describe some of the behavior problems that face any project team.

To our knowledge, it is rare for a PM to have much influence over the project's organizational form, choice of form usually being made by senior management. The PM's work, however, is strongly affected by the project's structure, and the PM should understand its workings. Experienced PMs do seem to mold the project's organization to fit their notions of what is best. One project team member of our acquaintance remarked at length about how different life was on two projects (both matrix organized) run by different PMs. A study of the subtle impacts of the PM on project structure are beyond the scope of this book and deserve more attention from researchers in the behavioral sciences. (For an excellent review of relevant research, see [28].)

4.1 THE PROJECT AS PART OF THE FUNCTIONAL ORGANIZATION

As one alternative for giving the project a "home," we can make it a part of one of the functional divisions of the firm. Figure 4-1 illustrates a purely functional organization. Figure 4-2 is the organization chart for the University of Cincinnati, a functionally organized institution. If the project in question involves a new technology, it might well be placed under the supervision of the vice-president of engineering. If it involves the introduction of a new product line, we would more likely find it under the control of the vice-president of marketing. If, on the other hand, the project concerns the installation of a new manufacturing process, it would probably be overseen by the vice-president of manufacturing. A project tends to be assigned to the functional unit that has most interest in ensuring its success or that can be most helpful in implementing it.

There are advantages and disadvantages of using functional elements of the parent organization as the administrative home for a project—assuming that one has chosen an appropriate function.

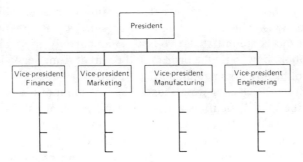

Figure 4-1 Functional organization.

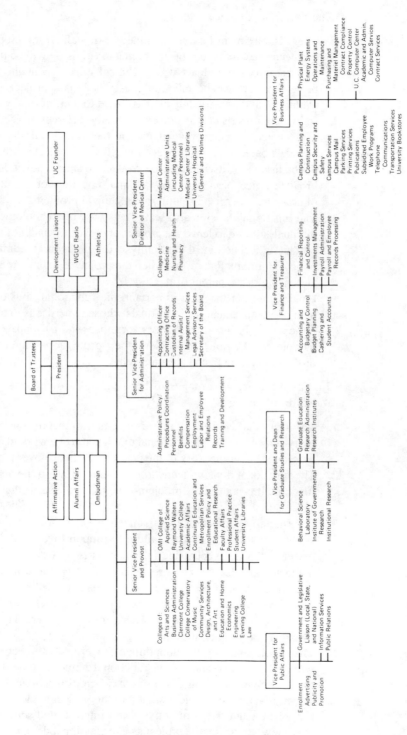

Figure 4-2 University of Cincinnati: Organization chart.

The major advantages are:

1. There is maximum flexibility in the use of staff. If the proper functional division has been chosen as the project's home, the division will be the primary administrative base for individuals with technical expertise in the fields relevant to the project. Experts can be temporarily assigned to the project, make the required contributions, and immediately be reassigned to their normal work.

2. Individual experts can be utilized by many different projects. With the broad base of technical personnel available in the functional divisions, people can be switched back and forth between the different projects with relative ease.

3. Specialists in the division can be grouped to share knowledge and experience. The broad technical base is not only a major repository of talent; it is a potential source of creative, synergistic solutions to technical problems.

4. The functional division also serves as a base of technological continuity when individuals choose to leave the project, and even the parent firm. Perhaps just as important as technological continuity is the procedural, administrative, and overall policy continuity that results when the project is maintained in a specific functional division of the parent firm.

5. Finally, and not the least important, the functional division contains the normal path of advancement for individuals whose expertise is in the functional area. The project may be a source of glory for those who participate in its successful completion, but the functional field is their professional home and the focus of their professional growth and advancement.

Just as there are advantages to housing the project in a functional area, there are also disadvantages:

1. A primary disadvantage of this arrangement is that the client is not the focus of activity and concern. The functional unit has its own work to do, which usually takes precedence over the work of the project, and hence over the interests of the client.

2. The functional division tends to be oriented toward the activities particular to its function. It is not usually problem-oriented in the sense that a project must be to be successful.

3. Occasionally in functionally organized projects, no individual is given full responsibility for the project. This failure to pinpoint responsibility usually means that the PM is made accountable for some parts of the project, but another person is made accountable for one or more other parts. Little imagination is required to forecast the lack of coordination and chaos that results.

4. The same reasons that lead to lack of coordinated effort tend to make response to client needs slow and arduous. There are often several layers of management between the project and the client.

5. There is a tendency to suboptimize the project. Project issues that are directly within the interest area of the functional home may be dealt with carefully, but those outside normal interest areas may be given short shrift, if not totally ignored.

6. The motivation of people assigned to the project tends to be weak. The project is not in the mainstream of activity and interest, and some project team members may view service on the project as a professional detour.

7. Such an organizational arrangement does not facilitate a holistic approach to the project. Complex technical projects such as the development of a jet transport aircraft or an emergency room in a hospital simply cannot be well designed unless they are designed as a totality. No matter how good the intentions, no functional division can avoid focusing on its unique areas of interest.

4.2 THE PROJECT ORGANIZATION

At the other end of the organizational spectrum is the pure project organization. The project is separated from the rest of the parent system. It becomes a self-contained unit with its own technical staff, its own administration, tied to the parent firm by the tenuous strands of periodic progress reports and oversight. Some parent organizations prescribe administrative, financial, personnel, and control procedures in detail. Others allow the project almost total freedom within the limits of final accountability. There are examples of almost every possible intermediate position. Figure 4-3 illustrates this pure project organization.

As with the functional organization, the pure project has its unique advantages and disadvantages. The former are:

1. The project manager has full line authority over the project. Though the PM must report to a senior executive in the parent organization, there is a complete work force devoted to the project. The PM is like the CEO of a firm that is dedicated to carrying out the project.

2. All members of the project work force are directly responsible to the PM. There are no functional division heads whose permission must be sought or whose advice must be heeded before making technological decisions. The PM is truly the project director.

3. When the project is removed from the functional division, the lines of communication are shortened. The entire functional structure is bypassed, and the PM communicates directly with senior corporate management. The shortened communication lines result in faster communications with fewer failures.

4. When there are several successive projects of a similar kind, the pure project organization can maintain a more or less permanent cadre of experts who develop

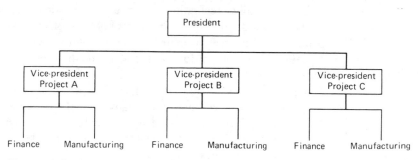

Figure 4-3 Project organization.

considerable skill in specific technologies. Indeed, the existence of such skill pools can attract customers to the parent firm. Lockheed's famous "Skonk Works" was such a team of experts who took great pride in their ability to solve difficult engineering problems. The group's name, taken from the *Li'l Abner* comic strip, reflects the group's pride, irreverent attitude, and strong sense of identity.

5. The project team that has a strong and separate identity of its own tends to develop a high level of commitment from its members. Motivation is high and acts to foster the task orientation discussed in Chapter 3.

6. Because authority is centralized, the ability to make swift decisions is greatly enhanced. The entire project organization can react more rapidly to the requirements of the client and the needs of senior management.

7. Unity of command exists. While it is easy to overestimate the value of this particular organizational principle, these is little doubt that the quality of life for subordinates is enhanced when each subordinate has one, and only one, boss.

8. Pure project organizations are structurally simple and flexible, which makes them relatively easy to understand and to implement.

9. The organizational structure tends to support a holistic approach to the project. A full explanation of the systems approach is beyond the scope of this book, but the dangers of focusing on and optimizing the project's subsystems rather than the total project are often a major cause of technical failure in projects.

While the advantages of the pure project organization make a powerful argument favoring this structure, its disadvantages are also serious:

1. When the parent organization takes on several projects, it is common for each one to be fully staffed. This can lead to considerable duplication of effort in every area from clerical staff to the most sophisticated (and expensive) technological support units.

2. In fact, the need to ensure access to technological knowledge and skills results in an attempt by the PM to stockpile equipment and technical assistance in order to be certain that it will be available when needed. Thus, people with critical technical skills may be hired by the project when they are available rather than when they are needed. Similarly, they tend to be maintained on the project longer than needed, "just in case."

3. Removing the project from technical control by a functional department has its advantages, but it also has a serious disadvantage if the project is characterized as "high technology." Though individuals engaged with projects develop considerable depth in the technology of the project, they tend to fall behind in other areas of their technical expertise. The functional division is a repository of technical lore, but it is not readily accessible to members of the pure project team.

4. Pure project groups seem to foster inconsistency in the way in which policies and procedures are carried out. In the relatively sheltered environment of the project, corner-cutting is common and easily justified as a response to the client or to technical exigency. "They don't understand our problems" becomes an easy excuse for ignoring dicta from headquarters.

5. In pure project organizations, the project takes on a life of its own. Team members

form strong attachments to the project and to each other. A disease known as *projectitis* develops. A strong we–they divisiveness grows, distorting the relationships between project team members and their counterparts in the parent organization. Friendly rivalry may become bitter competition, and political infighting between projects is common.

6. Another symptom of projectitis is the worry about "life after the project ends". Typically, there is considerable uncertainty about what will happen when the project is completed. Will team members be laid off? Will they be assigned to low-prestige work? Will their technical skills be too rusty to be successfully integrated into other projects? Will our team (that old gang of mine) be broken up?

4.3 THE MATRIX ORGANIZATION

In an attempt to couple some of the advantages of the pure project organization with some of the desirable features of the functional organization, and to avoid some of the disadvantages of each, the matrix organization was developed. In effect, the functional and the pure project organizations represent extremes. The matrix organization is a combination of the two. It is a pure project organization overlaid on the functional divisions of the parent firm.

Being a combination of pure project and functional organization structures, a matrix organization can take on a wide variety of specific forms, depending on which of the two extremes (functional or pure project) it most resembles. Because it is simpler to explain, let us first consider a strong matrix, one that is similar to a pure project. Rather than being a stand-alone organization, like the pure project, the matrix project is not separated from the parent organization. Consider Figure 4-4. The project manager of Project 1, PM_1, reports to a program manager who also exercises supervision over other projects.

Project 1 has assigned to it three people from the manufacturing division, one and one-half people from marketing, one-half of a person each from finance and

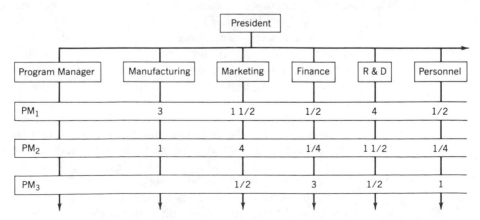

Figure 4-4 Matrix organization.

personnel, four individuals from R & D, and perhaps others not shown. These individuals come from their respective functional divisions and are assigned to the project full-time or part-time, depending on the project's needs. It should be emphasized that the PM controls when and what these people will do, while the functional managers control who will be assigned to the project and what technology will be used.

With heavy representation from manufacturing and R & D, project 1 might involve the design and installation of a new type of manufacturing process. Project 2 could involve a new product or, possibly, a marketing research problem. Project 3 might concern the installation of a new, computerized, financial control system.

If the organization conducts relatively few projects, there may be no program manager. Instead, the PMs may report to the head of the functional department with a major interest in the project—manufacturing, marketing, and finance in these examples. It is also common for PMs to report directly to the chief executive officer, the chief operating officer, or an executive vice-president in smaller firms with only a few projects.

At the other end of the spectrum of matrix organization is the weak matrix, one more like the functional organization. A project might, for example, have only one full-time person, the PM. Rather than having functional specialists assigned to the project, the functional departments may be asked to take on specific jobs required by the project. For example, the PM of a project set up to create a new database for personnel might request that the basic design be done by the systems analysis group in the administrative division. The personnel job would then be added to the normal workload of the systems group. The priority given to the design might be assigned by senior management or might be the result of negotiations between the PM and the head of the systems group. In some cases, the systems group's charges for the job might also be subject to negotiation.

Between these extremes, there are many different mixtures of project and functional responsibilities. When a functional group's work is frequently required by projects, it is common to operate it as a functional group rather than to transfer its people to the project. For instance, a toxicology unit in a cosmetic business, a quality assurance group in a multiproduct manufacturing firm, or a computer graphics group in a publishing firm might all be functionally organized and take on project work much like outside contractors. While the PM's control over the work is diminished by this arrangement, the project does have immediate access to any expertise in the group, and the group can maintain its technological integrity.

The impetus for the matrix organization was the fact that firms operating in high-technology areas had to integrate several functional specialties to work on a set of projects and wished to *time-share* expertise between individual projects in the set. Further, the technical needs of the projects often required a *systems* approach [6]. In earlier times, when a high-technology project was undertaken by a firm, it would start its journey through the firm in the R & D department. Concepts and ideas would be worked out and the result passed on to the engineering department, which would sometimes rework the whole thing. This result would then be forwarded to manufacturing, where it might be reworked once more in order to ensure that the output was manufacturable by the firm's current machinery. All of this required a great deal of time, and the emergent project might have scant resemblance to the original specifications.

In the meantime, another firm would be doing much the same thing on another project for the customer. These two projects might later have to be joined together, or to a third, and the combination was then expected to meet its intended function. For example, the first project might be a jet aircraft engine, the second a weapon system, and the third an airframe. The composite result rarely performed as originally conceived because the parts were not designed as a unified system. Military aircraft buffs may recall several World War II aircraft that used the Allison in-line engine (made by Rolls Royce). The P-39 (Airacobra) was a mediocre combat aircraft. The P-38 (Lightning) was a fairly good plane. The P-51 (Mustang) was an outstanding combat machine. In all three cases, the engine, armament, and airframe were designed separately. In one case this approach to design worked well; in one it did not. A systems approach to design would require that engine, airframe, and weapon system be designed as a unit. The attempt is to optimize the composite system rather than the parts. This improves the chance of developing a P-51 and decreases the likelihood of making a P-39. Indeed, given the complexity of the systems going into a combat aircraft today, it is doubtful if a plane *could* be designed using the old methods.

The systems approach was adopted as an alternative to the traditional method described above. This did not mean that the same firm had to manufacture everything, but it did mean that one organization had to take responsibility for the integrity of project design—to make sure that the parts were compatible and that the combination would function as expected. This required that R & D, engineering, manufacturing, etc., work closely together, and that all these work closely with the client, all the while coordinating efforts with other firms that were supplying subsystems for the project.

Housing the project in a functional organization was simply too constraining. Setting it up as a pure project was workable but expensive because of the need to duplicate expensive scientific talent when more than one project was involved. The matrix organization, which allowed the PM to draw temporarily on the technological expertise and assistance of all relevant functions, was a way out of the dilemma.

The matrix approach has its own unique advantages and disadvantages. Its strong points are:

1. The project is the point of emphasis. One individual, the PM, takes responsibility for managing the project, for bringing it in on time, within cost, and to specification. The matrix organization shares this virtue with the pure project organization.

2. Because the project organization is overlaid on the functional divisions, temporarily drawing manpower from them, the project has reasonable access to the entire reservoir of technical talent in the functional divisions. When there are several projects, the talents of the functional divisions are available to all projects, thus sharply reducing the duplication required by the pure project structure.

3. There is less anxiety about what happens when the project is completed than is typical of the pure project organization. Even though team members tend to develop a strong attachment for the project, they also feel close to their functional "home."

4. Response to client needs is as rapid as in the pure project case, and the matrix organization is just as flexible. Similarly, the matrix organization responds flexibly and rapidly to the demands made by those inside the parent system. A project nested within an operating firm must adapt to the needs of the parent firm or the project will not survive.

5. With matrix management, the project will have—or have access to—representatives from the administrative units of the parent firm. As a result, consistency with the policies, practices, and procedures of the parent firm tends to be preserved. If nothing else, this consistency with parent firm procedures tends to foster project credibility in the administration of the parent organization, a condition that is commonly undervalued.

6. Where there are several projects simultaneously under way, matrix organization allows a better companywide balance of resources to achieve the several different time/cost/performance targets of the individual projects. This holistic approach to the total organization's needs allows projects to be staffed and scheduled in order to optimize total system performance rather than to achieve the goals of one project at the expense of others.

In some cases there is another manager inserted into the system to oversee an

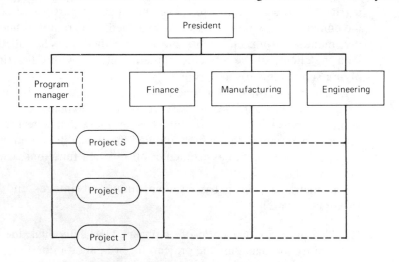

Figure 4-5 Matrix organization.

entire set of projects. This *program manager* is indicated by the dashed box in Figure 4-5. The aim, of course, is to reduce the number of managers reporting to the senior authority. The program manager usually holds the same status as the other functional managers. (Multiple-project scheduling and resource allocation, a major problem when the organization is working on more than one project at a time, is discussed in Chapter 9.)

7. While pure project and functional organizations represent extremes of the organizational spectrum, matrix organizations cover a wide range in between. When the PM of a matrix-organized project has considerable command authority over the project, it is said to be a *strong* matrix. If the PM is subject to extensive control by functional managers, the matrix is said to be *weak*. There is, therefore, a great deal of flexibility in precisely how the project is organized—all within the basic matrix structure—so that it can be adapted to a wide variety of projects, some of which might require strong support from functional heads and some of which might have PMs more or less ready to assume full control.

The advantages accruing to the matrix structure are potent. Unfortunately, the disadvantages are also serious:

1. In the case of functionally organized projects, there is no doubt that the functional division is the focus of decision-making power. In the pure project case, it is clear that the PM is the power center of the project. With matrix organizations, the power is more balanced. Often, the balance is fairly delicate. When doubt exists about who is in charge, the work of the project suffers.

2. While the ability to balance time, cost, and performance between several projects is an advantage of matrix organization, that ability has its dark side. The set of projects must be carefully monitored *as a set*, a tough job. Further, the movement of resources from project to project in order to satisfy the several schedules may foster political infighting among the several PMs, all of whom tend to be more interested in ensuring success for their individual projects than in helping the total system optimize organizationwide goals.

3. Problems associated with shutting down a project are almost as severe as those in pure project organizations. The projects, having individual identities, resist death. Even in matrix organizations, projectitis is still a serious disease.

4. In matrix-organized projects, the PM controls administrative decisions and the functional heads control technological decisions. The distinction is simple enough when writing about project management, but for the operating PM the division of authority and responsibility inherent in matrix management is complex. The ability of the PM to negotiate anything from resources to technical assistance to delivery dates is a key contributor to project success. Success is doubtful for a PM without strong negotiating skills.

5. Matrix management violates the management principle of unity of command. Project workers have at least two bosses, their functional heads and the PM. There is no way around the split loyalties and confusion that results. Anyone who has worked under such an arrangement understands the difficulties. Those who have

not done so cannot appreciate the discomforts it causes. To paraphrase Plato's comment on democracy, matrix management "is a charming form of management, full of variety and disorder."

4.4 MIXED ORGANIZATIONAL SYSTEMS

As noted in the introduction to this chapter, divisionalization is a means of dividing a large and monolithic organization into smaller, more flexible units. This enables the parent organization to capture some of the advantages of small, specialized organizational units while retaining some of the advantages that come with larger size.

Organizing projects by product involves establishing each product-project as a relatively autonomous, integrated element within the organization as a whole. Such primary functions as engineering and finance are then dedicated to the interests of the product itself.

Consider a firm making lawn furniture. The firm might be divisionalized into products constructed of plastic or aluminum. Each product line would have its own specialized staff. Assume now two newly designed styles of furniture, one plastic and the other aluminum, each of which becomes a project within its respective product division. (Should a new product be a combination of plastic and aluminum, the pure project form of organization will tend to forestall interdivisional battles for turf.)

Similarly, territorial form is especially attractive to national organizations whose activities are physically or geographically spread, and where the products have some geographical uniqueness, such as ladies' garments. Project organization across customer divisions is typically found when the projects reflect a paramount interest in the needs of different types of customers. Here customer preferences are more substantial than either territorial or product activities. The differences between consumer and manufacturer, or civilian and military, are examples of such substantial differences.

A special kind of project organization often found in manufacturing firms develops when projects are housed in process divisions. Such a project might concern new manufacturing methods, and the machining division might serve as the base for a project investigating new methods of removing metal. The same project might be housed in the machining division but include several people from the R & D lab, and be organized as a combination of functional and matrix forms.

Pure functional and pure project organizations may coexist in a firm. This results in the *mixed* form shown in Figure 4-6. This form is rarely observed with the purity we have depicted here, yet it is not uncommon. What is done, instead, is to spin off the large, successful long-run projects as subsidiaries or independent operations. Many firms nurture smaller projects that are not yet stable under the wing of an existing division, then wean them to pure projects with their own identity, and finally allow the formation of a *venture team*—or, for a

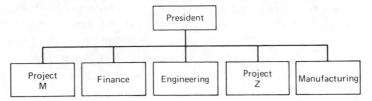

Figure 4-6 "Mixed" organization.

larger project, *venture firm*—within the parent company. For example, Texas Instruments has done this with the Speak and Spell toy that was developed by one of its employees.

The hybridization of the mixed form leads to flexibility. It enables the firm to meet special problems by appropriate adaptation of its organizational structure. There are, however, distinct dangers involved in hybridization. Dissimilar groupings within the same accountability center tend to encourage overlap, duplication, and friction because of incompatibility of interests.

Figure 4-7 illustrates another common solution to the problem of project organizational form. The firm sets up what appears to be a standard form of functional organization, but it adds a staff office to administer all projects. This frees the functional groups of administrative problems while it uses their technical talents. In a large specialty chemical firm, this organizational form worked so well that the staff office became the nucleus of a full-scale division of the firm. The division's sole purpose was to administer projects.

In many ways this organizational form is not distinguishable from matrix management, but it is typically used for small, short-run projects where the for-

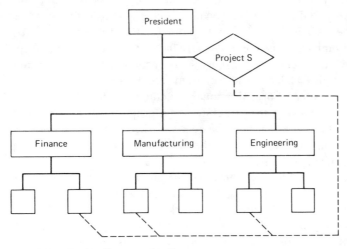

Figure 4-7 Staff organization.

mation of a full-fledged matrix system is not justified. This mixed form shares several advantages and disadvantages of the matrix structure, but the project life is usually so short that the disease of projectitis is rarely contracted. If the number or size of the projects being staffed in this way grows, a shift to a formal matrix organization naturally evolves.

4.5 CHOOSING AN ORGANIZATIONAL FORM

Even experienced practitioners find it difficult to explain how one should proceed when choosing the organizational structure for a project. The choice is determined by the situation, but even so is partly intuitive. There are few accepted principles of design, and no step-by-step procedures that give detailed instructions for determining what kind of structure is needed and how it can be built. All we can do is consider the nature of the potential project, the characteristics of the various organizational options, the advantages and disadvantages of each, and make the best compromise we can.

In general, the functional form is apt to be the organizational form of choice for projects where the major focus must be on the in-depth application of a technology rather than, for example, on minimizing cost, meeting a specific schedule, or achieving speedy response to change. Also, the functional form is preferred for projects that will require large capital investments in equipment or buildings of a type normally used by the function.

If the firm engages in a large number of similar projects (e.g., construction projects), the pure project form of organization is preferred. The same form would generally be used for one-time, highly specific, unique tasks that require careful control and are not appropriate for a single functional area—the development of a new product line, for instance.

When the project requires the integration of inputs from several functional areas and involves reasonably sophisticated technology, but does not require all the technical specialists to work for the project on a full-time basis, the matrix organization is the only satisfactory solution. This is particularly true when several such projects must share technical experts. But matrix organizations are complex and present a difficult challenge for the PM. They should be avoided when simpler organizational structures are feasible.

In choosing the structure for a project, the first problem is to determine the kind of work that must be accomplished. This is best done by first identifying the primary objective(s) of the project and then determining the major tasks associated with each objective. Next, this work can be decomposed into *work packages.* We can then consider just what individual organizational elements or subsystems will be contained within the project. Additional items to consider are the individuals doing the work and their personalities, the technology to be employed, and the clients to be served. Environmental factors inside and outside the parent organization must also be taken into account. By understanding the various structures, their advantages and disadvantages, a firm can select the organizational structure that seems to offer the most effective and efficient choice.

Since it is our objective in this chapter to provide criteria for the selection of a project organization, we shall illustrate the process with two examples. In each case, we use the following procedure.

1. Define the project with a statement of the objective(s) that identifies the major outcomes desired.
2. Determine the key tasks associated with each objective and locate the units in the parent organization that serve as functional "homes" for these types of tasks.
3. Arrange the key tasks by sequence and decompose them into work packages.
4. Determine which project subsystems are required to carry out the work packages and which subsystems will work particularly closely with which others.
5. List any special characteristics or assumptions associated with the project—for example, level of technology needed, probable length and size of the project, any potential problems with the individuals who may be assigned to the work, possible political problems between different functions involved, and anything else that seems relevant, including the parent firm's previous experiences with different ways of organizing projects.
6. In light of the above, and with full cognizance of the pros and cons associated with each structural form, choose a structure.

Example 1

Trinatronic, Inc.

Project objective: To design, build, and market a multitasking personal computer containing 8-, 16-, and 32-bit processors, 2 Mbytes RAM, and at least 30 Mbytes of memory to retail at $3,000 or less.

	Key Tasks	Organizational Units
A.	Write specifications.	Mktg. Div. and R & D
B.	Design hardware, do initial tests.	R & D
C.	Engineer hardware for production.	Eng. Dept., Mfg. Div.
D.	Set up production line.	Eng. Dept., Mfg. Div.
E.	Manufacture small run, conduct quality and reliability tests.	Mfg. Div. and Q. A. Dept., Exec. V.P. staff
F.	Write (or adopt) operating systems.	Software Prod. Div.
G.	Test operating systems.	Q. A. Dept., Exec. V. P. staff
H.	Write (or adopt) applications software.	Software Prod. Div.
I.	Test applications software.	Q. A. Dept., Exec. V. P. staff
J.	Prepare full documentation, repair and user manuals.	Tech. Writing Section (Eng. Div.) and Tech. Writing Section (Software Prod. Div.)
K.	Set up service system with manuals and spare parts.	Service Dept., Mktg. Div.
L.	Prepare marketing program.	Mktg. Div.
M.	Prepare marketing demonstrations.	Mktg. Div.

Without attempting to generate a specific sequence for these tasks, we note that they seem to belong to four categories of work.

1. Design, build, and test hardware.
2. Design, write, and test software.
3. Set up production and service/repair systems with spares and manuals.
4. Design marketing effort, with demonstrations, brochures, and manuals.

Based on this analysis, it would appear that the project will need the following elements:

- Groups to design the hardware and software.
- Groups to test the hardware and software.
- A group to engineer the production system for the hardware.
- A group to design the marketing program.
- A group to prepare all appropriate documents and manuals.
- And, lest we forget, a group to administer all the above groups.

These subsystems represent at least three major divisions and perhaps a half-dozen departments in the parent organization. The groups designing the hardware and the multiple operating systems will have to work closely together. The test groups may work quite independently of the hardware and software designers, but results seem to improve when they cooperate. We can prepare a simple responsibility chart for the tasks (Figure 4-8). In this particular case the verbal chart is sufficient, but when the set of tasks is large, the matrix is quite helpful.

Tasks	Executive V.P. Staff	Q.A. Dept.	Marketing Division	Serv. Dept.	Manufacturing Division	Eng. Dept.	Engineering Division	Tech. Writ.	Software Division	Tech. Writ.	Research & Development Division
A			x								x
B											x
C						x					
D						x					
E		x			x						
F									x		
G		x									
H									x		
I		x									
J								x		x	
K				x							
L			x								
M			x								

Figure 4-8 Trinatronics, Inc. product task/organization responsibility chart.

Trinatronics has people capable of carrying out the project. The design of the hardware and operating systems is possible in the current state of the art, but to design such systems at a cost that will allow a retail price of $3,000 or less will require an advance in the state of the art. The project is estimated to take between 18 and 24 months, and to be the most expensive project yet undertaken by Trinatronics.

Based on the sketchy information above, it seems clear that a functional project organization would not be appropriate. Too much interaction between major divisions is required to make a single function into a comfortable organizational home for everyone. Either a pure project or matrix structure is feasible, and given the choice, it seems sensible to choose the simpler pure project organization if the cost of additional personnel is not too high. Note that if the project had required only part-time participation by the highly qualified scientific professionals, the matrix organization might have been preferable. Also, a matrix structure would probably have been chosen if this project were only one of several such projects drawing on a common staff base.

Example

Urban Hospital

Project objective: To develop and implement a computerized scheduling system for the hospital's operating rooms.

Key Tasks		**Organizational Unit**
A.	Find and prioritize objectives of the system.	Syst. Anal., Admin. Dept., and Dept. of Surg.
B.	Build preliminary model.	Syst. Anal., Admin. Dept.
C.	Program and test preliminary model.	Syst. Anal., Admin. Dept.
D.	Use model in parallel with current scheduling system.	Syst. Anal., Admin. Dept.
E.	Compare results and present to Dept. of Surg.	Syst. Anal., Admin. Dept., and Dept. of Surg.
F.	If necessary, amend model and repeat tasks D and E.	Syst. Anal., Admin. Dept., and Dept. of Surg.
G.	Install model, including full documentation.	Syst. Anal., Admin. Dept.
H.	Train Dept. of Surg. clerks in operation of model.	Syst. Anal., Admin. Dept., and Dept. of Surg.

The order in which tasks should be performed is as shown above because all the work must be done sequentially. There are three major jobs.

1. Build the model based on input from the users.
2. Test model on an "as if" basis and amend if necessary.
3. Install model and train operators.

Only two units will be required for the project, a systems analysis group (housed in the Department of Administration) and a user group. Analysts and users will have to work together throughout the project. These groups each represent a different part of the parent organization.

Consideration was given to the use of an outside consultant to analyze the system and develop the model. The internal systems analysts are heavily involved in replacing an outside vendor's accounting software system with one of their own devising. They expect to be fully occupied for another six to eight months. On the other hand, some members of the Department of Surgery are worried that the hospital's own analysts will not be sensitive to the special needs of the department and would be even less likely to tolerate and trust outsiders. Indeed, several of the surgeons are doubtful about the entire project. They are not sure that it makes any sense to set priorities on the objectives for scheduling the operating rooms because "quality of patient care is our only priority."

While the analysis group is currently engaged in a major project, it is estimated that they will be able to release an analyst to the OR scheduling project within three months. The project does not appear particularly difficult, and they feel it should not require more than two or three months to complete, given that the surgeons will consider cooperating in the analysis.

In this case, it seems best to house the project in the Department of Surgery. The project is small and involves only two departments. It is easy to move the analytic skill to the Department of Surgery, and there is nothing here that requires a separate project or matrix organization with the concomitant need for separate administration. Further, housing the project in Surgery would give that department a sense of control, which might act to allay their fears. It would, of course, be feasible to organize this endeavor as a staff project under the CEO of the hospital or the chief of the medical staff, but the psychological and political advantages of housing it in the Department of Surgery warrant the use of the functional organization.

4.6 THE PROJECT TEAM

In this section we consider the makeup of the project team, bearing in mind that different projects have vastly different staff needs. Then we take up some problems associated with staffing the team. Last, we deal with a few of the behavioral issues in managing this team.

Before discussing these issues, there is a seemingly unimportant item that needs mention, but it is far more critical than it might seem. It is useful to have a *project office,* even for small projects—say, those having only a half-dozen people or so. The project office, sometimes called the *war room,* serves as a control center, chart room, conference room for visiting senior management and the project client, center for technical discussions, coffee shop, crisis center, and, in general, the focus of all project activity. It need not be sumptuous, but the PM's open cubicle will not suffice. (If space is tight, projects can share an office.) The war room represents the project "physically" and aids in instilling an esprit de corps in team members. If at all possible, the regular project team members should have their offices located near the project office. Certainly, the project manager's office should be nearby.

Now we continue with our discussion of the project team. To be concrete, let us use the example of an engineering project to determine how to form a project team. Assume that the size of our hypothetical project is neither particularly large nor small. In addition to the PM, the following key team members might be needed, plus an appropriate number of scientists, engineers, technicians, clerks, and the like.

- *Project Engineer*   The project engineer is in charge of product design and development and is responsible for functional analysis, specifications, drawings, cost estimates, quality/reliability, engineering changes, and documentation.

- *Manufacturing Engineer*   This engineer's task is the efficient production of the product or process the project engineer has designed, including responsibility for manufacturing engineering, design and production of tooling/jigs/fixtures, production scheduling, and other production tasks.

- *Field Manager*   This person is responsible for the installation, testing, and support of the product/process once it is delivered to the customer.

- *Contract Administrator*   The administrator is in charge of all official paperwork, keeping track of customer changes, billings, questions, complaints, legal aspects, costs, and other matters related to the contract authorizing the project. Not uncommonly, the contract administrator also serves as project historian and archivist.

- *Project Controller*   The controller keeps daily account of budgets, cost variances, labor charges, project supplies, capital equipment status, etc. The controller also makes regular reports and keeps in close touch with both the PM and the company controller. If the administrator does not serve as historian, the controller can do so.

- *Support Services Manager*   This person is in charge of product support, subcontractors, data processing, and general management support functions.

Of these top project people, it is most important that the project engineer and the project controller report directly to the PM (see Figure 4-9). This facilitates control over two of the main goals of the project: technical performance and budget. (The project manager is usually in personal control of the schedule.) For a large project, all six project officials could work out of the project office and report directly to the PM.

To staff the project, the PM works from a forecast of personnel needs over the life cycle of the project. This is done with the aid of some special charts. First, a *work breakdown structure* is prepared to determine the exact nature of the tasks required to complete the project. (This chart is described in detail and illustrated in Chapter 5.) The skill requirements for these tasks are assessed and like skills are aggregated to determine work force needs. From this base, the functional departments are contacted to locate individuals who can meet these needs.

On occasion, certain tasks may be subcontracted. This option may be adopted

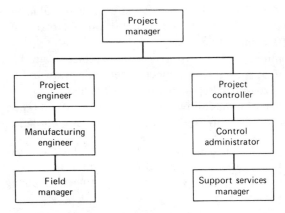

Figure 4-9 Typical organization for engineering projects.

because the appropriately skilled personnel are unavailable or cannot be located, or even because some special equipment required for the project is not available in-house. But if the proper people (and equipment) are found within the organization, the PM usually must obtain their services from their home departments. Many firms insist on using "local" resources when they are available, in order to maintain better control over resource usage and quality. Typically, the PM will have to negotiate with both the department head and the employee, trying to "sell" the employee on the challenge and excitement of working on the project and trying to convince the department head that lending the employee to the project is in the department head's best interest.

There are some people who are more critical to the project's success than others and should report directly to the PM or to the PM's deputy (often the project engineer):

- Senior project team members who will be having a long-term relationship with the project.
- Those with whom the PM will require continuous or close communication.
- Those with rare skills necessary to project success.

Remember that the PM must depend on reason when trying to convince a department head to lend these valuable people to the project. The department head, who sees the project as a more or less glamorous source of prestige in which the department cannot share, has little natural motivation to be cooperative. Once again, it is obvious that success depends on the political skill of the PM as much as on the technical skill of the team.

4.7 HUMAN FACTORS

With this reminder of the need for the PM to possess a high level of political sensitivity, we can discuss the other human factors in project management. We discuss them from the viewpoint of the PM as an individual who must cope with the personal as well as the technical victories and frustrations of life on a project.

Meeting schedule and cost goals without compromising performance appears to be a technical problem for the PM. Actually, it is only partly technical because it is also a human problem—more accurately, a technical problem with a human dimension. Project professionals tend to be perfectionists. It is difficult enough to meet project goals under normal conditions, but when, out of pride of workmanship, the professionals want to keep improving (and thus changing) the product, the task becomes almost impossible. Changes cause delays. Throughout the project, the manager must continue to stress the importance of meeting due dates. It also helps if the PM establishes, at the beginning of the project, a *technical change procedure* to ensure control over the incidence and frequency of change. (It would not, however, be wise for the PM to assume that everyone will automatically follow such a procedure.)

Another problem is the motivation of the project team members. As noted in Chapter 3, the PM usually does not control the normal economic rewards of work, but must stress its challenges and its possible accomplishments. Frederick Herzberg, who studied what motivates technical employees such as engineers, scientists, and professionals on a project team, contends [15] that recognition, achievement, the work itself, responsibility, and advancement are what motivate the technical worker. It is the PM's responsibility to make sure that project work is structured in such a way as to emphasize these motivational factors.

A program like Management by Objectives (MBO) helps. First suggested by Peter Drucker in 1954 [10], and advocated by many others [e.g., 24], MBO allows the worker to take responsibility for the design and performance of a task under controlled conditions. It gives the team members a chance to monitor their own progress and achievements while allowing full recognition by the PM. Some advantages of using MBO in a team setting are:

1. MBO is a *participative* mechanism. It harnesses the ability of the team members to manipulate tasks so that project objectives are met. The team is encouraged to find better ways to do things.
2. Professionals do not like being oversupervised. MBO does not tell them how to work but, given a goal, allows them to design their own methods.
3. The team members know what is expected of them.
4. The members have the opportunity to participate in deciding their own individual responsibilities.
5. The team members get timely feedback on their performance.
6. The project manager is provided a tool for evaluating and controlling performance.

MBO will succeed or fail depending largely on how the program is implemented. It is predicated on the philosophy that work is a natural, healthy human activity, and MBO will probably fail if it is implemented by a manager who basically believes that people must be forced to work—a so-called "Theory X" manager. In practice, a good MBO management system has much in common with Ouchi's [25] "Theory Z".

While often described as a management technique whereby objectives are (or should be) set from below by those who must do the work, in most of the successful implementations of MBO with which we are familiar, objectives were set from above. In superior-subordinate pairs, for example, the superior sets an objective in consultation with the subordinate to ensure that the latter agrees that the objective is challenging and at the same time feasible. The subordinate then develops an *action plan,* a detailed plan and schedule that will result in achieving the objective. The action plan is reviewed by the superior and any modifications of the plan result from joint discussion and mutual acceptance. The final plan then becomes a sort of contract between them.

In two particular applications we have seen, MBO was quite effective when used in project management. In both cases, the focus was on preparation of a written plan. In Chapter 5 we cover the planning process in detail and we emphasize the use of an action plan, a concept borrowed directly from MBO. The PM works with the senior members of the project team, usually as a group, to develop specific plans for meeting project objectives. Senior team members meet with their subordinates and a comprehensive set of written plans is generated by this process. The resulting document is a plan and a control mechanism. Because the system is participative and makes team members accountable for their specific parts of the overall plan, it not only motivates them, but also clearly denotes the degree to which team members are mutually dependent. This strongly reinforces the team feeling. The fear of "letting the team down" is also a strong motivator.

Another major element posing a behavioral problem for the PM is interpersonal conflict. Table 4-1, based on [31], relates the most likely sources of conflict to specific stages of the project life cycle. The table also suggests some solutions. When the project is first organized, priorities, procedures, and schedules all have roughly equal potential as sources of conflict. During the buildup phase, priorities become significantly more important than any other conflict factor; procedures are almost entirely established by this time. In the main program phase, priorities are finally established and schedules are the most important cause of trouble within the project, followed by technical disagreements. Getting adequate support for the project is also a point of concern. At project finish, meeting the schedule is the critical issue, but interpersonal tensions that were easily ignored early in the project can suddenly erupt into conflict during the last hectic weeks of the life cycle. Worry about reassignment exacerbates the situation. Both Tables 4-1 and 4-2 show conflict as a function of stage in the project life cycle as well as by source of the conflict, but Table 4-2 also shows the *frequency* of conflict by source and stage of the life cycle. Figure 4-10 illustrates these tables.

Conflict can be handled in several ways, but one thing seems sure: Conflict avoiders do not make successful project managers. On occasion, compromise appears to be helpful, but most often, gently confronting the conflict is the method of choice. Much has been written about conflict resolution and there is no need to summarize that literature here beyond noting that the key to conflict resolution rests on the manager's ability to transform a win–lose situation into win–

Table 4-1   Major sources of conflict during various stages of the project life cycle

| Life Cycle Phase | Major Conflict Source and Recommendations for Minimizing Dysfunctional Consequences | | |
	Conflict Source	Recommendations
Project formation	Priorities	Clearly defined plans. Joint decision making and/or consultation with affected parties. Stress importance of project to organization goals.
	Procedures	Develop detailed administrative operating procedures to be followed in conduct of project. Secure approval from key administrators. Develop statement of understanding or charter.
	Schedules	Develop schedule commitments in advance of actual project commencement. Forecast other departmental priorities and possible impact on project.
Buildup phase	Priorities	Provide effective feedback to support areas on forecasted project plans and needs via status review sessions.
	Schedules	Schedule work breakdown packages (project subunits) in cooperation with functional groups.
	Procedures	Contingency planning on key administrative issues.
Main program	Schedules	Continually monitor work in progress. Communicate results to affected parties. Forecast problems and consider alternatives. Identify potential trouble spots needing closer surveillance.
	Technical	Early resolution of technical problems. Communication of schedule and budget restraints to technical personnel. Emphasize adequate, early technical testing. Facilitate early agreement on final designs.
	Manpower	Forecast and communicate staffing requirements early. Establish staffing requirements and priorities with functional and staff groups.
Phaseout	Schedules	Close schedule monitoring in project life cycle. Consider reallocation of available staff to critical project areas prone to schedule slippages. Attain prompt resolution of technical issues which may affect schedules.
	Personality and manpower	Develop plans for reallocation of people upon project completion. Maintain harmonious working relationships with project team and support groups. Try to loosen up high-stress environment.

Source: Thamhain, Hans J., and David L. Wilemon, "Conflict Management in Project Life Cycles," *Sloan Management Review,* Summer 1975.

win. The Likerts have written [21] an interesting work on the nature and management of conflict, and Hill and White report [16] on how one particular project manager handled a difficult conflict:

Table 4-2 Number of conflicts during a sample project

PHASE OF PROJECT				SOURCES OF CONFLICT
Start	**Early**	**Main**	**Late**	
27	35	24	16	Project priorities
26	27	15	9	Admin. procedures
18	26	31	11	Technical trade-offs
21	25	25	17	Staffing
20	13	15	11	Support cost estimates
25	29	36	30	Schedules
16	19	15	17	Personalities

Source: Thamhain, Hans J., and David L. Wilemon, "Conflict Management in Project Life Cycles," *Sloan Management Review*, Summer 1975.

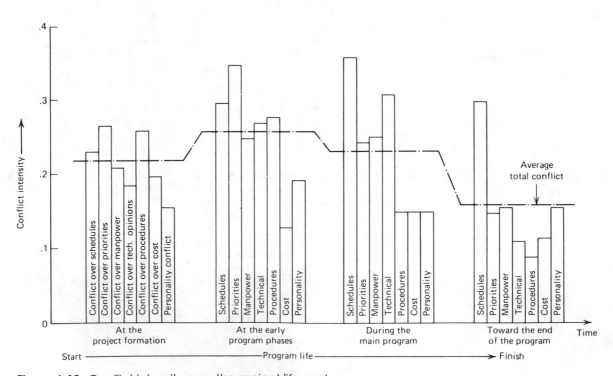

Figure 4-10 Conflict intensity over the project life cycle.
Source: Thamhain, H. J. and D. L. Wilemon, "Conflict Management in Project Life Cycles," *Sloan Management Review*, Summer, 1975.

The project manager did not flinch in the face of negative interpersonal feelings when listening to differences between people. "You have to learn to listen, keep your mouth shut, and let the guy get it off his chest."

- The project manager encouraged openness and emotional expression.
- The manager set a role model for reacting to personality clashes. It was observed that a peer would often intercede and act out a third party conciliation role much like the manager.
- The manager seemed to exhibit the attitude that conflict could he harnessed for productive ends.
- Although managers usually confronted conflicts, they also avoided face to face meetings when the outside pressure was too high.

4.8 SUMMARY

This chapter described the various organizational structures that can be used for projects, and detailed their advantages. An appropriate procedure for choosing the best form was described and two examples were given. The chapter then moved into a discussion of the project team itself, describing the organization of the project office staff and the human issues, such as motivation and conflict, the project manager will face.

Specific points made in the chapter were these:

If the project is to be included in a functional organization, it should be placed in that unit with the greatest interest in its success or the unit that can provide the most help. Though there are advantages in this mode of organizing, the disadvantages are greater.

The project form of organizing has its advantages and disadvantages. Though the disadvantages are not as severe as with the functional form, they are nevertheless significant.

The matrix organization combines the functional and project forms in an attempt to reap the advantages of each. While this approach has been fairly successful, it also has its own unique disadvantages.

There are many variants of the pure forms of organization, and special hybrids are commonly used to handle special projects. The best form for a particular case requires consideration of the characteristics of the project compared with the various advantages and disadvantages of each form.

A useful procedure for selecting an organizational form for a project is:

1. Identify the specific outcomes desired.
2. Determine the key tasks to attain these outcomes and identify the units within the parent organization where these tasks would normally be assigned.
3. Sequence the key tasks and group them into logical work steps.
4. Determine which project subsystems will be assigned which steps and which subsystems must closely cooperate.

5. Identify any special firm or project characteristics, constraints, or problems that may affect how the project should be organized.
6. Consider all the above relative to the pros and cons of each organizational form as a final decision is made.

Every project should have a project office, even if it must be shared with another project.

Larger, more complex projects may include, in addition to the PM, a project engineer, manufacturing engineer, field manager, contract administrator, project controller, and support service manager.

Those on the project team who should report directly to the PM are the project engineer and project controller. So also should:

1. Senior team members who will have a long-term relationship with the project.
2. Those with whom the PM will be continuously or closely communicating.
3. Those with rare skills needed for project success.

Perfectionism, motivation, and conflict are often the major behavioral problems facing the PM . Management by Objectives (MBO) is often a useful tool for addressing the first two, while gentle confrontation usually works best for the latter.

Sources of project conflict are often priorities and policies at first, schedule and technical problems during the main phase, and schedule and personal issues near termination.

In the next chapter we move from organizational issues to project planning tasks. We address the topics of coordination, interface management, and systems engineering. We also present some extremely useful concepts and tools such as the work breakdown structure and linear responsibility chart.

4.9 GLOSSARY

ACTION PLAN—A detailed plan of what needs to be done and when (see Chapter 5 for more discussion and some examples).

FUNCTIONAL MANAGEMENT—The standard departments of the organization that represent individual disciplines such as engineering, marketing, purchasing, and so on.

HOLISTIC—The whole viewed at one time rather than each piece individually.

MANAGEMENT BY OBJECTIVES (MBO)—A management approach popular during the 1960s that encouraged managers to give their subordinates more freedom in determining how to achieve task objectives.

MATRIX ORGANIZATION—A method of organizing that maintains both functional supervisors as well as project supervisors. A strong matrix operates closer to a pure project organization while a weak matrix operates more like a functional organization.

MIXED ORGANIZATION—This approach includes both functions (disciplines) and projects in its hierarchy.

PROGRAM MANAGER—This person is typically responsible for a number of projects, each with its own project manager.

PROJECTITIS—A social phenomenon, inappropriately intense loyalty to the project.

SUBCONTRACT—Subletting tasks out to smaller contractors.

SUBOPTIMIZATION—The optimization of a subelement of a system, perhaps to the detriment of the overall system.

WAR ROOM—A project office where the latest detail on project progress is available.

WORK BREAKDOWN STRUCTURE—A basic project document that describes all the work that must be done to complete the project and forms the basis for costing, scheduling, and work responsibility (see Chapter 5).

4.10 PROJECT TEAM ASSIGNMENT

In this exercise, you will have to determine how to organize the project team. An initial work breakdown structure will be needed to determine the tasks to be completed. Then tasks will have to be assigned to project personnel. Determine, based on the size of the project and the personnel available, whether single individuals can be assigned individualized tasks (such as project controller) or if tasks must be grouped. Finally, try to anticipate where potential conflicts may arise over the course of the project and how you might handle them at that time.

4.11 MATERIAL REVIEW QUESTIONS

1. What is a program manager? How does this job differ from that of a project manager?
2. Identify the advantages and disadvantages of the matrix form of organization.
3. Name the four basic types of project organization and list at least one characteristic, advantage, and disadvantage of each.
4. Give some major guidelines for choosing an organizational form for a project.
5. Why is the project office so important?
6. Identify three ways of dealing with a conflict associated with projects. Does dealing with conflict always need to be a zero-sum game?

4.12 CONCEPTUAL DISCUSSION QUESTIONS

1. Discuss some of the differences between managing professionals and managing other workers or team members.
2. Human factors loom large in the success of projects. Given the general lack of coverage of this subject in engineering and science education, how might such a PM gain these abilities?
3. A disadvantage of the pure project organization has to do with the tendency to fall behind in areas of technical expertise not used on the project. Name several ways that a project manager might approach this problem.
4. Discuss the effects of the various organizational forms on coordination and interaction, both within the project team and between the team and the rest of the firm.

5. Discuss the role of planning in the success of projects.
6. Can you think of any advantages other than those listed in the text associated with using MBO? Disadvantages?
7. How would you organize a project to develop a complex new product such as a new personal computer? How would you organize if the product was simpler, such as a new disk drive?
8. How should the following projects be organized?
   a. A bank's investment banking department.
   b. A firm's basic research laboratory.
   c. An international construction firm's project.
   d. A city's bus transportation project.
   e. A state's health service organization.
   f. A management consulting firm's project.
9. What do you think may be the purpose of a work breakdown structure? How might it aid the PM in organizing the project?

4.13 CHAPTER EXERCISE

Assume that you have been placed in charge of a project to educate the clerical staff in the advantages a microcomputer might offer them in their work. Assume that the organization is a large one and one you are familiar with, such as your own firm or school. Follow the procedure for selecting an organizational project form described in the chapter.

What special characteristics, constraints, or problems did you identify that a different project, or organization, might not have had? Were there any that seemed independent of the project? of the organization? What project form pros and cons did you find to be relevant in this exercise? Would they probably be relevant for any project or organization? Was the procedure effective? In your estimation, were there any unnecessary steps? Were there any missing steps?

4.14 INCIDENTS FOR DISCUSSION

Shaw's Strategy

Rick Shaw has been tapped to be a project manager for the third time this year. Although he enjoys the challenges and opportunity for personal development afforded to him as a project manager, he dreads the interpersonal problems associated with the position. Sometimes he feels like a glorified babysitter handing out assignments, checking on assignment progress, and making sure everyone is doing his or her fair share. Recently Rick read an article that recommended using MBO as an aid to the project manager in supervising and controlling team members. Rick thought this was a useful idea and decided to try it on his next project.

The project in question involved making a decision on whether to close one of the company's regional distribution centers. Rick had once been the manager of the distribution services department, so he felt very comfortable about his ability to lead the team and resolve this problem. He defined the objective of the project and detailed all the major tasks involved, as well as most of the subtasks. By the time the first meeting of the project team took place Rick felt more secure about the control and direction of the project than he had at the beginning of any of his previous projects. He had specifically defined objectives and tasks for each team member and had assigned completion dates for each task. He had even made up individual "contracts" for each team member to sign as an indication of their commitment to completion of the assigned tasks per schedule dates. The meeting went very smoothly, with almost no comments from team members. Everyone picked up a copy of his or her "contract" and went off to work on the project. Rick was ecstatic about the success of this new approach.

Question: Do you think he will feel the same way six weeks from now?

Better-Built

Better-Built Tape Recorder Company of Cleveland, Ohio, is planning to manufacture a new line of mini-tape recorders to compete with the small pocket recorders made by competitors. The company currently manufactures about 10,000 regular-size recorders per year and hopes to be manufacturing 5,000 of the smaller version beginning in two years. The new recorder will require a 25 percent enlargement of the existing facility. The president of the company feels he must set up a project team to handle the engineering, manufacturing, financing, and support services. After considering several project managers, he decided on the man he believes will get the job done and instructed that man to select his project team.

Question: Based on the above, what key people should the project manager try to enlist?

Hydrobuck

Hydrobuck is a medium-sized producer of gasoline-powered outboard motors. In the past it has successfully manufactured and marketed motors in the 3- to 40-horsepower range. Executives at Hydrobuck are now interested in larger motors and would eventually like to produce motors in the 50- to 150-horsepower range.

The internal workings of the large motors are quite similar to those of the smaller motors. However, large, high-performance outboard motors require *power trim*. Power trim is simply a hydraulic system that serves to tilt the outboard motor up or down on the boat transom. Hydrobuck cannot successfully market the larger outboard motors without designing a power trim system to complement the motor.

The company is financially secure and is the leading producer of small outboard motors. Management has decided that the following objectives need to be met within the next two years:

1. Design a quality power trim system.
2. Design and build the equipment to produce such a system efficiently.
3. Develop the operations needed to install the system on the outboard motor.

The technology, facilities, and marketing skills necessary to produce and sell the large motors already exist within the company.

Question: What type of project organization would best suit the development of the power trim system? Discuss your reasons for selecting this type of organization.

4.15 BIBLIOGRAPHY

1. Archibald, R. D. *Managing High Technology Programs and Projects.* Wiley, New York, 1976.
2. Argyris, C. "Today's Problems with Tomorrow's Organizations." *Journal of Management Studies,* Feb. 1967.
3. Barnes, L. B. *Project Management and the Use of Authority: A Study of Structure, Role, and Influence Relationships in Public and Private Organizations.* Ph.D. dissertation, University of Southern California, 1971.
4. Cicero, J. P., and D. L. Wilemon. "Project Authority: A Multidimensional View." *IEEE Transactions on Engineering Management,* May 1970.
5. Cleland, D. I. *Matrix Management Systems Handbook.* Van Nostrand Reinhold. New York, 1983.
6. Cleland, D. I., and W. R. King. *Systems Analysis and Project Management,* 3rd ed. McGraw-Hill, New York, 1983.
7. Crowston, W. B. "Models for Project Management." *Sloan Management Review,* Spring, 1971.
8. Davis, S. M., and P. R. Lawrence. *Matrix.* Addison-Wesley, Reading, MA, 1977.
9. Delbecq, A. L., and A. C. Filey. *Program and Project Management in a Matrix Organization: A Case Study.* Bureau of Business Research and Service, University of Wisconsin, 1974.
10. Drucker, P. *The Practice of Management.* Harper Brothers, 1954.
11. Forrester, J. W. "A New Corporate Design." *Industrial Management Review,* Fall 1965.
12. Galbraith, J. R. "Matrix Organization Designs—How to Combine Functional and Project Forms," *Business Horizons,* Feb. 1971.
13. Greiner, L. E. "Evolution and Revolution as Organizations Grow." *Harvard Business Review,* July–Aug. 1972.
14. Gunz, H. P., and A. Pearson. "How to Manage Control Conflicts in Project Based Organizations." *Research Management,* March 1979.
15. Herzberg, F. H. "One More Time: How Do You Motivate Employees?" *Harvard Business Review,* Jan.–Feb. 1968.
16. Hill, R., and B. J. White. *Matrix Organization and Project Management.* Michigan Business Paper #64, University of Michigan, 1979.
17. Janger, A. R. "Anatomy of The Project Organization." *Business Management Record,* Nov. 1963.
18. Kerzner, H., and D. I. Cleland. *Project/Matrix Management Policy and Strategy: Case and Situations.* Van Nostrand Reinhold, New York, 1984.
19. Killian, W. P. "Project Management—Future Organizational Concepts." *Marquette Business Review,* Feb. 1971.
20. Knight, K. *Matrix Management.* PBI-Petrocelli, 1977.

21. Likert, R., and J. G. Likert. *New Ways of Managing Conflict*. McGraw-Hill, New York, 1976.
22. Marquis, D. G., and D. M. Straight, Jr. "Organizational Factors in Project Performance." *School of Management Working Paper,* Massachusetts Institute of Technology, 1965.
23. Middleton, C. J. "How to Set Up a Project Organization." *Harvard Business Review,* March–April 1967.
24. Odiorne, G. S. *Managing by Objectives: A System of Management Leadership*. Pitman Publishing, New York, 1965.
25. Ouchi, W. *Theory Z: How American Business Can Meet the Japanese Challenge,* Addison-Wesley, Reading, MA, 1981.
26. Peart, A. T. *Design of Project Management Systems and Records.* Cahners Books, 1971.
27. Rogers, R. A. "Guidelines for Project Management Teams," *Industrial Engineering,* Dec. 1974.
28. Shaw, M. E. *Group Dynamics,* 3rd ed. McGraw-Hill, New York, 1981.
29. Shull, F. A. *Matrix Structure and Project Authority for Optimizing Organizational Capacity,* Business Science Monograph No. 1, Business Research Bureau, Southern Illinois University, 1965.
30. Smysler, C. H. *A Comparison of the Needs of Program and Functional Management.* Masters Thesis, School of Engineering, U.S. Air Force Institute of Technology, 1965.
31. Thamhain, H. J., and D. L. Wilemon. "Conflict Management in Project Life Cycles," *Sloan Management Review,* Summer 1975.
32. Tsai, M. C-P. *Contingent Conditions for The Creation of Temporary Management Organizations,* Masters Thesis, School of Management, Massachusetts Institute of Technology, 1976.
33. White, B. J. "Alternative Forms of Project Organization: Design and Evaluation." *Matrix Organization and Project Management*. Michigan Business Papers, Ann Arbor, 1979.
34. Wren, D. A., and D. Voich, Jr. *Management: Process, Structure and Behavior.* Wiley, New York, 1984.
35. Wright, N. H. "Matrix Management, A Primer for the Administrative Manager." *Management Review,* May 1979.

4.16 READING

This article reports on a survey of the use and effectiveness of matrix management. It identifies three different kinds of matrix organizations and describes the advantages and disadvantages of matrix management in general, and of each of the three kinds in particular.

After a description of the study situation, the results are reported in terms of the usage of each of the three types of matrix and their effectiveness in those situations. Though usage was rather evenly distributed across the types, effectiveness was higher for the project matrix and below average for the functional matrix.

Matrix Management: Contradictions and Insights

Erik W. Larson
David H. Gobeli

Matrix management has been championed by many as the best way to manage the development of new products and services [1]. Born out of the aerospace race, matrix management is a "mixed" organizational form in which normal hierarchy is "overlayed" by some form of lateral authority, influence, or communication. In a matrix, there are usually two chains of command, one along functional lines and the other along project lines. Perham published, during the early 1970s, a list of matrix users which included such prestigious companies as American Cyanamid, Avco, Carborundum, Caterpillar Tractor, General Telephone and Electronics, Hughes Aircraft, ITT, 3M, Monsanto Chemical, TRW, and Texas Instruments [2].

While matrix enjoyed widespread popularity in the seventies, discord has begun to surface in the eighties. For example, Texas Instruments reportedly dumped its matrix system, citing it as one of the principle reasons for economic decline [3]. Medtronic, one of the leading producers of cardiac pacemakers, scrapped its formal matrix system after two years of frustration [4]. Similarly, Xerox recently abandoned

matrix, claiming that it had created a stranglehold on product development [5]. Probably the most damning criticism can be found in the popular *In Search of Excellence,* in which Peters and Waterman assert that the tendency toward hopelessly complicated and ultimately unworkable structures "reaches its ultimate expression in the formal matrix organization structure [which] regularly degenerates into anarchy and rapidly becomes bureaucratic and noncreative." [6]

Is matrix management an unworkable system that eventually stifles the development of new products and services? Or is matrix management an effective mechanism for managing development projects in organizations? Hard evidence on the efficacy of matrix is virtually nonexistent. For the most part the literature consists of anecdotal success or failure stories. We believe that the issue has been obscured further by failing to recognize

©1987 by the Regents of the University of California. Reprinted from the *California Management Review,* Vol. 29, No. 4 by permission of the Regents.

that there are different types of matrix. We further contend that the mixed reviews of matrix pertain more to different types of matrix rather than to matrix management in general.

While matrix has been applied to a number of different contexts (i.e., financial services, hospitals, construction), our focus is on its application to product development. To pursue this issue, we sampled over 500 managers, experienced in the development of new products and services, and collected data regarding both the usage and effectiveness of different matrix structures in their company. Before reporting the results, three different forms of matrix structures will be described and their relative advantages and disadvantages discussed.

THREE MATRIX STRUCTURES

Galbraith has distinguished different forms of matrix on a continuum which ranges from the functional organization to the pure project organization [7]. The functional organization is the traditional hierarchical structure in which the organization is usually broken down into different functional areas, such as engineering, research, accounting, and administration. When applied to a product development effort, the project is divided into segments and assigned to relevant functional groups with the heads of the functional groups responsible for their segments of the project. Coordination is provided by functional and upper levels of management.

At the other end of the spectrum is the project organization, in which all the resources necessary to complete a project are separated from the regular functional structure and set up as a self-contained team headed by a project manager. The project manager has direct authority over all the personnel on the project.

Matrix organizations lie between these two extremes by integrating the functional structure with a horizontal project structure. Instead of dividing a project into separate parts or creating an autonomous team, project participants report simultaneously to both project and functional managers. The open violation of the principle of unity of command is the trademark of a matrix management.

Companies apply this matrix arrangement in a variety of different ways. Some organizations set up temporary matrix systems to deal with specific projects while matrix may be a permanent fixture in other organizations. In addition, specialists may work full-time on one project or contribute to a variety of projects. One useful way to examine different forms of matrix management is in terms of the relative influence of project and functional managers; three different forms of matrix can be identified.

A *Functional Matrix* occurs when the project manager's role is limited to coordinating the efforts of the functional groups involved. Functional managers are responsible for the design and completion of technical requirements within their discipline. The project manager basically acts as a staff assistant with indirect authority to expedite and monitor the project. Conversely, *Project Matrix* refers to a situation in which the project manager has direct authority to make decisions about personnel and work flow activities. Functional managers' involvement is limited to providing services and advisory support. Finally, a *Balanced Matrix* is one in which the project manager is responsible for defining what needs to be accomplished while the functional managers are concerned with how it will be accomplished. More specifically, the project manager establishes the overall plan for completing the project, integrates the contributions of the different disciplines, sets schedules, and monitors progress. The functional managers are responsible for assigning personnel and executing their segment of the project according to the standards and schedules set by the project manager. The merger of "how and what" requires both parties to share responsibility and authority over work flow operations. Table 1 summarizes these descriptions, as well as the functional and project organization for reference [8].

Matrix is essentially a compromise between the traditional functional organization and a pure project organization. It is more flexible than a functional organization but not as flexible as a project team. At the same time, it is more efficient than a project team, but incurs administrative cost which is unnecessary in a functional organization.

Table 2A summarizes the major advantages and disadvantages reported in the literature.

Many of the problems associated with matrix are in contradiction with its strengths. Critics have described matrix as being costly, cumbersome, and overburdening to manage, while proponents praise its efficiency and flexibility. Everyone agrees that matrix is a delicate system to manage, but few have discussed the relative efficacy of different types of matrix. With this in mind, the three types of matrix structures will be compared according to the advantages and disadvantages associated with matrix. Table 2B summarizes the tentative conclusions of this discussion.

Advantages:

- *Efficient Use of Resources*—All three forms of matrix allow specialists as well as equipment to be shared across multiple projects.
- *Project Integration*—Granting the project manager

more control over work activities should increase project integration, but at the same time quality may suffer since input from functional areas is less concentrated.

- *Flexibility*—The multidisciplinary involvement inherent in all three kinds of matrix should enhance flexibility and adaptive reactions. This should be especially true for the Balanced Matrix in which consensus through give-and-take are necessary to win joint approval. The Functional Matrix and Project Matrix are likely to be less flexible since authority is more clearly defined, making decisions less negotiable.
- *Information Flow*—Vertical information flow should be enhanced under all forms of matrix, since one of the roles of the project manager is to be a central communication link with top management. Lateral communication, however, should be strongest in a Balanced Matrix. This is probably due more to necessity than design. Shared decision making places a premium on close communication through which agreements are eventually shaped.

Table 1.
Project Management Structures

Functional Organization:	The project is divided into segments and assigned to relevant functional areas and/or groups within functional areas. The project is coordinated by functional and upper levels of management.
Functional Matrix:	A person is formally designated to oversee the project across different functional areas. This person has limited authority over functional people involved and serves primarily to plan and coordinate the project. The functional managers retain primary responsibility for their specific segments of the project.
Balanced Matrix:	A person is assigned to oversee the project and interacts on an equal basis with functional managers. This person and the functional managers jointly direct work flow segments and approve technical and operational decisions.
Project Matrix:	A manager is assigned to oversee the project and is responsible for the completion of the project. Functional ionalmanagers' involvement is limited to assigning personnel as needed and providing advisory expertise.
Project Team:	A manager is put in charge of a project team composed of a core group of personnel from several functional areas and/or groups, assigned on a full-time basis. The functional managers have no formal involvement.

Table 2A.
Advantages and Disadvantages of a Matrix Organization

Advantages

+ Efficient use of resources—Individual specialists as well as equipment can be shared across projects.
+ Project integration—There is a clear and workable mechanism for coordinating work across functional lines.
+ Improved information flow—Communication is enhanced both laterally and vertically.
+ Flexibility—Frequent contact between members from different departments expedites decision making and adaptive responses.
+ Discipline retention—Functional experts and specialists are kept together even though projects come and go.
+ Improved motivation and commitment—Involvement of members in decision making enhances commitment and motivation.

Disadvantages

− Power struggles—Conflict occurs since boundaries of authority and responsibility deliberately overlap.
− Heightened conflict—Competition over scarce resources occurs especially when personnel are being shared across projects.
− Slow reaction time—Heavy emphasis on consultation and shared decision making retards timely decision making.
− Difficulty in monitoring and controlling—Multidiscipline involvement heightens information demands and makes it difficult to evaluate responsibility.
− Excessive overhead—Double management by creating project managers.
− Experienced stress—Dual reporting relations contributes to ambiguity and role conflict.

Table 2B.
Comparative Advantages and Disadvantages of Three Types of Matrix Structures

Advantages	Functional Matrix	Balanced Matrix	Project Matrix
+ Resource efficiency	High	High	High
+ Project integration	Weak	Moderate	Strong
+ Discipline retention	High	Moderate	Low
+ Flexibility	Moderate	High	Moderate
+ Improved information flow	Moderate	High	Moderate
+ Improved motivation and commitment	Uncertain	Uncertain	Uncertain
Disadvantages			
− Power struggles	Moderate	High	Moderate
− Heightened conflict	Low	Moderate	Moderate
− Reaction time	Moderate	Slow	Fast
− Difficulty in monitoring and controlling	Moderate	High	Low
− Excessive overhead	Moderate	High	High
− Experienced stress	Moderate	High	Moderate

Conversely, lateral communication may suffer a bit under a project using Functional Matrix since the project manager and functional managers are not as dependent upon each other as in a Balanced Matrix.

- *Discipline Retention*—A key advantage that matrix has over the pure project team approach is that it allows participants to sustain their link with their functional area while working on multidisciplinary projects. This not only provides a home port for specialists to return to once work on the project is completed but also helps participants to remain technically sharp in their discipline. Still, the ability of participants to maintain ties with their specialty area is likely to decline as their involvement becomes more and more under the jurisdiction of the project manager.

- *Motivation and Commitment*—Inherent in all types of matrix is a high degree of involvement in decision making, which should enhance personal commitment and motivation. Team spirit, however, is likely to be high under a Project Matrix since participant involvement is more project focused. Still, many specialists find interacting with different types of people and performing a wide range of activities frustrating. It is difficult to conclude which structure will elicit the highest levels of commitment and motivation.

Disadvantages:

- *Power Struggles*—Matrix is predicated on tension between functional managers and project managers who are in competition for control over the same set of resources. Such conflict is viewed as a necessary mechanism for achieving an appropriate balance between complex technical issues and unique project requirements. While the intent is noble, the effect is sometimes analogous to opening Pandora's box. Legitimate conflict spills over to a more personal level, resulting from conflicting objectives and accountabilities, disputes about credit and blame, and attempts to redress infringements on professional domains. The Balanced Matrix is more susceptible to these kinds of problems since power and authority are more negotiable under this system. Power struggles should be reduced under functional and project matrices since the relative authority of each party is more clearly defined.

- *Heightened Conflict*—Any situation in which equipment and people are being shared across projects lends itself to conflict and competition for scarce resources. A Functional Matrix, however, should alleviate some of these problems since specialists can directly appeal to their functional superior to resolve conflicting demands on their time and energy.

- *Reaction Time*—While shared decision making enhances the flexibility of the Balanced Matrix, the drawback is the time necessary to reach agreement. The Project Matrix should produce faster results since the project manager is not necessarily bound to a consensus style of decision making, which is formalized in a Balanced Matrix. For the same reason, the Functional Matrix should be quicker than the Balanced Matrix, but not as fast as the Project Matrix since decision making has to be coordinated across functional lines.

- *Monitoring and Control*—Matrix is susceptible to passing the buck, abdication of responsibility, and cost accounting nightmares. This is particularly true for Balanced Matrix in which responsibility is explicitly shared across functional and project lines. While in principle each functional area is responsible for its particular segment of the project under a Functional Matrix, contributions naturally overlap, making it difficult to determine accountability. The Project Matrix centralizes control over the project, permitting more efficient cost-control and evaluation systems.

- *Excessive Overhead*—All three forms of matrix increase administrative overhead by instituting the role of project manager. Administrative costs, in the form of salaries, are likely to be higher for the Balanced and Project forms of matrix due to the greater roles of the project manager.

- *Experienced Stress*—The very nature of development projects tend to make it a very stressful experience for participants. Matrix management appears to exacerbate this problem. Multiple reporting relationships and divided commitment across projects heighten role conflict and ambiguity. Stress is likely to be a more serious problem where ambiguity is the greatest: the Balanced Matrix. Both the Functional Matrix and the Project Matrix are likely to reduce ambiguity and associated stress, since lines of authority and responsibility are more clearly defined.

Overall, these comparisons indicate that the advantages and disadvantages associated with matrix are not necessarily true for all three forms of matrix and that each type of matrix has its own unique set of strengths and weaknesses. The comparisons also suggest that the Project Matrix is superior in many ways to the other two forms of matrix. The Project Matrix is likely to enhance project integration, decrease reaction time, diminish power struggles, and improve the control and monitoring of project activities and costs. On the down side, technical quality may suffer since functional areas have less control over their contributions.

The Functional Matrix is likely to improve technical quality as well as provide a better system for managing conflict across projects. The Achilles' heel is that functional control is maintained at the likely expense of poor project integration. The Balanced Matrix represents a compromise between the two extreme approaches and as such shares to a lesser degree several of the advantages of the two other approaches. At the same time, it is the most delicate system to manage and is more likely to succumb to many of the problems associated with matrix.

The questions that need to be addressed are: What has been the experience of actual companies with these different matrix structures? Which form of matrix is the most widely used? More to the point, does practice support theory? Do practitioners support our conclusion that the Project Matrix is the most effective form of matrix for developing new products and services?

The Study

This study is part of a research program sponsored by the Project Management Institute (PMI). PMI is the professional association for practitioners of project management and has over 5,000 members worldwide. Data were collected by means of a mailed questionnaire which was sent to randomly selected PMI members in both Canada and the United States. Repeated mailings yielded a 64 percent response rate. This study is based on the 510 respondents who reported that they were primarily involved in development projects directed at creating new products, services, and/or processes.

Over 30 percent of the sample were either project managers or directors of project management programs within their firm. Sixteen percent were members of top management (i.e., president, vice-president, or division manager), while 26 percent were managers in functional areas such as marketing, operations, and accounting. Eighty percent share the common experience of having been a project manager at some time during their career.

The sample represents a wide variety of industries. For example, 14 percent were involved in developing pharmaceutical products, 10 percent were in aerospace, and 10 percent were involved in developing computer and data processing products. Among the other industries represented in lesser numbers are telecommunications, medical instruments, glass products, petrochemical products, software development, and housewares goods.

As we report our findings, we are keenly aware that individual perceptions do not provide the best basis for drawing inferences about effectiveness. Still, the breadth of the study provides a useful referent point for assessing the current status of matrix in North America.

Matrix: Usage In order to ascertain experience with matrix, respondents were asked two questions: Has your organization ever used matrix management to develop new products or services? If so, what is the likelihood matrix will be used again? If they responded that it would not be used again, then they were asked to state the reasons why. Figure 1 represents the results for these two questions.

Over three-quarters of respondents reported that their company has used matrix. Of those who responded yes, 89 percent felt that matrix would probably or definitely continue to be used. Only 1 percent reported that matrix would definitely not be used again. Among the reasons given for dropping matrix were breakdowns in coordination between functional and project managers, a shift towards using project teams to complete projects, and the size of their organization was too small to

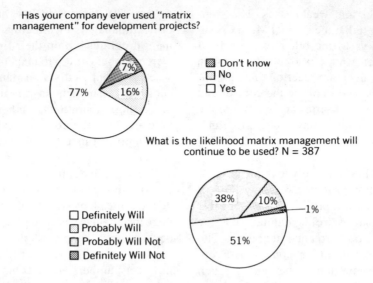

Figure 1.

take advantage of a matrix system. Still, the overwhelming opinion was that matrix is the dominant mode for managing development projects in the organizations sampled and will continue to be so.

These results address matrix in general. The usage of the three types of matrix was measured by having respondents indicate the number of current projects ("many," "few," or "none") in their organization that utilized each structure (see Figure 2). Respondents based their responses on a capsule description of each structure (as presented in Table 1).

All three forms of matrix were widely used. Project Matrix was the most popular, with over 78 percent of the respondents reporting that this form of matrix was being used to manage development projects in their company. Seventy-four percent reported that their firm used the

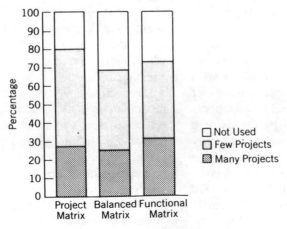

Figure 2. Usage of Different Matrix Structures

Functional Matrix while 68 percent reported using the Balanced Matrix.

Since size affects economies of scale, availability of resources, and integration requirements, usages rate for the different structures were compared to the size of the firm. The only significant variation occurred in companies with less than 100 employees. Over 84 percent of respondents working in small firms reported using a Project Matrix while the usage levels were lower for both the Balanced Matrix (62 percent) and Functional Matrix (56 percent). No differences were revealed in the usage patterns of large and medium-sized firms.

Matrix: Effectiveness Respondents were asked to rate the effectiveness of each of the matrix structures they had experienced. Controlling cost, meeting schedule, and achieving technical performance parameters were among the factors considered in evaluating the different structures. The average rating for each form of matrix is reported in Figure 3. The results indicate a strong preference for the Project Matrix, which was rated above effective. The Balanced Matrix was considered effective, while the Functional Matrix was rated below effective.

The ratings for the total sample are somewhat clouded by the fact that not all the respondents had direct experience with each of the three matrix structures. A more valid reference point can be obtained from the 123 respondents who had direct experience with all three structures. Their ratings are also reported in Figure 3, and here the pattern is further reinforced. The Project Matrix received the highest rating while the Functional Matrix was rated as ineffective. The Balanced Matrix received only a marginal rating.

Potential variations in the above results were examined for the size of the firm. One of the reasons mentioned for dropping matrix was that the organization was too small to sustain a matrix structure. However, when effectiveness ratings were examined according to size of the firm, size had little impact on the ratings. For example, both respondents in firms of less than one hundred employees and

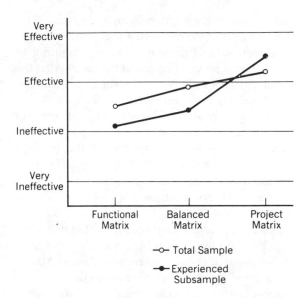

Figure 3. Rated Effectiveness of Different Matrix Structures

respondents in firms of greater than 1,000 employees rated Project Matrix as the most effective.

The results indicate a strong preference for a Project Matrix in which the project manager has primary responsibility and control over development activities. These results may have been tempered by self-interest since a significant portion of the sample was project managers. To examine this potential bias, the ratings of project managers were compared with those of top management and managers in other functional areas. These results revealed only minor differences in the ratings of the three groups. Top management, project managers, and even functional managers were in agreement that the Project Matrix is the most effective form of matrix. The Functional Matrix was considered the least effective, even by the functional managers.

Discussion and Conclusions

While matrix might be viewed as being cumbersome, chaotic, and anarchical by critics, it is still widely used by North American businesses. Over three-fourths of the respondents reported that their organization has tried matrix and will continue to use it. These results contradict the notion that the popularity of matrix is waning, suggesting instead that matrix is the dominant mode for completing development projects. The support is strong, but not without reservations. The following comment from one respondent is typical of the feelings toward matrix management: "Matrix management works, but it sure seems difficult at times. All matrix managers must keep up their health and take stress tabs."

More specifically, all three forms of matrix were popular, with the Project Matrix having a slightly higher usage rate than either the Balanced Matrix or the Functional Matrix. Size of the firm affected usage patterns only with regard to small firms which were found to have a much stronger preference for the Project Matrix. The effectiveness data confirmed our prediction concerning the relative efficacy of the different matrix structures. The Project Matrix was consistently rated superior to the other two forms of matrix. The Balanced Matrix received a marginal rating, while the Functional Matrix was considered ineffective. These effectiveness ratings were not affected by the size of the firm.

The results of this study reveal an interesting contradiction. If the Project Matrix form is considered the most effective, why are the other two forms used nearly as often?

One explanation for this contradiction can be found in the work of Davis and Lawrence[9]. They argue that matrix systems tend to evolve over time, beginning first with a Functional Matrix, followed by a shift towards a Balanced Matrix, and ultimately maturing into a Project Matrix. The comparable usage patterns among the matrix structures suggest that the organizations sampled may be at different stages of matrix development.

A related factor is resistance to change. Matrix management, especially the Project Matrix form, represents a radical departure from the conventional functional approach to organizing. Such change is likely to evoke strong resistance. This is especially true among functional managers, who perceive their authority being usurped by the project manager. Since authority typically resides along functional lines before the introduction of matrix, it would seem only natural that vested interests play a role in choosing a weaker form of matrix. Several project managers commented that their company's reliance on a Functional Matrix was politically motivated and that their functional counterparts strongly opposed expanding the role of project managers over projects.

This condition also underscores once again the need to recognize that not all matrix structures are the same. Our position is that much of the recent criticism leveled at matrix is more relevant to the balanced and functional forms of matrix. Conversely, much of the support for matrix probably comes from those using the Project Matrix form. While more rigorous studies are needed to substantiate this claim, the responses from practitioners in this study support this argument. The final lesson to be learned is a relatively simple one: managers who are concerned with the development of new products and services should consider moving to a Project Matrix if they haven't already done so, especially if they see the disadvantages of a Functional Matrix and a Balanced Matrix occurring in their firm.

REFERENCES

1. See, for example, Leonard Sayles, "Matrix Management: The Structure with a Future," *Organizational Dynamics* (Autumn 1976), pp. 2–17; W. C. Goggin, "How the Multi-Dimensional Structure Works at Dow-Corning," *Harvard Business Review* (January/February 1974), pp. 54–65; Jay Galbraith, ed., *Matrix Organizations: Organization Design for High Technology* (Cambridge, MA: MIT Press, 1971).

2. H. Perham, "Matrix Management: A Tough Game to Play," *Dun's Review* (August 1970), pp. 31–34.

3. *Business Week,* "An About Face in TI's Culture," July 5, 1982, p. 77.

4. David H. Gobeli and W. R. Rudelius, "Managing Innovation: Lessons from the Cardiac Pacing In-

dustry," *Sloan Management Review* (Summer 1985), pp. 29–43.

5. *Business Week*, "How Xerox Speeds Up the Birth of New Products," March 19, 1984, pp. 58–59.

6. Tom Peters and Robert Waterman, *In Search of Excellence* (New York, NY: Harper and Row, 1982), p. 49.

7. Jay Galbraith, "Matrix Organization Designs—How to Combine Functional and Project Forms," *Business Horizons* (February 1971), pp. 29–40.

8. For those readers interested in a more comprehensive description of matrix, we recommend: Stanley Davis and Paul Lawrence, *Matrix* (Reading, MA: Addison-Wesley Publishing Co., 1977); D. R. Kingdon, *Matrix Organization* (London: Tavistock, 1973); Lynn Stuckenbruck, "The Matrix Organization," *Project Management Quarterly* (1979), pp. 21–33.

9. Stanley Davis and Paul Lawrence, op. cit.

CHAPTER 5
Project Planning

In the previous chapter we laid out procedures for organizing the project and tying it to the parent organization. With a project team in place, it is now time to start planning the work. Project planning has been described [23] as a set of six planning sequences. First comes preliminary coordination where the various parties involved in the project get together and make preliminary decisions about what will be achieved (project objectives) and by whom. These preliminary plans serve as the basis for a detailed description of the various tasks that must be undertaken and accomplished in order to achieve the objectives of the project. In addition, the very act of engaging in the preliminary planning process increases member commitment to the project.

These work plans are used for the third and fourth sequences, deriving the project budget and schedule. Both the budget and the schedule directly reflect the detail (or lack of it) in the project work plan, the detailed description of project tasks. The fifth planning sequence is a precise description of all project status reports, when they are to be produced, what they must contain, and to whom they will be sent. Finally, plans must be developed that deal with project termination, explaining in advance how the project pieces will be redistributed once its purpose has been completed.

This chapter deals only with the first two of the six planning sequences, but we develop planning techniques that link the first two stages to each of the other sequences, which are covered in later chapters. Project budgets are discussed in Chapter 7, schedules in Chapter 8, status reports in Chapter 10, and project termination in Chapter 13.

But before we begin, we assume in this chapter that the purpose of planning is to facilitate later accomplishment. The world is full of plans that never become deeds. The planning techniques covered here are intended to smooth the path from idea to accomplishment. It is a complicated process to manage a project, and plans act as a map of this process. The map must have sufficient detail to determine what must be done next but be simple enough that workers are not lost in a welter of minutiae.

5.1 INITIAL PROJECT COORDINATION

It is crucial that the project's objectives be clearly tied to the overall mission of the firm. Senior management should define the firm's intent in undertaking the project, outline the scope of the project, and describe the project's desired results. Without a clear beginning, project planning can easily go astray. It is also vital that a senior manager call and be present at an initial coordinating meeting as a visible symbol of top management's commitment to the project.

At-the meeting, the project is discussed in sufficient detail that potential contributors develop a general understanding of what is needed. If the project is one of many similar projects, the meeting will be quite short and routine, a sort of "touching base" with other interested units. If the project is unique in most of its aspects, extensive discussion may be required.

Whatever the process, the outcome must be that: (1) technical objectives are established (though perhaps not "cast in concrete"), (2) basic areas of performance responsibility are accepted by the participants, and (3) some tentative schedules and budgets are spelled out. Each individual/unit accepting responsibility for a portion of the project should agree to deliver, by the next project meeting, a preliminary but detailed plan about how that responsibility will be accomplished. Such plans should contain descriptions of the required tasks, budgets, and schedules.

These plans are then reviewed by the group and combined into a composite *project plan*. The composite plan, still not completely firm, is approved by each participating group, by the project manager, and then by senior organizational management. Each subsequent approval hardens the plan somewhat, and when senior management has endorsed it, any further changes must be made by processing a formal *change order*. However, if the project is not large or complex, informal written memoranda can substitute for the change order. The main point is that no *significant* changes in the project are made, without written notice, following top management's approval. The definition of "significant" depends on the specific situation and the people involved.

The PM generally takes responsibility for gathering the necessary approvals and assuring that any changes incorporated into the plan at higher levels are communicated to, and approved by, the units that have already signed off on the plan. Nothing is as sure to enrage functional unit managers as to find that they have been committed by someone else to alterations in their carefully considered plans without being informed. Violation of this procedure is considered a betrayal of trust. Several incidents of this kind occurred in a firm during a project to design a line of children's clothing. The anger at this *change without communication* was so great that two chief designers resigned and took jobs with a competitor.

Because senior managers are almost certain to exercise their prerogative to change the plan, the PM should always return to the contributing units for consideration and reapproval of the plan as modified. The final, approved result of this procedure is the project plan, also known as the *master plan,* or the *baseline plan.*

Outside Clients

When the project is to deliver a product/service to an outside client (often referred to as the project's *deliverables),* the fundamental planning process in unchanged except for the fact that the specifications cannot be altered without the client's permission. A common "planning" problem in these cases is that marketing has promised deliverables that engineering does not know how to produce on a schedule that manufacturing cannot meet. This sort of problem usually results when the various functional areas are not involved in the planning process at the time the original proposal is made to a potential client.

Two objections to such early participation by engineering and manufacturing are likely to be raised. First, the sales arm of the organization is trained to sell and is expected to be fully conversant with all technical aspects of the firm's products/services. Further, salespeople are expected to be knowledgeable about design and manufacturing lead times and schedules. On the other hand, it is widely assumed by marketing (with some justice on occasion) that manufacturing and design engineers do not understand sales techniques, will be argumentative and/or pessimistic about client needs in the presence of the client, and are generally not "housebroken" when customers are nearby. Second, it is expensive to involve so much technical talent so early in the sales process—typically, prior to issuing a proposal. It can easily cost a firm $5,000 to $10,000 to send five technical specialists on a trip to consider a potential client's needs. The willingness to accept higher sales costs puts even more emphasis on the selection process.

The rejoinder to such objections is simple. It is usually cheaper, faster, and easier to do things right the first time than to redo them. When the product/service is a complex system that must be installed in a larger, more complex system, it is appropriate to treat the sale like a project. The sale *is* a project and deserves the same kind of planning. A great many firms that consistently operate in an atmosphere typified by design and manufacturing crises have created their own panics. In fairness, it is appropriate to urge that anyone meeting customers face to face should receive some training in the tactics of selling.

Project Plan Elements

Given the project plan, approvals really amount to a series of authorizations. The PM is authorized to direct activities, spend monies (usually within preset limits), request resources and personnel, and start the project on its way. Senior management's approval not only signals its willingness to fund and support the project, but also notifies subunits in the organization that they may commit resources to the project.

The process of developing the project plan varies from organization to organization, but any project plan must contain the following elements:

Overview   This is a short summary of the objectives and scope of the project. It is directed to top management and contains a statement of the goals of the project, a brief explanation of their relationship to the firm's objectives, a description of the managerial structure that will be used for the project, and a list of the major milestones in the project schedule.

Objectives   This contains a more detailed statement of the general goals noted in the overview section. The statement should include profit and competitive aims as well as technical goals.

General Approach   This section describes both the managerial and the technical approaches to the work. The technical discussion describes the relationship of the project to available technologies. For example, it might note that this project is an extension of work done by the company for an earlier project. The subsection on the managerial approach takes note of any deviation from routine procedure—for instance, the use of subcontractors for some parts of the work.

Contractual Aspects   This critical section of the plan includes a complete list and description of all reporting requirements, customer-supplied resources, liaison arrangements, advisory committees, project review and cancellation procedures, proprietary requirements, any specific management agreements (e.g., use of subcontractors), as well as the technical deliverables and their specifications and delivery schedule. Completeness is a necessity in this section. If in doubt about whether an item should be included or not, the wise planner will include it.

Schedules   This section outlines the various schedules and lists all milestone events. The estimated time for each task should be obtained from those who will do the work. The project master schedule is constructed from these inputs. The responsible person or department head should sign off on the final, agreed-on schedule.

Resources   There are two primary aspects to this section. The first is the budget. Both capital and expense requirements are detailed by task, which makes this a *project budget* (discussed further in Chapter 7). One-time costs are separated from recurring project costs. Second, cost monitoring and control procedures should be described. In addition to the usual routine elements, the monitoring and control procedures must be designed to cover special resource requirements for the project, such as special machines, test equipment, laboratory usage or construction, logistics, field facilities, and special materials.

Personnel   This section lists the expected personnel requirements of the project. Special skills, types of training needed, possible recruiting problems, legal or policy restrictions on work force composition, and any other special requirements, such as security clearances, should be noted here. (This reference to "security" includes the need to protect trade secrets and research targets from competitors as well as the need to protect the national security.) It is helpful to index personnel needs to the project schedule. This makes clear when the various types of contributors are needed and in what numbers. These projections are an important element of the budget, so the personnel, schedule, and resources sections can be cross-checked with one another to ensure consistency.

Evaluation Methods   Every project should be evaluated against standards and by methods established at the project's inception. This section contains a brief description of the procedure to be followed in monitoring, collecting, storing, and evaluating the history of the project.

Potential Problems   Sometimes it is difficult to convince planners to make a serious attempt to anticipate potential difficulties. One or more such possible disasters as subcontractor default, technical failure, strikes, bad weather, sudden required breakthroughs, critical sequences of tasks, tight deadlines, resource limitations, complex coordination requirements, insufficient authority in some areas, and new, complex, or unfamiliar tasks are certain to occur. The only uncertainties are which ones will occur and when. In fact, the timing of these disasters is not random. There are times, conditions, and events in the life of every project when progress depends on subcontractors, or the weather, or coordination, or resource availability, and plans to deal with unfavorable contingencies should be developed early in the project's life cycle. Some PMs disdain this section of the plan on the grounds that crises cannot be predicted. Further, they claim to be very effective firefighters. It is quite possible that when one finds such a PM, one has discovered an arsonist. No amount of current planning can solve the current crisis, but preplanning may avert some.

These are the elements that constitute the project plan and are the basis for a more detailed planning of the budgets, schedules, work plan, and general management of the project. Once this basic plan is fully developed and approved, it is disseminated to all interested parties. For an example of a project plan, see the case at the end of this chapter.

5.2 SYSTEMS INTEGRATION

Systems integration (sometimes called *systems engineering*) plays a crucial role in the performance aspect of the project. We are using this phrase to include any technical specialist in the science or art of the project who is capable of performing the role of integrating the technical disciplines to achieve the customer's objectives. As such, systems integration is concerned with three major objectives.

1. *Performance*   Performance is what a system does. It includes system design, reliability, quality, maintainability, and repairability. Obviously, these are not separate, independent elements of the system, but are highly interrelated

qualities. Any of these system performance characteristics is subject to over-design as well as underdesign but must fall within the design parameters established by the client. If the client approves, we may give the client more than the specifications require simply because we have already designed to some capability, and giving the client an overdesigned system is faster and less expensive than delivering precisely to specification. At times, the esthetic qualities of a system may be specified, typically through a requirement that the appearance of the system must be acceptable to the client.

2. Effectiveness   The objective is to design the individual components of a system to achieve the desired performance in an optimal manner. This is accomplished through the following guidelines:

- Require no component performance specifications unless necessary to meet one or more systems requirements.
- Every component requirement should be traceable to one or more systems requirements.
- Design components to optimize system performance, not the performance of a subsystem.

It is not unusual for clients to violate any or all of these seemingly logical dicta. Tolerances specified to far closer limits than any possible system requirement, superfluous "bells and whistles," and "off the shelf" components that do not work well with the rest of the system are so common they seem to be taken for granted by both client and vendor. The causes of these strange occurrences are probably associated with some combination of inherent distrust between buyer and seller, the desire to overspecify in order to be sure, and the feeling that "this part will do just as well." As we will see in Chapter 6, these attitudes can be softened and replaced with others that are more helpful to the process of system integration.

3. Cost   Systems integration considers cost to be a design parameter, and costs can be accumulated in several areas. Added design cost may lead to decreased component cost, leaving performance and effectiveness otherwise unchanged. Added design cost may yield decreased production cost, and production cost may be traded off against unit cost for materials. *Value engineering* examines all these cost tradeoffs and is an important aspect of systems integration. It can be used in any project where the relevant cost tradeoffs can be estimated. It is simply the consistent and thorough use of cost/effectiveness analysis. For an application of value engineering techniques applied to disease control projects, see [10].

Systems integration plays a major role in the success or failure of any project. If a risky approach is taken by systems integration, it may delay the project. If the approach is too conservative, we forego opportunities for enhanced project capabilities or advantageous project economics. A good design will take all these tradeoffs into account in the initial stages of the technical approach. A good design will also avoid locking the project into a rigid solution with little flexibility or adaptability in case problems occur later on or changes in the environment demand changes in project performance or effectiveness.

The details of systems integration are beyond the scope of this book. The interested reader is referred to [5]. In any case, the ability to do systems integration or engineering depends on at least a minimal level of technical knowledge about most parts of the project. It is one of the reasons project managers are expected to have some understanding of the technology of the projects they head.

5.3 SORTING OUT THE PROJECT

In the next section of this chapter, and in Chapters 7 and 8 on budgeting and scheduling, we move into a consideration of the details of the project. We need to know exactly what is to be done, by whom, and when. All activities required to complete the project must be precisely delineated and coordinated. The necessary resources must be available when and where they are needed, and in the correct amounts. Some activities must be done sequentially, but some may be done simultaneously. If a large project is to come in on time and within cost, a great many things must happen when and how they are supposed to happen. In this section, we propose a simple method to assist in sorting out and planning all this detail.

To accomplish any specified project, several major activities must be completed. First, list them in the general order in which they would normally occur. A reasonable number of major activities might be anywhere between 2 and 20. Break each of these major activities into 2 to 20 subtasks. There is nothing sacred about these limits. Two is the minimum possible breakdown and 20 is about the largest number of interrelated items that can be comfortably sorted and scheduled at a given level of task aggregation. Second, preparing a network from this information, as we will in Chapter 8, is much more difficult if the number of activities is significantly greater than twenty.

It is important to be sure that all items in the list are at roughly the same level of task generality. In writing a book, for example, the various chapters tend to be at the same level of generality, but individual chapters are divided into finer detail. Indeed, subdivisions of a chapter may be divided into finer detail still.

Sometimes a problem arises because some managers tend to think of outcomes (events) when planning and others think of specific tasks (activities). Many mix the two. The problem is to develop a list of both activities and outcomes that represents an exhaustive, nonredundant set of results to be accomplished (outcomes) and the work to be done (activities) in order to complete the project.

The procedure proposed here is a *hierarchical* planning system. First, the goals must be specified. This will aid the planner in identifying the set of required activities for the goals to be met, the *project action plan*. Each activity has an outcome (event) associated with it, and these activities and events can be decomposed into subactivities and subevents, which may, in turn, be subdivided again. The *project plan* is the set of these action plans. The advantage of the project plan is that it contains all planning information in one document.

Assume, for example, that we have a project whose purpose is to acquire and install a large machining center in an existing plant. In the hierarchy of work to be accomplished for the installation part of the project, we might find such tasks as "Develop a plan for preparation of the floor site" and "Develop a plan to maintain plant output during the installation and test period." These tasks are two of a larger set of jobs to be done. The task "...preparation of the floor site" is subdivided into its elemental parts, including such items as "Get specifics on machine center mounting points," "Check construction specifications on plant floor," and "Present final plan for floor preparation for approval." A form that may help to organize this information is shown in Figure 5-1. (Additional information about each element of the project will be added to the form later when budgeting and scheduling are discussed.) Figure 5-2 shows an action plan for a college "Career Day."

A tree diagram can be used to represent a hierarchical plan as in Figure 5-3. Professor Andrew Vazsonyi has called this type of diagram a *Gozinto chart* after the famous Italian mathematician, Prof. Zepartzat Gozinto, of Vazsonyi's invention. (Readers familiar with the Bill of Materials in a Materials Requirements Planning (MRP) system will recognize the parallel to nested hierarchical planning.)

The actual form of such plans varies. If the project does not involve capital equipment and special materials, estimates may not be necessary. Some projects require a long chain of tasks that are mostly sequential—for example, the real estate syndication of an apartment complex (see Figure 8-26 in Chapter 8) or the development and licensing of a new drug. Other projects require the coordination of many concurrent tasks that finally come together—for example, the design and manufacture of an aircraft engine or the construction of a house. Still others have the characteristics of both. An example of a plan to acquire a sub-

ACTION PLAN

Deliverables _____

_____

Measure(s) of accomplishment _____

_____

Key constraints and assumptions _____

TASKS	ESTIMATED RESOURCES	IMMEDIATE PREDECESSOR TASKS	ESTIMATED TIME DURATION(S)	ASSIGNED TO

Figure 5-1 A form to assist hierarchical planning.

Tasks 1	Responsibility	Time (weeks)	Precedent	Resources
ACTION PLAN, CONTACT ORGANIZATIONS.				
1. Print forms	credentials secretary	6	na	printing shop
2. Contact organizations	program manager	15	1.1	word processing
3. Collect display information	office manager	4	1.2	
4. Gather college/ major particulars	office manager	4	1.2	
5. Print programs	credentials secretary	6	1.4	printing shop
6. Print participation certificates	grad. assistant	8	na	off-campus printer

Tasks 2	Responsibility	Time	Precedent	Resources
ACTION PLAN, BANQUET AND REFRESHMENTS.				
1. Select guest speaker	program manager	14	na	
2. Organize food	program manager	3	1.2	caterer
3. Organize liquor	director	10	1.2	Department of Liquor Control
4. Organize refreshments	grad. assistant	7	1.2	University purchasing

Tasks 3	Responsibility	Time	Precedent	Resources
ACTION PLAN, PUBLICITY AND PROMOTION.				
1. Send invitations	director	2	na	word processing
2. Organize gift certificates	grad. assistant	5.5	na	
3. Arrange banner	grad. assistant	5	na	Campus Calendar
4. Contact faculty members	program manager	1.5	1.4	word processing
5. Advertise in *News Record*	credentials secretary	5	1.4	*News Record*
6. Class announcements	grad. assistant	1	3.4	registrar's office
7. Organize posters	credentials secretary	4.5	1.4	printing shop
8. Special promotions	open	TBD		

Tasks 4	Responsibility	Time	Precedent	Resources
ACTION PLAN, FACILITIES.				
1. Arrange facilities at TUC	program manager	2.5	1.3	Work Control
2. Transport materials	office manager	0.5	4.2	Work Control

Figure 5-2 Action plan for college "Career Day".

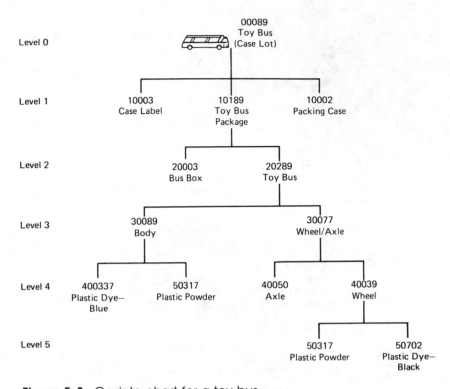

Figure 5-3 Gozinto chart for a toy bus.
Source: Harris, R.D. and R.F. Gonzalez, *The Operations Manager*, West Pub. Co., 1981, p. 267.

sidiary is illustrated in Figure 5-4. One page of a five-page plan is shown. The individuals and groups mentioned developed similar plans at a greater level of detail. (Names have been changed at the request of the firm.)

The importance of careful planning can scarcely be overemphasized. Schultz, Slevin, and Pinto [24] developed a list of ten factors that should be associated with success in implementation projects. The factors were split into strategic and tactical clusters. Of interest here are the strategic factors:

1. *Project mission.* It is important to spell out clearly defined and agreed-upon goals in the beginning of the project.
2. *Top management support.* It is necessary for top managers to get behind the project at the outset and make clear to all personnel involved that they support successful completion.
3. *Project schedule or plan.* A detailed plan of the required steps in the implementation process needs to be developed, including all resource requirements (money, raw materials, staff, and so forth).

Extensive empirical testing showed these factors to be required for implementation project success. (Tactical factors are also necessary for success, but they are not a consideration here.)

SEPTEMBER 10

To allow Ajax to operate like a department of Instat by April 1, 1986, we must do the following by dates indicated.

SEPTEMBER 24

Ajax Management advised of coming under Instat operation. The Instat sales department will begin selling Ajax Consumer Division production effective Jan. 1, 1986. There will be two sales groups: (1) Instat, (2) Ajax Builder Group.

OCTOBER 15

Instat Regional Managers advised—Instat sales dept. to assume sales responsibility for Ajax products to distribution channels, Jan. 1, 1986.

OCTOBER 15

Ajax regional managers advised of sales changes effective Jan. 1, 1986.

OCTOBER 15

Instat Management, Bob Carl, Van Baker, and Val Walters visit Ajax management and plant. Discuss how operations will merge into Instat.

OCTOBER 22

Ajax regional managers advised Ajax sales personnel and agents of change effective Jan. 1, 1986.

OCTOBER 24

Brent Sharp and Ken Roadway visit Instat to coordinate change over.

OCTOBER 29

Instat regional managers begin interviewing Ajax sales personnel for possible positions in Instat's sales organization.

NOVEMBER 5

Instat regional managers of Ajax for sales training session.

NOVEMBER 26

Walters visits Ajax to obtain more information.

NOVEMBER 30

DATA PROCESSING (Morrie Reddish) and MFG. ENGINEERING (Sam Newfield): Request DP tapes from Bob Cawley, Ajax, for conversion of Ajax to Instat eng. records: master inventory file, structure file, Bill of Materials file, where used file, cross-reference Instat to Ajax part numbers, etc.

Allow maximum two weeks until December 14, 1985, for tapes to be at Instat.

DECEMBER 3

ADMINISTRATIVE (Val Walters): Offer Norwood warehouse for sublease.

DECEMBER 3

SALES (Abbott and Crutchfield): Week of sales meeting . . . instruction of salespeople in Ajax line . . . including procedure in writing Ajax orders on separate forms from Instat orders . . . temporarily, adding weight and shipping information, and procedure below:

Crutchfield to write procedure regarding transmission of orders to Instat, credit check, and transmission of order information to shipping point, whether Norwood, San Francisco, or, later, Instat Cincinnati.

Figure 5-4 Action plan for merger of Ajax Hardware into Instat Corp. (page 1 of 5).

5.4 THE WORK BREAKDOWN STRUCTURE AND LINEAR RESPONSIBILITY CHARTS

The Work Breakdown Structure (WBS) used in project management is a type of Gozinto chart and is constructed directly from the project's action plans. The WBS may also be perceived as an organization chart with tasks substituted for people, as shown in Figure 5-5. It pictures a project subdivided into hierarchical units of tasks, work packages, and work units. The end result is a collection of work units each of which is relatively short in time span. Each has definite beginning and end points along with specific criteria for evaluating performance.

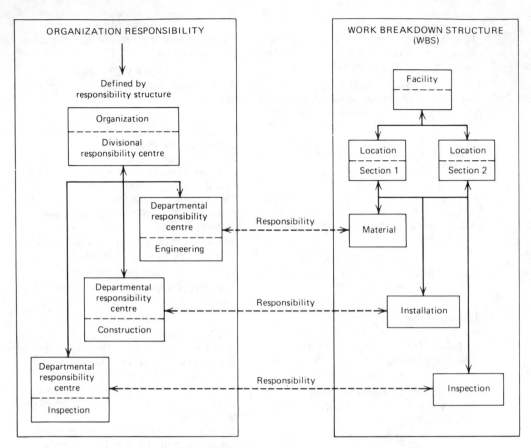

Figure 5-5 Responsibility/WBS relationship.
Source: Lavold, G. D., "Developing and Using the Work Breakdown Structure," in Cleland, D. I., and W. R. King, *Project Management Handbook.* Van Nostrand Reinhold, New York, 1983.

Each part of the project down to the smallest subtask element is budgetable in terms of money, labor hours, and other requisite resources. Each is a single, meaningful job for which individual responsibility can be assigned. Each can be scheduled as one of the many jobs that the organization must undertake and complete.

In constructing the WBS, it is wise to contact the managers and workers who will be directly responsible for each of the work packages. These people can develop a hierarchical plan for the package delegated to them, as explained in Section 5.3. It is from such documents that the PM develops the WBS shown in Figure 5-6. Using workers and managers to aid in this job is an important aspect of the entire process. According to our experience, a manager can effectively plan one or two levels below his/her position. Indeed, it is an implicit assumption of participative management that work beneath this level is too remote from the manager's recent experience, and critical detail will be lost.

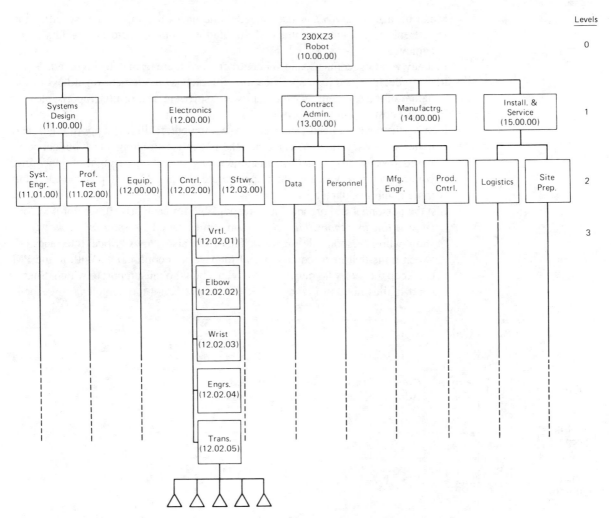

Figure 5-6 Work breakdown structure (account numbers shown).

The WBS can be used to illustrate how each piece of the project is tied to the whole in terms of performance, responsibility, budgeting, and scheduling. The following general steps explain the procedure for designing and using the WBS as it would be used on a large project. For small or moderate-size projects, some of the steps might be skipped, combined, or handled less formally than our explanation indicates, particularly if the project is of a type familiar to the organization.

1. Using information obtained from the people who will perform the work, break project tasks down into successively finer levels of detail. Continue until all meaningful tasks have been identified and each task can be individually planned, scheduled, budgeted, monitored, and controlled.

2. For each such work element:

Make up a *work statement* that includes the necessary inputs, the specification references, particular contractual stipulations, and specific end results to be achieved.

List any vendors, contacts, and subcontractors who are or may be involved.

Identify detailed end item specifications for each work element regardless of the nature of the end item, whether hardware, software, test results, reports, etc.

Establish cost account numbers.

Identify the resource needs, such as staff, equipment, facilities, support, funds, and materials. Cost estimators can assist the PM in constructing a task budget composed of costs for materials, manufacturing operations, freight, engineering, contingency reserves, and other appropriate charges. (This step is considered in more detail in Chapter 7.)

List the personnel and organizations responsible for each task. It is helpful to construct a *linear responsibility chart* (sometimes called a *responsibility matrix*) to show who is responsible for what. This chart also shows critical interfaces between units that may require special managerial coordination. With it, the PM can keep track of who must approve what and who must report to whom. Such a chart is illustrated in Figure 5-7. If the project is not too complex, the respon-

WBS / Responsibility		Project Office				Field Oper.	
Subproject	Task	Project Manager	Contract Admin.	Project Engrng.	Industrial Engrng.	Field Manager	
Determine Need	A1	⬡		●	▲		
	A2	■	⬡	▲	●		
Solicit Quotations	B1	⬡	■	▲		●	
Write Approp. Request	C1	■	▲	⬡	●		
	C2		●	⬡	▲		
	C3	●	■	▲		■	
"	"						
"	"						
"	"						

Legend:
▲ Responsible
● Support
■ Notification
⬡ Approval

Figure 5-7 Linear Responsibility Chart

sibility chart can be simplified (see Figure 5-8). Figure 5-9 shows one page of a project plan developed by a firm to reorganize its distribution system. In this case, the chart takes the form of a 30-page document covering 116 major activities.

Construct a preliminary list of the estimated times required to accomplish each of the tasks in the WBS, making sure that precedence relationships are noted for each. This requires a list of all immediate predecessor activities (or predecessor events) for each task. Such a list is the raw material from which the project schedule will be constructed.

	Vice-president	General manager	Project manager	Manager engineering	Manager software	Manager manufacturing	Manager marketing	Subprogram mgr mfg	Subprogram mgr sftwr	Subprogram mgr hdwr	Subprogram mgr svcs
Estb project plan	6	2	1	3	3	3	3	4	4	4	4
Define WBS		5	1	3	3	3	3	3	3	3	3
Establish hardware specs		2	3	1	4	4	4				
Establish software specs		2	3	4	1		4				
Estb interface specs		2	3	1	4	4	4				
Estb manufacturing specs		2	3	4	4	1	4				
Define documentation		2	1	4	4	4	4				
Establish market plan	5	3	5	4	4	4	1				
Prepare manpower est			3	1	1	1		4	4	4	4
Prepare eqpmt cost est			3	1	1	1		4	4	4	4
Prepare material costs			3	1	1	1		4	4	4	4
Make program assignments			3	1	1	1		4	4	4	4
Estb time schedules		5	3	1	1	1	3	4	4	4	4

1 Actual responsibility   4 May be consulted
2 General supervision   5 Must be notified
3 Must be consulted   6 Final approval

Figure 5-8 Simplified Linear Responsibility Chart.
Source: Paul Sjoquist, *Program Management Handbook.* Control Data Corporation, undated, p. 2–25.

Activities	Initiate Action	Responsible Individuals	
		Work With	**Clear Action With**
DISTRIBUTION SYSTEM AND ITS ADMINISTRATION			
1. Recommend distribution system to be used.	Mktg Officers	ILI & IHI LOB MCs M-A Cttee VP & Agcy Dir	Sr VP Mktg
	Mktg Officers	Group LOB MC M-A Cttee VP & Agcy Dir	Sr VP Mktg
	Mktg Officers	IA LOB MC M-A Cttee VP & Agcy Dir	Sr VP Mktg
Compensation			
2. Determine provisions of sales compensation programs (e.g., commissions, subsidies, fringes).	Compensation Task Force	Mktg, S&S & Eqty Prod Offrs	President
	Compensation Task Force	Mktg, S&S & Eqty Prod Offrs	
	Compensation Task Force	Mktg, S&S & Eqty Prod Offrs	President
3. Ensure cost-effectiveness testing of sales compensation programs.	Compensation Task Force	Mktg, S&S & Eqty Prod Offrs	President
Territory			
4. Establish territorial strategy for our primary distribution system.	VP & Agcy Dir	Dir MP&R M-A Cttee	Sr VP Mktg
5. Determine territories for agency locations and establish priorities for starting new agencies.	VP & Agcy Dir	Dir MP&R M-A Cttee	Sr VP Mktg
6. Determine agencies in which advanced sales personnel are to operate.	Dir Ret Pln Sls Dir Adv Sls	VP S&S	Sr VP Mktg

Legend: IA, ILI, IHI: Product lines.
  LOB: Line of business.
  MC: Management committee.
  M-A Cttee: Marketing administration committee.
  S&S: Sales and service.
  MP&R: Marketing planning and research.

Figure 5-9 Project Plan.

3. The WBS, budget, and time estimates are reviewed with the people or organizations who have responsibility for doing or supporting the work. The purpose of this review is to verify the WBS's accuracy, budget, schedule, and to check interdependency of tasks, resources, and personnel. The WBS may be revised as necessary, but the planner must be sure to check significant revisions with all individuals who have previously made inputs. When agreement is reached, individuals should sign off on their individual elements of the project plan.

4. Resource requirements, time schedules, and subtask relationships are now integrated to form the next higher level of the WBS; and so it continues at each succeeding level of the WBS hierarchy. Each succeeding level of the WBS will contain the same kinds of information regarding resources, budgets, schedules, and responsibilities as the levels below it. The only difference is that the information is aggregated to one higher level.

5. At the uppermost level of the WBS, we have a summary of the project budget. For the purpose of pricing a proposal, or determining profit and loss, the total project budget should consist of four elements: direct budgets from each task as described above; an indirect cost budget for the project, which includes general and administrative overhead costs (G & A), marketing costs, potential penalty charges, and other expenses not attributable to particular tasks; a project "contingency" reserve for unexpected emergencies; and any residual, which includes the profit derived from the project, which may, on occasion, be intentionally negative. In Chapter 7 we argue that the budget used for pricing should not be the same budget that the PM uses to control the project.

6. Similarly, schedule information and milestone (significant) events can be aggregated into a *project master schedule*. The master schedule integrates the many different schedules relevant to the various parts of the project. It is comprehensive and must include contractual commitments, key interfaces and sequencing, milestone events, and progress reports. In addition, a time contingency reserve for unforeseeable delays should be included. A graphic example of a master schedule is shown in Figure 5-10.

This series of steps completes the use of the WBS as a project planning document. The WBS is also a key document for implementing, monitoring, and controlling the project. The remaining steps concern its use for these purposes.

7. One can now compare required task performance and outputs specified in the WBS with those specified in the basic project plan in order to identify potential misunderstandings, problems, and schedule slippages, and then design corrective actions.

8. As the project is carried out, step by step, the PM can continually examine actual resource use, by work element, work package, task, and so on up to the full project level. By comparing actual against planned resource usage at a given point in time, the PM can identify problems, harden the estimates of final cost, and make sure that relevant corrective actions have been designed and are ready to implement if needed. It is necessary to examine resource usage in relation to results achieved because, while the project may be over budget, the results may be farther along than expected. Similarly, the expenses may be exactly as planned, or even

Subproject		Task	Responsible Dept.	Dependent Dept.	19x4 J	F	M	A	M	J	J	A	S	O	N	D	19x5 J	F	M	A	M	J	J	A	S	O	N	D
Determine Need	A1	Find operations that benefit most	Industrial			△ ▲																						
	A2	Approx. size and type needed	Project Engnrng.	I.E.				△		▲																		
Solicit Quotations	B1	Contact vendors & review quotes	P.E.	Fin., I.E. Prchsng.					○		●		○ ▲																
Write Appropriation Request	C1	Determine tooling costs	Tool Design	I.E.								○		●		△													
	C2	Determine labor savings	I.E.	I.E.									○	△ ▲															
	C3	Actual writing	P.E.	Tool Dsgn Fin, I.E.													△ ○												

		Purchasing	P.E.				
Purchs. Mach. Tooling, and Gauges	D1	Order robot	Purchasing	P.E.			
	D2	Design and order or manufacture tooling	Tool dsgn	Prchsng. Tool Mkr			
	D3	Specify needed gauges and order or mnufctr	Q.C.	Tool Dsgn Prchsng.			
Installation and Startup	E1	Install robot	Plant Layout	Mill-wrights			
	E2	Train employees	Personnel	P.E. Mnufctrng			
	E3	Runoff	Mnufctrng	Q.C.			

Note: As of Jan. 31, 19x5, the project is one month behind schedule. This is due mainly to the delay in task C1, which was caused by the late completion of A2.

Legend:
* Project Completion
□ Contractual Commitment
△ Planned Completion
▲ Actual Completion
○ Status Date
Milestone Planned
● Milestone Achieved
Planned Progress
Actual Progress

Figure 5-10   Project Master Schedule.

lower, but actual progress may be much less than planned. Control charts showing these *earned values* are described in more detail in Chapter 10.

9. Finally, the project schedule must be subjected to the same comparisons as the project budget. Actual progress is compared to scheduled progress by work element, package, task, and complete project, to identify problems and take corrective action. Additional resources may be brought to those tasks behind schedule to expedite them. These added funds may come out of the budget reserve or from other tasks that are ahead of schedule. This topic is discussed further in Chapter 9.

5.5 INTERFACE MANAGEMENT

The most difficult aspect of implementing the project plan is the coordination of the various elements of the project so that they meet their joint goals of performance, schedule, and budget. The PM must control the process and timing of this coordination as a part of the everyday task of managing the project. The term *interface* is used to denote both the process and fact of this coordination. The linear responsibility chart discussed above is clearly a useful aid to the PM in performing this managerial task because it displays the multiple ways the project's people must interact and what the rights, duties, and responsibilities of each will be.

A more formal and detailed approach to this problem has been developed [4] by Benningson. This analytic approach is called TREND (Transformed Relationships Evolved from Network Data) and was designed to illustrate important relationships between work groups, to alert the project manager to potential problems associated with interfaces, and to aid in the design of effective ways to avoid or deal with the potential interface problems.

Three key concepts are added in Benningson's approach: interdependence, uncertainty, and prestige. The project master schedule, the WBS, and task networks can be used to provide some of the information required to delineate the nature of these concepts, to understand their potential impacts on the interface between individuals and groups, and to denote task and group interdependencies. Figure 5-11 is an organizational chart that has been modified according to TREND procedures. Interdependencies are shown by lines, with the primary direction of the interdependence indicated by the arrows.

The uncertainty facing each task group or individual and the relative prestige levels of each of the task groups/individuals need to be established. Uncertainty levels are assumed to correlate with such factors as the length of the project time horizon, the level of reliance on formal authority, and the degree of task orientation of the work. If estimates are available, the spread between the optimistic and pessimistic time estimates reflects the level of uncertainty of the schedule. See the shaded boxes in Figure 5-11.

Prestige is inferred from organization charts or from known anecdotal information. See the right-hand scale in Figure 5-11. Although using position on the organization chart as a surrogate for organizational prestige is questionable, no better overall measure seems to be available. The analyst would be well advised

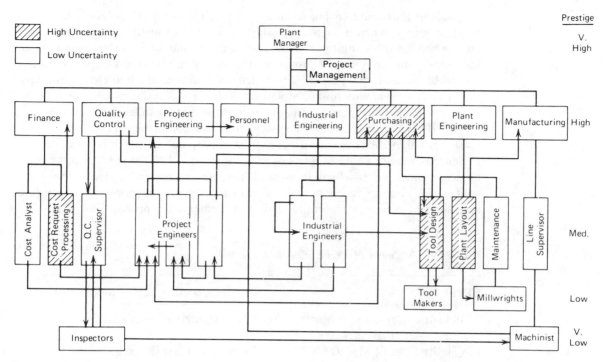

Figure 5-11 TREND organizational overlay.

to check this assumption for each particular case when employing this model. All three elements—prestige, uncertainty, and interdependence—can be depicted on an organization chart to illustrate potential coordination problems.

Dependence is shown by an arrow from the preceding task group/person to the following, dependent task group/person. Uncertainty is denoted by shading those groups/persons with high task uncertainty and not shading those with low uncertainty. Prestige is read directly off the chart by noting the level of the group/person in the organizational structure. See [4] for a detailed example.

A complete description of the project interfaces can be shown by mapping all dependencies in the project together with the average uncertainty faced by each group/person. Similarly, the different phases of the project life cycle can be displayed using TREND, and can be examined to see what problems might arise within particular time periods. For instance, the work of a particular group might consist mostly of work having low uncertainty, but at project startup, for example, the group may be assigned to some high uncertainty tasks. The PM would give this group special attention during startup in order to react quickly to problems that arose during that period, but could afford to relax attention to this specific group during other phases of the project's life cycle. This pattern of high uncertainty followed by low uncertainty is common. Design of the foundation for a large building may have high uncertainty until test borings are completed, and low uncertainty thereafter. The same is true for most R & D projects, there being high uncertainty until an approach is proven, and then low uncertainty.

Problems also tend to occur when a high-prestige group is dependent on a low-prestige group, when a high-uncertainty task follows another high-uncertainty task, when complex multiple uncertainties exist, and so on. The various combinations of uncertainty and group prestige differentials have various potentials for problems and can best be controlled by managerial strategies formulated specifically to deal with unique situations. Table 5-1 describes some potential interface problems in Figure 5-11 together with possible managerial solutions.

TREND is hardly a complete system for interface management and its full-scale, formal use is rarely justified, but the conceptual approach is valuable. Experienced PMs are aware of many of the problems TREND exposes, but the technique provides an excellent framework for the inexperienced and a check for "old hands." For an excellent discussion of the behavioral problems in interface management as well as the entire project implementation process, see [20].

Table 5-1 Analysis of TREND Overlay

EFFECT	COORDINATION REQUIRED
1. Industrial Engs. and Project Engs.—self-dependencies.	Monitor internal coordination.
2. Quality Control Mgr./Q.C. Supervisor—same functional areas, same low uncertainty, low status depends on high.	Depend on planning, regular coordination.
3. Q.C. Mgr./Tool Design—different functional areas, mixed uncertainty, low status depends on high status.	Set up interfunctional system for coordination. Monitor regularly.
4. Personnel Mgr./Machinist—different functional area, low uncertainty, high status depends on low status.	Interface as coordinator and translator.
5. Project Engineer/Purchasing Mgr.—different functional area, mixed uncertainty, reciprocal dependence, different status.	Set up regular review meetings for coordination. Project manager chairs meetings.
6. Tool designers/Purchasing Mgr.—different functional area, same high uncertainty, different status, reciprocal dependence.	Set up regular review meetings. Plant eng. mgr. and purch. mgr. to rotate chairing meeting. Perhaps include the project engineers in the meeting.
7. Project Eng. Mgr./Project Engineers—same functional area, high status depends on low, same low uncertainty.	Depend on regular authority and information structure. Stay informed. Encourage frequent discussion.

5.6 SUMMARY

In this chapter we initiated planning for the project in terms of identifying and addressing the tasks required for project completion. We emphasized the importance of initial coordination of all parties involved and the smooth interpretation of the various systems required to achieve the project objectives. Last, we described some tools such as TREND, the Work Breakdown Structure (WBS), the linear responsibility chart, and the Gozinto chart to aid in the planning process.

Specific points made in the chapter were these:

- The preliminary work plans are important because they serve as the basis for personnel selection, budgeting, scheduling, and control.
- Top management should be represented in the initial coordinating meeting where technical objectives are established, participant responsibility is accepted, and preliminary budgets and schedules are defined.
- The approval and change processes are complex and should be handled by the project manager.
- Common elements of the project plan are the overview, statement of objectives, general approach, contractual requirements, schedules, budget, cost control procedures, evaluation procedures, and potential problems.
- Systems integration concerns the smooth coordination of project systems in terms of cost, performance, and effectiveness.
- The hierarchical approach to project planning is most appropriate and can be aided by a tree diagram of project subsets, called a Gozinto chart, and a Work Breakdown Structure (WBS). The WBS relates the details of each subtask to its task and provides the final basis for the project budget, schedule, personnel, and control.
- A linear responsibility chart is often helpful to illustrate the relationship of personnel to project tasks and to identify where coordination is necessary.
- A tool particularly helpful in identifying potential interface and coordination problems is the TREND organization chart overlay, based on differences in status or prestige level, task dependence, and uncertainty.

Based on the now established project plan and WBS, we can consider the task of negotiating for the resources to implement the project. This topic completes Part I of the text.

5.7 GLOSSARY

BASELINE PLAN—The nominal plan to which deviations will be compared.

BILL OF MATERIALS—The set of physical elements required to build a product.

CONTROL CHART—A graph showing how a statistic is changing over time compared to its average and extreme values.

DELIVERABLES—The physical items to be delivered from a project. This typically includes reports and plans as well as physical objects.

EARNED VALUE—A measure of project progress, frequently related to tasks accomplished and milestones achieved.

EFFECTIVENESS—Achieving the objectives set beforehand; to be distinguished from efficiency, which is measured by the output realized for the input used.

ENGINEERING CHANGE ORDERS—Product improvements that engineering has designed after the initial product design was released.

GOZINTO CHART—A pictorial representation of a product that shows how the elements required to build a product fit together.

HIERARCHICAL PLANNING—A planning approach that breaks the planning task down into the activities that must be done at each managerial level. Typically, the upper level sets the objectives for the next lower level.

INTERFACE MANAGEMENT—Managing the problems that tend to occur between departments and disciplines, rather than within individual departments.

MATERIAL REQUIREMENTS PLANNING (MRP)—A planning and material ordering approach based on the known or forecast final demand requirements, lead times for each fabricated or purchased item, and existing inventories of all items.

SYSTEMS ENGINEERING—The engineering tasks involved in the complete system concerning the project and the integration of all the subsystems into the overall system.

VALUE ENGINEERING—An approach that examines each element of a product or system to determine if there is a better or cheaper way of achieving the same function.

WORK STATEMENT—A description of a task that defines all the work required to accomplish it, including inputs and desired outputs.

5.8 PROJECT TEAM ASSIGNMENT

For this exercise, initial project planning must be conducted. To construct the overall project plan, start with the work breakdown structure, construct a Gozinto chart, determine a linear responsibility chart, and assemble an action plan. Include the instructor in your plans as a representative of top management. From this set of information, build a project budget and determine a master schedule with major milestones. Finally, use the TREND procedure to build an organizational overlay, project potential problem areas, and suggest possible remedies.

5.9 MATERIAL REVIEW QUESTIONS

1. List the six component planning sequences of project planning.
2. Any successful project plan must contain nine key elements. List these items and briefly describe the composition of each.
3. What are the basic guidelines for systems design which assure that individual components of the system are designed in an optimal manner?
4. What are the general steps for managing each work package within a specific project?
5. How may the three key concepts in the TREND approach be depicted on an or-

ganizational chart, and how are potential problems recognized and possibly averted using this method?

6. What is shown on a linear responsibility chart? How is it useful to a PM?

5.10 CONCEPTUAL DISCUSSION QUESTIONS

1. What percentage of the total project effort do you think should be devoted to planning? Why?

2. Why do you suppose that the coordination of the various elements of the project is considered the most difficult aspect of project implementation?

3. What kinds of problem areas might be included in the project plan?

4. What is the role of systems integration in project management? What are the three major objectives of systems integration?

5. In what ways may the WBS be used as a key document to monitor and control a project?

6. Describe the process of subdivision of activities and events which composes the tree diagram known as the Work Breakdown Structure or Gozinto chart. Why is the input of responsible managers and workers so important an aspect of this process?

5.11 CHAPTER EXERCISE

Recall a recent or current project in a formal group, such as a church committee or social group, of which you are a member. Construct a detailed Gozinto chart and Work Breakdown Structure for the project. Then lay out a linear responsibility chart for the project along the lines of Figure 5-7. Next, design a general organization chart that includes all the parties identified on the linear responsibility chart.

5.12 INCIDENTS FOR DISCUSSION

Ringold's Pool and Patio Supply

John Ringold, Jr., just graduated from a local university with a degree in industrial management and joined his father's company as executive vice-president of operations. Dad wants to break Johnny in slowly and has decided to see how he can do on a project that John Sr. has never had time to investigate. Twenty percent of the company's sales are derived from the sale of above-ground swimming pool kits. Ringold's does not install the pools. John Sr. has asked John Jr. to determine whether or not they should get into that business. John Jr. has decided that the easiest way to impress Dad and get the project done is personally to estimate the cost to the company of setting up a pool and then call some competitors and see how much they charge. That will show whether or not it is profitable.

John Jr. remembered a method called the work breakdown structure (WBS)

Table 5-2 Pool Installation WBS

		Labor-hours (estimated)
Prepare ground surface		2.67
Clear	1	
Rake	$\frac{1}{3}$	
Level	1	
Sand bottom	$\frac{1}{3}$	
Lay out pool frame		2.50
Bottom ring	1	
Side panels	$\frac{1}{2}$	
Top ring	1	
Add plastic liner		0.50
Assemble pool		1.66
Build wooden support		3.00
Lay out	1	
Assemble	2	
Fill and test		2.00
Total		12.33

that he thought might serve as a useful tool to estimate costs. Also, the use of such a tool could be passed along to the site supervisor to help evaluate the performance of work crews. John Jr.'s WBS is shown in Table 5-2. The total cost John Jr. calculated was $185.00, based on 12.33 labor-hours at $15.00/labor-hour. John Jr. found that, on average, Ringold's competitors charged $229.00 to install a similar pool. John Jr. thought he had a winner. He called his father and made an appointment to present his findings the next morning. Since he had never assembled a pool himself, he decided to increase the budget by 10 percent, "just in case".

Question: Is John Jr.'s WBS projection reasonable?

HAC Computer Company

The board members of HAC Computer Company approved the building of a new facility approximately six months ago. The facility is to be constructed in South Carolina and will be used to manufacture a new line of microcomputers. The company is currently manufacturing only minicomputers and mainframes, but because of the tremendous market for the micro, they plan to enter this field also. The company has already selected the project manager and the project team. The project manager is ready to get the project under way and has begun work on the project master plan. The three aspects of the master plan that he is most concerned about are schedules, resources, and personnel. Since he is so concerned about scheduling, he decided to get a head start and do the project scheduling estimates for the milestone events himself. For the resource planning he developed some capital requirements for the various parts of the project that would be continuing throughout the project, and for personnel he developed a preliminary forecast of what skills he felt might be needed, and when, over the life of the project.

Question: If you were the project manager, would you handle these three aspects of the master plan the same or differently? Explain.

5.13 BIBLIOGRAPHY

1. Agarwal, J. C. "Project Planning at Kennecott." *Research Managment,* May 1974.
2. Anderson, J., and R. Narasimhan. "Assessing Project Implementation Risk: A Methodical Approach." *Management Science,* June 1979.
3. Baumgartner, J. S. *Project Management.* Irwin, Homewood, IL, 1963.
4. Benningson, L.A. "TREND: A Project Management Tool." *Proceedings of the Project Management Conference,* Philadelphia, Oct. 1972.
5. Blanchard, B.S., and W. Fabrycky. *Systems Engineering and Analysis.* Prentice-Hall, Englewood Cliffs, NJ, 1981.
6. Blanning, R. W. "How Managers Decide to Use Planning Models." *Long Range Planning,* April 1980.
7. Davis, E. W. *Project Management: Techniques, Applications, and Managerial Issues,* 2nd ed. Institute of Industrial Engineers, Norcross, GA., 1983.
8. Friend, F. L. "Be A More Effective Program Manager." *Journal of Systems Management,* Feb. 1976.
9. Goodman, L. J., and R. N. Love, eds. *Project Planning Management,* Pergamon Press Inc., New York, 1980
10. Gross, R. N. "Cost-Benefit Analysis and Social Planning." *Analysis of Planning Programming Budgeting.* M. Alfandary-Alexander, ed. Washington Operations Research Council, Potomac, MD., 1968.
11. Gunderman, J. R., and F. R. McMurry. "Making Project Management Effective." *Journal of Systems Management,* Feb. 1975.
12. Hughes, E. R. "Planning: The Essence of Control." *Managerial Planning,* June 1978.
13. Johnson, J. R. "Advanced Project Control." *Journal of Systems Management,* May 1977.
14. Kaherlas, H. "A Look at Major Planning Methods: Development, Implementation, Strengths and Limitations." *Long Range Planning,* Aug. 1978.
15. Kerzner, H. *Project Management: A Systems Approach to Planning, Scheduling, and Controlling,* 2nd ed. Van Nostrand Reinhold, New York, 1984.
16. Knutson, J., and M. Scott. "Developing a Project Plan." *Journal of Systems Management,* Oct. 1978.
17. Kondinell, D. A. "Planning Development Projects: Lessons from Developing Countries." *Long Range Planning,* June 1979.
18. Martin, J. "Planning: The Gap Between Theory and Practice." *Long Range Planning,* Dec. 1979.
19. Martyn, A. S. "Some Problems in Managing Complex Development Projects." *Long Range Planning,* April 1975.
20. Morris, W. T. *Implementation Strategies for Industrial Engineers.* Grid Publishing, Inc., Columbus, OH, 1979.

21. Nutt, P. C. "Hybrid Planning Methods." *Academy of Management Review,* July 1982.

22. Rolefson, J. F. "Project Management—Six Critical Steps." *Journal of Systems Management,* April 1975.

23. Roman, D. *R & D Management,* Appleton-Century-Crofts, New York, 1968.

24. Schultz, R. L., D. P. Slevin, and J. K. Pinto, "Strategy and Tactics in a Process Model of Project Implementation." *Interfaces,* May–June 1987.

25. Stewart, J. M. "Guides to Effective Project Management." *Management Review,* Jan. 1966

26. Wedley, W. C., and A. E. J. Ferrie. "Perceptual Differences and Effects of Managerial Participation on Project Implementation." *Operations Research,* March 1978.

27. Wheelwright, S. C., and R. L. Blank. "Involving Operating Managers in Planning Process Evaluation." *Sloan Management Review,* Summer 1979.

5.14 CASE: A Project Management and Control System for Capital Projects[*]

Herbert F. Spirer and A. G. Hulvey

This article describes a project system designed to plan and control capital projects at Heublein, Inc. It includes the WBS, responsibility charts, and other tools useful in planning and controlling projects.

INTRODUCTION

Heublein, Inc., develops, manufactures and markets consumer food and beverage products domestically and internationally. The businesses of Heublein, Inc., their sales revenue, and some of their better known products are shown in Figure 1. Highlights of Figure 1 include:

*Reprinted with permission from *Proceedings of PMI, Internet 81,* 1981, a publication of the Project Management Institute.

The four major businesses ("Groups") use different manufacturing plants, equipment and processes to produce their products. In the Spirits Group large, continuous-process bottling plants are the rule; in the Food Service and Franchising Group, small fast food restaurants are the "manufacturing plants."

The amount of spending for capital projects and support varies greatly among the Groups, as would be expected from the differences in the magnitude of sales revenues.

The engineering departments of the Groups have responsibility for operational planning and control of capital projects, a common feature of the Groups. However, the differences among the Groups are reflected in differences in the sizes of the engineering departments and their support services. Similarly, financial tracking support varies from full external support to self-maintained records.

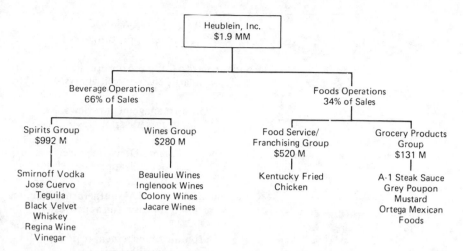

Figure 1   Heublein, Inc. (fiscal 1981).

Prior to the implementation of the Project Management and Control System (PM&C) described in this paper, the capital project process was chiefly concerned with the financial justification of the projects, as shown in Figure 2. Highlights include:

A focus on cost-benefit analysis.

Minimal emphasis on execution of the projects; no mechanism to assure that non-financial results were achieved.

In the late 1970s the following factors focused attention on the execution weaknesses of the process:

Some major projects went over budget.

The need for optimal utilization of capital funds intensified since depreciation legislation was not keeping pace with the inflationary rise in costs.

Responding to these factors, Heublein's corporate management called for a program to improve execution of capital projects by implementing PM&C. Responsibility for this program was placed with the Corporate Facilities and Manufacturing Department,

which, in addition to reviewing all Capital Appropriation Requests, provided technical consulting services to the corporation.

FEASIBILITY STUDY

Lacking specialized expertise in project management, the Director of Facilities and Manufacturing Planning decided to use a consultant in the field. Interviewing of three consultants was undertaken to select one who had the requisite knowledge, compatibility with the style and goals of the firm, and the ability to communicate to all levels and types of managers. The latter requirement was important because of the diversity of the engineering department structures and personnel involved. The first author was selected as the consultant.

With the consultant selected, an internal program manager for PM&C was selected. The deferral of this choice until after selection of the consultant was deliberate, to allow for development of interest and enthusiasm among candidates for this position and so that both the selected individual and the selection committee would have a clear picture of the nature of the

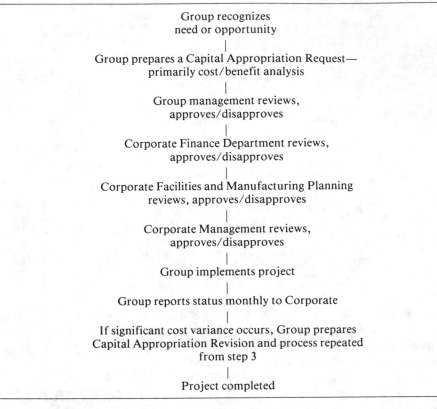

Group recognizes
need or opportunity
|
Group prepares a Capital Appropriation Request—
primarily cost/benefit analysis
|
Group management reviews,
approves/disapproves
|
Corporate Finance Department reviews,
approves/disapproves
|
Corporate Facilities and Manufacturing Planning
reviews, approves/disapproves
|
Corporate Management reviews,
approves/disapproves
|
Group implements project
|
Group reports status monthly to Corporate
|
If significant cost variance occurs, Group prepares
Capital Appropriation Revision and process repeated
from step 3
|
Project completed

Figure 2 Capital project process prior to PM&C.

program. A program manager was chosen from the corporate staff (the second author).

Having the key staff in place, ground rules were established as follows:

The PM&C program would be developed internally to tailor it to the specific needs of the Groups. A "canned" or packaged system would limit this flexibility, which was deemed essential in this application of project management principles.

The directors of the engineering departments of each of the Groups were to be directly involved in both the *design* and implementation of the PM&C system in total and for their particular Group. This would assure the commitment to its success that derives from ownership and guarantees that those who know the needs best determine the nature of the system.

To meet the above two ground rules, a thorough fun-

damental education in the basic principles of project management would be given to all involved in the system design.

The emphasis was to be project *planning* as opposed to project *control*. The purpose of PM&C was to achieve better performance on projects, not catch mistakes after they have occurred. Success was the goal, rather than accountability or identification of responsibility for failure.

PROGRAM DESIGN

The option of defining a uniform PM&C system, to be imposed on all engineering departments by corporate mandate, was rejected. The diversity of projects put the weight in favor of individual systems, provided planning and control was such that success of the projects was facilitated. The advantage to corporate staff of uniform planning and reporting was given second place to accommodation of the unique needs of each Group and the wholehearted commitment of each engineering manager to the effective use of the adopted system. Thus, a phased implementation of PM&C within Heublein was planned in advance. These phases were:

Phase I. Educational Overview for engineering department managers. A three-day seminar with two top-level educational objectives: (1) comprehension by participants of a maximal set of project management principles and (2) explanation of the corporate objectives and recommended approach for any PM&C system. Despite some expressed initial concern, the response to this session was positive. It was correctly perceived as the first step in a sincere attempt by corporate management to develop a jointly defined PM&C system that would be useful to the managers of projects, rather than to satisfy a corporate reporting need.

Phase II. PM&C system design. A "gestation period" of three weeks was deliberately introduced between Phases I and II to allow for absorption, discussion and review of the project management principles and objectives by the engineering department managers. At the end of this period a session was called for the explicit purpose of defining the system. The session was chaired by the consultant, a deliberate choice to achieve the "lightning rod" effect whereby any negative concern was directed to an outsider. Also, the consultant—as an outsider—could criticize and comment in ways that should not be done by the engineering department managers who will have long-term working relationships among each other. It was agreed in advance that a consensus would be sought to the greatest possible extent, avoiding any votes on how to handle particular issues which leaves the "nay" votes feeling that their interests have been overridden by the majority. If consensus could not be achieved, then the issue would be sidestepped to be deferred for later consideration; if sufficiently important then a joint solution could be developed outside the session without the pressure of a fixed closing time. The dynamics of this design session included the development of consensus into summary statements which were displayed immediately on overhead transparencies to be worked into shape. As soon as this was acceptable to the Group as a whole, one of two attending stenographers would record the agreement, leave the room and return later with a typed version for group consideration. The use of two stenographers assured that one was always in attendance. The enthusiasm expressed by the engineering department managers for this meeting was high.

Phase III. Project plan development. The output of Phase II (the set of consensus conclusions) represented both guidelines and specific conclusions concerning the nature of a PM&C system. Recognizing that the PM&C program will be viewed as a model project and that it should be used as such, serving as an example of what is desired, the program manager prepared a project plan for the PM&C program. The remainder of this paper is primarily concerned with the discussion of this plan, both as an example of how to introduce a PM&C system and how to make a project plan. The plan discussed in this paper and illustrated in Figures 3 to 11 is the type of plan that is now required before any capital project may be submitted to the approval process at Heublein.

Phase IV. Implementation. With the plan developed in Phase III approved, it was possible to move ahead with implementation. Implementation was in accordance with the plan discussed in the balance of this paper. Evaluation of the results was considered a part of this implementation.

PROJECT PLAN

A feature of the guidelines developed by the engineering managers in Phase II was that a "menu" of component parts of a project plan was to be established in the corporate PM&C system, and that elements of this menu were to be chosen to fit the situational or corporate tracking requirements. The menu is:

1. Introduction.
2. Project Objectives.
3. Project/Program Structure.
4. Project/Program Costs.

5. Network.
6. Schedule.
7. Resource Allocation.
8. Organization and Accountability.
9. Control System.
10. Milestones or Project Subdivisions.

In major or critical projects, the minimal set of choices from the menu is specified by corporate staff (the definition of a "major" or "critical" project is a part of the PM&C procedure). For "routine" projects, the choice from the menu is left to the project manager.

In the PM&C plan, items 6 and 7, Schedule and Resource Allocation, were combined into one section for reasons which will be described as part of the detailed discussions of the individual sections which follows.

Introduction

In this PM&C system, the Introduction is an executive summary, with emphasis on the justification of the project. This can be seen from the PM&C Program Introduction shown in Figure 3. It is to the advantage of everyone concerned with a project to be fully aware of the reasons

for its existence. It is as important to the technicians as it is to the engineers or the corporate financial department. When the project staff clearly comprehends the reason for the project's existence it is much easier to enlist and maintain their support and wholehearted efforts. In the Heublein PM&C system, it is expected that the introduction section of a project plan will include answers to these question: What type of project is involved? What is the cost/benefit relationship? What are the contingency plans? Why is it being done this way (that is, why were alternatives rejected)? Figure 3 not only illustrates this approach, but is the executive summary for the Heublein PM&C system.

Objectives

Both anecdotal and research inputs have established the importance of clearly stated objectives; von Clauswitz' "Principles of the Objective: A clearly defined, attainable goal" *(On War, the Modern Library, 1943)*, holds for projects in business. Goals for a project at Heublein must be stated in terms of *deliverable items*. To so state a project objective forces the definition of a clear, comprehensible, measurable and tangible objec-

---

External and internal factors make it urgent to ensure most efficient use of capital funds. Implementation of a project management and control ("PM&C") system has been chosen as one way to improve the use of capital funds. In March 1979, the Corporate Management Committee defined this need.

Subsequently, Corporate Facilities and Manufacturing Planning ("FM&P") performed a feasibility study on this subject. A major conclusion of the study was to develop the system internally rather than use a "canned" system. An internally-developed system can be tailored to the individual Groups, giving flexibility which is felt to be essential to success. Another conclusion of the study was to involve Group engineering managers in the design and implementation of the system for better understanding and acceptance.

This is the detailed plan for the design and implementation of a corporate-wide PM&C System. The short term target of the system is major capital projects; the long term target is other types of projects, such as new product development and R&D projects. The schedule and cost are:

Completion Date: June, 1980.

Cost: $200,000, of which $60,000 is out of pocket.

Figure 3 Introduction to PM&C program project plan.

tive. Often, deliverable items resulting from a project are documents. In constructing a residence, is the deliverable item "the house" or is it "the certificate of occupancy"? In the planning stages of a project (which can occur during the project as well as at the beginning) asking this question is as important as getting the answer. Also, defining the project in terms of the deliverables tends to reduce the number of items which are forgotten. Thus, the Heublein PM&C concept of objectives can be seen to be similar to a "statement of work" and is not meant to encompass specifications (detailed descriptions of the attributes of a deliverable item) which can be included as appendices to the objectives of the project.

Figure 4 shows the objectives stated for the Heublein PM&C program. It illustrates one of the principles set for objective statement: that they be hierarchically structured, starting with general statements and moving to increasingly more detailed particular statements. When both particular and general objectives are defined, it is imperative that there be a logical connection; the particular must be in support of the general. Ambiguity and confusion at this point is not unusual and where they exist, they are a source of considerable conflict among client, project management and staff.

A project (the PM&C Program) satisfying the broadly expressed needs of the Introduction (Figure 3) is more precisely defined in Figure 4. Here we see first that the primary thrust of this system is *General Objectives* item number 3, to provide Group personnel with the ability to do their jobs better. We believe it is important that

---

General Objectives.

1. Enable better communication between Group and Corporate management with regard to the progress of major projects.

2. Enable Group management to more closely monitor the progress of major projects.

3. Provide the capability for Group personnel to better manage and control major projects.

Specific Objectives.[a]

1. Reporting and Control System
—For communication of project activity within Group and between Group and Corporate.
––Initially for high-cost capital projects, then for "critical," then all others.

2. Procedures Manual
—Document procedures and policies.
—Preliminary manual available by October 20, 1979 for use in general educational seminars.

3. Computer Support Systems
—Survey with recommendations to establish need for and value of computer support.

4. General Educational Package
—Provide basic project planning and control skills to personnel directly involved in project management, to be conducted by academic authority in field.
—Technical seminars in construction, engineering, contract administration, and financial aspects of project management.

[a]Defined at the July 1979 PM&C Workshop, attended by representatives of Operating Groups.

Figure 4 Objectives of PM&C program.

these general objectives, which were set in a Corporate Management Committee meeting, are not concerned with assigning blame or setting the stage for tighter corporate control, but are in fact positive goals which not only answer desires of corporate and Group management, but also resolve issues often raised by the operational level personnel.

The specific objectives follow the general objectives in Figure 4, which is largely in accord with our own standards for expression of specific objectives in terms of deliverables. It is now apparent that this could have been carried further; but the success of the program supports the view that these objectives were good enough for their purpose.

Project Structure

Having a definition of deliverables, the project manager needs explicit structuring of the project to:

Relate the specific objectives to the general.

Define the elements which comprise the deliverables.

Define the activities which yield the elements and deliverables as their output.

Show the hierarchical relationship among objectives, elements and activities.

The WBS is the tool used to meet these needs. While the WBS may be represented in either indentured (textual) or tree (graphical) formats, the graphic tree format has the advantage of easy comprehension at all levels. The tree version of the WBS also has the considerable advantage that entries may be made in the nodes ("boxes") to indicate charge account numbers, accountable staff, etc.

Figure 5 is the WBS for the PM&C Program, showing the nature of the WBS in general and the structure of the PM&C Program project in particular. At this point we can identify the component elements and the activities necessary to achieve them. A hierarchical numbering system was applied to the elements of the WBS, which is always a convenience. The 22 Design Phase Reports (2100 series in Figure 5) speak for themselves, but it is important to note that this WBS is the original WBS: All of these reports, analyses, and determinations were defined prior to starting the program and there were no requirements for additional items. In this area, there was no change of scope problem because the cooperation of all involved functions was obtained at the start of the program. The breadth of the definition task for this company, which does not contract or subcontract to public agencies (with their own special requirements), gives some idea of the considerations that must be taken into account when setting up a PM&C System. The rest of the WBS is self-explanatory and it is hoped that it can serve as a starting point for others wishing to implement similar programs.

Project Costs

The WBS provides a listing of the tasks to be performed to achieve the project objectives; with only the WBS in hand it is possible to assemble a *preliminary* project estimate. The estimates based only on the WBS are preliminary because they reflect not only uncertainty (which varies considerably among types of projects), but because the allocation of resources to meet schedule difficulties cannot be determined until both the network and the schedule and resource evaluations have been completed. However, at this time the project planner can begin to hierarchically assemble costs for use at any level. First the lowest level activities of work (sometimes called "work packages") can be assigned values. These estimates can be aggregated in accordance with the WBS tree structure to give higher level totals. At the root of the tree there is only one element—the project—and the total preliminary estimated cost is available.

Figure 6 shows the costs as summarized for the PM&C program plan. This example is supplied to give the reader an idea of the nature of

HEUBLEIN PM&C PROGRAM

1000 Program Plan

2000 PM&C System

    2100 Design-Phase Reports
       2101 Analyze Project Scope
       2102 Define Performance Reports
       2103 Define Project Planning
       2104 Define Revision Procedure
       2105 Define Approval/Signoff Procedure
       2106 Define Opening/Closing Procedure
       2107 Define Authority/Responsibility Procedure
       2108 Define Recordkeeping Requirements
       2109 Define Estimating Requirements
       2110 Define Reporting and Control System
       2111 Determine Accounting Support Capabilities
       2112 Define Estimating Procedures
       2113 Define Recordkeeping Procedures
       2114 Prepare Organization Impact Analysis (Include Ongoing training)
       2115 Define Policy Requirements
       2116 Define Public Relations Policy
       2117 Define Legal Policies—Environmental, OSHA, EEO, Government Agencies, Land Use
       2118 Define Personal Liability Policy
       2119 Define Financial Policy—Capital Expense, Cash Flow
       2120 Define Purchasing Policy—Contracts vs PO, Contractor Qualification, $ Approvals
       2121 Define Record Retention Policy
       2122 Define Computer Support Systems Requirements
    2200 Procedures Manual
       2201 Preliminary Manual
       2202 Final Manual
    2300 Reporting and Control System
    2400 Computer Support Survey
       2401 PERT/CPM
       2402 Scheduling
       2403 Accounting

3000 General Training

    3100 Project Planning and Control Seminar
       3101 Objective Setting
       3102 WBS
       3103 Networks
       3104 Scheduling
       3105 Cost Estimating
       3106 Record Keeping
       3107 Control
    3200 Technical Seminars
       3201 Construction Engineering
       3202 Contract Administration
       3203 Financial Aspects
    3300 Ongoing Training

Figure 5 Project structure.

Labor costs	
Development & Design	$ 40,000
Attendees' time in sessions	60,000
Startup time of PM&C in Group	40,000
Basic Educational Package	
Consultants' fees	20,000
Attendees' travel & expenses	30,000
Miscellaneous	10,000
TOTAL PROGRAM COST	$200,000

Out-of-pocket costs: $60,000

Figure 6 Program costs.

the costs to be expected in carrying out such a PM&C program in this type of situation. Since a project-oriented cost accounting system does not exist, out-of-pocket costs are the only incremental charges. Any organization wishing to cost a similar PM&C program will have to do so within the framework of the organizational approach to costing indirect labor. As a guide to such costs, it should be noted that in the Heublein PM&C Program, over 80 percent of the costs—both out-of-pocket and indirect—were in connection with the General Training (WBS code 3000).

Seminars were limited to two and two-and-a-half days to assure that the attendees perceived the educational process as efficient, tight and not unduly interfering with their work; it was felt that it was much better to have them leaving with a feeling that they would have liked more rather than the opposite. Knowing the number of attendees, it is possible to determine the labor-days devoted to travel and seminar attendance; consultant/lecturer's fees can be obtained (expect preparation costs) and the incidentals (travel expenses, subsistence, printing, etc.) are easily estimated.

Network

The PM&C system at Heublein requires networks only for major projects, but encourages their use for all projects. The project manager is allowed the choice of whatever type of network (activity-on-node or event-on-node) he or she prefers to use. For this reason, all educational activities provided instruction in both types of network.

Figure 7 shows a segment of the network for the PM&C Plan. All the usual principles of network creation and analysis (for critical path, for example) may be applied by the project manager to the extent that it facilitates planning, implementation and control. Considerable emphasis was placed on network creation and analysis techniques in the educational phases of the PM&C Program because the network is the basis of the scheduling methods presented, is potentially of great value and is one of the hardest concepts to communicate.

In the Heublein PM&C system, *managerial* networks are desired—networks which the individual project managers will use in their own management process and which the staff of the project can use to self-direct where appropriate. For this reason, the view towards the network is that no one network should exceed 50 nodes. The top-level network represents the highest level of aggregation. Each activity on that network may well represent someone else's next lower level network consisting of not more than 50 nodes; any activity on that second-level network may represent someone else's third-level network consisting of not more than 50 nodes; and so on. Networks with hundreds of nodes are to be avoided because of the difficulty of read-

Act'y Short Descr.	Time (weeks)	Immediate Predecessors
4000 prepare final rpt	2	2000, 2122, 3200
2000 monitor system	6	2000: hold group workshops
2000 hold group w'shps	2	2000: obtain approval
2000 prepare final proc	2	2000: monitor system
2000 prepare final proc manual, revise syst	2	2116–2121: approvals
2000 monitor system	8	2000: hold group workshops
2000 prepares for impl'n	2	3100: hold PM&C seminar
2122 get approval	2	2122: define com'r supp needs
2122 def comp supp needs	4	3100: hold PM&C sem
3200 hold tech seminars	4	3200: prepare seminars
3200 prepare seminars	8	3200: obtain approvals
3200 obtain approvals	2	3200: def tech sem needs
3200 def tech sem needs	2	3100: hold PM&C sem
3100 hold PM&C seminar	3	3100: integrate proc man in sem
		2201: revise prel proc man
3100 int. proc man in sem	1	2201: prel. proc manual
2201 revise prel proc man	.6	2201–2300: get approval
2201–2300 get approval	1	2214: org impact analysis
2214 org impact analysis	.4	2201: prel. proc manual
2201 prepare prel. pm	1	2213: def recd kpng proc
2213 def recd kpng proc	1	2111: det acctg supp
2111 det acctg supp	2	2103, 2108, 2109
2112 def est proc	2	2103, 2108, 2109
2300 revise rep cont sys	6	2110: get approval
2110 get approval	1	2110: define rep/contr sys
2110 def rep/con sys	1	2101: analyze scopes
		1000: revise prog plan
		2104–7: def proc's
		2103, 2108, 2109
2116–21 get approval	2	2116–21: define policies
2116–21 define pol'y's	8	2115: def pol'y req'ts
2115 def pol'y req'ts	3	1000: prep. program plan
2101 analyze scopes	1	1000: ditto
1000 rev prog plan	.4	1000: get appr plan
1000 get appr plan	2	1000: prep. program plan
2104–7 4–revision 5–appr/signoff 6–open/close 7–auth/resp'y	1.8	2102: def perf repts
2102 def perf repts	1	1000: prep. program plan
2103, 2108, 2109 3–proj planning 8–recd-kpng 9–estimating	2	2102: def perf repts
3100 prepare PM&C sem	4	3100: get appr content
3100 get appr content	1	1000: prep. program plan

Note: Because of space limitations, the network is given in the form of a precedence table. An activity-on-node diagram may be directly constructed from this table. Numerical designations refer to the WBS of Figure 5.

Figure 7 Network of PM&C program.

ing them and also because of the negative attitudes towards formal network planning methods generated by experiences with huge (over 5000 nodes, for example) networks in the 1950s and 1960s. This is not to say that there are not thousands of activities possible in a Heublein project, but that at the working managerial level, each manager or project staff person responsible for a networked activity is expected to work from a single network of a scope that can be easily comprehended. It is not an easy task to aggregate skillfully to reduce network size, but the exercise of this discipline has value in planning and execution in its own right.

The network shown reflects the interdependencies of activities for Heublein's PM&C Program; they are dependent on the design of the Program and the needs of the organization. Each organization must determine them for themselves. But what is important is that institution of a PM&C Program be planned this way. There is a great temptation in such programs to put all activities on one path and not to take advantage of parallel activities and/or not to see just what is the critical path and to focus efforts along it. Even where there is no special urgency in completion, it is important that all parts of the program work smoothly. If the PM&C Program team cannot assure that all necessary materials are on hand when the seminar attendees arrive to be instructed in methods of assuring timely completion of projects, the PM&C system will be viewed with great cynicism.

Schedule and Resource Allocation

The network defines the mandatory interdependency relationships among the tasks on a project; the schedule is the realization of the *intent* of the project manager, as it shows when the manager has determined that tasks are to be done. The schedule is constrained in a way that the network is not, for the schedule must reflect calendar limitations (vacations, holidays, plant and vendor shutdowns, etc.) and also the limita-

tions on resources. It is with the schedule that the project manager can develop the resource loadings and it is the schedule which ultimately is determined by both calendar and resource constraints.

Organization and Accountability

Who is responsible for what? Without clear, unambiguous responses to this question there can be no assurance that the task will be done. In general, committees do not finish projects and there should be one organizational unit responsible for each element in the work breakdown structure and one person in that organizational unit who holds final responsibility. Thus responsibility implies a single name to be mapped to the task or element of the WBS, and it is good practice to place the name of the responsible entity or person in the appropriate node on the WBS.

However, accountability may have multiple levels below the top level of complete responsibility. Some individuals or functions may have approval power, veto power without approval power, others may be needed for information or advice, etc. Often, such multilevel accountability crosses functional and/or geographical boundaries and hence communication becomes of great importance.

A tool which has proved of considerable value to Heublein where multilevel accountability and geographical dispersion of project staff is common is the "accountability matrix." An accountability matrix for a part of the PM&C Program project is shown in Figure 8.

The accountability matrix reflects considerable thought about the *strategy* of the program. In fact, one of its great advantages is that it forces the originator (usually the project manager) to think through the process of implementation. Some individuals must be involved because their input is essential. For example, all engineering managers were essential inputs to establish the exact nature of their needs. On the other hand, some individuals or

Activity	PM&C Mgr	Consult	Managers of Engineering FSPS/F	GPGNES	WINRTS	SPIRTS	Dir F&MP
Program Plan	I	P					A
Design-Phase Reports	I	P	P	P	P	P	
Procedures Manual	I						A
Reporting & Control System	I	P	P	P	P	P	
Computer Support Survey	I	P					P
Project Planning & Control Seminar	A	I					P
Technical Seminars	I		P	P	P		A

Legend: I: Initiate/Responsibility
          A: Approve
          P: Provide input

Figure 8 Accountability matrix for PM&C program.

departments are formally involved to enlist their support, even though a satisfactory program could be defined without them.

Control System

The basic loop of feedback for control is shown in Figure 9. This rationale underlies all approaches to controlling projects. Given that a plan (or budget) exists, we then must know what is performance (or actual); a comparison of the two may give a variance. If a variance exists, then the cause of the variance must be sought. Note that any variance is a call for review; as experienced project managers are well aware, underspending or early completions may be as unsatisfactory as overspending and late completions.

The PM&C program did not involve large purchases, or for that matter, many purchases. Nor were large numbers of people working on different tasks to be kept track of and coordinated.

These reasons of scale made it possible to control the PM&C Program through the use of Gantt conventions, using schedule bars to show plan and filling them in to show performance. Progress was tracked on a periodic basis, once a week.

Figure 10 shows the timing of the periodic

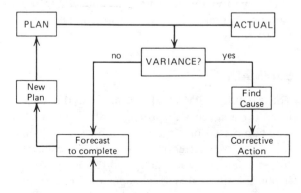

Figure 9 The basic feedback loop of control.

1. Periodic status checking will be performed monthly.
2. Labor costs will be collected manually and estimated where necessary from discussion with Group engineering management.
3. Out-of-pocket costs will be collected through commitments and/or invoice payment records.
4. Monthly status reports will be issued by the PM&C Program project manager including:
    a. Cost to date summaries.
    b. Cost variances.
    c. Schedule performance relative to schedule in Gantt format.
    d. Changes in scope or other modifications to plan.
5. Informal control will be exercised through milestone anticipation by the PM&C Program project manager.

Figure 10 Control system.

reviews for control purpose and defines the nature of the reports used.

Milestones and Schedule Subdivisions

Milestones and Schedule Subdivisions are a part of the control system. Of the set of events which can be defined (in the Event-on-Node network, or implicitly in the Activity-on-Node network), milestones form a limited subset of events, in practice rarely exceeding 20 at any given level. The milestones are predetermined times (or performance states) at which the feedback loop of control described above (Figure 9) should be exercised. Other subdivisions of the project are possible, milestones simply being a subdivision by events. Periodic time subdivisions may be made, or division into phases, one of the most common. Figure 11 shows the milestones for the PM&C Program.

SUMMARY

The Heublein PM&C Program met the conditions for a successful project in the sense that it was completed on time and within the budgeted funds. As is so often the case, the existence of a formal plan and continuing reference to it made it possible to deal with changes of scope. Initial reaction to the educational package was so favorable that the population of attendees was increased by Group executives and engineering managers; by reference to the original plan it was possible to predict cost increases in advance. Thus, there was no overrun in any sense.

To deliver on time and within budget, but to deliver a product which does not serve the client's needs is also unsatisfactory. Did this PM&C Program achieve the "General Objectives" of Figure 5? We all know the difficulties of quantifying and measuring such objectives within the real-world environment, where the concept of a proper research design is not allowable: We rarely deliberately experiment with organizations. This is a similar problem to that faced in medical research; if we have a methodology that can save or make millions of dollars, can we deny it to any Group, even if we are not absolutely certain of its value?

Thus, as is so often the case in managerial systems and educational programs, we are forced to rely on the perceptions of the clients. In this PM&C Program, the clients are Corporate Management, Group Management, and most importantly, the Managers of Engineering and their staffs. In the short run, the latter two operational clients are primary. In addition to informal feedback from them, formal feedback was obtained in the form of Impact Statements (item number 4000 in the WBS of Figure 5). The Impact Statements concerned the impact of the PM&C

Date	Description
09/05/79	Program plan approved by both Corporate & Groups
09/26/79	Reporting and control system approved by Corporate and Groups
10/05/79	Organizational impact analysis report issued
11/07/79	Basic project planning and control seminars completed
01/07/79	Reporting and control system implemented
03/24/80	Final procedures manual approved
05/19/80	Technical Seminars completed Computer support systems survey completed
06/30/80	Final impact assessment report issued

Figure 11 Milestones.

Program on the concerned organization ("How many labor-hours are expected to be devoted to the PM&C System?") and response to the PM&C Program ("Has this been of value to you in doing your job better?").

Clearly, the response of perceived value from the operating personnel was positive, or this paper would not have been written. Can we put any measure on it? We sought no formal instruments for measurement, relying instead on subjective, free form, and anecdotal responses. Can we measure the improvement which we believe to be taking place in the implementation of capital and other projects? It may be years before the impact (positive or negative) can be evaluated, and even then there may be such confounding with internal and external variables that no unequivocal, quantified response can be defined.

At this point we base our belief in the value of the PM&C Program on the continuing flow—starting with the Impact Statements—of positive perceptions. The following is an example of such a response, occurring one year after the exposure of the respondent:

...find attached an R&D Project Tracking Diagram developed as a direct result of the [PM&C] seminar...last year. [In the seminar we called it] a Network Analysis Diagram. The Product Development Group has been using this exclusively to track projects. Its value has been immeasurable. Since its inception, fifteen new products have gone through the sequence...

Questions

1. Which of the project planning aids (WBS, etc.) described in the chapter was used in the case?

2. For each of the aids used in the case, describe how they were constructed and if there were any modifications in form.

3. How were each of the aids applied in the case?

4. Would a TREND organizational overlay have been useful in this situation? What potential problems might it have shown?

5.15 READING

This article investigates the dual importance of strategy and tactics in project management. It uses a project life cycle framework to illustrate its points and postulates ten critical project success factors, some strategic and some tactical. Four types of major errors are described and illustrated with four example firms. Then the ten critical success factors are derived for each of the firms to show their interplay.

Balancing Strategy and Tactics in Project Implementation

Dennis P. Slevin
University of Pittsburgh
Jeffrey K. Pinto
University of Cincinnati

Successful project implementation is complex and difficult. Project managers must pay attention simultaneously to a wide variety of human, financial, and technical factors—and they are often made responsible for project outcome without being given sufficient authority, money, or manpower.

Project-based work tends to be very different from other organizational activities. Projects usually have a specific goal or goals, a defined beginning and end, and a limited budget. Often developed by a team of individuals with special expertise, projects usually consist of a series of complex tasks requiring high levels of coordination.

Perhaps not surprisingly, the project manager's job is characterized by role overload, frenetic activity, and superficiality. He or she needs tools that will help to identify critical issues and to prioritize them over the life of the project.

Project management tools must acknowledge that the manager is of necessity a generalist as well as a specialist: he or she must know how to *plan* effectively and *act* efficiently. Unfortunately, the "dreamers" who are effective strategists often lack the operational skills to realize their plans. Likewise, project managers who are uncomfortable with planning prefer to address concrete, well-defined problems. Balancing the interplay between planning and action—strategy and tactics—may be a project manager's most important job.

Despite the fact that many project managers are uneasy with either the strategic or the tactical side of their work, project management research to date has generally failed to address this important issue. This article provides some conceptual tools designed to do so. It proposes ten project management "critical success factors," defines their relationship to one another, and describes how they fit into a strategic-tactical framework. In addition, it pinpoints errors likely to occur if strategy is well managed but tactics are not, and vice versa. Finally, it offers some pragmatic advice about strategic and tactical project management.

Reprinted from *Sloan Management Review*, Fall 1987, pp. 33–41, by permission of the publisher. Copyright © 1987 by the Sloan Management Review Association. All rights reserved.

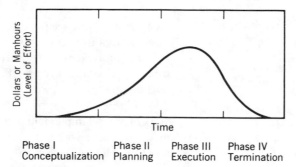

Phase I   Phase II   Phase III   Phase IV
Conceptualization Planning   Execution   Termination

Source: Adams and Barndt: ''Behavioral implications
of the Project Life Cycle.'' In *Project Management
Handbook*, ed. Cleland and King, Copyright © 1983
by Van Nostrand Reinhold Co. Inc. Reprinted by
permission of the publisher.

Figure 1 Stages in the project life cycle.

THE PROJECT LIFE CYCLE

The concept of a *project life cycle* provides a useful framework for looking at project dynamics over time. The idea is familiar to most managers; it is used to conceptualize work stages and the budgetary and organizational resource requirements of each stage[1]. As Figure 1 shows, this frame of reference divides projects into four distinct phases of activity.

- **Conceptualization.** The initial project stage. Top managers determine that a project is necessary. Preliminary goals and alternative project approaches are specified, as are the possible ways to accomplish these goals.
- **Planning.** The establishment of formal plans to accomplish the project's goals. Activities include scheduling, budgeting, and allocation of other specific tasks and resources.
- **Execution.** The actual "work" of the project. Materials and resources are procured, the project is produced, and performance capabilities are verified.
- **Termination.** Final activities that must be performed once the project is completed. These include releasing resources, transferring the project to clients, and, if necessary, reassigning project team members to other duties.

As Figure 1 shows, the project life cycle is useful for project managers because it helps to define the level of effort needed to perform the tasks associated with each stage. During the early stages, require-

ments are minimal. They increase rapidly during late planning and execution and diminish during termination. Project life cycles are also helpful because they provide a method for tracking the status of a project in terms of its stage of development.

PROJECT CRITICAL SUCCESS FACTORS

In recent years the authors and other researchers have focused on identifying those factors most critical to project success and have generated both theoretical models and lists of "success" factors[2]. Through a recent study, we have developed and refined a set of critical success factors that we believe will make conceptual sense to managers, and that is general enough to be supported across a wide range of project types[3]. As we shall see, these factors fit into a broader framework that models the dynamic project implementation process. They have also led to the development of a Project Implementation Profile (PIP) that can be used to monitor and update the factors' status throughout a project's life. First, though, we should define the factors[4].

- **Project Mission.** Initial clarity of goals and general direction.
- **Top Management Support.** Willingness of top management to provide the necessary resources and authority or power for project success.

- **Project Schedule/Plans.** Detailed specification of the individual action steps required for project implementation.
- **Client Consultation.** Communication and consultation with, and active listening to, all affected parties.
- **Personnel.** Recruitment, selection, and training of the necessary personnel for the project team.
- **Technical Tasks.** Availability of the required technology and expertise to accomplish the specific technical action steps.
- **Client Acceptance.** The act of "selling" the final project to its intended users.
- **Monitoring and Feedback.** Timely provision of comprehensive control information at each stage in the implementation process.
- **Communication.** Provision of an appropriate network and necessary data to all key actors in the project implementation.
- **Trouble Shooting.** Ability to handle unexpected crises and deviations from plan.

A fifty-item instrument has been developed to measure a project's score on each of the ten factors in comparison to over 400 projects studied. The Project Implementation Profile provides a quantitative way of quickly profiling a project on these ten key factors.

As Figure 2 shows, we have developed a framework of project implementation based on the ten factors. This framework is intended to demonstrate that these ten factors are not only all critical to project success, but that there is also a relationship *among* the factors. In other words, these factors must be examined in relation to each other as well as to their individual impact on successful implementation. Conceptually, the factors are sequenced logically rather than randomly. For example, it is important to set goals or define the mission and benefits of the program before seeking top management support. Similarly, unless consultation with clients occurs early in the process, chances of subsequent client acceptance will be lowered. In actual practice considerable overlap can occur among the various fac-

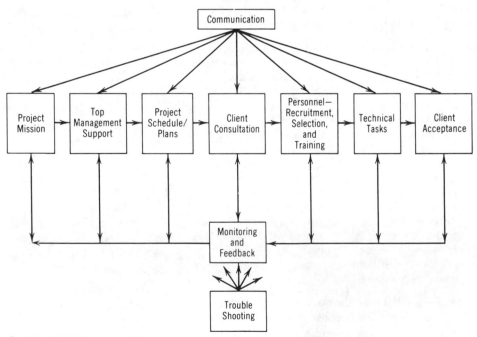

Copyright © 1984 Randall L. Schultz and Dennis P. Slevin. Used with permission.

Figure 2 Ten key factors of the Project Implementation Profile.

tors, and their sequencing is not absolute. The arrows in the model represent information flows and sequences, not causal or correctional relationships.

As Figure 2 shows, in addition to the seven factors that can be laid out on a sequential critical path, three additional factors are hypothesized to play a more overriding role in the project implementation. These factors, monitoring and feedback, communication, and trouble shooting, must all necessarily be present at each point in the implementation process. Further, a good argument could be made that these three factors are essentially different facets of the same general concern (i.e., project communication). Communication is vital for project control, for problem solving, and for maintaining beneficial contacts with both clients and the rest of the organization.

STRATEGY AND TACTICS

As one moves through the ten-factor model, it becomes clear that the factors' general characteristics change. The first three (mission, top management support, and schedule) are related to the early, "planning" phase of project implementation. The other seven are concerned with the actual implementation or "action" of the project. These planning and action elements can usefully be considered *strategic*—the process of establishing overall goals and of planning how to achieve those goals—and *tactical*—using human, technical, and financial resources to achieve strategic ends. Briefly, the critical success factors of project implementation fit into a strategic/tactical breakout in the following way:

- **Strategic:** mission, top management support, project schedule/plans.
- **Tactical:** client consultation, personnel, technical tasks, client acceptance, monitoring and feedback, communication, trouble shooting.

Strategy and Tactics over Time

While both strategy and tactics are essential for successful project implementation, their importance shifts as the project moves through its life

cycle. Strategic issues are most important at the beginning, tactical issues gain in importance toward the end. There should, of course, be continuous interaction and testing between the two—strategy often changes in a dynamic corporation, so regular monitoring is essential. Nevertheless, a successful project manager must be able to make the transition between strategic and tactical considerations as the project moves forward.

As Figure 3 shows, a recent study of more than 400 projects charted the shifting balance between strategic and tactical issues over the project's life cycle[5]. The "importance" value was measured by regression beta weights showing the relationships among strategy, tactics, and project success over the life cycle stages. During the two early stages, conceptualization and planning, strategy is significantly more important to project success than tactics. As the project moves toward the final stage, they achieve almost equal importance. Throughout the project, initial strategies and goals continue to "drive" or shape tactics.

These changes have important implications. A project manager who is a brilliant strategist but an ineffective tactician has a strong potential for commit-

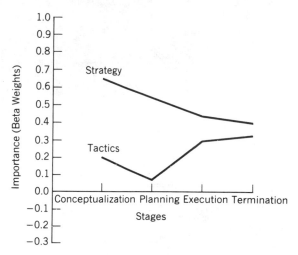

Figure 3 Changes in strategy and tactics across the Project Life Cycle (n = 418).

ting certain types of errors as the project moves forward. These errors may occur after substantial resources have been expended. In contrast, the project manager who is excellent at tactical execution but weak in strategic thinking has a potential for committing different kinds of errors. These will more likely occur early in the process, but may remain undiscovered because of the manager's effective execution.

Strategic and Tactical Performance

Figure 4 shows the four possible combinations of strategic and tactical performance and the kinds of problems likely to occur in each scenario. The values "high" and "low" represent strategic and tactical *quality,* i.e., effectiveness of operations performed.

A *Type I* error occurs when an action that should have been taken was not. Consider a situation in which strategic actions are adequate and suggest development and implementation of a project. A Type I error has occurred if tactical activities are inadequate, little action is subsequently taken, and the project is not developed.

A *Type II* error happens if an action is taken when it should not have been. In practical terms, a Type II error is likely to occur if the project strategy is ineffective or inaccurate, but goals and schedules are implemented during the tactical stage of the project anyway.

A *Type III* error can be defined as solving the wrong problem, or "effectively" taking the wrong action. In this scenario, a problem is identified, or a project is desired, but because of a badly performed strategic sequence, the wrong problem is isolated, so the implemented project has little value—it does not address the intended target. Such situations often involve large expenditures of human and budgetary resources (tactics) for which there is inadequate initial planning and problem recognition (strategy).

A *Type IV* is the final kind of error common to project implementation: the action taken does solve the right problem, but the solution is not used. That is, if project management correctly identifies a problem, proposes an effective solution, and implements that solution using appropriate tactics—but the project is not used by the client for whom it was intended—then a Type IV error has occurred.

As Figure 4 suggests, each of these errors is most likely to occur given a particular set of circumstances.

- **Cell 1: High Strategy/High Tactics.** Cell 1 is the setting for projects rated effective in carrying out both strategy and tactics. Not surprisingly, most projects in this situation are successful.
- **Cell 3: Low Strategy/Low Tactics.** The reciprocal of the first is the third cell, where both strategic and tactical functions are inadequately performed. Projects in this cell have a high likelihood of failure.
- **Cell 4: High Strategy/Low Tactics.** The results of projects in the first two cells are intuitively obvious. Perhaps a more intriguing question concerns the likely outcomes for projects found in the "off diagonal" of Figure 4, namely, High Strategy/Low Tactics and Low Strategy/High Tactics.

In Cell 4, the project strategy is effectively developed but subsequent tactics are ineffective. We would expect projects in this cell to have a strong tendency toward "errors of inaction" such

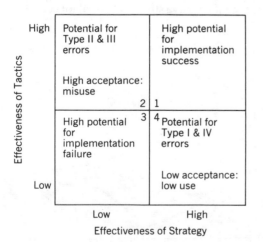

Type I error: Not taking an action when one should be taken.
Type II error: Taking an action when none should be taken.
Type III error: Taking the wrong action (solving the wrong problem).
Type IV error: Addressing the right problem, but solution is not used.

Figure 4 Strategy/tactics effectiveness matrix.
Source: Schultz, Slevin and Pinto (1987).

as low acceptance and low use by organization members or clients for whom the project was intended. Once a suitable strategy has been determined, little is done in the way of tactical follow-up to operationalize the goals of the project or to "sell" the project to its prospective clients.

- **Cell 2: Low Strategy/High Tactics.** The final cell reverses the preceding one. Here, project strategy is poorly conceived or planning is inadequate, but tactical implementation is well managed. Projects in this cell often suffer from "errors of action." Because of poor strategy, a project may be pushed into implementation even though its purpose has not been clearly defined. In fact, the project may not even be needed. However, tactical follow-up is so good that the inadequate or unnecessary project is implemented. The managerial attitude is to "go ahead and do it"; not enough time is spent early in the project's life assessing whether the project is needed and developing the strategy.

CASE STUDY ILLUSTRATIONS

In the section that follows, we discuss four instances in which strategic and tactical effectiveness were measured by project participants using the Project Implementation Profile. We caution that the results were reported in three instances by only one observer—the project manager—so they are obviously not meant as evidence in support of an argument, but rather as an illustration of distinct project-outcome types. In each case, a ten-factor profile is provided, using the actual scores from the PIP based on input from the project managers.

High Strategy/High Tactics:
The New Alloy Development

One department of a large organization was responsible for coordinating the development and production of new stainless steel alloys for the automotive exhaust market. This task meant overseeing the efforts of the metallurgy, research, and operations departments. The project grew out of exhaust component manufacturers' demands for more formable alloys. Because this product line represented a potentially significant portion of the company's market, the project was given high priority.

As Figure 5A demonstrates, the scores for this project as assessed by the project team member were uniformly high across the ten critical success factors. Because of the importance of the project, its high priority was communicated to all personnel, and this led to a strong sense of project mission and top management support. The strategy was clear and was conveyed to all concerned parties, including the project team, which was actively involved in early planning meetings. Because the project team would include personnel from research, metallurgy, operations, production, and commercial departments, great care was taken in its selection and coordination. Use throughout the project team of action plans and daily exception reports was reflected in high scores on Technical Tasks and Trouble Shooting.

In the new alloy development project, a strong, well-conceived strategy was combined with highly competent tactical follow-up. The seeds of project success were planted during the conceptual and planning stages and were allowed to grow to their potential through rigorous project execution. Success in this project can be measured in terms of technical excellence and client use, as well as project team satisfaction and commercial profitability. In a recent follow-up interview, a member of a major competitor admitted that the project was so successful that the company still has a virtual lock on the automotive exhaust market.

Low Strategy/Low Tactics:
The Automated Office

A small, privately owned company was attempting to move from a nonautomated paper system to a fully integrated, automated office that would include purchasing, material control, sales order, and accounting systems. The owner's son, who had no previous experience with computers, was hired as MIS director. His duties consisted of selecting hardware and software, directing installation, and learning enough about the company to protect the family's interests. Figure 5B shows a breakdown of the ten critical success factors as viewed by a project team member.

Several problems emerged immediately. Inade-

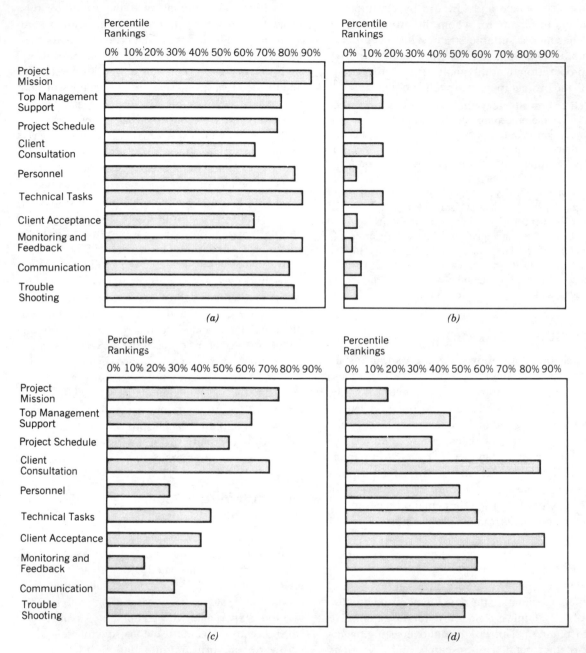

Figure 5 (a) High Strategy/High Tactics Project, (b) Low Strategy/Low Tactics Project, (c) High Strategy/Low Tactics Project, (d) Low Strategy/High Tactics Project.

quate "buy-in" on the part of organization members, perceived nepotism, and lack of interaction with other top managers in purchasing decisions were seen as problems while the project was still in its strategy phase. A total lack of a formal schedule or implementation plan emphasized other strategic inadequacies destined to lead to tactical problems as well.

Tactically, the project was handled no better. Other departments that were expected to use the system were not consulted about their specific needs; the system was simply forced upon them. Little effort was made to develop project control and trouble-shooting mechanisms, perhaps as a direct result of inadequate scheduling.

Project results were easy to predict. As the team member indicated and Figure 5B reinforces, the project was over budget, behind schedule, and coolly received—all in all, an expensive failure. The owner's son left the company, the manager of the computer department was demoted, the mainframe computers were found to be wholly inadequate and were sold, and upper management forfeited a considerable amount of employee goodwill.

High Strategy/Low Tactics: The New Bank Loan Setup

The purpose of this project was to restructure the loan procedures used at a major bank. The project was intended to eliminate duplicate work done by branches and the servicing department and to streamline loan processes. These goals were developed and strongly supported by upper management, which had clearly conveyed them to all concerned parties. The project was kicked off with a great deal of fanfare; there was a high expectation of speedy and successful completion. Trouble started when the project was turned over to a small team that had not been privy to the initial planning, goal setting, and scheduling meetings. In fact, the project team leader was handed the project after only three months with the company.

Project tactics were inadequate from the beginning. The team was set up without any formal feedback channels and with few communication links with either the rest of the organization or top management. The project was staffed on an ad hoc basis, often with nonessential personnel from other departments. This staffing method resulted in a diverse team with conflicting loyalties. The project leader was never able to pull the team together.

As the project leader put it, "Although this project hasn't totally failed, it is in deep trouble." Figure 5C illustrates the breakdowns for the project as reported by two team members. Almost from the start of its tactical phase, the project suffered from the team's inability to operationalize the initial goals. This failure caused frustration both within the project team and throughout the rest of the organization. The frustration resulted from having a clear idea of the initial goals without having prescribed the means to achieve them. As of this writing, the project continues to stagger along, with cost overruns and constantly revised schedules. Whether or not it achieves its final performance goals, this project will be remembered with little affection by the rest of the organization.

Low Strategy/High Tactics: The New Appliance Development

A large manufacturing company initiated the development of a new kitchen appliance to satisfy what upper management felt would be a consumer need in the near future. The project was perceived as the pet idea of a divisional president and was rushed along without adequate market research or technical input from the R&D department. A project team was formed to develop the product and rush it to the marketplace.

Figure 5D shows the breakdowns of the ten critical success factors for this project. Organizational and project team commitment was low. Other members of upper management felt the project was being pushed along too fast and refused to get behind it. Initial planning and scheduling developed

by the divisional president and his staff were totally unrealistic.

What happened next was interesting. It was
turned over to an experienced, capable manager
who succeeded in taking the project, which had
gotten off to such a shaky start, and successfully
implementing it. He reopened channels of communication within the organization, bringing
R&D and marketing on board. He met his revised
schedule and budget, using trouble-shooting and
control mechanisms. Finally, he succeeded in getting the project to the market in a reasonable time
frame.

In spite of the project manager's effective tactics, the product did not do well in the market. As it
turned out, there was little need for it at the time,
and second-generation technology would make it
obsolete within a year. This project was highly
frustrating to project team members, who felt,
quite correctly, that they had done everything possible to achieve success. Through no fault of their
own, this project was doomed by the poor strategic
planning. All the tactical competence in the world
could not offset the fact that the project was poorly conceived and indifferently supported, resulting in an "error of action"[6].

IMPLICATIONS FOR MANAGERS

These cases, and the strategy/tactics effectiveness matrix, suggest practical implications for
managers wishing to better control project implementation.

Use a multiple-factor model. Project management is a complex task requiring attention to many
variables. The more specific a manager can be
regarding the definition and monitoring of those
variables, the greater the likelihood of successful
project outcome. It is important to use a multiple-
factor model to do this, first to understand the
variety of factors affecting project success, then to
be aware of their relative importance across
project implementation stages[7]. This article offers such a model: ten critical success factors that
fit into a process framework of project implementation; within the framework, different factors be-

come more critical to project success at different
points in the project life cycle.

Additionally, both the project team and clients
need to perform regular assessments to determine
the "health" of the project. The time for accurate
feedback is when the project is beginning to
develop difficulties that can be corrected, not
down the road when the troubles have become insurmountable. Getting the project team as well as
the clients to perform status checks has the benefit
of giving insights from a variety of viewpoints, not
just that of the project manager. Further, it reinforces the goals the clients have in mind, as well as
their perceptions of whether the project satisfies
their expectations.

*Think strategically early in the project life
cycle.* It is important to consider strategic factors
early in the project life cycle, during conceptualization and planning. As a practical suggestion, organizations implementing a project should
bring the manager and his or her team on board
early. Many managers make the mistake of not involving team members in early planning and conceptual meetings, perhaps assuming that the team
members should only concern themselves with
their specific jobs. In fact, it is very important that
at an early stage both the manager *and* the team
members "buy in" to the goals of the project and
the means to achieve those goals. The more team
members are aware of the goals, the greater the
likelihood of their taking an active part in monitoring and trouble shooting.

*Think more tactically as the project moves for-
ward in time.* As Figure 4 shows in the later
project stages, strategy and tactics are of almost
equal importance to project implementation success. Consequently, it is important that the project
manager shift the team's emphasis from "What do
we do?" to "How do we want to do it?" The
specific critical success factors associated with
project tactics tend to reemphasize the importance
of focusing on the "how" instead of the "what."
Factors such as personnel, communication, and
monitoring are concerned with better managing
specific action steps in the project implementation
process. While we argue that it is important to

bring the project team on board during the initial strategy phase, it is equally important to manage their shift into a tactical, action mode in which their specific project duties are performed to help move the project toward completion.

Consciously plan for and communicate the transition from strategy to tactics. Project monitoring will include an open, thorough assessment of progress at several stages of implementation. The assessment must acknowledge that the transition from a strategic to a tactical focus introduces an additional set of critical success factors.

Project managers should regularly communicate with team members about the shifting status or focus of the project. Communication reemphasizes the importance of a joint effort, and it reinforces the status of the project relative to its life cycle. The team is kept aware of the degree of strategic versus tactical activity necessary to move the project to the next life-cycle stage. Finally, communication helps the manager to track the various activities performed by the project team, making it easier to verify that strategic vision is not lost in the later phases of tactical operationalization.

Make strategy and tactics work for you and your project team. Neither strong strategy nor strong tactics by themselves will ensure project success. When strategy is strong and tactics are weak, there is a potential for creating projects that never get off the ground. Cost and schedule overruns, along with general frustration, are often the side effects of projects that encounter "errors of inaction." On the other hand, a project that starts off with a weak or poorly conceived strategy and receives strong subsequent tactical operationalization is likely to be successfully implemented, but to address the wrong problem. New York advertising agencies can tell horror stories of advertising campaigns that were poorly conceived but still implemented, sometimes costing millions of dollars, and that were ultimately judged disastrous and scrubbed.

In addition to having project strategy and tactics working together, it is important to remember (again following Figure 3) that strategy should be used to "drive" tactics. Strategy and tactics are not independent of each other. At no point do strategic factors become unimportant to project success; instead, they must be continually assessed and reassessed over the life of the project in light of new project developments and changes in the external environment.

REFERENCES

The authors wish to acknowledge the comments of Robert W. Zmud and an anonymous reviewer on a draft of this article.

1. The four-stage project life cycle is based on work by J. Adams and S. Barndt, "Behavioral Implications of the Project Life Cycle," in *Project Management Handbook,* eds., D. I. Cleland and W. R. King (New York: Van Nostrand Reinhold, 1983), pp. 222–244.

2. For an alternative methodology for the development of critical success factors for the implementation of organizational systems, see the work of M. Shank, A. Boynton, and R. W. Zmud, "Critical Success Factor Analysis as a Methodology for MIS Planning," *MIS Quarterly,* June 1985, pp. 121–129. See further, A. Boynton and R. W. Zmud, "An Assessment of Critical Success Factors," *Sloan Management Review,* Summer 1984, pp. 17–27.

3. D. P. Slevin and J. K. Pinto, "The Project Implementation Profile: New Tool for Project Managers," *Project Management Journal,* 17 (1986): 57–70.

4. J. K. Pinto and D. P. Slevin, "Critical Factors in Successful Project Implementation," *IEEE Transactions on Engineering Management,* EM-34, Feb. 1987, pp. 22–27.

5. J. K. Pinto, "Project Implementation: A Determination of Its Critical Success Factors, Moderators, and Their Relative Importance across Stages in the Project Life Cycle" (Pittsburgh, PA: University of Pittsburgh, unpublished doctoral dissertation, 1986).

6. Pinto (1986).

7. For a copy of the full 100-item Project Implementation Profile, see Slevin and Pinto (1986).

8. R. L. Schultz, D. P. Slevin, and J. K. Pinto, "Strategy and Tactics in a Process Model of Project Implementation," *Interfaces,* May–June 1987, pp. 34–46.

CHAPTER 6
Negotiation and Conflict Resolution

As we noted in Chapter 5, the process of planning a project usually requires inputs from many people. Even when the project is relatively small and simple, planning involves the interaction of almost every functional and staff operation in the organization. It is virtually impossible for these interactions to take place without conflict, and when a conflict arises, it is helpful if there are acceptable methods to reduce or resolve it.

Conflict has been defined as "...the process which begins when one party perceives that the other has frustrated, or is about to frustrate, some concern of his" [16, p. 891]. While conflict can arise over issues of belief or feelings or behavior, our concern in this chapter is focused for the most part on goal conflicts that occur when an individual or group pursues goals different from those of other individuals or groups [13, Ch. 12]. A party to the conflict will be satisfied when the level of frustration has been lowered to the point where no action, present or future, against the other party is contemplated. When all parties to the conflict are satisfied to this point, the conflict is said to be resolved.

There are, of course, many ways to resolve conflict. Brute force is a time-honored method, as is the absolute rule of the monarch, but the rule of law is the method of choice for Western societies—in spite of occasional lapses. Conflict resolution is the ultimate purpose of law.

Organizations establish elaborate and complex sets of rules and regulations to settle disputes between the organization itself and the individuals and groups with whom it interacts. Contracts between a firm and its suppliers, its trade unions, and its customers are written to govern the settlement of potential conflicts. But the various parties-at-interest do not always agree about the meaning of a law or a provision in a contract. No agreement, however detailed, can cover all the circumstances that might arise in the extensive relationships between the buyer and the seller of complicated industrial equipment, between the user and the supplier of engineering consulting services—the list of potential conflicts is endless. Our overcrowded courts are witness to the extent and variety of conflict. More than 500,000 lawyers in the United States [19] are employed in helping conflicting parties to adjudicate or settle their differences.

In this chapter we examine the nature of negotiation as a means of reducing or resolving the kinds of conflict that typically occur within projects. But *before we begin the discussion, it must be made quite clear that this chapter is not a primer on how to negotiate;* a course in negotiation is beyond the scope of this book and beyond our expertise (for such information, the reader is referred to the bibliography). Rather, this chapter focuses on the roles and applications of negotiation in the *management* of projects. Note also that we have excluded negotiations between the organization and outside vendors. In our experience, this type of negotiation is conducted sometimes by the project manager, sometimes by the project engineer, but most often by members of the organization's purchasing department. In any case, negotiations between buyer and seller are admirably covered by [5 and 13].

Of course, conflict may produce positive outcomes for the organization. Debate over the proper technical approach to a problem often generates a collaborative solution that is superior to any solution originally proposed. Conflict often educates individuals and groups about the goals/objectives of other individuals and groups in the organization, thereby satisfying a precondition for valuable win–win negotiations (see Section 6.3). Indeed, the act of engaging in win–win negotiations serves as an example of the positive outcomes that can result from such an approach to conflict resolution.

In Chapter 3 we noted that negotiation was a critical skill required of the project manager. In this chapter we describe typical areas of project management where this skill is mandatory. In addition, we will cover some of the appropriate and inappropriate approaches to negotiation, as well as a few of the characteristics of successful negotiation suggested by experts in the field or indicated by our experience. Unlike other chapters, we will use comparatively few illustrative examples throughout the body of this one. Successful negotiation tends to be idiosyncratic to the actual situation, and most brief examples do little to help transform theory into practice. We have, however, included a vignette at the end of the chapter. This vignette was adapted from "real life;" the names were changed to protect innocent and guilty alike.

No project manager should attempt to practice his/her trade without explicit training in negotiation. We are appalled that the subject is rarely mentioned in books on project management, excepting [5] on buyer-seller negotiations. (We are chagrined that it received less than minimal attention in our first edition.)

6.1 THE NATURE OF NEGOTIATION

The favored technique for resolving conflict is *negotiation*. What is negotiation? Wall [20, Preface] defines negotiation as "...the process through which two or more parties seek an acceptable rate of exchange for items they own or control." Dissatisfied with this definition, he spends part of a chapter extending and discussing the concept [20, Chapter 1], without a great deal of improvement. Cohen [2, p. 15] says that "Negotiation is a field of knowledge and endeavor that focuses on gaining the favor of people from whom we want things." Other authors define negotiation differently, but do not appreciably extend Cohen's definition. Even if no single definition neatly fits all the activities we label "negotiation," we do recognize that such terms as "mediate," "conciliate," "make peace," "bring to agreement," "settle differences," "moderate," "arbitrate," "adjust differences," "compromise," "bargain," "dicker," and "haggle," [14, pp. 504–505, 534, 545] are synonyms for "negotiate" in some instances.

Most of the conflicts that involve the organization and outsiders have to do with property rights and contractual obligations. In these cases, the parties to negotiation see themselves as opponents. Conflicts arising inside the organization may also appear to involve property rights and obligations, but they typically differ from conflicts with outsiders in one important way: As far as the firm is concerned, they are conflicts between allies, not opponents. Wall [20, pp. 149–50] makes this point neatly:

Organizations, like groups, consist of interdependent parts that have their own values, interests, perceptions, and goals. Each unit seeks to fulfill its particular goal...and the effectiveness of the organization depends on the success of each unit's fulfillment of its specialized task. Just as important as the fulfillment of the separate tasks is the integration of the unit activities such that each unit's activities aid or at least do not conflict with those of the others.

One of the ways in which organizations facilitate this integration is to establish *"lateral relations* [which] allow decisions to be made horizontally across lines of authority" [20, p. 150]. Because each unit will have its own goals, integrating the activities of two or more units is certain to produce the conflicts that Wall says should not take place. The conflicts may, however, be resolved by negotiating a solution, if one exists, that produces gains (or minimizes losses) for all parties. Raiffa [13, p. 139] defines a Pareto optimal solution to the two-party conflict and discusses the nature of the bargaining process required to reach optimality, a difficult and time-consuming process. While it is not likely that the conflicting parties will know and understand the complex tradeoffs in a real world, project management, many-persons/many-issues conflict [see 13, Chapters 17–23], the general objective is to find a solution that makes no party better off without making another party worse off—i.e., a Pareto optimal solution.

Approaching intraproject conflicts with a desire to win a victory over other parties in inappropriate. The proper outcome of this type of negotiation should be to optimize the outcome in terms of overall organizational goals. Although it is not always obvious how to do this, negotiation is clearly the correct approach.

6.2 CONFLICT AND THE PROJECT LIFE CYCLE

In this section, following a brief discussion of the project life cycle, we will categorize the types of conflicts that frequently occur in the project environment, and then amplify the nature of these conflicts. Finally, we will link the project life cycle with the fundamental conflict categories and discover that certain patterns of conflict are associated with the different periods in the life of a project. With this knowledge, the PM can do a faster and more accurate job of diagnosing the nature of the conflicts he/she is facing, thereby reducing the likelihood of escalating the conflict by dealing with it ineffectually.

More on the Project Life Cycle

Various authors define the stages of the project life cycle (see Figures 1-2 and 1-3 in Chapter 1) in different ways. Two of the most commonly cited definitions are those of Thamhain and Wilemon [16] and Adams and Barndt [1]. The former use a four-stage model with project formation, buildup, main program, and phaseout identified as the stages of the life cycle. Adams and Barndt also break the project life cycle into four stages: conceptualization, planning, execution, and termination.

For our purposes, these two views of the cycle are not significantly different. During the first stage, senior management tentatively, sometimes unofficially, approves preliminary planning for a project. Often, this management recognition is preceded by some strictly unofficial "bootleg" work to test the feasibility of an idea. Initial planning is undertaken, basic objectives are often adopted, and the project may be "scoped copedout." The second stage is typified by detailed planning, budgeting, scheduling, and the aggregation of resources. In the third stage, the lion's share of the actual work on the project is accomplished. During the final stage of the life cycle, work is completed and products are turned over to the client or user. This stage also includes disposition of the project's assets and personnel. It may even include preparation for the initial stage of another related project to follow.

Categories of Conflict

All stages of the project life cycle appear to by typified by conflict. In Chapter 4, we discussed some of the human factors that require the PM to be skilled at reducing interpersonal tensions. In that chapter we also introduced the work of Thamhain and Wilemon [16, 17] on conflict in the project. These conflicts center on such matters as schedules, priorities, staff and labor requirements, technical factors, administrative procedures, cost estimates, and, of course, personality conflicts. Thamhain and Wilemon collected data on the frequency and magnitude of conflicts of each type during each stage of the project life cycle. Multiplying frequency by a measure of conflict magnitude and adjusting for the proportion of PMs who reported each specific type of conflict, they derived an estimate of the "intensity" of the conflicts (see Tables 4-1 and 4-2). Figure 4-10 illustrates these conflicts and is repeated here as Figure 6-1 for the reader's convenience.

On examination of the data, it appears that the conflicts fall into three fundamentally different categories:

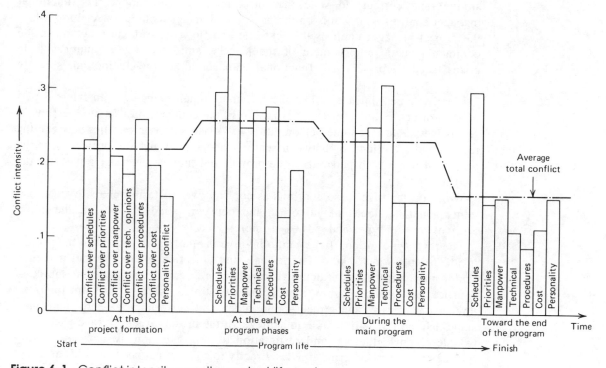

Figure 6-1   Conflict intensity over the project life cycle.
Source: Thamhain, H. J. and D. L. Wilemon, "Conflict Management in Project Life Cycles," *Sloan Management Review*, Summer, 1975.

1. Groups working on the project may have different goals and expectations.
2. There is considerable uncertainty about who has the authority to make decisions.
3. There are interpersonal conflicts between people who are parties-at-interest in the project.

Some conflicts reflect the fact that the day-to-day work on projects is usually carried out by many different units of the organization, units that often differ in their objectives and technical judgments. The result is that these units have different expectations about the project, its costs and rewards, its relative importance, and its timing. Conflicts about schedules, intra- and interproject priorities, cost estimates, and staff time tend to fall into this category. At base, they arise because the project manager and the functional managers have very different goals. The PM's concern is the project. The primary interest of the functional manager is the daily operation of his/her function.

Other conflicts reflect the fact that both technical and administrative procedures are important aspects of project management. Uncertainty about who has the authority to make decisions on resource allocation, on administrative procedures, on communication, on technological choices, and on all the other matters affecting the project produces conflict between the PM and the other parties. It is simple (and correct) to state that in a matrix organization, the functional manager controls who works on the project and makes technical decisions, while the project manager controls the schedule and flow of work. In practice, in the commonly hectic environment of the project, amid the day's countless little crises faced by project and functional manager alike, the distinction is rarely clear.

Finally, some conflicts reflect the fact that human beings are an integral part of all projects. In an environment that forces the cooperation of many persons, it seems inevitable that some personalities will clash. Also, in conflict between the project and the client, or between senior management and the project, it is the project manager who personifies the project and thus is generally a party to the conflict.

We can categorize these conflicts as conflict over differing goals, over uncertainty about the locus of authority, and between personalities. For the entire array of conflict types and parties-at-interest, see Table 6-1.

The three types of conflict seem to involve the parties-at-interest to the project in identifiable ways. The different goals and objectives of the project manager, senior management, and functional managers are a major and constant source of conflict. For example, senior management (at times, arbitrarily) is apt to fix all three parameters of the project—time, cost, and performance—and then to assume that the PM will be able to achieve all the preset targets. As we will see in Chapter 7 on budgeting, underestimation of cost and time is a natural consequence of this practice, and it leads directly to conflict between the PM, as a representative of the project team, and senior management. A second consequence is that the PM tries to pass the stringent cost and time estimates along to functional managers whose units are expected to perform certain work on the project. More conflict arises when the functional managers complain that they cannot meet the time and cost restrictions. All this tends to build failure into the job of managing a project, another source of conflict between the PM and senior management.

Functional managers also may not see eye to eye with the PM on such issues

Table 6-1 Project Conflicts by Category and Parties-at-Interest

| Parties-at-Interest | Categories of Conflict | | |
	Goals	Authority	Interpersonal
Project team	Schedules Priorities	Technical	Personality
Client	Schedules Priorities	Technical	
Functional and senior management	Schedules Priorities Manpower Cost	Technical Administrative	Personality

as the project's priority or the desirability of assigning a specifically named individual to work on the project, or even the applicability of a given technical approach to the project. In addition, the client's priorities and schedule, whether an inside or outside client, may differ radically from those of senior management and the project team. Finally, the project team has its own ideas about the appropriateness of the schedule or level of project staffing. The Thamhain and Wilemon data show that these goal-type conflicts occur in all stages of the project's life cycle, though they are particularly serious in the early stages (see Figure 6-1). Regardless of the timing, in many cases it is not certain just whose priorities are ruling.

There are, of course, a number of methods for settling conflicts about priorities between projects, as well as intraproject conflicts. Often, the project selection model used to approve projects for funding will generate a set of projects ranked by some measure of value. It is also common for senior management to determine interproject priorities. The relative importance of the various tasks in an individual project is set by the project manager, who allocates scarce resources depending on the requirements of schedule, task difficulty, resource availability, and similar considerations. The existence of these methods for resolving priority conflicts is all too often irrelevant, because there is a powerful tendency for both project and functional managers to optimize their interests, with little regard for the total organization.

In matrix organizations, the center of authority is particularly unclear. Locus-of-authority conflicts are endemic to matrix-organized projects. The project team and the client tend to focus on the technical procedures, debating the proper approach to the project, or perhaps how to solve individual problems that can occur at any stage. Senior management has other fish to fry. Not only do they insist that the project manager adopt and maintain a set of administrative procedures that conform to organizational and legal standards, but they also are quite concerned with who reports to whom and whose permission is required to take what action. The astute reader will note that such concerns are not entirely appropriate for matrix-organized projects. Our discussions with senior managers lead us to the not-surprising conclusion that it is common for senior management to want the efficiency and other advantages of matrix management but simultaneously to attempt to maintain the managerial comforts of traditional hierarchical structures—a sure source of conflict.

Project managers will often find themselves arguing for scheduling or resource priorities from functional managers who outrank them by several levels. Neither the functional nor the project managers are quite sure about who has what authority. (The reader will recall that the pure project form of organization has a tendency to breed deviant administrative behaviors, and that matrix organization is characterized by superior-subordinate confusion.) A constant complaint of project managers is "I have to take the responsibility, but I have no authority at all."

People problems arise, for the most part, within the project team, though functional managers may clash with PMs—the former accusing the latter of being "pushy," and the latter accusing the former of "foot dragging." In our experience, most personality clashes on the project team result from differences in technical approach or philosophy of problem solving, and in the methods used to implement the project results. Of course, it is quite possible that a personality conflict *causes* a technical conflict. It is also possible that any type of conflict will appear, at first blush, to be a personality clash.

Next we put these conflicts into the chronological perspective of the project life cycle.

Project Formation

In the initial stage of the project life cycle, most of the conflict centers around the inherent confusion of setting up a project in the environment of matrix management. Almost nothing about the project or its governance has been decided. Even the project's technical objectives, not clearly defined or established, are apt to be understood only in the most general sense. Moving from this state of semi-chaos to the relatively ordered world of the buildup stage is difficult. To make this transition, four fundamental issues must be handled, although not necessarily in the order presented here.

First, the technical objectives of the project must be specified to a degree that will allow the detailed planning of the buildup stage to be accomplished. Second, commitment of resources to the project must be forthcoming from senior management and from functional managers. Third, the priority of the project, relative to the priorities of the parent organization's other projects, must be set and communicated. Fourth, the organizational structure of the project must be established to an extent sufficient for the WBS and a linear responsibility chart, or its equivalent, to be prepared during the next stage of the life cycle.

These conditions are not sufficient, but they are most certainly necessary if the conflicts typical of the formation stage are to be resolved—at least at a reasonable level—and not simply carried forward to the buildup stage in an exacerbated state.

The project manager who practices conflict avoidance in this stage is inviting disaster in the next. The four fundamental issues above underlie such critical but down-to-earth matters as these: Which of the functional areas will be needed to accomplish project tasks? What will be the required level of involvement of each of the functional areas? How will conflicts over resources/facility usage between this and other projects be settled? What about those resource/facility conflicts between the project and the routine work of the functions? *Who* has the authority to decide the technical, scheduling, personnel, and cost questions that will arise? Most important, how will changes in the parent organization's priorities be communicated to everyone involved?

Note that three of the four fundamental issues—delimiting the technical objectives, getting management commitment, and setting the project's relative priority—must be resolved irrespective of what organizational form is selected for the project. It should also be noted that the organizational structure selected will have a major impact on the ways in which the conflicts are handled. The stronger the matrix, having the pure project as its limit, the more authoritative the role played by the PM. The weaker the matrix, having functional organization as its limit, the more authority is embedded in the functional managers. Lack of clarity about the relative power/influence/authority of the PM and the functional managers is a major component of all conflicts involving technical decisions, resource allocation. and scheduling.

Project Buildup

Thamhain and Wilemon note that conflict occurring in the buildup stage "over project priorities, schedules, and administrative procedures...appears as an extension from the previous program phase"[16, pp. 39]. This is the period during which the project moves (or should move) from a general concept to a highly detailed set of plans. If the project's organizational format is a strong matrix, the PM seeks a commitment of *people* from the functional departments. If the project if organized as a weak matrix, the PM seeks a commitment of *work* from the functional departments. In either case, the PM seeks commitment from functional managers who are under pressure to deliver support to other projects as well as, and in addition to, the routine, everyday demands made on their departments.

As the project's plans become detailed, conflicts over technical issues build—again, conflicts between the PM and the functional areas tend to predominate. Usually, ine functional departments can claim more technical expertise than the PM, who is a "generalist." On occasion, however, the PM is also a specialist. In such situations, discussions between the functional manager and the project manager about the best technical approach often result in conflict. The total level of conflict is at its highest in this transition period.

Main Program

Schedules are still a major source of conflict in the main program phase of the project life cycle, though the proximate cause of schedule-related conflict is usually different than in the earlier stages. Project plans have been developed and approved by everyone involved (although, perhaps, grudgingly), and the actual work is under way. Let us make an assumption that is certain to be correct; let us assume that some activity runs into difficulty and is late in being completed. Every task that is dependent on this late activity will also be delayed. Some of these subsequent activities will, if sufficiently late and if the late work is not made up, delay the entire project.

In order to prevent this consequence, the PM must try to get the schedule back on track. But catching up is considerably more difficult than falling behind. Catching up requires extra resources that the functional groups who are doing the "catching up" will demand, but which the PM may not have.

The more complex the project, the more difficult it is to trace and estimate the impact of all the delays, and the more resources that must be consumed to get things back on schedule. Throughout this book we have referred to the PM's job of managing time/cost/performance trade-offs. Maintaining the project schedule is precisely an exercise in managing tradeoffs, but adding to the project's cost or scaling down the project's technical capabilities in order to save time are tradeoffs the PM will not take if there is any viable alternative. The PM's ability to make tradeoffs is often constrained by contract, company policy, and ethical considerations. In reality, tradeoff decisions are extremely difficult.

Like schedule conflicts, technical conflicts are frequent and serious during the main program stage. Also like schedule conflicts, the source of technical conflict is somewhat different than in earlier stages. Just as a computer and a printer must be correctly linked together in order to perform properly, so must the many parts of a project. These linkages are known as *interfaces*. The number of interfaces increases rapidly as the project gets larger, which is to say that the system gets more complex. The need to manage these interfaces and to correct incompatibilities is the key to the technical conflicts in the main program phase.

Project Phaseout

As in the main program stage, schedule is the major source of conflict during project phaseout. If schedule slippage has occurred in the main program stage (and it most certainly will have), the consequences will surely be felt in this final stage. During phaseout, projects with firm deadlines develop an environment best described as hectic. The PM, project team, and functional groups often band together to do what is necessary to complete the project on time and to specification. Cost overruns, if not outrageously high, are tolerated—though they may not be forgiven and they will certainly be remembered.

Technical problems are comparatively rare during phaseout because most have been solved or bypassed earlier. Similarly, working interfaces have been developed and put in place. If the project involves implementing a technology in an outside client's system, technical conflicts will probably arise, but they are usually less intense.

Thamhain and Wilemon [16, p. 41] note that personality conflicts are the second-ranked source of conflict during phaseout. They ascribe these conflicts to interpersonal stress caused by the pressure to complete the project, and to individuals' natural anxiety about leaving the project either to be assigned to another, or be returned to a functional unit. In addition, we have observed conflict, sometimes quite bitter, focused on the distribution of the project's capital equipment and supplies when the project is completed. Conflict also arises between projects phasing out and those just starting, particularly if the latter need resources or personnel with scarce talents being used by the former.

The upshot is simple. As we noted in the first section of Chapter 1, conflict is an inherent characteristic of projects, and the project manager is constantly beset by conflict. The ability to reduce and resolve conflict in ways that support achievement of the project's goals is a prime requisite for success as a PM. The primary tool to accomplish conflict resolution and reduction is negotiation, and the method of handling conflict established in the project formation stage will set the pattern for the entire project. Therefore, the style of negotiation adopted by the PM is critical.

6.3 SOME REQUIREMENTS AND PRINCIPLES OF NEGOTIATION

The word "negotiation" evokes many images: Reagan and Gorbachev, a player's agent and the owner of an NFL team, the buyer and seller of an apartment complex, attorneys for husband and wife in a divorce settlement, union and management working out a collective bargaining agreement, tourist and peddler haggling over a rug in an Ankara market. But as we noted in the introduction to this chapter, none of these images is appropriate for the project manager who must resolve the sorts of conflicts we have considered in the previous section.

The key to understanding the nature of negotiation as it applies to project management is the realization that few of the conflicts arising in projects have to do with *whether* or not a task will be undertaken or a deliverable produced; rather, they have to do with *how* results will be achieved, by *whom, when,* and at *what cost.* The implication is clear: *The work of the project will be done.* If conflicts between any of the parties to the project escalate to the point where negotiations break down and work comes to a halt, everyone loses. *One requirement for the conflict reduction/resolution methods used by the PM is that they must allow the conflict to be settled without irreparable harm to the project's objectives.*

A closer consideration of the attorneys negotiating the divorce settlement makes clear a second requirement for the PM negotiating conflicts between parties-at-interest to the project. While the husband and wife (or the rug peddler and tourist) may employ unethical tactics during the negotiation process and, if not found out, profit from them at the expense of the other party, it is much less likely for the attorneys representing the husband and wife to do so—particularly if they practice law in the same community. The lawyers know they will have to negotiate on other matters in the future. Any behavior that breeds mistrust will make future negotiations extremely difficult, perhaps impossible. The rug peddler assumes no further contact with the tourist, so conscience is the sole governor of his ethics. *A second requirement for the conflict resolution/reduction methods used by the PM is that they allow (and foster) honesty between the negotiators.*

The conflicting parties-at-interest to a project are not enemies or competitors, but rather allies—members of an alliance with strong common interests. *It is a requirement of all conflicting parties to seek solutions to the conflict that not only satisfy their own individual needs, but also satisfy the needs of other parties to the conflict, as well as the needs of the parent organization.* In the language of negotiation, this is called a "win–win" solution. Negotiating to a win–win solution is the key to conflict resolution in project management.

Fisher and Ury [4] have developed a negotiation technique that tends to maintain these three requirements. They call it "principled negotiation." The method is straightforward; it is defined by four points [4, p. 11].

1. *Separate the people from the problem.* The conflicting parties are often highly emotional. They perceive things differently and feel strongly about the differences. Emotions and objective fact get confused to the point where it is not clear which is which. Conflicting parties tend to attack one another rather than the problem. To minimize the likelihood that the conflict will become strictly in-

terpersonal, the substantive problem should be carefully defined. Then everyone can work on it rather than each other.

2. *Focus on interests, not positions.* Positional bargaining occurs when the PM says to a functional manager: "I need this subassembly by November 15." The functional manager responds: "My group can't possibly start on it this year. We might be able to deliver it by February 1." These are the opening lines in a dialogue that sounds suspiciously like the haggling of the tourist and the rug peddler. A simple "Let's talk about the schedule for this subassembly" would be sufficient to open the discussion. Each party develops a high level of ego involvement in his/her position and the negotiation never focuses on the real interests and concerns of the conflicting parties—the central issues of the conflict. The exchange deteriorates into a series of positional compromises that do not satisfy either party and leave both feeling that they have lost something important.

In positional negotiation, the "positions" are statements of immediate wants and assume that the environment is static. Consider these positional statements: "I won't pay more than $250,000 for that property." Or, as above, "We might be able to deliver it by February 1." The first position assumes that the bidder's estimates of future property values are accurate, and the second assumes that the group's current workload (or a shortage of required materials) will not change. When negotiation focuses on interests, the negotiator must determine the underlying concern of the other party. The real concerns or interests of the individuals stating the positions quoted above might be to earn a certain return on the investment in a property, or to not commit to delivery of work if delivery on the due date cannot be guaranteed. Knowledge of the other party's interests allows a negotiator to suggest solutions that satisfy one party's interests without agreeing with the other's position.

3. *Before trying to reach agreement, invent options for mutual gain.* The parties-in-conflict usually enter negotiations knowing the outcome they would like. As a result, they are blind to other outcomes and are not particularly creative. Nonetheless, as soon as the substantive problems are spelled out, some effort should be devoted to finding a wide variety of possible solutions—or elements thereof—that advance the mutual interests of the conflicting parties. Success at finding options that produce mutual gain positively reinforces win–win negotiations. Cohen [2] reports on a conflict between a couple in which "he" wanted to go to the mountains and "she" wanted to go to the shore. A creative win–win solution sent them both to Lake Tahoe.

4. *Insist on using objective criteria.* Rather than bargaining on positions, attention should be given to finding standards (e.g., market value, expert opinion, law, company policy) that can be used to determine the quality of an outcome. Doing this tends to make the negotiation less a contest of wills or exercise in stubbornness. If a functional manager wants to use an expensive process to test a part, it is acceptable for the PM to ask if such a process is required to ensure that the parts meet specified quality standards.

Fisher and Ury have had some success with their approach, "principled negotiation," in the Harvard (Graduate School of Business) Negotiation Project. Use of their methods increases the chance of finding win–win solutions.

There are many books on negotiation, some of which are listed in the bibliography of this chapter. Most of these works are oriented toward negotiation between opponents, not an appropriate mindset for the project manager, but all of them contain useful, tactical advice for the project manager. Wall's book [20] is an excellent academic treatment of the subject. Fisher and Ury [4] is a clear presentation of principled negotiation, and contains much that is relevant to the PM. In addition, Herb Cohen's *You Can Negotiate Anything* [2] is an outstanding guide to win–win negotiation.

Among the tactical issues covered by most books on negotiation are things the project manager, as a beginning negotiator, needs to know. For example, what should a negotiator who wishes to develop a win–win solution do if the other party to the conflict adopts a win–lose approach? What do you do if the other party tries to put you under psychological pressure by seating you so that a bright light shines in your eyes? What do you do if the other party refuses to negotiate in order to put you under extreme time pressure to accept whatever solution he/she offers? How do you settle what you perceive to be purely technical disputes? How should you handle threats? What should be your course of action if a functional manager, with whom you are trying to reach agreement about the timing and technology of a task, goes over your head and attempts to enlist the aid of your boss to get you to accept a solution you feel is less than satisfactory? How can you deal with a person you suspect dislikes you?

In addition, the reader will find books on body language and communication in the bibliography. These works explain the nonverbal aspects of communication. At times, nonverbal messages are at variance with verbal messages, providing proof of that old adage, "actions speak louder than words". When negotiating, the PM must be sensitive to *all* the messages being communicated, not merely those arriving in verbal form.

Almost every writer on negotiation emphasizes the importance of understanding the interests of the person with whom you are negotiating. As we noted above, the positions taken by negotiators are not truly understandable without first understanding the interests and concerns that prompt those positions. The statement that a test requested for May 15 cannot be run until June 2 may simply mean that the necessary test supplies will not be delivered until the latter date. If the PM can get the supplies from another source in time for the May 15 deadline, the test can be run on schedule. But the ability to do this depends on knowing *why* the test was to be delayed. If the negotiation remains a debate on positions, the PM will never find out that the test could have been run on time. *The key to finding a negotiator's interests and concerns is to ask "Why?" when he/she states a position.* The following vignette demonstrates the maintenance of a nonpositional negotiating style. This vignette is based on an actual event and was described to the authors by an "actor" in the case.

6.4 NEGOTIATION IN ACTION—The Quad Sensor Project

Dave Rogers, an experienced project manager, was assigned the project of designing and setting up a production system for an industrial instrument. The instrument would undoubtedly be quite delicate, so the design and fabrication methods for the shipping container were included in the project. Production of containers capable of meeting the specifications in this case were outside the experience of the firm, but one engineer in the container group had worked with this type of package in a previous job. This engineer, Jeff Camm, was widely recognized as the top design engineer in the container group.

During the initial meetings on the project, which was organized as a weak matrix, Rogers asked Tab Raturi, manager of the Container Group, to assign Camm to the project because of his unique background. Raturi said he thought they could work it out, and estimated that the design, fabrication of prototypes, and testing would require about four weeks. The package design could not start until several shape parameters of the instrument had been set and allowable shock loadings for the internal mechanisms had been determined. The R&D group responsible for instrument design thought it would require about nine months of work before they could complete specifications for the container. In addition to the actual design, construction, and test work, Camm would have to meet periodically with the instrument design team to keep track of the project and to consult on design options from the container viewpoint. It was estimated that the entire project would require about eighteen months.

Seven months into the project, at a meeting with Dave Rogers, the senior instrument design engineer, Richard Morey, casually remarked: "Say, Dave, I thought Jeff Camm was going to do the package for the Quad Sensor?"

"He is, why?" Rogers replied.

"Well," said the engineer, "Camm hasn't been coming to the design team meetings. He did come a couple of times at the start of the project, but then young McCutcheon showed up saying that he would substitute for Camm and would keep him informed. I don't know if that will work. That package is going to be pretty tricky to make."

Rogers was somewhat worried by the news the engineer had given him. He went to Camm's office, as if by chance, and asked, "How are things coming along?"

"I'm up to my neck, Dave," Camm responded. "We've had half a dozen major changes ordered from Baker's office (V.P. Marketing) and Tab has given me the three toughest ones. I'm behind, getting behinder, and Baker is yelling for the new container designs. I can't possibly do the Quad Sensor package unless I get some help—quick. It's an interesting problem and I'd like to tackle it, but I just can't. I asked Tab to put McCutcheon on it. He hasn't much experience, but he seems bright."

"I see," said Rogers. "Well, the Quad Sensor package may be a bit much for a new man. Do you mind if I talk to Tab? Maybe I can get you out from under some of the pressure."

"Be my guest!" said Camm.

The next day Rogers met with Tab Raturi to discuss the problem. Raturi seemed depressed. "I don't know what we're supposed to do. No sooner do I get a package design set and tested than I get a call changing things. On the Evans order, we even had production schedules set, had ordered the material, and had all the setups figured out. I'm amazed they didn't wait till we had completed the run to tell us to change everything."

Raturi continued with several more examples of changed priorities and assignments. He complained that he had lost two draftsmen and was falling further and further behind. He concluded: "Dave, I know I said you could use Camm for the Quad Sensor job, but I simply can't cut him loose now. He's my most productive person, and if anyone can get us out from under this mess, he can. I know Mc-Cutcheon is just out of school, but he's bright. He's the only person I can spare, and I can only spare him because I haven't got the time to train him on how we operate around here—if you can call this 'operating.'"

The two men talked briefly about the poor communications and the inability of senior management to make up its collective mind. Then Rogers suggested: "Look, Tab, Quad Sensor is no more screwed up than usual for this stage of the project. How about this? I can let you borrow Charlotte Better for three or four weeks. She's an excellent draftsman and she's working on a low-priority job that's not critical at the moment. Say, I'll bet I can talk Anderson into letting you borrow Levy, too, maybe half time for a month. Anderson owes me a favor."

"Great, Dave, that will help a lot, and I appreciate the aid. I know you understand my problem and you know that I understand yours." Raturi paused and then added, "You realize that this won't take much pressure off Jeff Camm. If you can get him the drafting help he needs he can get more done, but I can't release him for the amount of time you've got allocated for the Quad Sensor."

They sat quietly for a while, then Rogers said, "Hey, I've got an idea. Container design is the hard problem. The production setup and test design isn't all that tough. Let me have Camm for the container design. I'll use McCutcheon for the rest of the project and get him trained for you. I can get Carol Matthews to show him how to set up the shock tests and he can get the word on the production setup from my senior engineer, Dick Morey."

Raturi thought a moment. "Yeah, that ought to work," he said. "But Camm will have to meet with your people to get back up to speed on the project. I think he will clean up Baker's biggest job by Wednesday. Could he meet with your people on Thursday?"

"Sure, I can arrange that," Rogers said.

Raturi continued. "This will mean putting two people on the package design. McCutcheon will have to work with Camm if he is to learn anything. Can your budget stand it?"

"I'm not sure," Rogers said, "I don't really have any slack in that account, but..."

"Never mind," interrupted Raturi, "I can bury the added charge somewhere. I think I'll add it to Baker's charges. He deserves it. After all, he caused our problem."

6.5 SUMMARY

This chapter addressed the need for negotiation as a tool to resolve project conflicts. We first discussed the nature of negotiation and its purpose in the organization. We then described various categories of conflict and related them to the project life cycle. We followed this by identifying a number of requirements and principles of negotiation. Finally, we presented a short vignette illustrating an actual negotiation situation.

Specific points made in the chapter were these:

- Negotiation within the firm should be directed at obtaining the best outcome for the organization, not winning.
- There are three major categories of conflict: goal-oriented, authority-based, and interpersonal.
- There are also three primary sources of conflict. They are the project team itself, the client, and functional and senior management.
- Critical issues to handle in the project formation stages are delimiting technical objectives, getting management commitment, setting the project's relative priority, and selecting the project organizational structure.
- The total level of conflict is highest during the project buildup stage.
- Scheduling and technical conflicts are most frequent and serious in the project buildup and main program stages, and scheduling conflicts in particular during the phaseout stage.
- Project negotiation requirements are that conflicts must be settled without permanent damage, the methodology must foster honesty, and the solution must satisfy both individuals' and the organization's needs.
- One promising approach to meeting the requirements of project negotiation is called principled negotiation.

This chapter concludes the subject of project initiation. In the next part of the text we address project implementation, starting with the subject of budgeting. We look at various budgeting methods. The chapter also addresses the issue of cost estimation and its difficulty.

6.6 GLOSSARY

INTERFACES—The boundaries between departments or functions.

LATERAL RELATIONS—Communication across lines of equivalent authority.

PARETO OPTIMAL SOLUTION—A solution where at least one element is better and no element is worse than before.

POSITIONAL NEGOTIATION—Stating immediate wants on the assumption that the environment is static.

PRINCIPLED NEGOTIATION—A process of negotiation that aims to achieve a win–win result.

PARTIES-AT-INTEREST—Those who have a vested interest in the outcome of the negotiations.

WIN–WIN—When both parties are better off in the outcome.

6.7 PROJECT TEAM ASSIGNMENT

As your project progresses, record the negotiation process that group members encounter throughout the term of the project. Consider both negotiations between members of the team as well as negotiations with outsiders, such as for resources, information, or even time. Make note if the principles of good negotiation were used and how the outcome evolved. Was it a "win–win" process or not? At what point in the project life cycle did the issue arise?

6.8 MATERIAL REVIEW QUESTIONS

1. Construct a definition of negotiation that generally encompasses all the meanings discussed in the chapter.
2. Review and justify the placement of the seven types of conflicts into the nine cells of Table 6.1.
3. Discuss each of the four fundamental issues for potential conflict during the project formation stage.
4. Identify the types of likely conflicts during the project buildup, main program, and phaseout stages.
5. What are the three main requirements of project negotiation?
6. Describe the four points of principled negotiation.

6.9 CONCEPTUAL DISCUSSION QUESTIONS

1. Summarize the vignette in the chapter in terms of the negotiation skills used. Comment on the appropriateness and ethical aspects related to "burying" the cost.
2. What will be the likely result of a win–win style manager negotiating with a win–lose style manager? What if they are both win–lose styled?
3. Reallocate the placement of the seven types of conflicts into the nine cells of Table 6.1 according to your own logic.
4. Describe the effect of using "conflict avoidance" in the project formation stage in terms of the resulting problems during the buildup stage.
5. How does the type of project organization affect each of the types of conflicts that occur over the project life cycle?
6. Project managers are primarily concerned with project interfaces. At what rate do these interfaces increase with increasing project size?
7. The critical term in the concept of principled negotiation is "position." Elaborate on the multiple meanings of this term relative to negotiation. Can you think of a better term?

6.10 CHAPTER EXERCISE

Review two recent incidents where you had a conflict with another person, one a success and one a failure. Describe the incidents in terms of the types of conflicts discussed in the chapter and the approaches to negotiation that were used. Were the requirements of project negotiation followed? Would the points of principled negotiation have helped?

6.11 INCIDENTS FOR DISCUSSION

Pritchard Soap Co.

Sam Calderon is manager of a project that will completely alter the method of adding perfume to Pritchard Soap's "Queen Elizabeth" gift soap line. The new process will greatly extend the number of available scents and should result in a significant increase in sales. The project had been proceeding reasonably well, but fell several weeks behind when the perfume supplier, the Stephen Marcus Parfumissary, was unable to meet its delivery deadline because of a wildcat strike.

Under normal circumstances this would not have caused problems, but the project had been subject to a particularly long evaluation study and now was in danger of not being ready for the Christmas season. The major scheduling problem concerned the toxicity lab. Mike Lee, lab manager, had been most cooperative in scheduling the Queen Elizabeth perfumes for toxicity testing. He had gone out of his way to rearrange his own schedules to accommodate Calderon's project. Because of the strike at Marcus, however, Calderon cannot have the perfumes ready for test as scheduled, and the new test date Lee has given him will not allow him to make the new line available by Christmas. Calderon suspects that the project might not have been approved if senior management had known that they would miss this year's Christmas season.

Question: What should Sam Calderon do?

Sutton Electronics

Harold Frank was still basking in the glory of his installation as a new project manager for Sutton Electronics Corp., manufacturer of fire alarm systems for motels, offices, and other large-scale installations. Frank's first project involved the development of an alarm system based on sophisticated circuitry that would detect and identify a large number of dangerous gases as well as smoke and very high temperatures. The device was the brainchild of Ira Magoo, Vice-President of Research and the technical wizard responsible for many of Sutton's most successful products.

It was unusual for so young and relatively inexperienced an employee as Frank to be given control of such a potentially important project, but he had shown skill in handling several complex, though routine, jobs. In addition, he had the necessary scientific background to allow him to understand the nature of Magoo's proposed gas detection system.

Four weeks into the project, Frank was getting quite worried. He had tried to set up an organizational and basic planning meeting several times. No matter when he scheduled the meeting, the manager of the marketing department, Jake Benken, was unable to attend. Finally, Frank agreed that marketing could be represented by young Bill Powell, a Benken protégé who had just graduated from college and joined Sutton Electronics. Frank was doubtful that Powell could contribute much to the project.

Frank's worry increased when Powell missed the first planning meeting completely and did not appear at the second meeting until it was almost over. Powell seemed apologetic and indicated that departmental crises had kept him away from both meetings. The project was now seven weeks old and Frank was almost five weeks late with the master plan. He was thinking about asking Ira Magoo what to do.

Question: Do you think that Frank should involve Magoo at this point? If so, what outcome would you expect? If not, what should he do?

6.12 BIBLIOGRAPHY

1. Adams, J. R., and S. E. Barndt. "Behavorial Implications of the Project Life Cycle." In *Project Management Handbook,* D. I. Cleland and W. R. King, eds. Van Nostrand Reinhold. New York, 1983.
2. Cohen, H. *You Can Negotiate Anything.* Lyle Stuart Inc., 1980.
3. Fast, J. *Body Language.* Pocket Books, 1971.
4. Fisher, R., and W. Ury, *Getting to Yes.* Penguin Books, 1983.
5. Hajek, V. G. *Management of Engineering Projects.* McGraw Hill, New York, 1977.
6. Ilich, J. *The Art and Skill of Successful Negotiation.* Prentice-Hall, 1973.
7. Ilich, J. *Power Negotiating.* Addison-Wesley, Reading, MA, 1980.
8. Jandt, F. E. *Win–Win Negotiating.* Wiley, New York, 1985.
9. Kuhn, R. L. *Deal Maker.* Wiley, New York, 1988.
10. Nierenberg, G. I. *Fundamentals of Negotiating.* Hawthorn Books, 1973.
11. Nierenberg, G. I., and H. H. Calero, *How to Read a Person Like a Book.* Cornerstone Library, 1971.
12. Nierenberg, G. I., and H. H. Calero, *Meta-talk.* Cornerstone Library, 1973.
13. Raiffa, H. *The Art and Science of Negotiation.* Belknap/Harvard Press, 1982.
14. *Roget's International Thesaurus.* Thos. Y. Crowell, 1946.
15. Steer, R. M. *Introduction to Organizational Behavior,* 3rd ed. Scott, Foresman, 1988.
16. Thamhain, H. J., and D. L. Wilemon. "Conflict Management in Project Life Cycles." *Sloan Management Review,* Vol. 26, No. 3, Summer 1975.
17. Thamhain, H. J., and D. L. Wilemon. "Diagnosing Conflict Determinants in Project Management." *IEEE Transactions on Engineering Management,* February 1975.
18. Thomas, K. W. "Conflict and Conflict Management." In M.D. Dunnette, ed., *Handbook of Industrial and Organizational Psychology.* Rand McNally, 1976.
19. U.S. Bureau of the Census. *Statistical Abstract of the United States: 1987.* Washington, DC, 1986.
20. Wall, J. A., Jr. *Negotiation: Theory and Practice.* Scott, Foresman, 1985.

6.13 READING

This article investigates the use of a number of standard methods for negotiating and handling conflicts. The authors identify effective and ineffective methods ranging from withdrawal to forcing. Each method is then illustrated with a number of examples. Finally, the most effective method, confrontation-problem solving, is described in terms of its many characteristics.

Methods of Resolving Interpersonal Conflict

Ronald J. Burke

The management of conflict in creative and useful ways, rather than its containment or abolition, has been proposed by many writers. Various strategies for dealing with conflict at different levels and for managing disagreements have also been proposed. Most of these methods have not been experimentally evaluated. Given the central and inevitable role of conflict in human affairs, a high priority of importance is to be placed on learning the most effective way to resolve it.

PURPOSE OF THIS STUDY

In a previous investigation, Burke (1969a) collected questionnaire data from 74 managers, in which they described the way they and their superiors dealt with conflict between them. It was possible to relate five different methods of conflict resolution originally proposed by Blake and Mouton (1964)—Withdrawing, Smoothing, Compromising, Forcing, and Confrontation or Problem Solving—to two major areas of the superior-subordinate relationship. These were (1) constructive use of differences and disagreements, and (2) several aspects of the superior-subordinate relationship in planning job targets and evaluating accomplishments.

In general, the results showed that Withdrawing and Forcing behaviors were consistently negatively related to these two areas. Compromising was not related to these two areas. Use of Smoothing was inconsistently related, sometimes positive and sometimes negative. Only Confrontation or Problem Solving was always related positively to both. That is, use of Confrontation was associated with constructive use of differences and high scores on various measures of the superior-subordinate relationship.

This study has the dual purpose of attempting to specify more precisely the characteristics of the Confrontation or Problem Solving method of conflict resolution, and replicating the earlier study (Burke, 1969a) using different methodology.

METHOD

Subjects: The respondents were managers from various organizations who were enrolled in a university course emphasizing behavioral science concepts relevant to the functions of management. Their organizational experience ranged from one year to over thirty years.

©1969 International Personnel Management Association. Reprinted from *Personnel Administration*, July-August 1969, by permission.

Procedure: Each respondent was asked to describe a time when he felt particularly GOOD (or BAD) about the way in which an interpersonal conflict was resolved. The specific instructions stated:

"Think of a time when you felt especially GOOD (or BAD) about the way an interpersonal conflict or disagreement (e.g., boss-subordinate, peer-peer, etc.) in which you were involved was resolved. It may have been on your present job, or any other job, or away from the work situation.

"Now describe it in enough detail so a reader would understand the way the conflict or differences were handled."

This statement appeared at the top of a blank sheet of paper.

Approximately half the respondents were first to describe the instance when they felt particularly good, followed by the instance when they felt particularly bad. The remaining respondents described the instances in the reverse order. No apparent effects were observed from the change in order, so the data from both groups will be considered together in this report.

RESULTS

Fifty-three descriptions of effective resolution of conflict (felt especially GOOD) and 53 descriptions of ineffective resolutions of conflict (felt especially BAD) were obtained. These were provided by 57 different individuals. Some individuals provided only one example. The response rate was about 70 percent of the total available population.

The written descriptions were then coded into one of the five methods of conflict resolution proposed by Blake and Mouton, (1964) (1) *Withdrawing*—easier to refrain than to retreat from an argument; silence is golden. "See no evil, hear no evil, speak no evil". (2) *Smoothing*—play down the differences and emphasize common interests; issues that might cause divisions or hurt feelings are not discussed. (3) *Compromising*—splitting the difference, bargaining, search for an

intermediate position. Better half a loaf than none at all; no one loses but no one wins. (4) *Forcing*—a win–lose situation; participants are antagonists, competitors, not collaborators. Fixed positions, polarization. Creates a victor and a vanquished. (5) *Confrontation or Problem-Solving*—open exchange of information about the conflict or problem as each sees it, and a working through of their differences to reach a solution that is optimal to both. Both can win.

Table 1 presents the method of conflict resolution associated with effective resolution (left half of Table 1) and ineffective resolution (right half of Table 1). Considering the left half of the table, Confrontation or Problem Solving was the most common method for effective resolution (58.5%), followed by Forcing (24.5%), and Compromise (11.3%). The prominence of Confrontation as an effective method is consistent with the earlier study (Burke, 1969a) but the value for Forcing was higher than expected. When these 13 cases are considered as a group, 11 of them are similar in that the party providing the written description benefited as a result of the Forcing. That is, Forc-

Table 1

Methods Associated with Effective and Ineffective Conflict Resolution

	Effective Resolution (N=53)		Ineffective Resolution (N=53)	
	N	%	N	%
Withdrawal	0	0.0*	5	9.4*
Smoothing	0	0.0	1	1.9
Compromise	6	11.3	3	5.7
Forcing	13	24.5*	42	79.2*
Confrontation- Problem Solving	31	58.5*	0	0.0*
Other (Still unresolved; Unable to determine how resolved; Irrelevant to assignment; etc.)	3	5.7	2	3.8

*Percentage difference between groups is significant at the 0.5 level of confidence.

ing was perceived as an effective method of resolving conflict by the victor, but not by the vanquished.

Moving to the right half of Table 1, Forcing was the most commonly used method for ineffective resolution, followed in second place by Withdrawal with only 9.4 percent. The vast majority of individuals providing written descriptions of Forcing methods were victims or "losers" as a result of Forcing behavior.

In summary, the major differences in methods of conflict resolution found to distinguish effective versus ineffective examples were: (1) significantly greater use of Confrontation or Problem Solving in the effective examples (58.5% vs. 0.0%); (2) significantly less use of Forcing in the effective examples (24.5% vs. 79.2%); and, (3) significantly less use of Withdrawing in the effective examples (0.0% vs. 9.4%).

When Forcing was seen to be effective, the authors of the examples were "winners" of a win–lose conflict; when Forcing was seen to be ineffective, the authors of the examples were "losers" of a win–lose conflict. Whether the resolution of conflict via Forcing would actually be perceived to be effective by members of the organization outside the conflict (i.e., objectively seen as effective), as it was perceived to be effective by the "winners," remains to be determined by future research.

EFFECTIVE CONFLICT RESOLUTION

A few of the examples of effective conflict resolution are provided to highlight specific features of Confrontation or Problem Solving. These were taken verbatim from the written descriptions.

1. *This example highlights the presentation of a problem of mutual interest—meeting deadlines more often at the earliest opportunity (when the problem is observed). Superior is open-minded and asking for help.*

"I once was given the responsibility for managing a small group of technicians engaged in turning out critical path schedules. I spent some time trying to get organized and involved with the group, but I sensed a hostile atmosphere, accompanied by offhand sarcastic remarks. At the end of the day very little work had been accomplished.

"The next day when I came in, I called the group together and told them that we were falling behind, and asked them to help me find a solution. After the initial distrust had been dissipated, the group produced some good ideas on work re-allocation, office arrangement, priorities and techniques. I told the group that all of their agreed upon suggestions would be implemented at once, and their reply was that backlog would be cleared in three days and would not build up again.

"Within three days the backlog was gone, the group worked together better, and for the six months I was in charge, schedules were always ready before they were required."

2. *This example highlights emphasis on facts in determining the best resolution of conflict. Both had strong convictions but one willingly moved to the other's position when facts indicated that this position was best.*

"The project engineer and I disagreed about the method of estimating the cost of alternative schemes in a highway interchange. Neither of use could agree on the other's method. Eventually I was able to satisfy him using algebra. We were both happy with the result."

3. *Like Example 2, this one highlights an emphasis on facts and the conviction that by digging and digging, the truth will be discovered. Although the superior had a vested interest in the "old" system (a product of his thinking), the discussion was never personalized. That is, it did not involve "me" versus "you", but rather a comparison of two systems, two concepts or two ideas.*

"About a year ago I developed a new system for processing the accounting of the inventory of obsolete material on hand in our plant. It was my estimation that it would prove to be an easier system to operate and control and would also involve a considerable monetary saving for the company.

"When I approached my boss with the system, he immediately turned it down as he had developed the present system and was sure it was the best possible system. As I was sure my new system was superior to the present one, I then convinced him to join me in analyzing a comparison of the two systems, pointing out the strengths and weaknesses of the two. After a period of evaluation involving many differences of opinion, we were able to resolve that my system had definite merit and should be brought into operation."

4. *This example highlights the fact that through problem solving both parties can benefit. Instead of compromising, the issues are discussed until a solution completely satisfactory to both is found. Often this is superior to the ones initially favored by the separate parties.*

"In the —— Board of Education, there were eight inspectors of Public Schools and four superintendents. Last February the inspectors were given the assignment of developing an in-service plan for the training of teachers for the school year 1968–69. The inspectors gave the assignment to a group of three of their number who were to bring a report to the next inspectors' meeting. I was not a member of the in-service committee but in conversations with the committee members I discovered that they contemplated having an in-service program for two teachers from each school (there are about 85 schools) once a month for the entire year in mathematics. I felt that this would be a very thin coverage of our 2,000 or so teachers.

"Consequently I worked on a plan whereby utilizing two Thursday mornings a month and the specialized teaching help available in ——, every teacher would have the opportunity to become involved in an in-service training session in a subject of his or her choice once during the year. At the inspectors' meeting the sub-committee presented its report and after some procedural wrangling I was permitted to present my plan. The two were diametrically opposed and it looked as if my plan would be voted down except the chairman suggested that both plans be presented to the superintendents.

"At the meeting of the superintendents, the sub-committee made its report and I presented my plan. As the meeting progressed there was some give and take and instead of one or the other being discarded both plans were adopted. For this school year mathematics is stressed for the first, eight Thursday mornings (their plan in a rather concentrated form) then for the next eight months on the second and fourth Thursday my plan is used. We came out of this meeting with a combination of the two plans which was better than either one individually."

INEFFECTIVE CONFLICT RESOLUTION

Examples 5, 6 and 7 illustrate Forcing methods of conflict resolution. A win–lose situation is set up, and usually the superior wins. The individual with the greater power triumphs (a personalized disagreement) rather than the one whose position is supported by the most factual evidence.

5. "In a previous job, I worked for a major management consulting group as a consultant. One assignment, lasting four months, was to use a simulation technique to evaluate the most preferable investment decision using defined quantitative criteria. At the end of the job two alternatives were shown to be marginally better than the other. However, later sensitivity tests also showed that the analytical technique could not rate one to be substantially better than the other.

"Therefore, I wrote a 'technically honest' report stating that our analysis could not provide the one best alternative. My manager, feeling that we were hired to recommend a 'one best' alternative, wanted to cover up the limitations of our methodology.

"We disagreed and I was overruled. The manager wrote a 'technically dishonest' version of the report and the devised report was sent to the client indicating the 'one best' alternative."

6. "Recently in my firm, management had sprung a secrecy agreement contract upon all of the technical people. No word of introduction or explanation was given. It was simply handed out and we were asked to sign it. Most of us found objection in several clauses in the agreement. However, management officials stated that the agree-

ment would probably not stand up in a court of law. They further stated that it was something that was sent up from the U.S. and was not their idea. The employees continued to show reluctance.

"The vice-president called on everyone individually and stated that there would be no room for advancement for anyone who did not sign the contract. As a result everyone signed."

7. "I was assigned a project by my boss to determine the optimum way, using predetermined times, to lay out an assembly line. It would have to provide optimum efficiency with the following variables: (a) different hourly production rates (e.g., 100/hr. Mon., 200/hr. Tues.) which would mean different numbers of operators on the line; (b) different models of the product (electric motors). The group was on group incentive.

"After much research and discussion, the system was installed utilizing the floating system of assembly (operators could move from station to station in order to keep out of the bottleneck operation). This system was working out well. However, at this time I was informed by my boss that he and the foreman of the area decided that they wished to use the 'paced' system of assembly. This would mean the conveyor belt would be run at set speeds and that the stripes would be printed on the belt indicating that one device would have to be placed on each mark and operators would not float.

"I was dead against this since I had considered it and rejected it in favor of the implemented method. I was, however, given the order to use their proposed system *or else*. There was *no* opportunity for discussion or justification of the method."

8. *This example is a classic description of Withdrawal as a mode of Conflict resolution. Clearly the problem is not resolved.*

"On the successful completion of a project which involved considerable time and effort, I was praised and thanked for a job well done by my immediate supervisor and his supervisor, the vice president in charge of manufacturing. They promised me that on my next salary review I would receive a substantial increase.

"The next salary review came up and my im-

mediate supervisor submitted an amount that he and I felt was a good increase. The amount I received was one-third of this figure. I felt insulted, cheated, and hurt that the company considered I was worth this 'token' amount.

"I had a personal interview with the vice president where I argued that I felt I should receive more. He agreed in sort of an offhanded way—he felt the whole salary schedule should be reviewed and that my area of responsibility should be increased. He said the company wants people to 'prove themselves' before they give them increases; and he suggested a salary review. I felt I had just done this in my last project—I felt I was being put off, but agreed to the salary review.

"One month passed and nothing happened. I became frustrated—I purposely slowed down the amount of work I turned out.

"Another month passed and still no action. I became disillusioned with the company and resolved at this point to look for another position. Several months later with still no action, I resigned and accepted another position."

INABILITY TO RESOLVE CONFLICT

These descriptions of ineffective resolution of conflict indicate that an impressive number of respondents included termination or change of employment of one member in the situation (19 of 53, 26%). These cases tended to be of two types.

The first is represented by Example 8. Here an employee decides to quit because he felt the problem was not resolved in a satisfactory manner. Forcing is likely to be associated with instances of voluntary termination.

The second centered around an inability to resolve the conflict. Then the "problem employee" (a visible symptom of the conflict) was dismissed.

9. *The following example illustrates this:*

"This concerned a young girl about 18 years old who was a typist in our office. This girl lacked a little maturity, but was not really all that bad. She was tuned to all the latest fashions in both dress and manners.

"I felt and still feel that this girl was a potentially good employee. But it was decided that she should be let go. The argument used was that she was not a good worker and lacked the proper attitude for office work. Rather than spend a little time and effort to understand the girl and perhaps develop her into a good employee, the easy way was taken and the girl was fired."

There were two other clear cases of "effective" conflict resolution resulting in voluntary employee terminations. In both instances a Forcing mode was employed and the "loser" resigned from the organization soon after. Our finding is that these were given as examples of effective conflict resolution by the "winner". In another effective example of Forcing, the "loser" was dismissed.

CONCLUSIONS

The results of this investigation are consistent with an earlier study (Burke, 1969a), and the data of Lawrence and Lorsch (1967a, 1967b) in showing the value of Confrontation and Problem Solving as methods of conflict resolution. About 60 percent of the examples of effective conflict resolution involved use of this method, while no examples of ineffective conflict resolution did. The poorest method of conflict resolution was Forcing. This method accounted for 80 percent of the examples of ineffective conflict resolution and only 24 percent of the examples of effective conflict resolution. The latter conclusion is somewhat at odds with Lawrence and Lorsch's findings that Forcing was an effective backup method to Confrontation, from an organizational effectiveness standpoint. In fact, the earlier study (Burke, 1969a) found that the use of these methods tended to be negatively correlated. Managers high in use of one of them tended to be low in use of the other.

CHARACTERISTICS OF PROBLEM SOLVING

Let us now consider more specific features of Confrontation, the most effective method of resolving interpersonal conflict. Insights from the present investigation and the writings of others (e.g., Blake, Shepard and Mouton, 1964; Maier, 1963; Maier and Hoffman, 1965) becomes relevant. The following then are characteristics of Confrontation or Problem Solving as a method of managing conflict:

(1) Both people have a vested interest in the outcome. (Examples 1, 2, 3 and 4).

(2) There is a belief on the part of the people involved that they have the potential to resolve the conflict and to achieve a better solution through collaboration.

(3) There is a recognition that the conflict or the problem is mainly in the relationship between the individuals and not in each person separately. If the conflict is in the relationship, it must be defined by those who have the relationship. In addition, if solutions are to be developed, the solutions have to be generated by those who share the responsibility for assuring that the solution will work and for making the relationship last.

(4) The goal is to solve the problem, not to accommodate different points of view. This process identifies the causes of reservation, doubt, and misunderstanding between the people confronted with conflict and disagreement. Alternative ways of approaching conflict resolution are explored and tested (Examples 2 and 3).

(5) The people involved are problem-minded instead of solution-minded; "fluid" instead of "fixed" positions. Both parties jointly search out the issues that separate them. Through joint effort, the problems that demand solutions are identified, and later solved.

(6) There is a realization that both aspects of a controversy have potential strengths and potential weaknesses. Rarely is one position completely right and the other completely wrong. (Example 4).

(7) There is an effort to understand the conflict or problem from the other person's point of view, and from the standpoint of the "real" or legitimate needs that must be recognized and met before problem solving can occur. Full acceptance of the other is essential.

(8) The importance of looking at the conflict objectively rather than in a personalized sort of way is recognized. (Example 3).

(9) An examination of one's own attitudes (hostilities, antagonisms) is needed before interpersonal contact on a less effective basis has a chance to occur.

(10) An understanding of the less effective methods of conflict resolution (e.g., win–lose, bargaining, etc.) is essential.

(11) One needs to prevent "face-saving" situations. Allow people to "give" so that a change in one's viewpoint does not suggest weakness or capitulation.

(12) There is need to minimize effects of status differences, defensiveness, and other barriers which prevent people from working together effectively.

(13) It is important to be aware of the limitations of arguing or presenting evidence in favor of your own position while downgrading the opponent's position. This behavior often stimulates the opponent to find even greater support for his position (increased polarization). In addition, it leads to selective listening for weakness in opponent's position rather than listening to understand his position.

ATTITUDE, SKILL, AND CREATIVITY

Two related themes run through these characteristics, one dealing with attitudes, and the other with skills (interpersonal, problem solving) of the individuals involved. As the research of Maier and his associates has shown, differences and disagreements need not lead to dissatisfaction and unpleasant experiences but rather can lead to innovation and creativity. One of the critical variables was found to be leader's attitudes toward disagreement. The person with different ideas, especially if he is a subordinate, can be seen as a problem employee and troublemaker or he can be seen as an idea man and innovator, depending on the leader's attitude. There are some people that go through

life attempting to sell their ideas, to get others to do things they do not want to do. They set up a series of win–lose situations, and attempt to emerge victorious. Many of these people are able to accomplish their ends. There are others who are more concerned with the quality and effectiveness of their operations, and who, with creative solutions to problems, are genuinely openminded and able and willing to learn from others (and to teach others), in a collaborative relationship.

The interpersonal skills are related to the development of a "helping relationship" and include among others, mutual trust and respect, candid communication, and awareness of the needs of the others. The problem solving skills center around locating and stating the problem, seeking alternatives, exploring and testing alternatives, and selecting the best alternative. Knowledge and insight gained through experience with the benefits of problem solving and the dysfunctional effects of other strategies would be valuable in developing interpersonal skills.

FURTHER RESEARCH NEEDED

Two additional areas need immediate research consideration. The first needs to explore the notions of conflict resolution from the organizational as well as the individual viewpoint. Lawrence and Lorsch report that Forcing was an effective back-up mode to Confrontation from the organization's standpoint, because at least things were being done. Our data in two separate investigations indicate that this mode of conflict resolution is very unsatisfactory from the standpoint of the one forced, the "loser," and may also have dysfunctional consequences.

The second research area concerns the application of these principles of effective conflict resolution (Confrontation and Problem Solving, with their more specific attitudinal and skill components) in an attempt to arrive at more constructive use of disagreement. Preliminary results from an experiment simulating conflict situations using role playing suggest that knowledge of these principles and some limited practice in their use increases one's ability to use differences constructively in obtaining a quality solution, and decreases the tendency to engage in "limited war" (Burke, 1969b).

REFERENCES

Blake, R. R., and Mouton, J. S., *The Managerial Grid,* Houston: Gulf Publishing Company, 1964.

Blake, R. R.; Shepard, H. A., and Mouton, J. S., *Managing Intergroup Conflict in Industry,* Houston: Gulf Publishing Company, 1964.

Boulding, K., A pure theory of conflict applied to organization—In R. I. Kahn and E. Boulding (Eds.), *Power and Conflict in Organizations,* New York: Basic Books, Inc., 1964, pp. 136–145.

Burke, R. J., Methods of managing superior-subordinate conflict: Their effectiveness and consequences, Unpublished manuscript, 1969a.

Burke, R. J., Effects of limited training on conflict resolution effectiveness, Unpublished manuscript, 1969b.

Kata, D., Approaches to managing conflict—In R. L. Kahn and E. Boulding (Eds.), *Power and Conflict in Organizations,* New York: Basic Books, Inc., 1964, pp. 105–114.

Lawrence, P. R., and Lorsch, J. W., Differentiation and Integration in Complex Organizations, *Administrative Science Quarterly,* 1967a, 12, 1–47.

Lawrence, P. R., and Lorsch, J. W., *Organization and Environment,* Boston: Division of Research, Harvard Business School, Harvard University, 1967b.

Maier, N. R. F., *Problem-Solving Discussions and Conferences,* New York: McGraw-Hill, 1963.

Maier, N. R. F., and Hoffman, L. R., Acceptance and quality of solutions as related to leaders' attitudes toward disagreement in group problem-solving, *Journal of Applied Behavioral Science,* 1965, 1, 373–386.

McGregor, D., *The Professional Manager,* New York: McGraw-Hill, 1967.

Shepard, H. A., Responses to situations of competition and conflict—In R. L. Kahn and E. Boulding (Eds.), *Power and Conflict in Organizations,* New York: Basic Books, Inc., 1964, pp. 127–135.

Part II
Project Implementation

At this point in the book we turn to a detailed description of project implementation. Chapter 7 initiates our discussion with a description of budgeting as a logical extension of the planning techniques from Chapter 5. Project scheduling, considered by some to be the meat of project management, and certainly the most written-about area of the field, is addressed in Chapter 8. Such well-known techniques as PERT and Gantt charts are described with illustrations. Chapter 9 then covers the topic of resource allocation, both within a single project and among multiple projects.

Chapter 10 is devoted to the linkage between planning and control: monitoring and information systems. This chapter includes a brief description of many of the commonly used computerized Project Management Information Systems (PMIS).

Chapter 11 concludes this part of the text with a full description and discussion of the control processes for project management. Standards for comparison, common control techniques, and the basic role of control are covered here.

CHAPTER 7
Budgeting

In Chapter 5 we reviewed the planning process, gave some guidelines for designing the project plan, and then discussed the art of negotiation to achieve that plan in Chapter 6. We are now ready to begin implementation. First priority is, of course, obtaining resources with which to do the work. Senior management approval of the project budget does exactly that. A budget is a plan for allocating resources. Thus, the act of budgeting is the allocation of scarce resources to the various endeavors of an organization. The outcomes of the allocation process often do not satisfy managers of the organization who must live and work under budget constraints. It is, however, precisely the pattern of constraints in a budget that embodies organizational policy. The degree to which the different activities of an organization are fully supported by an allocation of resources is one measure of the importance placed on the outcome of the activity. Most of the senior managers we know try hard to be evenhanded in the budgetary process, funding each planned activity at the "right" level—neither overfunding, which produces waste and encourages slack management, nor underfunding, which inhibits accomplishment and frustrates the committed.

The budget is not simply one facet of a plan, nor is it merely an expression of organizational policy; it is also a control mechanism. The budget serves as a standard for comparison, a baseline from which to measure the difference between the actual and planned uses of resources. As the manager directs the deployment of resources to accomplish some desired objective, resource usage should be monitored carefully. This allows deviations from planned usage to be checked against the progress of the project, and exception reports can be generated if resource expenditures are not consistent with accomplishments. Indeed, the pattern of deviations (variances) can be examined to see if it is possible, or reasonable, to forecast significant departures from budget. With sufficient warning, it is sometimes possible to implement corrective actions. In any event, such forecasting helps to decrease the number of undesirable surprises for senior management.

Budgets play an important role in the entire process of management. It is clear that budgeting procedures must associate resource use with the achievement of organizational goals or the planning/control process becomes useless. If budgets are not tied to achievement, management may ignore situations where funds are being spent far in advance of accomplishment but are within budget when viewed by time period. Similarly, management may misinterpret the true state of affairs when the budget is overspent for a given time period but outlays are appropriate for the level of task completion. Data must be collected and reported in a timely manner, or the value of the budget in identifying and reporting current problems or anticipating upcoming problems will be lost. The reporting process must be carefully designed and controlled. It is of no value if the data are sent to the wrong person or the reports take an inordinately long time to be processed through the system. For example, one manager of a large computer company complained that, based on third-quarter reports, he was instructed to act so as to alter the fourth-quarter results. However, he did not receive the instructions until the first quarter of the following year.

In Chapter 5 we described a planning process that integrated the planning done at different levels of the project. At the top level is the overall project plan, which is then divided and divided again and, perhaps, still again into a "nest" of plans. Project plans were shown to be the verbal equivalents of the WBS. If we cost the WBS, step by step, we develop a project budget. If we cost project plans, we achieve exactly the same end. Viewed in this way, *the budget is simply the project plan in another form.*

Let us now consider some of the various budgeting methods used in organizations. These are described in general first, then with respect to projects. We also address some problems of cost estimation, with attention to the details and pitfalls. We consider some of the special demands and concerns with budgeting for projects. Finally, we present a method for improving one's skills at budget estimation, or estimation and forecasting of any kind.

7.1 BUDGETING METHODS

To prepare a budget, the manager must adopt a method for gathering data as well as a method for presenting it. In this section, we examine ways to do both and briefly indicate some of the implications of these methods.

Before discussing such issues, however, it is helpful to know that developing project budgets is much more difficult than developing budgets for more permanent organizational activities. The influence of history is strong in the budget of an ongoing activity and many entries may ultimately become just "last year's figure plus X percent," where X is any number the budgeter feels "can be lived with," and is probably acceptable to the person or group who approves the budgets. No single item in the budget for an ongoing activity is apt to be crucial, because over the course of years the budget has gained sufficient slack that internal adjustments will probably take care of minor shortages in the key accounts.

But the project budgeter cannot depend on tradition. At project inception, there are no past budgets to use as a base. At times, the budgeter may have budgets and audit reports for similar projects to serve as guides, but these are rough guides at best. Tradition, however, has another impact on budgeting, this time a helpful one. In the special case of R & D projects, it has been found [10] that project budgets are stable over time when measured as a percent of the total allocation to R & D from the parent firm, though within the project the budget may be reallocated among activities. There is no reason to believe that the situation is different for other kinds of projects, and we have some evidence that shows stability similar to R & D projects.

Even if the project has survived its first year, the extensive planning and time-phasing of the project means that budgets for the entire life must often be set at the beginning. As if that were not enough, the degree of executive oversight and review is usually much higher for projects than for ongoing operations, so the budgeter must expect to defend any and all budget entries.

Tradition has still another impact on project budgeting. Every organization has its idiosyncrasies. One firm charges the project's R & D budget with the cost of training sales representatives on the technical aspects of a new product. Another adopts special property accounting practices for contracts with the government. Unless the PM understands the organizational accounting system, there is no way to exercise budgetary control over the project. The methods for project budgeting described below are intended to avoid these problems as much as possible, but complete avoidance is out of the question. Further, it is not politically feasible for the PM to plead a special case with the accountants, who have their own problems. The PM simply must be familiar with the organization's accounting system!

Another aspect of preparing budgets is especially important for project budgeting. Every expenditure (or receipt) must be identified with a specific project task (and with its associated milestone, as we will see in the next chapter). Referring back to Figure 5-6, we see that each element in the WBS has a unique account number to which charges are accrued as work is done. These identifiers are needed for the PM to exercise budgetary control.

With these things in mind, the issue of how to gather input data for the budget becomes a matter of some concern. There are two fundamentally different strategies for data gathering, top-down and bottom-up.

Top-down Budgeting

This strategy is based on collecting the judgments and experiences of top and middle managers, and available past data concerning similar activities. These managers estimate overall project cost as well as the costs of the major sub-projects that comprise it. These cost estimates are then given to lower-level managers, who are expected to continue the breakdown into budget estimates for the specific work packages that comprise the subprojects. This process continues to the lowest level.

The process parallels the hierarchical planning process described in the last chapter. The budget, like the project, is broken down into successively finer detail, starting from the top, or most aggregated, level. It is presumed that lower-level managers will argue for more funds if the budget allocation they have been granted is, in their judgment, insufficient for the tasks assigned. However, this presumption is often incorrect. Instead of reasoned debate, argument sometimes ensues, or simply sullen silence. When senior managers insist on maintaining their budgetary positions—based on "considerable past experience"—junior managers feel forced to accept what they perceive to be insufficient allocations to achieve the objectives to which they must commit.

Discussions between the authors and a large number of managers support the contention that lower-level managers often treat the entire budgeting process as if it were a zero-sum game, a game in which any individual's gain is another individual's loss. Competition among junior managers is often quite intense.

The advantage of this top-down process is that aggregate budgets can often be developed quite accurately, though a few individual elements may be significantly in error. Not only are budgets stable as a percent of total allocation, the statistical distribution of the budgets is also stable, making for high predictability [10]. Another advantage of the top-down process is that small yet costly tasks need not be individually identified, nor need it be feared that some small but important aspect has been overlooked. The experience and judgment of the executive is presumed automatically to factor all such elements into the overall estimate.

Bottom-up Budgeting

In this method, elemental tasks, their schedules, and their individual budgets are constructed through the work breakdown structure. The people doing the work are consulted regarding times and budgets for the tasks to ensure the best level of accuracy. Initially, estimates are made in terms of resources, such as man-hours and materials. These are later converted to dollar equivalents. Standard analytic tools such as learning curve analysis (discussed in the next section) and work sampling are employed where appropriate to improve the estimates. Differences of opinion are resolved by the usual discussions between senior and junior managers. If necessary, the project manager and the functional manager(s) may enter the discussion in order to ensure the accuracy of the estimates. The resulting task budgets are aggregated to give the total direct costs of the project. The PM adds such indirect costs as general and administrative (G & A), a project reserve for contingencies, and a profit figure to arrive at the final project budget.

Bottom-up budgets should be, and usually are, more accurate in the detailed tasks, but it is critical that all elements be included. It is far more difficult to develop a complete list of tasks when constructing that list from the bottom up than from the top down. Just as the top-down method may lead to budgetary game playing, the bottom-up process has its unique managerial budget games.

For example, individuals overstate their resource needs because they suspect that higher management will probably cut all budgets by some percentage. Their suspicion is, of course, quite justified, as Gagnon [13, 14] and others have shown. Managers who are particularly persuasive sometimes win, but those who are consistently honest and have high credibility win more often.

The advantages of the bottom-up process are those generally associated with participative management. Individuals closer to the work are apt to have a more accurate idea of resource requirements than their superiors or others not personally involved. In addition, the direct involvement of low-level managers in budget preparation increases the likelihood that they will accept the result with a minimum of grumbling. Involvement also is a good managerial training technique, giving junior managers valuable experience in budget preparation as well as the knowledge of the operations required to generate a budget.

While top-down budgeting is common, true bottom-up budgets are rare. Senior managers see the bottom-up process as risky. They tend not to be particularly trusting of ambitious subordinates who may overstate resource requirements in an attempt to ensure success and build empires. Besides, as senior managers note with some justification, the budget is the most important tool for control of the organization. They are understandably reluctant to hand over that control to subordinates whose experience and motives are questionable. This attitude is carried to an extreme in one large corporation that conducts several dozen projects simultaneously, each of which may last 5 to 8 years and cost in excess of $1 million. Project managers do not participate in the budgeting process in this company, nor do they have access to project budgets during their tenure as PMs. (At the time of writing, the firm has just decided to give PMs access to project budgets but they are still not allowed to participate in the budgetary process.)

The Budget Request Process

For the most part, a sensible mixture of top-down and bottom-up budgeting is used. The budget process often begins with an invitation from top management for each division to submit a *budget request* for the coming year. Division heads pass the invitation along to departments, sections, and subsections, each of which presumably collects requests from below, aggregates them, and passes the result back up the organizational ladder.

This sounds like bottom-up budgeting, but there is an important difference between this procedure and a true bottom-up system. Along with the formal invitation for submission of a budget request, in the *mixed* system another message is passed down—a much less formal message that carries the following kinds of information: the percent by which the wage bill of the organization will be allowed to be increased, organizational policy on adding to the work force, the general attitude toward capital expenditures, knowledge about which projects and activities are considered to be high priority and which are not, and a number of other matters that, in effect, prescribe a set of limits on lower-level managers. As the budget requests are passed back up the organization, they are carefully inspected for conformity to guidelines. If they do not conform, they are "adjusted," often with little or no consultation with the originating units.

The less autocratic the organization (and the less pressured it is by current financial exigencies), the greater the probability that this process will allow dialogue and some compromise between managerial levels. But Gagnon's finding [13] still holds true, that the farther you move up the organizational chart away from immediate responsibility for doing the work, the easier, faster, and cheaper the job appears to that level of manager.

Even the most *participative* firms will not long tolerate lower-level managers who are not sensitive to messages relating to budget limitations. It makes little difference whether budget policy is passed down the system by means of formal, written policy statements or as a haphazard set of oral comments informally transmitted by some senior managers and practically neglected by others; the PM's budget request is expected to conform to policy. Ignorance of the policy is no excuse. Repeated failure to conform will be rewarded with a ticket to corporate Siberia. It is the budget originator's responsibility to find out about budget policy. Again we see the importance of political sensitivity. The PM's channels of communication must be sensitive enough to receive policy signals even in the event that a noncommunicative superior blocks those signals.

Activity vs. Task-Oriented Budgets

Thus far we have discussed one facet of an organization's philosophy of budgeting. Another facet has to do with the degree to which a budget is activity-oriented or task-oriented, a distinction we have mentioned before. The traditional organizational budget is activity-oriented. Individual expenses are classified and assigned to basic budget *lines* such as phone, materials, personnel-clerical, utilities, direct labor, etc. These expense lines are gathered into more inclusive categories, and are reported by organizational unit—for example, by section, department, and division. In other words, the budget can be overlaid on the organizational chart. Table 7-1 shows one page of a.typical monthly budget report for a real estate project. Table 7-2 shows a project budget divided by task and expected time of expenditure.

With the advent of project organization, it became necessary to organize the budget in ways that conformed more closely to the actual pattern of fiscal responsibility. Under traditional budgeting methods, the budget for a project could be split up among many different organizational units, which diffused control so widely that it was frequently nonexistent. It was often almost impossible to determine the actual size of major expenditure categories in a project's budget. In light of this problem, ways were sought to alter the budgeting process so that budgets could be associated directly with the projects that used them. This need gave rise to *program budgeting*.

Program budgeting is the generic name given to a budgeting system that aggregates income and expenditures across programs (projects). In most cases, aggregation by program is in addition to, not instead of, aggregation by organizational unit. The project has its own budget. In the case of pure project

Table 7-1 Typical Monthly Budget for a Real Estate Project (Page 1 of 6)

	Current			
	Actual	**Budget**	**Variance**	**Pct**
Corporate—Income Statement				
Revenue				
8430 Management fees				
8491 Prtnsp reimb—property mgmt	7,410.00	6,222.00	1,188.00	119.0
8492 Prtnsp reimb—owner acquisition	.00	3,750.00	3,750.00–	.0
8493 Prtnsp reimb—rehab	.00	.00	.00	.0
8494 Other income	.00	.00	.00	.0
8495 Reimbursements—other	.00	.00	.00	.0
Total revenue	7,410.00	9,972.00	2,562.00–	74.3
Operating expenses				
Payroll & P/R benefits				
8511 Salaries	29,425.75	34,583.00	5,157.25	85.0
8512 Payroll taxes	1,789.88	3,458.00	1,668.12	51.7
8513 Group ins & med reimb	1,407.45	1,040.00	387.45–	135.3
8515 Workmens compensation	43.04	43.00	.04–	100.0
8516 Staff apartments	.00	.00	.00	.0
8517 Bonus	.00	.00	.00	.0
Total payroll & P/R benefits	32,668.12	39,124.00	6,457.88	83.5
Travel & entertainment expenses				
8521 Travel	456.65	300.00	156.65–	152.2
8522 Promotion, entertainment & gift	69.52	500.0	430.48	13.9
8523 Auto	1,295.90	1,729.00	433.10	75.0
Total travel & entertainment exp	1,822.07	2,529.00	706.93	72.1
Professional fees				
8531 Legal fees	419.00	50.00	369.00–	838.
8532 Accounting fees	289.00	.00	289.00–	.0
8534 Temporary help	234.58	200.00	34.58–	117.2
8535 Commissions & consulting	4,398.50	2,532.00	1,866.50–	173.7
8536 Data processing services	61.46	125.00	63.54	49.1
Total professional fees	5,402.54	2,907.00	2,495.54–	185.8
Facility expense				
8541 Rent & parking	8,860.60	8,816.00	44.60–	100.5
8542 Telephone	1,306.26	800.00	506.26–	163.2
8543 Office supplies & expense	664.62	700.00	35.38	94.9
8544 Photocopy	.00	.00	.00	.0
8545 Postage	302.45	200.00	102.45–	151.2
8546 Repairs & maintenance	440.00	350.00	90.00–	125.7
8547 Insurance	67.50	.00	67.50–	.0

Table 7-2 Project Budget by Task and Month

Task	I	J	Estimate	Monthly Budget (£)							
				1	2	3	4	5	6	7	8
A	1	2	7000	5600	1400						
B	2	3	9000		3857	5143					
C	2	4	10000		3750	5000	1250				
D	2	5	6000		3600	2400					
E	3	7	12000				4800	4800	2400		
F	4	7	3000				3000				
G	5	6	9000			2571	5143	1286			
H	6	7	5000					3750	1250		
I	7	8	8000						2667	5333	
J	8	9	6000								6000
			75000	5600	12607	15114	14192	9836	6317	5333	6000

Source: Harrison, F. L., *Advanced Project Management,* Gower, 1983.

organizations, the budgets of all projects are aggregated to the highest organizational level. When functional organization is used for projects, the functional department's budget will be arranged in whatever manner is standard for the organization, but the income/expense associated with each project will be shown. The physical arrangement of such budget reports varies widely, but usually takes the form of a spread sheet with the standard budget categories listed down the left-hand side of the sheet and category totals disaggregated into "regular operations" and charges to the various projects. Project charges will be split out and spread across the page, with special columns devoted to each project. For example, the columns shown in Table 7-1 would be repeated for each project.

Two special forms of program budgeting have received considerable notoriety in the recent past. One is Planning-Programming-Budgeting Systems (PPBS) and the other is Zero-Base Budgeting (ZBB). While neither PPBS nor ZBB is now widely used, both have influenced managerial thinking. We know of no organizations that currently use ZBB and only a few that have permanently adopted PPBS, mainly social service agencies. But we do know of several corporations that occasionally require PPBS-type cost/benefit analyses. We even know a few senior managers who considered preparing zero-base budgets, but none have actually done so yet. Again, because these concepts have influenced managerial thinking in ways that are important to PMs, they are briefly discussed here.

Planning-Programming-Budgeting System(PPBS)

PPBS was developed in the late 1960s through then Secretary of Defense Robert McNamara's efforts to deal rationally with the budget of the Department of Defense. PPBS is basically a program budgeting (and planning) system oriented to identifying, planning, and controlling projects that will maximize achievement of the organization's long-run goals. The system focuses on funding those projects that will bring the greatest progress toward organizational goals for the least cost. The PPBS budgeting process entails four major steps:

1. The identification of goals and objectives for each major area of activity. This is the "planning" portion of PPBS.
2. Analysis of the programs proposed to attain organizational objectives; multiyear programs are considered as well as short-term programs. This step requires a good description of the nature of each project so that its intent and the character of its proposed contribution to the organization are understood. This is the "programming" part of PPBS.
3. Estimation of total costs for each project, including indirect costs. Time phasing of costs is detailed for multiyear projects.
4. Final analysis of the alternative projects and sets of projects in terms of expected costs, expected benefits, and expected project lives. Cost/benefit analyses are performed for each program so that the programs can be compared with one another in preparation for selecting a set of projects, i.e., a "portfolio," for funding.

PPBS was mandated by the Department of Defense for contractors, and at the time was deemed useful and effective. In recent years, however, it has fallen from grace and now enjoys only limited use by a few state and local government agencies and some social service organizations. Its precepts, however, have been embodied in the budgeting procedures of many organizations.

Zero-Base Budgeting (ZBB)

ZBB came into favor in the 1970s as a reaction to the automatic budget increases given year after year to government agencies. As a form of program budgeting, the goal of ZBB was to link the level of funding directly to the achievements associated with specific programs. As opposed to making incremental changes in programs and their accompanying budget allocations, the philosophy of ZBB is that the fundamental desirability of every program should be reviewed and justified each year before the program receives any funding at all. The objective is to cut waste by culling out projects that have outlived their utility and are continuing simply because of the inertia of policymakers.

The ZBB procedure is to describe each project/program, evaluate each one, and rank them in terms of cost/benefit or some other appropriate measure. Funds can then be allocated in accordance with this ranking.

As PPBS is associated with Robert McNamara, ZBB is associated with President Jimmy Carter. He employed ZBB as governor of Georgia and promised (threatened) to do so as president. Like PPBS, ZBB has had no great success. Whereas PPBS involved difficult implementation problems, particularly in the area of measuring costs and benefits (see[27], among many other critiques), ZBB raises a different problem. The primary effect of ZBB is to challenge the existence of every budgetary unit every budget period. Any project that cannot justify continued funding is sentenced to administrative death. The threat of ZBB is so great that organizations subjected to this budget process tend to devote more and more of their energies to defending their existence.

ZBB has a great deal of opposition and little support from the people who must supply the data for the analyses. Few governments have sufficient political clout to adopt and operate a true ZBB system, but some executives employ the logic of ZBB to challenge the continuation of projects they see as inefficient or ineffective. We feel this use of ZBB has considerable merit. For most cases, we feel that use of ZBB is rarely a cost-effective means of project budget control, but the concept is useful for helping to make decisions about whether or not to terminate projects. In Chapter 13 we illustrate an approach to the termination decision based on ZBB. Please note, however, that ZBB is not applied to projects that are clearly successful or are obvious failures, but to projects that cannot be identified as belonging to either group.

7.2 COST ESTIMATION

The cooperation of several people is required to prepare cost estimates for a project. If the firm is in a business that regularly requires bids to be submitted to its customers, it will have "professional" cost estimators on its staff. In these cases, it is the job of the PM to generate a description of the work to be done on the project in sufficient detail that the estimator can know what cost data must be collected. Frequently, the project will be too complex for the PM to generate such a description without considerable help from experts in the functional areas.

At times, the job of cost estimation for complex projects may be relatively simple because experience has shown that some formula gives a good *first approximation* of the project's cost. For example, the Goodyear Aircraft Co. makes an initial estimate of the cost of building a blimp by multiplying the estimated weight of the blimp by a specific dollar factor. (The weight is estimated in pounds, presumably prior to the blimp's inflation with helium.) The cost of buildings is commonly estimated as dollars per square foot times the square feet of floor area. Obviously these approximations must be adjusted for any special characteristics associated with each individual project, but this adjustment is far easier than making an estimate from scratch.

Turning now to the problem of estimating direct costs, project managers often find it helpful to collect direct cost estimates on a form that not only lists the level of resource needs, but also indicates *when* each resource will be needed, and notes whether or not it is available (or will be available at the appropriate time.) Figure 7-1 shows such a form. It also has a column for identifying the person to contact in order to get specific resources. This table can be used for collating the resource requirements for each task element in a project, or for aggregating the information from a series of tasks onto a single form.

Note that Figure 7-1 contains no information on overhead costs. The matter of what overhead costs are to be added and in what amounts is unique to the firm, beyond the PM's control, and generally a source of annoyance and frustration to one and all. The allocation of overhead is arbitrary by its nature, and when the

PROJECT NAME_____

DATE_____

TASK NUMBER_____

RESOURCES NEEDED

Resources	Person to Contact	How Many Much Needed	When Needed	Check ( ) If Available
People: Managers, Supervisors				
Professional & Technical				
Nontechnical				
Money				
Materials: Facilities				
Equipment				
Tools				
Power				
Space				
Special services: Research & Test				
Typing/clerical				
Reproduction				
Others				

Figure 7-1 Form for gathering data on project resource needs.

addition of overhead cost causes an otherwise attractive project to fail to meet the organization's economic objectives, the project's supporters are apt to complain bitterly about the "unfairness" of overhead cost allocation.

At times, firms fund projects that show a significant incremental profit over direct costs but are not profitable when fully costed. Such decisions can be justified for a number of reasons, such as:

* To develop knowledge of a technology
* To get the organization's "foot in the door"
* To obtain the parts or service portion of the work
* To be in a good position for a follow-on contract
* To improve a competitive position
* To broaden a product line or a line of business.

All of these are adequate reasons to fund projects that, in the short term, may lose money but provide the organization with the impetus for future growth and profitability. It is up to senior management to decide if such reasons are worth it.

Learning Curves

If the project being costed is one of many similar projects, the estimation of each cost element is fairly routine. If the project involves work in which the firm has little experience, cost estimation is more difficult, particularly for direct labor costs. For example, consider a project that requires 25 units of a complex electronic device to be assembled. The firm is experienced in building electronic equipment but has never before made this specific device, which differs significantly from the items it routinely assembles.

Experience might indicate that if the firm were to build many such devices, it would use about seventy hours of direct labor per unit. If labor is paid a wage of $12 per hour, and if benefits equal 28 percent of the wage rate, the estimated labor cost for the 25 units is

$$(1.28)(\$12/hr.)(25 \text{ units})(70 \text{ hours/unit})=\$26,880.$$

In fact, this would be an underestimate of the actual labor cost because more time per unit output is used early in the production process. Studies have shown that human performance usually improves when a task is repeated. In general, performance improves by a fixed percent each time production doubles. If an individual requires 10 minutes to accomplish a certain task the first time it is attempted and only 8 minutes the second time, that person is said to have an 80 percent learning rate. If output is doubled again from two to four, we would expect the fourth item to be produced in

$$8(.8)=6.4 \text{ minutes.}$$

Similarly, the eighth unit of output should require

$$6.4(.8)=5.12 \text{ minutes}$$

and so on. The time required to produce a unit of output follows a well-known formula:

$$T_n = T_o n^r$$

where T_n = the time required for the nth unit of output,
T_o = the time required for the initial unit of output,
n = the number of units to be produced, and
r = log percent learning rate/log 2.

The total time required for all units of a production run of size N is

$$\text{Total Time} = T_o \sum_{n=1}^{N} n^r.$$

Tables are widely available with both unit and total values for the learning curves, and have been calculated for many different improvement ratios (learning rates).

In the example given above, assume that after producing the twentieth unit, there is no significant further improvement i.e., assembly time has reached a steady state. Further assume that previous study established that the usual learning rate for assemblers in this plant is about 85 percent. We can estimate the time required for the first unit by letting T_n = 70 hours. Then

$$70 = T_o(20)^r$$

$$T_o = 141.3 \text{ hours.}$$

Now we know the time for the initial unit. Using the table that shows the total time multiplier (see [23, p. 127-128] for example), we can find the appropriate total time multiplier for this example—the multiplier for 20 units given a learning rate of 85 percent. With this multiplier, 12.40, we can calculate the total time required to build all 20 units. It is

$$(12.40)(141.3 \text{ hrs.}) = 1752.12 \text{ hours.}$$

The last 5 units are produced in the steady-state time of seventy hours each. Thus the total assembly time is

$$1752.12 + 5(70 \text{ hrs.}) = 2102.12 \text{ hours.}$$

We can now refigure the direct labor cost.

$$2102.12(\$12)(1.28) = \$32,288.56.$$

Our first estimate, which ignored learning effects, understated the cost by

$$\$32,288.56 - \$26,880 = \$5,408.56$$

or about 17 percent. Figure 7-2 illustrates this source of the error.

The conclusion is simple. For any task where labor is a significant cost factor and the production run is reasonably short, the PM should take the learning curve into account when estimating costs. The implications of this conclusion should not be overlooked. We do not often think of projects as "production," but they are. Recent research [14] has shown that the learning curve effect is impor-

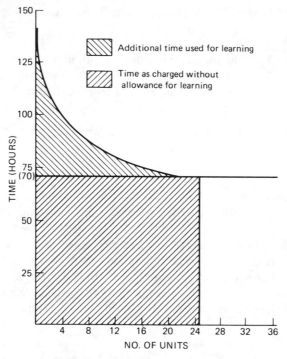

Figure 7-2 Effect of ignoring learning curve.

tant to decisions about the role of engineering consultants on computer-assisted design (CAD) projects. The failure to consider performance improvement is a significant cause of project cost underestimation.

Other Factors

The number of things that can produce errors in cost estimates is almost without limit, but some problems occur with particularly high frequency. Changes in resource prices is one of these. The most commonly used solution to this problem is to increase all cost estimates by some fixed percentage. A more useful approach is to identify each input that accounts for a significant portion of project cost and estimate the direction and rate of price change for each.

The determination of which inputs account for a "significant" portion of project cost is not difficult, though it may be somewhat arbitrary. Suppose, for example, that our initial, rough cost estimate (with no provision for future price changes) for a project is $1 million and is to be spent over a three-year period in approximately equal amounts per year. If we think personnel costs will comprise about 40 percent of that total, also spread equally over time, the wage/salary bill will be about $400,000. Split into three equal amounts, we have expenditures of $133,333 per year. If we estimate that wage/salary rates will increase by 6 percent per year, our expense for the second year rises to $141,333 (an increase of $8,000), and to $149,813 in the third year (an increase of $8.480). Failure to account for wage/salary inflation would result in an underestimate of project cost of about $16,500. This is an error of slightly more than 4 percent of the personnel cost and almost 2 percent of the total project budget.

Further improvements can be made by taking into account the fact that the prices of different inputs often change at very different rates. A quick examination of the Bureau of Labor Statistics (BLS) wage and price indices, which cover a very large number of specific commodities and wage rates, will reveal that even in periods of stable prices, the prices of some things rise while others fall and still others do not change appreciably. Thus, the PM may wish to use different *inflators* for each of several different classes of labor or types of commodities.

The proper level of breakdown in estimating the impact of price changes simply depends on the organization's willingness to tolerate error. Assume that management is willing to accept a 5 percent difference between actual and estimated cost for each major cost category. In the example above, expected increases in wage/salary costs will use four-fifths of that allowance. That leaves 1 percent ($40,000) of allowable error, and the need to add one engineer to the project for a single year would more than use the remaining allowance.

Other elements that need to be factored into the estimated project cost include an allowance for waste and spoilage. No sane builder would order "just enough" lumber to build a house. Also, personnel costs can be significantly increased by the loss and subsequent replacement of project professionals. Not only must new people go through a learning period—which, as we have seen, will have a negative effect on production—but professional starting salaries often rise faster than the general rate of annual salary increases. Thus, it may well cost more to replace a person who leaves the project with a newcomer who has approximately the same level of experience.

Finally, there is plain bad luck. Delays occur for reasons that cannot be predicted. Machinery with the reliability of a railroad spike suddenly breaks down. That which has never failed fails. Every project needs an "allowance for contingencies."

Some writers and instructors differentiate four bases for estimating costs: experience, quantitative (statistical) methods, constraints, and worksheets. They discuss the advantages and disadvantages of each and then, typically, decide that one or another gives the best results. We feel strongly that all four are useful and that no approach to cost estimation should be accepted as the best or rejected out of hand. The best estimators seem to employ an eclectic approach that uses, as one said, "anything that works." The wise PM takes into account as many known influences on the project budget as can be predicted. What cannot be predicted must then, by experience, simply be "allowed for."

Improving the Cost Estimation Process

Cost overruns are so frequent for all types of projects that senior managers often develop a cynical attitude when examining a project budget. They assume it is significantly understated. A common explanation for this phenomenon is that the PM purposely underestimates the project budget in order to improve its benefit-cost ratio, thereby increasing the probability that the project will be funded. Once the project is underway, the reasoning goes, and a monetary and psychic investment has been made in the work, the firm will not let a "good" project die and will make up for budget shortages, albeit grudgingly.

Let us assume, for the moment, that budget estimation errors are not the result of a conspiracy to mislead senior managers, but rather derive from honest errors on the part of the PM, the project cost estimators, or anyone else involved in the estimation process. As we have already noted, there are a number of reasons why "honest" underestimation errors occur. Furthermore, to senior managers the job even looks easier, faster, and less expensive than it appears to the person who must do the job. Non-expert cost estimators tend to overlook details necessary to the completion of a set of tasks. Neophyte and expert project managers alike seem to assume that Murphy's Law has been repealed in the case of their personal project.

Ambrose Bierce, in *The Devil's Dictionary,* defined "experience" as "The wisdom that enables us to recognize as an undesirable old acquaintance the folly that we have already embraced." It is axiomatic that we should learn through experience. It is a truism that we do not. Nowhere is this more evident than in project management, and yet it is not difficult to improve one's estimation/forecasting skills.

Using the ubiquitous Lotus 1-2-3®, we can construct a spreadsheet that captures the essence of a person's performance as an estimator. Two simple statistical measures are used; the mean absolute deviation (MAD), and the tracking signal (TS). The printout of such a Lotus 1-2-3® spreadsheet is shown in Figure 7-3.

Figure 7-3 assumes that for each period (Column A) someone has made an estimate of a variable (Column B), and that the actual value of that variable is, sooner or later, known (Column C). (It should be noted that Column A need not be time periods. This column simply counts the number of estimates made and links estimates with their respective actuals.) Column D calculates the difference between the actual value, A(t), and the estimate or forecast for that period, F(t). Column E contains the absolute value of that difference. We can now calculate a statistic known as the *Mean Absolute Deviation* (MAD).

As the information in Row 3 of the spreadsheet shows:

$$\text{MAD} = \Sigma \left(\left| A(t) - E(t) \right| \right) / n$$

where *n* is the number of differences. The MAD is therefore the arithmetic average of the absolute values of the differences—the mean absolute deviation.

Students of statistics may note that the MAD has certain logical similarities to the standard deviation. Assuming that the forecast errors are normally distributed, the MAD is approximately 80 percent of a standard deviation (see [9] and elsewhere). Thus, if the MAD is a sizable fraction of the variable being estimated, the average error is large and the forecast or estimate is not very accurate.

Now, consider Column D. The sum of the entries in this column for any number of periods is the sum of the forecast errors, often referred to as the "running sum of the forecast errors" (RSFE). If the estimator's errors are truly random, their sum should approach zero; that is, the RSFE should be a small number be-

```
A1:  'This is a template for improving one's estimating skills          READY

          A          B          C          D              E          F          G
1   This is a template for improving one's estimating skills
2
3   MAD = SUM(|A(t) - F(t)|)/n   (The Average Error)
4   Tracking Signal = SUM (A(t) - F(t))/MAD  (A Measure of Bias)
5                                                                             Tracking
6   Period    Estimate    Actual (A(t) - F(t))   |A(t) - F(t)|    MAD        Signal
7   ======================================================================================
8
9      1        155        163         8              8
10     2        242        240        -2              2           5.00        1.20
11     3         46         67        21             21          10.33        2.61
12     4         69         78         9              9          10.00        3.60
13     5         75         71        -4              4           8.80        3.64
14     6        344        423        79             79          20.50        5.41
15     7         56         49        -7              7          18.57        5.60
16     8        128        157        29             29          19.88        6.69
17
18                                   133            159
19
20
22-Dec-87   02:55 PM
```

Figure 7-3 Lotus 1-2-3® template for improving cost estimation.

cause positive errors should be offset by negative errors. If either positive or negative errors are more numerous or consistently larger than the other, the estimation process is said to be biased and the errors are not random. In Figure 7-3, RSFE = 133, so the forecast is quite positively biased.

The tracking signal measures the estimator's bias. It is easily found:

$$TS = RSFE/MAD$$

Note that it calculates the number of MADs in the RSFE (see column G in Figure 7-3, and recall the similarity between MAD and standard deviation). If the RSFE is small, approaching zero, the TS will also approach zero. As the RSFE grows, the TS will grow, indicating bias. Division of the RSFE by the MAD creates a sort of "index number," the TS, that is independent of the size of the variables being considered. We cannot say just how much bias is acceptable in an estimator/forecaster. We feel that a TS ≥ 3 is too high unless the estimator is a rank beginner. Certainly, an experienced estimator should have a much lower TS.

Perhaps more important than worrying about an acceptable limit on the size of the tracking signal is the practice of keeping track of it and analyzing why the estimator's bias, if there is one, exists. Similarly, the estimator should consider how to reduce the MAD, the average estimation error. Such analysis is the embodiment of "learning by experience." The Lotus 1-2-3® template makes the analysis simple to conduct, and should result in decreasing the size of both the

MAD and the TS. (For those familiar with Lotus 1-2-3®, the formulas used for Figure 7-3 are shown in Figure 7-4.)

A final note: At the beginning of this discussion, we made the assumption that estimation errors were "honest." That assumption is not necessary. If a manager suspects that costs are purposely being under- or overestimated, it is usually not difficult to collect appropriate data and calculate the tracking signal for an individual estimator—or even for an entire project team. If it is known that such information is being collected, one likely result is that the most purposeful bias will be sharply reduced.

```
A1:    'This is a template for improving one's estimating skills
A3:    'MAD = SUM (|A(t) - F(t)|)/n  The Average Error
A4:    'Tracking Signal = SUM (A(t) - F(t))/MAD  A Measure of Bias
G5:    [W12] ^Tracking`
A6:    'Period
B6:    "Estimate
C6:    "Actual
D6:    [W13] "A(t) - F(t)
E6:    [W13] "|A(t) - F(t)|
F6:    ^MAD
G6:    [W12] ^Signal
A7:    '=============
B7:    '=============
C7:    '=============
D7:    [W13] '=============
E7:    [W13] '=============
F7:    '=============
G7:    [W12] '=============
A9:    1
B9:    155
C9·    163
D9:    [W13] +C9-B9
E9:    [W13] @ABS(C9-B9)
A10:   2
B10:   242
C10:   240
D10:   [W13] +C10-B10
E10:   [W13] @ABS(C10-B10)
F10:   (F2) (@SUM($E$9..E10))/A10
G10:   (F2) [W12] (@SUM($D$9..D10))/F10
A11:   3
B11:   46
C11:   67
D11:   [W13] +C11-B11
E11:   [W13] @ABS(C11-B11)
F11:   (F2) (@SUM($E$9..E11))/A11
G11:   (F2) [W12] (@SUM($D$9..D11))/F11
```

Figure 7-4 Lotus 1-2-3® formulas for Figure 7-3.

7.3 SUMMARY

This chapter initiated the subject of project implementation by focusing on the project budget, which authorizes the project manager to obtain the resources needed to begin work. Different methods of budgeting were described along with their impacts on project management. Then, a number of issues concerning cost estimation were discussed, particularly the effect of learning on the cost of repetitive tasks and how to use the concept of the learning curve.

Specific points made in the chapter were these:

- The intent of a budget is to communicate organizational policy concerning the organization's goals and priorities.
- There are a number of common budgeting methods: top-down, bottom-up, the budget request, PPBS, ZBB.
- The intent of PPBS is to focus on cost/benefit relative to the organization's goals for selecting projects to fund.
- The intent of ZBB is to avoid automatic percentage budgeting in each budget period by focusing on the total value of each project to the organization's goals.
- A form identifying the level of resource need, when it will be needed, who the contact is, and its availability is especially helpful in estimating costs.
- It is common for organizations to fund projects whose returns cover direct but not full costs in order to achieve long-run strategic goals of the organizations.
- If projects include repetitive tasks with significant human input, the learning phenomenon should be taken into consideration when preparing cost estimates.
- The learning curve is based on the observation that the amount of time required to produce one unit decreases a constant percentage every time the cumulative output doubles.
- A method for determining whether or not cost estimations are biased is described. The method can be used to improve any estimation/forecasting process.
- Other major factors, in addition to learning, that should be considered when making project cost estimates are inflation, differential changes in the cost factors, waste and spoilage, personnel replacement costs, and contingencies for unexpected difficulties.

In the next chapter we address the subject of task scheduling, a topic of major importance in project management. More research and investigation has probably been conducted on the subject of scheduling than any other element of project management.

7.4 GLOSSARY

BOTTOM UP—A budgeting method that begins with those who will be doing the tasks estimating the resources needed. The advantage is more accurate estimates.

PLANNING-PROGRAMMING-BUDGETING-SYSTEM (PPBS)—A system developed in the 1960s for dealing rationally with budgeting through maximization of the chances for attaining the organization's long-run goals.

PROGRAM BUDGETING—Aggregating income and expenditures by project or program, often in addition to aggregation by organizational unit.

TOP DOWN—A budgeting method that begins with top managers' estimates of the resources needed for a project. Its primary advantage is that the aggregate budget is typically quite accurate because no element has been left out. Individual elements, however, may be quite inacurate.

VARIANCES—The pattern of deviations in costs and usage used for exception reporting to management.

ZERO-BASED BUDGETING—A budgeting method from the 1970s that was devised as an alternative to the incremental approach. Every program budget had to be totally justified every budget cycle.

7.5 PROJECT TEAM ASSIGNMENT

At this point, the team must establish the project budget. Start with the work breakdown structure and estimate, both from the bottom up and the top down, what the appropriate budget will be. Examine any discrepancies between the two budgets for errors, misunderstandings, or oversights. If any of the tasks are repetitious, use the learning curve to predict their cost by unit. If the task is mechanical, use a 75–80 percent rate; if more mental, use a 65–70 percent rate. Finally, describe how a PPBS and ZBB approach might apply to your project.

7.6 MATERIAL REVIEW QUESTIONS

1. What are the advantages of top-down budgeting? Of bottom-up budgeting? What is the most important task for top management to do in bottom-up budgeting?
2. In preparing a budget, what indirect costs should be considered?
3. What is the procedure for zero-base budgeting? Is it a good method to use in planning a state or national budget? Why, or why not?
4. List the four main steps involved in PPBS. Why has it become obsolete?

7.7 CONCEPTUAL DISCUSSION QUESTIONS

1. Discuss ways in which to keep budget planning from becoming a game.
2. List some of the pitfalls in cost estimating. What steps can a manager take to correct cost overruns?
3. Why do consulting firms frequently subsidize some projects?
4. What steps can be taken to make controlling costs easier? Can these steps also be used to control other project parameters, such as performance?

7.8 CHAPTER EXERCISE

Use the work breakdown structure from the chapter exercise in Chapter 5 to design a project budget for that project. Organize it hierarchically by task, etc. How would a top-down budgeting process proceed for this project? Compare it to a bottom-up process.

Then consider the tasks within the WBS itself. Are any of the tasks repetitive, with a high labor content? Might the learning curve apply here? If mechanical tasks requiring tools or machinery follow an 80 percent learning rate whereas simply memory/learning tasks follow a 60 percent learning rate, what rate would you estimate for these tasks?

7.9 INCIDENTS FOR DISCUSSION

Preferred Widget Company

Larry Cole has been appointed project manager of the Preferred Widget Company's new widget manufacturing process project. Widgets are extremely price-sensitive and Preferred has done a great deal of quantitative work so it can accurately forecast changes in sales volume relative to changes in pricing.

The company president, J. R. Widget, has considerable faith in the firm's sensitivity model and insists that all projects that affect the manufacturing cost of widgets be run against the sensitivity model in order to generate data to calculate the return on investment. The net result is that project managers, like Larry, are put under a great deal of pressure to submit realistic budgets so go/no-go project decisions can be made quickly. Mr. Widget has canceled several projects that appeared marginal during their feasibility stages and recently fired a project manager for overestimating project costs on a new model widget. The project was killed very early in the design stage and six months later a competitor introduced a similar widget that proved to be highly successful.

Larry's dilemma is how to go about constructing a budget that accurately reflects the cost of the proposed new manufacturing process. Larry is an experienced executive and feels comfortable with his ability to come close to estimating the cost of the project. However, the recent firing of his colleague has made him a bit gun-shy. Only one stage out of the traditional four-stage widget manufacturing process is being changed, so he has detailed cost information about a good percentage of the process. Unfortunately, the tasks involved in the process stage being modified are unclear at this point. Larry also believes that the new modification will cause some minor changes in the other three stages, but these changes have not been clearly identified. The stage being addressed by the project represents almost 50 percent of the manufacturing cost.

Question: Under these circumstances, would Larry be wise to pursue a top-down or a bottom-up budgeting approach? Why?

General Ship Company

General Ship Company has been building nuclear destroyers for the Navy for the last twenty years. It has recently completed the design of a new class of nuclear destroyer and will be preparing a detailed budget to be followed during construction of the first destroyer.

The total budget for this first destroyer is $90 million. The controller feels the initial project cost estimate prepared by the planning department was too low because the waste and spoilage allowance was underestimated. Thus, he is concerned that there may be a large cost overrun on the project, and he wants to work closely with the project manager to control the costs.

Question: How would you monitor the costs of this project?

7.10 BIBLIOGRAPHY

1. Austin, A. L. *Zero-Based Budgeting: Organizational Impact and Effects.* AMACOM, 1977.
2. Bacon, J. *Managing the Budget Function.* National Industrial Conference Board, 1970.
3. Bartizal, J. R. *Budget Principles and Procedures.* Prentice-Hall, 1940.
4. Block, E. B. "Accomplishment/Cost: Better Project Control." *Harvard Business Review,* May 1971
5. Briggs, G. R. *The Theory and Practice of Management Control.* American Management Association, 1970.
6. Brown, R., and J. D. Suver. "Where Does Zero-Base Budgeting Work?" *Harvard Business Review,* Dec. 1977.
7. Bunge, W. R. *Managerial Budgeting for Profit Improvement.* McGraw-Hill, 1968.
8. Burkhead, J. *Budgeting and Planning.* General Learning Press, 1971.
9. Chase, R. B., and N. J. Aquilano. *Production and Operations Management,* 4th ed. Irwin, 1985.
10. Dean, B. V., S. J. Mantel, Jr., and L. A. Roepcke. "Research Project Cost Distributions and Budget Forecasting." *IEEE Transactions on Engineering Management,* Nov. 1969.
11. Deardon, J. *Cost and Budget Analysis.* Prentice-Hall, 1962
12. Eiteman, J. W. *Graphic Budgets,* Masterco Press, 1949.
13. Gagnon, R. J. *An Exploratory Analysis of The Relevant Cost Structure of Internal and External Engineering Consulting.* Ph.D. dissertation, University of Cincinnati, 1982.
14. Gagnon, R. J., and S. J. Mantel, Jr. "Strategies and Performance Improvement for Computer-Assisted Design." *IEEE Transactions on Engineering Management,* Nov. 1987.
15. Heckert, J. B. *Business Budgeting and Control.* Ronald Press, 1967.
16. Hitch, C. J. "Plans, Programs and Budgets in The Department of Defense" *Operations Research,* Jan.–Feb. 1963.
17. Hitch, C. J. "A Planning-Programming-Budgeting System." In *Science, Technology and Management,* F. E. Kast and J. E. Rosensweig, eds. McGraw-Hill, 1963.

18. Hover, L. D. *A Practical Guide to Budgeting and Management Control Systems: A Functional and Performance Evaluation Approach.* Lexington Books, 1979.
19. Lin, T. "Corporate Planning and Budgeting: An Integrated Approach." *Managerial Planning,* May 1979.
20. Maciariello, J. A. "Making Program Management Work." *Journal of Systems Management,* July 1974.
21. Maclead, R. K. "Program Budgeting Works in Non-Profit Institutions." *Harvard Business Review,* Sept. 1971
22. McKean, R. N. "Remaining Difficulties in Program Budgeting." In Enke, S., ed., *Defense Management,* Prentice-Hall, 1967.
23. Meredith, J. R. *The Management of Operations,* 3rd ed. Wiley, 1987.
24. Ntuen, M. "Applying Artificial Intelligence to Project Cost Estimates." *Cost Engineering,* 29, 5, 1987.
25. Pyhrr, Peter A. *Zero-Base Budgeting: A Practical Management Tool for Evaluating Expenses.* Wiley, 1973.
26. Stedry, Andrew C. *Budget Control and Cost Behavior.* Prentice-Hall, 1960
27. Steiner, G. "Program Budgeting Business Contribution to Government Management." *Business Horizons,* Spring 1965.

7.11 READING

This article clearly describes the importance and impact of cost-related issues on a project. These issues can significantly alter the profitability and even success of a project. Costs are discussed from three viewpoints: that of the project manager, the accountant, and the controller. Not only are the amounts of expenditures and encumbrances important, but their timing is critical also. And perhaps most important is having a project cost system that accurately reports costs and variances in a way that can be useful for managerial decisions.

Three Perceptions Of Project Cost—
Cost Is More Than A Four Letter Word

David H. Hamburger
Management Consultant

Project cost seems to be a relatively simple expression, but "cost" is more than a four letter word. Different elements of the organization perceive cost differently, as the timing of project cost identification affects their particular organizational function. The project manager charged with on-time, on-cost, on-spec execution of a project views the "on cost" component of his responsibility as a requirement to stay within the allocated budget, while satisfying a given set of specified conditions (scope of work), within a required time frame (schedule). To most project managers this simply means a commitment to project funds in accordance with a prescribed plan (time based budget). Others in the organization are less concerned with the commitment of funds. The accounting department addresses expense recognition related to a project or an organizational profit and loss statement. The accountant's ultimate goal is reporting profitability, while positively influencing the firm's tax liability. The comptroller (finance department) is primarily concerned with the organization's cash flow. It is that person's responsibility to provide the funds for paying the bills, and putting the unused or available money to work for the company.

To be an effective project manager, one must understand each cost, and also realize that the timing of cost identification can affect both project and corporate financial performance. The project manager must be aware of the different cost perceptions and the manner in which they are reported. With this knowledge, the project manager can control more than the project's cost of goods sold (a function often viewed as the project manager's sole financial responsibility). The project manager can also influence the timing of cost to improve cash flow and the cost of financing the work, in addition to affecting revenue and expense reporting in the P&L statement.

THREE PERCEPTIONS OF COST

To understand the three perceptions of cost—commitments, expenses and cash flow—consider the purchase of a major project component. Assume that a $120,000 compressor with delivery quoted at six months was purchased. Figure 1 depicts the order execution cycle. At time 0 an order is placed. Six months later the vendor makes two shipments, a large box containing the compressor and a small envelope containing an invoice. The received invoice is processed immediately, but payment is usually delayed to comply with corporate payment policy (30, 60, 90 or more days may pass before a check is actually mailed to the vendor). In this example, payment was made 60 days after receipt of the invoice or 8 months after the order for the compressor was given to the vendor.

©1986 by the Project Management Institute. Reprinted by permission from *Project Management Journal*, June 1986, pp. 51–58.

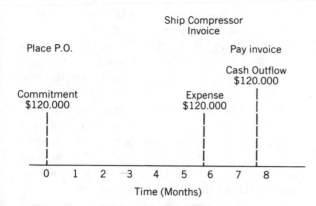

Figure 1 Three Perceptions of Project Cost.

Commitments—The Project Manager's Concern

Placement of the purchase order represents a *commitment* to pay the vendor $120,000 following satisfactory delivery of the compressor. As far as the project manager is concerned, once this commitment is made to the vendor, the available funds in the project budget are reduced by that amount. When planning and reporting project costs the project manager deals with commitments. Unfortunately, many accounting systems are not structured to support project cost reporting needs and do not identify commitments. In fact, the value of a purchase order may not be recorded until an invoice is received. This plays havoc with the project manager's fiscal control process, as he cannot get a "handle" on the exact budget status at a particular time. In the absence of a suitable information system, a conscientious project manager will maintain personal (manual or computer) records to track his project's commitments.

Expenses—The Accountant's Concern

Preparation of the project's financial report requires identification of the project's revenues (when applicable) and all project *expenses*. In most conventional accounting systems, expenses for financial reporting purposes are recognized upon receipt of an invoice for a purchased item (not when the payment is made—a common misconception). Thus, the compressor would be treated as an expense in the sixth month.

In a conventional accounting system, revenue is recorded when the project is completed. This can create serious problems in a long term project in which expenses are accrued during each reporting period with no attendant revenue, and the revenue is reported in the final period with little or no associated expenses shown. The project runs at an apparent loss in each of the early periods and records an inordinately large profit at the time revenue is ultimately reported—the final reporting period. This can be seriously misleading in a long term project which runs over a multi-year period.

To avoid such confusion, most long term project P&L statements report revenue and expenses based on a "percentage of completion" formulation. The general intent is to "take down" an equitable percentage of the total project revenue (approximately equal to the proportion of the project work completed) during each accounting period, assigning an appropriate level of expense to arrive at an acceptable period gross margin. At the end of each accounting year and at the end of the project, adjustments are made to the recorded expenses to account for the differences between actual expenses incurred and the theoretical expenses recorded in the P&L statement. This can be a complex procedure. The misinformed or uninformed project manager can place the firm in an untenable position by erroneously misrepresenting the project's P&L status; and the rare unscrupulous project manager can use an arbitrary assessment of the project's percentage of completion to manipulate the firm's P&L statement.

There are several ways by which the project's percentage of completion can be assessed to avoid these risks. A typical method, which removes subjective judgments and the potential for manipulation by relying on strict accounting procedures is to be described. In this process a theoretical period expense is determined, which is divided by the total estimated project expense budget to compute the percentage of total budget expensed for the period. This becomes the project's percentage of completion which is then used to determine the revenue to be "taken down" for the period. In this process, long delivery purchased items are not expensed on receipt of an invoice, but have the value of their purchase order prorated over the term of order execution. Figure 2 shows the $120,000 compressor in the example being expensed over the six month delivery period at the rate of $20,000 per month.

Cash Flow—The Comptroller's Concern

The comptroller and the finance department are responsible for managing the organization's funds, and also assuring the availability of the appropriate amount of cash for payment of the project's bills. Unused funds are put to work for the organization in interest bearing accounts or in other ventures. The finance department's primary concern is in knowing when funds will be needed for invoice payment in order to minimize the time that these funds are not being used productively. Therefore, the comptroller really views project cost as a *cash outflow*. Placement of a purchase order merely identifies a future cash outflow to the comptroller, requiring no action on his part. Receipt of the invoice generates a little more interest, as the comptroller now knows that a finite amount of cash will be re-

quired for a particular payment at the end of a fixed period. Once a payment becomes due, the comptroller provides the funds, payment is made, and the actual cash outflow is recorded.

It should be noted that the compressor example is a simplistic representation of an actual procurement cycle, as vendor progress payments for portions of the work (i.e., engineering, material and delivery) may be included in the purchase order. In this case, commitment timing will not change, but the timing of the expenses and cash outflow will be consistent with the agreed upon terms of payment.

The example describes the procurement aspect of project cost, but other project cost types are treated similarly. In the case of project labor, little time elapses between actual work execution (a commitment), the recording of the labor hours on a time sheet (an expense), and the payment of wages (cash outflow). Therefore, the three perceptions of cost are treated as if they each occur simultaneously. Subcontracts are treated in a manner similar to equipment purchases. A commitment is recorded when the subcontract is placed and cash outflow occurs when the monthly invoice for the work is paid. Expenses are treated in a slightly different manner. Instead of prorating the subcontract sum over the performance period, the individual invoices for the actual work performed are used to determine the expense for the period covered by each invoice.

Thus the three different perceptions of cost can result in three different time-based cost curves for a given project budget. Figure 3 shows a typical relationship between commitments, expenses and cash outflow. The commitment curve leads and the cash outflow curve lags, with the expense curve falling in the middle. The actual shape and the degree of lag/lead between the curves are a function of several factors, including: the project's labor, material and subcontract mix; the firm's invoice payment policy; the delivery period for major equipment items; subcontract performance period and the schedule of its work; and the effect of the project schedule on when and how labor will be expended in relation to equipment procurement.

The conscientious project manager must under-

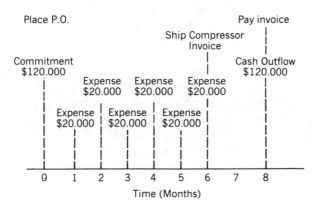

Figure 2 Percentage of Completion Expensing.

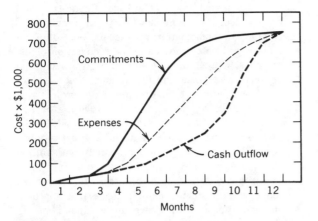

Figure 3 Three Perceptions of Cost.

stand these different perceptions of cost and should be prepared to plan and report on any and all approaches required by management. The project manager should also be aware of the manner in which the accounting department collects and reports "costs." Since the project manager's primary concern is in the commitments, he should insist on an accounting system which is compatible with the project's reporting needs. Why must a project manager resort to a manual control system when the appropriate data can be made available through an adjustment in the accounting department's data processing system?

PUTTING YOUR UNDERSTANDING OF COST TO WORK

Most project managers believe that their total contribution to the firm's profitability is restricted by the ability to limit and control project cost, but they can do much more. Once the different perceptions of cost have been recognized, the project manager's effectiveness is greatly enhanced. The manner in which the project manager plans and executes the project can improve company profitability through influence on financing expenses, cash flow and the reporting of revenue and expenses. To be a completely effective project manager one must be totally versed

in the cost accounting practices which affect the firm's project cost reporting.

Examination of the typical project profit & loss statement (See Table 1) shows how a project sold for profit is subjected to costs other than the project's costs (cost of goods sold). The project manager also influences other areas of cost as well, addressing all aspects of the P&L to influence project profitability positively.

Specific areas of cost with examples of what a project manager can do to influence cost of goods sold, interest expense, tax expense and profit are given below:

Cost of Goods Sold (Project Cost).

- Evaluation of alternate design concepts and the use of "trade-off" studies during the development phase of a project can result in a lower project cost, without sacrificing the technical quality of the project's output. The application of value engineering principles during the initial design period will also reduce cost. A directed and controlled investment in the evaluation of alternative design concepts can result in significant savings of project cost.
- Excessive safety factors employed to ensure "on-spec" performance should be avoided. Too frequently the functional members of the project team will apply large safety factors in their effort to meet or exceed the technical specifications. The project team must realize that such excesses increase the project's cost. The functional staff should be prepared to justify an incremental investment which

Table 1
Typical Project Profit & Loss Statement

Revenue (project sell price)	$1,000,000
(less) cost of goods sold (project cost)	($ 750,000)
Gross margin	$ 250,000
(less) selling, general & administrative expenses	($ 180,000)
Profit before interest and taxes	$ 70,000
(less) financial expense	($ 30,000)
Profit before taxes	$ 40,000
(less) taxes	($ 20,000)
Net profit	$ 20,000

was made to gain additional performance insurance. Arbitrary and excessive conservatism must be avoided.

- Execution of the project work must be controlled. The functional groups should not be allowed to stretch out the project for the sake of improvement, refinement or the investigation of the most remote potential risk. When a functional task has been completed to the project manager's satisfaction (meeting the task's objectives), cut off further spending to prevent accumulation of "miscellaneous" charges.

- The project manager is usually responsible for controlling the project's contingency budget. This budget represents money that one expects to expend during the term of the project for specific requirements not identified at the project onset. Therefore, these funds must be carefully monitored to prevent indiscriminate spending. A functional group's need for a portion of the contingency budget must be justified and disbursement of these funds should only be made after the functional group has exhibited an effort to avoid or limit its use. It is imperative that the contingency budget be held for its intended purpose. Unexpected problems will ultimately arise, at which time the funds will be needed. Use of this budget to finance a scope change is neither advantageous to the project manager nor to management. The contingency budget represents the project manager's authority in dealing with corrections to the project work. Management must be made aware of the true cost of a change so that financing the change will be based on its true value (cost/benefit relationship).

- In the procurement of equipment, material and subcontract services, the specified requirements should be identified and the lowest priced, qualified supplier found. Adequate time for price "shopping" should be built into the project schedule. The Mercury project proved to be safe and successful even though John Glenn, perched in the Mercury capsule atop the Atlas rocket prior to America's first earth orbiting flight, expressed his now famous concern that "all this hardware was built by the low bidder." The project manager should ensure that the initial project budget is commensurate with the project's required level of reliability. The project manager should not be put in the position of having to buy project reliability with unavailable funds.

- Procurement of material and services based on par-

tially completed drawings and specifications should be avoided. The time necessary for preparing a complete documentation package before soliciting bids should be considered in the preparation of the project schedule. Should an order be awarded based on incomplete data and the vendor then asked to alter the original scope of supply, the project will be controlled by the vendor. In executing a "fast track" project, the project manager should make certain that the budget contains an adequate contingency for the change orders which will follow release of a partially defined work scope.

- Changes should not be incorporated in the project scope without client and/or management approval and the allocation of the requisite funds. Making changes without approval will erode the existing budget and reduce project profitability; meeting the project manager's "on-cost" commitment will become extremely difficult, if not impossible.

- During periods of inflation, the project manager must effectively deal with the influence of the economy on the project budget. This is best accomplished during the planning or estimating stage of the work, and entails recognition of planning and an inflationary environment for its effect by estimating the potential cost of two distinct factors. First, a "price protection" contingency budget is needed to cover the cost increases that will occur between the time a vendor provides a firm quotation for a limited period and the actual date the order will be placed. (Vendor quotations used to prepare an estimate usually expire long before the material is actually purchased.) Second, components containing certain price volatile materials (e.g., gold, silver, etc.) may not be quoted firm, but will be offered by the supplier as "price in effect at time of delivery." In this case an "escalation" contingency budget is needed to cover the added expense that will accrue between order placement and material delivery. Once the project manager has established these inflation related contingency budgets, his role becomes one of ensuring controlled use.

Financial Expense.

- The project's financial cost (interest expense) can be minimized by the project manager through the timing of order placement. Schedule slack time can be used to defer the placement of a purchase order so that the material is not available too early and the related cash outflow is not premature. There are several risks associated with this concept. Delaying an order too long could backfire if the desired material is unavailable when needed. Allowing a reasonable margin for error in the delivery cycle, saving some of the available slack time for potential delivery problems, will reduce this risk. Waiting too long to place a purchase order could result in a price increase which can more than offset the interest savings. It is possible to "lock-up" a vendor's price without committing to a required delivery date, but this has its limitations. If vendor drawings are a project requirement, an "engineering only" order can be placed to be followed by hardware release at the appropriate time. Deferred procurement which takes advantage of available slack time should be considered in the execution of all projects, especially during periods when the cost of money is excessively high.

- Vendors are frequently used to help "finance the project" by placing purchase orders which contain extended payment terms. The financially astute vendor will build the cost of financing the project into his sell price, but only to the extent that he can remain competitive. A vendor's pricing structure should be checked to determine if progress payments would result in a reduced price and a net project benefit. A discount for prompt payment should be taken if the discount exceeds the interest savings that could result from deferring payment.

- Although frequently beyond the project manager's control, properly structured progress payment terms can serve to negate most or all project financial expenses. The intent is simple. A client's progress payment terms can be structured to provide scheduled cash inflows which offset the project's actual cash outflow. In other words, maintenance of a zero net cash position throughout the period of project execution will minimize the project's financial expense. In fact, a positive net cash position resulting from favorable payment terms can actually result in a project which creates interest income rather than one that incurs an interest expense. Invoices to the client should be processed quickly, to minimize the lost interest resulting from a delay in receiving payment.

- Similarly, the project manager can influence receipt of withheld funds (retention) and the project's final payment to improve the project's rate of cash in-

flow. A reduction in retention should be pursued as the project nears completion. Allowing a project's schedule to indiscriminately slip delays project acceptance, thereby delaying final payment. Incurring an additional expense to resolve a questionable problem should be considered whenever the expense will result in rapid project acceptance and a favorable interest expense reduction.

- On internally funded projects, where retention, progress payments and other client related financial considerations are not a factor, management expects to achieve payback in the shortest reasonable time. In this case, project spending is a continuous cash outflow process which cannot be reversed until the project is completed and its anticipated financial benefits begin to accrue from the completed work. Unnecessary project delays, schedule slippages and long term investigations extend system startup and defer the start of payback. Early completion will result in an early start of the investment payback process. Therefore, management's payback goal should be considered when planning and controlling project work, and additional expenditures in the execution of the work should be considered if a shortened schedule will adequately hasten the start of payback.

Tax Expense and Profit.

- On occasion, management will demand project completion by a given date to ensure inclusion of the project's revenue and profit within a particular accounting period. This demand usually results from a need to fulfill a prior financial performance forecast. Delayed project completion by only a few days could shift the project's entire revenue and profit from one accounting period to the next. The volatile nature of this situation, large sums of revenue and profit shifting from one period to the next, results in erratic financial performance which negatively reflects on management's ability to plan and execute their efforts.

- To avoid the stigma of erratic financial performance, management has been known to suddenly redirect a carefully planned, cost effective project team effort to a short term, usually costly, crash exercise, directed towards a project completion date, artificially necessitated by a corporate financial reporting need. Unfortunately, a project schedule driven by influences external to the project's fundamental objectives usually results in additional cost and reduces profitability.

- In this particular case, the solution is simple if a percentage of completion accounting process can be applied. Partial revenue and margin take-down during each of the project's accounting periods, resulting from this procedure (rather than lump sum take down in a single period at the end of the project, as occurs using conventional accounting methods) will mitigate the undesirable wild swings in reported revenue and profit. Two specific benefits will result. First, management's revenue/profit forecast will be more accurate and less sensitive to project schedule changes. Each project's contribution to the overall forecast will be spread over several accounting periods and any individual performance change will cause the shift of a significantly smaller sum from one accounting period to the next. Second, a project nearing completion will have had 90–95% of its revenue/profit taken down in earlier periods which will lessen or completely eliminate management pressure to complete the work to satisfy a financial reporting demand. Inordinate, unnecessary spending to meet such unnatural demands can thereby be avoided.
- An Investment Tax Credit[1] a net reduction in corporate taxes gained from a capital investment project (a fixed percentage of the project's installed cost), can be earned when the project actually provides its intended benefit to the owner. The project manager should consider this factor in scheduling the project work, recognizing that it is not necessary to complete the entire project to obtain this tax benefit as early as possible. Failure to substantiate beneficial use within a tax year can shift this savings into the next tax year. The project manager should consider this factor in establishing his project's objectives, diligently working towards attainment by scheduling the related tasks to meet the tax deadline. Consideration should also be given premium expenditures (to the extent they do not offset the potential tax savings) to reach this milestone by the desired date.
- In managing the corporate P&L statement, the need to shift revenue, expenses and profit from one tax period to the next often exists. By managing the project schedule (expediting or delaying major component procurements or shifting expensive activities) the project manager can support this requirement. Each individual project affords a limited benefit, but this can be maximized if the project manager is given adequate notice regarding the necessary scheduling adjustments.
- Revenue/profit accrual based on percentage of completion can create a financial problem if actual expenses greatly exceed the project budget. In this case the project's percentage of completion will accumulate more quickly than justified and the project will approach a theoretical 100% completion before all work is done. This will "front load" revenue/profit take down and will ultimately require a profit reversal at project completion. Some managers may find this desirable, since profits are being shifted into earlier periods, but most reputable firms do not wish to overstate profits in an early period which will have to be reversed at a later time. Therefore, the project manager should be aware of cost overruns and, when necessary, reforecast the project's "cost on completion" (increasing the projected cost and reducing the expected profit) to reduce the level of profit taken down in the early periods to a realistic level.

CONCLUSION

Cost is not a four letter word to be viewed with disdain by the project manager. It is a necessary element of the project management process which the project manager must comprehend despite the apparent mysteries of the accounting systems employed to report cost. The concept of cost is more than the expenses incurred in the execution of the project work: the manner in which cost is treated by the organization's functional elements can affect project performance, interest expenses and profitability. Therefore, the conscientious project manager must develop a complete understanding of project cost and the accounting systems used to record and report costs. The project manager should also recognize the effect of the timing of project cost, and

---

[1]The proposed tax law revisions under consideration in Congress at the time this article was written include a provision which eliminates the Investment Tax Credit.

the differences between commitments, expenses and cash flow. The project manager should insist on the accounting system modifications needed to accommodate project cost reporting and control requirements. Once an appreciation for these concepts has been gained, the project manager can apply this knowledge towards positively influencing project and organizational profitability in all areas of cost through control of the project schedule and the execution of the project's work.

CHAPTER 8
Scheduling

The previous chapter initiated our discussion of project implementation. In this and the following three chapters, we continued with the implementation of the project plans we made in Chapter 5. In this chapter we examine some scheduling techniques that have been found to be useful in project management. We cover the Program Evaluation and Review Technique (PERT), the Critical Path Method (CPM), Gantt charts, and briefly discuss Precedence Diagramming, the Graphical Evaluation and Review Technique (GERT), and report-based methods.

In Chapter 9, we consider the special problems of scheduling when resource limitations force conflicts between concurrent projects, or even between two or more tasks in a single project. We also look at ways of expediting activities by adding minimal amounts of resources through the use of CPM. Following a discussion of the monitoring and information system function in Chapter 10, we discuss the overall topic of project control in Chapter 11.

8.1 BACKGROUND

A schedule is the conversion of a project action plan into an operating timetable. As such, it serves as a fundamental basis for monitoring and controlling project activity and, taken together with the plan itself, is probably the major tool for the management of projects. In a project environment, the scheduling function is more important than it would be in an ongoing operation because projects lack the continuity of day-to-day operations and often present much more complex problems of coordination. Indeed, project scheduling is so important that a detailed schedule is sometimes a customer-specified requirement. In later chapters we discuss the fact that a properly designed, detailed schedule can also serve as a key input in establishing the monitoring and control systems for the project.

Not all project activities need to be scheduled at the same level of detail. In face, there may be several schedules: the master schedule, the development and testing schedule, the assembly schedule, and so on. These schedules are typically based on the previously determined Work Breakdown Structure, and it is good practice to create a schedule for each major task level in the WBS which will cover the work packages. It is rarely necessary to list all work packages. One can focus mainly on those that need to be monitored for maintaining adequate control over the project. Such packages are usually difficult, expensive, or have a relatively short time frame for their accomplishment.

When making a schedule, it is important that the dates and time allotments for the work packages be in precise agreement with those set forth in the project master schedule. It is also important that the work units that aggregate into work packages be in agreement with the times in the master schedule. These times are control points for the PM. It is the project manager's responsibility to insist on and maintain this consistency, but the actual scheduling of the task and work packages is usually done by those responsible for their accomplishment—after the PM has established and checked appropriate due dates for all tasks. This procedure ensures that the final project schedule reflects the interdependencies among all the tasks and departments involved in the project, and maintains consistency among them.

The basic approach of all scheduling techniques is to form an actual or implied network of activity and event relationships that graphically portrays the sequential relations between the tasks in a project. Tasks that must precede or follow other tasks are then clearly identified, in time as well as function. Such a network is a powerful tool for planning and controlling a project and has the following benefits:

- It is a consistent framework for planning, scheduling, monitoring, and controlling the project.
- It illustrates the interdependence of all tasks, work packages, and work units.
- It aids in ensuring that the proper communications take place between departments and functions.
- It determines an expected project completion date.
- It identifies so-called critical activities which, if delayed, will delay the project completion time.
- It also identifies activities with slack that can be delayed for specified periods without penalty, or from which resources may be temporarily borrowed without harm.
- It determines the dates on which tasks may be started—or must be started if the project is to stay on schedule.
- It illustrates which tasks must be coordinated to avoid resource or timing conflicts.
- It also illustrates which tasks may be run, or must be run, in parallel to achieve the predetermined project completion date.

- It may, depending on the network form used, allow an estimate of the probability of project completion by various dates, or the date corresponding to a particular a priori probability.

8.2 NETWORK TECHNIQUES: PERT AND CPM

With the exception of Gantt charts, to be discussed below, the most common approach to project scheduling is the use of network techniques such as PERT and CPM. The Program Evaluation and Review Technique was developed by the U.S. Navy in cooperation with Booz-Allen Hamilton and the Lockheed Corporation for the Polaris missile/submarine project in 1958. The Critical Path Method was developed by DuPont, Inc., during the same time period.

In application, PERT has primarily been used for R & D projects, the type of projects for which it was developed, though its use is more common on the "development" side of R & D than it is on the "research" side. CPM was designed for construction projects and has been generally embraced by the construction industry. (There are many exceptions to these generalities. The Eli Lilly Co., for example, uses CPM for its research projects.)

The two methods are quite similar and are often combined for educational presentation. Throughout most of this chapter we will not distinguish between them except where the differences are of direct interest to us. We will write "PERT/CPM" whenever the distinction is not important. Originally, however, PERT was strictly oriented to the time element of projects and used probabilistic activity time estimates to aid in determining the probability that a project could be completed by some given date. CPM, on the other hand, used deterministic activity time estimates and was designed to control both the time and cost aspects of a project, in particular, time/cost trade-offs. In CPM, activities can be "crashed" (expedited) at extra cost to speed up the completion time. Both techniques identified a project *critical path* whose activities could not be delayed, and also indicated *slack* activities that could be somewhat delayed without lengthening the project completion time.

We might note in passing that the *critical* activities in real-world projects typically constitute less than 10 percent of the total activities. In our examples and simplified problems in this chapter, the critical activities constitute a much greater proportion of the total because we use smaller networks to illustrate the techniques.

Before explaining the mechanics of these methods, we must note that their value in use is not totally accepted by everyone. Research [9, 22, 23] into the use of PERT/CPM does not indicate any significant difference in the technological performance of projects where PERT/CPM was used and in those where it was not. There *was,* however, a significantly lower probability of cost and schedule overruns when PERT/CPM was used. We now define some terms that are used in our discussion.

Terminology

Activity—A specific task or set of tasks that are required by the project, use up resources, and take time to complete.

Event—The result of completing one or more activities. An identifiable end state occurring at a particular point in time.

Network—The combination of all activities (usually drawn as *arcs*) and events (usually drawn as *nodes* at the beginning and end of each arc) define the project and the activity precedence relationships. Networks are usually drawn starting on the left and proceeding to the right. Arrowheads placed on the arcs are used to indicate the direction of flow—that is, to show the proper precedences. Before an event can be *realized,* that is, achieved, all activities that immediately precede it must be completed. These are called its *predecessors.* Thus, an event represents an instant in time when each and every predecessor activity has been finished. Events themselves have no time duration and use no resources. They are merely points on the network, conditions of the system that can be recognized.

Path—The series of connected activities (or intermediate events) between any two events in a network.

Critical—Activities, events, or paths which, if delayed, will delay the completion of the project. A project's critical path is understood to mean that sequence of critical activities (and critical events) that connect the project's start event to its finish event.

A network is constructed by linking arc (activity) to node (event) as specified by the precedence relationships and shows the interrelationships between the activities and events. Figure 8-1 is a typical (simplified) project network. (Ignore the dashed arrows for the moment.) This figure shows an activity-on-arc (AOA) network. An alternative way of drawing the same set of relationships is to draw an activity-on-node (AON) network (see Figure 8-2). In this case the nodes represent activities and the arcs show the precedence relationships.

It is not difficult to convert AOA networks to AON networks. The procedure* is to connect each predecessor–successor pair of activities by an arrow—the dashed arrows in Figure 8-1. Each activity in Figure 8-1 becomes a node in

*We thank our colleague James Evans for showing us this technique.

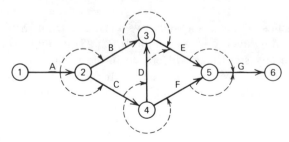

Figure 8-1 Sample AOA network.

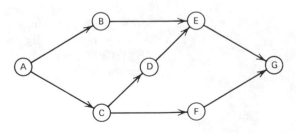

Figure 8-2 Sample AON network.

Figure 8-2. These nodes are connected by the dashed arrows we drew on Figure 8-1, which become the solid arrows of Figure 8-2. The AOA network has now become an AON network. (Unfortunately, going from an AON to an AOA network is not so simple. It must be done by trial and error.)

The choice between AOA and AON representation is largely a matter of personal preference. Our impression is that users of PERT favor AOA and users of CPM favor AON, but both approaches appear in the educational literature. Both are also used in commercially available computer packages. AOA networks are slightly harder to draw, but they identify events (milestones) clearly. AON networks do not require the use of *dummy* activities (defined below) and are easier to draw. Throughout most of this chapter we adopt the AOA form of PERT. In Section 8.4, we use the AON representation that is standard with that method. In this way, the reader can become familiar with both types of networks. This chapter is intended as an introduction to project scheduling at a level sufficient for the PM who wishes to use most commercial computerized project scheduling packages. For a deeper understanding of PERT/CPM, we refer the reader to [10, 15, 32, 35, 45].

Recall the planning documents we developed in Chapter 5. In particular, the Action Plan contains the information we need. It is a list of all activities that must be undertaken in order to complete a specified task, the time each activity is expected to take, any nonroutine resources that will be used by the activity, and the predecessor activities for each activity. For example, we might have an Action Plan like that shown in Figure 8-3.

Constructing the Network

Let us start by assuming the node numbered 1 denotes the event called "START." Activities **a** and **b** have no predecessors, so we assume their source is at START (node 1) and their destination at nodes we will number 2 and 3, respectively (Figure 8-4). As explained above, the arrowheads show the direction of flow.

ACTION PLAN

OBJECTIVE: To complete. . . . .
. . . .
MEASURES OF PERFORMANCE. . . . .
. . . .
CONSTRAINTS . . . .

Tasks	Precedence	Time	Cost	Who Does
a	—	5 days	—	—
b	—	4 days	—	—
c	a	6 days	—	—
d	b	2 days	—	—
e	b	5 days	—	—
f	c,d	8 days	—	—

Figure 8-3 Sample Action Plan.

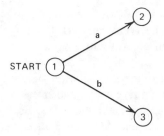

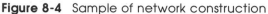

Figure 8-4 Sample of network construction

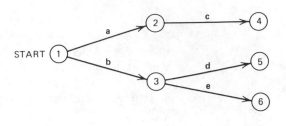

Figure 8-5 Sample of network construction.

Activity **c** follows **a**, activity **d** follows **b**, and activity **e** also follows **b**. Let's add these to our network in Figure 8-5. Note that we number the event nodes sequentially from left to right as we construct the network. No great damage occurs if we do not use this convention, but it is convenient.

Now note that activity **f** must follow both **c** and **d**, but *any given activity must have its source in one, and only one, node*. Therefore, it is clear that **c** and **d**, both of which must precede **f**, must conclude in the same node from which **f** originates. We can now redraw the network, collapsing nodes 4 and 5 (and renumbering them) as in Figure 8-6.

The Action Plan does not indicate any further activity is required to complete the task, so we have reached the end of this particular plan. Once again, we can redraw the network to show that the final activities (those with no successors) end in a single node, Figure 8-7.

This process of drawing and redrawing the network may seem a bit awkward, and is. If the list of activities associated with a project is long, with complicated interrelationships, this way of constructing the network would be too time-consuming to be practical. In Chapter 10 we will describe some computer routines that can automatically generate the network.

Construction of **a** network may not be straightforward in some cases. For instance, there may be a need for a dummy activity to aid in indicating a particular precedence, via a dashed arc. Figure 8-8 illustrates the proper way to use a dummy activity if *two* activities occur between the same *two* events. Figure 8-8 also shows why dummy activities may be needed for AOA networks. An activity is identified by its starting and ending nodes as well as its "name." For example, activities **a** and **b** both start from node 1 and end at node 2. Many computer programs that are widely used for finding the critical path and time for networks

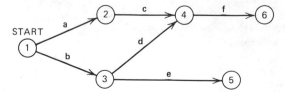

Figure 8-6 Sample of network construction.

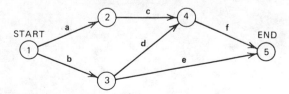

Figure 8-7 Sample of network construction.

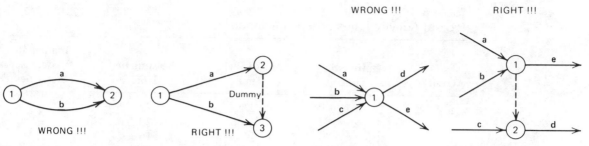

Figure 8-8 Networking concurrent activities.

Figure 8-9 Activity c not required for e.

require the nodes to identify which activity is which. In our example, **a** and **b** would appear to be the same, both starting at node 1 and ending during period 2.

Figure 8-9 illustrates how to use a dummy activity when activities **a**, **b**, and **c** must precede activity **d**, but only **a** and **b** must precede activity **e**. Last, Figure 8-10 illustrates the use of dummy activities in **a** more complex setting.

Let us now consider a small project with ten activities in order to illustrate the network technique. Table 8-1 lists the activities, their most likely completion times, and the activities that must precede them. The table also includes optimistic and pessimistic estimates of completion time for each activity in the list. Actual activity time is expected rarely to be less than the optimistic time or more than the pessimistic time (More on this matter shortly.)

As above, we start the network by finding those activities that have no predecessors. In the table **a**, **b**, and **c** meet the test. Therefore, they can all be drawn emerging from our starting node.

Next, we look for activities that only require **a**, **b**, or **c**, or some combination of **a**, **b**, and **c**, to precede them. Activity **d** requires that **a** be completed, and **e**, **f**, and **g** all require that **b** and **c** be completed. Note that a dummy will be necessary unless we begin the network from separate nodes for **b** and **c**. Last, **h** requires only that **c** be completed. To this point, the network might look like Figure 8-11.

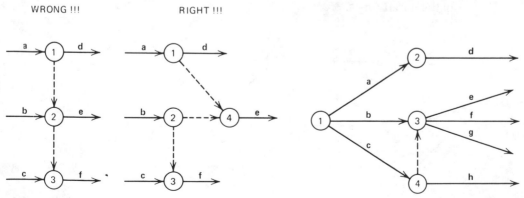

Figure 8-10 **a** precedes **d**. **a** and **b** precede **e**. **b** and **c** precede **f** (**a** does not precede **f**).

Figure 8-11 Partial network.

Table 8-1
Project Activity Times and Precedences

Activity	Optimistic Time	Most Likely Time	Pessimistic Time	Immediate Predecessor Activities
a	10	22	22	—
b	20	20	20	—
c	4	10	16	—
d	2	14	32	a
e	8	8	20	b,c
f	8	14	20	b,c
g	4	4	4	b,c
h	2	12	16	c
i	6	16	38	g,h
j	2	8	14	d,e

The last two activities, **i** and **j**, are drawn in the same manner. Activity **i** requires that both **g** and **h** be completed, so **g** and **h** are directed to a single node (node 5). Similarly, activity **j** requires the completion of both **d** and **e**, which are directed to node 6. Since no activities require that **f**, **i**, or **j** precede them, these activities are directed to the project completion node, 7. The complete project network is shown in Figure 8-12.

Calculating Activity Times

The next step is to calculate expected activity completion times from the data in Table 8-1. These expected completion times are found by using the three time estimates (optimistic, pessimistic, and most likely) in the table. The most likely time, m, is exactly that, the time most likely to occur—i.e., the mode of the distribution of all times.

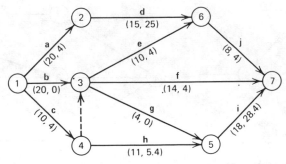

Figure 8-12 The complete network from Table 8-1.

The expected time, *TE,* is found by

$$TE = (a + 4m + b)/6$$

where *a* = optimistic time estimate,
b = pessimistic time estimate, and
m = most likely time estimate, mode.

Note in Table 8-1 that some activity durations are known with certainty, which is to say that *a, b,* and *m* are the same (see activity **b,** for instance). Note further that the most likely time may be the same as the optimistic time ($a = m$) as in activity **e,** or that the most likely time may be identical to the pessimistic time ($m = b$) as in activity **a.** The range about *m* may be symmetric where

$$m - a = b - m$$

as in activity **c,** or may be quite asymmetric, as in activities **h** and **i.**

The above formula for calculating expected times is usually said to be based on the beta statistical distribution. This distribution is used rather than the more common normal distribution because it is highly flexible in form and can take into account such extremes as where $a = m$ or $b = m$.

Recently, Sasieni noted [40] that writers (including himself) have been using the formula used here to estimate *TE.* He pointed out that it could not be derived from the formula for the beta distribution without several assumptions that were not necessarily reasonable, and he wondered about the original source of the formula. Fortunately for two generations of writers on the subject, Littlefield and Randolph [25] cited a U.S. Navy paper that derives the approximations used here and states the not unreasonable assumptions on which they are based. Gallagher [14] makes a second derivation of the formula using a slightly different set of assumptions.

Estimates of *a* and *b* are made such that there is a very small probability (such as one chance in a hundred) that the time actually required for an activity will fall outside the range of *a* to *b.* Most estimators, however, are uncomfortable dealing with extreme values. Occasionally, if an observer has witnessed a given activity repeatedly over the course of years, for example, the pouring of a foundation for a building, the observer may be willing to make such estimates. But where the observations are made less frequently, such as in the installation of a machining center, there will be a great reluctance to estimate extreme values for *a* and *b.*

Fortunately, the precision is not critical. Unless the distribution is highly asymmetric, *TE* is not particularly sensitive to the errors that will result from an estimate made at the 5 percent level (one out of twenty times outside the range *a* to *b*) or even at the 10 percent level (one out of ten times outside the range). Indeed, the estimate of total network duration is usually not seriously affected by the typical case in which different estimators have somewhat different probability levels in mind when making their estimates of *a* and *b* for different activities in the same project.

The results of the expected value calculations are shown in Table 8.2 and are included on Figure 8.12 as well. Also included in the table and on the network are measures of the *uncertainty* of activity duration, the *variance, V,* that is given by

Table 8-2
Expected Activity Times (*TE*), Variances (*V*), and Standard Deviations (σ)

Activity	Expected Time, TE	Variance, V	Standard Deviation, σ
a	20	4	2
b	20	0	0
c	10	4	2
d	15	25	5
e	10	4	2
f	14	4	2
g	4	0	0
h	11	5.4	2.32
i	18	28.4	5.33
j	8	4	2

$$V = ((b - a)/6)^2$$

and the *standard deviation*, σ, which is given by

$$\sigma = \sqrt{V}.$$

Critical Path and Time

Consider the hypothetical project shown in Figure 8.12. Assume, for convenience, that the time units involved are days. How long will it take to complete the project? (For the moment we will treat the expected times as if they were certain.) If we start the project on day zero, we can begin simultaneously working on activities **a**, **b**, and **c**, each of which have no predecessor activities. We will reach event 2 in twenty days, event 3 in twenty days, and event 4 in ten days. In Figure 8-13 we have redrawn the network with these times shown just above their respective nodes. They are labelled EOT (earliest occurrence time) because they represent the earliest times that the event can occur. Activity **d**, for

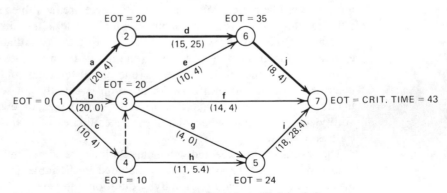

Figure 8-13 The complete network from Table 8-2.

example, cannot begin before event 2 has occurred, which means that all activities that precede event 2 must be completed. In this case, of course, activity **a** is the only predecessor of event 2.

Note that event 3 not only requires the completion of activity **b**, but also requires the completion of activity **c**, as shown by the dummy activity. (Refer to Figure 8-8 for a refresher.) The dummy requires neither time nor resources, so it does not affect the network time in any way. Event 3 does not occur until the *longest* path leading to it has been completed. The path from event 1 to event 3 requires the completion of activity **b** (twenty days) *and* the completion of activities **c** and **dummy** (ten + zero days). Because the two paths may be followed simultaneously, we can reach event 3 in twenty days. Therefore, the earliest starting time (EST) for any activity emanating from event 3 is twenty days.

Proceeding similarly, we see that event 6 has two predecessor activities, **d** and **e**. Activity **d** cannot start until day 20, (EST = 20) and it requires fifteen days to complete. Thus, its contribution to event 6 will require a total of thirty-five days from the start of the project. Activity **e** may also start after 20 days, the EOT for event 3, but it requires only ten days, a total of thirty days from the project start. Because event 6 requires the completion of both activities **d** and **e**, the EOT for event 6 is thirty-five days, the *longest* of the paths to it. Event 5 has an EOT of twenty-four days, the longest of the two paths leading to it, and event 7, the completion event of the network, has a time of forty-three days. The EOTs are shown in Figure 8-13.

There are eight activity paths leading to event 7. They are

a-d-j = 20 + 15 + 8 = 43 days **c-dummy-e-j** = 10 + 0 + 10 + 8 = 28 days
b-e-j = 20 + 10 + 8 = 38 days **c-dummy-f**   = 10 + 0 + 14   = 24 days
  b-f = 20 + 14   = 34 days **c-dummy-g-i** = 10 + 0 + 4 + 18 = 32 days
b-g-i = 20 + 4 + 18 = 42 days
c-h-i = 10 + 11 + 18 = 39 days

The longest of these paths is **a-d-j** using forty-three days, which means that forty-three days is the *shortest* time in which the entire network can be completed. This is called the *critical time* of the network, and **a-d-j** is the critical path, usually shown as a heavy line.

In a simple network such as our example, it is easy to find and evaluate every path between start and finish. Many real networks are considerably more complex, and finding all paths can be taxing. Using the method illustrated above, there is no need to worry about the problem. Every node is characterized by the fact that one or more activities lead to it. Each of these activities has an expected duration and originates in an earlier node. As we proceed to calculate the EOT of each node, beginning at the start, *we are actually finding the critical path and time to each of the nodes in the network.* Note that event 5 has an EOT (critical time) of twenty-four days, and its critical path is **b-g** rather than **c-h** which requires twenty-one days, or **c-dummy-g** which takes fourteen days.

The number of activities leading to an event tells us the number of paths we must evaluate to find the EOT for that event. Here, *path* is defined as originating at immediate predecessor events, not at the network origin. With event 5, that number is two, so we find the EOT and activity times for the two immediate predecessors. For event 7, we have three evaluations to do, the EOT of event 6 plus the duration of activity **j** (forty-three days), the EOT of event 3 plus the duration of **f** (thirty-four days), and the EOT of event 5 plus the duration of **i** (forty-two days). There is, therefore, no need to find, list, and evaluate all possible start-to-finish paths in the network.

Slack

Thus far in this discussion we have focused mostly on the events in the network. We found the EOTs for the project milestones. It is now helpful to focus on the activities by finding their earliest starting times (EST) and latest possible starting times (LST). As noted in the previous section, the EST for an activity is equal to the EOT for the event from which the activity emanates. Activity **i** cannot start until event 5 has occurred. Event 5 has an EOT of twenty-four days, and so activity **i** has an EST of twenty-four days. An important question for the PM is this: What is the latest time (LST) activity **i** could start without making the entire project late?

Refer again to Figure 8-13. The project has a critical time of forty-three days. Activity **i** requires eighteen days to be accomplished. Therefore, **i** must be started no later than day 25 (43 – 18 = 25) if the project is to be complete on day 43. The LST for activity **i** is day 25. Because **i** cannot begin until event 5 has occurred, the latest occurrence time (LOT) for event 5 is also day 25. The difference between the LST and the EST for an activity is called its *slack* or *float*. In the case of activity **i**, it *must* be started no later than day 25, but *could* be started as early as day 24, so it has one day of slack. It should be immediately obvious that all activities on the critical path have zero slack. They cannot be delayed without making the project late.

For another example, consider activity **f**. Its EST is day 20, which is equal to the EOT for event 3 from which it emanates. The LST for activity **f** is 43 – 14 = 29. If **f** is started later than day 29, it will delay the entire project. Activity **f** has slack of LST – EST = 29 – 20 = 9 days.

To find the slack for any activity or the LOT for any event, we make a backward pass (right to left) through the network just as we made a forward pass (left to right) to find the critical path and time and the EOTs for all events (which are also the ESTs for successor activities). There is one simple convention we must adopt: *When there are two or more noncritical activities on a path, it is conventional to calculate the slack for each activity as if it were the only activity in the path.* Thus, when finding the slack for activity **i**, for example, we assume that none of **i**'s predecessors are delayed, and that event 5 occurred on its EOT of day 24. Of course, if some activity, **x**, had six days of slack (given a specific EOT for the immediate preceding event), and if an earlier activity was late, causing the event to be delayed say two days, then activity **x** would have only four days of slack, having lost two days to the earlier delay.

It is simple to calculate slack for activities that are immediate predecessors of the final node. As we move to earlier activities, it is just a bit more complicated.

Consider activity **g**. Remembering our assumption that the other activities in the same path use none of the available slack, we see that activity **i** must follow **g**, and that **g** emanates from event 3. Starting with the network's critical time of forty-three days, we subtract eighteen days for activity **i** and four more days for **g** (43 − 18 − 4 = 21). Thus **g** can begin no later than day 21 without delaying the network. The EST for **g** (EOT for event 3) is day 20, so **g** has one day of slack.

To find the LOT for event 3, we must investigate each path that emanates from it. We have already investigated two paths, one with activity **g** and one with activity **f**. Recall that **f** could start as late as day 29. For **f** not to delay the network, event 3 would have to be complete not later than day 29. But activity **g** must start no later than day 21, so event 3 must be complete by day 21 or the **g-i** path will cause a delay. Now consider activity **e**, the only remaining activity starting from event 3. Activity **e** must be completed by day 35 or event 6 will be late and the network will be delayed. (Note that we do not have to work backward from the end of the network to find the slack for any activity that ends at a node on the critical path. All events and activities on the critical path have zero slack, so any activity ending on this path must arrive at event 6 not later than day 35.) The LST for **e** is 35 − 10 = 25. Its EST is day 20, so activity **e** has five days of slack.

We now can see that the LOT for event 3 is day 21, the most restrictive (earliest) time required, so that no activity emanating from it will cause the network to be late. Table 8-3 shows the LST, EST, and slack for all activities, and the LOT, EOT, and slack for all events.

Table 8-3 Times and Slacks for Network in Figure 8-3

Event	LOT	EOT	Slack
1	0	0	0
2	20	20	0
3	21	20	1
4	14	10	4
5	25	24	1
6	35	35	0
7	43	43	0

Activity	LST	EST	Slack
a	0	0	0
b	1	0	1
c	4	0	4
d	20	20	0
e	25	20	5
f	29	20	9
g	21	20	1
h	14	10	4
i	25	24	1
j	35	35	0

On occasion, the PM may negotiate an acceptable completion date for a project which allows for some slack in the entire network. If, in our example, an acceptable date was fifty working days after the project start, then the network would have a total of 50 − 43 = 7 days of slack. This is the latest occurrence time minus the earliest occurrence time for the ending node, 7, of the network.

Uncertainty of Project Completion Time

When discussing project completion dates with senior management, the PM should try to determine the probability that a project will be completed by the suggested deadline—or find the completion time associated with a predetermined level of risk. With the information in Table 8-2, this is not difficult.

If we assume that the activities are independent of each other, then the variance of a set of activities is equal to the sum of the variances of the individual activities comprising the set. Those who have taken a course in statistics will recall that the variance of a population is a measure of the population's dispersion and is equal to the square of the population's standard deviation. The variances in which we are interested are the variances of the activities on the critical path.

The critical path of our example includes activities **a**, **d**, and **j**. From Table 8-2 we find that the variances of these activities are four, twenty-five, and four, respectively; and the variance for the critical path is the sum of these numbers, thirty-three days. Assume, as above, that the PM has promised to complete the project in fifty days. What are the chances of meeting that deadline? We find the answer by calculating Z, where

$$Z = (D - S)/\sqrt{V}$$

and

D = the desired project completion time
S = the scheduled project completion time, that is, the critical time
V = the variance of the critical path
Z = the number of standard deviations of a normal distribution (the *standard normal deviate*)

Z, as calculated above, can be used to find the probability of completing the project on time.

Using the numbers in our example, $D = 50$, $S = 43$, and $V = 33$ (the square root of V is 5.745), we have

$$Z = (50 - 43)/5.745$$
$$= 1.22 \text{ standard deviations.}$$

We turn now to Table 8-4, which shows the probabilities associated with various levels (Table 8-4 also appears as Appendix **c**. It is shown here for the reader's convenience.) We go down the left-hand column until we find $Z = 1.2$, and then across to column .02 to find $Z = 1.22$. The probability value of $Z = 1.22$

shown in the table is .8888. which is the likelihood that we will complete the critical path of our sample project within fifty days of the time it is started. Figure 8-14 shows the resulting probability distribution of the project completion times.

We can work the problem backward, too. What deadline is consistent with a .95 probability of on-time completion? First, we go to Table 8-4 and look

Table 8-4 Cumulative Probabilities of the Normal Probability Distribution (Areas under the Normal Curve from $-\infty$ to Z)

z	00	.01	.02	.03	.04	.05	.06	.07	.08	.09
.0	.5000	.5040	.5080	.5120	.5160	.5199	.5239	.5279	.5319	.5359
.1	.5398	.5438	.5478	.5517	.5557	.5596	.5636	.5675	.5714	.5753
.2	.5793	.5832	.5871	.5910	.5948	.5987	.6026	.6064	.6103	.6141
.3	.6179	.6217	.6255	.6293	.6331	.6368	.6406	.6443	.6480	.6517
.4	.6554	.5691	.6628	.6664	.6700	.6736	.6772	.6808	.6844	.6879
.5	.6915	.6950	.6985	.7019	.7054	.7088	.7123	.7157	.7190	.7224
.6	.7257	.7291	.7324	.7357	.7389	.7422	.7454	.7486	.7517	.7549
.7	.7580	.7611	.7642	.7673	.7704	.7734	.7764	.7794	.7823	.7352
.8	.7881	.7910	.7939	.7967	.7995	.8023	.8051	.8078	.8106	.8133
.9	.8159	.8186	.8212	.8238	.8264	.8289	.8315	.8340	.8365	.8389
1.0	.8413	.8438	.8461	.8485	.8508	.8531	.8554	.8577	.8599	.8521
1.1	.8643	.8665	.8686	.8708	.8729	.8749	.8770	.8790	.8810	.8880
1.2	.8849	.8869	.8888	.8907	.8925	.8944	.8962	.8980	.8997	.9015
1.3	.9032	.9049	.9066	.9082	.9099	.9115	.9131	.9147	.9162	.9177
1.4	.9192	.9207	.9222	.9236	.9251	.9265	.9279	.9292	.9306	.9319
1.5	.9332	.9345	.9357	.9370	.9382	.9394	.9406	.9418	.9429	.9441
1.6	.9452	.9463	.9474	.9484	.9495	.9505	.9515	.9525	.9535	.9545
1.7	.9554	.9564	.9573	.9582	.9591	.9599	.9608	.9616	.9625	.9633
1.8	.9641	.9649	.9656	.9664	.9671	.9678	.9686	.9693	.9699	.9706
1.9	.9713	.9719	.9726	.9732	.9738	.9744	.9750	.9756	.9761	.9767
2.0	.9772	.9778	.9783	.9788	.9793	.9798	.9803	.9808	.9812	.9817
2.1	.9821	.9826	.9830	.9834	.9838	.9842	.9846	.9850	.9854	.9857
2.2	.9861	.9864	.9868	.9871	.9875	.9878	.9881	.9884	.9887	.9890
2.3	.9893	.9896	.9898	.9901	.9904	.9906	.9909	.9911	.9913	.9916
2.4	.9918	.9920	.9932	.9925	.9927	.9929	.9931	.9932	.9934	.9936
2.5	.9938	.9940	.9941	.9943	.9945	.9946	.9948	.9949	.9951	.9952
2.6	.9953	.9955	.9956	.9957	.9959	.9960	.9961	.9962	.9963	.9964
2.7	.9965	.9966	.9967	.9968	.9969	.9970	.9971	.9972	.9973	.9974
2.8	.9974	.9975	.9976	.9977	.9977	.9978	.9979	.9979	.9980	.9981
2.9	.9981	.9982	.9982	.9983	.9984	.9984	.9985	.9985	.9986	.9986
3.0	.9987	.9987	.9987	.9988	.9988	.9989	.9989	.9989	.9990	.9990
3.1	.9990	.9991	.9991	.9991	.9992	.9992	.9992	.9992	.9993	.9993
3.2	.9993	.9993	.9994	.9994	.9994	.9994	.9994	.9995	.9995	.9995
3.3	.9995	.9995	.9995	.9996	.9996	.9996	.9996	.9996	.9996	.9997
3.4	.9997	.9997	.9997	.9997	.9997	.9997	.9997	.9997	.9997	.9998

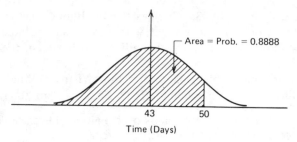

Figure 8-14 Probability distribution of project completion times.

through the table until we find .95. The Z value associated with .95 is 1.645. (The values in the table are not strictly linear, so our interpolation is only approximate.) We know that S is forty-three days, and that the square root of V is 5.745. Solving the equation for **d**, we have

$$D = S + 5.745(1.645)$$
$$= 43 + 9.45$$
$$= 52.45 \text{ days.}$$

Thus, there is a 95 percent chance of finishing the project by 52.45 days.

Note that as D approaches S, Z gets smaller, approaching zero. Table 8-4 shows that for $Z = 0$, the chance of on-time completion is fifty-fifty. The managerial implications are all too clear. If the PM wants a reasonable chance of meeting a project deadline, there must be some slack in the project schedule. When preparing a project budget, it is quite proper to include some allowance for contingencies. The same principle holds for preparing a project schedule. The allowance for contingencies in a schedule is network slack, and the wise PM will insist on some.

Finally, to illustrate an interesting point, let's examine a noncritical path, activities **b-g-i**. The variance of this path (from Figure 7-12) is $0 + 0 + 28.4 = 28.4$, which is slightly less than the variance of the critical path. The path time is 45 days. The numerator of the fraction $(D-5)/\sqrt{V}$ is larger, and in this case the denominator is smaller. Therefore, Z will be larger, and the probability of this path delaying project completion is less than for the critical path. But consider the noncritical path **c-h-i** with a time of $10 + 11 + 18 = 39$ days, and a total variance of 37.8. (Remember, we are trying to find the probability that this noncritical path with its higher variance but shorter completion time will make us late, given that the critical path is 43 days.)

$$Z = (50 - 39)/6.15$$
$$Z = 1.79$$

The result is that we have a 96 percent chance for this noncritical path to allow the project to be on time.

If the desired time for the network equaled the critical time, forty-three days, we have seen that the critical path has a fifty-fifty chance of being late. What are the chances that the noncritical path c-h-i, will make the project late? D is now forty-three days, so we have

$$Z = \frac{(43 - 39)}{6.15}$$

$$= .65$$

$Z = .65$ is associated with a probability of .74 of being on time, or $1 - .74 = .26$ of being late.

Assuming that these two paths (**a-d-j** and **c-h-i**) are independent, the probability that both paths will be completed on time is the product of the individual probabilities, $(.50)(.74) = .37$, which is considerably less than the fifty-fifty we thought the chances were. (If the paths are not independent, the calculations become more complicated.) Therefore, it is a good idea to consider noncritical paths that have activities with large variances and/or path times that are close to critical in duration (i.e., those with little slack).

Another Lotus 1-2-3® File

Just as we did in Chapter 7 on budgeting, we can construct a Lotus 1-2-3® template to do the calculations for finding the expected times, variances, and standard deviations associated with a series of three-time estimates for PERT/CPM networks. Figure 8-15 shows the file itself and Figure 8-16 shows the formulas used.

```
A1: 'This is a template for three-time PERT schedule estimates            READY


         A         B         C         D         E         F         G         H
1    This is a template for three-time PERT schedule estimates
2
3    a = optimistic time estimate (9/10)
4    b = pessimistic time estimate (1/10)
5    m = typical (modal) time estimate
6
7    Activity                      a         m         b        te    Variance Std. Dev.
8    ================================================================================
9
10       a                         5         6         8      6.17     0.250     0.500
11       b                         4         7         8      6.67     0.444     0.667
12       c                         6         8        12      8.33     1.000     1.000
13       d                         7         7         7      7.00     0.000     0.000
14       e                         6         7         8      7.00     0.111     0.333
15       f                         4         5        12      6.00     1.778     1.333
16       g                         4         6         9      6.17     0.694     0.833
17
18
19
20
22-Dec-87  02:57 PM
```

Figure 8-15 A spreadsheet template for PERT schedules.

```
A1:  'This is a template for three-time PERT schedule estimates
A3:  'a = optimistic time estimate (9/10)
A4:  'b = pessimistic time estimate (1/10)
A5:  'm = typical (modal) time estimate
A7:  'Activity
C7:  "a
D7:  "m
E7:  "b
F7:  ^te
G7:  ^Variance
H7:  'Std. Dev.
A8:  '==============
B8:  '==============
C8:  '==============
D8:  '==============
E8:  '==============
F8:  '==============
G8:  '==============
H8:  '==============
A10: ^a
C10: 5
D10: 6
E10: 8
F10: (F2) (C10+(4*D10)+E10)/6
G10: (F3) (((E10-C10)/6)^2)
H10: (F3) +G10^0.5
A11: ^b
C11: 4
D11: 7
E11: 8
F11: (F2) (C11+(4*D11)+E11)/6
G11: (F3) (((E11-C11)/6)^2)
H11: (F3) +G11^0.5
A12: ^c
C12: 6
D12: 8
E12: 12
F12: (F2) (C12+(4*D12)+E12)/6
G12: (F3) (((E12-C12)/6)^2)
H12: (F3) +G12^0.5
```

Figure 8-16 Template formulas for PERT spreadsheet.

Most of the widely used project management software will not accept three-time estimates or do the necessary calculations to use such estimates, but a large majority of such software packages will routinely exchange information with Lotus 1-2-3®. It is therefore quite simple to enter the three-time estimates into a Lotus 1-2-3® file and transfer the expected activity times, *TE*s, into a project management scheduling package where they can be used as if they were deterministic times in finding a project's critical path and time. Calculations of the probability of completing a project on or before some elapsed time can easily be done by hand.

8.3 GANTT CHARTS

One of the oldest and still one of the most useful methods of presenting schedule information is the Gantt chart, developed around 1917 by Henry L. Gantt, a pioneer in the field of scientific management. The Gantt chart shows planned and actual progress for a number of tasks displayed against a horizontal time scale. It is a particularly effective and easy-to-read method of indicating the actual current status for each of a set of tasks compared to the planned progress for each item of the set. As a result, the Gantt chart can be helpful in expediting, sequencing, and reallocating resources among tasks, as well as in the valuable but mundane job of keeping track of how things are going. In addition, the charts usually contain a number of special symbols to designate or highlight items of special concern to the situation being charted.

There are several advantages to the use of Gantt charts. First, even though they may contain a great deal of information, they are easily understood. While they do require frequent updating (as does any scheduling/control device), they are easy to maintain *as long as task requirements are not changed or major alterations of the schedule are not made.* Gantt charts provide a clear picture of the current state of a project.

Another significant advantage of Gantt charts is that they are easy to construct. While they may be constructed without first drawing a PERT diagram, there is a close relationship between the PERT/CPM network and the Gantt chart. We use the example in the previous section to illustrate this relationship and, at the same time, demonstrate how to construct such a chart.

First, the PERT/CPM network of Figure 8-13 is redrawn so that the lengths of each arc are in proportion to the respective task times. In essence, we redraw the network along a horizontal time scale. This modified network is shown in Figure 8-17. The heavy line, **a-d-j** is the critical path, and the horizontal dashed line segments indicate slack times. The vertical dashed line segments are dummy activities (as between events 3 and 4), or merely connectors (as elsewhere in the drawing). Note that to transform the network in this manner requires that we "explode" single nodes into multiple nodes when multiple activities emanate from the single node. In this modified network, each activity must originate from an individual node, although several activities still can have a common destination node.

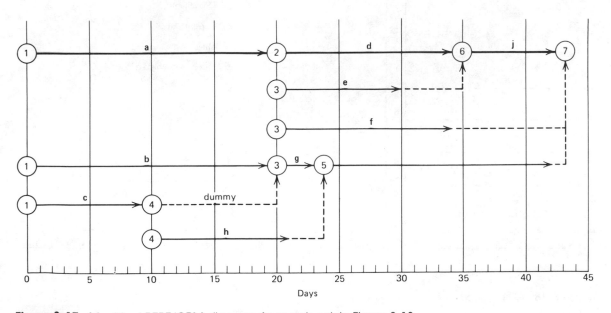

Figure 8-17 Modified PERT/CPM diagram from network in Figure 8-13.

The nodes of Figure 8-13 are placed at their EOTs (the early start times for ensuing activities), and the slack is shown *after* the activity duration. (We have used an arrowhead to separate the activity duration from its slack.) To draw the modified diagram only requires that the nodes be placed at their EOTs listed on the PERT/CPM network and the activity durations drawn out from them as solid lines. Precedence is shown by connecting the duration lines with dashed line segments, showing each specific connection to the appropriate nodes.

The Gantt chart can be drawn directly from the modified PERT/CPM diagram. A list is made of all activities required to complete the project. Activities are usually listed in alphabetic (or numeric) order—which is most often the order in which they were listed in the Action Plan or whatever source document was originally used. As Figure 8-18 shows, activity times are superimposed on a linear calendar, much as in Figure 8-17. Precedence relationships are preserved by not allowing the activity line or bar for a successor activity to begin until its predecessors are complete. Scheduled activity times are drawn as light lines or hollow bars. A heavy line or a filled-in bar indicates actual progress. Color is sometimes used for easy visibility.

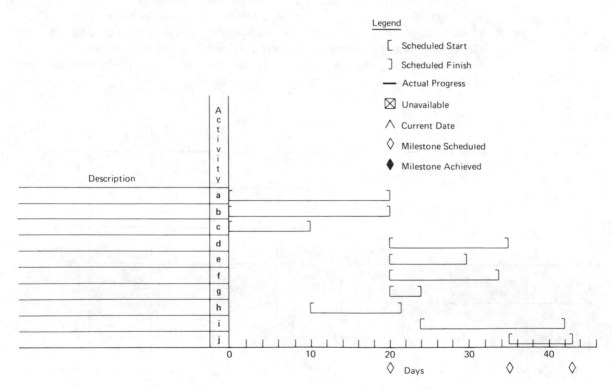

Figure 8-18 Gantt project chart from Figure 8-13.

Figure 8-18 transforms the modified PERT/CPM network into a Gantt chart. Note that three milestones are shown as diamonds below the baseline. These are the events that occur along the critical path. While there is no particular rule mandating the use of critical path events as project milestones, it is common for them to be chosen in this way. (If there are many critical events, some may be ignored and only the particularly noteworthy critical events are selected as milestones.) We can also see that while all precedence relationships must be preserved, it is not possible to distinguish easily their technical relationships simply by observing the chart itself. For example, activities **a** and **b** both have a duration of twenty days. Activities **d**, **e**, **f**, and **g** begin on the twentieth day. But it is not possible to determine which of the latter set of activities are successors to which of the former. If a single activity is completed at some point in time, it is reasonable to assume that other activities starting at that point are dependent on the first one; but if two or more activities end at the same time, the relationships between them and subsequent activities are unclear.

Figure 8-19 pictures the project as it might appear on its twenty-second day. Actual progress is shown as a heavy line added just below the scheduled progress line. Activity **a** started and finished on time, while **b** started on time but was completed one day late. Activity **c** was begun two days late and finished

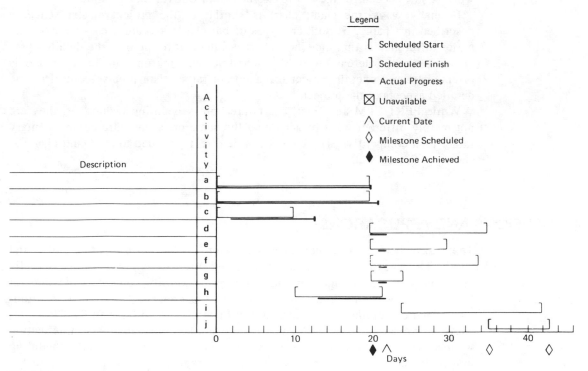

Figure 8-19 Gantt chart showing progress of project on Day 22.

three days late, which delayed the start of **h**. (In this case, the predecessor relationship of **c** to **h** is clear.) Activity **d** is under way and was started on time. Activities **e**, **f**, and **g** were all started one day late. Even with some activities starting late, nothing has happened to delay the actual critical path. While it is not clear from the Gantt chart, the network (Figure 8-13) shows that the delay in **b** means that the **b-g-i** path has gone critical.

This example illustrates both the strength and weakness of the Gantt chart. Its major strength is that it is easy to read. Gantt charts are often mounted on the wall of the project office and updated frequently. Anyone interested in the project can see the state of progress easily, even if the interested party knows little about the actual nature of the work being done. The weakness of the Gantt chart is simply that one needs the PERT/CPM network (or the WBS) to interpret what appears on the Gantt chart beyond a cursory level—or to plan how to compensate for lateness.

Another advantage is the ease of construction of the chart. In our example, we converted the PERT/CPM network in Figure 8-13 to a Gantt chart by modifying the network as in Figure 8-17. In practice, this intermediate stage is not necessary, and one can easily go from network to chart in a single step. On balance, ease of construction and ease of use have made the Gantt chart the most popular method for displaying a project schedule [23]. Nonetheless, a PERT/CPM network is still needed for the PM to exercise control over the schedule.

In many ways, the Gantt chart is similar to the project master schedule described in Chapter 5. Both are types of bar charts and are used similarly. The major difference is that the Gantt chart is intended to monitor the detailed progress of work, whereas the master schedule contains only major tasks and is oriented toward overall project management rather than precise control of the detailed aspects of the project.

While PERT/CPM and Gantt charts are both scheduling techniques, they are not merely different ways of achieving the same ends; they are complementary rather than competitive. The budget can be directly related to the Gantt chart, as shown in Figure 8-20.

8.4 EXTENSIONS AND APPLICATIONS

There have been a large number of extensions to the basic ideas of PERT and CPM. These extensions are often oriented toward handling rather specific problem situations through additional program flexibility, computerizing some of the specific problems, fine-tuning some of the concepts for special environments, and combining various management approaches with the PERT/CPM concepts—for example, the TRENT approach discussed in Chapter 5. In this section we discuss some of these extensions and look at the utility of network scheduling models in general. However, we delay our coverage of extensions aimed primarily at resource allocation and formal applications of CPM until Chapter 9.

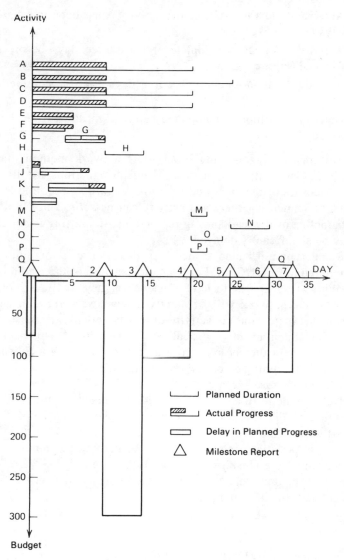

Figure 8-20 Relating the budget to the Gantt chart schedule.

Precedence Diagramming

One shortcoming of the PERT/CPM network method is that it does not allow for leads and lags between two activities without greatly increasing the number of subactivities to account for this. In construction projects, in particular, it is extremely common for the following restrictions to occur.

- Activity B must not start before activity A has been in progress for at least two days (Figure 8-21a).
- Activity A must be complete at least three days before activity B can be finished (Figure 8-21b).
- Activity B cannot begin before four days after the completion of A (Figure 8-21c).
- Activity B cannot be completed before eight days from the start of A (Figure 8-21d).

Precedence diagramming is an AON network method that allows for these leads and lags within the network. Node designations are illustrated in Figure 8-21e. Because of the increased flexibility regarding required lead and lag times, it must be known whether each activity can be *split* or not. Splitting allows easier satisfaction of the lead and lag restrictions. If splitting is not allowed, the project may be significantly delayed.

Some anomalies tend to occur in precedence diagramming that are not encountered in PERT/CPM. For example, because of the lead and lag requirements, activities may appear to have slack when they really do not. Also, the critical path of the network will frequently go backward through an activity, with the result that increasing the activity time may actually decrease the project completion time. Such an activity is called *reverse critical*. This happens when the critical path enters the completion of an activity through a finish constraint (Figure 8-21b or d), continues backward through the activity, and leaves through a start constraint (Figure 8-21a or d).

Network node times are calculated in a manner similar to PERT/CPM times. Because of the lead and lag restrictions, it is often helpful to lay out a Gantt chart to see what is actually happening.

Precedence diagramming seems to be gaining in popularity. The richer set of precedence relationships it allows is pertinent for a variety of projects, particularly for construction projects. For more details on this technique, see [10, Chapters 6 and 17], and [32].

GERT

The Graphical Evaluation and Review Technique (GERT) is a network model developed to deal with more complex modeling situations than can be handled by PERT/CPM. GERT combines signal flowgraph theory, probabilistic networks, PERT/CPM, and decision trees all in a single framework. Its components consist of *logical nodes* (defined below) and directed arcs (or branches) with *two* parameters; the probability that a given arc is taken (or "realized") and the distribution function describing the time required by the activity. Evaluation of a GERT network yields the probability of each node being realized and the elapsed time between all nodes.

At this point, it may be useful to compare GERT and PERT/CPM in order to focus on what is different about GERT.

GERT	PERT/CPM
Branching from a node is probabilistic.	Branching from a node is deterministic.
Various possible probability distributions for time estimates.	Only the beta distribution for time estimates.
Flexibility in node realization.	No flexibility in node realization.
Looping back to earlier events is acceptable.	Looping back is not allowed.
Difficult to use as a control tool.	East to use for control.
Arcs may represent time, cost, reliability, etc.	Arcs represent time only.

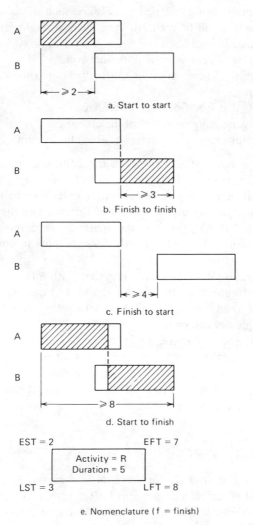

a. Start to start

b. Finish to finish

c. Finish to start

d. Start to finish

e. Nomenclature (f = finish)

Figure 8-21 Precedence diagramming conventions.

While there are computer programs that optimize PERT/CPM problems, GERT and its various enhancements are computer simulations. Most of the programs (and the enhancements) are the result of work conducted by Pritsker [37]. His latest GERT modeling package (at this writing) is called Q-GERT and simulates queues, or waiting lines, in the network. (There are other extensions of PERT that have some features similar to GERT and Q-GERT—VERT, for example— but GERT seems to be the most widely used extension.)

The steps employed in using GERT are these:

1. Convert the qualitative description of the project Action Plan into a network, just as in the use of PERT/CPM.
2. Collect the necessary data to describe the arcs of the network, focusing not only on the specific activity being modeled, but also on such characteristics of the activity as the likelihood it will be realized, the chance it might fail, any alternative activities that exist, and the like.
3. Determine the *equivalent function* of the network.
4. Convert the equivalent function of the network into the following two performance measures:
   The probability that specific nodes are realized
   The "moment generating function" of the arc times.
5. Analyze the results and make inferences about the system.

It is not appropriate to deal here with the complex solution techniques employed for GERT networks. They make use of topology equations, equivalent functions, moment generating functions, and extensive calculation. The interested reader is urged to consult the papers of Pritsker and his associates [37], for instance, for formal descriptions of the methods involved in formulating and solving GERT networks. Instead, we will describe how to construct a GERT network of a simple situation.

The list of common GERT symbols, together with a few examples, is given in Figure 8-22. This figure describes the left-hand, or input, side of the nodes first, and then the right-hand, output, side next. All combinations of input and output symbols are feasible, as shown in the examples.

Now let us describe a manufacturing project situation developed by Pritsker and portray it through the GERT approach. This situation concerns the initiation of a new production process developed by manufacturing engineering for an electronic component. The resulting GERT model could just as well describe an R & D project, a government project, or a Girl Scout project.

Sample Problem, Modeled with GERT

A part is manufactured on a production line in 4 hours. Following manufacture, parts are inspected. There is a 25 percent failure rate, and failed parts must be reworked. Inspection time is a stochastic variable, exponentially distributed, with a mean of 1 hour. Rework takes 3 hours, and 30 percent of the reworked parts fail

Symbol	Name	Explanation
	INPUT	
K	Exclusive—or	Any branch leading into the node causes the node to be realized, but only one branch can occur.
$<$	Inclusive—or	Any branch causes the node to be realized and at the time of the earliest branch.
$($	And	The node is realized only after ALL branches have occurred.
	OUTPUT	
$)$	Deterministic	All branches out must occur if the node is realized.
$>$	Probabilistic	Only one of the branches may occur if the node is realized.
	EXAMPLES	
	Beginning node with branches that must occur.	
	Ending node that occurs whenever **a** or **b** occurs.	
	Intermediate node that occurs if **a** occurs with either **b** or **c** following.	
	Intermediate node that occurs when all **a**, **b**, and **c** occur with either **d** or **e** following.	

Figure 8-22 GERT symbols.

the next inspection and must be scrapped. Parts that pass their original inspection or pass inspection after rework are sent to a finishing, a process that requires 10 hours 60 percent of the time and 14 hours otherwise. A final inspection rejects 5 percent of the finished parts, which are then scrapped.

We can now model this situation as a GERT network so that it can be solved for the expected percentage of good parts, and the expected time required to produce a good part. This GERT network is illustrated in Figure 8-23.

Activity **a** represents the output of the 4-hour manufacturing process. The outputs enter an inspection from which 75 percent are passed, **c**, and 25 percent fail, **b**. The latter go to rework, with flow **d** emerging. Another inspection takes place—**e** (30 percent of 25 percent = 7.5%) flows to scrap, while the successfully reworked parts (70 percent of 25 percent = 17.5 percent), represented by **f**, go with the other good parts, **c**, to the finishing process. Sixty percent of this input requires 10 hours of work, **g**, and the remainder (40 percent) needs 14 hours, **h**,

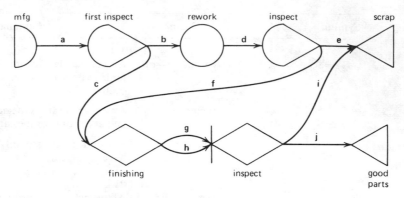

Figure 8-23 Sample GERT network.

the final inspection process discards 5 percent of the output, which goes through finishing, **i** goes to scrap, and the remainder (which is 87.875 percent of the original input) is sent to "good parts," **j**.

The time for an "average" part to proceed through the network can be found in much the same way as we calculated the output. The result of the entire analysis is therefore considerably richer than the simpler PERT/CPM. It should, however, be obvious that the input information requirements for GERT are more extensive and the computational requirements are far more extensive than for PERT/CPM, particularly for large networks. As always, the PM should adopt the simplest scheduling technique consistent with the needs of the project.

Other Methods

Two straightforward methods for project scheduling that do not use networks or Gantt charts are employed by some agencies of the U.S. government. The Goddard Space Flight Center develops its project schedules in three phases. Phase I is Advanced Schedule Planning, where the basic project schedule is developed directly from the Work Breakdown Structure. Phase I lists all major elements of the project. This is used for presenting the proposed project to NASA and to the Congress and its many committees.

Phase II consists of the preparation of the Operational Schedule. This is the equivalent of the project master schedule. Phase III is Schedule Administration. In this last phase, the project is monitored and the master schedule is updated through the use of biweekly reports. Any necessary corrections and alterations to the project master schedule are made as a result of this process.

The Department of General Services uses a project scheduling system that provides planning, scheduling, and control in three distinct but closely related stages. Activity scheduling is the initial stage. At this point the planner attempts to develop optimum timing for the start and completion of all tasks associated with the project. Labor-hour and progress scheduling is carried out in the second stage. This identifies the labor (and other resources) required to initiate project activities on time and to sustain the necessary rate of progress to keep the project on schedule. Progress reporting takes place in the final stage. In this third stage, the project is monitored and a more or less constant stream of reports are filed so that appropriate action can be taken to keep the project on schedule. The information reported to senior management shows the project status relative to activity milestones and actual progress relative to planned progress. The value of the progress achieved as well as the estimated value of progress remaining is used to calculate (forecast) the labor-hours required to complete the remaining work on schedule.

Note that these methods parallel the basic concept of the project Action Plan with its specific steps to be taken, its estimate of resource requirements, times, and precedences, and most important, with each step in the higher-level plans broken down into lower-level Action Plans.

A Mild Caveat

Many researchers, most recently Richard Schonberger [41], have exposed some interesting anomalies in PERT/CPM networks which show that deterministic times are optimistically biased. In essence, the effect comes about when one or more paths in the network have times that are close to the critical path time. If the non-critical path is delayed and becomes critical, it may extend the average completion time for the network. Schonberger develops a simple example to illustrate this finding. His critique extends to the three time estimate method, which allows for activity time variance on a path-by-path analysis, but does not consider delays caused by path interaction. (Remember that the ability to calculate path variance as the sum of the variances of individual activities is based on the assumption of independence between activities—and paths.)

Several possible conclusions may be drawn from Schonberger's insight:

- Projects will probably be late—relative to the deterministic critical path.
- Network simulation is probably not worth the added expense.
- Deterministic time estimates should be used in place of the three time estimates.
- The network developed from these deterministic time estimates should be subjectively reevaluated for any path interaction factors that would tend to make the project late.
- Critical or near-critical activities should be intensively managed, the usual practice of project managers.

While it is helpful to be aware of these issues, we are not entirely in agreement with Schonberger's conclusions. The costs of simulation techniques are decreasing rapidly. GERT is an example of a simulation-based technique that is quite valuable *if the required information base and computational power are readily available*. GERT and other computer programs come in sufficient variety to have a great many applications in project management.

A stronger area of disagreement is our belief that three time estimates are far more informative to the PM than deterministic time estimates. The degree of activity variability is a clear indicator of the need for adaptive planning. In any case, for most project managers, the use of deterministic times does not mean that they estimate the variance of each and every activity to be zero, but rather that they assume that optimistic and pessimistic times are symmetrically distributed around the most likely times and cancel out. The distinction between a deterministic time and an average time is easily ignored by the unsophisticated. Further, this error is compounded because it leads to the false assumption that the expected time approach is the same as the deterministic approach. Clearly, the critical times would be the same in either case, which leads the unwary to the error.

As we illustrated earlier with Lotus 1-2-3®, readily available and inexpensive computer software makes the additional computational cost of three time estimates a trivial matter. Perhaps more serious is the advice to increase the calculated network time by subjective evaluation of the effects of path interaction. This will extend the network time by some arbitrary amount, usually in the form of network slack, a time-consuming but non-resource-consuming "activity" added to the end of the project, which automatically adds duration to the critical path. (In Chapter 9 we will define a similar activity as a "pseudo-activity".)

This practice makes the operation of *Parkinson's Law* a clear and present danger. The work done on project elements is almost certain to "expand to fill the additional time," as Schonberger himself and many others have observed. We favor a different way of handling the problem. If three time estimates are used, and if various completion dates with their associated probabilities are calculated, and, finally, if the PM and senior management can agree on a mutually acceptable completion date for the project, the PM can be held accountable for on-time delivery. If an additional allowance is needed for path interdependence, some mutually acceptable network slack can be added. It should not, however, make the PM any less accountable for project performance.

Using These Tools

We have heard differing opinions on the value of each of the tools we have described, including many of the computerized Project Management Information Systems (PMISs). We have been told, "No one uses PERT/CPM/Precedence Diagramming," "No one uses three-time PERT," and "No one uses ————— computer package." But we have first-hand knowledge of PERT users, of CPM users, of precedence diagram users. We know PMs who collect and use three time PERT. For example, refer to Figures 8-24 and 8-25. Figure 8-24 is a forty-eight step Action Plan for the syndication of an apartment complex. Note that several of the steps are obvious composites of multistep Action Plans designed for a lower level. Figure 8-25 is an AON network of Figure 8-24. The firm also

	TASK	A	M	B	T(e)	V	T(hr)	V(hr)
1.	Product package received by Secy. in Real Estate (R.E.) Dept.	n/a	(.3)	(.4)				
2.	Secy. checks for duplicates. and forwards all packages in Atlanta region (but not addressed to R.E. staff member) to Atl. via fast mail. Atl. office sends copy of submittal log to L.A. office on weekly basis.	n/a	(.2)	(.3)				
3.	Secy. date stamps, logs, checks for duplication, makes new file, checks for contact source, adds to card file all new packages. Sends criteria letter to new source. Send duplication letter. Forwards package to Admin. Asst. (AA)	(.7)	(.7)	(.9)				
4.	AA reviews package, completes Property Summary Form, forwards to L.A. Reg. Acquisit. Director (RAD) officer or to R.E. staff member to whom package is addressed.	(.5)	(.5)	(.7)				
Total 1-4		1(1.7)	1(1.7)	3(2.3)	1.3	0.11	1.8	0.01
5.	Person to whom package forwarded determines action. (May refer to other or retain for further review.) "Passes" sent to Secy. for files. "Possibles" retained by RAD for further review.	1(.5)	1(.5)	1(1)	1.0		.58	0.01
6.	RAD gets add'l data as needed, gets demographics and comparables. Rough numbers run. Looks for the "opportunities." If viable, continue.	4(3)	5(3)	3(2.3)	5.5	0.69	3.83	0.69
7.	RAD (with input from Prop.Mgt.) does prelim. projections, and structures price, terms, rehab, and syndic. based on discussions with seller. Determines viability	1(6)	1(8)	3(20)	1.3	0.11	8.33	5.44
8.	Prelim site visit by RAD or high confidence other. Verify opportunity aspects.	2(16)	2(16)	3(24)	2.2	0.33	17.33	1.78
9.	RAD refers prop. to Acquisition Manager (AM) with assumptions for analysis. Add'l data from RAD as needed by AM.	1(3)	2(5)	10(30)	3.2	2.25	8.83	20.25
10.	AM does computer analysis of projections and structure.	1(3)	2(6)	3(18)	2.0	0.11	7.5	6.25
11.	RAD and AM review analysis with Prop. Mgt. (PM)	1(2)	1(4)	1(8)	1.0		4.33	1.0
12.	RAD maintains contact with seller	5(0)	10(0)	12(0)	9.5	1.36		
13.	RAD and AM review property, numbers and terms with VPs Legal or RE for possible issuance of Letter of Intent (LOI)	1(1)	3(2)	8(3)	3.5	1.36	2.0	0.11
14.	VP-Leg. and/or VP-RE issue LOI. (RAD may issue LOI with VP approval)	1(3)	1(6)	2(10)	1.2	0.03	6.17	1.36
15.	AA (RE) requests, and Finance issues Sprint code.	1(1)	1(1)	3(1)	1.3	0.11	1.0	
16.	If not already done, VP briefs Pres. on deal and projections	1(1)	1(1)	1(2)	1.0		1.17	0.03
17.	RAD transfers call with potential counteroffer from seller to VP to receive the counteroffer.	3(0)	4(0)	10(0)	4.8	1.36		
18.	Negotiating responsibility shifts from RAD to VP	1(1)	1(1)	1(2)	1.0		1.2	0.03
19.	VP negotiates deal	3(1)	5(3)	15(5)	6.3	4.0	3.0	0.44
20.	RAD, AM and VP restructure deal as needed	1(2)	3(4)	5(6)	3.0	0.44	4.0	0.44
21.	VP Leg. determines Marketing, timing, banking, etc. and reviews with Pres. Arranges escrow deposit.	1(3)	10(16)	15(25)	9.3	5.44	15.3	13.44
22.	Acceptance of LOI by seller	1(0)	3(0)	5(0)	3.0	0.44		
23.	Conduct due diligence on prop.							
	A. Legal dept.	1(2)	5(3)	20(10)	6.8	10.03	4.0	1.78
	B. Prop. Mgt. dept.	4(40)	6(60)	8(80)	6.0	0.44	60.0	44.44

Figure 8-24

C. Pres. visits prop. if not previously visited.	1(0)	2(0)	5(0)	2.3	0.44		
24. Legal prepares initial Deal Memo	1(2)	2(3)	3(3)	2.0	0.11	2.8	0.03
25. VP Leg. gets preliminary Mktg. and banking commitments.	1(1)	1(1)	2(1)	1.2	0.03	1.0	
26. Prop. Manager prepares narrative sections for PPM.	3(30)	5(40)	8(60)	5.2	0.69	41.7	25.0
A. Prop. description, site plan, vicinity map, attach good photo of prop.							
B. Gather info. for descript. of city area-wide economy, gen'l econ. condits., demographics.							
C. Describe competitive props. including map of competition							
D. Rent schedules/lease summaries note nature of leases/contracts							
27. Controller (PM) prepares prop. operating projections, based on due diligence and corrections from VP Leg. and Pres.	3(20)	3(20)	8(50)	3.8	0.69	25.0	25.0
28. Fin. and RE (F/RE) prepare initial deprec. and amortization schedules, and tax and cash flow projections.	3(18)	4(23)	10(65)	4.8	1.36	29.2	61.40
29. Legal prepare initial draft of contract	1(0)	1(0)	1(0)	1.0	1.78		
30. A. Structure partnership, includ. number and size of units, min. purchase, investor's contributs., spread equity alternative. G.P. compensation. B. Limited partner's return and allocations, rate and period of accrual for annual priority return; describe cum. and non-cumulative returns							
Finance dept.	8(24.2)	12(40)	20(80)	12.7	4.0	44.0	86.49
Legal dept.	2(4)	3(6)	5(12)	3.2	0.25	6.67	1.78
Real Estate dept.	2(16)	4(20)	10(40)	4.7	1.78	22.67	16.0
C. Fin./RE does following: 1. PPM projections 2. Prep. footnotes for projections 3. Prep. supplemental projections and footnotes for GPs 4. Description of offering 5. All tables and charts							
Fin. portion of work	13(90.4)	20(120)	40(160)	22.2	20.25	121.73	134.56
RE portion of work	3(20)	3(20)	3(20)	3.0		20.0	
31. VPs L/RE and Pres. approve deal then, deliver contract to seller, negotiate, Pres. final approval,	5(0)	25(0)	65(0)	28.3	100.0		
32. Get final GP commitment	2(0)	5(0)	10(0)	5.3	1.78		
33. Legal writes, assembles material for PPM A. Describe specific goals for prop. How attained. Projected renovation, value-added program. B. Draft Terms of Offerings, G.P. Comp., Risk Factors, Investment Goals, Descript. of Property, Competition							
C. Supervise counsel's prep. of Fed. Income Tax Consequences D. Prepare Summary of Partnership Agreement E. Notes: Subscriber promissory, Other F. Prep. of tables, graphs, chart G. PPM Review	20(250)	25(300)	30(500)	25.0	2.78	291.7	1736.11
34. Legal does following: A. Prepare, execute, and record Certif. of Ltd. Prtnrshp.							
B. Leg. does first revision, then supervises counsel's prep. of partnership agreement.	3(20)	4(30)	5(40)	4.0	0.11	30.0	11.11
C. Prep. ficticious business name statement D. Get names of states in which offering will be made from Mktg. Send to counsel.							

Figure 8-24 Continued.

	E. Supervise counsel's prep. of selling agreement							
	F. Draft Descript. of Acquisition							
35.	Execute contract.	2(1)	4(2)	6(2)	4.0	0.11	1.83	0.03
36.	Fin. arrange escrow deposit and bridge (gap) financing	5(0)	8(0)	20(0)	9.5	6.25		
37.	Fin. makes "Good faith deposit"	1(2)	5(8)	20(16)	6.8	10.03	8.3	5.44
38.	Get final GP approvals, if any changes or disclosures from final contract.	2(1)	5(3)	7(5)	4.8	0.69	3.0	0.44
39.	President reviews Selling Agreement and GP representations	1(1)	1(1)	2(1)	1.2	0.03	1.0	
40.	Prepare Mktg. brochure	5(20)	10(25)	15(35)	10.(	2.78	25.8	6.25
41.	If "we.have a deal," Finance does: A. Open cash accounts B. Get Fed. Tax Ident. No. C. Arrange spread equity finance. D. Describe bank acct. estab. in name of prtnrshp, and amount deposited	1(4)	5(20)	60(120)	13.5	96.69	34.0	373.78
42.	Legal dept. arrange printing	2(2)	3(2)	8(4)	3.7	1.0	2.3	0.11
43.	Commence marketing process Marketing brochure	10(20)	15(25)	20(35)	15.0	2.78	25.83	6.25
44.	Legal/Mktg. does following: A. Coordinate number of circulars, distribution, tracking of offerees B. Blue Sky filing	2(4)	4(5)	7(7)	4.2	0.69	5.17	0.25
45.	Prop. Mgt./Fin. prepares for closing and take-over. At closing, prorations of taxes, rents, service contracts.	3(4)	5(8)	10(24)	5.5	1.36	10.0	11.11
46.	PM final inspect. On-site at close.	1(4)	1(8)	2(12)	1.2	0.03	8.0	1.78
47.	Legal closes	2(8)	2(14)	4(25)	2.3	0.11	14.83	8.03
48.	Legal issues Post Closing Memorandum	2(5)	5(8)	10(10)	5.3	1.78	7.83	0.69

Figure 8-24 Concluded.

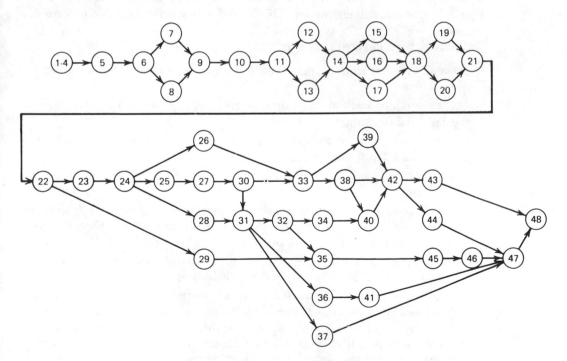

Figure 8-25 Apartment complex network

has a Gantt chart version of the network that is used for tracking each project. Figure 8-24 also contains three time estimates of the "calendar" time used for each step and of the "resource" time used for each step. The time estimate *2(10)* is read, "2 days, 10 labor-hours." The data are useful for scheduling work loads.

We are reluctant to give advice about which tools to use. If the PM indulges in a bit of experimentation with the major systems, their relative advantages and disadvantages *in a given application* will become evident. Digman and Green [12] have developed an interesting and useful framework for evaluating the various planning and control techniques. It is included as a reading at the end of this chapter. The PM should opt for the simplest method sufficient to the needs of the project and its parent firm. If a computerized PMIS is used, the problem is avoided. Most require inputs of specific form and produce their own unique outputs. Again, a thorough demonstration of the PMIS should be a prerequisite to purchase or lease. In the end, these tools are intended to help the PM manage the project. The PM should select those that seem most useful—and most comfortable. The PMIS will be discussed in more detail in Chapter 11.

8.5 SUMMARY

In this chapter the scheduling aspect of project implementation was addressed. Following a description of the benefits of using a network for planning and controlling a project, the PERT/CPM approach was described. Next, Gantt charts were described and their relation to the PERT/CPM diagram was illustrated. Finally, precedence diagramming, GERT, and a few other extensions were discussed.

Specific points covered in the chapter were these:

- Scheduling is particularly important to projects because of complex coordination problems.
- The network approach to scheduling offers a number of specific advantages of special value for projects.
- In origination, and subsequent applications as well, PERT was for R & D projects and CPM for construction projects.
- Critical project tasks typically constitute fewer than 10 percent of all the project tasks.
- Although research indicates technological performance is not significantly affected by the use of PERT/CPM, there did seem to be a significantly lower probability of cost and schedule overruns.
- Network techniques can adopt either an activity-on-node or activity-on-arc framework without significantly altering the analysis.
- Networks are usually constructed from left to right, indicating activity precedence and event times as the network is constructed. Through use of the network, critical activities and events are identified, early and late activity start times are found, available slacks for each activity are determined, and probabilities of project completion by various times are calculated.

- Gantt charts, a monitoring technique, are closely related to network diagrams, but are more easily understood and provide a clearer picture of the current state of the project. However, while offering some advantages, they also have some drawbacks, such as not clearly indicating task precedence and dependencies.
- GERT is one of the more common extensions of PERT/CPM and allows:
  Probabilistic branching from nodes
  Various probability distributions for the activity times
  Looping in the network
  Representation of project elements other than time, such as cost or reliability.

In the next chapter we investigate the scheduling problem further when multiple projects require a set of common resources to be shared. Again, a number of techniques are useful for resource allocation and activity expediting under such circumstances.

8.6 GLOSSARY

ACTIVITY—A specific project task that requires resources and time to complete.

ACTIVITY-ON-ARC (NODE)—The two ways of illustrating a network: placing the activities on the arcs or on the nodes.

ARC—The line connecting two nodes.

CRASH—In CPM, an activity can be conducted at a normal pace or at an expedited pace, known as *crashed,* at a greater cost.

CRITICAL—An activity or event that, if delayed, will delay some other important event, commonly project completion.

EVENT—A end state for one or more activities that occurs at a specific point in time.

GANTT CHART—A manner of illustrating multiple, time-based activities on a horizontal time scale.

MILESTONE—a clearly identifiable point in a project or set of activities that commonly denotes a reporting requirement or completion of a large or important set of activities.

NETWORK—A combination of interrelated activities and events depicted with arcs and nodes.

NODE—An intersection of two or more lines or arrows, commonly used for depicting an event or activity.

PATH—A sequence of lines and nodes in a network.

PROJECT MANAGEMENT INFORMATION SYSTEM (PMIS)—The systems, activities, and data that allow information flow in a project, frequently computerized but not always.

TRADE-OFF—The amount of one factor that must be sacrificed in order to achieve more or less of another factor.

8.7 PROJECT TEAM ASSIGNMENT

The task for the project team is to formulate the schedule for the project from the work breakdown structure. Use optimistic, most likely, and pessimistic times for each activity; construct the PERT diagram; and conduct a full analysis of the data, including likelihoods of delay by certain amounts of time and 80, 90, and 99 percent likelihood of completion times. Identify the project's critical path, the critical path to each event, the slacks for each activity, and the earliest and latest occurrence times. Show the schedule as an AON and an AOA network, as well as a Gantt chart with milestones. Graph the budget from Chapter 7 on the Gantt chart to illustrate cash flow needs. Finally, comment on the applicability of one of the other network approaches such as GERT or precedence diagramming to your project.

8.8 MATERIAL REVIEW QUESTIONS

1. Define *activity, event,* and *path* as used in network construction. What is a dummy activity?
2. What characteristic of the critical path times makes them critical?
3. What two factors are compared by Gantt charting? How does the Gantt chart differ in purpose from the project master schedule?
4. How is the GERT technique different from the PERT technique?
5. When is each scheduling technique appropriate to use?

8.9 CONCEPTUAL DISCUSSION QUESTIONS

1. How do you think the network technique could be used to estimate costs for manufacturing?
2. What are some benefits of the network approach to project planning? What are some drawbacks?
3. What is your position on the conclusions in the Caveat section?
4. Why is PERT of significant value to the project manager?

8.10 PROBLEMS

1. Given the following activities and precedents, draw a PERT/CPM diagram:

Activity	Immediate Predecessor
A	—
B	—
C	A
D	A,B
E	A,B
F	C
G	D,F
H	E,G

2. Given the following network:

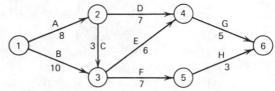

(a) What is the critical path?
(b) How long will it take to complete this project?
(c) Can activity **B** be delayed without delaying the completion of the project? If so, how many days?
(d) Convert the PERT diagram to a Gantt chart.

3. Given the estimated activity times below and the network in 2. above:

Activity	a	m	b
A	6	7	14
B	8	10	12
C	2	3	4
D	6	7	8
E	5	5.5	9
F	5	7	9
G	4	6	8
H	2.5	3	3.5

What is the probability that the project will be completed within:
(a) 21 days?
(b) 22 days?
(c) 25 days?

4.

Activity*	a	m	b
AB	3	6	9
AC	1	4	7
CB	0	3	6
CD	3	3	3
CE	2	2	8
BD	0	0	6
BE	2	5	8
DF	4	4	10
DE	1	1	1
EF	1	4	7

Find:
(a) the critical path;
(b) all event slacks;
(c) critical path to event D;
(d) probability of completion in 14 days;
(e) the effect if CD slips to 6 days; to 7 days; to 8 days.

*The nomenclature AB means the activity *between* events A and B.

5.

Activity*	TE
AB	1
AC	2
AD	3
DC	4
CB	3
DE	8
CF	2
BF	4
IJ	2
CE	6
EF	5
FG	10
FH	11
EH	1
GH	9
EJ	3
GI	8
HJ	6

(a) Draw the PERT diagram.
(b) Find the critical path.
(c) Find the completion time.

*See nomenclature note in Problem 4.

6. The Denver Iron & Steel Company is expanding its operations to include a new drive-in weigh station. The weigh station will be a heated/air-conditioned building with a large floor and small office. The large room will have the scales, a 15-foot counter, and several display cases for its equipment.

Before erection of the building, the project manager evaluated the project using PERT/CPM analysis. The following activities with their corresponding times were recorded:

#	Activity	Times			Preceding Tasks
		Optimistic	Most Likely	Pessimistic	
1	Lay foundation	8	10	13	—
2	Dig hole for scale	5	6	8	—
3	Insert scale bases	13	15	21	2
4	Erect frame	10	12	14	1,3
5	Complete building	11	20	30	4
6	Insert scales	4	5	8	5
7	Insert display cases	2	3	4	5
8	Put in office equipment	4	6	10	7
9	Finishing touches	2	3	4	8,6

Using PERT/CPM analysis, find the critical path, the slack times, and the expected completion time.

7. The Dock B Shipbuilding Company received a contract from the government to build the prototype of a new U.S. Navy destroyer. The destroyer is to be nuclear-powered, have advanced weapon systems, and have a small crew. The Dock B Shipbuilding Company has assigned to the task a project manager who, in turn, has delegated minor subprojects to subordinate managers.

The project was evaluated using PERT/CPM analysis. Due to the extensive length of the project, many activities were combined. The following is the result.

Activity*	Time
AB	3
BC	6
BD	2
BF	5
BE	4
CD	9
DG	20
FG	6
EH	11
EI	19
GJ	1
HK	3
IL	9
LM	12
KN	7
JO	4
MN	15
NP	13
OP	10

Find the critical path and expected completion date.
*See nomenclature note in Problem 4.

8. The following PERT chart was prepared at the beginning of a small construction project.

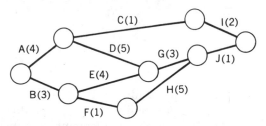

The duration, in days, follows the letter of each activity. What is the critical path? Which activities should be monitored most closely?

At the end of the first week of construction, it was noted that activity **A** was completed in 2.5 days, but activity **B** required 4.5 days. What impact does this have on the project? Are the same activities critical?

9. Given the following project find the probability of completion by 17 weeks. By 24 weeks. By what date is management 90 percent sure completion will occur?

Times(weeks)

Activity	Optimistic	Most likely	Pessimistic
1–2	5	11	11
1–3	10	10	10
1–4	2	5	8
2–6	1	7	13
3–6	4	4	10
3–7	4	7	10
3–5	2	2	2
4–5	0	6	6
5–7	2	8	14
6–7	1	4	7

If the firm can complete the project within 18 weeks it will receive a bonus of $10,000. But if the project delays beyond 22 weeks it must pay a penalty of $5,000. If the firm can choose whether or not to bid on this project, what should its decision be if the project is only a breakeven one normally?

10. Given a project with the following information:

Activity	Standard Deviation	Critical?	Duration
a	2	yes	2
b	1		3
c	0	yes	4
d	3		2
e	1	yes	1
f	2		6
g	2	yes	4
h	0	yes	2

Find:

a. The probability of completing this project in 12 weeks (or less).
b. The probability of completing this project in 16 weeks (or less).
c. The probability of completing this project in 13 weeks (or less).
d. The number of weeks required to assure a 92.5 percent chance of completion.

11. Given a PERT network:

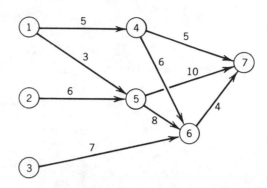

Note that four activities can start immediately.

Find:
a. The critical path.
b. The earliest time to complete the project.
c. The slack on activities **4-6, 5-6,** and **4-7**.
d. Draw the network on a Gantt chart.

12. The events of the project below are designated as 1, 2, and so on.
a. Draw the PERT network and the Gantt chart.
b. Find the critical path.
c. Find the slacks on all the events and activities.

Activity	Preceding Event	Succeeding Event	t_e (weeks)	Preceding Activities
a	1	2	3	none
b	1	3	6	none
c	1	4	8	none
d	2	5	7	a
e	3	5	5	b
f	4	5	10	c
g	4	6	4	c
h	5	7	5	d,e,f
i	6	7	6	g

13. Given the following PERT network (times are in weeks):

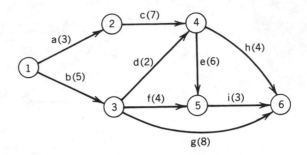

Determine:

a. The EOT and LOT for each event.
b. The slacks on all events and activities.
c. The critical activities and path.

14. Given the following schedule for a liability work package done as part of an accounting audit in a corporation:

Activity	Duration (days)	Preceding Activities
a. Obtain schedule of liabilities	3	None
b. Mail confirmation	15	a
c. Test pension plan	5	a
d. Vouch selected liabilities	60	a
e. Test accruals and amortization	6	d
f. Process confirmations	40	b
g. Reconcile interest expense to debt	10	c,e
h. Verify debt restriction compliance	7	f
i. Investigate debit balances	6	g
j. Review subsequent payments	12	h,i

Find:

a. The critical path
b. The slack time on "process confirmations."
c. The slack time on "test pension plan."
d. The slack time on "verify debt restriction compliance."

15. In the project network shown in the figure below, the number alongside each activity designates the activity duration (t_e) in weeks.

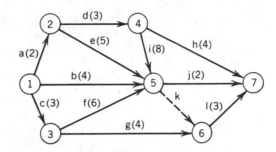

Determine:

a. The EOT and LOT for each event.
b. The earliest time that the project can be completed.
c. The slack on all events and activities.
d. The critical events and activities.
e. The critical path.

16. Given the following information regarding a project:

Activity	t_e (weeks)	Preceding Activities
a	3	none
b	1	none
c	3	a
d	4	a
e	4	b
f	5	b
g	2	c,e
h	3	f

a. Draw the PERT network and the Gantt chart.
b. What is the critical path?
c. What will the scheduled (earliest completion) time for the entire project be?
d. What is the critical path to event 4 (end of activities **c** and **e**)? What is the earliest time that this event can be reached?
e. What is the effect on the project if activity **e** takes an extra week? Two extra weeks? Three extra weeks?

17. Construct a network for the project below and find its critical path.

Activity	t_e (weeks)	Preceding Activities
a	3	None
b	5	a
c	3	a
d	1	c
e	3	b
f	4	b,d
g	2	c
h	3	g,f
i	1	e,h

18. Construct a network for the project:

Activity	t_e (weeks)	Preceding Activities
a	3	None
b	5	None
c	14	a
d	5	a
e	4	b
f	7	b
g	8	d,e
h	5	g,f

a. Draw the PERT network and the Gantt chart.

b. Find the critical path.

c. Assume activity **a** took five weeks. Replan the project.

d. From where would you suggest transferring resources, and to what activities so that the original target date may be maintained?

8.11 INCIDENTS FOR DISCUSSION

Yankee Chair Company

The Yankee Chair Company was anxious to get a new model rocking chair onto the market. Past efforts to introduce new models had resulted in frustrating failures. Jim Ricks, president of Yankee Chair, was determined that it would not happen again with the newest model. He had no confidence in his current management team, so he hired Stan Dymore, a local consultant, to organize and manage this project. He assigned a Yankee Chair manager, Tom Gort, to work with Dymore to start developing some talent for project management within the company. Dymore decided to set up a PERT network and guided Gort through the process of listing activities, assigning precedence, and estimating completion times. He also explained the critical path concept to Gort, who by this time had a reasonable grasp of the project direction. At the first review session with Mr. Ricks, the PERT approach was accepted enthusiastically, but toward the end of the review Dymore made some critical remarks about the product design and was subsequently released from the project.

Ricks then asked Gort if he could carry on the PERT approach by himself. Gort jumped at the chance, but later in his office he began to question whether or not he really could use the PERT network effectively. Dymore had made a guess at what the critical path would be and how long the project would take, but he had also told Gort that several other calculations had to be made in order to calculate the exact time estimates for each activity and the variances of those activity times. Gort really did not understand the mathematics involved and certainly did not want to look bad in Rick's eyes, so he decided to take Dymore's guess at the critical path and get the best possible estimates of those activity times. By concentrating his attention on the critical path activities and ignoring the variance issues, he figured he could bring the project in on time.

Question: Will Gort's approach work? How much more of a gamble is Gort taking than any project manager normally takes?

Cincinnati Equipment Company

Cincinnati Equipment Company, which specializes in the manufacture of modern construction equipment, will be building a facility to house a new foundry. The company has selected a project manager and team to follow the project through to completion. The project team is very interested in selecting an appropriate scheduling technique for the project. The project manager has thus set the following guidelines for the selection process: simple; able to show durations of events, the flow of work, and the relative sequence of events; able to indicate planning and actual flow, which items may proceed at the same time, and how far they are from completion. The assistant project manager favors the Gantt chart, the finance representative likes PERT, and the construction supervisor prefers CPM.

Question: If you were the project manager, which method would you use, and why?

8.12 BIBLIOGRAPHY

1. Archibald, R. D., and R. L. Villoria. *Network Based Management Systems (PERT/CPM)*. Wiley, 1967.
2. Ayers, R. H., R. M. Walsh, and R. G. Staples. "Project Management by the Critical Path Method." *Research Management,* July 1970.
3. Baker, B. N., and R. L. Eris. *An Introduction to PERT-CPM*. Irwin, 1964.
4. Bennington, L. A. *TREND—New Management Information from Networks*. Sandoz Co. Reprint, 1974.
5. Berkwitt, G. W. "Management Rediscovers CPM" *Dun's Review,* May 1971.

6. Blystone, E. E., and R. G. Odum. "A Case Study of CPM in a Manufacturing Situation." *Journal of Industrial Engineering,* Nov.–Dec. 1964.

7. Brennan, J. *Applications of Critical Path Techniques.* American Elsevier, 1968.

8. Clark, C. G., D. G. Malcom, J. H. Rosenbloom, and W. Fazar. "Applications of a Technique for Research and Development Program Management." *Operations Research,* Sept.–Oct. 1959.

9. Davis, E. W. "Networks: Resource Allocation." *Industrial Engineering,* April 1974.

10. Dean, B. V. *Project Management: Methods and Studies.* Elsevier, 1985.

11. DeCoster, D. T. "PERT/Cost—The Challenge." *Management Services,* May–June 1964

12. Digman, L. A., and G. I. Green. "A Framework of Evaluating Network Planning and Control Techniques." *Research Management,* Jan. 1981.

13. Evarts, H. E. *Introduction to PERT.* Allyn and Bacon, 1964.

14. Gallagher, C., "A Note on Pert Assumptions," *Management Science,* October 1987.

15. Gido, J. *An Introduction to Project Planning,* 2nd ed. Industrial Press, 1986.

16. Golfarb, N., and W. K. Kaiser. *Gantt Charts and Statistical Quality Control.* Hofstra University Press, 1964.

17. Horowitz, J. *Critical Path Scheduling: Management Control Through CPM and PERT.* Ronald Press, 1967.

18. Jenett, E. "Experience with and Evaluation of Critical Path Methods." *Chemical Engineering,* Feb. 1969.

19. Karns, L. A., and L. A. Swanson. "The Effect of Activity Time Variance on Critical Path Scheduling." *Project Management Quarterly,* Dec. 1973.

20. Kelly, J. E., and M. R. Walker, "Critical Path Planning and Scheduling." *Proceedings, Eastern Joint Computer Conference,* 1959.

21. Kerzner, H. *Project Management: A Systems Approach to Planning, Scheduling, and Controlling.* Van Nostrand Reinhold, 1984.

22. Kirkpatrick, C. A. and R. C. Levine. *Planning and Control with PERT/CPM.* Mc-Graw-Hill, 1966.

23. Levy, J. E., G. L. Thompson, and J. D. Wiest. "The ABC's of the Critical Path Method." *Harvard Business Review,* Sept.–Oct. 1963.

24. Liberatore, M. J., and G. J. Titus. "The Practice of Management Science in R & D Project Management," *Management Science,* Aug. 1983.

25. Littlefield, T. K., Jr., and P. H. Randolph. "An Answer to Sasieni's Question on PERT Times." *Management Science,* Oct. 1987.

26. Lockyer, K. G. *An Introduction to Critical Path Analysis.* Pitman, London, 1964.

27. Lowe, C. W. *Critical Path Analysis by Bar Chart.* Business Books, London, 1966.

28. MacCrimmon, K. R., and C. R. Ryavec. "An Analytical Study of PERT Assumptions." *Operations Research,* Jan.–Feb. 1964.

29. Marquis, D. C. "A Project Team Plus PERT=Success. Or Does It?" *Innovation,* 1969.

30. Martino, R. L. *Project Management and Control, Vol. I.* American Management Association, 1964.

31. Meyer, W. C., J. B. Ritter, and L. R. Shaffer. *The Critical Path Method.* McGraw-Hill, 1965.

32. Moder, J. J., C. R. Phillips, and E. W. Davis. *Project Management with CPM, PERT, and Precedence Diagramming,* 3rd ed. Van Nostrand Reinhold, 1983.

33. Morris, L. N. *Critical Path, Construction and Analysis.* Pergamon Press, 1967.

34. Muth, J. F., and G. L. Thompson. *Industrial Scheduling.* Prentice-Hall, 1963.

35. Naik, B. *Project Management: Scheduling and Monitoring by PERT/CPM.* Advent Books, 1984.

36. Pazer, H. H., and L. A. Swanson. *PERTsim, Text and Simulation.* International Textbook Co., 1969.

37. Pritsker, A. A. B. "GERT Networks." *The Production Engineer,* Oct. 1968.

38. Raithe, A. W., ed. *Gantt on Management.* American Management Association, 1961.

39. Saitow, A. R. "CSPC: Reporting Project Progress to the Top." *Harvard Business Review,* Jan.–Feb. 1969.

40. Sasieni, M. W. "A Note on PERT Times." *Management Science,* Dec. 1986.

41. Schonberger, R. J. "Why Projects are Always Late: A Rationale Based on Manual Simulation of a PERT/CPM Network." *Interfaces,* Oct. 1981.

42. Turban, E. "The Line of Balance—A Management By Exception Tool." *Journal of Industrial Engineering,* Sept. 1968.

43. Vazsonyi, A. "L'Histoire de Grandeur et la Decadence de la Methode PERT." *Management Science,* April 1979.

44. Wiest, J. D. "A Heuristic Model for Scheduling Large Projects with Limited Resources." *Management Science,* Feb. 1967.

45. Wiest, J. D., and F. K. Levy, *A Management Guide to PERT/CPM,* 2nd ed. Prentice-Hall, 1977.

46. Woodgate, H. S. *Planning by Network.* Business Publications, 1964.

8.13 Case: The Sharon Construction Corporation*

The Sharon Construction Corporation has been awarded a contract for the construction of a 20,000-seat stadium. The construction must start by February 15 and be completed within one year. A penalty clause of $15,000 per week of delay beyond February 15 of next year is written into the contract.

Jim Brown, the president of the company, called a planning meeting. In the meeting he expressed great satisfaction at obtaining the contract and revealed that the company could net as much as $300,000 on the project. He was confident that the project could be completed on time with an allowance made for the usual delays anticipated in such a large project.

Bonnie Green, the director of personnel, agreed that in a normal year only slight delays might develop due to a shortage of labor. However, she reminded the president that for such a large project, the company would have to use unionized employees and that the construction industry labor agreements were to expire on November 30. Past experience indicated a fifty-fifty chance for a strike.

Jim Brown agreed that a strike might cause a problem. Unfortunately, there was no way to change the contract. He inquired about the prospective length of a strike. Bonnie figured that such a strike would last at least eight weeks (70 percent chance) and possibly twelve weeks (30 Percent chance).

Jim was not too pleased with these prospects. However, before he had a chance to discuss contingency plans he was interrupted by Jack White, the vice president for engineering. Jack commented than an extremely cold December had been predicted. This factor had not been taken into considera-

tion during earlier estimates since previous forecasts called for milder weather. Concrete pouring in a cold December would require in one out of every three cases (depending on the temperature) special heating that cost $500 per week.

This additional information did not please Jim at all. The chances for delay were mounting. And an overhead expense of $500 per week would be incurred in case of any delay.

The technical details of the project are given in the appendix to this case.

The management team was asked to consider alternatives for coping with the situation. At the end of the week five proposals were submitted.

1. Expedite the pouring of seat gallery supports. This would cost $20,000 and cut the duration of the activity to six weeks.
2. The same as proposal 1, but in addition, put a double shift on the filling of the field. A cost of $10,000 would result in a five-week time reduction.
3. The roof is very important since it precedes several activities. The use of three shifts and some overtime could cut six weeks off the roofing at an additional cost of only $9,000.
4. Do nothing until December 1. Then, if December is indeed cold, defer the pouring until the cold wave breaks, schedule permitting, and heat whenever necessary. If a strike occurs, wait until it is over (no other choice) and then expedite *all* remaining activities. In that case, the duration of any activity could be cut to no less than one third of its normal duration. The additional cost per activity for any week which is cut would be $3,000.
5. Do not take any special action; that is, hope and pray that no strike and no cold December occur (no cost).

Analyze the five proposals and make recommendations.

*Source: E. Turban and J. R. Meredith, *Fundamentals of Management Science,* 3rd ed., Business Publications, Inc., 1977, 1981, and 1985. Reproduced by permission.

APPENDIX: TECHNICAL DETAILS OF THE STADIUM

The stadium is an indoor structure with a seating capacity of 20,000. The project begins with clearing the site, an activity that lasts eight weeks. Once the site is clear, the work can start simultaneously on the structure itself and on the field.

The work in the field involves subsurface drainage which lasts 8 weeks, followed by filling for the playing field and track. Only with the completion of the filling (14 weeks) can the installation of the artificial playing turf take place, an activity that consumes 12 weeks.

The work on the structure itself starts with excavation followed by the pouring of concrete footings. Each of these activities takes 4 weeks.

Next comes the pouring of supports for seat galleries (12 weeks), followed by erecting pre-cast galleries (13 weeks). The seats can then be poured (4 weeks) and are ready for painting. However, the painting (3 weeks) cannot begin until the dressing rooms are completed (4 weeks). The dressing rooms can be completed only after the roof is erected (8 weeks). The roof must be erected on a steel structure which takes 4 weeks to install. This activity can start only after the concrete footings are poured.

Once the roof is erected, work can start simultaneously on the lights (5 weeks) and on the scoreboard and other facilities (4 weeks). Assume there are 28 days in February and that February 15 falls on a Monday.

8.14 READING

This article describes a framework that integrates the existing variety of network techniques: GERT, VERT, PERT/COST, PERT/CPM, and LOB. Evaluations of the applicability of each of the various techniques are included, as well as their advantages and limitations. The criteria for applicability include schedule, cost, performance, and risk. The criteria for evaluation include flexibility, reporting, ease of updating, operating cost, database capability, focus, and preparation requirements. The value of this article for managers is the knowledge gained concerning which technique is most appropriate for which situations and what the strengths of each technique are in those situations.

A Framework for Evaluating Network Planning and Control Techniques

L.A. Digman and Gary I. Green
University of Nebraska-Lincoln.

With the advent of project management some twenty years ago, a single manager was made responsible for the totality of actions required to complete the project, with responsibility cutting across the various phases required for project completion as well as the various functional groups in-

© 1981. Reprinted from *Research Management*, January 1981, by permission.

volved in the task. Prior to employment of this approach, several functional managers were responsible for portions of a project, with overall coordination taking a back seat. The success of the single manager concept is well known, and has been greatly facilitated (perhaps made possible) by the concurrent availability of certain planning and control techniques—notably the Program Evaluation and Review Technique and the Critical Path Method (PERT/CPM).

Network-based management techniques (such as PERT/CPM) enabled the project manager to plan diverse undertakings on an integrated basis, as well as to coordinate project tasks and to control work accomplishment. A major advantage of the networking techniques is that they assisted the manager in assessing two critical interrelationships: (1) the interface between various elements and work groups involved in the project; and (2) the relation between current status and likely status at some future point. Thus, the manager was able to plan and institute corrective actions on a more timely and effective basis.

However, as we know, PERT-type systems are most effective in the developmental, design-oriented stages of a project, as opposed to the more repetitive actions required during later project phases. Also, PERT systems, while of decided value in managing time-related concerns, proved to be cumbersome at best in managing costs (PERT/Cost), and of little direct benefit in achieving performance related variables or in managing risks inherent in project-type undertakings. For these reasons, other techniques have typically been employed in conjunction with PERT systems, some in parallel and some sequentially. For example, Line of Balance (LOB) type systems have been used to monitor production and deliveries, the Graphical Evaluation and Review Technique (GERT) adds to PERT the ability to explicitly deal with uncertainties in flow through the network, and newer approaches such as the Venture Evaluation and Review Technique (VERT) expanded GERT to include performance, as well as time and cost factors. (However, VERT's applicability is still primarily in the concept, design and development stages of a project).

The point is that the project manager is faced with an array of systems and techniques which may be used to manage the time, cost, performance, and risk parameters of the project during its life-cycle. The much heralded "total management system" of a few years back has never materialized. This array of somewhat ad-hoc systems may cause problems, inefficiencies, overlaps, and voids if not properly integrated, particularly for the relatively inexperienced management team. A conceptual framework is required to provide project managers with a "roadmap" through the morass of information and decision needs, parameters, phases, techniques, and processing requirements. Providing that framework is the objective of this article.

THE PROJECT LIFE-CYCLE

The normal life-cycle of a product progresses through several somewhat distinct but partially overlapping stages or phases. For example, most new products begin as a concept that is evaluated in various ways, progressing to a design and development phase where the concept is transformed into a product, then to a phase where a quantity of the product or item is produced for sale or use. Use of the item constitutes an operational phase, which terminates when the product or item is rendered obsolete, discontinued, or phased-out in some manner. The relative duration of these stages may vary greatly depending upon the product in question (for example, high volume, long relative production and operational stages may occur for consumer products; a moderate volume, short operational phase for military hardware; a moderate volume, long operating phase for items such as commercial airliners; and, low volume for items such as nuclear reactors). In consumer product parlance, most go through an "invest/grow" stage to be followed later by a "harvest/divest" stage.

Treating the product life-cycle stages as phases of a project, then, results in four basic steps:

1. *Concept Phase*—The phase during which

potentially feasible and profitable candidate products are investigated. Included is: (a) an assessment of the likelihood that competing candidates will operate as desired when designed and manufactured; (b) ′that the candidate will meet the real or perceived needs of the ultimate consumers or users; (c) the extent of likely demand; and, (d) the likelihood that the product can be designed, developed, produced, and operated as desired within time and cost constraints, given acceptable levels of risk. At completion of this phase, schedule, cost, and performance estimates and characteristics should exist for the product/item, plus an identification of the inherent risks. In addition, a specific plan for completion of the remaining phases should exist.

2. *Design and Development Phase*—Upon selection of a concept, detailed design and development activities can begin. This includes engineering work resulting in the building of test models, or prototypes, for design revision and refinement. The output of this phase should be a set of detailed drawings and specifications (including data pertaining to expected reliability of the product) which are sufficient to manufacture the product as designed and specified.

3. *Production Phase*—While the production phase normally follows design and development, the two may overlap—at increased risk—if time is a critical parameter. In any event, this phase includes manufacture and on-time delivery of specified quantities of an item with acceptable quality, operational performance, and unit cost. Learning curve effects and necessary engineering changes occur as this phase progresses.

4. *Operational Phase*—This phase typically overlaps with production, beginning with the deployment or delivery of the item to the ultimate user. Successful operation includes possession of the desired performance characteristics by the user, with acceptable reliability and maintainability, at acceptable costs. This phase is concluded when the product or item is rendered obsolete by changing user/customer needs, existence of more desirable alternative products/items, or failure of the item to perform satisfactorily. Disposal of the item completes its life-cycle.

While the above phases represent the normal life-cycle of a successful product or item, few items are project-managed throughout all phases. Transition may occur to product management or conventional management at any time, heightening the need for a conceptual framework which can facilitate and ease this "hand-off" from the project management group.

Many key decisions must be made by the manager over the life-cycle of the item. Upon closer inspection, those decisions are largely represented by four key interrelated parametric groupings—time, cost, performance, and risk. The major information needs to manage each of these four parameters in each of the life-cycle phases are shown in Table 1 (and are described in a later paragraph). The parameters themselves may be defined as follows:

Time—The time parameter initially includes the need to accurately estimate the length of time required and available to accomplish the various activities comprising the early phases of the project, the objective being the development of a realistic and attainable schedule. Once underway, attention is focused on meeting scheduled dates and milestones. In the production phase, the time parameter shifts to concern for setting and meeting production rates and delivery schedules and, in the operational phase, with logistics.

Costs—Funding availability and levels are key resource inputs in the early stages of planning. While the level of resource availability constrains what can be accomplished during each phase, a major output of each phase is the further refinement of cost and resource estimates for subsequent phases. Holding costs and resources within approved levels is one of the manager's main responsibilities.

Performance—The product or item must possess an acceptable level of operational

Table 1 Life-Cycle Management Information Needs

Project Parameters	Project Phase			
	Concept	Design & Development	Production	Operational
Time	Completion and quantity guidance; required for each concept.	Milestone accomplishment; estimates to complete.	Output rates; delivery schedules.	Supply & logistical data.
Cost	Budget guidance; "should cost for each concept".	Development costs; cost to complete.	Unit cost.	Cost of operation.
Performance	Desired operational characteristics; likely performance for each concept.	Design achievement; performance of prototypes.	Conformance to specifications.	Reliability and maintainability.
Risk	Probability of achieving time, cost, and performance desired for each concept.	Probability of successful accomplishment of above.	Probability of successful accomplishment of above.	Evaluation of potential successor concepts.

capability, or the effort and resource expenditures are wasted. Design activities must result in specifications which permit prototypes and later units to meet test criteria. Production items must also perform adequately and must conform to design specifications. In addition, specified reliability must be proven and, since service is required and breakdowns will occur, the item must be able to be maintained under realistic conditions and procedures. Drawings and documentation describing each of these areas must be completed.

Risk—Since uncertainties exist and unfavorable results may occur, risks are inherent in the very nature of new product/item developments. Acceptable levels of risk must be determined for the many factors comprising the time, cost, and performance parameters. Also, continuous monitoring of the likelihood of achieving unacceptable values of time, cost, and performance must occur.

It is difficult to categorize the decisions made by the project manager, even when classifying them by the parameters or phases. At the risk of oversimplification, one may conclude that the most difficult planning decisions occur in the concept stage, involving the evaluation and selection of competing candidates. Usually, performance characteristics are the driving factor at this point,

with estimates of time, cost, and risk being developed for desired levels of performance. The implicit and/or explicit relative importance of the parameters comes into play as required trade-offs are made between them during the concept stage.

At this point, an objective or goal has been created, and a detailed plan (usually based upon a network) is developed to accomplish the goal. Design, development, and testing activities begin, and the focus of the project manager shifts to control and corrective action, which remains a major focus from this point forward. It is not the only focus, however, as progressively more detailed planning for the production and operational phases are major outputs of the design and development phase.

The management information required to adequately plan and control each of the project parameters during each life-cycle phase (depicted in Table 1) offers a framework for management. This framework provides a roadmap for the manager in charge of the item during any of the phases, enabling him to focus on critical areas as well as appreciate what precedes and follows the current phase. For the project manager with multiphase responsibility, this perspective is critical. He can make sure that the information requirements of future phases of the project are planned, with systems developed and implemented to provide information as required when needed.

KEY NETWORK-BASED TECHNIQUES

While numerous network techniques exist, the manager is interested only in those which provide a planning and/or control capability. Further, the project manager's interest is primarily network-based management techniques that assist him in managing the time, cost, performance, and risk parameters over the project life-cycle. Thus, a review of the major variations of the key network methods would be helpful in illustrating the need for a modularity framework, enabling the project manager to decide which technique(s) would be most relevant, given the project parameter and project stage. Included are the basic critical path techniques—PERT/CPM and PERT/Cost; a basic production phase technique—Line of Balance (LOB); and two decision-oriented techniques—GERT and VERT.

PERT/CPM—The Program Evaluation and Review Technique (PERT) and the Critical Path Method (CPM) represent a generic form of network planning and control techniques. Granted, there are differences between PERT and CPM. The major difference is that PERT is event-oriented and CPM is activity-oriented. But the similarities far outweigh the differences. In fact, many of the more recent computer programs will accommodate either approach. For example, the choice between using traditional PERT's three time estimates or CPM's single estimate for activity times is left to the user (1). In any case, the PERT/CPM approach is as follows:

1. Determine the tasks (activities) required for project completion and associated descriptors of project progress (events).
2. Construct a deterministic precedence chart (network) or the activities and events required for project completion. Included are time estimates for each of the activities, plus required dates for completion of any of the key activities or events (milestones).
3. Perform the network calculations, yielding initial values of activity or event slack and criticality.
4. Reallocate resources between activities as required or desired, resulting in a schedule of activities and events which efficiently utilizes resources and meets schedule constraints (to the extent possible).
5. Begin work accomplishment and control progress using actual activity times and updated time estimates for future activities.

In summary, PERT/CPM systems have proven their worth in managing non-repetitive projects with a number of activities that must be efficiently scheduled and coordinated. A major shortcoming is the inability to handle decision-type events, where one of several possible activities is selected, for example (in PERT/CPM, *each* activity in the network must be accomplished) (2).

PERT/Cost—PERT/Cost was an attempt to include the cost parameter in the PERT/CPM system. Beginning with a project tree diagram—or Work Breakdown Structure (WBS)—the project was divided into progressively more detailed components, assemblies, parts, or functions. At the most detailed level of breakout, cost categories called work packages were developed, consisting of one or more network activities. Costs were estimated at this level, with the ability to summarize at higher levels of the WBS, plus by functional cost category. After work commenced, actual costs were to be accumulated, remaining costs re-estimated, and estimates-to-complete developed for control purposes. The network portion of PERT/Cost remained the same as in basic PERT/CPM (3).

In practice, it was soon found that the project management effort to operate the PERT/Cost system was too great. The amount of updating, reestimating, changes due to technical and performance problems, and the need to estimate actual costs to be met and report cut-off dates caused the system to fail. Today, project management techniques allow costs to be assigned at higher levels of indenture, or by activity, resulting in effect a modified PERT/CPM system with an associated cost capability (4).

Line of Balance—Line of Balance (LOB) is a management-oriented charting tool for collecting and presenting information relating to time and accomplishment during production. It shows the progress, status, timing, and phasing of the interrelated activities of the production process; these data provide management with a means of comparing actual with planned performance. In addition, management receives timely information concerning the critical areas where the process is, or will be, behind schedule. LOB differs from other network techniques in that it is utilized mainly in the production process, from the point when incoming or raw materials arrive to the shipment of the end product. It is basically a means of integrating and monitoring the flow of materials, components, and subcomponents into manufacturing in accordance with delivery requirements (5).

As originally conceived, LOB was a graphical technique. As such, it had little capability to accommodate changing production cycle times due to learning, complex production sequences caused problems, and the use of common parts in several subassemblies required separate analysis. Today, the graphical technique has been replaced and the LOB type of analysis can be provided by Materials Requirements Planning (MRP) Systems.

Stochastic Networking Techniques (GERT)— PERT, CPM, PERT/Cost, and LOB are deterministic network models; that is, they do not permit probabilistic occurrence of activities. Each activity in the network must occur, with all precedence relationships specified by the persons preparing the network. In the real world, however, risk and uncertainty exist, and certain chance events may occur in the course of a project; for example, a certain test may be successful, unsuccessful, or partly successful, each with a certain likelihood. PERT/CPM could not accommodate this type of stochastic outcome.

Stochastic networking techniques broaden the applicability to include probabalistic nodes (events); that is, each branch (activity) emanating from a node has associated with it the probability that it will be taken. (In PERT/CPM networks, this probability = 1; each branch *must* be taken).

Perhaps the best known and most widely used stochastic networking technique is the Graphical

Evaluation and Review Technique (GERT). GERT networks may contain probabilistic branching, deterministic branching, or some combination of the two. Nodes are considered to have an input and output side, which specify how they interrelate to incoming and outgoing actions (branches). The four types of input logic specify how many incoming activities are required for first and subsequent releases of the node, and the two types of output logic determine the type of branching—deterministic or probabilistic—emanating from the node. GERT has the capability to include repetitive, or recurring, activities as well as cost information.

One of the main advantages of the probabilistic network (in addition to its added realism) is the ability to simulate project outcomes. Since the network can incorporate probabilistic occurrences— both favorable and unfavorable—it is possible to develop a distribution of likely outcomes through repeated runs of the network. This is particularly valuable in the planning stages of a project, and gives the manager a picture of the probability of success and the risk of failure, as well as which activities are critical to these outcomes. Furthermore, managers might desire to simulate the project impact of varying policies with respect to production loads, materials availability, work scheduling, and so on GERT would appear to be an excellent vehicle for such analysis. GERT may also include cost analysis by enabling fixed, variable, and total cost to be assigned to each activity with events serving as cost centers. Halting of activities, partial completion of precedent activities with the next event's activities being released (production of a product with components missing or partially completed), and activities which are resource constrained (not enough time, labor, materials, equipment) may be treated by some of the many members of the GERT family (6).

*VERT—*The Venture Evaluation and Review Technique (VERT) is, like GERT, a stochastic networking technique. It is similar in basic concept to GERT, but specifically treats time, cost and performance parameters for nodes and activities (arcs).

Numerical values for each activity's time, cost

and performance parameters may be assigned in terms of: (1) one of thirteen standard statistical distributions embedded in the VERT model; or (2) a histogram; or (3) a mathematical relationship if the time and/or cost and/or performance of this activity is dependent upon other nodes and/or arcs which are to be processed (completed) prior to this arc. Performance can be modeled in terms of any meaningful unit of measure, such as quantities produced, return on investment, or a dimensionless index that combines the many required diverse characteristics needed to fully define the resultant output of the resource expenditure.

Arcs and nodes are similar in that both have time, cost and performance attributes. Arcs have a primary and cumulative set of time, cost and performance values associated with them while nodes have only the cumulative set. The primary set represents the time expended, the cost incurred and the performance generated to complete the specific activity this arc represents. The cumulative set represents the total time expended, cost incurred, and composite performance generated to process all the arcs encountered along the path the network flow came through in order to complete the processing of the arc or node in question.

VERT has two types of nodes, that either start, stop or channel the network flow. The most commonly used type is split-node logic. It has separate input and output operations. The second, more specialized and less frequently used type of node has a single-unit logic, which covers both input and output operations simultaneously. There are four basic input logics available for the split-logic nodes. There are six basic split-node output logics available to distribute the network flow to the appropriate output arc(s). The cumulative time, cost and performance values computed for the active output arcs consist of the sum of the time, cost and performance values derived for those arcs, plus the time, cost, and performance carried by the arc's input node.

After the problem situation has been adequately modeled via VERT's arcs and nodes to achieve the desired level of realism, the problem is ready to simulate. VERT simulation involves the creation of a network flow which traverses the network from initial node(s) to create one trial solution of the problem being modeled. This simulation process is repeated as required to create a sufficiently large sample of possible outcomes. Node completion time, cost, and performance values may be obtained in any of eight desired forms. VERT optionally produces a critical-optimum path index for nodes

Table 2 Summary Evaluation of Network-Based Management Techniques

Criterion	PERT/CPM	PERT/COST	LOB	GERT	VERT
1. Project Phase Applicability	Design & development	Design & development	Production	Concept, design & devel., production	Concept, des. & dev., production operational
2. Parametric Focus	Time	Time and cost	Time	Time, cost, risk	Time, cost, performance, risk
3. Preparation Requirements	Moderate	Appreciable	Simple	Can be appreciable	Appreciable
4. Data Base	Moderate	Large	Low	Can be large	Large
5. System Operating Cost	Moderate	High	Very low	Moderate to high	High
6. Comprehensiveness	One-time activities only	One-time activities only	Repetitive activities only	One-time plus repetitive	One-time plus repetitive
7. Flexibility	Deterministic situations only	Deterministic situations only	Deterministic fixed procedure	Stochastic orientation	Stochastic orientation
8. Ease of Update	Moderate	Burdensome	Easy	Appreciable requirement	Appreciable requirement
9. Focus Reporting	Very Good	Excellent	Very Good	Outstanding	Outstanding

and arcs. The critical path is chosen as the path through the network with the longest completion time, highest cost, lowest performance or the least desirable weighted combination of these factors, based upon user-developed weights.

While VERT has direct application to project management, it has further application to the general area of strategic design analysis. To date, it has been successfully utilized to assess the risks involved in new ventures and projects, in the estimation of future capital requirements, in control monitoring, and in the overall evaluation of ongoing projects, programs, and systems. It has been helpful to management in cases where there is a requirement to make decisions with incomplete or inadequate information about the alternatives (7).

Comparison of Techniques

Table 2 provides a summary comparison of key network-based management techniques evaluated against nine criteria important to managers. Table 3 provides a more thorough treatment of each of the five techniques versus the evaluation criteria. The criteria are defined as follows:

1. *Project Phase Applicability*—Phases during the normal product/item life-cycle for which the technique offers significant applicability.
2. *Parametric Focus*—For which of the parametric areas does the technique offer planning and/or control information?
3. *Preparation Requirements*—The amount of time, effort and resources required to implement the technique, including network preparation, estimating and other input preparation, etc.
4. *Data Base*—How large a data base is required to operate the system?
5. *System Operating Cost*—What are the costs of utilizing the technique, including processing time, analytical effort, etc.?
6. *Comprehensiveness*—Breadth of applicability of the technique to varying types of activities.
7. *Flexibility*—Ability to handle varying types of situations occurring during the project life-cycle.
8. *Ease of Update*—The amount of time, effort and

resources required to produce subsequent outputs reflecting changing conditions.

9. *Focus Reporting*—Ability of the technique to highlight areas or situations of critical importance to the manager.

In short, PERT-type systems possess the advantages of serving as integrated planning and control systems, but their limitations reduce their applicability to one-time deterministic activities, largely in the Design and Development Phase; the performance parameter is not treated. LOB is exclusively a Production Phase technique, which is simple and economical to use, but at the cost of rather severe limitations. In practice, LOB-type information can be generated by Materials Requirement Planning (MRP) systems. The stochastic, decision-oriented, and simulation features of GERT and VERT provide significantly more powerful analysis than other techniques, particularly in planning (their forte is not as control systems). They allow management to much more fully assess potential outcomes—particularly VERT with its impressive array of input and output logics, thirteen statistical distributions, histogram capability and output displays. The technique accommodates all of the basic parameters, with performance broadly defined to accept any meaningful unit of measure, such as return on investment or dimensionless indices of combined objectives, as well as individual performance characteristics. The technique can work within specified yearly expenditure levels, and has particular application to the evaluation of strategic design alternatives for the firm in addition to the more familiar project applications.

INTEGRATED MODULAR FRAMEWORK.

Condensing the preceding evaluation of network-based management techniques in terms of their applicability to manage key parameters during project life-cycle phases results in the modular framework shown in Table 4. The criterion for inclusion of a technique in the framework is its ability to serve as a management system, possessing both planning and control strengths. While it appears from the chart that the stochastic network

Table 3 Evaluation of Major Network-Based Project Management Techniques

Criterion	PERT/CPM	PERT/COST	LOB	GERT	VERT
Project Phase Applicability	Prime application to one-time projects, largely Design & Development phase.	Same as basic PERT/CPM	Production only.	Most value in Concept phase; usable in all phases to some degree.	Same comment as for GERT.
Parametric Focus	Time-oriented; treats performance & costs as objectives, constraints, or by-products.	Adds cost planning & control feature to basic PERT/CPM.	Time-oriented (schedule & quantity)	Time-oriented with addition cost feature; analyzes time & cost risks.	Fully treats time, cost, & various performance measures; analyzes risks in all three.
Preparation Requirements	Network & time estimating is significant, but is planning which should be done anyway.	Cost estimating by work package or activity is significant addition to PERT preparation, but should be done anyway.	Main requirement is production flow chart and cycle times.	Networking requires special familiarity; multitude of features adds complexity.	Same comment as for GERT; use of optional features increases requirement.
Data Base	By-product of preparation, as is quality of data.	Cost accumulation & control requires extensive data input.	Requires only times & quantities at selected control points	Direct function of the number of features selected; large, if technique fully utilized.	Same comment as for GERT.
System Operating Cost	Programs easy to use; main cost is effort of preparation & updating.	Canned programs expand basic PERT; largest cost by far is preparation and updating.	Practically nonexistent, especially if part of MRP or other system.	Function of database simulation requires multiple runs; input preparation appreciable.	Same comment as for GERT; to use additional features increases cost.
Comprehensiveness	Limited to time parameter & non-repetitive activities.	Limited to time & cost parameters for non-repetitive activities.	Limited to repetitive situations only.	Accommodates most types of activities.	Accommodates most activities plus numerous input modes.
Flexibility	Handles deterministic situations only; no ability to accommodate decision alternatives or chance events.	Deterministic only; same as PERT.	Deterministic situations only; fixed production cycle required; learning curve presents problems.	Accommodates stochastic & deterministic activities.	Significantly more optional input and ouput features than has budgeting capability.
Ease of Update	Relatively simple; requires discipline to insure that future activities are reevaluated. Actual times present little problem.	Theoretically simple but major effort in practice; "estimating actual" cost data and constant changes are problems.	Requires only a physical count of cumulative production.	Appreciable, but value of technique in planning, rather than control.	Same comment as for GERT.
Focus Reporting	Highlighting of critical activities & problem areas is strong point; forecasts status at completion.	Adds to PERT the ability to trace cost problems to the source.	Highlights potential delivery schedule problem areas.	Risk analysis focuses attention on what is likely to occur and its probability.	Analyzes & highlights outcomes in time, costs, & performance; can be used in non-project strategic planning.

Table 4 A Modular Framework of Technique Applicability for Life-Cycle Management Needs

Parameter	Concept	Phase Design and Development	Production	Operational
Time	VERT, GERT	PERT/CPM, VERT,** GERT,**	VERT,** GERT,** LOB, others such as MRP	VERT,** GERT,** others required
Cost	VERT,GERT	PERT/Cost, VERT,** GERT**	VERT,** GERT,** others required	VERT,** GERT,** others required
Performance	VERT	VERT,** other techniques required	VERT,** other techniques required	VERT,** others required
Risk	VERT, GERT*	VERT, GERT*	VERT,GERT*	VERT,GERT*

*Time and cost only.
**Primarily for planning.

techniques—GERT and, particularly, VERT—are the answer to the project manager's prayer, one must not forget that they are primarily techniques for planning and evaluating alternatives, rather than control techniques. Thus, other techniques may be required once a plan has been chosen and accomplishment is underway.

The optimal approach would appear to be to use VERT to evaluate alternatives during the Concept phase (including likely results during the ensuing three phases of the life-cycle). After a concept is selected and planned, a great deal (but not all) of the uncertainty will be eliminated; therefore, more traditional techniques could be employed for the duration of the life-cycle. However, it should be noted that Design and Development activities may have considerable stochastic features, and this may necessitate a trade-off between using a PERT system for its control features and/or VERT because of its decision-tree capabilities. Perhaps the optimal approach would be to use a VERT-type stochastic network at the macro level, with specific control systems used for the major work efforts in each of the project phases; this approach would appear to yield the best of both worlds.

SUGGESTIONS FOR THE FUTURE

While the preceding analysis and modular framework was intended to serve as a guide for the life-cycle manager, it is apparent that certain areas exist for future technique improvement and development. Those areas include the following:

1. While stochastic networking techniques (especially VERT) have advanced the planning capability of the manager, further improvement is possible in the control area. Whether such techniques are modularized or broadened to include this capability or whether they are used as macro-systems for existing techniques is an open question and an area for further research.

2. Critical planning and control problems occur during the transition from one life-cycle phase to another. Previous attempts to manage phase interfaces and overlaps (e.g., PERT/LOB) have not been wholly successful. However, the VERT/GERT ability to combine single and repetitive activity offers promise.

3. While numerous applications of the techniques exist, further refinement is undoubtedly possible and will result in additional types of applications.

4. Comparative data concerning each technique's effectiveness, cost, and other criteria should be accumulated to evaluate the techniques on a more definitive basis.

5. Key advantages of PERT systems are their conceptual simplicity and understandability by managers. Stochastic approaches are not as familiar to the practitioner, although many managers are familiar with the decision-tree con-

cept. Stochastic approaches need to be publicized to the practitioner. One approach would be to illustrate the applicability to strategic planning, showing the compatibility with the managers' concerns and their decision processes.

REFERENCES

1. *Project Management System (PMS) 360: Application Description Manual,* Second Edition, No. GH200210, IBM Corporation, 1968.

2. Jerome D. Wiest and Ferdinand K. Levy, *A Management Guide to PERT/CPM, Second Edition (Englewood Cliffs, New Jersey: Prentice-Hall, 1977).*

3. *DOD/NASA Guide to PERT/COST Systems Design* (Washington, D.C.: Office of the Secretary of Defense and National Aeronautics and Space Administration, June 1972).

4. For example, see IBM PMS 360 manual.

5. Peter P. Schoderbek and Lester A. Digman, "Third Generation, PERT/LOB," *Harvard Business Review,* Volume 45, No. 5, September–October 1967, pp 100–110.

6. Laurence J. Moore and Edward R. Clayton, *GERT Modeling and Simulation: Fundamentals and Applications* (New York: Petrocelli/Charter, 1976).

7. Gerald L. Moeller and Lester A. Digman, "VERT: A Technique to Assess Risks," *Proceedings of 10th Annual Conference, American Institute for Decision Sciences,* Volume II, October 1978, p. 292.

CHAPTER 9
Resource Allocation

In the previous chapter we looked at a special type of resource allocation problem, that of allocating time among project tasks, better known as *scheduling*. Now we consider the allocation of physical resources as well. Also, we are concerned with using resources in both individual and in multiple, simultaneous projects. The subject relates directly to the topic of scheduling because altering schedules can alter the need for resources and—just as important—alter the timing of resource needs. At any point in time, the firm may have a fixed level of various resources available for its projects. The fixed resources might include man-hours of various types of special professional or technical services, machine-hours of various types of machinery or instrumentation, hours of computing time, and similar scarce resources needed for accomplishing project tasks. For example, if the need for some resource varies between 70 and 120 percent of resource capacity, then that resource will be wasted at one point in the project and in insufficient supply at another. If the project schedule can be adjusted to smooth the use of the resource, it may be possible to avoid project delay and, at the same time, not saddle the project with the high cost of excess resources "just to make sure."

This chapter addresses situations that involve resource problems. We discuss the trade-offs involved, the difference between allocation to one project and allocation between multiple projects, the relationship between resource loading and leveling, and some of the approaches employed to solve allocation problems, including the Critical Path Method (CPM) and several other well-known techniques. Although CPM is not actually a resource allocation method, we include it here because we view time as a resource, and trade-offs between time and other resources are a major problem in resource management.

9.1 CRITICAL PATH METHOD

In Chapter 8 we mentioned that CPM is similar to PERT. In the original versions of CPM and PERT there was one important difference: CPM included a way of relating the project schedule to the level of physical resources allocated to the project. This allowed the PM to trade time for cost, or vice versa. In CPM, two activity times and two costs are specified, if appropriate, for each activity. The first time/cost combination is called *normal* and the second set is referred to as *crash*. Normal times are "normal" in the same sense as the *m* time estimate of the three times used in PERT. Crash times result from an attempt to expedite the activity by the application of additional resources—for example, overtime, special equipment, additional staff or material, and the like.

It is standard practice with PERT/CPM to estimate activity times under the assumption of resource loadings that are normal. To discuss a time requirement for any task without some assumption about the level of resources devoted to the task makes no real sense. At the same time, it does not make sense to insist on a full list of each and every resource that will be spent on each of the hundreds of activities that may comprise a PERT/CPM network. Clearly, there must have been some prior decision about what resources would be devoted to each task, but much of the decision making is, in practice, relegated to the common methods of standard practice and rules of thumb. The allocation problem requires more careful consideration if it is decided to speed up the accomplishment of tasks and/or the total project. We need to know what additional resources it will take to shorten completion times for the various activities making up the project.

While standard practice and rules of thumb are sufficient for estimating the resource needs for normal progress, careful planning is critical when attempting to expedite (crash) a project. Crash plans that appear feasible when considered activity by activity may incorporate impossible assumptions about resource availability. For example, we may need to crash some activities on the Wild Horse Dam Project. To do so, we have all the labor and materials required, but we will need a tractor-driven crawler crane on the project site not later than the eighth of next month. Unfortunately, our crane will be in Decatur, Illinois, on that date. No local contractor has a suitable crane for hire. Can we hire one in Decatur or Springfield and bring ours here?

And so it goes. When we expedite a project, we tend to create problems; and the solution to one problem often creates several more problems that require solutions.

Difficulties notwithstanding, the wise PM adopts the Scout's motto: "Be Prepared." If deterministic time estimates are used, and if project deadlines are firm, there is a high likelihood that it will be necessary to crash the last few activities of most projects. Use of the three probabilistic time estimates of PERT may reduce the chance that crashing will be needed because they include uncertainties that are sometimes forgotten or ignored when making deterministic time estimates. Even so, many things make crashing a way of life on some projects—

Table 9-1 An Example of CPM

Activity	Precedence	Duration, Periods (normal, crash)	Cost (normal, crash)
a	—	3,2	$40,80
b	a	2,1	20,80
c	a	2,2	20,20
d	a	4,1	30,120
e	b	3,1	10,80

things such as last-minute changes in client specifications, without permission to extend the project deadline by an appropriate increment.

Consider the data in Table 9-1. First, we compute a cost/time *slope* for each activity that can be expedited (crashed). Note that activity **c** cannot be expedited. A clear implication of this calculation is that activities can be crashed in increments of one day (or one period). Often, this is not true. A given activity may have only two or three technically feasible durations. The "dollars per day" slope of such activities is relevant only if the whole crash increment is useful. For example, if an activity can be carried out in eight days or in four days with no feasible intermediate times, and if an uncrashable parallel path goes critical when the first activity is reduced to six days, then the last two days of time reduction are useless. (Of course, there are times when the PM may expedite activities that have little or no impact on the network's critical time, such as when the resources used must be made available to another project.) Table 9-2 shows the time/cost slopes for our example.

To use CPM, we develop a table or graph of the cost of a project as a function of the project's various possible completion dates. This can be obtained by either of two logics.

The first approach is to start with the normal schedule for all project activities, and then to crash selected activities, one at a time, to decrease project duration at the minimum additional cost. This approach is illustrated in Figure 9-1. The normal schedule is shown in network 9-1a. (Note the required dummy activity. We

Table 9-2 Activity Slopes—Cost per Period for Crashing

Activity	Slope ($/period)
a	40/1=40
b	60/1=60
c	—
d	90/3=30
e	70/2=35

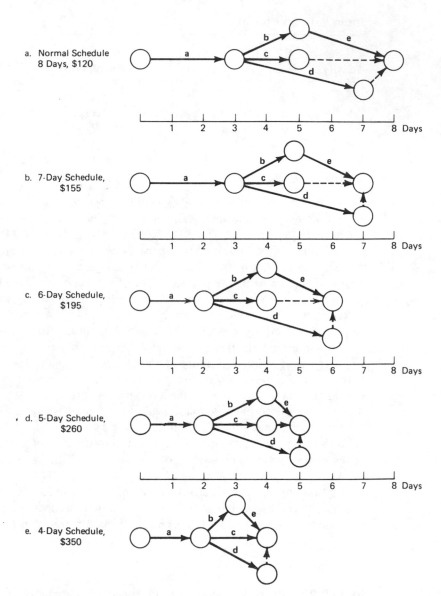

Figure 9-1 A CPM example.

use the AOA representation to illustrate that this procedure can be used with PERT as well as with CPM.)

The critical path of network 9-1 is **a–b–e**. To reduce the total network duration, we must reduce the time required by one of the activities along this critical path. Inspecting Table 9-2 to see which critical activity can be reduced at the least cost, we find it is **e**, at a cost of $35 per day. If we crash **e** by one day, we have a seven-day project duration at a cost of $155, as shown in Figure 9-1b.

Crashing e by a day has created a second critical path, **a–d–dummy.** To reduce project duration further, we might cut one day off this new critical path in addition to another day from activity **e.** (Remember that the path **a–b–e** is also critical.) Activity **d** has the most favorable cost-per-day rate among the critical activities. This adds $30 to the $35 required to reduce **e,** for a total cost increment of $65. We will still have two critical paths. Another alternative, however, is to crash an activity common to both critical paths, activity **a.** Reducing **a** by one day at a cost of $40 is less expensive than crashing both **e** and **d,** so this is preferred (see Figure 9-1c). Because **a** cannot be further reduced, we now cut **e** and **d** to lower total project duration to five days and raise project cost to $260 (see Figure 9-1d).

Activity **e** has now been crashed to its maximum (as has **a**), so additional cuts will have to be made on **b** to reduce the **a–b–e** critical path. Cutting one day from **b** (which is expensive) and **d** results in the final network that now has a time of four days and a cost of $350, more than 200 percent of the cost for normal time. The project duration cannot be reduced further, since both critical paths have been crashed to their limits.

The second approach to CPM is to start with an all-crash schedule, compute its cost, and "relax" activities one at a time. Of course, the activities relaxed first should be those that do not extend the completion date of the project—that is, those not on the critical path. In our example, this is possible. The all-crash cost is $380, and the project duration is four days. Activity **d,** however, could be extended by one day at a cost saving of $30 without altering the project's completion date. This can be seen in Figure 9-1e, where activity **d** is shown taking two days. Continuing in this manner would eventually result in the all-normal schedule of eight days and a cost of $120, as shown in Figure 9-1a.

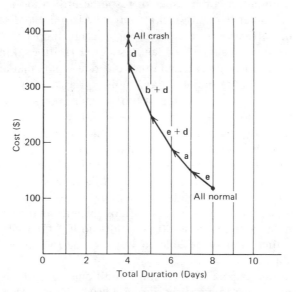

Figure 9-2 CPM cost-duration history.

The time/cost relationships of crashing are shown in Figure 9-2. Starting at the right (all-normal), note that the curve of cost per unit of duration gets steeper and steeper the more the project duration is reduced. It becomes increasingly costly to squeeze additional time out of the project. Economists will recognize that attempts to expedite a project are subject to decreasing marginal returns.

Charts such as the one shown in Figure 9-2 are useful to the PM in exercising control over project duration and cost. They are particularly helpful in dealing with senior managers who may argue for early project completion dates with little understanding of the costs involved. Similarly, such data are of great benefit when clients plead for early delivery. If the client is willing to pay the cost of crashing, or if the firm is willing to subsidize the client, the PM can afford to listen with a sympathetic ear.

Some organizations have more than one level of crash. Table 9-3 illustrates such a case. In this example, the firm has two distinct levels of expediting a project, rush and blitz. The differences in the precedence relationships between tasks are noted in the table, as are differences in resource commitments. The last two rows of the table show the expected changes in cost and time if the project is expedited.

Finally, if a project has a penalty clause that makes the organization liable for late delivery, the cost/duration trade-off curve contains the information the PM needs to know in order to determine whether crashing the project or paying the penalty is the more economic course of action.

9.2 THE RESOURCE ALLOCATION PROBLEM

A shortcoming of the scheduling procedures covered in the previous chapter is that they do not address the issues of resource utilization and availability. They focus on time rather than physical resources. Also, in the discussion that follows it will not be sufficient to refer to resource usage simply as "costs." Instead, we must refer to individual types of labor, specific facilities, kinds of materials, individual pieces of equipment, and other discrete inputs that are relevant to an individual project but are limited in availability. Last, we must not forget that time itself is always a critical resource in project management, one that is unique because it can neither be inventoried nor renewed.

The relationship between progress, time, and resource availability/usage is the major focus of this chapter. Schedules should be evaluated not merely in terms of meeting project milestones, but also in terms of the timing and use of scarce resources. A fundamental measure of the PM's success in project management is the skill with which the trade-offs among performance, time, and cost are managed. It is a continuous process of cost/benefit analysis: "I can shorten this project by a day at a cost of $400. Should I do it?" "If I buy 300 more hours of engineering time, I may be able to improve performance by 2 or 3 percent. Should I do it?"

Occasionally it is possible that some additional (useful) resources can be added at little or no cost to a project during a crisis period. At other times, some re-

Table 9-3   Official Pace of a Project

Title	Normal	Rush	Blitz
Approved Project Definition	Full.	Some abbreviations from normal pace.	Only as necessary for major management decisions, purchasing and design engineering.
Study of Alternates	Reasonable.	Quick study of major profitable items.	Only those not affecting schedule.
Engineering Design	Begins near end of Approved Project Definition.	Begins when Approved Project Definition 50–75% complete.	Concurrently with such Approved Project Definition as is done.
Issue Engineering to Field	Allow adequate time for field to plan and purchase field items. Usually 1/2–2 months lead time between issue and field erection.	Little or no lead time between issue and field erection.	No lead time between issue and field erection.
Purchasing	Begins in latter stages of Approved Project Definition.	Done concurrently with Approved Project Definition. Rush purchase of all long delivery items. Many purchases on "advise price" basis.	Done concurrently with such Approved Project Definition as is done. Rush buy anything that will do job. Overorder and duplicate order to guarantee schedule.
Premium Payments	Negligible.	Some to break specific bottlenecks.	As necessary to forestall any possible delays.
Field Crew Strength	Minimum practical or optimum cost.	Large crew with some spot overtime.	Large crew; overtime and/or extra shifts.
Probable Cost Difference compared with Normal Pace, as a result of:			
*Design and Development	Base	5–10% more	15% and up, more
*Engineering and construction costs	Base	3–5% more	10% and up, more
Probable Time	Base	Up to 10% less	Up to 50% less

sources in abundant supply may be traded for scarce ones (à la M.A.S.H.'s "Radar"). Most of the time, however, these trades entail additional costs to the organization, so a primary responsibility for the PM is to make do with what is available.

The extreme points of the relationship between time use and resource use are these:

- *Time Limited:* The project must be finished by a certain time, using as few resources as possible. But it is time, not resource usage, that is critical.
- *Resource Limited:* The project must be finished as soon as possible, but without exceeding some specific level of resource usage or some general resource constraint.

The points between these two extremes represent time/resource-use trade-offs. As in Figure 9-2, they specify the times achievable at various resource levels. Equivalently, they specify the resources associated with various completion times. Clearly, the range of time or resource variability is limited.

On occasion, it may be that one or more tasks in a project are *system-constrained*. A system-constrained task requires a fixed amount of time and known quantities of resources. Some industrial processes—heat treating, for instance—are system-constrained. The material must "cook" for a specified time to achieve the desired effect. More or less "cooking" will not help. When dealing with a system-constrained task or project, no trade-offs are possible. The only matter of interest in these cases is to make sure that the required resources are available when needed.

In the following sections we discuss approaches for understanding and using these relationships in various project situations.

9.3 RESOURCE LOADING

Resource loading describes the amounts of individual resources an existing schedule requires during specific time periods. Therefore, it is irrelevant whether we are considering a single work unit or several projects; the loads (requirements) of each resource type are simply listed as a function of time period. Resource loading gives a general understanding of the demands a project will make on a firm's resources. It is an excellent guide for early, rough project planning. Obviously, it is also a first step in attempting to reduce excessive demands on certain resources, regardless of the specific technique used to reduce the demands.

The PERT/CPM network technique is well suited for the job of generating time-phased resource requirements. A Gantt chart could be adapted, but the PERT/CPM diagram, particularly if modified to illustrate slacks, will be helpful in the analysis used for resource leveling. Let us illustrate with the PERT/CPM network used as an example in the previous chapter. The network (Table 8-2) reappears as Figure 9-3, and resource usage is illustrated for two hypothetical resources, A and B, on the arcs. The expected activity time is shown above the arc and resource usage is

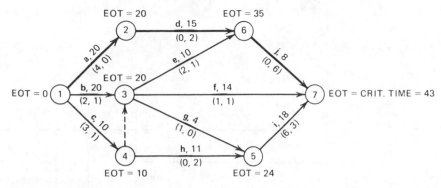

Figure 9-3 The complete network from Figure 8-13.

shown in parentheses just below the arc, with the use of A shown first and B second; e.g., (5,3) would mean that five units of A and three units of B would be used on the activity represented by the arc. Figure 9-4 shows the "calendarized" PERT/CPM diagram, similar to the familiar Gantt chart. Resource demands can now be summed by time period across all activities.

The loading diagram for resource A is illustrated in Figure 9-5a, and that for resource B in Figure 9-5b. The loads are erratic and vary substantially over the duration of the project. Resource A, used in tasks **a, b,** and **c,** has a high initial demand that drops through the middle of the project and then climbs again. Resource B, on the other hand, has low initial use but increases as the project

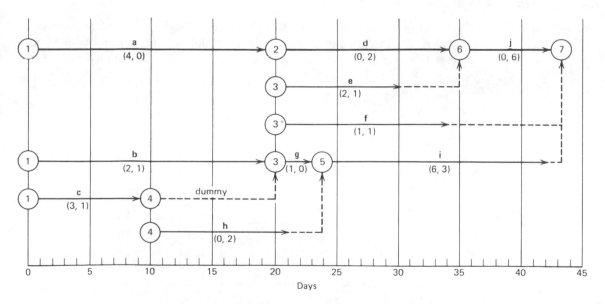

Figure 9-4 Modified PERT/CPM diagram showing resource usage (from Figure 9-3).

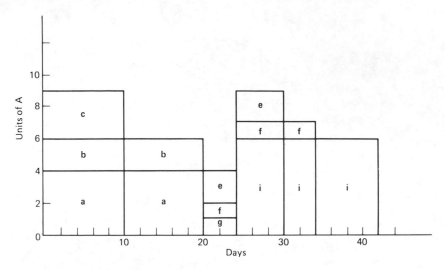

Figure 9-5a Load diagram for resource A.

develops. The PM must be aware of the ebbs and flows of usage for each input resource throughout the life of the project. It is the PM's responsibility to assure that the required resources, in the required amounts, are available when and where they are needed. In the next three sections, we will discuss how to meet this responsibility.

9.4 RESOURCE LEVELING

In the example above, we noted that the project began with the heavy use of resource A, used smaller amounts during the middle of the project, and then continued with rising usage during the project's latter stages. Usage of B started low

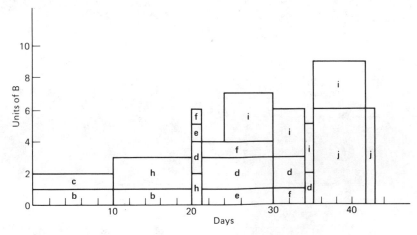

Figure 9-5b Load diagram for resource B.

and rose throughout the project's life. Large fluctuations in the required loads for various resources are a normal occurrence—and are undesirable from the PM's point of view. Resource leveling aims to minimize the period-by-period variations in resource loading *by shifting tasks within their slack allowances.* The purpose is to create a smoother distribution of resource usage.

There are several advantages to smoother resource usage. First, much less hands-on management is required if the use of a given resource is nearly constant over its period of use. The PM can arrange to have the resource available when needed, can have the supplier furnish constant amounts, and can arrange for a backup supplier if advisable. Moreover, the PM can do this with little error. Second, if resource usage is level, the PM may be able to use a "just-in-time" inventory policy without much worry that the quantity delivered will be wrong. If the resource being leveled is people, leveling improves morale and results in fewer problems in the personnel and payroll offices.

The basic procedure for resource leveling is straightforward. For example, consider the simple network shown in Figure 9-6a. The activity time is shown above the arc, and resource usage (one resource, workers) is in parentheses below the arc. Activities **a, b,** and **c** follow event 1, and all must precede event 4. Activity **a** requires two workers and takes two days, **b** requires two workers and takes three days, and **c** needs four workers and five days. (We addressed the problem of trade-offs between labor and activity time in the first section of this chapter.) If all these tasks are begun on their early start dates, the resource loading diagram appears as shown in Figure 9-6b, steps of decreasing manpower demand varying from eight workers to four workers. If, however, task **b** is delayed for two days, the full length of its slack in this particular case, the resource loading diagram is smoothed, as shown in Figure 9-6c. The same result would have occurred if **b** were started as early as possible and task **a** were delayed until day 3.

Resource leveling is a procedure that can be used for almost all projects, whether or not resources are constrained. If the network is not too large and there are only a few resources, the leveling process can be done manually. For larger networks and multiple resources, resource leveling becomes extremely complex, far beyond the power of manual solutions. Fortunately, a number of computer programs can handle most leveling problems efficiently (discussed in Chapter 10).

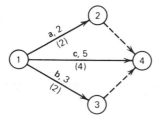

Figure 9-6a The network.

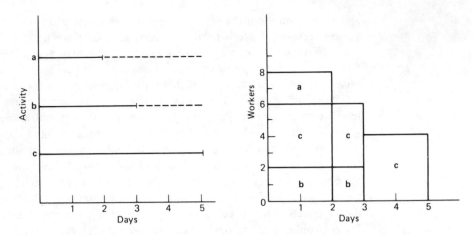

Figure 9-6b Before resource leveling.

Reconsider the load diagrams of Figures 9-5a and b. Assume it is desired to smooth the loading of resource B, which is particularly jagged. Both activities **e** and **f** can be delayed (**e** has five days of slack and **f** has nine). If we delay both for one day, we remove the peak on day 20 without increasing any of the other peaks (see Figure 9-7b). If we do this, however, it also alters the use of resource A and deepens the "valley" on day 20 (see Figure 9-7a). If we further delay **f** another seven days in order to level the use of A toward the end of the project, we would deepen the valley between days 20 and 24, and the resultant use of A would be as shown by the dotted lines on Figure 9-7a. Activity **f** would begin on day 29 (and would become critical). The effect on the usage of B is easy to see (Figure 9-7b). The change would lower usage by one unit beginning on day 21 (remember that we have already delayed **f** one day), and increase usage by one

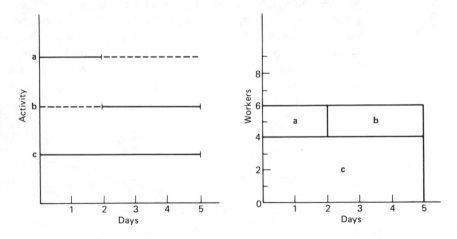

Figure 9-6c After resource leveling.

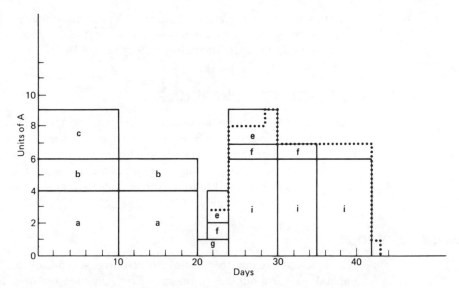

Figure 9-7a   Load diagram for resource A with activities **e** and **f** delayed by one day each.

unit beginning on day 35, continuing to the end of the project. This action increases peak use of B from nine to ten units.

It is important to emphasize that if the network under consideration is more complex and the number of resources to be leveled is realistically large, a manual leveling process is out of the question. Computer-aided leveling is not only mandatory, it is also helpful because it allows the PM to experiment with various patterns of resource usage through simulation.

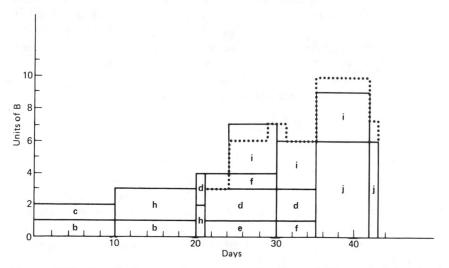

Figure 9-7b   Load diagram for resource B with activities **e** and **f** delayed by one day each.

Let us now raise the most general problem of minimizing resource usage while still achieving various completion dates—or the inverse problem, minimizing completion times while operating with specified limits on resources.

9.5 CONSTRAINED RESOURCE SCHEDULING

There are two fundamental approaches to constrained allocation problems: heuristics and optimization models. Heuristic approaches employ rules of thumb that have been found to work reasonably well in similar situations. They seek better solutions. Optimization approaches seek the best solutions but are far more limited in their ability to handle complex situations and large problems. We will discuss each separately.

Heuristic Methods

Heuristic approaches to constrained resource scheduling problems are in wide, general use for a number of reasons. First, they are the only feasible methods of attacking the large, nonlinear, complex problems that tend to occur in the real world of project management. Second, while the schedules heuristics generate may not be optimal, they are usually quite good—certainly good enough for most purposes. Commercially available computer programs handle large problems and have had considerable use in industry. Further, modern simulation techniques allow the PM to develop many different schedules quickly and to determine which, if any, are significantly better than current practice. If a reasonable number of simulation runs fails to produce significant improvement, the PM can feel fairly confident that the existing solution is a good one.

Most heuristic solution methods start with the PERT/CPM schedule and analyze resource usage period by period, resource by resource. In a period when the available supply of a resource is exceeded, the heuristic examines the tasks in that period and allocates the scarce resource to them sequentially, according to some priority rule. The major difference among the heuristics is in the priority rules they use. *Remember that the technological necessities always take precedence.* Some of the more common priority rules are these:

Shortest Task First Tasks are ordered in terms of duration, with the shortest first. In general, this rule will maximize the number of tasks that can be completed by a system during some time period.

Most Resources First Activities are ordered by use of a specific resource, with the largest user heading the list. The assumption behind this rule is that more important tasks usually place a higher demand on scarce resources.

Minimum Slack First This heuristic orders activities by the amount of slack, least slack going first. (It is common, when using this rule, to break ties by using the shortest-task-first rule.)

Most Critical Followers Tasks are arranged by number of critical activities following them. The ones with the greatest number of critical followers go first.

Most Successors This is the same as the previous rule, except that *all* followers, not merely critical ones, are counted.

There are many such priority rules employed in scheduling heuristics. Most of them are simple adaptations and variations of the heuristics used for the traditional "job shop scheduling" problem of production/operations management, a problem that has much in common with multiproject scheduling and resource allocation. Also, most heuristics use a combination of rules—a primary rule, with a secondary rule used to break ties.

Several researchers [19, 25, 26] have conducted tests of the more commonly used schedule priority rules. Although their findings vary somewhat because of slightly different assumptions, the minimum slack rule was found to be best or near-best quite often and rarely caused poor performance. It usually resulted in the minimum amount of project schedule slippage, the best utilization of facilities, and the minimum total system occupancy time.

As the scheduling heuristic operates, one of two events will result. The routine runs out of activities (for the current period) before it runs out of the resources, or it runs out of resources before all activities have been scheduled. (While it is theoretically possible for the supply of resources to be precisely equal to the demand for such resources, even the most careful planning rarely produces such a tidy result.) If the former occurs, the excess resources are left idle, assigned elsewhere in the organization as needed during the current period, or applied to future tasks required by the project—always within the constraints imposed by the proper precedence relationships. If one or more resources are exhausted, however, activities requiring those resources are slowed or delayed until the next period when resources can be reallocated.

If the minimum slack rule is used, resources would be devoted to critical or nearly critical activities, delaying those with greater slack. Delay of an activity uses some of its slack, so the activity will have a better chance of receiving resources in the next allocation. Repeated delays move the activity higher and higher on the priority list. We consider later what to do in the potentially catastrophic event that we run out of resources before all critical activities have been scheduled.

The heuristic procedure just described is probably the most common. There are, however, other heuristic procedures that work in a similar manner. One works in reverse and schedules jobs from the end of the project instead of from its beginning. Activities that just precede the project finish are scheduled to be completed just barely within their latest finish times. Then, the next-to-last tasks are considered, and so on. The purpose of this approach is to leave as much flexibility as possible for activities that will be difficult to schedule in the middle and early portions of the project. This logic seems to rest on the idea that flexibility early in the project gives the best chance of completing early and middle activities on time and within budget, thereby improving the chances of being on time and budget with the ending activities.

Other heuristics use the *branch and bound* approach. They generate a wide variety of solutions, discard those that are not feasible and others that are feasible but poor solutions. This is done by a *tree search* that prunes infeasible solutions and poor solutions when other feasible solutions dominate them. In this way, the heuristic narrows the region in which good, feasible solutions may be found. If the "tree" is not too large, this approach can locate optimal solutions, but more computer search time will be required. See [49] for further details.

These heuristics are usually embedded in a computer simulation package that describes what will happen to the project(s) if certain schedules or priority rules are followed. A number of different priority rules can be tried in the simulation in order to derive a set of possible solutions. Simulation is a powerful tool and can also handle unusual project situations. Consider, for example, the following project scheduling problem.

Given the network and resource demand shown in Figure 9-8, find the best schedule using a constant crew size. Each day of delay beyond 15 days incurs a penalty of $1,000. Workers cost $100 per day, and machines cost $50 per day. Workers are interchangeable, as are machines. Task completion times vary directly with the number of workers, and partial work days are acceptable. The critical time for the project is 15 days, given the resource usage shown in Figure 9-8. (There are other jobs in the system waiting to be done.)

Figure 9-8 lists the total man-days and machines per day normally required by each activity (below the activity arc). Because activity times are proportional to worker input, the critical path is **b–c–e–i,** and this path uses 149 man-days.

The fact that completion times vary with the number of workers means that activity **a** could be completed in 6 days with ten workers or in 10 days with six workers. Applying some logic and trying to avoid the penalty, which is far in excess of the cost of additional resources, we can add up the total man-days required on all activities, obtaining 319. Dividing this by the 15 days needed to

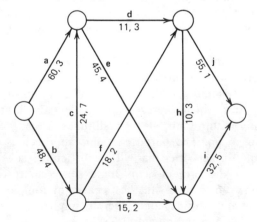

Figure 9-8 Network for resource load simulation.

Note: The numbers on the arcs represent, respectively, worker-days, machine-days.

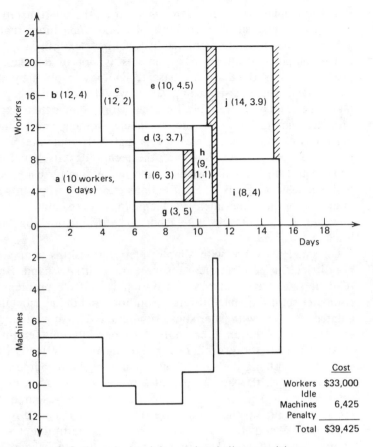

Figure 9-9 Load chart for a simulation problem.

complete the project results in a requirement of slightly more than twenty-one workers—say, twenty-two. How should they be allocated to the activities? Figure 9-9 shows one way, arbitrarily determined. Workers are shown above the "days" axis and machines below. We have 22 workers at $100 per day for 15 days ($33,000) and 128.5 machine days at $50 per day ($6425). The total cost of this particular solution is $39,425.

We could remove some manpower from those tasks not on the critical path. If a given activity has slack, we could trade some or all of the slack for a resource saving. Take activity **j**, for example. It has 1.2 days of slack. Our basic assumption is that 10 workers can do activity **j** in 5.5 days. If we use the slack, **j** can take up to 6.7 days without delaying the project. Using this slack, we can reduce the manpower required from 10 to 8.2, saving 1.8 workers for use on a critical task. If the manpower loading on task **i** is increased by 1.8 workers, the task time is cut to 3.1 days. (It is reduced to 33/34.8 or 98.4 percent of its original value.) The path **b–c–d–j** is now critical. Activity slack in other activities can be used in a similar way. (Note that we have implicitly assumed that machine use is proportional to manpower usage. If this is not true, the relationship must be known activity by activity, and the amounts of workers/machines that can be shifted are subject to the constraints implied by machine flexibility.)

The purpose of these reassignments is not to decrease labor cost in the project. This is fixed by the base technology implied by the worker/machine usage data. The reassignments do, however, shorten the project duration and make the resources available for other work sooner than expected. If the trade-offs are among resources, for instance, trading more manpower for fewer machines or more machines for less material input, the problem is handled in the same way. Always, however, the technology itself constrains what is possible. The Chinese build roads in the mountains by using labor. In the United States machines are used. Both nations exercise an option because either labor-intensive or machine-intensive technology is feasible. The ancient Israelites, however, could not substitute labor for straw in making bricks: No straw, no bricks.

On small networks with simple interrelationships among the resources, it is not difficult to perform these resource trade-offs by hand. But for networks of a realistic size, a computer is clearly required. If the problem is programmed for computer solution, many different solutions and their associated costs can be calculated. But, as with heuristics, simulation does not guarantee an optimal, or even feasible, solution. It can only test those solutions fed into it.

Another heuristic procedure for leveling resource loads is based on the concept of minimizing the sum of the squares of the resource requirements in each period. That is, the smooth use of a resource over a set of periods will give a smaller sum of squares than the erratic use of the resource that averages out to the same amount as the smooth use. This approach, called *Burgess's method,* was applied by Woodworth and Willie [55] to a multiproject situation involving a number of resources. The method was applied to each resource sequentially, starting with the most critical resource first.

Next, we briefly discuss some optimizing approaches to the constrained resource scheduling problem.

Optimizing Methods

The methods to find an optimal solution to the constrained resource scheduling problem fall into two categories: mathematical programming (linear programming for the most part) and enumeration. In the 1960s, the power of LP improved from being able to handle three resources and fifteen activities to four resources and fifty-five activities. But even with this capacity, LP is usually not feasible for reasonably large projects where there may be a dozen resources and thousands of activities. (See [18] and [35] for more detail.)

In the late sixties and early seventies, limited enumeration techniques were applied to the constrained resource problem with more success. Tree search and branch and bound methods [44] were devised to handle up to five resources and perhaps two hundred activities, but sizable problems are still beyond the reach of true optimizing procedures.[1]

More recent approaches have combined programming and enumeration methods. Patterson and Huber [36], for example, employ an integer programming approach combined with a minimum bounding procedure to reduce the computation time for minimizing project duration. Similarly, Talbot [46] uses integer programming and implicit enumeration to formulate and solve problems where the completion time is a function of the resources allocated to the project.

One problem with even the newer combination of approaches is that the characteristics of problems that can be usefully addressed with these methods is still largely unknown. Why various methods will work on one problem and not on a similar problem is still being researched.

9.6 MULTIPROJECT SCHEDULING AND RESOURCE ALLOCATION

Scheduling and allocating resources to multiple projects is much more complicated than for the single-project case. The most common approach is to treat the several projects as if they were each elements of a single large project. (A more detailed explanation is given below when we consider a specific multiproject scheduling heuristic.) Another way of attacking the problem is to consider all projects as completely independent; see [25 & 26], for example. As [25] shows, these two approaches lead to different scheduling and allocation outcomes. For either approach, the conceptual basis for scheduling and allocating resources is essentially the same.

There are several projects, each with its own set of activities, due dates, and resource requirements. In addition, the penalties for not meeting time, cost, and performance goals for the several projects may differ. Usually, the multiproject problem involves determining how to allocate resources to, and set a completion time for, a new project that is added to an existing set of ongoing projects. This requires the development of an efficient, dynamic multiproject scheduling system.

To describe such a system properly, standards are needed by which to measure scheduling effectiveness. Three important parameters affected by project scheduling are: (1) schedule slippage, (2) resource utilization, and (3) in-process inventory. The organization (or the PM) must select the criterion most appropriate for its situation.

Schedule slippage, often considered the most important of the criteria, is the time past a project's due date or delivery date when the project is completed. Slippage may well result in penalty costs that reduce profits. Further, slippage of one project may have a ripple effect, causing other projects to slip. Indeed, expediting a project in order to prevent slippage may, and usually does, disturb the overall organization to the point where slippage is caused in other projects. The loss of goodwill when a project slips and deliveries are late is important to all producers. As is the case with many firms, Grumman Aircraft jealously guards

---

[1]Recent advances in LP techniques may allow LP to be used on large constrained resource scheduling problems.

its reputation for on-time delivery. During a project to install a new machine control system on a production line, Grumman insisted that the project be designed to minimize disturbance to operations in the affected plant and avoid late shipments. This increased the cost of the project, but the firm maintained delivery schedules.

A second measure of effectiveness, resource utilization, is of particular concern to industrial firms because of the high cost of making resources available. A resource allocation system that smooths out the peaks and valleys of resource usage is ideal, but it is extremely difficult to attain while maintaining scheduled performance because all the projects in a multiproject organization are competing for the same scarce resources. In particular, it is expensive to change the size of the human resource pool on which the firm draws.

While it is relatively easy to measure the costs of excess resource usage required by less than optimal scheduling in an industrial firm, the costs of uncoordinated multiproject scheduling can be high in service-producing firms, too. In the real estate syndication firm used as an example of an AON network in Chapter 8 (see Figure 8-22), the scarce resource is executive judgment time. If two deals arrived at the same point in time, one would have to wait. This is undesirable because other potential buyers are seeking properties, and the process must move along without delay.

The third standard of effectiveness, the amount of in-process inventory, concerns the amount of work waiting to be processed because there is a shortage of some resource(s). Most industrial organizations have a large investment in in-process inventory, which may indicate a lack of efficiency and often represents a major source of expense for the firm. The remedy involves a trade-off between the cost of in-process inventory and the cost of the resources, usually capital equipment, needed to reduce the in-process inventory levels. It is almost axiomatic that the most time-consuming operation in any production system involving much machining of metals is an operation called "wait." If evidence is required, simply observe parts sitting on the plant floor or on pallets waiting for a machine, or for jigs, fixtures, and tools.

All these criteria cannot be optimized at the same time. As usual, trade-offs are involved. A firm must decide which criterion is most applicable in any given situation, and then use that criterion to evaluate its various scheduling and resource allocation options.

At times, the demands of the marketplace and the design of a production/distribution system may require long production runs and sizable levels of in-process inventory. This happens often when production is organized as a continuous system, but sales are organized as projects, each customized to a client order. Items may be produced continuously but held in a semifinished state and customized in batches.

A mattress manufacturing company organized to produce part of its output by the usual continuous process; but the rest of its production was sold in large batches to a few customers. Each large order was thought of as a project and was organized as one. The customization process began after the metal frames and springs were assembled. This required extensive in-process inventories of semi-finished mattresses.

As noted earlier, experiments by Fendley [19] revealed that the minimum-slack-first rule if the best overall priority rule, generally resulting in minimum project slippage, minimum resource idle time, and minimum system occupancy time (i.e., minimum in-process inventory) for the cases he studied. But the most commonly used priority rule is first come, first served—which has little to be said for it except that it fits the client's idea of what is "fair." In any case, individual firms may find a different rule more effective in their particular circumstances and should evaluate alternative rules by their own performance measures and system objectives.

Fendley found that when a new project is added to a multiproject system, the amount of slippage is related to the average resource load factor. The load factor is the average resource *requirement* during a set time period divided by resource *availability* for that time period. When the new project is added, the load factor for a resource increases and slippage rises. Analysis of resource loads is an important element in determining the amount of slippage to expect when adding projects.

Given these observations, let us examine some examples of the various types of multiproject scheduling and resource allocation techniques. We begin with a short description of one optimization method, briefly cover several heuristics, and then discuss one heuristic in greater detail.

Mathematical Programming

Mathematical programming [16, 18, 35, 49] can be used to obtain optimal solutions to certain types of multiproject scheduling problems. These procedures determine when an activity should be scheduled, given resource constraints. In the following discussion, it is important to remember that each of the techniques can be applied to the activities in a single project, or to the projects in a partially or wholly interdependent set of projects. Most models are based on integer programming that formulates the problem using 0–1 variables to indicate (depending on task early start times, due dates, sequencing relationships, etc.) whether or not an activity is scheduled in specific periods. The three most common objectives are these:

1. Minimum total throughput time (time in the shop) for all projects
2. Minimum total completion time for all projects
3. Minimum total lateness or lateness penalty for all projects

Constraint equations ensure that every schedule meets any or all of the following constraints, given that the set of constraints allow a feasible solution.

1. Limited resources
2. Precedence relationships among activities
3. Activity-splitting possibilities
4. Project and activity due dates
5. Substitution of resources to assign to specified activities
6. Concurrent and nonconcurrent activity performance requirements

In spite of its ability to generate optimal solutions, mathematical programming has some serious drawbacks when used for resource allocation and multiproject scheduling. As noted earlier, except for the case of small problems, this approach has proved to be extremely difficult and computationally expensive.

Heuristic Techniques

Because of the difficulties with the analytical formulation of realistic problems, major efforts in attacking the resource-constrained multiproject scheduling problem have focused on heuristics. We touched earlier on some of the common general criteria used for scheduling heuristics. Let us now return to that subject.

There are scores of different heuristic-based procedures in existence. A great many of the procedures have been published (see [18] and [34], for example), and descriptions of some are generally available in commercial computer programs.

The most commonly applied rules were discussed in Section 9.5. The logical basis for these rules predates PERT/CPM. They represent rather simple extensions of well-known approaches to job shop scheduling. Some additional heuristics for resource allocation have been developed that draw directly on PERT/CPM. All these are commercially available for computers, and most are available from several different software vendors in slightly different versions.

Resource Scheduling Method In calculating activity priority, give precedence to that activity with the minimum value of d_{ij} where

$$d_{ij} = \text{increase in project duration resulting when activity } j \text{ follows activity } i,$$
$$= \text{Max } [0; (EFT_i - LST_j)]$$

where EFT_i = early finish time of activity i
LST_j = latest start time of activity j

The comparison is made on a pairwise basis among all activities in the *conflict set*.

Minimum Late Finish Time This rule assigns priorities to activities on the basis of activity finish times as determined by PERT/CPM. The earliest late finishers are scheduled first.

Greatest Resource Demand This method assigns priorities on the basis of total resource requirements, with higher priorities given for greater demands on resources. Project or task priority is calculated as:

$$\text{Priority} = d_j \sum_{i=1}^{m} r_{ij}$$

where d_j = duration of activity j
r_{ij} = per period requirement of resource i by activity j
m = number of resource types

Resource requirements must be stated in common terms, usually dollars. This heuristic is based on an attempt to give priority to potential resource bottleneck activities.

Greatest Resource Utilization   This rule gives priority to that combination of activities that results in maximum resource utilization (or minimum idle resources) during each scheduling period. The rule is implemented by solving a 0–1 integer programming problem, as described earlier. This rule was found to be approximately as effective as the minimum slack rule for multiple project scheduling, where the criterion used was project slippage. Variations of this rule are found in commercial computer programs such as RAMPS (see [31].

Most Possible Jobs   Here, priority is given to the set of activities that results in the greatest number of activities being scheduled in any period. This rule also requires the solution of a 0–1 integer program. It differs from the greatest-resource-utilization heuristic in that the determination of the greatest number of possible jobs is made purely with regard to resource feasibility (and not with regard to any measure of resource utilization).

Heuristic procedures for resource-constrained multiproject scheduling represent the only practical means for finding workable solutions to the large, complex multiproject problems normally found in the real world. Let us examine a multiproject heuristic in somewhat more detail.

A Multiproject Scheduling Heuristic

To attack this problem, recall the hierarchical approach to project planning we adopted in Chapter 5. A project plan is a nested set of plans, composed of a set of generalized tasks, each of which is decomposed into a more detailed set of work packages that are, in turn, decomposed further. The decomposition is continued until the work packages are simple enough to be considered "elemental." A PERT/CPM diagram of a project might be drawn for any level of task aggregation. A single activity (arrow) at a high level of aggregation would represent an entire network of activities at a lower level (see Figure 9-10). Another level in the planning hierarchy is shown as a Gantt chart in Figure 9-11.

If an entire network is decomposed into subnetworks, we have the equivalent of the multiproject problem where each of the projects (subnetworks) is linked to predecessor and successor projects (other subnetworks). In this case, the predecessor/successor relationships depend on the technology of the parent project. In the true multiproject case, these relationships may still depend on technological relationships—for example, a real estate development project being dependent on the outcome of a land procurement project. The relationships may, however, be determined more or less arbitrarily, as when projects are sequenced on a first-come, first-served basis, or by any other priority-setting rule, or undertaken simultaneously in the hope that some synergistic side effects might occur. Or the relationship among the projects may simply be that they share a common pool of resources.

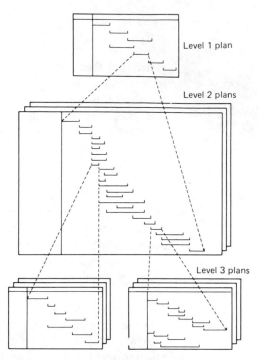

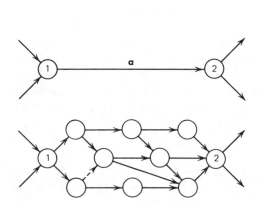

Figure 9-10 Task **a** decomposed into a network of subtasks.

Figure 9-11 Hierarchy of Gantt charts.
Source: F. L. Harrison, *Advanced Project Management,* Gower, 1983.

With this conceptual model, assume we have a set of projects. Each individual project is represented by a network of tasks. We can form a single network of these projects by connecting them with dummy activities (no resources, no duration) and/or pseudoactivities (no resources, some duration). Both dummy activities and pseudoactivities represent dependency relationships, but these dependencies, as noted above, may be technological or quite arbitrary.[2]

As usual, and excepting dummy and pseudoactivities, each task in each network requires time and resources. The amount of time required may or may not vary with the level of resources applied to it. The total amount of resources and/or amounts of individual resources are limited in successive scheduling periods. Our problem is to find a schedule that satisfies the sequence constraints and minimizes the overall duration of the entire network. The resulting schedule should indicate when to start any activity and at what level of resources it should be maintained while it is active.

Weist's heuristic (SPAR-1, Scheduling Program for Allocation of Resources) allocates resources to activities in order of their early start times. In the first period, we would list all available tasks and order them by their slack, from least

---

[2] This exposition is based on Weist's work [53], and on Corwin's application of Weist's papers to resource allocation among multiple R & D projects [11].

to most. (Calculation of slack is based on the assumption that activities will be supported at *normal* resource levels.) Activities are selected for support and scheduling one by one, in order. As activities at the top of the list are supported, the relevant resource stocks are debited. Tasks are scheduled sequentially until the list of available jobs is completed, or until the stock of one or more resources is depleted. If we deplete resources before completing the task list, remaining tasks are delayed until the next period. Postponed activities lose slack and rise toward the top of the priority list.

The information requirements for this heuristic are straightforward. Each period, we need a period-by-period updating of the list of currently active tasks continued from the previous period, including the resource usage level for each active task, the current scheduled (or expected) completion date, and the current activity slack. We need to know the currently available stocks of each type of resource, less the amounts of each in use. We also need a list of all available tasks together with their slacks and normal resource requirements. As activities are completed, their resources are "credited" to the resource pool for future use.

Thus, resources are devoted to activities until the supply of available resources or activities is exhausted. If we use up the resources before all critical activities are scheduled, we can adopt one of two subheuristics. First, we may be able to borrow resources from currently active, but noncritical, tasks. Second, we may "deschedule" a currently active, noncritical task. The former presumably slows the progress of the work, and the latter stops it. In both cases, some resources will be released for use on critical tasks. Obviously, if a critical task is slowed, descheduled, or not supported, the duration of the associated project will be extended.

If the size of the resource pool is more than sufficient for the list of active and available tasks, the extra resources may be used to crash critical activities in order to put some slack in the critical path as insurance against project delays caused by last-minute crises. In fact, it is often possible to borrow resources from tasks with plenty of slack in order to crash critical items that are frequent causes of project delay.

As a result of this scheduling process, each task from the previous period, along with any tasks newly available for support, will be:

1. Continued as is, or newly funded at a normal level
2. Continued or funded at a higher level of resources as a result of criticality
3. Continued or funded at a lower-than-normal level as a result of borrowing
4. Delayed because of a resource shortage

If there is more than one scarce resource, a separate activity can be created for each type of scarce resource. These "created" activities must be constrained to start in the same period as the parent activity, and to have the same level of resource assignment (normal, crash, or minimal.) Figure 9-12 shows a flow diagram for SPAR-1.

There are a number of alternatives to SPAR-1, such as McAuto's Management Scheduling and Control System (MSCS). This system is described in more detail in the next chapter.

Several commercially available software packages have the ability to schedule

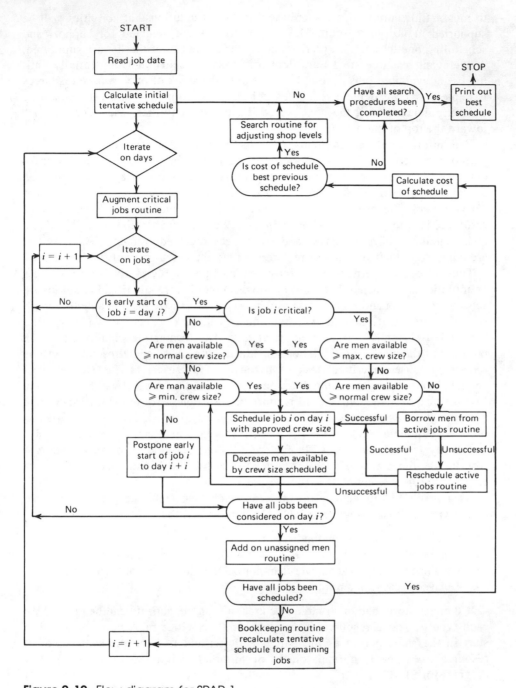

Figure 9-12 Flow diagram for SPAR-1.

Source: Wiest, J. D., "A Heuristic Model for Scheduling Large Projects with Limited Resources," *Management Science,* Feb. 1967.

constrained resources among multiple projects—for example, Scitor Corporation's PS5000® [20], and ARTEMIS Project Management® [51]. Many others will allow the user to solve the problem by trial and error. If a set of projects is linked together by dummy activities so that it can be treated like a single project, the software will report resource usage conflicts; that is, cases in which the scheduled utilization of a resource is greater than the supply of that resource. The *Project Management Journal* published five times a year by the Project Management Institute is an excellent source of reviews on project management software. These reviews typically include a discussion of the package's capabilities.

9.7 SUMMARY

In this chapter we looked at the problem of allocating physical resources, both among the multiple activities of a project and among multiple projects. The continuous problem to the PM is finding the best trade-offs among resources, particularly time. We considered resource loading, allocation, and leveling, and presented methods and concepts to aid in all these tasks.

Specific points made in the chapter were these:

- The critical path method (CPM) is a network constructed in the same manner as PERT but considers the possibility of adding resources to tasks (called crashing) to shorten their duration, thereby expediting the project.

- The resource allocation problem is concerned with determining the best trade-offs between available resources, including time, throughout the duration of a project.

- Resource loading is the process of calculating the total load from project tasks on each resource for each time period of the project's duration.

- Resource leveling is concerned with evening out the demand for various resources required in a project by shifting tasks within their slack allowances. The aid of a computer is mandatory for realistic projects.

- There are two basic approaches to addressing the constrained resources allocation problem.

Heuristic methods are realistic approaches that may identify feasible solutions to the problem. They essentially use simple priority rules, such as shortest task first, to determine which task should receive resources and which task must wait.

Optimizing methods, such as linear programming, find the best allocation of resources to tasks but are limited in the size of problems they can efficiently solve.

- For multiproject scheduling, three important measures of effectiveness are schedule slippage, resource utilization, and level of in-process inventory.

- When a new project is added to a multiproject system, the amount of slippage is directly related to the average resource load.

- Mathematical programming models for multiproject scheduling aim either to minimize total throughput time for all projects, minimize the completion time for all projects, or minimize the total lateness (or lateness penalty) for all projects. These models are limited to small problems.

There are a number of heuristic methods, such as the resource scheduling method, available for the multiproject scheduling problem.

In the next chapter we move to the ongoing implementation of the project and consider the project information systems used for monitoring progress, costs, performance, and so on. The chapter also describes a number of available computer packages for this function.

9.8 GLOSSARY

COST/TIME SLOPE   The ratio of the increased cost for expediting to the decreased amount of time for the activity.

FOLLOWERS   The tasks that logically follow a particular task in time.

HEURISTIC   A formal process for solving a problem, like a rule of thumb, that results in an acceptable solution.

MATHEMATICAL PROGRAMMING   A general term for all the mathematical approaches to solving constrained optimization problems, including linear programming, integer programming, and so on.

PREDECESSORS   The tasks that logically precede a particular task in time.

PRIORITY RULES   Formal methods, such as ratios, that rank items to determine which one should be next.

RESOURCE LEVELING   Approachs to even out the peaks and valleys of resource requirements so that a fixed amount of resources can be employed over time.

RESOURCE LOADING   The amount of resources of each kind that are to be devoted to a specific activity in a certain time period.

SUCCESSORS   *See* followers.

TREE SEARCH   The evaluation of a number of alternatives that logically branch from each other like a tree with limbs.

9.9 PROJECT TEAM ASSIGNMENT

The project team now is to address the problem of identifying and allocating resources for the project. First, determine what the resource loads are for each activity and what the resource availabilities are. Also determine whether activities can be speeded up by the allocation of additional resources; that is, the cost/time trade-offs. Conduct a CPM analysis to see where crashing may be desirable to meet an expedited completion and derive the cost-duration history graph.

Next, plot the multiple resource needs for the project on a Gantt chart and evaluate their loadings. Use various heuristics and priority rules to level the loads and evaluate the time-resource trade-offs. Are there "natural" points of high efficiency or resource usage? What heuristics and priority rules seem to work best? Might any of the programming or optimizing methods seem applicable for your project? Might the SPAR heuristic be useful for your project? Why or why not?

9.10 MATERIAL REVIEW QUESTIONS

1. Identify several resources that may need to be considered when scheduling projects.
2. What is resource loading? How does it differ from resource leveling?
3. Why is CPM superior to PERT when scheduling with respect to resource allocation? What is an activity slope and what does it indicate?
4. Name four priority rules. What priority rule is best overall? How would a firm decide which priority rule to use?
5. Name three efficiency criteria that might be considered when choosing a multi-project scheduling system.
6. What is the average resource load factor? How is it used to determine project completion times?

9.11 CONCEPTUAL DISCUSSION QUESTIONS

1. Why are large fluctuations in the demands for particular resources undesirable? What are the costs of resource leveling? How would a PM determine the "best" amount of leveling?
2. When might a firm choose to crash a project? What factors must be considered in making this decision?
3. Why is the impact of scheduling and resource allocation more significant in multi-project organizations?
4. How much should a manager know about a scheduling or resource allocation computer program to be able to use the output intelligently?
5. With the significantly increased power of today's computers, do you think the mathematical programming optimization approaches will become more popular?

9.12 PROBLEMS

1. Consider the following network:

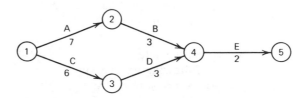

(a) Construct a schedule showing
    ESTs for all activities
    LSTs for all activities

EOTs for all events
LOTs for all events
Slacks for all activities and events
Critical path

(b) Given the following:

Activity	Crash Time	Normal Cost	Total Crash Cost	Maximum Crash days
A	4	$500	$ 800	3
B	2	200	350	1
C	4	500	900	2
D	1	200	500	2
E	1	300	550	1
			$3100	

1. Find the crash cost per day.
2. Which activities should be crashed to meet a project deadline of 10 days with a minimum cost?
3. Find the new cost.

2. Given the following:

Activity	Immediate Predecessor	Activity time (months)
A	—	4
B	—	6
C	A	2
D	B	6
E	C,B	3
F	C,B	3
G	D,E	5

(a) Draw the network.
(b) Find the ESTs, LSTs, EOTs, LOTs, and Slacks.
(c) Find the critical path.
(d) If the project has a 1 1/2 year deadline, should we consider crashing some activities? Explain.

3. Given the data in Problem 1, determine the first activities to be crashed by the following priority rules:
(a) Shortest task first.
(b) Most resources first (use normal cost as the basis).
(c) Minimum slack first.
(d) Most critical followers.
(e) Most successors.

4. Given the following network with resource demands, construct a modified PERT chart with resources and a resource load diagram. Suggest how to level the load if you can split operations. The project is due at day 36.

Code: $\dfrac{\text{activity, time}}{\text{resource units}}$

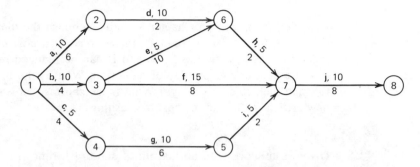

5. Reconsider Problem 12 in Chapter 8 under the constraint that the project *must* be completed in 16 weeks. This time, however, activities *c, f, h,* and *i* may be crashed as follows:

Activity	Crash Time (weeks)	Additional Cost per Week
c	7	$ 40
f	6	20
h	2	10
i	3	30

Find the best schedule and its cost.

6. The following data were obtained from a study of the times required to overhaul a chemical plant:

Activity	Crash Schedule Time	Cost	Normal Schedule Time	Cost
1–2	3	$ 6	5	$ 4
1–3	1	5	5	3
2–4	5	7	10	4
3–4	2	6	7	4
2–6	2	5	6	3
4–6	5	9	11	6
4–5	4	6	6	3
6–7	1	4	5	2
5–7	1	5	4	2

Note: Costs are given in thousands of dollars, time in weeks.

a. Find the all-normal schedule and cost.

b. Find the all-crash schedule and cost.

c. Find the total cost required to expedite all activities from all-normal (case *a*) to all-crash (case *b*).

d. Find the *least-cost* plan for the all-crash time schedule. Start from the all-crash problem *(b)*.

7. Consider Problem 8 in Chapter 8 again. Suppose the duration of both activities A and D can be reduced to one day, at a cost of $15 per day of reduction. Also, activities E, G, and H can be reduced in duration by one day at a cost of $25 per day of reduction. What is the least cost approach to crash the project two days? What is the shortest "crashed" duration, the new critical path, and the cost of crashing?

8. Given a network with normal times and crash time (in parentheses), find the optimal time-cost plan. Assume indirect costs are $100 per day. The data are:

Activity	Time reduction direct cost per day
1–2	$30 first, $50 second
2–3	$80 each
3–4	$25 first, $60 second
2–4	$30 first, $70 second, $90 third

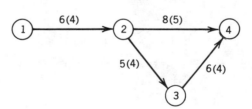

9. The network shown in the table has a fixed cost of $90 per day, but money can be saved by shortening the project duration. Find the least cost schedule.

Activity	Normal Time	Crash Time	Cost Increase (1st, 2nd, 3rd day)
1–2	7	4	$30, 50, 70
2–3	9	6	40, 45, 65
1–3	12	10	60, 60
2–4	11	9	35, 60
3–4	3	3	—

9.13 INCIDENTS FOR DISCUSSION

Bryce Power Tool Company

George Ertle is the director of engineering for the Bryce Power Tool Company. A decision was made recently to modernize Bryce's entire tool line. The president of Bryce has indicated that he expects the modernization program to result in a significant improvement in design technology. Mr. Ertle is concerned with the possibility that his department will not have adequate resources to support the modernization program. Mr. Ertle believes he has enough staff to handle the aggregate engineering requirements, but he is not too sure he will be able to supply engineering personnel at the times and quantities requested by the company's project manager.

To complicate matters further, the tool modernization program will be under the control of four different project managers. Each major market segment has been recognized as a separate business unit with the authority to modernize the key tools for that segment based on a schedule that makes sense for it.

Mr. Ertle knows a little bit about resource allocation techniques. He remembers that one of the most effective allocation techniques is to work first on the activity with the minimum slack, so he has instructed his staff to approach any tasks they are assigned as members of a project team on that basis.

Question: Is this technique a reasonable way to schedule the engineering resources of Bryce? Why or why not?

Critical Care Hospital

Critical Care Hospital will be purchasing a CATSCAN (computerized axial tomography scanner) in the next six months. The CATSCAN equipment will be installed in the radiology department and will require a significant renovation for the area. The scanner will arrive in about five months, but the construction project cannot be started until the unit is set in place. This will result in a project length of approximately twelve months. The hospital estimates the equipment will generate an income of $25,000 per month and is therefore in a hurry to complete the project. The project manager feels she may be able to cut the time on some aspects of the project, but at an increased cost. She has decided, in an effort to make the best decision, to use a resource allocation version of CPM.

Question: What information must the project manager gather to use this method properly?

9.14 BIBLIOGRAPHY

1. Anderson, D. R., D. J. Sweeney, and T. A. Williams. *An Introduction To Management Science.* Boulder, CO: West Publishing, 1981.
2. Arrow, K. J., and L. Hurwicz. *Studies In Resource Allocation Processes.* New York: Cambridge Univ. Press, 1977.

3. Balas, E. "Project Scheduling with Resource Constraints." *Applications of Mathematical Programming Techniques.* Carnegie-Mellon Univ., 1970.

4. Benson, L. A., and R. F. Sewall, "Dynamic Crashing Keeps Projects Moving." *Computer Decisions,* Feb. 1972.

5. Berman, E. B. "Resource Allocation in a PERT Network Under Continuous Activity Time-Cost Functions." *Management Science,* July 1964.

6. Bildson, R. A., and J. R. Gillespie. "Critical Path Planning PERT Integration." *Operations Research.* Nov.–Dec. 1962.

7. Buffa, E. S., and J. G. Miller. *Production-Inventory Systems: Planning and Control,* 3rd ed., Homewood, IL: Irwin, 1979.

8. Carruthers, J. A., and A. Battersby. "Advances in Critical Path Methods." *Operational Research Quarterly,* Dec. 1966.

9. Charnes, A., and W. W. Cooper. "A Network Interpretation and a Direct Subdual Algorithm for Critical Path Scheduling." *Journal of Industrial Engineering,* July–Aug. 1962.

10. Clark, E. "The Optimum Allocation of Resources among the Activities of a Network." *Journal of Industrial Engineering,* Jan.–Feb. 1961.

11. Corwin, B. D. "Multiple R and D Project Scheduling with Limited Resources." *Technical Memorandum No. 122,* Dept. of Operations Research, Case Western Reserve University, 1968.

12. Croft, F. M. "Putting a Price Tag on PERT Activities." *Journal of Industrial Engineering,* July 1966.

13. Crowston, W., and G. L. Thompson. "Decision CPM: A Method for Simultaneous Planning, Scheduling, and Control of Projects." *Operations Research,* May–June 1967.

14. Davies, E. M. "An Experimental Investigation of Resource Allocation in Multiactivity Projects." *Operational Research Quarterly,* Dec. 1973.

15. Davis, E. W. "Networks: Resource Allocation." *Industrial Engineering,* April 1974.

16. Davis, E. W. *Project Management: Techniques, Applications, and Managerial Issues,* 2nd ed. Institute of Industrial Engineers, 1983.

17. Davis, E. W., and G. E. Heidorn. "An Algorithm for Optimal Project Scheduling Under Multiple Resource Constraints." *Management Science,* Aug. 1971.

18. Davis, E. W., and J. H. Patterson. "A Comparison of Heuristic and Optimum Solutions in Resource-Constrained Project Scheduling." *Management Science,* April 1975.

19. Fendley, L. G. "Towards the Development of a Complete Multiproject Scheduling System." *Journal of Industrial Engineering,* Oct. 1968.

20. Glauber, L. W. "Project Planning With Scitor's PS5000." *Project Management Journal,* June 1985.

21. Gorenstein, S. "An Algorithm for Project (Job) Sequencing with Resource Constraints." *Operations Research,* July–Aug. 1972

22. Hastings, N. A. J. "On Resource Allocation in Networks." *Operational Research Quarterly,* June 1972.

23. Kelley, J. "Critical Path Planing and Scheduling: Mathematical Basis." *Operations Research,* May–June 1961.

24. Krone, W. T. B., and H. V. Phillips. "SCRAPP, a Reporting and Allocation System for a Multi-Project Situation." *Applications of Critical Path Techniques.* The English Universities Press Ltd., London, 1968.

25. Kurtulus, I., and E. W. Davis. "Multi-Project Scheduling: Categorization of Heuristic Rules Performance," *Management Science,* Feb. 1982.

26. Kurtulus, I., and S. C. Narula. "Multi-Project Scheduling: Analysis of Project Performance," *IEEE Transactions on Engineering Management,* March 1985.

27. Lamberson, L. R., and R. R. Hocking. "Optimum Time Compression in Project Scheduling." *Management Science,* June 1970.

28. Marchbanks, J. L. "Daily Automatic Rescheduling Technique." *Journal of Industrial Engineering,* March 1966.

29. Moder, J. J., C. R. Phillips, and E. W. Davis. *Project Management With CPM, PERT and Precedence Diagramming,* 3rd ed. New York: Van Nostrand Reinhold, 1983.

30. Moodie, C. L., and D. E. Mandeville. "Project Resource Balancing by Assembly Lines Balancing Techniques." *Journal of Industrial Engineering,* July 1965.

31. Moshman, J., J. Johnson, and M. Larsen. "RAMPS—A Technique for Resource Allocation and Multiproject Scheduling." *Proceedings,* Spring Joint Computer Conference, 1963.

32. Parncutt, G. "Concepts of Resource Allocation and Cost Control and Their Utility in Project Management." *Project Management Quarterly,* 1974.

33. Parris, T. P. E. "Practical Manpower Allocation of a Project Mix Via Zero-Float CPM Networks." *Project Management Institute Proceedings,* 1972.

34. Pascoe, T. L. "An Experimental Comparison of Heuristic Methods for Allocating Resources." Ph.D. Dissertation, Department of Engineering, Cambridge University, 1965.

35. Patterson, J. H. "Alternate Methods of Project Scheduling with Limited Resources." *Naval Research Logistics Quarterly,* Dec. 1973.

36. Patterson, J. H., and W. D. Huber. "A Horizon-Varying, Zero-One Approach to Project Scheduling." *Management Science,* Feb. 1974.

37. Pritsker, A. A. B., L. J. Walters, and P. M. Wolfe. "Multi-Project Scheduling with Limited Resources: A Zero-One Programming Approach." *Management Science,* Sept. 1969.

38. Robinson, D. R. "A Dynamic Programming Solution to Cost-Time Trade-off for CPM." *Management Science,* Oct. 1975.

39. Sakarev, I., and M. Demirov. *Solving Multi-Project Planning by Network Analysis.* Amsterdam: North-Holland Publishing Co., 1969.

40. Schrage, L. "Solving Resource-Constrained Network Problems by Implicit Enumeration—Non-Preemptive Case." *Operations Research,* 1970.

41. Shih, W. "A New Application of Incremental Analysis in Resource Allocations." *Operational Research Quarterly,* Dec. 1974.

42. Shih, W. "A Branch and Bound Procedure for a Class of Discrete Resource Allocation Problems with Several Constraints." *Operational Research Quarterly,* June 1977.

43. Stinson, J. P. "A Branch and Bound Algorithm for a General Class of Resource

Constrained Scheduling Problems." *AIIE Conference Proceedings,* Las Vegas, 1975.

44. Stinson, J. P., E. W. Davis, and B. Khumawala. "Multiple Resource-Constrained Scheduling Using Branch and Bound." *AIIE Transactions,* Sept. 1978.

45. Sunage, T. "A Method of the Optimal Scheduling for a Project with Resource Restrictions." *Journal of The Operations Research Society of Japan,* March 1970.

46. Talbot, F. B. "Project Scheduling with Resource-Duration Interactions: The Non-preemptive Case." Working paper No. 200, Graduate School of Business Administration, University of Michigan, Jan. 1980.

47. Talbot, B. F., and J. H. Patterson. "Optimal Methods for Scheduling Under Resource Constraints." *Project Management Quarterly,* Dec. 1979.

48. Tonge, F. M. *A Heuristic Program for Assembly Line Balancing.* Prentice-Hall, 1961.

49. Turban, E., and J. R. Meredith. *Fundamentals of Management Science,* 4th ed. Plano, TX: Business Publications, 1988.

50. Walton, H. "Administration Aspects of Network Analysis." *Applications of Critical Path Techniques.* London: The English Universities Press Ltd., 1968.

51. Weaver, J. "Mainframe ARTEMIS: More Than a Project Management Tool." *Project Management Journal,* April 1988.

52. Whitehouse, G. E., and J. R. Brown. "GENRES: An Extension of Brook's Algorithm for Project Scheduling with Resource Constraints." *Computers and Industrial Engineering,* No. 3, 1979.

53. Wiest, J. D. "A Heuristic Model for Scheduling Large Projects with Limited Resources." *Management Science,* Feb. 1967.

54. Wiest, J. D. "Heuristic Programs for Decision Making." *Harvard Business Review,* Sept.–Oct. 1965.

55. Woodworth, B. M., and C. T. Willie. "A Heuristic Algorithm for Resource Levelling in Multi-Project, Multi-Resource Scheduling." *Decision Sciences,* 1975.

9.15 Case: D. U. Singer Hospital Products Corp.*

D. U. Singer Hospital Products Corp. has done sufficient new product development at the research and development level to estimate a high likelihood of technical success for a product of assured commercial success: A long-time antiseptic. Management has instructed Singer's Antiseptic Division to make a market entry at the earliest possible time; they have requested a complete plan up to the startup of production. Marketing and other plans following startup of production are to be prepared separately after this plan has been completed.

Project responsibility is assigned to the division's Research and Development Group; Mike Richards, the project scientist who developed the product, is assigned responsibility for project management. Assistance will be required from other parts of the company: Packaging Task Force, R & D Group; Corporate Engineering; Corporate Purchasing; Hospital Products Manufacturing Group; Packaged Products Manufacturing Group.

Mike was concerned about the scope of the project. He knew from his own experience that a final formula had yet to be developed, although such development was really a "routine" function. The remaining questions had to do with color, odor and consistency additives rather than any performance-related modification. Fortunately, the major regulatory issues had been resolved and he believed that submission of regulatory documentation would be followed by rapid approval as they already had a letter of approval contingent on final documentation.

But there were also issues in packaging that had to be resolved; development of the packaging design was one of his primary concerns at this time. Ultimately, there will have to be manufacturing procedures in accordance with corporate policies and standards; capital equipment selection and procurement, installation of this equipment and startup.

Mike was concerned about defining the project unambiguously. To that end, he obtained an interview with S. L. Mander, the Group Vice President.

When he asked Mander where his responsibility should end, the executive turned the question back to him. Mike had been prepared for this and said that he would like to regard his part of the project as done when the production process could be turned over to manufacturing. They agreed that according to Singer practice, this would be when the manufacturing operation could produce a 95% yield of product (fully packaged) at a level of 80% of full production goal of 10 million liters per year.

"But I want you to remember," said Mander, "That you must meet all current FDA, EPA and OSHA regulations and you must be in compliance with our internal specification—the one I've got is dated September and is RD78/965. And you know that manufacturing now—quite rightly, I feel—insists on full written manufacturing procedures."

After this discussion, Mike felt that he had enough information about this aspect to start to pin down what had to be done to achieve these results. His first step in this effort was to meet with P. H. Docent, the Director of Research.

"You are naive if you think that you can just start right in finalizing the formula," said Docent. "You must first develop a product rationale (a).[1] This is a formally-defined process according to company policy. Marketing expects inputs at this stage, manufacturing expects their voice to be heard and you will have to have ap-

*Reproduced with the kind persmission of Herbert F. Spirer, Professor of Management and Administrative Sciences, MBA Program at Stamford, University of Connecticut. Copyright © 1980 Herbert F. Spirer.

[1]Tasks which must be accounted for in a network plan are identified by lower-case alphabetic symbols in parentheses. Refer to Exhibit 1.

provals from every unit of the company that is involved; all of this is reviewed by the Executive Committee. You should have no trouble if you do your homework, but expect to spend a good eight weeks to get this done."

"That certainly stretches things out," said Mike. "I expected to take 12 weeks to develop the ingredient formula (b) and you know that I can't start to establish product specifications (c) until the formula is complete. That's another three weeks."

"Yes, but while you are working on the product specifications you can get going on the regulatory documentation (d). Full internal specifications are not required for that work, but you can't start those documents until the formula is complete."

"Yes, and I find it hard to believe that we can push through both preparation of documents *and* getting approval in three weeks, but Environmental swears it can be done."

"Oh, it can be done in this case because of the preparatory work. Of course, I won't say that this estimate of three weeks is as certain as our other time estimates. All we need is a change of staff at the Agency and we are in trouble. But once you have both the specifications and the approval, you can immediately start on developing the processing system (g)."

"Yes, and how I wish we could get a lead on that, but the designers say that there is too much uncertainty and they won't move until they have both specifications and regulatory documentation and approval. They are offering pretty fast response; six weeks from start to finish for the processing system."

"They are a good crew, Mike. And of course, you know that you don't have to delay on starting the packaging segment of this project. You can start developing the packaging concept (e) just as soon as the product rationale has been developed. If my experience is any judge, it will take a full eight weeks; you'll have to work to keep the process from running forever."

"But as soon as that is finished we can start on the design of the package and its materials (f)

which usually takes about six weeks. Once that is done we can start on the packaging system (h) which shouldn't take longer than eight weeks," concluded Mike. At this point he realized that although Docent would have general knowledge, he needed to talk directly to the Director of Manufacturing.

"The first step, which follows the completion of the development of processing and packaging systems," said the Director of Manufacturing, "is to do a complete study of the facilities requirements (i). You won't be able to get that done in less than four weeks. And that must precede the preparation of the capital equipment list (j) which should take about three-quarters as long. Of course, as soon as both the process system and packaging system are completed, you could start on preparing the written manufacturing procedures (q)."

"But," said Mike, "Can I really finish the procedures before I have installed and constructed the facilities (p)?"

"No, quite right. What you can do is get the first phase done, but the last three of the ten weeks it will take to do that will have to wait for the installation and construction."

"Then this means that I really have two phases for the writing, that which can be completed without the installation and construction (q), and that which has to wait for those inputs (q')."

"True. Now you realize that the last thing you have to do is to run the equipment in a pilot test (r) which will show that you have reached a satisfactory level?"

"Yes. Since that must include debugging, I've estimated a six-week period as adequate." The Director of Manufacturing assented. Mike continued, "What I'm not sure of is whether we can run all the installation tasks in parallel."

"You can let the purchase orders and carry out the procurement of process equipment (k), packaging equipment (l), and facilities (m) as soon as the capital equipment list is complete. The installation of each of these types of equipment and facilities can start as soon as the goods are on hand (n,o,p)."

"What do you estimate for the times to do these

Activity	Packaging Task Force	R+D Group	Corp. Eng.	H-P Manuf.	Pack. Prod. Manuf.	Maint.	Purchasing	Material & Other Direct Charges
a—prod. rationale	1	12	1	1	2	0	0	$ 0
b—dev formula	0	16	4	2	0	0	0	500
c—prod spec	1	6	3	1	1	0	↖	0
d—reg. document.	0	12	4	2	0	0	0	0
e—dev. pkg. conc.	12	8	4	2	8	0	2	4000
f—design pkg.	12	2	3	0	3	0	3	2000
g—dev. proc. sys.	0	18	12	12	0	0	0	0
h—dev. pkg. sys.	24	8	8	0	8	0	2	0
i—study fac. req.	0	4	16	2	2	0	0	0
j—cap. equip. list	0	1	3	0	0	0	1	0
k—procure proc. e.	0	1	1	1	0	0	7	40000
l—procure pkg e.	1	0	1	0	1	0	9	160000
m—procure facil.	0	0	1	1	1	1	6	30000
n—install proc. e	0	2	4	8	0	4	1	4000
o—install pkg. e.	2	0	4	0	8	4	1	8000
p—install fac. e.	0	0	5	5	5	10	1	6000
q,q'—written procedures	5	5	5	10	15	10	0	5000
r—pilot test	3	6	6	6	6	6	0	

tasks?" asked Mike. The Director of Manufacturing estimated 18, 8 and 4 weeks for the purchasing phases for each of the subsystems in that order and four weeks for each of the installations. "Then I can regard my job as done with the delivery of the procedures and when I show my 95% yield," said Mike, and the Director of Manufacturing agreed, but reminded Mike that none of the purchasing cycles could start until the capital equipment list had been prepared and approved (j) which he saw as a three-week task.

The Executive Committee of D. U. Singer Hospital Products Corp. set a starting date for the project of December 10 and asked Mike to project a completion date with his submission of the plan. The Committee's request implied that whatever date Mike came up with was acceptable, but Mike knew that he would be expected to show how to shorten the time to complete the project. However, his task in making the schedule was clear; he had to establish the resource requirements and deal with calendar constraints as best as he could.

To this end, Mike had to get an estimate of resources which he decided to do by making a list of the activities and asking each group involved what was their level of input. The results of this survey are shown in Exhibit 1.

For the purposes of overall planning, the Accounting Department told Mike that he could estimate a cost of $600 per week per employee. This would enable him to provide a cash flow forecast along with his plan; which the Chief Accountant said would be expected, something that Mike had not realized.

Mike knew that it was customary at D. U. Singer to provide the following as parts of a plan to be submitted to the Executive Committee:

1. Statement of Objectives.
2. Work Breakdown Structure.
3. A Network, either activity-on-node (CPM) or event-on-node (PERT).
4. A determination of the critical path or paths and the duration along the critical path.
5. An Early-Start Schedule, in which every activity would be started at its Early Start, regardless of resource constraints.
6. A period labor requirements graph for:
   a. Each group.
   b. Project as a whole.
7. Cumulative labor requirements plot for:
   a. Each group.
   b. Project as a whole.
8. A schedule based on the best leveling of labor requirements that could be achieved without lengthening project duration by more than 15% in calendar days.
9. A cash flow requirements graph for the project when leveled, assuming that commitments for materials and other direct charges are made at the start of the activity but that arrivals of purchased goods are uniformly distributed through the first two-thirds of the activity.

9.16 READING

This article describes the evaluation of four resource allocation software packages on a test network of 15 activities requiring five different resources. Four resource cases were tested for each of the packages: unlimited resources, resource A constrained, resource B constrained, and all resources constrained. The basic criterion used to compare the packages was the minimum project duration. Results of each of the packages were compared with the known optimal results. Some packages did well and others less well; none was perfect.

The value of this article for managers is the information concerning the capabilities of commercially available software packages for addressing the resource allocation problem. Both the benefits as well as the limitations are noted. Just as important, a methodology for evaluating such packages that managers can use for conducting their own tests is presented.

Resource Allocation: A Comparative Study

Luis F. Suarez *Coopers & Lybrand*

INTRODUCTION

Project managers face a challenge in every project assignment: executing a project with the highest quality standards, and with the minimum possible time, cost and resources. Social and economic factors dictate that every project manager make optimal use of the limited available resources, both in terms of manpower and materials supply. Various resource allocation techniques have been developed to facilitate the allocation of resources and generation of schedules that satisfy resource constraints and produce optimal use of limited resources.

This article summarizes the results of a comparative study [1] of the resource allocation packages found in four widely used mainframe computer packages: ARTEMIS, CIPREC, PREMIS and PROJECT/2.[*]

BACKGROUND

Projects are becoming increasingly complex because of the large number of resources and the need for tighter controls of the always scarce available resources. Resources may include: personnel,

materials, money and time. Project management makes use of a variety of techniques to help the project manager plan and control the project tasks. These techniques include: barcharts, networks, CPM and PERT diagrams, resource allocation and resource leveling.

Typical network, CPM and PERT techniques are limited to scheduling of activities based on a logical order of precedence usually dictated by technology constraints. The outcome of these calculations includes time computations of early and late start, early and late finish, float times, critical activities, etc.

In real life cases, the project manager is always concerned not only with the logic and time constraints but also with the availability of resources. And even if the availability of resources is not critical, it is unlikely that the resource schedules are optimal in terms of project time or cost.

Resource allocation and resource leveling techniques have been developed to determine feasible and optimal schedules that include both time and resource availability factors. Even if a resource appears to be unlimited (such as labor or materials), it may be beneficial to consider the resource as being of limited amount, especially if there are other projects competing for the same resources.

Various textbooks and papers describe the

---

[*]ARTEMIS is a registered trademark of Metier Management Systems, Inc. CIPREC is a registered trademark of IBM. PREMIS is a registered trademark of K&H Project Systems, Inc. PROJECT/2 is a registered trademark of Project Software & Development, Inc.

© 1987 by Project Management Institute. Reprinted from *Project Management Journal,* March 1987, by permission.

various models, algorithms and detailed steps involved in resolving the resource allocation problem. Basically, any resource availability conflict is resolved by examining on a consecutive fashion, each two conflicting activities at one time and making changes in the sequence of activities until the resource constraint is satisfied. It follows that any postponement in the start of an activity may result in an extension of the project duration. The optimal solution may be found by performing an iterative analysis.

Of course, the minimum project duration is not always the optimal solution since the project manager must also consider the issue of resource leveling. For example, one cannot dismiss and rehire personnel on an intermittent pattern just to satisfy a theoretical optimal resource loading solution. Manual implementation of the theoretical approach becomes extremely cumbersome for projects or networks involving more than a dozen activities, and two or three resources per activity. Various computer programs have been developed to facilitate the use of the resource allocation technique for large projects. Brief descriptions of the characteristics and the resource allocation results from four readily available mainframe computer programs follow.

RESOURCE ALLOCATION PACKAGES

Four software packages were selected for this study: ARTEMIS, CIPREC, PREMIS and PROJECT/2. These programs were selected as a basis for comparison because of the availability of a previous comparative study [2], and because these programs are both well known in the project management field and widely used in industry.

ARTEMIS is a management information system that uses a relational data base for handling network data, report formats and data sets created by the user. It allows both precedence notation and activity on the arrow notation for network modeling. Resource scheduling is made by the serial method. Available options for resource scheduling include: definition of activity priorities, activity splitting, use of alternative resource levels, and resource leveling. Results are accessible by creating report models which can be stored and used continuously.

CIPREC is a project management system created by IBM as a replacement product for PROJACS and PMS IV. It is made up of two packages: the central processor and the extended function package. The extended function package is an optional package that includes the Resource Allocation Processor, an Activity-Oriented Cost-Processor, and a Work Package Oriented Cost Processor. Both activity on the arrow and precedence notation are allowed. Allocation of resources is made by performing a simulation analysis with the forward parallel scheduling algorithm. CIPREC offers an extensive list of options for the priority rules that will govern the allocation of available resources among the competing activities.

PREMIS allows both precedence notation and activity on the arrow notation for network modeling. There is no limit on the number of types of resources per activity, and the number of total resources per project is subject only to memory size of available computer. Resource scheduling is made by the serial method. Available options for resource scheduling include: definition of activity priorities, activity splitting, and resource leveling. Results are accessible by creating report models (to be used indefinitely) or by requesting one of the many standard reports available. Some of the available reports include: time scheduling activity check lists, time scheduling event listing, project bar-chart, resource scheduling, resource usage tables, and resource schedule histograms.

PROJECT/2 allows both precedence notation and activity on arrow notation for network modeling. Resource scheduling can be made by the serial or by the parallel heuristic algorithms. Available options for resource scheduling include: definition of activity priorities, activity splitting, resource leveling, and use of alternative resource levels. The program is made up of eight processors: Network and CPM Schedule Processor, Target Processor, Resource and Cost Allocation Processor, Project Cost Processor, Resource Constraining Processor, Multiproject Processor, Graphic Processor, and Interactive Processor.

TEST PROJECT

A test network was used to compare the results of the various resource allocation packages. The test project consists of building a garage. It has fifteen activities, including one dummy activity. The network uses the activity on the arrow notation. Some activities require more than one resource, and a total of five resources are specified. Duration and required resources for each activity are indicated in the network shown in Fig. 1. The project start day is Monday, October 4.

A working calendar of five days per week was specified for all the programs. All five resources are of a carried-forward nature and the maximum available levels are: A=15, B=4, C=2, D=2 and E=2. Carried-forward resources are those that are carried over from one operation to another once the first operation is completed, i.e. personnel or equipment. In contrast, used-by-job resources are those that are entirely consumed during the execu-

tion of a particular operation, such as building materials, fuel and paint.

COMPARISON CRITERIA

The basic criteria used in this study for comparing the results of resource allocation analysis was the minimum project duration within given resource constraints for the following cases:

a. unlimited resources
b. constant constraint on resource A
c. constant constraint on resource B
d. constant constraint on all resources

Additionally, differences in the scheduling of individual activities will be indicated. Three different scheduling priorities were specified when using the CIPREC program: minimum late start (default), minimum early start (ES) and minimum late finish (LF).

UNLIMITED RESOURCES

Simulation of unlimited resources was made by specifying a maximum resource availability level of 50 units for each of the resources. The three

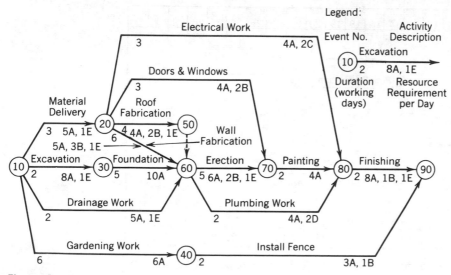

Figure 1.   Test Network

resource schedules produced by CIPREC using the three separate scheduling priorities (default, ES and LF) are identical with a minimum project duration of 18 days.

The optimal manual solution for the unlimited resources case is 18 days. This case was included only for the purpose of verifying CIPREC's schedule with the optimal manual solution. It is expected that all programs should provide the same schedule in the absence of resource constraints.

CONSTANT CONSTRAINT ON RESOURCE A

This case was simulated by specifying a maximum resource availability level of 15 units for resource A while maintaining a level of 50 units for each of the remaining resources. With the CIPREC program, project duration using the default priority (LS) is 26 days, with the minimum early start priority (ES) 24 days, and with the minimum late finish priority (LF) also 24 days. The optimal manual solution has a duration of 20 days and the other three computer programs gave a minimum duration of 23 days.

The schedules produced by CIPREC are longer than those produced by the other three programs.

The difference is because of CIPREC's early scheduling of activity Doors and Windows which forces the activity Foundation (with a duration of 5 days and resource requirement of 10 units) to be postponed.

CONSTANT CONSTRAINT ON RESOURCE B

This case was simulated by specifying a maximum resource availability level of 4 units for resource B while maintaining a level of 50 units for each of the remaining resources.

Resource schedules produced by CIPREC using the three separate scheduling priorities (default, ES, and LF) indicate a minimum project duration of 22 days. The minimum early start (ES) and minimum late finish (LF) resource schedules are identical for all activities. Schedules for the manual solution, ARTEMIS, PREMIS, and PROJECT/2 are identical with a minimum project duration of 22 days. Fig. 2 illustrates the sequencing of activities when there is a constant constraint on Resource B. These schedules are identical to the resource schedule produced by CIPREC using the minimum late start (default) priority.

All solutions, except for CIPREC's minimum

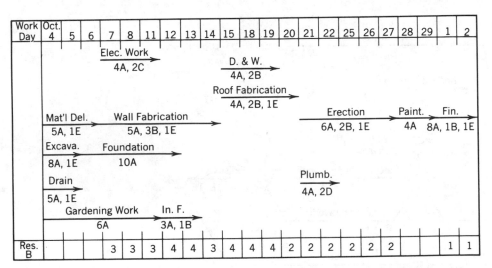

Figure 2. Optimal Manual Solution, ARTEMIS, PREMIS, and PROJECT/2 Schedules: Constant Constraint on Resource B

early start (ES) and minimum late finish (LF), have the same minimum project duration of 22 days and the same scheduling of activities. CIPREC's (ES) and (LF) schedules choose the activities Doors and Windows and Roof Fabrication before scheduling Wall Fabrication even though Wall Fabrication has an earlier late finish than Doors and Windows. This may be explained by the fact that on October 7, the first activity to receive B resources was probably Roof Fabrication, leaving only 2 unused B units which were insufficient for Wall Fabrication.

CONSTANT CONSTRAINT ON ALL RESOURCES

This case was simulated by specifying the following maximum resource availability levels: A=15, B=4, C=2, D=2, and E=2. Resource schedules produced by CIPREC using three separate scheduling priorities (default, ES, and LF) indicate minimum project durations of 24, 25 and 24 days respectively.

Schedules for the optimal manual solution and PROJECT/2 were identical and had a minimum project duration of 22 days; ARTEMIS and PREMIS had a project duration of 25 and 23 days respectively.

CIPREC's schedule with all resources constrained, default scheduling priority (LS) has a project duration of 24 days which compares better than CIPREC's schedule with constraint on resource A only, default priority which has a minimum project duration of 26 days. This may be explained by the fact that when all resources are constrained, CIPREC scheduled Electrical Work instead of Roof Fabrication on October 11. Thus, Foundation could be scheduled on October 14 which made better use of all the available resources.

CONCLUSIONS

A test network with 15 activities and 5 different resource requirements was used to compare the performance of various resource allocation computer programs. Three different resource alloca-tion schedules were produced using CIPREC's Resource Allocation Package. Resource scheduling priorities chosen for this study were: minimum late start (default option), minimum early start (ES) and minimum late finish (LF). These scheduling priorities were selected because they represent some of the most common resource scheduling priorities used.

The programs included in this study used the serial or the parallel method for allocating constrained resources. The serial method allocates resources (for the entire activity duration) by examining activities in series, i.e. one activity at a time and using the established priority rules. The parallel method allocates resources (only for one day at a time) by examining resource availability on a daily basis regardless of activity duration and the scheduler has the option of specifying whether execution of the activity may be interrupted before its completion. The schedules produced by CIPREC were compared with those produced by ARTEMIS, PREMIS and PROJECT/2. ARTEMIS uses the serial algorithm with minimum early start as the priority rule for resource allocation. PREMIS uses the serial algorithm with the minimum late finish as priority rule. PROJECT/2 uses the parallel algorithm with the minimum slack as the priority rule.

A summary of the minimum project durations produced by the different resource allocation programs is given in Table 1.

When comparing the results obtained by the computer programs, one must keep in mind that any comparisons made between different schedules are valid only for the specific network and resource requirements specified. Generalizations about the performance of a program cannot be made relying exclusively on the results of one test network.

For the test network analyzed and with the specified resource requirements, CIPREC's resource schedules yielded generally longer project durations than those made by ARTEMIS, PREMIS and PROJECT/2. Only for the case of constant constraint on resource B, the programs gave the same minimum project duration which was also the optimal manual solution.

Table 1 Minimum Project Durations (days)

| | Priority | Sequence | Constant Constraint On Resource: | | | Unlimited Resources |
			A (15)	B (4)	All (15,4,2,2,2)	
CIPREC	LS	Parallel	26	22	24	18
CIPREC	ES	Parallel	24	22	25	18
CIPREC	LF	Parallel	24	22	24	18
ARTEMIS	ES	Serial	23	22	25	18
PREMIS	LF	Serial	23	22	23	18
PROJECT/2	Slack	Parallel	23	22	22	18
Optimal Manual Solution			20	22	22	18

Comparison of other relevant features such as user friendliness, speed of computation, documentation, etc. was not made.

REFERENCES

1. IBM Conversational and Interactive Project Evaluation and Control. *Program Reference Manuals and User's Guide,* 1982.

2. Suarez, L.F., Resource Allocation Using the IBM CIPREC Program. *MBA Professional Report,* Graduate School of Business, The University of Texas at Austin, 1984.

3. Yoo, H., Resource Scheduling with CPM—Comparative Study of Three Existing Software Packages. M.S. Thesis, Civil Engineering, The University of Texas at Austin, 1983.

CHAPTER 10
Monitoring and Information Systems

In Chapter 9 we looked at the resource allocation-scheduling interactions in project implementation. This chapter is the link between planning and control—namely, *monitoring*. Monitoring is collecting, recording, and reporting information concerning any and all aspects of project performance that the project manager or others in the organization wish to know. In our discussion it is important to remember that monitoring, as an activity, should be kept distinct from controlling (which uses the data supplied by monitoring to bring actual performance into approximate congruence with planned performance), as well as from evaluation (through which judgments are made about the quality and effectiveness of project performance).

First we expand on the nature of this link between planning and control, including a brief discussion of the various aspects of project performance that need to be monitored. We also examine some of the problems associated with monitoring a project. Finally, we report on several computer software packages that can greatly increase the speed and effectiveness of project monitoring.

This chapter is addressed to practicing PMs as well as students of project management. Students resist the idea that PMs do not have immediate access to accurate information on every aspect of the project. But PMs know it is not always easy to find out what's going on when working on a project. Records are frequently out of date, incomplete, in error, or "somewhere else" when needed.

Throughout the chapter, our primary concern is to ensure that all parties interested in the project have available, *on a timely basis,* the information needed to exercise effective control over the project. The other uses for monitoring (e.g., auditing, learning from past mistakes, or keeping senior management informed), important as they are, must be considered secondary to the control function when constructing the monitoring system. The key issue, then, is to create an information system that gives project managers the information they need to make informed, timely decisions that will keep project performance as close as possible to the project plan.

One final note. In this chapter we frequently refer to a "project monitor," a "project controller," or even to the "group" responsible for monitoring. These individuals and groups do in fact exist on most large projects. On a small project, it is likely that the person in charge of monitoring is the same person as the project controller—and the same person as the PM. That is, when we refer to the project monitor and controller, we are referring to roles needed in project management, not necessarily to different individuals.

10.1 THE PLANNING-MONITORING-CONTROLLING CYCLE

Throughout this book we have stressed the need to plan, check on progress, compare progress to the plan, and take corrective action if progress does not match the plan. There is no doubt that some organizations do not spend sufficient time and effort on planning and controlling projects. If is far easier to focus on doing, especially because it appears to be more effective to "stop all the talk and get on with the work." We could cite firm after firm that incurred great expense (and major losses) because the planning process was inadequate for the tasks undertaken.

A major construction project ran over budget by 63 percent and over schedule by 48 percent because the PM decided that, since "he had managed similar projects several times before, he knew what to do without going into all that detail that no one looks at anyway." A large industrial equipment supplier took a bath on a project designed to develop a new area of business because it applied the same planning and control procedures to the new area that it had used (successfully) on previous, smaller, less complex jobs. A computer store won a competitive bid to supply a computer, five terminals, and associated software to the Kansas City office of a national firm. Admittedly insufficient planning made the installation significantly late. Performance of the software was not close to specified levels. This botched job prevented the firm from being invited to bid on more than twenty similar installations planned by the client.

The planning (budgeting and scheduling) methods we propose "put the hassles up front." They require a significantly greater investment of time and energy early in the life of the project, but they significantly reduce the extent and cost of poor performance and time/cost overruns. Note that this is no guarantee of a trouble-free project, merely an improvement in the risk of failure.

It is useful to perceive the control process as a *closed loop* system, with revised plans and schedules (if warranted) following corrective actions. We delay a detailed discussion on control until the next chapter, but the planning-monitoring-controlling cycle is continuously in process until the project is completed. The information flows for such a cycle are illustrated in Figure 10-1. Note the direction of the flows, information flowing from the bottom toward the top and authority flowing from the top down.

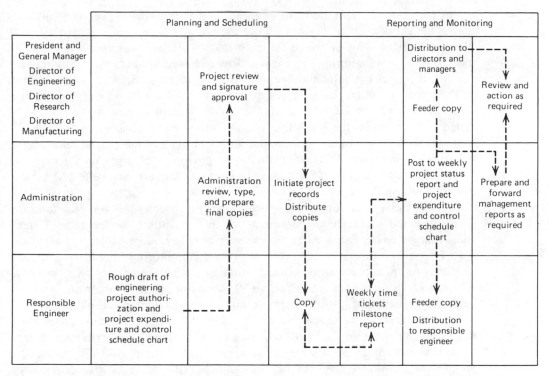

Figure 10-1 Project authorization and expenditure control system information flow.

Source: B. V. Dean, *Evaluating, Selecting, and Controlling R & D Projects,* American Management Association Research Study 89, 1968.

It is also useful to construct this process as an internal part of the organizational structure of the project, not something external to and imposed on it or, worse, in conflict with it. Finally, experience tells us that it is also desirable, though not mandatory, that the planning-monitoring-controlling cycle be the normal way of life in the parent organization. What is good for the project is equally good for the parent firm. In any case, unless the PM has a smoothly operating monitoring/control system, it will be difficult to manage the project effectively.

Designing the Monitoring System

The first step in setting up any monitoring system is to identify the key factors to be controlled. Clearly, the PM wants to monitor performance, cost, and time but must define precisely which specific characteristics of performance, cost, and time should be controlled and then establish exact boundaries within which control should be maintained. There may also be other factors of importance worth noting, at least at milestone or review points in the life of the project. For example, the number of labor hours used, the number or extent of engineering changes, the level of customer satisfaction, and similar items may be worthy of note on individual projects.

But the best source of items to be monitored is the project Action Plan—actually, the set of Action Plans that describe what is being done, when, and the planned level of resource usage for each task, work package, and work unit in the project. The monitoring system is a direct connection between planning and control. If it does not collect and report information on some significant element of the plan, control can be faulty or missing. The Action Plan furnishes the key items that must be measured and reported to the control system, but it is not sufficient. For example, the PM might want to know about changes in the client's attitudes toward the project. Information on the morale of the project team might be useful in preparing for organizational or personnel changes on the project. These two latter items may be quite important, but are not reflected in the project's Action Plans.

Unfortunately, it is common to focus monitoring activities on data that are easily gathered—rather than important—or to concentrate on "objective" measures that are easily defended at the expense of softer, more subjective data that may be more valuable for control. Above all, monitoring should concentrate primarily on measuring various facets of output rather than intensity of activity. It is crucial to remember that effective PMs are not primarily interested in how hard their project teams work. They are interested in achieving results.

Given all this, performance criteria, standards, and data collection procedures must be established for each of the factors to be measured. The criteria and data collection procedures are usually set up for the life of the project. The standards themselves, however, may not be constant over the project's life. They may change as a result of altered capabilities within the parent organization or a technological breakthrough made by the project team; but, perhaps more often than not, standards and criteria change because of factors that are not under the control of the PM.

For example, they may be changed by the client. One client who had ordered a special piece of audio equipment altered performance specifications significantly when electronic parts became available that could filter out random noises.

Standards may also be changed by the community as a response to some shift in public policy—witness the changes in the performance standards imposed on nuclear power installations. Shifts in the prime rate of interest or in unemployment levels often alter the standards that the PM must use for making project related decisions. The monitoring process is based on the criteria and standards because they dictate, or at least constrain, the set of relevant measures.

Next, the information to be collected must be identified. This may consist of accounting data, operating data, engineering test data, customer reactions, specification changes, and the like. The fundamental problem is to determine precisely which of all the available data should be collected. It is worth repeating that the typical determinant for collecting data too often seems to be simply the ease with which they can be gathered. Of course the nature of the required data is dictated by the project plan, as well as by the goals of the parent organization, the needs of the client, and by the fact that it is desirable to improve the process of managing projects.

Perhaps the most common error made when monitoring data is to gather information that is clearly related to project performance but has little or no probability of changing significantly from one collection period to the next. Prior to its breakup, the American Telephone and Telegraph Co. used to collect monthly statistics on a very large number of indicators of operating efficiency. The extent of the collection was such that it filled a telephone-book-sized volume known as "Ma Bell's Green Book". For a great many of the indicators, the likelihood of a significant change from one month to the next was extremely small. When asked about the matter, one official remarked that the mere collection of the data kept the operating companies "on their toes." We feel that there are other, more positive and less expensive ways of motivating project personnel. Certainly, "collect everything" is inappropriate as a monitoring policy.

Therefore, the first task is to examine the project plans in order to extract performance, time, and cost goals. These goals should relate in some fashion to each of the different levels of detail; that is, some should relate to the project, some to its tasks, some to the work packages, and so on. Data must be identified that measure achievement against these goals, and mechanisms designed that gather and store such data.

Similarly, the process of developing and managing projects should be considered and steps taken to ensure that information relevant to the diagnosis and treatment of the project's organizational infirmities and procedural problems are gathered and collected. A reading of the fascinating book, *The Soul of a New Machine* [18], reveals the crucial roles organizational factors, interpersonal relationships, and managerial style play in determining project success.

How to Collect Data

Given that we know *what type* of data we want to collect, the next question is *how* to collect this information. At this point in the construction of a monitoring system, it is necessary to define precisely what pieces of information should be gathered and *when*. In most cases, the PM has options. Questions arise. Should cost data be gathered before or after some specific event? Is it always mandatory to collect time and cost information at exactly the same point in the process? What do we do if a specific item is difficult to collect because the data source (human) fears reporting any information that might contribute to a negative performance evaluation? What do we do about the fact that some use of time is reported as "hours charged" to our project, and we are quite aware that our project has been charged for work done on another project that is over budget? Are special forms needed for data collection? Should we set up quality control procedures to ensure the integrity of data transference from its source to the project information system? Such questions merely indicate the broad range of knotty issues that must be handled.

A large proportion of all data collected take one of the following forms, each of which is suitable for some types of measures.

1. *Frequency counts* A simple tally of the occurrence of an event. This type of measure is often used for "complaints," "number of times a project report is late," "days without an accident," "bugs in a computer program" and similar items. The

data are usually easy to collect and are often reported as events per unit time or events as a percent of a standard number.

2. *Raw numbers* Dates, dollars, hours, physical amounts of resources used, and specifications are usually reported in this way. These numbers are reported in a wide variety of ways, but often as direct comparisons with an expected or standard number. Also, "variances" are commonly reported as the ratios of actual to standard. Comparisons or ratios can also be plotted as a time series to show changes in system performance.

3. *Subjective numeric ratings* These numbers are subjective estimates, usually of a quality, made by knowledgeable individuals or groups. They can be reported in most of the same ways that objective raw numbers are, but care should be taken to make sure that the numbers are not manipulated in ways only suitable for quantitative measures. (See Chapter 2 comments on measurements.) Ordinal rankings of performance are included in this category.

4. *Indicators* When the PM cannot measure some aspect of system performance directly, it may be possible to find an indirect measure or indicator. The speed with which change orders are processed and changes are incorporated into the project is often a good measure of team efficiency. Response to change may also be an indicator of the quality of communications on the project team. When using indicators to measure performance, the PM must make sure that the linkage between the indicator and the desired performance measure is as direct as possible.

5. *Verbal measures* Measures for such performance characteristics as "quality of team member cooperation," "morale of team members," or "quality of interaction with the client" frequently take the form of verbal characterizations. As long as the set of characterizations is limited and the meanings of the individual terms consistently understood by all, these data serve their purposes reasonably well.

After data collection has been completed, reports on project progress should be generated. These include project status reports, time/cost reports, and variance reports, among others. Causes and effects should be identified and trends noted. Plans, charts, and tables should be updated on a timely basis. Where known, "comparables" should be reported, as should statistical distributions of previous data if available. Both help the PM (and others) to interpret the data being monitored. Figures 10-2 and 10-3 illustrate the use of such data. Figure 10-2 shows the results of a count of "bugs" found during a series of tests run on a new piece of computer software. (Bugs found were fixed prior to subsequent tests.) Figure 10-3 shows the percent of the time a computer program retrieved data within a specified time limit. Each point represents a series of trials.

The PM can fit a statistical function to the data shown in Figure 10-2 and make a rough estimate of the number of tests that will have to be run to find some predetermined number of additional bugs in the program. By fitting a curve (formally or "by eyeball") to the data in Figure 10-3, the PM can estimate the cost and time (the number of additional trials and adjustments) required to get system performance up to the specified level.

The nature of *timeliness* will be amplified below, but it is important that the

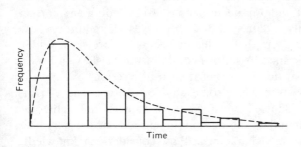

Figure 10-2 Number of bugs found during test of Datamix program.

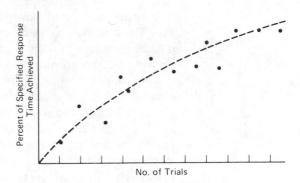

Figure 10-3 Percent of specified performance met during repeated trials.

PM make sure that the PERT/CPM and Gantt charts in the project war room (office) are frequently updated. Monitoring can serve to maintain high morale on the project team as well as to alert team members to problems that will have to be solved.

The purpose of the monitoring system is to gather and report data. The purpose of the control system is to act on the data. To aid the *project controller,* it is helpful for the *monitor* to carry out some data analysis. Significant differences from plan should be highlighted or "flagged" so that they cannot be overlooked by the controller. The methods of statistical quality control are very useful for determining what size variances are "significant" and sometimes even help in determining the probable cause(s) of variances. Where causation is known, it should be noted. Where it is not known, an investigation may be in order. The decisions about when an investigation should be conducted, by whom, and by what methods are the prerogative of the project controller, although the actual investigation may be conducted by the group responsible for monitoring.

At base, this provides a *management by exception* reporting system for the PM. But management by exception has its flaws as well as it strengths. It is essentially an "after-the-fact" approach to control. Variances occur, are investigated, and only then is action taken. The astute PM is far more interested in preventing problems than curing them. Therefore, the monitoring system should develop data streams that indicate variances yet to come. Obviously, such indicators are apt to be statistical in nature, hinting at the likelihood of a future problem rather than predicting it with certainty. An example would be a trend in the data showing a system heading out of control. The PM may waste time and effort trying to deal with trouble that will not actually occur. This may be frustrating, but the costs of dealing with some nonproblems is usually minor when compared to the costs of dealing with real problems too late.

In creating the monitoring system, some care should be devoted to the issues of honesty and bias. The former is dealt with by setting in place an internal audit. The audit serves the purpose of ensuring that the information gathered is honest. No audit, however, can prevent bias. All data are biased by those who report them, advertently or inadvertently. The controller must understand this fact of life. The first issue is to determine whether or not the possibility of bias in the data matters significantly. If not, nothing need be done. Bias finding and correcting activities are worthwhile only if data with less or no bias are required.

The issue of creating an atmosphere that fosters honesty on a project is widely ignored, but it is of major importance. A set of instructions to the PM on how to do this is not beyond the scope of this book, but if such instructions exist, we do not know of them. We do, however, have some advice to offer. The PM can tolerate almost any kind of behavior except dishonesty. Projects are vulnerable to dishonesty, far more vulnerable than the ongoing operations of the parent organization. Standard operations are characterized by considerable knowledge about expected system performance. When the monitoring system reports information that deviates from expectations, it is visible, noteworthy, and tends to get attention. In the case of many projects, expectations are not so well known. Deviations are not recognized for what they are. The PM is often dependent on team members to call attention to problems. To get this cooperation, the PM must make sure that the bearer of bad news is not punished; nor is the admitter-to-error executed. On the other hand, the hider-of-mistakes may be shot with impunity.

There is some tendency for project monitoring systems to include an analysis directed at the assignment of blame. This practice has doubtful value. While the managerial dictum "rewards and punishments should be closely associated with performance" has the ring of good common sense, it is actually not good advice. Instead of motivating people to better performance, the practice is more apt to result in lower expectations. If achievement of goals is directly measured and directly rewarded, tremendous pressure will be put on people to understate goals and to generate plans that can be met or exceeded with minimal risk and effort.

10.2 INFORMATION NEEDS AND THE REPORTING PROCESS

Everyone concerned with the project should be appropriately tied into the project reporting system. The monitoring system ought to be constructed so that it addresses every level of management, but reports need not be of the same depth or at the same frequency for each level. Lower-level personnel have a need for detailed information about individual tasks and the factors affecting such tasks. Report frequency is usually high. For the senior management levels, overview reports describe progress in more aggregated terms with less individual task detail. Reports are issued less often. In both cases, the structure of the reports should reflect the WBS, with each managerial level receiving reports that allow the exercise of control at the relevant managerial level. At times it may be necessary to move information between organizations, as illustrated in Figure 10-4, as well as between managerial levels.

The relationship of project reports to the project WBS is the key to the determination of both report content and frequency. Reports must contain data relevant to the control of specific tasks that are being carried out according to a

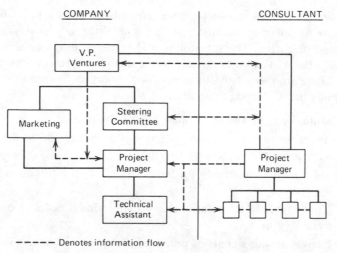

COMPANY   CONSULTANT

----- Denotes information flow

Figure 10-4 Reporting and information flows between organizations working on a common project.

specific schedule. The frequency of reporting should be great enough to allow control to be exerted during or before the period in which the task is scheduled for completion. For example, efficacy tests of drugs do not produce rapid results in most cases. Thus, there is no reason for weekly (and perhaps not even monthly) reports on such tests. When test results begin to occur, more frequent reports and updates may be required.

In addition to the criterion that reports should be available in time to be used for project control, the timing of reports should generally correspond to the timing of project milestones. This means that project reports may not be issued periodically—excepting progress reports for senior management. There seems to be no logical reason, except for tradition, to issue weekly, monthly, quarterly, etc., reports. Few projects require attention so neatly consistent with the calendar. This must not be taken as advice to issue reports "every once in a while." Reports should be scheduled in the project plan. They should be issued on time. The report schedule, however, need not call for *periodic* reports.

Identification of project milestones depends on who is interested. For senior management, there may be only a few milestones, even in large projects. For the PM there may be many critical points in the project schedule at which major decisions must be made, large changes in the resource base must be initiated, or key technical results achieved. The milestones relevant to lower levels relate to finer detail and occur with higher frequency.

The nature of the monitoring reports should be consistent with the logic of the planning, budgeting, and scheduling systems. The primary purpose is, of course, to ensure achievement of the project plan through control. There is little reason to burden operating members of the project team with extensive reports on matters that are not subject to control—at least not by them. For example, overhead costs or the in-house rental cost of the project war room are simply not appropriate considerations for a team member who is supervising a research experiment in polymer chemistry or designing the advertising campaign for a new brand of coffee. The scheduling and resource usage columns of the project Action Plan will serve as the key to the design of project reports.

There are many benefits of detailed reports delivered to the proper people on a timely basis. Among them are:

- Mutual understanding of the goals of the project
- Awareness of the progress of parallel activities and of the problems associated with coordination among activities
- More realistic planning for the needs of all groups and individuals working on the project
- Understanding the relationships of individual tasks to one another and to the overall project
- Early warning signals of potential problems and delays in the project
- Minimizing the confusion associated with change by reducing delays in communicating the change
- Faster management action in response to unacceptable or inappropriate work
- Higher visibility to top management, including attention directed to the immediate needs of the project
- Keeping the client and other interested outside parties up to date on project status, particularly regarding project costs, milestones, and deliverables.

Report Types

For the purposes of project management, we can consider three distinct types of reports: routine, exception, and special analysis. The routine reports are those issued on a regular basis; but, as we noted above, *regular* does not necessarily refer to the calendar. For senior management, the reports will usually be periodic, but for the PM and lower-level project personnel, milestones may be used to trigger routine reports. At times, it may be useful to issue routine reports on resource usage periodically, occasionally on a weekly or even daily basis.

Exception reports are useful in two cases. First, they are directly oriented to project management decision making and should be distributed to the team members who will have prime responsibility for decisions or who have a clear "need to know." Second, they may be issued when a decision is made on an exception basis and it is desirable to inform other managers as well as to document the decision—in other words, as part of a sensible procedure for protecting oneself. (PMs should be aware that overuse of exception reporting will be perceived by top management as sheeplike, overly cautious behavior.)

Special analysis reports are used to disseminate the results of special studies conducted as part of the project or as a response to special problems that arise during the project. Usually they cover matters that may be of interest to other PMs, or make use of analytic methods that might be helpful on other projects. Studies on the use of substitute materials, evaluation of alternative manufacturing processes, availability of external consultants, capabilities of new software, and descriptions of new governmental regulations are all typical of the kinds of subjects covered in special analysis reports. Distribution of these reports is usually made to anyone who might be interested.

Common Reporting Problems

There are three common difficulties in the design of project reports. First, there is usually too much detail, both in the reports themselves and in the input being solicited from workers. Unnecessary detail usually results in the reports not being read. Also, it prevents project team members from finding the information they need. Furthermore, the demand for unnecessary, highly detailed input information often results in careless preparation of the data, thereby casting doubt on the validity of reports based on such data. Finally, the preparation and inclusion of unnecessary detail is costly, at the very least.

A second major problem is the poor interface between the project information system and the parent firm's information system. Data are rarely comparable, and interaction between the PM and the organization's accountants is often strained. In our experience, the PM may try to force a connection. It rarely works well. The parent organization's information system must serve as the definitional prototype for the project's information system. In effect, this means that the parent's accounting, engineering, marketing, finance, personnel, and production information systems should be used as the base on which the project's information system is built. Obviously, different types of reports must be constructed for managing the project, but they can be built by using standard data for the most part. The PM can feel free to add new kinds of data to the information base but cannot insist that costs, resource usage, and the like be reported in the project differently from how they are reported in the parent organization.

The third problem concerns a poor correspondence between the planning and the monitoring systems. If the monitoring system is not tracking information directly related to the project's plans, control is meaningless. This often happens when the firm's existing information system is used for monitoring rather than a special system specifically designed for project management. For example, an existing cost tracking system oriented to shop operations would be inappropriate for a project with major activities in the area of research and development. But as we noted just above, the option of running the project from a different database is generally not viable. The PM's problem is to fit standard information into a reporting and tracking system that is appropriate for the project.

The real message carried by project reports is in the comparison of actual activity to plan and of actual output to desired output. Variances are reported by the monitoring system, and responsibility for action rests with the controller. Because the project plan is described in terms of performance, time, and cost, variances are reported for those same variables. Project variance reports usually follow the same format used by the accounting department, but at times they may be presented differently. An aircraft company specializing in the construction of landing gears underestimated the quantity of material needed on a project. The shortage caused a late delivery that resulted in a severe monetary penalty. Following this project, several unsuccessful proposals were submitted. Then the program manager (who coordinated all landing gear projects) noticed that on the next two proposals the material usage appeared to be overestimated. This raised the firm's cost estimate, thereby raising its bid, and it lost both contracts to proposals with lower bids. Discussions with purchasing (and with the engineer in charge of estimating material) produced the chart in Figure 10-5.

This variance report shows the ratio of the material estimated to the material used in six successive projects. As a result of this information, the program manager decided it would be less expensive for the company to carry small inventories in a few of the commonly used high alloys, and to estimate (and price) material use closer to actual expectations.

The Earned Value Chart

Thus far, our examples have covered monitoring for parts of projects. The monitoring of performance for the entire project is also crucial because performance is the raison d'être of the project. *Individual* task performance must be monitored carefully because the timing and coordination between individual tasks is important. But *overall* project performance is the crux of the matter and must not be overlooked. One way of measuring overall performance is by using an aggregate performance measure called *earned value*.

A serious difficulty with comparing actual expenditures against budgeted or *baseline* expenditures for any given time period is that the comparison fails to take into account the amount of work accomplished relative to the cost incurred. The earned value of work performed for those tasks in progress is found by multiplying the estimated percent completion for each task by the planned cost for that task. The result is the amount that should have been spent on the task thus far. This can then be compared with the actual amount spent. A graph such as that shown in Figure 10-6 can be constructed and provides a basis for evaluating cost and performance to date. If the total value of the work accomplished is in

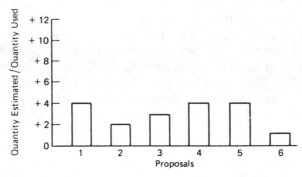

Figure 10-5 Material estimate-to-use ratio in projects to manufacture aircraft landing gears.

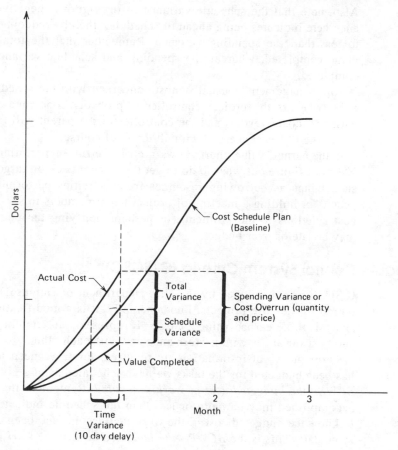

Figure 10-6 Earned value chart.

balance with the planned (baseline) cost (i.e., minimal scheduling variance), then top management has no particular need for a detailed analysis of individual tasks. Thus the concept of earned value combines cost reporting and aggregate performance reporting into one comprehensive chart.

Four variances can be identified on the earned value chart. The time variance is found by subtracting the actual time from the time scheduled for the value completed. The spending variance is the actual cost less the value completed. The schedule variance is the value completed less the baseline plan. The total variance is then the sum of the latter two, as shown below.

$$\begin{aligned}
\text{Spending variance} &= \text{actual cost} - \text{value completed} \\
+ \text{Schedule variance} &= \text{value completed} - \text{baseline cost} \\
\hline
= \text{Total variance} &= \text{actual cost} - \text{baseline cost}
\end{aligned}$$

Notice in Figure 10-6 that the time variance is negative, indicating a delay.

Also, note that the schedule variance in the figure is negative (a positive variance here indicates being ahead of schedule), thereby reducing the total variance to less than the spending variance. Remember that the total variance ignores value completed, whereas the spending and schedule variances consider value completed.

Top management is usually most concerned with the schedule (or time) variance, whereas the project controller is probably concerned with the spending variance (cost overrun) and the controller of the parent will track the total variance. The PM is concerned with all three, of course.

If the earned value chart shows a cost overrun or performance underrun, the PM must figure out what to do to get the system back on target. Options include such things as borrowing resources from activities performing better than expected, or holding a meeting of project team members to see if anyone can suggest solutions to the problems, or perhaps notifying the client that the project may be late or over budget.

Cost/Schedule Control System Criteria (C/SCSC)

C/SCSC was developed by the U.S. Department of Defense and is generally required for defense projects. Fundamentally, it is a modification of earned value analysis. Like earned value analysis, it represents an attempt to relate both time and cost variances with performance and with each other.

Three pieces of information are required. First, we need to know how much has been budgeted for the tasks we have scheduled as of a given date. This is the *BCWS—the budgeted cost of work scheduled*. Remember that the work actually accomplished may be more or less than the schedule indicates, so we also need to know the budgeted cost of the work that has, in fact, been completed as of the same date. This is the *BCWP—the budgeted cost of the work performed*. Finally, we need to know whether or not the amount actually spent differs from the amount we budgeted for whatever tasks we have carried out as of the same date. This is the *ACWP—the actual cost of work performed*. Note that

$$BCWS - BCWP = \text{the schedule variance}$$
$$BCWP - ACWP = \text{the cost variance}$$

The need to keep project performance, cost, and schedule related when monitoring projects has been emphasized in this chapter. This emphasis will be reinforced in Chapter 11. For purposes of control, it is just as important to emphasize the need to relate the realities of time, cost, and performance with the project's Master Plan. C/SCSC takes just such an approach, but there is a major caveat that must be heeded: *The set of project action plans (the project Master Plan) must be kept up to date*. These plans contain descriptions of each task together with estimations of the time and resources required by each. The plans are therefore the primary source of the BCWSs and BCWPs and the framework within which the ACWPs are collected.

Differences between work scheduled and work planned can develop from several different causes; for example, official change orders in the work elements required to accomplish a task, informal alterations in the methods used to accomplish specific tasks, or official or unofficial changes in the tasks to be accomplished. Similarly, cost variances can result from any of the above as well as from changes in input factor prices, changes in the accounting methods used by the project, or changes in the mix of input factors needed to accomplish a given task. If the plan is not altered to reflect such changes, comparisons between plan and actual are not meaningful.

Milestone Reporting

We referred earlier to milestone reports. A typical example of such a report is shown in Figure 10-7a, b, and c. In this illustration, a sample network with milestones is shown, followed by a routine milestone report form. A model top management project status report is illustrated in the next chapter. When filled out, these reports show project status at some point in time. They serve to keep all parties up to date on what has been accomplished. If accomplishments are inadequate or late, these reports serve as starting points for remedial planning.

Figures 10-7a and b show the network for a new product development project for a manufacturer. A steady flow of new products is an essential feature of this firm's business, and each new product is organized as a project as soon as its basic concept is approved by a project selection group. If we examine Figures 10-7a and b closely, we see that the sign-off control boxes at the top of the page correspond with sequences of events in the network. For example, look at the bottom line of the network in Figure 10-7a. The design of this product requires a sculpture that is formed on an armature. The armature must be constructed, and the sculpture of the product completed and signed off. Note that the sculpture is used as a form for making models that are, in turn, used to make the prototype product. The completion of the sculpture is signed off in the next-to-last box in the lower line of boxes at the top of the page.

A careful examination of Figure 10-7b reveals that it is a continuation of the previous page. Figure 10-7a is primarily concerned with product design and Figure 10-7b with production. The expected times for various activities are noted on the network, along with the various operations that must be performed. Figure 10-7c is a summary milestone report that covers several concurrent projects—four, in the case of this page. Each project has a series of steps that must be completed. Each has an original schedule that may have been amended to be a current schedule. Steps are completed in actual times. This form helps program managers coordinate several projects by trying to schedule the various steps to minimize the degree to which the projects interfere with one another by being scheduled for the same facilities at the same time.

The next section of this chapter, which discusses computerized project management information systems, contains several other examples of project reports.

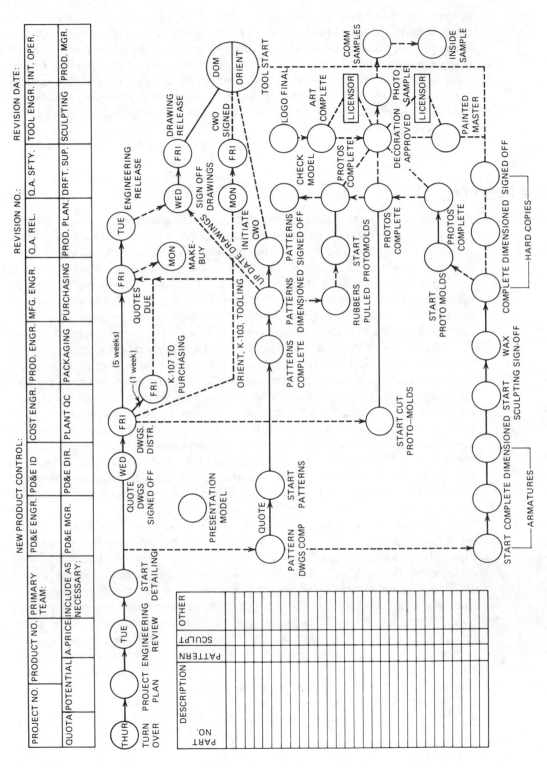

Figure 10-7a Sample project network with sign-off control.

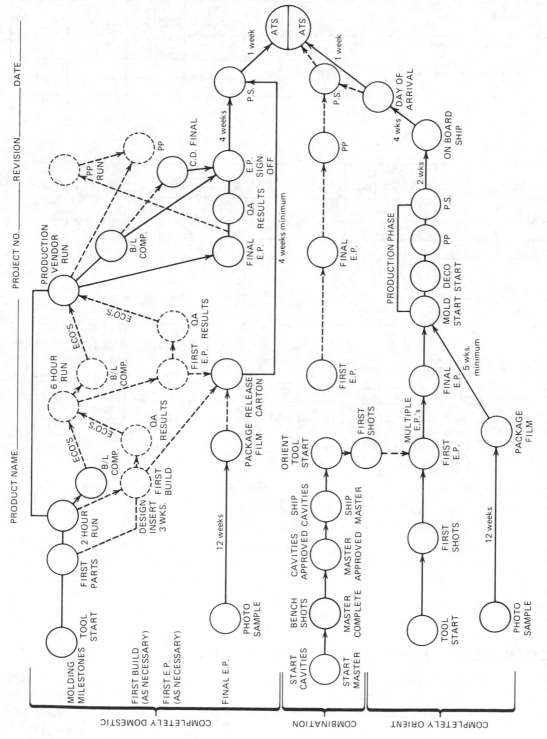

Figure 10-7b Continuation of Figure 10-7a.

NAME					PROJECT PLAN	ENGR. REVIEW	DESIGN REVIEW	QUOTE QUES.	PAT SCULP COMPL	PAT SCULP COMPL	QUOTES DUE	MAKE BUY
PROJECT NO	PRODUCT NO	MFG SOURCE	TURN OVER	ORIGINAL								
A-PRICE	QUOTA	POTENTIAL		CURRENT								
				ACTUAL								

ENGR. RELEASE	PROJECT REVIEW	RELEASE DWGS.	TOOL START	PHOTO SAMPLES	INSIDE SAMPLES	PKG. FILM	INSTR. LAYOUT	INSTR. FIM. ART	FINAL PARTS	FIRST EP	FINAL EP	EP SIGN-OFF	ORIENT PS	OBS	PROD. PILOT	PP SIGN-OFF	PROD. START	ATS

NAME					PROJECT PLAN	ENGR. REVIEW	DESIGN REVIEW	QUOTE QUES.	PAT SCULP COMPL	PAT SCULP COMPL	QUOTES DUE	MAKE BUY
PROJECT NO	PRODUCT NO	MFG SOURCE	TURN OVER	ORIGINAL								
A-PRICE	QUOTA	POTENTIAL		CURRENT								
				ACTUAL								

ENGR. RELEASE	PROJECT REVIEW	RELEASE DWGS.	TOOL START	PHOTO SAMPLES	INSIDE SAMPLES	PKG. FILM	INSTR. LAYOUT	INSTR. FIM. ART	FINAL PARTS	FIRST EP	FINAL EP	EP SIGN-OFF	ORIENT PS	OBS	PROD. PILOT	PP SIGN-OFF	PROD. START	ATS

Figure 10-7c Milestone monitoring chart for Figures 10-7a and b.

10.3 COMPUTERIZED PMIS (PROJECT MANAGEMENT INFORMATION SYSTEMS)

The project examples used in Chapters 8 and 9 were small, so that the concepts could be demonstrated. But real projects are often extremely large, with many hundreds or thousands of tasks. Diagramming, scheduling, and tracking all these tasks is clearly a job for the computer, and computerized PMISs were one of the earlier business applications for computers (e.g., see [31]). Initially, the focus was on simple scheduling packages, but this quickly extended to include costs, earned values, variances, management reports, and so on.

The earlier packages were typically written in FORTRAN and ran on large, expensive mainframe computers; thus, only the larger firms had access to them. Still, the use of these packages for managing projects on a day-to-day basis was not particularly successful, except perhaps in construction and contracting firms. This was because of the inability of project managers to update plans in real time, mainframe computers typically being run in a batch rather than online mode. With the development and proliferation of microcomputers, and the corresponding availability of a wide variety of project management software, project managers are showing a renewed interest in PMIS.

These new microcomputer-based PMIS are considerably more sophisticated than earlier systems and use the microcomputer's graphics, color, and other features more extensively. The systems are available for small, medium, and even large firms. They also offer much more support capability. The current trend in PMIS is integration of software, including spreadsheets, databases, word processing, communications, graphics, and other such capabilities. In this section we will describe one of the larger, more complex packages as well as some of the micropackages. Yet this area is developing so rapidly that any information given must be considered dated by the time it reaches print. The reader interested in current capabilities would be wise to refer to recent annual or monthly software reviews, such as [22, 36, and 44]. Finally, it is worth noting that these systems can be misused or inappropriately applied—as can any tools. The most common error of this type is managing the PMIS rather than the project itself. This and other such errors are described by Thamhain [40] and listed below.

- *Computer paralysis.* Excessive computer involvement with computer activity replacing project management; loss of touch with the project and its realities.
- *PMIS verification.* PMIS reports mask real project problems, are massaged to look good, or simply verify that real problems exist, yet are not acted upon.
- *Information overload.* Too many reports, too detailed, or the distribution of reports, charts, tables, data, and general information from the PMIS to too many people overwhelms managers and effectively hides problems.
- *Project isolation.* The PMIS reports replace useful and frequent communication between the project manager and top management, or even between the PM and the project team.
- *Computer dependence.* PM or top management wait for the computer reports/results to react to problems rather than being proactive and avoiding problems in the first place.
- *PMIS misdirection.* Due to the unequal coverage of the PMIS, certain project subareas are overmanaged and other areas receive inadequate attention; symptoms of problems are monitored and managed (budget overruns, schedule slippages), rather than the problems themselves.

Large PMIS Capabilities

Current PMISs that run on mainframes are intended for large, complex, engineering-based projects such as major defense or aerospace contracts. In these situations, the firm is a prime contractor or major subcontractor and is facing years of work involving thousands of tasks, perhaps millions of man-hours, and multiple interfaces with many subcontractors. The entire project must be well coordinated and tightly controlled if performance requirements are to be achieved and schedules met.

The first step in such projects is to *scope out* the work in a major work phase diagram. Such a chart is illustrated in Figure 10-8. The scope document is usually a RFP (Request for Proposal) or the firm's proposal in response to RFP. From this, phase I of project definition is initiated. This includes constructing a summary WBS for the project, laying out the major project milestones, and getting an estimate of the general order of magnitude of the project in terms of total man-hours required.

The next phase (II) is the definition of the work package in more detail. This involves determining exactly what must be done (the WBS), when, who will do it, and how much it will cost. Following this, baseline input data requirements are specified in phase III. This includes such items as estimates of activity duration, budgets, manpower requirements, constraints, and the other items listed in Figure 10-8.

Phase IV is ongoing monitoring where input data on project status are collected through system modules for schedules, costs, cash flows, and so forth. The final phase (V) is the definition of output management reports for the control function. This consists of defining the data analyses that must be conducted and report formatting and generation. Example outputs would be exception, earned value, cost status, schedule status, variance, and other such reports described earlier and in the following chapter.

The flows between these work phases and their interrelationships are shown in Figure 10-9 for the McAuto™ project management system. This system consists of three proprietary PMISs. The first is the Management Scheduling and Control System (MSCS), which simply creates a model of the complete work plan on a time-phased scale. This is the driver package in the system and interfaces heavily with other system packages. It also creates the reports concerned with tasks and schedules.

The second major PMIS is the cost package Cost Planning and Evaluation System (COPES). This package maintains historical costs, monitors current progress, and forecasts future costs. It creates those reports concerned with costs and variances. The third package is the Line Item Status System (LISS). This system tracks and reports on the status of engineering, materials, vendors, and other such routine line items. LISS also handles the voluminous set of discrete project deliverables such as drawings and specifications that require planning and tracking through the complex production process.

It is clear that such large packages require the use of a mainframe computer to handle the mass of routine data generated in large, defense-type engineering projects. Also, customer requirements for complex and thorough reporting

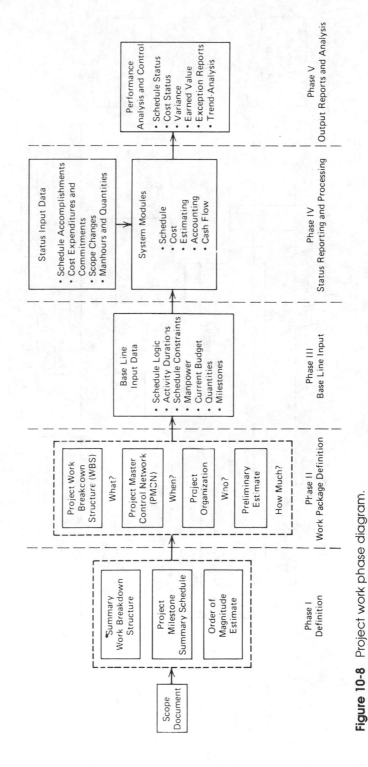

Figure 10-8 Project work phase diagram.

Source: Reproduced by permission of the McDonnel-Douglas Automation Co., St. Louis, MO.

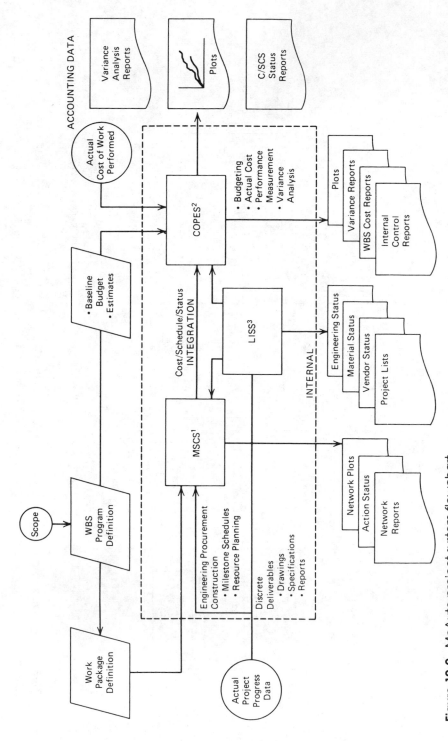

Figure 10-9 McAuto project system flowchart.

Source: Reproduced by permission of the McDonnel-Douglas Automation Co., St. Louis, MO.

Key 1. MSCS = Management Scheduling and Control System

2. COPES = Cost Planning and Evaluation System

3. LISS = Line Item Status System

throughout the project are easily handled by these expensive, large-scale packages. But such projects, though they require the most rigorous and extensive capabilities of PMISs, are not typical of the majority of projects, which are smaller and have less extensive requirements. PMISs for these projects can typically fit on a mini- or microcomputer.

Small PMIS Capabilities

The explosive growth in PMIS has, of course, occurred in the area of small systems intended for the microcomputer. There are now over 200 such packages on the market, and the number continues to grow. These packages come in a wide variety of capabilities and prices [11], from $20 (TASKPLAN® by Williams Software & Services) to $49,975 (Personal Project/2® by PSDI). Evaluations of these packages are common and plentiful (e.g., see [10, 11, 12, 28, 36, 37, 44]) but, of course, become outdated quickly. The annual project management software review [44] is thus helpful to check on current capabilities.

Our approach here will be to describe PMIS needs and capabilities generically, leaving individual package descriptions to more current surveys and articles. We then illustrate some typical outputs available with these packages by including hard copy reports, graphs, and tables generated with Microsoft's PROJECT®. It is worth noting, however, that many survey articles are written by software authorities rather than project managers and the comments may be from a different perspective than the user looking for insight from a PM's perspective. Thus, the capabilities reported in a PMIS evaluation may not indicate the difficulty of using these features on a day-to-day basis or their practicality in a project management environment. Avots [2] maintains that because of this, system reviews and comparative evaluations in trade journals are not a dependable basis for comparing PMIS.

Before delving into the wide variety of capabilities of these PMISs, it is worthwhile identifying the features project managers have indicated they desire. Two surveys [37, 48] were conducted of PMs, and all respondents mentioned the following features:

- *Friendliness.* For the novice user, this included clear and logical manuals, help screens, tutorials, a menu-driven structure, easy editing, and so on. For the advanced user, this meant well-documented and easy-to-program commands.
- *Schedules.* Gantt charts were mandatory, as well as automatic recalculation with updates of times, costs, and resources. Plots of earliest start, scheduled start, slack/float, latest finish, planned finish, and actual finish times were desired.
- *Calendars.* Either a job shop and/or calendar dates are necessary, plus the ability to indicate working days, non-working days, and holidays.
- *Budgets.* The ability to include a budget for planning, monitoring, and control was deemed necessary. Especially desirable was the ability to interface this with a spreadsheet program.

- *Reports.* Individualizing of report formats was considered most desirable. Again, having the ability to interface the reports with a word processing package was highly desired.

Half the respondents also mentioned the desirability of the following, more sophisticated features:

- *Graphics.* The ability to see the schedule and interactions was especially important.
- *Network.* The depiction of the network was deemed desirable by those familiar with this mode of project presentation.
- *Charts.* Charts for responsibility and histograms for resources were deemed particularly useful.
- *Migration.* The ability to migrate other software systems such as databases, spreadsheets, word processing, other project management packages, the organization's mainframe programs, graphics programs, and engineering and manufacturing software to and from the PMIS was considered valuable. Furthermore, general telecommunications and the ability to upload and download were deemed useful as well.
- *Integration/complexity.* Akin to user friendliness, an *appropriate* level of one-key-does-it-all integration and package complexity was considered important. Extensive integration makes errors difficult to correct, and overcomplexity, while adding capability, makes the PMIS less easy to use.

A number of respondents also mentioned the desirability of the PMIS supporting appropriate output devices (color printers, plotters, high-speed printers), having windowing capability, allowing three-time PERT estimates, and including precedence relationships and activity-on-arrow diagrams.

In terms of PMIS capabilities, it is important to remember that no one package will meet all needs, particularly at the same level. That is, numerous trade-offs exist not only between price and capability but also between functional capability, ease of use, complexity, and speed. The following discussion is summarized from [2, 10, 22, 28, 37, 40, 47], and the interested reader is referred to these sources for more detail.

In general, there are five areas of PMIS internal capabilities, separate from the ability to migrate data and communicate externally, that should be considered. These are project planning, resource management, tracking/monitoring, report generation, and decision making. We discuss each below.

Project Planning. In this initial area, consideration should be given to the number of activities per project, the use of various calendars and time units, data recording and organization, time estimation, graphics generations, Gantt chart and PERT chart capabilities, early and late starts, and the ability to handle subnetworks (i.e., nested networks). Of particular interest in this category is the ability to reschedule/update automatically.

Resource Management. The issues here are similar and include the number of resource types, the number of resources per project, sharing of resources, resource leveling, scheduling by resource load, resource updating, resource usage conflicts, multiproject resource analysis, resource planning and analysis, cost estimating, and financial modeling and analysis.

Tracking/monitoring. This area includes critical path analysis, subnetwork analysis, early warning systems, baseline and actual schedule updating and display, resource updating and display, and similar items.

Report Generation. This topic includes project status summaries, computer-assisted report generation, sophisticated data evaluation, resource lists and histograms, schedule lists, task detail, updating of report periods, resource detail, resource assignments, and current Gantt and PERT diagrams.

Decision Making. This area includes a number of capabilities, some involving external software packages. Generally, what-if analysis, expert system capability, multiproject tracking with cross analysis and other such types of capabilities are useful.

Davis [10] notes that there are three basic kinds of PMIS: those that permit planning only, those that also allow updating and progress monitoring, and those that additionally perform some type of automatic resource scheduling, including multiproject planning/scheduling with resource sharing. Clearly, the advanced capabilities are more expensive than the simple planning PMIS.

Avots [2] and Wheelwright [47] divide these PMIS into two general categories: low (mass market, $500) end and upper (advanced, full-powered, over $3,000) end. The main differences are, of course, in their capabilities in the five areas detailed above. It was noted, however, that price is not always an indication of overall quality or capability and that the user should investigate each package according to his or her own needs. The general superiority of upper-end PMIS is not necessarily always in system capabilities, but may be in the ease of use of these capabilities for ongoing project management. That is, low-end PMIS frequently had the capability to do a particular task but to accomplish it was an onerous, time-consuming chore. The weakest features of the low-end system were inadequate progress tracking and data sorting and selection for reports.

The potential purchaser of a PMIS would be wise to consider the intended use of the package, the background and needs of all the potential users, and the organizational setting where the package is to be employed, including the needs and orientation of those who will be receiving the reports and graphics. In terms of need, for example, is it really necessary to monitor costs or update schedules or resource usage? Are we dealing with large projects, or ones with large numbers of critical resources? How complex are the activity interrelationships? All these questions need to be addressed before selecting a final package.

A general PMIS selection process based on Levine's excellent work [22] is as follows:

1. Establish a comprehensive set of selection criteria, considering the questions and five areas of capabilities detailed above.
2. Set priorities for the criteria, separating "must have" items from "nice to have" items and "not needed" items.
3. Conduct a preliminary evaluation of the software packages relative to the criteria using vendor-supplied data, product reviews (see references noted earlier), and software surveys.
4. Narrow the candidate packages to three and obtain demos of each, evaluating the vendors at the same time in terms of interest, software maintenance, and support.
5. Evaluate each package with a standard project typical of your current and projected future needs. Make note of any weaknesses or strengths that are particularly relevant to your situation.
6. Negotiate on price, particularly if you are making a volume purchase or contemplating a site license. Include descriptions of vendor support, training, and product maintenance in the contract.

Figures 10-10 to 10-15 illustrate some typical outputs available from a microcomputer PMIS. The software package used to generate these outputs was Microsoft PROJECT®. Figure 10-10 gives a sequential listing of the project's activities by initiation date (and by completion date for activities with the same initiation date). It lists only the activity, its scheduled start and finish times, duration, and indicates critical activities with an asterisk. The advantage of this

```
                          LIST OF STARTBAR

Project: STARTBAR                          Date: Mar 13, 1987  2:06 PM
----------------------------------------------------------------------
*  1 CLEAN INTERIOR                        7.0 Days
     Sched   Start: Mar 13, 1987   2:00 PM   Sched Finish: Mar 21, 1987  1:00 PM
----------------------------------------------------------------------
   2 BLUEPRINTS                            6.0 Days
     Sched   Start: Mar 13, 1987   2:00 PM   Sched Finish: Mar 20, 1987  1:00 PM
----------------------------------------------------------------------
*  3 LIGHTING                              3.0 Days
     Sched   Start: Mar 21, 1987   2:00 PM   Sched Finish: Mar 25, 1987  1:00 PM
----------------------------------------------------------------------
*  4 FLOORPLN.ACT                          13.8 Days
     Sched   Start: Mar 25, 1987   2:00 PM   Sched Finish: Apr 10, 1987 12:00 PM
----------------------------------------------------------------------
   5 STOCKBAR.ACT                          7.0 Days
     Sched   Start: Apr 10, 1987  12:00 PM   Sched Finish: Apr 18, 1987 12:00 PM
----------------------------------------------------------------------
   6 MUSIC                                 5.0 Days
     Sched   Start: Apr 10, 1987  12:00 PM   Sched Finish: Apr 16, 1987 12:00 PM
----------------------------------------------------------------------
*  7 STAFF                                 14.0 Days
     Sched   Start: Apr 10, 1987  12:00 PM   Sched Finish: Apr 27, 1987 12:00 PM
```

Figure 10-10 Listing of project activities.

```
                            STARTBAR
                       TABLE OF ACTIVITIES

Project: STARTBAR                          Date: Mar 13, 1987  2:06 PM
-----------------------------------------------------------------------
*  1 CLEAN INTERIOR

      Early  Start: Mar 13, 1987  2:00 PM   Early Finish: Mar 21, 1987  1:00 PM
      Late   Start: Mar 13, 1987  2:00 PM   Late  Finish: Mar 21, 1987  1:00 PM
      Sched  Start: Mar 13, 1987  2:00 PM   Sched Finish: Mar 21, 1987  1:00 PM

      Duration:      7.0 Days               Slack:        None
      Predecessors: None
      Successors:    3

      Resource:     BRIAN, MIKE, PAT, TRUCK, BROOM, MOP, BUCKET
-----------------------------------------------------------------------
   2 BLUEPRINTS

      Early  Start: Mar 13, 1987  2:00 PM   Early Finish: Mar 20, 1987  1:00 PM
      Late   Start: Mar 14, 1987  2:00 PM   Late  Finish: Mar 21, 1987  1:00 PM
      Sched  Start: Mar 13, 1987  2:00 PM   Sched Finish: Mar 20, 1987  1:00 PM

      Duration:      6.0 Days               Slack:        1.0 Day
      Predecessors: None
      Successors:    3

      Resource:     BRIAN, MARTHA, PAPER, PENCIL, RULER
-----------------------------------------------------------------------
*  3 LIGHTING

      Early  Start: Mar 21, 1987  2:00 PM   Early Finish: Mar 25, 1987  1:00 PM
      Late   Start: Mar 21, 1987  2:00 PM   Late  Finish: Mar 25, 1987  1:00 PM
      Sched  Start: Mar 21, 1987  2:00 PM   Sched Finish: Mar 25, 1987  1:00 PM

      Duration:      3.0 Days               Slack:        None
      Predecessors: 1, 2
      Successors:    4

      Resource:     LIGHTS, ELECTRICIAN, EQUIPMENT
```

Figure 10-11 Activity table of characteristics.

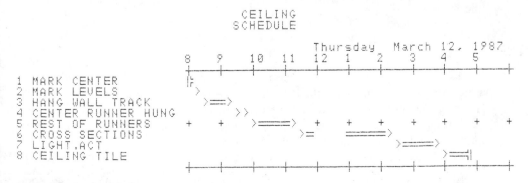

Figure 10-12 Gantt chart of activity times.

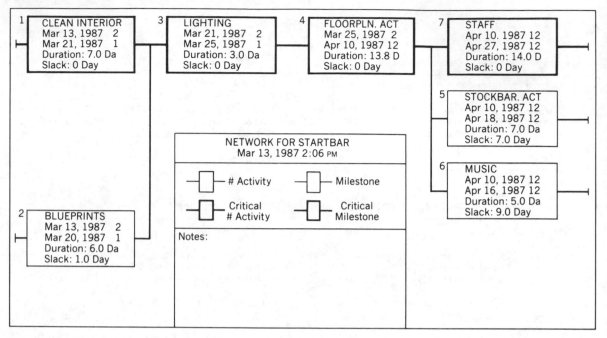

Figure 10-13 Project activity network.

list is the ability to oversee the entire project and its general order of flow. Figure 10-11, on the other hand, gives all the detailed information about each of these activities, but less succinctly in terms of the overall project. In addition to times, the table includes resource requirements and predecessor and successor activities. Activity slack is also shown. Figures 10-12 and 10-13 then show the project Gantt chart and network for easier visualization.

Resource use is depicted in Figures 10-14 and 10-15. In Figure 10-14 the resources are listed and their unit cost rates, capacities, and requirements are given. In Figure 10-15 a histogram of use for one of the resources is shown for each day of the project. The figure also gives supplementary information about the resource.

10.4 SUMMARY

In this chapter we reviewed the monitoring function, relating it to project planning and control, and described its role in the project implementation process. The requirements for monitoring were discussed, in addition to data needs and reporting considerations. Last, some techniques for monitoring progress were illustrated and some computerized PMISs were described.

Specific points made in the chapter were these:

• It is important that the planning-monitoring-controlling cycle be a closed loop cycle based on the same structure as the parent system.

COSTS FOR REMODEL

Project: REMODEL   Date: Mar 12, 1987 1:30 AM

# Resource	Capacity	Unit Cost	Per	Days to Complete	Cost to Complete
1 CLARK	1.0	$10.00	Hour	3.8	$305.00
2 TOOLS	4.0	$0.50	Hour	6.8	$27.22
3 DELIVERY MAN	No limit	$0.00	Hour	0.0	$0.00
4 ALEX	1.0	$5.00	Hour	5.1	$207.50
5 DELIVERY MEN	2.0	$0.00	Hour	2.0	$0.00
6 DELIVERY TRUCK	1.0	$0.00	Hour	1.0	$0.00
7 8 FT 2X4'S	60.0	$1.50	Use	75.0	$90.00
8 NAILS	1000.0	$0.03	Use	390.0	$10.20
9 HEAT DUCT	1.0	$50.00	Fixed	0.7	$50.00
10 DUCT GRILL	1.0	$5.00	Fixed	0.7	$5.00
11 SCREWS	700.0	$0.06	Use	945.0	$39.60
12 ELECTRICIAN	1.0	$15.00	Hour	0.3	$45.00
13 OUTLETS/SWITCH	5.0	$2.50	Use	1.8	$12.50
14 ELECTRICAL WIRE	100.0	$0.19	Use	30.0	$15.20
15 INSULATION ROLL	5.0	$16.00	Use	1.8	$80.00
16 STAPLES	500.0	$0.01	Use	75.0	$2.00
17 DRYWALL	22.0	$8.00	Use	30.0	$160.00
18 DON	1.0	$18.00	Hour	1.5	$216.00

Cost to complete: $2081.14   Total cost of project: $2081.14

Figure 10-14 Resource list for the project.

- The first task in designing the monitoring system is to identify the key factors in the project Action Plan to be monitored and to devise standards for them. The factors should concern results, rather than activities.
- The data collected are usually either frequency counts, numbers, subjective numeric ratings, indicators, or verbal measures.
- Project reports are of three types: routine, exception, and special analysis.
- Project reports should include an amount of detail appropriate to the target level of management with a frequency appropriate to the need for control, i.e.,

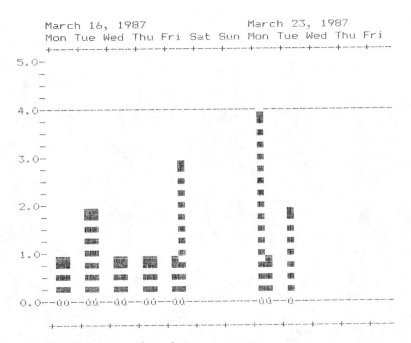

Figure 10-15 Histogram of use for one resource.

probably not weekly or other such regular basis. More commonly, reports occur near milestone dates.

- Three common project reporting problems are too much detail, poor correspondence to the parent firm's reporting system, and a poor correspondence between the planning and monitoring systems.

- The earned value chart depicts scheduled progress, actual cost, and actual progress (earned value) to allow the determination of spending, schedule, and total variances.

- There currently exist a number of computerized PMISs that are available for PMs, the greatest growth occurring in microcomputer PMIS.

- Project managers' preferred PMIS features were friendliness, schedules, calendars, budgets, and reports, with graphics, networks, charts, migration, and integration also frequently being mentioned.

- The five areas of internal PMIS capabilities are project planning, resource management, tracking/monitoring, report generation, and decision making.

In the next chapter we move into the final phase of project implementation, project control. We discuss the different types of control and describe some techniques useful to the PM in controlling the project.

10.5 GLOSSARY

COMPUTER PARALYSIS   Excessive fascination or activity with the computer rather than the project itself such that the project suffers.

EARNED VALUE   An approach for monitoring project progress that relies on the budgeted cost of activities completed to ascribe value.

FRIENDLINESS   When applied to computer use, this term refers to how easy it is to learn and/or use a computer or software package.

HARD COPY   Printed information output, as opposed to screen output.

INFORMATION OVERLOAD   Having an excess of information so that the information desired is difficult to locate.

MIGRATION   The ability to move files and data between software packages.

MONITOR   To keep watch in order to take action when progress fails to match plans.

SCHEDULE VARIANCE   The value completed less the planned value at this time.

SOFTWARE   The instructions for running a computer.

SPENDING VARIANCE   Cost overrun equal to the actual cost less the value completed.

SPREADSHEET   A matrix of data used with a computer. As the data in particular cells are changed, the results of other cells change also to keep in accordance.

TIME VARIANCE   The time overrun equal to the actual time less the time scheduled for the value completed.

TOTAL VARIANCE   The sum of the spending and schedule variance.

VARIANCE   A deviation from plan or expectation.

WINDOWING   A computer software feature that allows different functions to be conducted in a separate section of the screen, called a window.

10.6 PROJECT TEAM ASSIGNMENT

At this point, the project team should determine how progress will be monitored and reported. This includes the PMIS as well as the description of the regular (e.g., milestone) and exception reports that will be generated. The team must decide here what will be measured and reported. One of the reports must be the earned value chart, so the cost of planned work must be determined as well as the time schedule for the project. All variances should be computed and reported separately, as well as shown on the chart.

The team should determine and describe the PMIS features that will be important for the project. For example, is file migration or resource leveling important for the project? Will a microcomputer package be acceptable or will a mini or mainframe package be required? Follow the PMIS selection process described in the chapter and recommend one of the available packages. Then employ such a package in the project, using its features and reporting on a regular basis.

10.7 MATERIAL REVIEW QUESTIONS

1. Define *monitoring*. Are there any additional activities that should be part of the monitoring function?
2. Identify the key factors that need to be considered when setting up a monitoring system.
3. List some factors that would be difficult to monitor.
4. Describe routine reports and some problems with them.
5. What are the primary difficulties experienced in the design of project reports?
6. Describe the three variances of an earned value chart and explain their significance.
7. Contrast the Microsoft PROJECT® system with McAuto's PMIS.
8. Can you identify other symptoms of computer misuse?
9. Compare the PMIS features desired by PMs with the capabilities of microcomputer PMIS. Which are available; which are not?
10. Contrast Davis's kinds of PMIS with that of Avots and Wheelwright. Is there any overlap?

10.8 CONCEPTUAL DISCUSSION QUESTIONS

1. Discuss the benefits of timely, appropriate, detailed information. How can a value be assigned to those characteristics?
2. What are the advantages of having a computerized system over a manual one? The disadvantages?
3. A project is usually a one-time activity with a well-defined purpose. What is the justification of setting up a PMIS for such a project?
4. A more intensive, and extensive, monitoring system is needed in project management than in a functional organization. Why?
5. The earned value chart is an attempt to put the three-dimensional concept of Figure 1-1 (see Chapter 1) into a two-dimensional format. Is it successful? What is missing?
6. Will all future PMISs eventually be microcomputer-based?

10.9 PROBLEMS

1. Find the schedule variance for a project that has an actual cost at month 22 of $540,000, a scheduled cost of $523,000, and an earned value of $535,000.

2. A project at month 5 had an actual cost of $34,000, a planned cost of $42,000, and a value completed of $39.000. Find the total, spending, and schedule cost variances.
3. A project at day 70 exhibits an actual cost of $78,000, a scheduled cost of $84,000, and a value completed of $81,000. What are the total, spending, and schedule cost variances? Estimate the time variance.

10.10 INCIDENTS FOR DISCUSSION

Jackson Excavating Company

Donald Suturana joined Jackson Excavating Company six months ago. He is an experienced management information systems executive who has been given the task of improving the responsiveness of Jackson's data processing group to the end user. After several months of investigation, Suturana felt certain he understood the current situation clearly enough to proceed. First, approximately 90 percent of all end user requests came to data processing (DP) in project form, with the DP output either the final product of the project, or, more commonly, one step of a project. Accordingly, Don felt he should initially direct his efforts toward integrating DP's approach to projects with the company's formal project management system.

It has been Don's experience that most problems associated with DP projects revolve around poor project definition and inadequate participation by the end user during the system design phase. Typically, the end user does not become heavily involved in the project until the new system is ready to install. At that point, a great deal of work is required to adapt the system to meet end-user requirements. Don decided to institute a procedure that put end-user cooperation and participation on the front end of the project. The idea was to define the objective and design of the system so thoroughly that implementation would become almost mechanical in nature rather than an introduction to the end user of "his new system."

Don also recognized that something had to be done to control the programming quality of DP's output. A more effective front-end approach to DP projects would subject DP managers to more intense pressure to produce results within user's needs, including time constraints. Don was concerned that the quality of the DP output would deteriorate under those conditions, especially given the lack of technical expertise on the part of end users and outside project managers. To solve this problem, Don recommended the creation of a DP quality assurance (QA) manager who would approve the initial steps of the projects and review each additional step. The QA manager would have the authority to declare any step or portion of the output inadequate and to send it back to be reworked.

Question: Is this a good control system for DP? Does it also represent a good control point for company projects using DP to accomplish one portion of the project objective? What would your answer be if you were a non-DP project manager?

Guillotine Company

The Guillotine Razor Blade Company recently decided to replace eight metal-cutting machines with computerized machines to update its plant. Management feels that one of the existing machines should be replaced every two months for the duration of the project rather than attempting to replace all the machines at once. The project manager has been setting up the project for the last couple of weeks and is now trying to develop an effective way to monitor the project to ensure it proceeds according to plan. The monitoring system he has developed is based on certain key factors in the project progress. Also, he has developed performance criteria to keep himself abreast of the project performance. He believes that with these two elements, he can effectively monitor the project.

Question: If you were the project manager, would you be satisfied with these two elements? If not, explain the changes you would make.

The U.S. Army Corps of Engineers

The U.S. Army Corps of Engineers has contracted with a medium-size excavation firm to construct a small series of three earthen dams as part of a flood control project in North Carolina. For economic reasons, dams #1 and #2 had to be constructed at the same time and dam #3 could only be built after #1 and #2 were completed. There was also a very important scheduled completion date that had to be met (this related to next year's flood season). The project was handled by Bill Johnson, who had been with the company for about a year.

This was a new job for Mr. Johnson in that he had never before headed more than one project at a time. About three months into the building of dams #1 and #2, he began to notice an information problem. He had foremen from dams #1 and #2 reporting to him, but he never knew how far along they were in relation to each other. Since dam #3 could not be built until both dams were fully complete, he could not tell if it would be started on time and therefore completed on time. Realizing the situation was becoming serious, he began to wonder about how he could coordinate the projects. How could he tell where the projects were in relation to each other? How far were they jointly behind? Bill's major problem was his inability to monitor and record the dual projects effectively.

Question: What would you recommend to Bill?

10.11 BIBLIOGRAPHY

1. Anthony, R. N. *Planning and Control Systems: A Framework for Analysis.* Division of Research, Graduate School of Business Administration, Harvard University, 1965.
2. Avots, I. "How Useful Are the Mass Market Project Management Systems?" *Project Management Journal,* Aug. 1987.

3. Barnes, N. M. L. "Cost Modelling—An Integrated Approach to Planning and Cost Control." *American Association of Chemical Engineers Transactions,* March 1977.
4. Berger, W. C. "What A Chief Executive Should Know about Major Project Management." *Price Waterhouse Review,* Summer–Autumn 1972.
5. Brandon, D. H., and M. Gray. *Project Control Standards.* Brandon/Systems Press, 1970.
6. Caspe, M. S. "Monitoring People to Perform on Design and Construction Projects." *Project Management Quarterly,* Dec. 1979.
7. Caspe, M. S. "Developing A Management Support System for Performing Design and/or Construction Management." *Project Management Quarterly,* Sept. 1981.
8. Clarke, W. "The Requisites for a Project Management System." *Project Management Institute Proceedings,* 1979.
9. Cleland, D. I., and W. R. King. *Systems Analysis and Project Management,* 3rd ed. New York: McGraw-Hill, 1983.
10. Davis, E. W., and R. D. Martin. "Project Management Software for the Personal Computer: An Evaluation." *Project Management Journal,* Dec. 1985.
11. Filley, R. D. "1986 Project Management Software Buyer's Guide." *Industrial Engineering,* Jan. 1986.
12. Gido, J. *Project Management Software Directory.* Industrial Press, 1986.
13. Hodge, B., and R. Hodgson. *Management and the Computer in Information and Control Systems.* New York: McGraw-Hill, 1969.
14. Howard. D. C. "Cost/Schedule Control Systems." *Management Accounting,* Oct. 1976.
15. Johnson, J. R. "Advanced Project Control." *Journal of Systems Management,* May 1977.
16. Kelly, J. F. *Computerized Management Information Systems.* New York: Macmillan, 1970.
17. Khatian, G. A. "Computer Project Management—Proposal, Design, and Programming Phases." *Journal of Systems Management,* Aug. 1976.
18. Kidder, T. *The Soul of a New Machine.* Boston: Little, Brown, 1981.
19. Koemtzopoulos, G. A. "Matrix Based Cost Control Systems for the Construction Industry." *Project Management Institute Proceedings,* 1979.
20. Krakow, I. H. *Project Management with the IBM Personal Computer.* Bowie, MO: Brady Communications, 1985.
21. Levine, H. A. *Project Management Using Microcomputers.* Berkeley, CA: Osborne/McGraw-Hill, 1986.
22. Levine, H. A. "PM Software Forum." *Project Management Journal,* 1987, 1988 (all issues). See "Hints for Software Selection," June and December 1987.
23. Mandakovic, T., and L. A. Smith. "Defining Project Management Software." *Proceedings,* Decision Sciences Institute, November 1986.
24. Marchbanks, J. L. "Daily Automatic Rescheduling Technique." *Journal of Industrial Engineering,* March 1976.
25. Matthews, M. D. "A Conceptual Framework for Project Management Software." *Project Management Journal,* Aug. 1987.
26. McFarlan, W. "Portfolio Approach to Information Systems." *Journal of Systems Management,* Jan. 1982.

27. Meredith, J. R., and T. E. Gibbs. *The Management of Operations,* 3rd ed. New York: Wiley, 1987.

28. Palla, R. W. "Introduction to Microcomputer Software Tools for Project Information Management." *Project Management Journal,* Aug. 1987.

29. Peart, A. T. *Design of Project Management Systems and Records.* London: Gower Press, 1971.

30. Prince, T. *Information Systems for Management Planning and Control.* Homewood, IL: Irwin, 1970.

31. Saitow, A. R. "CSPC: Reporting Project Progress to the Top." *Harvard Business Review,* Jan.–Feb. 1969.

32. Sanders, J. "Effective Estimating Process Outlined." *Computer World,* April 7, 14, and 21, 1980.

33. Seaton, S. J. "Field Product Performance Reports." *Journal of Systems Management,* Oct. 1978.

34. Sethi, N. K. "Project Management." *Industrial Management,* Jan.–Feb. 1980.

35. Shull, F., and R. J. Judd. "Matrix Organizations and Control Systems." *Management International Review,* June, 1971.

36. Smith, L. A. (Ed.) "Project Management Software Review." *Project Management Journal,* 1986–87.

37. Smith, L. A., and S. Gupta. "Project Management Software in P&IM." *P&IM Review and APICS News,* June 1985.

38. Smith, M. G. "PCS: A Project Control System." Doctoral dissertation, Massachusetts Institute of Technology, Cambridge, 1973.

39. Spinner, M. *Elements of Project Management: Plan, Schedule, and Control.* Englewood Cliffs, NJ: Prentice-Hall, 1981.

40. Thamhain, H. J. "The New Project Management Software and Its Impact on Management Style." *Project Management Journal,* Aug. 1987.

41. Turban, E. "The Line of Balance—a Management by Exception Tool." *Journal of Industrial Engineering,* Sept. 1968.

42. van Gigch, J. P. *Applied General Systems Theory,* 2nd ed. New York: Harper & Row, 1978.

43. Voich, M. S. *Information Systems for Operations and Management.* South Western, 1975.

44. Webster, F. M., Jr. *Survey of Project Management Software Packages,* Drexel Hill, PA: Project Management Institute, 1987.

45. Wadsworth, M. D. *EDP Project Management Controls.* Englewood Cliffs, NJ: Prentice-Hall, 1972.

46. Wetzel, J. J. "Project Control at the Managerial Level in the Automotive Engineering Industry." Masters dissertation, Sloan School of Management, Massachusetts Institute of Technology, 1973.

47. Wheelwright, J. C. "How to Choose the Project Management Microcomputer Software That's Right for You." *Industrial Engineering,* Jan. 1986.

48. Witte, O. R. "Software for Project Management." *Architecture,* April 1987.

10.12 READING

This article describes the evaluation of eleven microcomputer project management software packages on a test project of 29 activities. Typical reports are depicted and features or faults are discussed in the process. It is found that there is no one package superior on most features and that trade-offs are very common among the features. A brief evaluation of some of the individual packages is given. The article ends with a suggested procedure for evaluation of software packages.

The value of this article for managers is probably the description of the procedure followed for evaluating the packages more than the evaluations themselves. Available features and common shortcomings are discussed in detail and give excellent background information. The thoughts and guidelines concerning software selection are also helpful.

Project Management Software for the Personal Computer: An Evaluation[1]

Edward W. Davis
Russell D. Martin
Colgate Darden Graduate School of Business
University of Virginia

INTRODUCTION

Judging from the number of new programs introduced by software vendors in the past three years, project management software for microcomputers appears to be taking its place alongside electronic spreadsheet and graphics packages as a "must" for managers.

Business organizations and government agencies have been using mainframe computer project management programs since the 1960's to help manage large projects such as found in construction, aerospace-defense and new product development activities. Unfortunately, however, the application of computer-based project management techniques to such projects has typically required a substantial infrastructure of project management professionals and EDP staff, with a large computer and high overhead costs. Because of such factors, and the inconvenience and need for extensive training in use of systems and procedures, the use of these potentially effective project management techniques was limited to a relatively small cadre of managers and professionals.

The emergence of personal computers and wide availability of easy-to-use project management software has changed all of this. Many of the old barriers which inhibited effective use of computer based systems for project management no longer

[1]This article was previously published in *Industrial Management*, January-February 1985, pp. 1-21, and has been updated. Reprinted by permission.

© 1985 by Project Management Institute. Reprinted from *Project Management Journal*, Dec. 1985, by permission.

exist. Any manager or engineer with access to a personal computer can now use these techniques easily and at very low cost. Project management software packages for personal computers have impressive power and many "extra" features. They use the Critical Path Method (CPM) to identify the critical activities of a project, allow planning of resources such as labor and equipment, provide cost tracking, and permit updating of plans with actual times and costs as the project progresses. Considering the power and features offered, these programs are available at surprisingly low cost; they are literally within budgetary reach of even the smallest organization.

Today there are at least 35 different project management software packages available for the microcomputer, the majority having appeared only within the past two years. Sorting through this mass of offerings is a taxing and time-consuming process, even for experienced managers. A number of helpful survey articles have been published recently, but many of these are essentially listings or summaries of technical features and costs of various packages. The study upon which this article is based was an attempt to go further and provide comparative performance information and evaluations, based upon actual use of the software in scheduling a common sample project.

Some of the available project management software packages are for "high-end" microcomputer configurations such as hard disks, extended memory, high-speed plotting printers, etc. with prices up to $5000. The packages evaluated in this study were limited to programs selling for less than $1,000; the majority actually sell for less than $400. All can be run on a "basic" version of the IBM PC with one or two floppy disk drives, IBM Disk Operating System, and less than 380K of memory.

SOFTWARE EVALUATION PROCEDURE

Since potential user's needs vary so widely, software packages are often compared by simply listing the technical features and characteristics of the available offerings. However, most users are concerned with what the program can do, what, if any, special features or advantages it has, what shortcomings, and how easy it is to learn and use. The procedure followed in this study was designed to produce this type information through the use of a "benchmark" project with each program evaluated. The actual evaluation procedure consisted of four separate steps:

1. Review of the program documentation and instruction manual, with special attention given to organization and clarity;
2. Study and experimentation with a tutorial exercise, if included in the manual, to become generally familiar with the program;
3. Entering data for the same 29-activity project, including times, costs and resource units required, as needed by the program to produce a project schedule and other information, such as costs and resource usage;
4. Entering "actual" progress data for a portion of the project's activities, in order to evaluate the program's updating and progress monitoring features.

Use of the same sample project to test each software package highlighted small differences between the programs. For example, the ease and speed of entering and revising the required data could be easily compared, and program flaws or weaknesses were occasionally found that were not apparent from reading the manual or simply operating the tutorial.

The sample project used for the test involves a hypothetical industrial equipment manufacturing company planning a sales campaign to promote a new piece of equipment. A total of 29 activities are involved; the project can be completed in 36 weeks if all activities are performed as planned. A network diagram of the project (shown in activity-on-node format) is provided in Figure 1.

A scheduled start date of July 2, 1984, was used for the project. A standard five-day, forty-hour work week was specified, and November 22, December 25, and January 1 designated as holidays. Since the project requires 36 weeks to complete, the CPM-calculated early finish date was

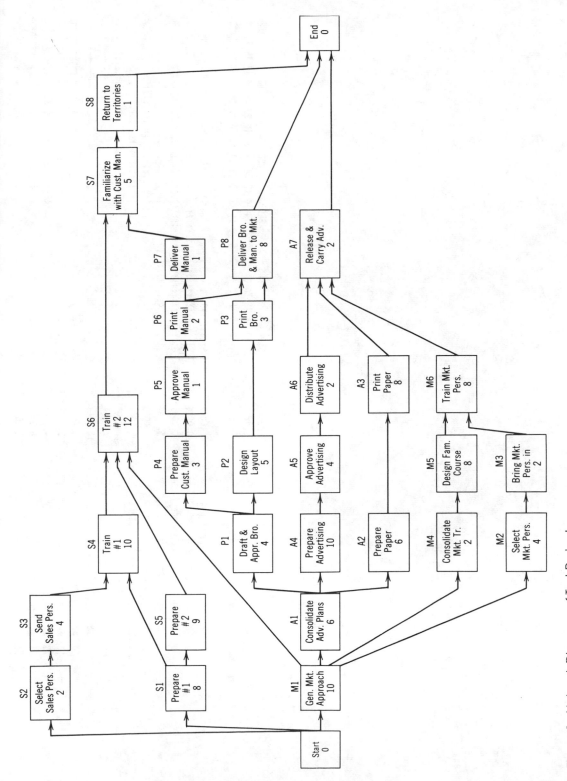

Figure 1 Network Diagram of Test Project.

THE DARDEN SCHOOL
Saaple Report#2- Gantt Chart

Name Of Project: Test Program
Project Leader: Martin

	JUL84		AUG			SEP			OCT			NOV			DE
	02 09 16 23	30 06 13 20	27 03 10 17	24 01 08 15	22 29 05 12	19 26 03

Task Ref No.	Code	Description	Total Task Cost
1	s2	select sales personnel	3,000$
2	s1	prepare #1	10,000$
3	a1	general marketing approach	10,000$
4	s3	send sales personnel	5,000$
5	s5	prepare #2	9,000$
6	a1	consolidate adv. plans	7,000$
7	s4	train #1	80,000$
8	p1	draft & approve brochure	4,000$
9	a4	prepare advertising	10,000$
10	a2	prepare paper	3,400$
11	m4	consolidate marketing trng.	2,000$
12	m2	select mktg. pers.	4,000$
13	s6	train #2	96,000$
14	p4	prepare customer manual	6,000$

15	p2	design layout	5,000$
16	a5	approve advertising	4,000$
17	a5	design fam. course	8,000$
18	a3	bring mktg. personnel in	2,500$
19	p5	approve manual	2,000$
20	a6	distribute advertising	500$
21	a3	print paper	4,200$
22	a6	train marketing personnel	32,000$
23	p6	print manual	1,800$
24	p3	print brochure	1,200$
25	p7	deliver manual	500$
26	p8	deliver broch. & man. to mkt.	500$
27	a7	release and carry adv.	10,000$
28	s7	familiarize with cust. manual	30,000$
29	s8	return to territories	5,000$
30	end	end	
			356,600$

Symbol Legend:

===	CRITICAL TASK	<	Task Has Dependencies
---	Non-Critical Task	>	Task Has Successors
...	Float Time	S	Task Has No Dependencies
:::	Completed Task	X	Task Has No Successors
$	Project Milestone	+	Current Run Date

Figure 2 Project 6 Gantt Chart Report for Portion of Test Project Showing Task Costs.

March 13, 1985. However, some of the programs ignored the effect of single-day holidays if activity durations were entered in weeks. In these cases the completion date was later than March 13.

Most of the project activities had specific manpower resource requirements of up to eight different types (e.g., sales manager, salesman, designer, etc.), which were each assigned weekly salary costs (variable costs). Fixed costs were also assigned some activities: the "total task cost" shown for each task in Figure 2 is a combination of variable and fixed costs. It might be noted that some of the activities required fractional units of resources, but some programs permitted resources to be entered only in integer amounts. In these cases resource requirements were rounded to the nearest whole number.

After entering all of the initial project data, the project completion date was checked to determine the accuracy of the program. In addition, sample reports were generated to check for versatility and ease of use. Finally, the progress updating capability of the programs was examined by entering hypothetical actual completion times and costs for seven of the tasks. Delays in three of these activities extended the project completion date to March 25 or March 27, 1985, depending upon how the programs dealt with holidays. These delays also increased the variable cost component of each delayed task.

SOFTWARE FEATURES

Microcomputer software available for project management falls into three broad categories: (A) programs which permit *planning* only and (B) programs which also permit *updating and progress monitoring*. Within these categories further subdivisions can be made according to whether costs and resources can be included. A final category (C) consists of programs which also perform some type of *automatic resource scheduling* and which permit planning/scheduling of *multiple projects* linked through usage of shared resources.

None of the programs evaluated in this study fall into category C, which includes the more expensive packages (up to $5,000) operating on "high end" hardware configurations. Of the eleven programs evaluated, eight fall into category A and only three into category B, as indicated below:

Category A:	Harvard Project Manager, Micro-Gantt, MicroPert, Microsoft Project, Milestone, Category PERTmaster, Pro-Ject 6, VisiSchedule
Category B:	Plan/Trax, Project Scheduler, Qwiknet

The features offered by these programs are shown in the comparison chart at the end of this article. The significance of these features is discussed below.

Maximum project size is a basic consideration. Some packages, such as Project 6, will handle only one project with a maximum of only 150 activities with the basic memory configuration. Others, like PERTmaster will handle 1,000 activities or more for one project. Some programs, like Project Scheduler, allow linking a large number of subprojects of tasks, each with essentially unlimited capacity.

Network Scheme refers to the approach used in the program for constructing the network "model" of the project, activity-on-arrow approach often requires creation of extra "dummy" activities in the network but may be logically appealing to some users; the activity-on-node approach is good when network revisions are required and when working with resources. Precedence diagramming is a newer approach which is more flexible in assumptions about activity precedence relationships than the traditional critical path methods.

In addition to considering the type of approach used, potential users should also be aware of the constraints on network characteristics inherent in the program. MicroGantt, for example, allows only four immediate predecessors per activity and Harvard Project Manager requires the use of "milestone" events (essentially summary points of activity completion) and dummy activities. In both cases dummy nodes must be created whenever an

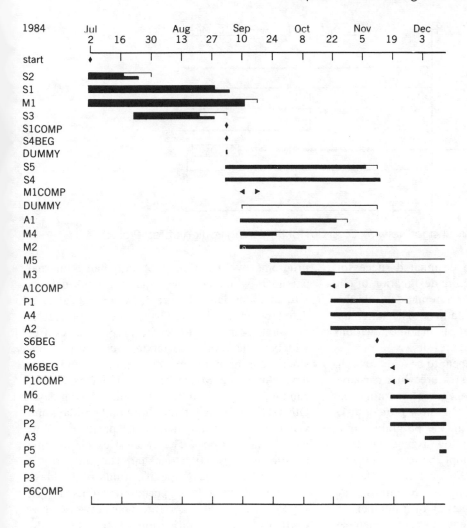

Figure 3 Harvard Project Manager Bar Chart Report.

activity has more than the allowable predecessors of successors, which is cumbersome.

For example, Figure 3 shows the Schedule Report (bar chart) produced by Harvard Project Manager for the test project, with identifying activity reference codes at the left. Codes with a suffix "COMP" or "BEG" (e.g., SICOMP, S4BEG) indicate completion and beginning events (nodes in the network diagram) required by the program. Similarly, "DUMMY" indicates artificial activities required by the program's logic. Some of these user-created events can be seen in Figure 4, which shows a portion of the activity-on-arrow network diagram produced by Harvard Project Manager for the test project. Most programs have more flexible constraints on the number of predecessor/successor activities allowed, but all impose some limit. While there are usually technical ways to work around these limits, it is frustrating and time-consuming to discover in the middle of entering data for a project that the program you are working with will allow only 5 predecessors per task, and you have several tasks with 7 or more predecessors. Also, some programs allow multiple

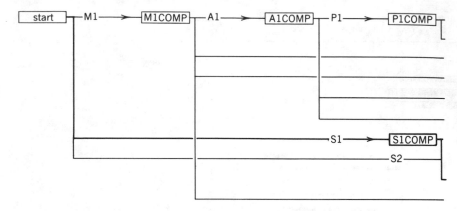

Figure 4 Harvard Project Manager Network Diagram for Beginning Portion of Test Project.

ending activities with no designated successor, while others explicitly require designation of one artificial ending activity or automatically do this in making schedule calculations. The latter approach is less desirable and can in some situations produce inaccurate schedule results.

Task Labeling would appear to be a minor technical consideration, but is a feature which can have important implications on ease of learning and ease of use. The item refers to how project tasks (activities) are identified in the program. Some programs, like Qwiknet, allow a generous combination of labeling with alphabetic and numeric descriptions and codes. Others, like Pro-Ject 6, allow no alphabetic labeling and require that all activities be identified in terms of a number between 1 and 150 or 250, depending upon memory used. The latter approach, of course, means that all reports produced will identify the various activities only in terms of numbers and not easily-understood alphabetic abbreviations or descriptions. Depending upon the number of persons using the program and how important reports will be as a communications device, this could be an important limitation. Some programs also require that task numbering be continuous and sequential between one and some highest number, which can limit flexibility with respect to network revisions and modifications.

Calendar dates refers to how the program keeps track of and reports the project schedule. All of the programs evaluated in this study have internal calendars which convert sequential work periods into calendar dates. Figure 5, showing a calendar date tabular schedule report for the test project, is one such example. However, the programs differ widely in their ability to handle such real-life considerations as non-working weekends and holidays. Some, like MicroPert and Plan/Trax, simply cannot allow for holidays and non-working days. Others, like MicroGantt, require that holidays and vacations be scheduled into the project as non-work time periods. The more flexible in this regard, such as Milestone and Harvard Project Manager, allow easy specifications of holidays and nonwork periods and permit time units in days, weeks, months or quarters, etc. One or two, such as Qwiknet, allow specification of specific start/-completion "target" dates for individual activities, with automatic schedule measurement against these dates. Potential users should also be aware that many programs have particular "quirks" or requirements regarding the calendar/schedule feature which may affect the project schedule obtained. For example, several will not allow fractional time units; others, like MicroGantt, may require all projects to start on a Monday, if daily time units are specified. Again, this feature is one which would appear to be a minor technical detail but actually has important implications for ease of use and schedule accuracy.

Types of Reports produced on screen and printer

THE DARDEN SCHOOL

Frame: 1

Sample Report#1 - Date Planning

Page: 1

Name of Project: **Test Program**
Project Leader: **Martin**
Sorted By: **Task Number**

Task No.	Ref Code	Description	Task Status	Dur	Early Start Date	Early Finish Date	Late Start Date	Late Finish Date	Float Time	Sched Start Date	Task Begin Offset
1	s2	select sales personnel	Complete	3	7/02/84	7/23/84	7/02/84	7/23/84			
2	s1	prepare #1	Complete	10	7/02/84	9/10/84	7/02/84	9/10/84			
3	a1	general marketing approach	Complete	10	7/02/84	9/10/84	7/02/84	9/10/84			
4	s3	send sales personnel	Complete	4	7/23/84	8/20/84	8/13/84	9/10/84	3		
5	s5	prepare #2	Complete	9	9/10/84	11/12/84	9/17/84	11/19/84	1		
6	a1	consolidate adv. plans	Complete	7	9/10/84	10/29/84	9/10/84	10/29/84			
7	s4	train #1	Complete	10	9/10/84	11/19/84	9/10/84	11/19/84			
8	p1	draft & approve brochure	Normal	4	20/19/84	11/26/84	10/29/84	11/26/84			
9	a4	prepare advertising	Normal	10	10/29/84	1/07/85	10/29/84	1/07/85			
10	a2	prepare paper	Normal	6	10/29/84	12/10/84	10/29/84	12/10/84			
11	a4	consolidate marketing trng.	Normal	2	9/10/84	9/24/84	9/10/84	9/24/84			
12	a2	select mktg. pers.	Normal	4	9/10/84	10/08/84	9/10/84	10/08/84			
13	s6	train #2	CRITICAL	12	11/19/84	2/11/85	11/19/84	2/11/85			
14	p4	prepare customer manual	Normal	3	11/26/84	12/17/84	11/26/84	12/17/84			
15	p2	design layout	Normal	5	11/26/84	12/31/84	11/26/84	12/31/84			
16	a5	approve advertising	Normal	4	1/07/85	2/04/85	1/07/85	2/04/85			
17	a5	design fam. course	Normal	8	9/24/84	11/19/84	9/24/84	11/19/84			
18	a3	bring mktg personnel in	Normal	2	10/08/84	10/22/84	11/05/84	11/19/84	4		
19	p5	approve manual	Normal	1	12/17/84	12/24/84	12/17/84	12/24/84			
20	a6	distribute advertising	Normal	2	2/04/85	2/18/85	2/04/85	2/18/85			
21	a3	print paper	Normal	8	12/10/84	2/04/85	12/24/84	2/18/85	2		
22	m6	train marketing personnel	Normal	8	11/19/84	1/14/85	12/24/84	2/18/85	5		
23	p6	print manual	Normal	2	12/24/84	1/07/85	12/24/84	1/07/85			
24	p3	print brochure	Normal	3	12/31/84	1/21/85	12/31/84	1/21/85			
25	p7	deliver manual	Normal	1	1/07/85	1/14/85	2/04/85	2/11/85	4		
26	p8	deliver broch. & man. to mkt.	Normal	8	1/21/85	3/18/85	1/28/85	3/25/85	1		
27	a7	release and carry adv.	Normal	2	2/18/85	3/04/85	3/11/85	3/25/85	3		
28	s7	familiarize with cust. manual	CRITICAL	5	2/11/85	3/18/85	2/11/85	3/18/85			
29	s8	return to territories	CRITICAL	1	3/18/85	3/25/85	3/18/85	3/25/85			
30	end	end	CRITICAL	0	3/25/85	3/25/85	3/25/85	3/25/85			

Symbol Legend:

===	CRITICAL TASK	< Task Has Dependencies
---	Non-Critical Task	> Task Has Successors
...	Float Time	S Task Has No Dependencies
:::	Completed Task	X Task Has No Successors
⇑	Project Milestone	+ Current Run Date

Figure 5 Calendar Date Tabular Schedule Report for Test Project (from Project Scheduler).

is another feature which exhibits wide variation from program to program. Some produce a few standard reports and allow no user modification or customization. Others automatically produce standard reports but allow modification or variation of the information or formats involved. One package (Pro-Ject 6) produces no standard reports, but allows the user to create a wide range of reports from the available combinations of information generated.

All of the programs in this study produce some form of bar-chart schedule and some type of tabular report with early-late calendar dates, as shown earlier in Figures 2 and 5. Beyond these two reports, the repertory varies greatly, depending upon whether resources and/or cost planning features are included.

While most of the programs evaluated in this study will print all reports which can be viewed on the screen, some will not. Others will not allow previewing of some or any reports before printing. Most print some form of bar-chart schedule or graph which is horizontally oriented and thus is produced in printer-paper-width segments which must be pasted together for comprehension. One or two have options to print these reports sideways, but the printing time may be greatly increased. Some programs permit use of the program while printing is in progress, others do not; the reports in several of the packages required as much as 5–8 minutes each to print out on an Epson-type printer for our small project. Obviously, users who desire numerous or frequent printed reports must give some thought to the timing of report requests when working with these programs to schedule larger projects.

With respect to *graphing capabilities,* three of the programs evaluated in this study will produce graph-like reports with the Epson-type printer used. Project Scheduler has an optional graphics package which produces outstanding graphical reports of such factors as resource usage and dollar expenditures, as does Plan/Trax. An example of a resource usage report from each of these programs is shown in Figures 6 and 7. Harvard Project Manager, MicroPert, Qwiknet and Microsoft's Project will produce chart-like versions of the

project network diagram, which some users value highly. Figure 8 shows a portion of the activity-on-node diagram for the test project produced by Quiknet, for comparison with the example from Harvard Project Manager shown earlier.

Resources Capability refers to the ability of the program to accent and provide information about resource requirements such as the units of labor and equipment required to perform the project activities. For example, resource summaries, or profiles, or resource requirements over the project's duration, like those shown in Figures 6 and 7, can be extremely valuable in project planning and even a necessity in situations involving limited or very costly resources. Several of the programs provide this capability. Automatic "leveling" of resources is a feature typically found only in more expensive programs, but, surprisingly, one of the Category A programs in this study, VisiSchedule, offers this capability on a limited basis: activities are rescheduled to level resource requirements, insofar as possible, within limits of available activity slack, without increasing project duration. Users who are interested in resource planning features are advised to check carefully program constraints in this area. For example, some programs allow only one or two different resource types per activity, while others allow up to 24 types. Some permit lengthy alphanumeric resource descriptions and codes, others only a one or two-number identifying label; some permit fractional resource units, others only integer units.

Cost control features are those relating to cost planning and monitoring. Dollar cost is considered another resource and tracked as such in packages like Pert-Master, but packages with more complete cost control features treat costs separately from resources, and allow differentiation between variable direct and fixed costs and permit tracking of actual versus planned costs. Figure 9 provides an example of one such graphical tracking report, produced by Plan/Trax. Most of the packages with cost control features permit each resource to have its own charge rate and some also accommodate rate changes during the life of the project (e.g., in case of overtime work, etc.). None, however, per-

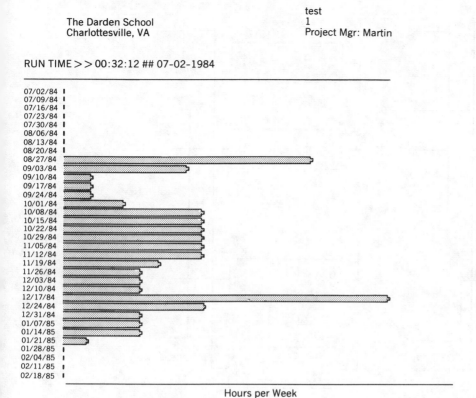

test
1
The Darden School
Charlottesville, VA
Project Mgr: Martin

RUN TIME > > 00:32:12 ## 07-02-1984

Hours per Week

Figure 6 Resource Distribution Report for Sales Manager (from Plan/Trax).

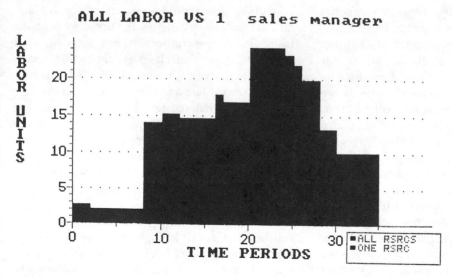

Figure 7 Resource Profile Diagram for Sales Manager Requirements versus Requirements of All Labor Types (from Project Scheduler).

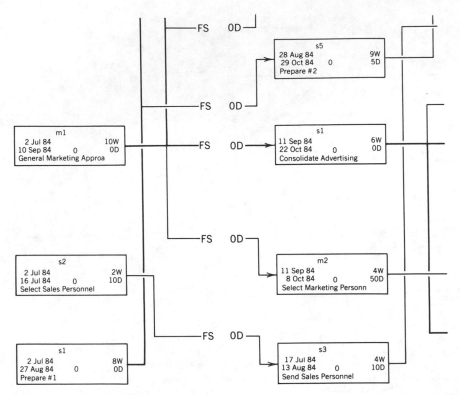

Figure 8 Network Diagram for Beginning Portion of Test Project (from Qwiknet).

mit breaking fixed costs into separate categories and only a few, such as Microsoft's Project, will provide estimated cost to complete the project based on the latest revision date. Programs with good cost control features contain provisions for using responsibility or cost account codes to permit use of the hierarchical Work Breakdown Structure (WBS) concept in aggregating and summarizing costs. The Harvard Project Manager, Pro-Ject 6 and Qwiknet are in the latter category.

Updating features are important to users who want to change the original plan and monitor project progress against the original or revised plan. The program should be capable of accepting update information on an exception basis. For example, inputs might consist of changes in the network and actual progress, such as activity start and finish dates since the last update. The entire set of network data should not have to be entered again.

Potential users should note that there are significant differences in how the updating function is handled by these programs. For example, some programs ignore activity start times and accept only the activity finish times. This means that if an activity started late and is not finished at the time of updating, that the late condition will not be recognized by the program, and the program's schedule output may be incorrect. Also, if only activity finish dates are accepted for updating, it may not be possible to compute and record the actual duration of each activity for comparison with the original estimated duration.

Some programs allow tasks to be indicated as finished but actual completion dates cannot be used and project duration is not updated on reports if the actual dates differ from planned. Others, like Qwiknet, accept both target start and finish dates and actual finish dates and actual costs, automati-

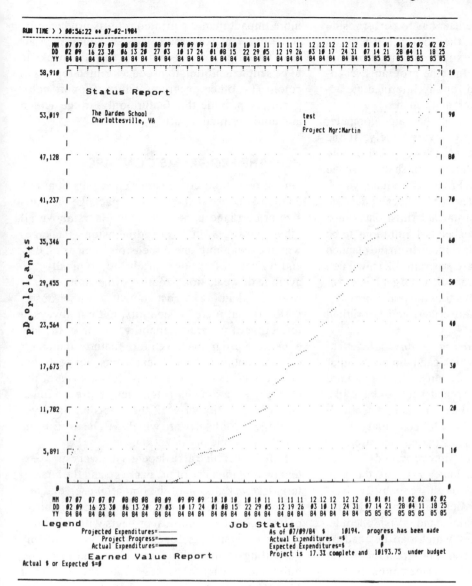

Figure 9 Cost Status Report Produced by Plan/Trax.

cally revise the project schedule and compare actual finish dates versus the target dates and actual costs versus planned costs to date. Most of the packages fall somewhere in between these two extremes.

Scheduled dates capability: most mainframe and mini-computer programs for project management will accept scheduled dates assigned to the terminal activities in the network, and project schedule computations are made from these dates rather than simply from the final activity's earliest expected date computed from the "forward pass" procedure of the critical path method. This means that the slack values calculated by the program will be related to the scheduled dates, and the critical path may have positive, zero or negative float.

Without this feature, the user has to perform side calculations to determine the relationship between the program-calculated expected completion date and the scheduled date. In some programs scheduled dates are permitted for any intermediate activity between project start and finish.

Again, the capabilities of the microcomputer programs in our sample group vary widely. At one extreme are programs like Milestone, which simply do not allow scheduled start and finish dates. In the middle are packages like Project Scheduler, which will accept scheduled dates, but not in calendar date format (period number for start and finish dates must be used), and require finished task durations to be changed when there are deviations from the planned values. At the upper end are programs like Qwiknet, which permit entering scheduled "target" dates for both end and intermediate activities, and provides schedule calculations based on these and the original estimated dates.

File format and interfacing options include features for creating files which can be read by other software programs, such as spreadsheet and word processing packages. A spreadsheet package like 1-2-3 can graph project data and also be useful in progress tracking and "what if" cost analyses. A data base management package can be used for creating custom reports not provided by the project management package. Five of the programs in this study provide this capability: Harvard Project Manager, Microsoft Project, Micro-Gantt, Project Scheduler and VisiSchedule. Qwiknet will create files which can be read by "Project/2," a large mainframe program for project management produced by the same company.

Color features and printing considerations are details which affect ease of use and may impact the usefulness of the reports and other information produced by the package. For example, Visi-Schedule's use of color on the screen to highlight critical activities, delineate slack, and emphasize predecessors on its schedule report greatly enhances the legibility and comprehension of that report. Likewise, the well-designed graph-like reports produced by Project Scheduler, PERTmaster, Plan/Trax and Qwiknet are easier to read and have more impact than the printed reports produced by some other packages. Project Scheduler also allows the output from its optional graphics package to be sent to a plotter, to produce printed reports in color. The other programs which support color generally provide this feature only on the screen and not in printed reports.

HOW THE PROGRAMS COMPARE

One of our major conclusions emerging from this comparison is that no one package in this size/price range is head and shoulders above all other packages in every dimension. Packages which excel along one dimension, such as quality and variety of reports produced, typically are average or weak along another dimension, such as resource planning or cost control. Another observation is that price is generally, but not always, a reflection of program capability: some of the less expensive programs have more features than their costlier counterparts. These facts suggest that potential users would be well-advised to carefully compare program characteristics before making a purchase, particularly if the decision involves multiple sets of software which will be used as the standard for one organization.

Software choice also depends to a very great extent on intended use of the package and the characteristics/background of the potential user, and his/her organizational setting. An engineer/manager of large complex technical projects with important resource constraints, for example, would probably be willing to invest the extra time and effort required to master a package like Pro-Ject 6 or MicroGantt. On the other hand, a marketing product manager temporarily involved with management of less complex projects might well decide to sacrifice power and features for simplicity and ease of use.

The comparison chart of program features in this article also contains our subjective evaluations of ease of learning and ease of use, and gives an overall summary evaluation of each program. Because program choice is so situational, it would be impractical for us to attempt to recommend some software packages over others for all potential users. We were, however, particularly impressed during this study with the features and performance of three of the packages, which deserve some brief mention here.

VisiSchedule, one of the earliest entrants in the field, is also among the least expensive programs available, and surely one of the best values. Extremely easy to learn and use, it would be a good choice for anyone who is willing to accept the relatively limited types of reports produced, the constraint of 8 resource types, and limited cost control features.

Microsoft's Project is somewhat more expensive than VisiSchedule and compares favorably on general performance. Employing an optional "mouse," it is also extremely easy to learn to use, can handle larger and more complex projects, and will construct a chart of the network diagram. The program's use of predefined resource tables and resource viewing function facilitates resource planning.

Qwiknet, one of the newest entrants in the project management field, is the most expensive package tested in this study and appropriately contains more powerful and innovative features than the other programs. It is one of three Category "B" programs evaluated, with features for progress reporting, which will generate current status reports and produce a revised project schedule based upon latest update information. Also employing a "mouse," it uses multiple windows and pop-down menus for exceptionally easy program interaction and viewing of reports. It is extremely fast in operation, and provides a good variety of well-designed printed reports. Unlike the initial version, the new version 2.0 permits reasonably fast data entry for updating project progress and revising the network.

SOFTWARE SELECTION: SOME THOUGHTS AND GUIDELINES

The process of software selection for project management should begin by looking at the user and his/her situation, instead of at the software itself. Here are some questions to assist in the process.

What Are the Characteristics of Your Projects?

Are your projects large, or small? How long do they last? How much money is involved? How many different people? What type of resources? How complex are the activity sequencing relationships: many interdependencies, or relatively few?

Research to date on use of microcomputers in project management suggests that most applications involve fewer than 200 activities per project, with the majority probably closer to 50–75. There are managers who truly need a capability for handling 1000 or more activities in a project, but we have thus far discovered none in this category who are using microcomputer-based software. Most large-project management is still being done with mainframe or mini-computer systems. In general, if the projects to be managed contain approximately 25–200 activities, with budgets of $50,000 and more, involving several different types of resources, several different organizational functions, with durations of several months or more, and reasonably complex activity interdependencies, then you should consider using a micro-computer-based software package. This assumes, of course, that good planning input data for the program is available or can be obtained.

Who Will Be Using the Software?

Will one person in the organization be responsible for entering and updating project information, or will several different people be using the program? How familiar are the users with personal computers? How familiar are they with critical path concepts? Will engineers, managers or clerical staff be using the program?

Questions like these are important when evaluating ease of learning and ease of use of a potential package. If a number of different people will have to learn the system or if the users have little or no technical background, emphasis should probably be placed on a user-friendly program rather than computing power and an imposing array of features.

Who Will Be Using the Reports?

Generally, users of the package can be broken into three categories according to level of authority: those who report to you, other managers at your level, and those to whom you report. Reports going to subordinates generally will contain more detail than reports going to superiors. Also, if there are more than two subordinates, involving different responsibilities, it might be desirable to have a capability for responsibility coding to permit sorting of the information produced, according to responsibility. Reports to managers at the same or higher level might simply contain highlights and summaries of the information produced, so a reporting capability of this sort could be desirable.

Of course, *how* the information is presented is also important, and depends upon the intended audience. Software packages with graphical reports features may be particularly useful in producing reports which provide quick visual impressions of project status for top managers. On the other hand, a detailed "map" of the project, such as provided by a computer-produced activity network diagram, might be helpful. It is vitally important that the potential user try to identify not only *what* information will be needed, but *who* will be using it and how *they* would like to see it presented.

The frequency of reporting and locations of persons using the reports are factors which can have much to do with the decision whether to use microcomputers at all, as well as the choice of particular software. For example, if project planning is to be done in successive phases, with sets of reports produced as the plan is revised, the report-producing capability of a microcomputer software package could be extremely advantageous. Likewise, if persons at several different locations are involved in project planning or implementation, it is relatively easy and inexpensive to distribute reports to these locations via telephone connections to the microcomputer. Alternatively, diskette copies can be distributed quickly and reliably via Federal Express or other express mail services, for use in creating individually-tailored reports at each location.

Do You Really Need to Monitor Costs?

One of the areas in which the available software differs most is in the ability to update and monitor costs against an original plan. But this capability may not actually be needed, if the cost monitoring function can be provided separately from the planning/controlling of schedule *time*. In many cases, for example, cost collection and reporting is handled through established channels and simply reported to the project manager. In such cases the project manager may need only a capability in the software for entering data to obtain estimates of the overall cost of a proposed project plan. Surprisingly, some of the packages in this study do not have such capability; if needed, it is something to look for early in the decision process.

If the project manager truly needs a capability for periodically updating the project plan with actual cost/schedule information to compare actual versus planned costs, the search has been narrowed considerably: only three of the programs in this study have such capability. Other recent comparisons of software indicate that most programs on the market do *not* have this capability, so this is again one of the first features to look for in cases where this need exists.

Do You Need Resource Planning/Scheduling?

Several of the packages in this study have good resource *planning* features, e.g., summaries of resource requirements, etc. But there is great difference in the number of resources allowed, and how easy the resource planning features are to use. If resource planning is important, this feature should be an important consideration. Note that there is a difference between resource *planning* and automatic resource *scheduling*. Of the packages in this study, only VisiSchedule makes an attempt at the latter, by providing the capability to automatically shift activities so as to obtain more "level" resource profiles. Situations involving a need for resource scheduling typically also involve multiple projects which are linked through use of common resource pools. If the project manager has a need for such capability, the search must be extended to Category "C" software packages not included in this study. Several such packages are available, generally at prices exceeding $2,000. Evidence from conversations with software developers and others suggests that resource scheduling and multi-project features will characterize the next round of software releases in this field, perhaps at prices considerably less than what is currently available, so this is something to look for.

What Are Your Hardware Limitations?

Memory and number of disk drives are two requirements you need to check before you buy. Most programs in our study require only one disk drive and a nominal amount of memory. Some packages, however, require two disk drives and/or a significant amount of memory, particularly as project size increases. Do you have a color monitor? Will color really be useful? This should not be your most important selection criterion, but it would be a deciding factor if you have narrowed the field to a few otherwise comparable packages. The color features of some programs are outstanding, and can be of considerable value in improving the legibility and impact of on-screen reports particularly if projection equipment is available for display of information on large screens.

SUMMARY

Software packages such as those reviewed in this study will not turn inept project managers into superheroes. Use of any of them may require the collection of more data and a higher degree of discipline and organization in project planning than has been necessary in the past. But their use can dramatically decrease the manual effort required in project management, and facilitate improved management decision making. Microcomputers appear to be ideal for small to medium-sized project management; their interactive nature permits fast development of "what if?" analyses to test alternative actions.

While the eleven software packages covered in this study are only about one-third of the total number in existence, they are representative of what exists in the way of Category "A" and Category "B" software. Several of the packages included here are, in fact, among the most popular packages in use today. However, the rate of change in this field is astonishing: over a five-month period in the fall of 1984, three new versions of existing programs and two entirely new programs were released. If your particular requirements cannot be met by existing packages, they probably will be in several months!

Vendor Addresses of Project Management Software Programs Evaluated in this Study

	Product	Vendor
1.	Harvard Project Manager	Harvard Software, Inc. 521 Great Road Littleton, MA 01460 617-486-8431
2.	MicroGANTT	Earth Data Corporation P.O. Box 13168 Richmond, VA 23225 804-231-0300
3.	MicroPERT	Sheppard Software Co. 4750 Clough Creek Road Redding, CA 96002 916-222-1553
4.	PROJECT	Microsoft Corporation 10700 Northrup Way P.O. Box 97200 Bellevue, WA 98004 206-328-8080
5.	Milestone	Digital Marketing Co. 236 Boulevard Circle Walnut Creek, CA 94596 800-826-2222
6.	PERTmaster	Westminster Software 660 Hansen Way, Suite 2 Palo Alto, CA 94303 415-424-8300

7. Plan/Trax Omicron Software
       57 Executive Park
       Atlanta, GA 30329

8. Project Scheduler SCITOR Corporation
       256 Gibraltar Drive, Bldg. 7
       Sunnyvale, CA 94086
       408-730-0400

9. Pro-ject 6 SoftCorp, Inc.
       2340 State Road 580, Suite 244
       Clearwater, FL 33575

            800-255-PLAN

10. Qwiknet Project Software & Development
       20 University Place
       Cambridge, MA 02138
       617-661-1444

11. VisiSchedule VisiCorp
       2895 Zanker Road
       San Jose, CA 95134
       408-946-9000

CHAPTER 11
Project Control

In the previous chapter we described the monitoring and information gathering process that would help the PM to control the project. *Control* is the last element in the implementation cycle of planning-monitoring-controlling. Information is collected about system performance, compared with the desired (or planned) level, and action taken if actual and desired performance differ enough that the *controller* (manager) wishes to decrease the difference. Note that reporting performance, comparing the differences between desired and actual performance levels, and accounting for why such differences exist are all parts of the control process. In essence, control is the *act* of reducing the difference between plan and reality.

As has been emphasized throughout this book, control is focused on three elements of a project—performance, cost, and time. The PM is constantly concerned with these three aspects of the project. Is the project delivering what it promised to deliver or more? Is it making delivery at or below the promised cost? Is it making delivery at or before the promised time? It is strangely easy to lose sight of these fundamental targets, especially in large projects with a wealth of detail and a great number of subprojects. Large projects develop their own momentum and tend to get out of hand, going their own way independent of the wishes of the PM and the intent of the proposal.

Think, for a moment, of a few of the things that can cause a project to require the control of performance, time, or cost.

Performance:

Unexpected technical problems arise.

Insufficient resources are available when needed.

Insurmountable technical difficulties are present.

Quality or reliability problems occur.

Client requires changes in system specifications.

Interfunctional complications arise.

Technological breakthroughs affect the project.

Costs:

Technical difficulties require more resources.

The scope of the work increases.

Initial bids or estimates were too low.

Reporting was poor or untimely.

Budgeting was inadequate.

Corrective control was not exercised in time.

Input price changes occurred.

Time:

Technical difficulties took longer than planned to solve.

Initial time estimates were optimistic.

Task sequencing was incorrect.

Required inputs of material, personnel, or equipment were unavailable when needed.

Necessary preceding tasks were incomplete.

Customer-generated change orders required rework.

Governmental regulations were altered.

These problems, among many others, may call for intervention and control by the project manager. There are infinite "slips 'twixt cup and lip," especially in projects where things are new and unfamiliar, and PMs, like most managers, find control is a difficult function to perform. There are two main reasons why this is so. Even in a large project, the project team is an in-group. It is "we," while outsiders are "they." It is difficult to criticize friends, to subject them to control. Second, many PMs see control as an ad hoc process. Each need to exercise control is seen as special, rather than as ongoing and recurring.

In this chapter we examine the purposes of control in their most general form. Following this, the basic structure of a control process is examined. Three distinct types of control processes are discussed, together with the nature of appropriate applications for each in the field of project management. We then consider some specific techniques of control that are particularly useful for project management and briefly examine some mechanisms that PMs find very helpful.

11.1 THE FUNDAMENTAL PURPOSES OF CONTROL

The two fundamental objectives of control are:

1. The regulation of results through the alteration of activities
2. The stewardship of organizational assets

Most discussions of the control function are focused on regulation. The PM needs to be equally attentive to both regulation and conservation. Because the main body of this chapter (and much of the next) concerns the PM as regulator, let us emphasize the conservationist role here. The PM must guard the physical assets of the organization, its human resources, and its financial resources. The processes for conserving these three different kinds of assets are different.

Physical Asset Control

Physical asset control requires control of the *use* of the physical assets. It is concerned with asset maintenance, whether preventive or corrective. At issue also is the timing of maintenance or replacement as well as the quality of maintenance. Some years ago, a New England brewery purchased the abandoned and obsolete brewing plant of a newly defunct competitor. It put a project manager in charge of this old facility with the instruction that the plant should be completely "worn out" over the next five-year period, but that it should be fully operational in the meantime. This presented an interesting problem: the controlled deterioration of a plant while at the same time maintaining as much of its productive capability as possible. Clearly, both objectives could not be achieved simultaneously, but the PM met the spirit of the project quite well.

If the project uses considerable amounts of physical equipment, the PM also has the problem of setting up maintenance schedules in such a way as to keep the equipment in operating condition while minimizing interference with ongoing work. It is critical to accomplish preventive maintenance prior to the start of that final section of the project life cycle known as the Last Minute Panic (LMP). (Admittedly, the timing of the LMP is not known, which makes the planning of pre-LMP preventive maintenance somewhat difficult.)

Physical inventory, whether equipment or material, must also be controlled. It must be received, inspected (or certified), and possibly stored prior to use. Records of all incoming shipments must be carefully validated so that payment to suppliers can be authorized. The same precautions applied to goods from external suppliers must also be applied to suppliers from inside the organization. Even such details as the project library, project coffee maker, project room furniture, and all the other minor bits and pieces must be counted, maintained, and conserved.

• Human Resource Control

Stewardship of human resources requires controlling and maintaining the growth and development of people. Projects provide particularly fertile ground for cultivating people. Because projects are unique, differing one from another in many ways, it is possible for people working on projects to gain a wide range of experience in a reasonably short time.

Measurement of physical resource conservation is accomplished through the familiar audit procedures. The measurement of human resource conservation is far more difficult. Such devices as employee appraisals, personnel performance indices, and screening methods for appointment, promotion, and retention are not particularly satisfactory devices for ensuring that the conservation function is being properly handled. The accounting profession has worked for some years on the development of *human resource accounting,* and while the effort has produced some interesting ideas, human resource accounting is not well accepted by the accounting profession.

Financial Resource Control

Though accountants have not succeeded in developing acceptable methods for human resource accounting, their work on techniques for the conservation (and regulation) of financial resources has most certainly resulted in excellent tools for financial control. This is the best developed of the basic areas needing control.

It is difficult to separate the control mechanisms aimed at conservation of financial resources from those focused on regulating resource use. Most financial controls do both. Capital investment controls work to conserve the organization's assets by insisting that certain conditions be met before capital can be expended, and those same conditions usually regulate the use of capital to achieve the organization goal of a high return on investments.

The techniques of financial control, both conservation and regulation, are well known. They include current asset controls, and project budgets as well as capital investment controls. These controls are exercised through a series of analyses and audits conducted by the accounting/controller function for the most part. Representation of this function on the project team is mandatory. The structure of the techniques applied to projects does not differ appreciably from those applied to the general operation of the firm, but the context within which they are applied is quite different. One reason for the differences is that the project is accountable to an outsider—an external client, or another division of the parent firm, or both at the same time.

The importance of proper conformance to both organizational and client control standards in financial practice and recordkeeping cannot be overemphasized. The parent organization, through its agent, the project manager, is responsible for the conservation and proper *use of* resources owned by the client or owned by the parent and charged to the client. Clients, and the courts, insist on the practice of *due diligence* in the exercise of such responsibility.

One final note on the conservationist role of the controller. The attitudes or mind sets of the conservationist are often antithetical to the mind set of the PM, whose attention is naturally on the use of resources rather than their conservation. The conservationist reminds one of the fabled librarian who is happiest when all the books are ordered neatly on the library shelves. The PM, manager and controller at one and the same time, is subject to this conflict and has no choice but to live with it. The warring attitudes must be merged and compromised as best they can.

11.2 THREE TYPES OF CONTROL PROCESSES

The process of controlling a project (or any system) is far more complex than simply waiting for something to go wrong and then, if possible, fixing it. We must decide at what points in the project we will try to exert control, what is to be controlled, how it will be measured, how much deviation from plan will be tolerated before we act, what kinds of interventions should be used, and how to spot and correct deviations before they occur, among a great many other things. In order to keep these and other such issues sorted out, it is helpful to begin a consideration of control with a brief exposition on the theory of control.

No matter what our purpose in controlling a project, there are three basic types of control mechanisms we can use: cybernetic control, go/no-go control, and postcontrol. In this section we will describe these three types and briefly discuss the information requirements of each.

Cybernetic Control

Cybernetic, or steering, control is by far the most common type of control system. *(Cyber* is the Greek word for "helmsman.") The key feature of cybernetic control is its automatic operation. Consider the diagrammatic model of a cybernetic control system shown in Figure 11-1.

As Figure 11-1 shows, a system is operating with inputs being subjected to a process that transforms them into outputs. It is this system that we wish to control. In order to do so, we must monitor the system output. This function is performed by a sensor that measures one or more aspects of the output, presumably those aspects one wishes to control. Measurements taken by the sensor are transmitted to the comparator, which compares them with a set of predetermined standards. The difference between actual and standard is sent to the decision maker, which determines whether or not the difference is of sufficient size to deserve correction. If the difference is large enough to warrant action, a signal is sent to the effector, which acts on the process or on the inputs to produce outputs that conform more closely to the standard.

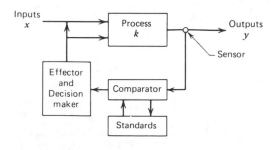

Figure 11-1 A cybernetic control system.

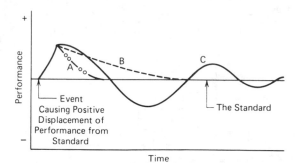

Figure 11-2 Typical paths for correction of deviation of performance from standard.

A cybernetic control system that acts to reduce deviations from standard is called a *negative feedback loop*. If the system output moves away from standard in one direction, the control mechanism acts to move it in the opposite direction. The speed or force with which the control operates is, in general, proportional to the size of the deviation from standard. (Mathematical descriptions of the action of negative feedback loops are widely available. See for example [36].) The precise way in which the deviation is corrected depends on the nature of the operating system and the design of the controller. Figure 11-2 illustrates three different response patterns. Response path A is direct and rapid, while path B is more gradual. Path C shows oscillations of decreasing amplitude. An aircraft suddenly deflected from a stable flight path would tend to recover by following pattern C.

Types of Cybernetic Control Systems

Cybernetic controls come in three varieties, or *orders,* differing in the sophistication with which standards are set. Figure 11-1 shows a simple *first-order* control system, a goal-seeking device. The standard is set and there is no provision made for altering it except by intervention from the outside. The common thermostat is a time-worn example of a first-order controller. One sets the standard temperature and the heating and air-conditioning systems operate to maintain it.

Figure 11-3 shows a *second-order* control system. This device can alter the system standards according to some predetermined set of rules or program. The complexity of second-order systems can vary widely. The addition of a clock to the thermostat to allow it to maintain different standards during day and night makes the thermostat a second-order controller. An interactive computer program may alter its responses according to a complex set of preprogrammed rules, but it is still only a second-order system. Many industrial projects involve second-order controllers—for example, robot installations, flexible manufacturing systems, and automated record-keeping or inventory systems.

A *third-order* control system (Fig. 11-4) can change its goals without specific

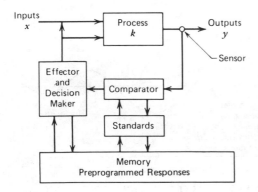

Figure 11-3 A second-order feedback system—preprogrammed goal changer.

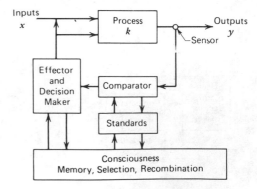

Figure 11-4 A third-order feedback system—reflective goal changer.

preprogramming. It can reflect on system performance and decide to act in ways that are not contained in its instructions. Third-order systems have reflective consciousness and, thus, must contain humans. Note that a second-order controller can be programmed to recognize patterns, and to react to patterns in specific ways. Such systems are said to "learn." Third-order systems can learn without explicit preprogramming, and therefore can alter their actions on the basis of thought or whim. An advantage of third-order controllers is that they can deal with the unforeseen and unexpected. A disadvantage is that, because they contain human elements, they may lack predictability and reliability. Third-order systems are of great interest to the PM, for reasons we discuss below.

Information Requirements for Cybernetic Controllers

In order to establish total control over a system, the controller must be able to take a counteraction for every action the system can take. This statement is a rough paraphrase of Ashby's Law of Requisite Variety [30]. This implies that the PM/controller is aware of the system's full capabilities. For complex systems, particularly those containing a human element, this is simply not possible. Thus, we need a strategy to aid the PM in developing a control system. One such strategy is to use a cost/benefit approach to control—to control those aspects of the system for which the expected benefits of control are greater than the expected costs. We are reminded of a firm that manufactured saw blades. It set up a project to reduce scrap losses for the high-cost steel from which the blades were made. At the end of the one-year project, the firm had completed the project—cost $9,700, savings $4,240. (Of course, if the savings were to be repeated for several years, the rate of return on the project would be acceptable. The president of the firm, however, thought that the savings would decline and disappear when the project ended.)

Relatively few elements of a project (as opposed to the elements of a standard system that operates more or less continuously) are subject to automatic control. An examination of the WBS or the details of an Action Plan will reveal which of the project's tasks are largely mechanistic and represent continuous types of systems. If such systems exist, and if they operate across a sufficient time period to justify the initial expense of creating an automatic control, then a cybernetic controller is useful.

Given the decisions about what to control, the information requirements of a cybernetic controller are easy to describe, if not to meet. First, the PM must define precisely what characteristics of an output (interim output or final output) are to be controlled. Second, standards must be set for each characteristic. Third, sensors must be built that will measure those characteristics at the desired level of precision. Fourth, measurements must be transformed to a signal that can be compared to a "standard" signal. Fifth, the difference between the two is sent to the decision maker, which detects it, if it is sufficiently large, and sixth, transmits a signal to the effector that causes the operating system to react in a way that will counteract the deviation from standard. If the control system is designed to allow the effector to take one or more of several actions, an additional piece of information is needed. There must be built-in criteria that instruct the effector on which action(s) to take.

Knowledge of cybernetic control is important because all control systems are merely variants, extensions, or nonautomatic modifications of such controls. Because most projects have relatively few mechanistic elements that can be subjected to classic cybernetic controls, this concept of control is best applied to tracking the system and automatically notifying the PM when things threaten to get out of control. Almost any item that can be monitored can be tracked by a cybernetic controller that can alert the PM when a measure is out of bounds, is approaching a boundary, or has occurred a specific number of times. In such cases, the control device does not act on the system to return it to control, but on the PM who takes care of the matter.

Go/No-go Controls

Go/no-go controls take the form of testing to see if some specific precondition has been met. This type of control can be used on almost every aspect of a project. For many facets of performance, it is sufficient to know that the predetermined specifications for project output have been met. The same is often true of the cost and time elements of the project plan.

It is, of course, necessary to exercise judgment in the use of go/no-go controls. Certain characteristics of output may be required to fall within precisely determined limits if the output is to be accepted by the client. Other characteristics may be less precisely defined. In regard to time and cost, there may be penalties associated with nonconformance with the approved plans. Penalty clauses that make late delivery costly for the producer are often included in the project contract. At times, early delivery can also carry a penalty. Cost overruns may be shared with the client or borne by the project. Some contracts arrange for the first $X of cost overrun to be shared by client and producer, with any further overrun being the producer's responsibility. The number and type of go/no-go controls on a project is limited only by the imagination and desire of the contracting parties.

The project plan, budget, and schedule are all control documents, so the PM has a predesigned control system complete with prespecified milestones as control checkpoints. Control can be exercised at any level of detail that is supported by detail in the plans, budgets, and schedules. The parts of a new jet engine, for instance, are individually checked for quality conformance. These are go/no-go controls. The part passes or it does not, and every part must pass its own go/no-go test before being used in an engine.

While cybernetic controls are automatic and will check the operating systems continuously or as often as designed to do so, go/no-go controls operate only when and if the controller uses them. In many cases, go/no-go controls function periodically, at regular, preset intervals. The intervals are usually determined by clock, calendar, or the operating cycles of some machine system. Such periodicity makes it easy to administer a control system, but it often allows errors to be compounded before they are detected. Things begin to go awry just after a quarterly progress check, for instance, and by the time the next quarterly check is made, some items may be seriously out of control.

Project milestones do not occur at neat, periodic intervals; thus, *controls should be linked to the actual plans and to the occurrence of real events, not simply to the calendar.* This is not to say that periodic reports are inappropriate. All projects should be reviewed by senior management at reasonably frequent intervals. We will discuss such reports shortly, but the PM cannot control the project properly with a periodic reporting system.

The PM must keep abreast of all aspects of the project, directly or through deputies. Competent functional managers understand the importance of *follow-up,* and the project manager's work provides no exception. Control is best exerted while there is still time for corrective action. To this end, the PM should establish an *early warning system* so that potential problems can be exposed and dealt with before they metamorphose into full-fledged disasters. One way to construct such an early warning system is to set up a project forecast data sheet. On this sheet, outputs or progress are forecast by period. Actual output or progress is then checked against the forecast, period by period. Figure 11-5 illustrates such a data sheet.

For an early warning system to work, it must be clear that the messenger who brings bad news will not be shot, and that anyone caught sweeping problems and mistakes under the rug will be. An important rule for any subordinate is the Prime Law of Life on a project: Never let the boss be surprised!

Controls have a tendency to terrorize the insecure and to induce high anxiety in everyone else. The result is avoidance, and avoidance is exactly what the PM cannot tolerate. Unless deviation from plan is discovered, it cannot be corrected. Therefore, a spirit of trust between superior and subordinate at all levels of the project is a prime requisite for the effective application of control.

Information Requirements for Go/No-Go Controls

Most of the input information needed to operate go/no-go project control has already been referenced directly or implied by the previous discussion. The project proposal, plans, specifications, schedules, and budgets (complete with approved change orders) contain all the information needed to apply go/no-go controls to the project. Milestones are the key events that serve as a focus for ongoing control activity. These milestones are the project's deliverables in the form of in-process output or final output. If the milestones occur on time, on budget, and at the planned level of quality, the PM can take comfort from the fact that things are proceeding properly. Perhaps just as important to the PM, senior management can be equally comfortable with the project—and with the project manager as well.

Except for a few important projects, senior management usually cannot keep up with the day-to-day or week-to-week progress of work; nor should they try. Senior management does, however, need a monthly or quarterly status review for all projects. The project status report contains a list of the important milestones for each project together with the status of each. If many of the projects are similar—such as construction projects or marketing projects, for example—the

TPFC-2664   PRINTED IN U.S.A.

	DATE

PROD. OR PROG. TITLE		CUSTOMER

DATE REC'D.	CONTRACT START DATE	SUBMISSION OR COMPLETE DATE	CUST. CONT. OR REQ. NO.	BUYER

CUST. - ENG. - DEPT.		T.E.P. NO.	REL. G & A PROJ. NO'S.		G & A CODE

CAPITAL EQUIPMENT	REL. ACCTG. CODE NO.	TOTAL G & A

DESCRIPTION OF PRODUCT OR PROGRAM:

REASON FOR   INTEREST:

EXPLOITATION PLAN SUMMARY - (ATTACH SHEETS FOR DETAIL AND PROGRESS)

FORECAST PERIOD	REQ. G & A	TOTAL R & D	TOTAL PRODUCT	PLAN R & D	PLAN PRODUCT	PROB. FACT.	VAL. FACT.	FIG. OF MERIT	COMPETITIVE POSITION						
									1	2	3	4	5	6	7
1															
2															
3															
4															
1															
2															
3															
4															
1															
2															
3															
4															
1															
2															
3															
4															

TOTAL BEYOND DETAILED FORECAST PERIODS					PLAN APPROVAL	DATE	ASSIGNED TO	DATE
					R.E.R.			
DATE					SALES:			
					ENG.:			
							SUMMARY INDEX NO.	

(SEE REVERSE SIDE FOR DETAIL G & A CODE)

Figure 11-5

Task	Project #1	#2	#3
	Project		
	#1	#2	#3
Priorities set	C	C	C
PM selected	C	C	C
Key members briefed on RFP	C	C	C
Proposal sent	C	C	C
Proposal accepted as negotiated	C	C	C
Preliminary design developed	C	W/10	C
Design accepted	C	W/12	C
Software developed	C	NS/NR	N/A
Product test design	C	W/30	W/15
Manufacturing scheduled	C	NS/HR	W/8
Tools, jigs, fixtures designed	W/1	NS/HR	W/2
Tools, jigs, fixtures delivered	W/2	NS/HR	W/8
Production complete	NS/HR	NS/HR	NS/HR
Product test complete	NS/NR	NS/HR	NS/HR
Marketing sign-off on product	NS/HR	NS/HR	NS/HR

Notes:

N/A—Not applicable	W—Work in progress (number refers to month required)	NS—Not started NR—Need resources
C—Completed		HR—Have resources

Figure 11-6 Sample project status report.

milestones will be of similar type, and one table can show the status of several projects in spite of the fact that each milestone may not be applicable to each and every project. The Elanco Products Company (the agricultural products division of Eli Lilly and Company) uses such a report. A generalized version of Elanco's Project Status Report is shown in Figure 11-6. The Gantt chart (see Chapter 8) is also a convenient way to present senior managers with information on project status.

Either of these report forms can be altered to contain almost any additional information that might be requested. For example, the Gantt chart can be annotated with footnotes indicating such matters of interest as the resources required to get a late milestone back on schedule, or a statement of how an activity must be changed if it is to be approved by a regulatory agency. The information requirements for such extensions of standard reports must be set on an ad hoc basis. For the most part, such information will be readily available within the project, but occasionally, external sources must be utilized. If the PM ensures that the status reports given to senior management contain information that is current enough to be actionable (and always is as accurate as required for control), little else can be done to furnish the decision makers with the proper data for them to exercise control. The PM is well advised to insist that status reports make clear the implications of specific conditions where those implications might be overlooked—or not understood—by senior managers.

Postcontrol

Postcontrols (also known as postperformance controls or postproject controls) are applied after the fact. One might draw parallels between postcontrol and "locking the barn after the horse has been stolen," but postcontrol is not a vain attempt to alter what has already occurred. Instead, it is a full recognition of George Santayana's observation that "Those who cannot remember the past are condemned to repeat it." Cybernetic and go/no-go controls are directed toward accomplishing the goals of an ongoing project. Postcontrol is directed toward improving the chances for future projects to meet their goals.

Postcontrol is applied through a relatively formal document that is usually constructed with four distinct sections.

The Project Objectives The postcontrol will contain a description of the objectives of the project. Usually, this description is taken from the project proposal, and the entire proposal often appears as an appendix to the postcontrol report. As reported here, project objectives include the effects of all change orders issued and approved during the project.

Because actual project performance depends in part on uncontrollable events (strikes, weather, failure of trusted suppliers, sudden loss of key employees, and other acts of God), the key initial assumptions made during preparation of the project budget and schedule should be noted in this section. A certain amount of care must be taken in reporting these assumptions. They should not be written with a tone that makes them appear to be excuses for poor performance. While it is clearly the prerogative, if not the duty, of every PM to protect himself politically, he or she should do so in moderation to be effective.

Milestones, Checkpoints, and Budgets This section of the postcontrol document starts with a full report of project performance against the planned schedule and budget. This can be prepared by combining and editing the various project status reports made during the project's life. Significant deviations of actual schedule and budget from planned schedule and budget should be highlighted. Explanations of why these deviations occurred will be offered in the next section of the postcontrol report. Each deviation can be identified with a letter or number to index it to the explanations. Where the same explanation is associated with both a schedule and budget deviation, as will often be the case, the same identifier can be used.

The Final Report on Project Results When significant variations of actual from planned project performance are indicated, no distinction is made between favorable and unfavorable variations. Like the tongue that invariably goes to the sore tooth, project managers focus their attention on trouble. While this is quite natural, it leads to complete documentation on why some things went wrong and little or no documentation on why some things went particularly well. Both sides, the good and the bad, should be chronicled here.

Not only do most projects result in outputs that are more or less satisfactory, most projects operate with a *process* that is more or less satisfactory. The concern here is not on what the project did but rather on *how* it did it. Basically descriptive, this part of the final report should cover project organization, an explanation of the methods used to plan and direct the project, and a review of the communication networks, monitoring systems, and control methods, as well as a discussion of intraproject interactions between the various working groups.

Recommendations for Performance and Process Improvement   The culmination of the postcontrol report is a set of recommendations covering the ways that future projects can be improved. Many of the explanations appearing in the previous section are related to one-time happenings—sickness, weather, strikes, or the appearance of a new technology—that themselves are not apt to affect future projects, although other, different one-time events may affect them. But some of the deviations from plan were caused by happenings that are very likely to recur. Provision for such things can be factored into future project plans, thereby adding to predictability and control.

Just as important, the process of organizing and conducting projects can be improved by recommending the continuation of managerial methods and organizational systems that appear to be effective, together with the alteration of practices and procedures that do not. In this way, the conduct of projects will become smoother, just as the likelihood of achieving good results, on time and on cost, is increased.

Postcontrol can have a considerable impact on the way projects are run. A large, market-driven company in consumer household products developed new products through projects that were organized in matrix form, but had a functional tie to the marketing division. PMs were almost always chosen from the marketing area. Members of the project team who represented R & D had argued that they should be given a leadership role, particularly early in the project's life. Marketing resisted this suggestion on the grounds that R & D people were not market-oriented, did not know what would sell, and were mainly interested in pursuing their own "academic" interests. After reading the perennial R & D request in a postcontrol report, the program manager of one product line decided to reorganize a project as requested by R & D. The result was not merely a successful project, but was the first in a series of related projects based on extensions of ideas generated by an R & D group not restricted to work on the specific product sought by marketing. Following this successful experiment, project organization was modified to include more input from R & D at an earlier stage of the project.

There is no need to repeat the information requirements for postcontrol here. It should be noted, however, that we have not discussed the postcontrol audit, a full review and audit of all aspects of the project. This is covered in Chapter 12.

11.3 COMMENTS ON THE DESIGN OF CONTROL SYSTEMS

Irrespective of the type of control used, there are some important questions to be answered when designing any control system: Who sets the standards? How realistic are the standards? How clear are they? Will they achieve the project's goals? What output, activities, behaviors should be monitored? Should we monitor people? What kinds of sensors should be used? Where should they be placed? How timely must the monitoring be? How rapidly must it be reported? How accurate must the sensors be? How great must a difference between standard and actual be before it becomes actionable? What corrective actions are available? What are the most appropriate actions for each situation? What rewards and penalties can be used? Who should take what action?

If the control system is to be acceptable to those who will use it and those who will be controlled by it, the system must be designed so that it appears to be sensible. Standards must be achievable by the mechanical systems used. Control limits must be appropriate to the needs of the client—that is, not merely set to show "how good we are." Like punishment, rewards and penalties should "fit the crime."

In addition to being sensible, a good control system should also possess some other characteristics.

- The system should be flexible. Where possible, it should be able to react to and report unforeseen changes in system performance.
- The system should be cost-effective. The cost of control should never exceed the value of control. As we noted above, control is not always less expensive than scrap.
- The control system must be truly useful. It must satisfy the real needs of the project, not the whims of the PM.
- The system must operate in a timely manner. Problems must be reported while there is still time to do something about them, and before they become large enough to destroy the project.
- Sensors and monitors should be sufficiently accurate and precise to control the project within limits that are truly functional for the client and the parent organization.
- The system should be as simple to operate as possible.
- The control system should be easy to maintain. Further, the control system should signal the overall controller if it goes out of order.
- The system should be capable of being extended or otherwise altered.
- Control systems should be fully documented when installed and the documentation should include a complete training program in system operation.

No matter how designed, all control systems we have described use feedback as a control process. Let us now consider some more specific aspects of control. To a large extent, the PM is trying to anticipate problems or catch them just as they begin to occur. The PM wants to keep the project out of trouble because upper management often bases an incremental funding decision on a review of the project. This review typically follows some particular milestone and, if acceptable, leads to a follow-on authorization to proceed to the next review point. If all is not going well, other technological alternatives may be recommended; or

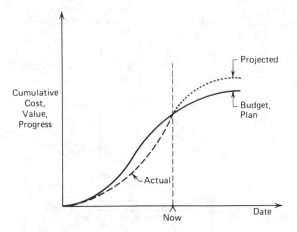

Figure 11-7 Trend projection.

if things are going badly, the project may be terminated. Thus, the PM must monitor and control the project quite closely.

The control of performance, cost, and time usually requires different input data. To control performance, the PM may need such specific documentation as engineering change notices, test results, quality checks, rework tickets, scrap rates, and maintenance activities. For cost control, the manager compares budgets to actual cash flows, purchase orders, labor hour charges, amount of overtime worked, absenteeism, accounting variance reports, accounting projections, income reports, cost exception reports, and the like. To control the schedule, the PM examines benchmark reports, periodic activity and status reports, exception reports, PERT/CPM networks, Gantt charts, the master project schedule, earned value graphs, and probably reviews the WBS and Action Plans.

Some of the most important analytic tools available to the project manager to use in controlling the project are variance analysis and trend projection, both of which have been discussed earlier in this book. The essence of these tools is shown in Figure 11-7. A budget, plan, or expected growth curve of time or cost for some task is plotted. Then actual values are plotted as a dashed line as the work is actually finished. At each point in time a new projection from the actual data is used to forecast what will occur in the future if the PM does not intervene. Based on this projection, the manager can decide if there is a problem, what action alternatives exist, what they will cost and require, and what they will achieve. Based on this analysis, the PM will decide what to do. Trend projection charts can even be used for combined performance/cost/time charts, as illustrated in Figure 11-8.

Earned value analysis was also described earlier. On occasion it may be worthwhile, particularly on large projects, for the PM to calculate a set of *critical ratios* for all project activities. The critical ratio is

$$(\text{Actual progress/scheduled progress}) \times (\text{budgeted cost/actual cost})$$

If this ratio is exactly 1, then the activity is probably on target. If the ratio differs

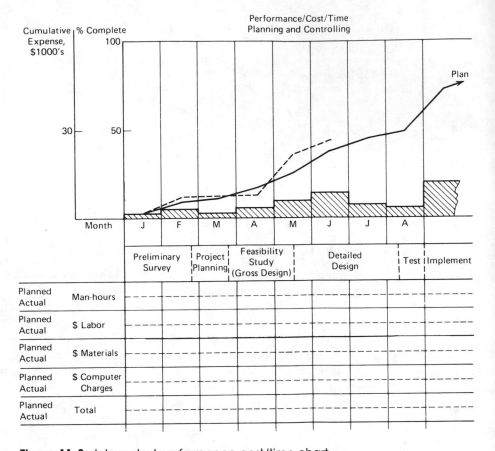

Figure 11-8 Integrated performance cost/time chart.
Source: Murdick, R.G. et al., *Information Systems for Modern Management,* 3rd ed., Prentice-Hall, 1984.

from 1, then the activity may need to be investigated. The closer the ratio is to 1, the less important is the investigation.

Consider Table 11-1. We can see that the first task is behind schedule but below budget. If lateness is no problem for this activity, the PM need take no action. The second task is on budget but its physical progress is lagging. Even if there is slack in the activity, the budget will probably be overrun. The third task is on schedule but cost is running higher than budget, creating another probable cost overrun. The fourth task is on budget but ahead of schedule. A cost saving may result. Finally, the fifth task is on schedule and is running under budget, another probable cost saving.

Tasks 4 and 5 have critical ratios greater than 1 and might not concern some PMs, but the thoughtful manager wants to know why they are doing so well (and the PM may also want to check the information system to validate the unexpectedly favorable findings). The second and third activities need attention, and the

Table 11-1 (Actual Progress/Scheduled Progress) × (Budgeted Cost/Actual Cost)

Task Number	Actual Progress		Scheduled Progress		Budgeted Cost		Actual Cost		Critical Ratio
1	(2	/	3)	×	(6	/	4)	=	1.0
2	(2	/	3)	×	(6	/	6)	=	.67
3	(3	/	3)	×	(4	/	6)	=	.67
4	(3	/	2)	×	(6	/	6)	=	1.5
5	(3	/	3)	×	(6	/	4)	=	1.5

first task may need attention also. The PM may set some critical-ratio control limits intuitively.

Charts can be used to monitor and control the project through the use of these ratios. Figure 11-9 shows an example. Note that the PM will ignore critical ratios in some ranges, and that the ranges are not necessarily symmetric around 1.0. Different types of tasks may have different control limits. Control charts can also

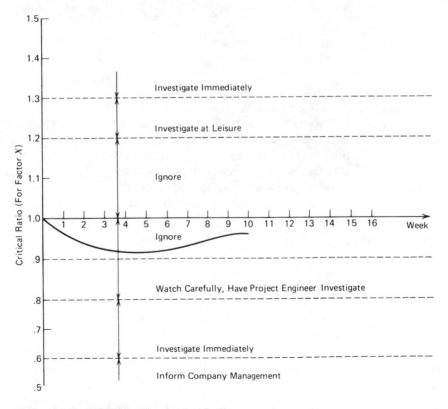

Figure 11-9 Critical ratio control limits.

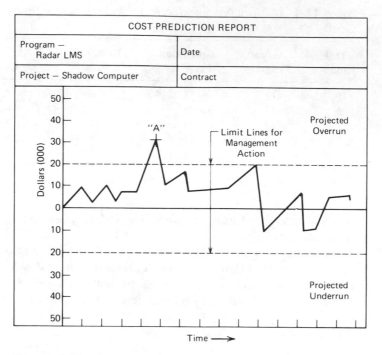

Figure 11-10 Cost control chart.
Source: Hajek, V.G., *Management of Engineering Projects,* Mc-Graw Hill, 1977.

be used to aid in controlling costs (Figure 11-10), work force levels, and other project parameters.

Auditing will be discussed in Chapter 12, but it needs a brief mention here. It is basically an investigation and count to identify and locate all elements of a project. The PM may find a particular activity perplexing or not understand why it is taking longer than it should or costing more than expected. An audit would provide the data to explain the unusual nature of the discrepancy. The PM may choose to do the audit or have the organization's accountant perform the work.

11.4 CONTROL AS A FUNCTION OF MANAGEMENT[1]

The PM is always subject to such eternal verities as the law of gravity, the laws of thermodynamics, and the brute fact that the exercise of managerial control will result in distorting the behavior of subordinates. The job of the PM/controller is to set controls that will encourage those behaviors/results that are deemed desirable and discourage those that are not. The unspoken assumption here is that control systems motivate individuals to behave in certain ways. While this may seem obvious, it is not the bland assertion it appears. The entire subject of

[1]Several of the matters mentioned in this and the following two sections are discussed at greater length in Newman's excellent work on control, *Constructive Control* [26].

motivation is a complex and rich field for research. there are several theories about the nature of motivation. Each has its supporters and critics. We adopt no particular theory here; we do, however, argue that the control mechanisms described in this chapter provide a context within which motivation takes place. Thus, while control does not provide a good explanation for the presence or absence of motivation, control does indicate the direction toward which the motivated person will move [22].

Though control does not ensure motivated behavior, individual reactions to the various types of control systems do affect levels of motivation. By and large, people respond to the goal-directedness of control systems in one of three general ways: (1) by active and positive participation and goal seeking, (2) by passive participation in order to avoid loss, and (3) by active but negative participation and resistance—usually not active resistance to the goal, but failure to undertake those activities that will result in goal achievement. Which of the three resemble a given individual's reaction to control depends on several variables, including such things as the specific control mechanism used, the nature of the goal being sought, the individual's self-image, assessment of the value of the goal, expectation of being able to achieve the goal, and basic tolerance for being controlled.

While human response to specific types of control is typified by its variety, some generalizations are possible.

Cybernetic Controls   Human response to steering controls tends to be positive. Steering controls are usually viewed as helpful rather than as a source of unwelcome pressure if the controllees perceive themselves as able to perform inside the prescribed limits. Contrary to the popular song, it is not the "impossible dream" that motivates goal-seeking behavior, but rather a moderately good chance of success.

Of course, response to steering control is dependent on the individual's acceptance of the goal as appropriate. Indeed, no control system is acceptable if the objective of control is not acceptable. Further, the source of control must be seen as legitimate for the control mechanism to be accepted.

Go/No-go Controls   Response to go/no-go controls tends to be neutral or negative. The reason appears to be related to the inherent nature of this type of control system. With go/no-go control systems, "barely good enough" results are just as acceptable as "perfect" results. The control system itself makes it difficult for the worker to take pride in high-quality work because the system does not recognize gradations of quality. In addition, it is all too common to be rather casual about setting the control limits for a go/no-go control; the limits should be very carefully set. The fact that this kind of control emphasizes "good enough" performance is no excuse for the nonchalant application of careless standards.

Postcontrols   Postcontrols are seen as much the same as a report card. They may serve as a basis for reward or punishment, but they are received too late to change current performance. Whether reaction to postcontrol is positive, neutral, or negative seems to depend on the "grade" received. In cases where a series of similar projects must be undertaken, postcontrols are regarded as helpful in planning for future work, but considerable care must be devoted to ensuring that controls are consistent with changing environmental conditions. To be effective, management must provide an incentive for project managers to study postcontrol reports, and to determine corrective procedures for problems exposed by the reports, as well as procedures that will replicate the techniques and systems that appear particularly helpful.

Because postcontrols are placed on the process of conducting a project, as well as on the usual time, cost, and performance standards, they may be applied to such areas as interproject communications, cooperation between the groups working on related task elements, the quality of project management, and the nature of interaction with the client. Application of control to such matters presents severe measurement problems. Often it is difficult to detect gross differences in the quality of intergroup communications, for example, or to relate these differences, if detected, to aspects of the project that can be controlled. To say that these matters are difficult to measure and control is not, of course, to obviate the need for control. The soft side of project performance is no less important in the longer run than the easier-to-measure hard side.

11.5 BALANCE IN A CONTROL SYSTEM

When developing a control system, it is important that the system be well *balanced*. Unfortunately, the concept of balance is fuzzy—difficult to explain, difficult to achieve, and difficult to recognize. Though precise definition is impossible, we can describe some general features of a balanced control system, and also indicate some of the things a controller can do to achieve good balance in a system.

- A balanced control system is built with cognizance of the fact that investment in control is subject to sharply diminishing returns. Costs increase exponentially as the degree of control increases.

- A balanced control system recognizes that as control increases past some point, innovative activity is more and more damped, and then finally shut off completely.

- A balanced control system is directed toward the correction of error rather than toward punishment. This requires a clear understanding of the fact that the past cannot be changed, no matter how loudly the manager yells.

- A balanced system exerts control only to the degree required to achieve its objectives. It rarely pays to spend dollars to find lost pennies, nor is it sensible to machine a part to the ten-thousandth if the client's requirements are to the tenth.

- A balanced system utilizes the lowest degree of hassle consistent with accomplishing its goals. The controller should avoid annoying those people whose cooperation is required to reach system objectives.

To sum up, a balanced control system is cost-effective, well geared for the end results sought, and not overdone. The causes of imbalance are legion. For example, the application of across-the-board controls is usually not a good idea. Treating everyone alike appeals to a naive sense of equity, but better results are usually achieved by treating everyone individually.

Across-the-board freezes on expenditures or on hiring tend to reward those who have already overspent or overhired and to penalize the frugal and efficient. The side effects of this are often quite odd. Several years ago, Procter & Gamble put a freeze on hiring into effect for an engineering development laboratory. Project managers who were shorthanded hired temporary labor, including highly skilled technicians, from Manpower and similar firms. P & G's accounting system allowed temporary labor to be charged to material accounts rather than to the salary account. The lesson to be learned is that results-oriented, creative project managers tend to see the across-the-board controls as a challenge and a barrier to be circumvented.

Other common causes of imbalance are these:

1. Placing too much weight on easy-to-measure factors and too little weight on difficult-to-measure, soft factors (the so-called "intangibles").
2. Emphasizing short-run results at the expense of longer-run objectives.
3. Ignoring the changes in the structure of organizational goals that result from the passage of time or changes in the firm's circumstances. For example, high quality and strict adherence to delivery schedules might be extremely important to a new firm. Later, perhaps, expense control might be more important.
4. Overcontrol by an aggressive executive often causes trouble. In an attempt to create a reputation for on-time delivery, one overly zealous PM put so much pressure on the project team that on-time shipments took precedence over proper test procedures. The result was serious malfunctions of the product and its subsequent recall.

Achieving balance in a control system is rather easy to discuss but quite difficult to accomplish. Several principles must be simultaneously upheld. Perhaps most important is the need to tie controls directly to project objectives. Occasionally, firms establish tortuous, indirect linkages between control and objective, apparently on the theory that people should not be aware of or understand the controls under which they must operate. It is as if the firm were trying to trap employees. Such control systems rarely work because they rest on two fallacious assumptions: (1) that people are generally perverse and will avoid trying to accomplish a known objective, and (2) that people are too stupid to see through the misdirection.

In addition to linking controls to objectives, controls should be closely and directly related to specific performance outcomes. Start by defining the desired results as precisely as possible. System actions that can cause deviation from the desired results are then examined and controls are designed for these actions, beginning with those that can be the source of serious deviation, particularly those that cause trouble with high frequency.

The PM should also examine all controls in terms of the probable reactions of individuals to the proposed controls. One asks, "How will the various members of the project team react to this control?" If negative reaction is likely, the control should be redesigned.

The problem of developing a good balance between long-run and short-run control objectives is delicate, not because the blending is inherently difficult, but because the PM is often preoccupied with urgent short-run problems rather than longer-run problems that can always be "temporarily" set aside no matter how important the results may be at some later date.

A good rule for the controller is to place the control as close as possible to the work being controlled and to design the simplest possible mechanism to achieve control. Giving the worker direct control over quality has had impressive results in Japanese production processes as well as at the Lincoln Electric Company in the United States. Similar results were achieved by a major producer of housing units. Carpenters, masons, electricians, and other workers were given considerable discretion over specific production methods. Projects on which this approach was employed showed significantly improved quality when compared to projects built by standard methods.

The most important step in constructing a balanced control system must be taken far in advance of the time when control systems are usually designed. Every step of project planning must be undertaken with the understanding that *whatever work is planned will also have to be controlled.* As we have emphasized, planning and control are opposite sides of the same coin. No amount of planning can solve the current crisis, but planning combined with the design and installation of appropriate control mechanisms can go a long way toward crisis prevention.

An excellent example of integrating the planning and control functions is provided by Mead Data Central, a producer of large-scale database systems and a subsidiary of Mead Corporation. In its *Project Management Development Guide,* Mead describes six stages of the project life cycle as seen from its point of view. For each stage, the purpose is carefully explained and the deliverables for that stage are listed. For example, the list of deliverables for the feasibility stage contains these items: project description, project number, preliminary business case, project requirements document, and so forth. For each deliverable, the individual(s) and/or groups responsible are noted.

An extensive glossary of terms is included in the document so that inexperienced project workers can understand what is meant by such diverse terms as "escalation document," "functional audit," "milestone," "not-to-do list," "project cost tracking," and "release readiness statement." In addition, the *Development Guide* summarizes the tasks that must be performed by each of the functional areas or individuals during each stage of the life cycle. The work of the Idea Champion, the Market Managers, the Business Management Process Director, the Project Review Committee, and so on is well defined. The result is an effective integration of planning and control that is available to anyone working on the organization's projects.

A senior executive at a large industrial firm that carries out many projects each year sees control in a slightly different light. Noting that differences between plan and reality usually represent problems for project managers, he remarked: "If you are solving problems faster than they are arriving to be solved, you have the project under control. If not, you haven't."

11.6 CONTROL OF CREATIVE ACTIVITIES

Some brief attention should be paid to the special case of controlling research and development projects, design projects, and similar processes that depend intimately on the creativity of individuals and teams. First, the more creativity involved, the greater the degree of uncertainty surrounding outcomes. Second, too much control tends to inhibit creativity. But neither of these dicta can be taken without reservation. As noted in Appendix A, control is not necessarily the enemy of creativity [34]; nor, popular myth to the contrary, does creative activity imply complete uncertainty. While the exact outcomes of creative activity may be more or less uncertain, the process of getting the outcome is usually not uncertain.

In order to control creative projects, the PM must adopt one or some combination of three general approaches to the problem: (1) progress review, (2) personnel reassignment, and (3) control of input resources.

Progress Review The progress review focuses on the process of reaching outcomes rather than on the outcomes per se. Because the outcomes are partially dependent on the process used to achieve them—uncertain though they may be— the process is subjected to control. For example, in research projects the researcher cannot be held responsible for the outcome of the research, but can most certainly be held responsible for adherence to the research proposal, the budget, and the schedule. The process is controllable even if the precise results are not.

Control should be instituted at each project milestone. If research results are not as expected or desired, milestones provide a convenient opportunity to assess the state of progress, the value of accomplishment to date, the probability of valuable results in the future, and the desirability of changes in the research design. Again, the object of control is to insure that the research design is sound and is being carried out as planned or amended. The review process should be participative. Unilateral judgments from the superior are not apt to be accepted or effective. Care must be taken not to overstress method as opposed to result. Method is controllable, and should be controlled, but results are still what count.

Personnel Reassignment This type of control operates in a very straightforward way. Individuals who are productive are kept. Those who are not are moved, to other jobs or to other organizations. Problems with this technique can arise because it is easy to create an elite group. While the favored few are highly motivated to further achievement, everyone else tends to be demotivated. It is also important not to apply control with too fine an edge. While it is not particularly difficult to identify those who fall in the top and bottom quartiles of productivity, it is usually quite hard to make clear distinctions between people in the middle quartiles.

Control of Input Resources In this case, the focus is on efficiency. The ability to manipulate input resources carries with it considerable control over output. Obviously, efficiency is not synonymous with creativity, but the converse is equally untrue. Creativity is not synonomous with extravagant use of resources.

The results flowing from creative activity tend to arrive in batches. Considerable resource expenditure may occur with no visible results, but then, seemingly all of a sudden, many outcomes may be delivered. The milestones for application of resource control must therefore be chosen with great care. The controller who decides to withhold resources just before the fruition of a research project is apt to become an ex-controller.

Sound judgment argues for some blend of these three approaches when controlling creative projects. The first and third approaches concentrate on process because process is observable and can be affected. But process is not the matter of moment; results are. The second approach requires us to measure (or at least to recognize) output when it occurs. This is often quite difficult. Thus, the wise PM will use all three approaches: checking process and method, manipulating resources, and culling those who cannot or do not produce.

11.7 SUMMARY

As the final subject in the project implementation part of the text, this chapter described the project control process in the planning-monitoring-controlling cycle. The need for control was discussed and the three types available were described. Then the design of control systems was addressed, including management's role, achieving the proper balance, and attaining control of creative activity.

Specific points made in chapter were these:

- Control is directed to performance, cost, and time.
- The two fundamental purposes of control are to regulate results through altering activity and to conserve the organization's physical, human, and financial assets.
- The three main types of control processes are cybernetic (either first-, second-, or third-order), go/no-go, and postcontrol.
- The postcontrol report contains four sections:
    Project objectives
    Milestones and budgets
    Final project results
    Recommendations for improvement
- The trend projection curve, critical ratios, and the control chart are useful control tools.
- Control systems have a close relationship to motivation and should be well-balanced; that is, cost-effective, appropriate to the desired end results, and not overdone.
- Three approaches to the control of creativity are progress review, personnel reassignment, and control of inputs.

In the next chapter we initiate the project termination part of the text, beginning with evaluation and auditing. This topic is closely related to the postcontrol topic in this chapter.

11.8 GLOSSARY

CHAMPION—A person who takes on personal responsibility (though not usually day-to-day management) for the successful completion of a "visionary project" for the organization. It may involve a product launch, a process innovation, or any other type of project.

CONTROL—Assuring that reality meets expectations or plans. Usually involves the process of keeping actions within limits to assure that certain outcomes will in fact happen.

CONTROL CHART—A chart of a measure—commonly a quality characteristic—over time, showing how it changes compared to a desired mean and upper and lower limits.

CRITICAL RATIO—A ratio that measures an important characteristic and is plotted or tracked in some fashion to determine priorities among items or events.

CYBERNETIC—Automatic guidance or steering. A cybernetic control system typically includes negative feedback loops to exert control.

EARLY WARNING SYSTEM—A monitoring system that forewarns the project manager if trouble arises.

GO/NO-GO—Initially, a type of gauge that quickly tells an inspector if an object's dimension is within certain limits. In the case of project management, this can be any measure that allows a manager to decide whether to continue, change, or terminate an activity or a project.

11.9 PROJECT TEAM ASSIGNMENT

For this assignment, design and use a project control system for your team project. Determine how you will control performance, cost, and time. Will you use go/no-go, postcontrol, or cybernetic controls, and if the latter, a first-, second-, or third-order system? Are these dynamic or static controls? What will you measure? What tools will you employ: control charts, critical ratios, trend projections? Will you attempt to control creativity? If so, how? Justify your control system in terms of cost effectiveness, appropriateness, and ability to motivate team members.

11.10 MATERIAL REVIEW QUESTIONS

1. What is the purpose of control? To what is it directed?
2. What are the three main types of control systems? What questions should a control system answer?
3. What tools are available to the project manager to use in controlling a project? Identify some characteristics of a good control system.
4. What is the mathematical expression for the critical ratio? What does it tell a manager?
5. Describe the relationship between motivation and control.
6. How is creativity controlled?

11.11 CONCEPTUAL DISCUSSION QUESTIONS

1. How could MBO be used in project control?
2. How might the project manager integrate the various control tools into a project control system?
3. How could a negative feedback control system be implemented in project management to anticipate client problems?
4. Compare the trend projection curve and the earned value chart. Could they be combined to aid the PM's control?
5. What other project parameters might a control chart be used for? How would their limits be set?
6. Control systems are sometimes classified into two categories, preventive and feedback. How do the three types of systems described in the chapter relate to these two categories?

11.12 PROBLEMS

1. Calculate the critical ratios for the following activities and indicate which activities are probably on target and which need to be investigated.

Activity	Actual Progress	Scheduled Progress	Budgeted Cost	Actual Cost
A	4 days	4 days	$60	$40
B	3 days	2 days	$50	$50
C	2 days	3 days	$30	$20
D	1 day	1 day	$20	$30
E	2 days	4 days	$25	$25

2. Given the following information, which activities are on time, which are early, and which are behind schedule?

Activity	Budgeted Cost	Actual Cost	Critical Ratio
A	$60	$40	1.0
B	$25	$50	0.5
C	$45	$30	1.5
D	$20	$20	1.5
E	$50	$50	0.67

3. Design and plot a critical ratio for a project that had planned constant, linear progress from 0 to an earned value of 200 over a 100 day duration. In fact, progress for the first 20 days has been: 2, 3, 4, 6, 7, 9, 12, 14, 15, 17, 20, 21, 21, 22, 24, 26, 27, 29, 31, 33. What can you conclude about this project?

4. Design and plot a critical ratio for a project that has planned constant, linear spending from 0 to a total of 1000 over a 100 day duration. In fact, daily spending for the first 15 days has been: 11, 10, 9, 10, 11, 12, 11, 9, 8, 9, 10, 12, 14, 11, 7. What can you conclude about this project?

5. Empire State Building, Inc., has two project teams installing virtually identical buildings for a customer in two separate cities. Both projects have a planned daily

cost of 100 and a planned daily earned value of 100. The first six days for each team have progressed as follows:

Day	Team A: Earned Value	Team B: Earned Value	A: Cost	B: Cost
1	90	90	95	95
2	92	88	98	94
3	94	95	101	102
4	98	101	106	109
5	104	89	116	99
6	112	105	126	118

Compare the two projects in terms of general progress and according to critical ratios.

6. World Trade Building, Ltd., is also constructing an identical building for the same customer as in Problem 5 and has the following earned values and costs for the first six days: EV: 90, 88, 95, 101, 89, 105; Cost: 92, 88, 93, 98, 85, 100. Compare this project to the two in Problem 5.

11.13 INCIDENTS FOR DISCUSSION

Speciality Pak, Inc.

Speciality Pak, Inc., is a custom packing operation serving the chemical industry in seven states. S.P. has one operation in each state, and they vary in size from 50 to 240 employees. A disturbing trend has been developing for the last couple of years that S.P. management wishes to stop. The incidence of tardiness and absenteeism is on the increase. Both are extremely disruptive in a custom packing operation. S.P. is nonunion in all seven locations, and since management wants to keep this situation, it wants a careful, low-key approach to the problem. Roger Horn, assistant personnel manager, has been appointed project manager to recommend a solution. All seven operations managers have been assigned to work with him on this problem.

Roger has had no problem interfacing with the operations managers. They have very quickly agreed that three steps must be taken to solve the problem:

1. Institute a uniform daily attendance report that is summarized weekly and forwarded to the main office. (Current practice varies from location to location, but comments on attendance are normally included in monthly operations reports.)
2. Institute a uniform disciplinary policy, enforced in a uniform manner.
3. Initiate an intensive employee education program to emphasize the importance of good attendance.

The team has further decided that the three-point program should be tested before a final recommendation is presented. They have decided to test the program at one location for two months. Roger wishes to control and evaluate the test by having the daily attendance report transmitted to him directly at headquarters, from which he will make the final decision on whether to present the program in its current format or not.

Question: Does this monitoring and control method appear adequate?

Night Tran Construction Company

Night Tran Construction Company specializes in building small power plants, mostly for utility companies. The company was awarded a contract approximately two years ago to build such a power plant. The contract stated a project duration of three years, after which a 1 percent penalty was invoked for each additional month of construction. Project records indicate the utility plan is only 50 percent completed and is encountering continuous problems. The owner of Night Tran Company, concerned over the potential losses, investigated the project and found the following: There were an excessive number of engineering design changes; there was a high work rejection rate; and the project was generally understaffed. As a result, he directed the project manager to develop a better system of project control and present this method to the board members in one week.

Question: If you were the project manager, what characteristics would you be looking for in the new control system? Will a new control system be adequate for the problem? Explain.

11.14 BIBLIOGRAPHY

1. Adams, J. R., S. E. Barndt, and M. Martin. *Managing by Project Management.* Universal Technology Corp., Dayton, OH, 1979.
2. Amrine, H. T., J. A. Ritchey, and O. S. Hulley. *Manufacturing Organization and Management,* 3rd ed. Englewood Cliffs, NJ: Prentice-Hall, 1975.
3. Archibald, R. D. *Managing High Technology Programs and Projects.* New York: Wiley, 1976.
4. Barnes, N. M. L. "Cost Modelling—An Integrated Approach to Planning and Cost Control." *American Association of Chemical Engineers Transactions,* March 1977.
5. Bent, J. A. "Project Control Concepts." *Project Management Proceedings,* 1979.
6. Block, E. B. "Accomplishment/Cost: Better Project Control." *Harvard Business Review,* May 1971.
7. Buffa, E. S. *Basic Production Management,* 2nd ed. New York: Wiley, 1975.
8. Cammann, C., and D. A. Nadler. "Fit Control Systems to Your Management Style." *Harvard Business Review,* Jan.–Feb. 1976.
9. Cestin, A. A. "What Makes Large Projects Go Wrong." *Project Management Institute Quarterly,* March 1980.
10. Davis, S. M., and P. Lawrence. *Matrix.* Boston: Addison Wesley, 1977.
11. Elliott, D. P. "Paper and Cost Control." *Project Management Proceedings,* 1979.
12. Frazier, Haugg, and Thackery. "Developing A Project Management Package." *Journal of Systems Management,* Dec. 1976.
13. Higgins, J. C., and R. Finn. "Managerial Attitudes Toward Computer Models for Planning and Control." *Long Range Planning,* Dec. 1976.
14. Hollander, G. L. "Integrated Project Control, Part II: TCP/Schedule: A Model for Integrated Project Control." *Project Management Quarterly.* June 1973.

15. Horovitz, J. H. "Strategic Control: A New Task for Top Management." *Long Range Planning,* June 1979.

16. Howard, D. C. "Cost Schedule Control Systems." *Management Accounting,* Oct. 1976.

17. Johnson, J. R., "Advanced Project Control," *Journal of Systems Management,* May 1977.

18. Keane, A. "Timing for Project Management Control." *Data Management,* 1979.

19. Kerzner, H. "Evaluation Techniques in Project Management." *Journal of Systems Management,* Feb. 1980.

20. Larsen, S. D. "Control of Construction Projects: An Integrated Approach," *The Internal Auditor,* Sept. 1979.

21. Likierman, A., "Avoiding Cost Escalation on Major Projects." *Management Accounting,* Feb. 1980.

22. Livingston, J. L., and R. Ronen. "Motivation and Management Control Systems." *Decision Sciences,* April 1975.

23. Martyn, A. S. "Some Problems in Managing Complex Development Projects." *Long Range Planning,* April 1975.

24. Moravec, M. "How Organizational Development Can Help and Hinder Project Managers." *Project Management Quarterly,* Sept. 1979.

25. Myers, G. "Forms Management; Part 5—How to Achieve Control." *Journal of Systems Management,* Feb. 1977.

26. Newman, W. H. *Constructive Control,* Englewood Cliffs, NJ: Prentice-Hall, 1975.

27. Newnem, A. "Planning Ahead with An Integrated Management Control System." *Project Management Proceedings,* 1979.

28. Saitow, A. R. "CSPC: Reporting Project Progress to The Top." In *Project Management: Techniques, Applications and Managerial Issues,* E. W. Davis, ed. Norcross, GA: American Institute of Industrial Engineers, 1976.

29. Sanders, J. "Effective Estimating Process Outlined." *Computer World,* April 7, 14, and 21, 1980.

30. Schoderbek, C. G., P. P. Schoderbek, and A. G. Kefalas. *Management Systems,* 3rd ed. Plano, TX: Business Publications, 1985.

31. Schoof, G. "What is The Scope of Project Control?" *Project Management Proceedings,* 1979.

32. Sethi, N. K. "Project Management." *Industrial Management,* Jan–Feb. 1980.

33. Snowdon, M. "Measuring Performance in Capital Project Management." *Long Range Planning,* Aug. 1980.

34. Souder, W. E. "Autonomy, Gratification, and R & D Outputs: A Small-Sample Field Study." *Management Science,* April 1974.

35. Toellner, J. D. "Project Management: A Formula for Success." *Computer World,* Dec. 1978.

36. van Gigch, J. P. *Applied General Systems Theory,* 2nd ed. New York: Harper & Row, 1978.

37. Weber, F. M. "Ways to Improve Performance on Projects." *Project Management Quarterly,* Sept. 1981.

38. Zeldman, M. *Keeping Technical Projects on Target.* New York: American Management Association, 1978.

11.15 Case: Corning Glass Works: The Z-Glass Project

After several highly successful years, 1977 had been a difficult one at Corning Glass Work's Harrisburg plant. In July the yields and productivity of the Z-Glass process had begun a long decline, and the entire plant organization was working overtime trying to correct the problem. Morale was plummeting as yields continued to decline throughout the summer and fall. In December of 1977, a team of engineers from the corporate Manufacturing and Engineering (M&E) staff had been assigned to the plant; its charter was to focus on long-term process improvement while the line organization concentrated on day-to-day operations.

On the morning of March 24, 1978, Eric Davidson, leader of the M&E project team at Harrisburg, sat in his office and reflected on the group's first three months in the plant. The project had not gone well, and Davidson knew that his team members were discouraged. The technical problems they faced were difficult enough, but it seemed that the line organization had resisted almost everything the M&E team had tried to do. In addition to conflicts over responsibility and authority, there were deep disagreements about the sources of the problems and how best to deal with them. Real cooperation was almost nonexistent, and the relationships between team and line personnel in some departments were tense. Davidson felt that a change in the direction of the project had to be made immediately.

As he began to sift through the comments and memos from his team, he recalled what David Leibson, vice president of Manufacturing and Engineering, had said to him shortly after he accepted the Harrisburg assignment:

Eric, this is the M&E group's first major turnaround project and the first real project of any kind in the In-

dustrial Products division. I picked you for this job because you're the kind of guy who gets things done. This is a key one for our group, and I think a big one for the company. In situations like this, you either win big or you lose big. There's very little middle ground.

CORNING GLASS WORKS IN THE 1970s

During the late 1960s and early 1970s Corning Glass Works was a corporation in transition: long a leader in the development of glass and ceramic products for industrial and commercial uses, Corning had entered several consumer goods markets during the 1960s. Under the direction of Lee Waterman, president from 1962 to 1971, Corning developed a strong marketing emphasis to go along with several new consumer products.

Although the public's perception of Corning in the 1960s was no doubt dominated by its well-known Pyrex and Ovenware cooking products, and Pyroceram dinnerware, its most successful consumer-oriented product was actually TV tube casings. Utilizing an innovative glass-forming process, Corning entered the market for TV tube funnels and front plates in 1958 and soon developed a strong market position. Throughout the mid- to late 1960s, growth in TV at Corning was rapid, and the profits at the TV division constituted the backbone of the income statement.

During the heyday of TV, Corning's organization was decentralized. The operating divisions had considerable control over marketing and manufacturing decisions, and corporate staffs in these areas were relatively small. Only in research and development did corporate staff personnel play a major role in the direction of the company. The Technical Staffs Division was responsible for all research and development activities, as well as for manufacturing engineering. New products were regarded as the lifeblood of the corporation, and the director of new product development, Harvey Blackburn, had built a creative and energetic staff. It was Blackburn's group that developed the glass-forming process that

Copyright © 1981 by the President and Fellows of Harvard College. This case was prepared by Kim B. Clark as a basis for class discussion rather than to illustrate either effective or ineffective handling of an administrative situation. Reprinted by permission of the Harvard Business School.

made TV tube production possible, and it was to this group that the corporation looked when growth in the TV division and other consumer products began to slow in the late 1960s.

CHANGES IN TV AND CORPORATE REORGANIZATION

The critical year for the TV division at Corning was 1968. Up to that point, sales and profits had grown rapidly, and Corning had carved out a substantial share of the market. In 1968, however, RCA (a major Corning customer) opened a plant in Ohio to produce glass funnels and front plates. Several of the engineering and management personnel at the new RAC plant were former Corning employees. RCA's decision to integrate backward into glass production had a noticeable effect on the performance of the TV division. Although the business remained profitable, growth over the next three years was much less rapid, and Corning's market share declined.

Slower growth in TV in the 1969–72 period coincided with reduced profitability in other consumer products as costs for labor and basic materials escalated sharply. These developments resulted in weaker corporate financial performance and prompted a reevaluation of the basic direction of the company.

The outcome of these deliberations was a reemphasis of the technical competence of the company in new project development and a focus on process excellence and productivity. A major step in the new approach to operations and production was the establishment of the Manufacturing and Engineering Division (M&E) at the corporate level. This reorganization brought together staff specialists in processes, systems, and equipment under the direction of David Leibson, who was promoted from the job of director of manufacturing at the TV division and was named a corporate vice president.

Shortly after the M&E Division was formed, Thomas MacAvoy, who was the general manager of the Electronics Division and the former direc-

tor of physical research on Corning's technical staff, was named president of the company. MacAvoy was the first Corning president in recent times with a technical background; he had a Ph.D. in chemistry and a strong record in research and development. An internal staff memorandum summed up the issues facing Corning under MacAvoy:

Our analysis of productivity growth at Corning from 1960 to 1970 shows that we performed no better than the average for other glass products manufacturers (2-4 percent per year) and in the last two years have actually been below average. With prices on the increase, improved productivity growth is imperative. At the same time, we have to improve our ability to exploit new products. It appears that research output has, if anything, increased in the last few years (Z-Glass is a prime example), but we have to do a much better job of transferring products from the lab into production.

THE MANUFACTURING AND ENGINEERING DIVISION

Much of the responsibility for improved productivity and the transfer of technology (either product or process) from research to production fell to the new and untried M&E division. Because of the company's historical preference for a small, relatively inactive manufacturing staff, building the M&E group into a strong and effective organization was a considerable challenge. Looking back on the early days, David Leibson reflected on his approach.

I tried to do two things in the first year:

1. Attract people with very strong technical skills in the basic processes and disciplines in use at Corning; and
2. Establish a working relationship with the manufacturing people in the operating divisions. I think the thing that made the difference in that first year was the solid support we got from Tom MacAvoy. It was made clear to all of the division general managers that productivity growth and cost reduction were top priorities.

From 1972 to 1977 engineers from the M&E division were involved in numerous projects throughout Corning involving the installation of new equipment and process changes. A typical project might involve four to five M&E engineers working with a plant organization to install a new type of conveyor system, possibly one designed in the M&E division. The installation project might last three to four months, and the M&E team would normally serve as consultants thereafter.

In addition to equipment projects and internal consulting, the M&E group became involved in the transfer of products from R&D to production. After laboratory development and prototype testing, new products were assigned to an M&E product team which took responsibility for the design of any new equipment required and for engineering and implementing the new process. Leibson felt that successful transfer required people who appreciated both the development process and the problems of production. In many respects M&E product teams served as mediators and translators; especially in the first few projects, their primary task was to establish credibility with R&D group and with the manufacturing people in the operating divisions.

By 1976, the M&E division had conducted projects and helped to transfer new products in most of Corning's divisions, although its role in industrial products was still quite limited. The manufacturing organization in that division had been relatively strong and independent, but Leibson felt that the reputation and expertise of his staff was increasing and that opportunities for collaboration were not far off. He also felt that M&E was ready to take on a completely new kind of responsibility: a turnaround project. From time to time parts of a production process, even whole plants, would experience a deterioration in performance. In some instances, these situations would last for several months and could have serious competitive consequences. It was Leibson's view that a concentrated application of engineering expertise could shorten the turnaround time significantly and could have a measurable impact on overall corporate productivity.

THE Z-GLASS PROJECT

The opportunity for M&E involvement in a major turnaround effort and for collaboration with the Industrial Products division came in late 1977. Since June of that year, yields on the Z-Glass process at the division's Harrisburg plant had experienced a sharp decline (see Exhibit 1). Substantial effort on the part of the plant organization failed to change the downward drift in yields, and in October, Oliver Williams, director of manufacturing for industrial products, met with David Leibson to establish an M&E project at Harrisburg.

Williams, a chemical engineer with an M.B.A. from NYU, had been named director of manufacturing in November of 1976, after 18 years of experience in various engineering and operations positions at Corning. He felt that the importance of the product (corporate expectations for Z-Glass were very high) and the seriousness of the problem warranted strong measures. The agreement he worked out with Leibson called for an M&E project team to work in the plant under the general supervision of a Review Board composed of Leibson, Williams, Martin Abramson, head of process engineering in the M&E division, and Bill Chenevert, head of M&E equipment development

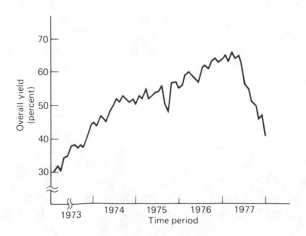

Exhibit 1
Overall Yield 1973–1977

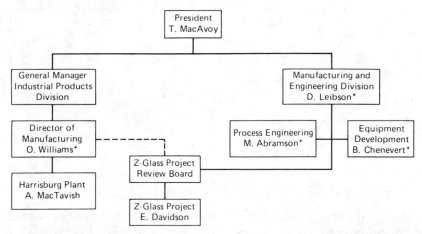

*Indicates members of Review Board.

Exhibit 2
Organization Chart

group. (See Exhibit 2 for an organization chart.) The team's charter was to increase yields, define and document the process and train the operating people (see Exhibit 3). A budget, the size of the team, specific goals, and timetable were to be developed in the first month of the team's operation.

While the plant manager and his staff had not been involved in the decision to bring in the M&E team, Williams and Leibson agreed that their involvement and support were essential. A decision was made to allocate all M&E charges to the Industrial Products division in order to relieve the plant of the extra overhead expense. Moreover, M&E specialists assigned to the project would be located in the plant on a full-time basis.

Since this was M&E's first turnaround project, Leibson was personally involved in the selection of the team leader and key project engineers. He had no trouble finding people willing to work on the project. It was clear to everyone in the M&E group that "turnarounds" were the next major activity for the group and that those working on the first team would be breaking a lot of new ground. Leibson chose Eric Davidson to lead the Harrisburg project. He was 32 years old, had a

masters degree in mechanical engineering from Cornell, and six years of experience at Corning. Davidson had completed several projects in the M&E division, including one in France, and had also worked as an assistant plant manager. A close friend and colleague commented on Davidson's reputation.

To say that Eric is on the fast track is a bit of an understatement. He has been given one challenging assignment after another and has been very successful. The word around M&E is that if you have a tough problem you want solved, just give it to Eric and get out of the way.

Working under Leibson's direction, Davidson spent the first two weeks of his assignment meeting with the plant management and selecting members of the M&E team. At the outset, he chose four specialists to work on the first phase of the project—data collection and problem definition:

Richard Grebwell: 35 years old, an expert in statistical process analysis with 10 years of experience at Corning. While Grebwell was considered by some to be a bit eccentric, his characteristically brilliant use of statistical analysis was vital to the project.

MEMORANDUM

To: E. Davidson E. D.   November 24, 1977
From: Harrisburg project team
Re: Team charter

The charter of the project team is yield improvement as a top priority, definition and documentation of the process, and operator training. Enclosed is a copy of the proposed Process Definition and Documentation Program; it will serve as the framework for process diagnosis and control. Its main elements are as follows:

Priority

1. Define best known *operating setpoint* for each major variable.
2. Establish auditing system to track variables daily with built-in feedback loop.
3. Develop and implement *process troubleshooting* guides.
4. Write and implement *Operating Procedures*.
5. *Train* operating personnel in procedure usage.
6. *Audit* operating procedures on random frequency.
7. Write and implement *Machine Specification Procedures*.

Your comments on the program are encouraged.

Exhibit 3

Jennifer Rigby: 28 years old, with a master's degree in industrial engineering from the University of Texas. She had worked in the Harrisburg plant for six months on her first assignment at Corning.

Arthur Hopkins: 40 years old, a mechanical engineer with 12 years of Corning experience. Hopkins had worked with Davidson on the French project and was, in Davidson's words, a "wizard with equipment."

Frank Arnoldus: 37 years old, a chemist with Corning for six years. He also had worked on the French project and had earned Davidson's admiration for his ability to solve processing problems.

Davidson's plan for the first two to three weeks was to use the small group to identify problems and then expand the team as specific tasks and subprojects were established. His objectives were focused on the long term:

I'm after increases in yields as soon as we can get them, but what I'm really shooting for is permanent improvements in the process. To do what we've got to do to define the process and document its operation.

My whole approach is based on the idea of "receivership": whatever solutions we come up with have to be received, or accepted, by the plant organization. And I mean really accepted; they have to "own" the changes. That's why I will be taking a team approach—each project we do will have two co-leaders, one from M&E (the transferer) and one from the plant (the receiver).

After a brief period to get acquainted and develop a plan, Davidson and his M&E team began working in the plant on December 10, 1977.

Z-GLASS: PRODUCT AND PROCESS

Z-Glass was Corning's code name for a multilayered, compression-molded glass product which was exceptionally strong and impact-resistant for its weight. Its durability and hardness, combined with its low weight and competitive cost, made it an attractive substitute for ceramic and plastic products used in the construction and auto industries. Introduced in 1973, Z-Glass products were an immediate success. From 1973 to 1977 production capacity grew 35 to 40 percent per year and still had failed to keep up with demand (see Exhibit 4). Many people thought that the current array of products was only the beginning of Z-Glass applications.

To Corning's knowledge, no other company in the world had yet developed the capability to make a product like Z-Glass, and if one did, it was assumed that they would have to license the technology from Corning. In fact, much of this technology was still an artform in the sense that a number of the characteristics of most Z-Glass products were not completely explainable in terms of known glass technology: people knew what it could do and roughly why it could do it but were still utilizing trial-and-error methods to perfect existing products and develop new ones.

Z-Glass had been developed by Harvey Blackburn and his staff during the early 1970s. In every sense of the word, the product was Blackburn's "baby." He not only conceived of the idea, but typical of the way Corning operated before the M&E division was created, he and his staff solved numerous technical problems, built all the machinery and equipment needed for prototype production, and even worked in the plant during startup. Furthermore, Blackburn had championed the product in discussions with top management. Several times when the project was not going well, his reputation and skills of persuasion were what kept funding going. When yields began to fall in 1977, engineers at Harrisburg had consulted Blackburn on an ad hoc

	Z1*		Z4†		Z10		Z35		Z12		Total	
	Pieces	Amount	Pieces	Amount	Pieces	Amount	Pieces	Amount	Pieces	Amount	Pieces	Amount
1973	—	—	—	—	119	$2,220.1	495	$5,217.8	—	—	614	$ 7,431.9
1974	—	—	—	—	232	4,315.2	549	6,313.5	—	—	781	10,628.7
1975	384	$ 5,161.5	—	—	239	4,983.2	552	6,513.6	—	—	1,175	16,658.3
1976	784	11,514.2	45	$ 552.3	268	5,831.9	591	7,541.7	82	$1,213.2	1,770	26,653.3
1977	803	12,005.0	407	5,372.4	264	6,087.6	671	8,689.5	534	8,410.5	2,679	40,565.0
1978‡	171	2,565.1	35	493.5	145	1,957.5	250	2,975.2	61	988.3	662	8,979.6

*Introduced in early 1975.
†Introduced in late 1976.
‡Data for 1978 cover reporting periods 1–3 (i.e., first 12 weeks of 1978). Note that because of seasonal factors it is not possible to arrive at an accurate indication of annual output of a particular product by multiplying the 1978 (1–3) results by 13/3.

Exhibit 4
Harrisburg Plant Sales by Product Line 1973–1978 (000s)

basis; he still felt responsible for the product and was a walking encyclopedia of information on its nuances and subtleties.

The Process

The production of Z-Glass products consisted of three main steps: melting, molding, and finishing, which were closely linked and had to be carried out in a fixed time sequence. The process required precise control over the composition and thicknesses of the various glass layers, as well as careful timing and monitoring during the molding and finishing operations. Maintaining this precision in a high-volume environment required continuous, tight controls as well as a "feel" for the process.

Melting

The first step was the preparation of the different types of molten glass which composed the various layers. These mixtures were prepared in separate electrically heated vats, which were designed and built by Corning. Each vat had to be carefully monitored to ensure that the ingredients of the glass were in correct proportion, distributed evenly throughout the vat, and at the appropriate temperature.

The "base" layer was poured continuously onto a narrow (two-three feet) moving strip. The outer layers were poured on top of each other at precisely controlled intervals so that when the layered strip arrived at the molding stage each layer of the multilayered glass sandwich was at the proper temperature and thickness for molding. Minor (and, at the beginning of process development, almost unmeasurable) deviations from the "recipe" could lead to major problems, which often could be solved only on an ad hoc basis utilizing the unprogrammable skill of the operators and technicians.

Some of these problems were clearly identifiable with the melting operation. For example, the existence of "blisters" (tiny bubbles in one or more of the glass layers), "stones" (unmelted bits of sand), and "streaks" (imperfectly melted or mixed ingredients) were observable visually and were obvious indicators of problems. Separation of the different layers, either after the

molding or finishing operations, often could also be traced to improper execution during melting. But when the glass sandwich did not mold properly, there was usually some question as to which operation was at fault.

A process engineer explained the difficulty of melting control:

The secret to avoiding problems at the melting state is maintaining its stability. Sometimes it's easy to tell when something has gone wrong there, but more often you don't find out until something goes wrong at a later stage. And usually it takes a long time to determine whether you've really solved the problem or are simply treating a symptom of a larger problem. It's tough to keep on top of what is going on in each of those melting vats because it's largely a chemical operation.

Despite the difficulty of maintaining control over the melting operation and of correcting it when problems developed, Corning had been able to achieve yields of as high as 95 percent at this stage of the process.

Molding

In contrast to melting, molding was basically a physical operation: rectangles of the soft glass sandwich were cut off the moving strip and moved onto a series of separated conveyor belts. Each slab was inserted between the jaws of a compression-molding device which contained a number of molds for the particular parts being produced. After the parts were stamped out, they continued down the conveyor line while the glass trim was discarded. Depending on the product mix, several conveyors might pool their contents before the parts entered the finishing stage.

Despite the apparent simplicity of this process (problems could be detected quickly and usually corrected quickly), so many different kinds of problems arose and so many different variables could be manipulated that it was generally considered to be even more of a problem to control this stage than the melting stage. Typical problems included the basic dimensional specifications of the product, its edge configuration, and "buckling" and "flattening" after molding. The occurrence of these problems, together with machine downtime associated both with correcting problems and changing the product mix, made it difficult to achieve more than an 80 percent efficiency (good output to rated machine capacity) during this stage of the process.

Finishing

The finishing operation consisted of heat treating the molded objects, then applying one of a variety of possible coatings to them. Heat treating both stabilized the internal tensions generated by the molding operation and appeared to improve the lamination between the various layers of the glass sandwich as well. Since it required a precise sequence of temperatures and their duration, this operation took place while the objects passed through long ovens on their conveyor belts. It usually did not present a problem, but if cracks or layer separation occurred, the heat-treating operation was sometimes the cause.

The application of coatings, on the other hand, was more of a job-shop operation and could be done off-line. There were a number of possible kinds of coatings that could be applied, from either purely practical (improving the reflective, insulating, or electrical conducting properties of surface) to purely ornamental. Sometimes decals were also applied either in place of or in addition to a coating. The number of possible coatings was steadily increasing, and one process engineer characterized the process as "a continual bother: lots of short runs but a necessity to maintain high speeds." The target yield was 95 percent, but it was seldom attained.

The differing characteristics of the three stages made overall control and fine-tuning of the total process quite difficult. The backgrounds and skills of the "hot end" workers were very different from those at the "cold end," and completely different branches of engineering were involved. When problems arose, many of them were undetectable for some time and often only showed up during destructive testing of parts after they had proceeded completely through the process. Then it was often difficult to isolate which part of the process was at fault because there appeared to be a high degree of interrelation between them. And finally, once a problem and its cause were identified, it sometimes took a long period of trial-and-error fiddling until people could be convinced that it was indeed corrected.

THE HARRISBURG PLANT

The decision to put Z-Glass into the Harrisburg plant had been based on its availability. Long devoted to the production of headlights and other auto products (the plant was built in 1958), the plant had experienced several years of excess capacity in the late 1960s. In 1972, headlight production was consolidated in the Farwell, Ohio, plant, and Harrisburg was set up for Z-Glass production. Several of the production foremen and manufacturing staff members were transferred to Farwell and replaced by individuals who had been involved in Z-Glass prototype production. (Exhibit 5 contains a profit and loss statement for the Harrisburg plant in 1975–76.)

The plant manager at Harrisburg was Andrew MacTavish, a 54-year-old native of Scotland. He came to the United States shortly after World War II and began working at Corning as a helper on a shipping crew at the old main plant. Over the years, MacTavish had worked his way up through various supervisory positions to production superintendent and finally to plant manager. He was a large man with a ruddy complexion and a deep booming voice. Although his temper was notorious, most people who had worked with him felt that some of his notorious tirades were more than a little calculated. Whatever peoples' perceptions of his personality might be, there was no question as to who was in charge at Harrisburg.

In mid-1977 MacTavish had been at Harrisburg for six years. From the beginning he had developed a reputation as a champion of the "little people," as he called them. He wore what the workers wore and spent two to three hours each day on the factory floor talking with foremen, supervisors, and production workers. If he had a philosophy of plant operations, it was to keep

Z-Glass Project
Harrisburg Plant
Profit and Loss Statement, 1976–77
($000)

	1976	1977
Sales*	$26,653.3	$40,565.0
Direct expenses		
Materials	9,947.2	16,214.2
Labor	3,714.3	6,194.7
Gross profit	12,991.8	18,156.1
Manufacturing overhead		
Fixed†	6,582.6	11,016.9
Variable‡	1,429.3	2,114.4
Plant administrative expenses	1,784.5	2,715.2
Plant profit	$ 3,195.4	$ 2,219.6

*Capacity utilization (on a nominal sales basis) was 92 percent in 1976 and 84 percent in 1977.
†Includes depreciation, insurance, taxes, maintenance, utilities, and supervision.
‡Includes fringe benefits, indirect labor and tools, and supplies.

Exhibit 5

management as close to the people as possible and to rely on the experience, judgment, and skill of his workers in solving problems.

The Harrisburg plant was organized along department lines, with a production superintendent responsible for three general foremen who managed the melting, forming, and finishing departments. Ron Lewis, production superintendent, had come to the plant in 1975 after eight years of Corning experience. He was quietly efficient and had developed a good rapport with the foremen and supervisors. Besides Lewis, three other managers reported to MacTavish: Al Midgely, director of maintenance and engineering; Arnie Haggstrom, director of production planning and inventory control; and Royce Ferguson, head of personnel.

By June of 1977 the management group at the Harrisburg plant had worked together for two years and had established what MacTavish thought was a solid organization. Speaking to a visitor in May of 1977 he commented:

I've seen a lot of plant organizations in my time, but this one has worked better than any of them. When we sit down in staff meetings every morning, everyone is on top of their situation, and we've learned to get to the heart of our problems quickly. With the different personalities around here you'd think it would be a dogfight, but these people really work together.

Of all the managers on his staff, MacTavish worked most closely with Al Midgely. Midgely, 46 years old, had come to the plant with Mac-Tavish, had a B.S. in mechanical engineering, and was regarded as a genius when it came to equipment ("He can build or fix anything," Mac-Tavish claimed). He was devoted to MacTavish:

Ten years ago, Andy MacTavish saved my life. I had some family problems after I lost my job at Bausch and Lomb, but Andy gave me a chance and helped me pick up the pieces. Everything I have I owe to him.

Several other people in the Harrisburg plant gratefully acknowledge MacTavish's willingness to help his people.

THE M&E PROJECT AT HARRISBURG

Davidson's first priority in the first two weeks of the project was to define the problem. Overall yields had declined, but there had been no analysis of available information to identify the major causes. It seemed clear to the M&E group that the plant organization had spent its time on firefighting during the past six months, and there had been little overall direction. Richard Grebwell concerned himself with analyzing the historical data collected by the production control department. The rest of the team spent the first two weeks familiarizing themselves with the process, meeting with their counterparts in the plant organization, and meeting together to compare notes and develop hypotheses about what was going on.

One problem surfaced immediately: the relative inexperience of the department supervisors. As MacTavish explained to them, four of the six supervisors had been in the plant less than nine months. The people they replaced had been with the Z-Glass process since its prototype days. MacTavish felt that part of the explanation for the decline in yields was the departure of people who knew and understood the process extremely well. He expressed confidence in the new people and indicated that they were rapidly becoming quite knowledgeable.

Grebwell's preliminary statistical work (see Exhibit 6) pointed to the molding department as the primary source of defects, with finishing the second major source. The team identified four areas for immediate attention: overall downtime, trim settings, glass adhesion, and layer separation. As Grebwell's work proceeded, other projects in other departments were identified, and additional staff members were added to the team. By the middle of January it was evident that the overall project would have to encompass activities throughout the plant. It was decided that the only way to measure performance equitably was to use overall yield improvement. A timetable for improved yields was established and approved by the Review Board in late January of 1978.

Davidson commented on the first six weeks of the project:

Our initial reception in the plant was lukewarm. People were a little wary of us at first, but we did establish a pretty good relationship with Ron Lewis and some of the people in the production control group. I was con-
fident that with time we could work together with MacTavish and people in other departments, but I wasn't as confident that the problems themselves could be solved. My objective was to obtain long-term improvements by defining and documenting the process, but when I arrived I found an inadequate data base and a process more complex than anyone had imagined.

Davidson also found resistance to the very idea of process documentation. The view of MacTavish and other people in the plant was aptly summarized by Harvey Blackburn, who appeared in Harrisburg off and on throughout the first three months of the M&E project. On one such visit he took Davidson into a conference room and had the following conversation:

Blackburn (after drawing on the blackboard): Do you know what this is? This is a corral and inside the corral is a bucking bronco. Now what do you suppose this is?

Davidson: It looks like a cowboy with a book in his hand.

Blackburn: That's right, sonny, it's a greenhorn cowboy trying to learn how to ride a bucking bronco by reading a book. And that's just what you are trying to do with all your talk about documentation. And you'll end right where the greenhorn is going to end up: flat on your face.

THE EMERGENCE OF CONFLICT

Following the Review Board's acceptance of the proposed timetable, it was Davidson's intent to create subproject teams, with an M&E specialist and a plant representative as co-leaders. Despite Blackburn's lecture, Davidson pressed ahead with plans for process definition and documentation. A key element of the program was the development of instrumentation to collect information on the critical operating variables (glass temperature, machine speeds, timing, and so forth). Beginning in early January, Frank Arnoldus had spent three weeks quietly observing the process, asking questions of the operators, and working on the development of instruments. He had decided to debug and confirm the systems on one production line (there were five separate lines in the plant) before transferring the instruments to other lines.

MEMORANDUM

To: M&E Project Team
From: R. Grebwell
Re: Yield report for December 1977

Below are data on yields in period 13 (provided by the production control department) along with notes based on preliminary observations. Rejects are based on 100 percent inspection. Note that selecting a reason for rejection is based on the concept of "principal cause"—if more than one defect is present, the inspector must designate one as the primary reason for rejection.

Harrisburg Plant
Yield Report Period 13, 1977

	Good Output as a Percent of Rated Capacity[a]					Downtime[b] as a Percent of Total Available Time
	Z1	Z4	Z10	Z35	Z12	
I. Melting:						
Glass	70.4	65.4	72.3	73.5	66.9	—
Equipment downtime	—	—	—	—	—	10.3

	Percent Rejected by Product, Reason, and Department[c]					Downtime[b] as a Percent of Total Available Time
	Z1	Z4	Z10	Z35	Z12	
II. Molding and finishing:						
A. Molding						
Trim[d]	6.4	12.8	4.1	3.4	10.2	—
Structural	3.7	6.2	1.7	2.8	5.7	—
Adhesion	4.5	8.3	2.5	3.1	8.5	—
Downtime	—	—	—	—	—	15.2
B. Finishing						
Cracks	0.8	4.2	.03	1.2	3.6	—
Separation	2.6	3.8	1.5	2.2	4.4	—
Coatings	1.9	2.4	0.6	1.7	2.1	—
Downtime	—	—	—	—	—	12.6

Exhibit 6

	Good Output as a Percent of Rated Capacity					
	Z1	**Z4**	**Z10**	**Z35**	**Z12**	**Total**
III. Summary:[e]						
Melting	70.4	65.4	72.3	73.5	66.9	—
Molding	72.4	61.6	77.8	76.9	64.1	—
Finishing	82.8	78.3	85.3	82.9	78.6	—
Overall	42.2	31.5	48.0	46.9	33.7	40.7

[a] This is overall yield and includes the effects of glass defects as well as downtime.

[b] No data are available on equipment downtime by product; the overall figure is applied to each product.

[c] The data are presented by department. They indicate the percentage of *department* output rejected and the principal reason for rejection. Total overall process yield (good output as a percent of rated capacity) depends on both product defects and downtime.

[d] The reasons for rejection breakdown as follows:

Molding:

Trim: This is basically two things—dimensions and edge configuration. It looks to me like the biggest problem is with the edges. The most common cause of defects in the runs I have watched is that the settings drift out of line. Apparently this depends on where the settings are established, how they are adjusted, and the quality of the glass.

Structural: Pieces are rejected if they buckle or if the surface has indentations. This one is a real mystery—it could be a problem with the equipment (not right specs) or the operating procedures. Without some testing it's hard to tell. One possibility we need to check is whether the temperature of the incoming glass is a factor.

Adhesion: If compression ratios are too low or if the glass temperature is not "just right" or the glass has stones, then the glass adheres to the surface of the molds. The operators check the ratios, but the ideal range is marked on the gauges with little bits of tape, and I suspect the margin of error is pretty large.

Finishing:

Cracks: Pieces sometimes develop cracks after heat treating. The principal suspect is consistency of temperature and flame zone. It is very hard to tell whether this is due to poor initial settings or changes in flames once the process starts. Inconsistencies in the material may be another source of cracks.

Layer separation: Layer separation seems to be caused by same factors as cracks.

Coatings: This is almost entirely a problem of operator error—handling damage, poor settings on the equipment, inattention to equipment going out of spec, and so forth.

[e] There are four steps to calculating overall yield:

1. For a given product in a given department, add up reject rates by reason and subtract from 1.
2. Then multiply by (1 – percent downtime) to get department yield for that product (e.g., molding yield for Z12 = (1 – .244) (1 – .152) = .641).
3. Multiply department yields to get overall yield by product (e.g., yield for Z12 = .669 × .641 × .786 = 337).
4. To get overall yield, take a weighted average of product yields, with share in total output (on a total-pieces basis) as weights: in period 13 these weights were Z1 = .3, Z4 = .15, Z10 = .10, Z35 = .25, and Z12 = .2.

Exhibit 6
Continued

The instrumentation project was scheduled to begin on February 1, with the installation of sensors to monitor glass temperature in the molding process. However, no plant representative for the project had been designated by that time, and Davidson postponed the installation. A series of meetings between Davidson and MacTavish then followed, but it was not until two days before the next Review Board meeting on February 23 that plant representatives for each subproject were chosen. Even then, things did not go smoothly. Frank Arnoldus described his experience:

I didn't want to impose the instrumentation program on the people; I wanted them to understand that it was a tool to help them do their jobs better. But I had a terrible time getting Hank Gordel (the co-leader of the project team) to even talk to me. He claimed he was swamped with other things. The thing of it is, he *was* busy. The plant engineering group had several projects of their own going, and those people were working 15 hours a day. But I knew there was more to it than that when people stopped talking to me and even avoided me in elevators and the cafeteria.

The other subprojects suffered a similar fate. The only team to make any progress was the group working on materials control. Ron Lewis thought the program was a good one, and he supported it; he had appointed one of his better supervisors to be co-leader. In the other areas of the plant, however, little was accomplished. Attempts to deal with people in the plant organization on an informal basis (lunch, drinks after work) were not successful, and Davidson's meetings with MacTavish and his requests for support were not fruitful. Indeed, it was MacTavish's view that the M&E team was part of the problem. His view was expressed forcefully in a meeting with Davidson in late March of 1978:

I've said right from the beginning that this yield problem is basically a people problem. My experienced production people were promoted out from under me, and it has taken a few months for the new people to get up to speed. But this kind of thing is not going to happen again. I've been working on a supervisor backup training program that will give me some bench strength.

I'm not saying we don't have problems. I know there are problems with the process, but the way to solve them is to get good people and give them some room. What this process needs now is some stability. Last year two new products were introduced, and this year I've got you and your engineers out there with your experiments and your projects, fiddling around with my equipment and bothering my people.

And then there's Blackburn. He blows in here with some crazy idea and goes right out there on the floor and gets the operators to let him try out his latest scheme. The best thing for this plant right now would be for all of you to just get out and let us get this place turned around.

I am convinced we can do it. In fact, we've already been doing it. You've seen the data for the last 12 weeks.[1] Yields have been increasing steadily, and we're now above average for last year. While you people have been making plans and writing memos, we've been solving the problem.

RESOLVING THE CRISIS

Eric Davidson sat at his desk in the Harrisburg plant on March 24, 1978, and reviewed the events of the last three months. He realized that he also had been guilty of excessive firefighting and had not taken the time to step back from the situation and plot out a course of action. The situation demanded careful thought.

He was genuinely puzzled by the recent improvement in yield performance; since the M&E team had done very little beyond data analysis, the improvement must have come from somewhere else. All his training and experience supported the concept of definition and documentation, but he had never encountered such a complex process. Perhaps MacTavish was right ...but he just couldn't bring himself to believe that.

Several options came to mind as he thought of ways to resolve the crisis; none of them were appealing. He could go to Leibson and Williams and ask (demand?) that MacTavish be replaced with someone more supportive. He could continue to try to build alliances with supporters in the plant (there were a few such people) and get a foothold in the organization. Or he could develop a new approach to the problem (perhaps new people?) and attempt to win over MacTavish. Davidson knew that his handling of this situation could have important consequences for the M&E Division, for the company, and for the careers of several people, including his own.

---

[1]Data from the preliminary yield report are presented in Exhibits 7 and 8.

Exhibit 7
Yields and Downtime, 1976–1978

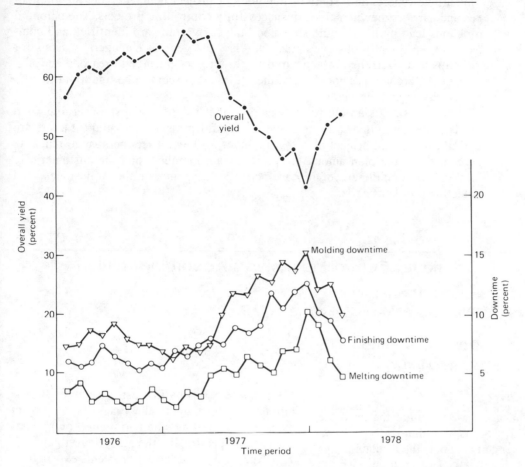

Exhibit 8
Harrisburg Plant Summary of Yields, Period 3, 1978

Department	Z1	Z4	Z10	Z35	Z12	Total
	Product Lines					
Melting	74.6	69.3	76.6	77.9	70.9	—
Molding	79.7	71.3	83.5	83.8	72.4	—
Finishing	85.8	83.7	88.7	87.6	84.9	—
Overall	51.0	41.4	56.7	57.2	43.6	53.4

11.16 READING

This article reports on a study of hundreds of project managers and the challenges and barriers they perceived in successfully controlling projects. The potential problems leading to schedule slips and budget overruns are identified and compared to the directly observed reasons. Also, the general managers' reasons for the slips and overruns are compared to the project managers' reasons and significant differences are noted. Last, the criteria that seem to be important to control are listed and discussed.

The value of this article for managers is the insight it gives concerning what needs to be controlled to bring about successful projects. The major factors are defining a detailed project plan that includes all key project personnel, reaching agreement on the plan among the project team members and the customer, obtaining the commitment of management, defining measurable milestones, and detecting problems early.

Criteria for Controlling Projects According to Plan

Hans J. Thamhain
Worchester Polytechnic Institute

David L. Wilemon
Syracuse University

INTRODUCTION

Few project managers would argue the need for controlling their projects according to established plans. The challenge is to apply the available tools and techniques effectively. That is, to manage the effort by leading the multifunctional personnel toward the agreed-on objectives within the given time and resource constraints. Even the most experienced practitioners often find it difficult to control programs in spite of apparent detail in the plan, personnel involvement, and even commitment. As summarized in Table 1, effective program management is a function of properly defining the work, budgets and schedules and then monitoring progress. Equally important, it is related to the ability to keep personnel involved and interested in the work, to obtain and refuel commitment from the team as well as from upper management, and to resolve some of the enormous complexities on the technical, human and organizational side.

Responding to this interest, a field study was initiated to investigate the practices of project managers regarding their project control experiences. Specifically, the study investigates:

1. Type of project control problems experienced by project managers.
2. Project management practices and performance.
3. Criteria for effective project control.

METHOD OF INVESTIGATION

Data were collected over a period of three years from a sample of over 400 project leaders in predominantly technical undertakings, such as electronics, petrochemical, construction, and pharmaceutical projects. The data were collected mostly by questionnaires from attendees of project manage-

© 1986 by the Project Management Institute. Reprinted from *Project Management Journal,* June 1986, pp. 75–81, by permission.

Table 1
Challenges of Managing Projects According to Plan

Rank	Challenge	Frequency (Mentioned by % of PMs)
1	Coping with End-Date Driven Schedules	85%
2	Coping with Resource Limitations	83%
3	Communicating Effectively among Task Groups	80%
4	Gaining Commitment from Team Members	74%
5	Establishing Measurable Milestones	70%
6	Coping with Changes	60%
7	Working Out Project Plan Agreement with Team	57%
8	Gaining Commitment from Management	45%
9	Dealing with Conflict	42%
10	Managing Vendors and Subcontractors	38%
11	Other Challenges	35%

ment workshops and seminars, as well as during in-plant consulting work conducted by the authors. Selectively, questionnaires were followed up by personal interviews. All data were checked for relevant sourcing to assure that the people who filled in the questionnaire had the minimum project leadership qualifications we established. These included: Two years of experience in managing multidisciplinary projects, leading a minimum of three other project professionals, and being formally accountable for final results.

SAMPLE CHARACTERISTICS

The final qualifying sample included 304 project leaders from 183 technical projects. Each leader had an average of 5.2 years of project management experience. As shown by the sigma/standard deviation[1] the sample data are distributed widely:

Number of Project Leaders in Sample   304
Number of Projects in Sample   183
Number of Project Leaders
  per Project   1.66 ($\sigma = 1$)
Project Size (Average) $850K ($\sigma = 310K$)
Project Duration (Average)   12 Months ($\sigma = 4$)
Multidisciplinary Nature
  (Average)   8 Team Members ($\sigma = 5$)
Project Management
  Experience/PM   5.2 Years ($\sigma = 2.5$)

[1]The distribution of the sample data is skewed. The sigma/standard deviation listed in parentheses corresponds to the positive side only.

Number of Previous
  Projects/PM   6 ($\sigma = 4.5$)

Data were collected in three specific modes: (1) Open-ended questions leading to a broad set of data, such as condensed in Table 2, and used for broad classifications and further, more detailed investigations; (2) Specific questions, requested to be answered on a tested five-point scale, such as shown in Figure 1. The scores enabled subsequent data ranking and correlation analysis; and (3) Interviews leading to a discussion of the previous findings and further qualitative investigations into the practices and experiences of project managers and their superiors.

All associations were measured by utilizing Kendall's Tau rank-order correlation. The agreement between project managers and their superiors on the reason for project control problems was tested by using the nonparametric Kruskal-Wallis one-way analysis of variance by ranks, setting the null-hypothesis for agreement at various confidence levels depending on the strength of the agreement or disagreement as specified in the write-up.

DISCUSSION OF RESULTS

The results of this study are being presented in four parts. First, the reasons for poor project control are analyzed as they relate to budget overruns and schedule slips. Second, the less tangible criteria

Table 2
Potential Problems* (Subtle Reasons) Leading
to Schedule Slips and Budget Overruns

01 Difficulty of Defining Work in Sufficient Detail
02 Little Involvement of Project Personnel During Planning
03 Problems with Organizing and Building Project Team
04 No Firm Agreement to Project Plan by Functional Management
05 No Clear Charter for Key Project Personnel
06 Insufficiently Defined Project Team Organization
07 No Clear Role/Responsibility Definition for P-Personnel
08 Rush into Project Kick-off
09 Project Perceived as Not Important or Exciting
10 No Contingency Provisions
11 Inability to Measure True Project Performance
12 Poor Communications with Upper Management
13 Poor Communications with Customer or Sponsor
14 Poor Understanding of Organizational Interfaces
15 Difficulty in Working across Functional Lines
16 No Ties between Project Performance and Reward System
17 Poor Project Leadership
18 Weak Assistance and Help from Upper Management
19 Project Leader Not Involved with Team
20 Ignorant of Early Warning Signals and Feedback
21 Poor Ability to Manage Conflict
22 Credibility Problems with Task Leaders
23 Difficulties in Assessing Risks
24 Insensitivity to Organizational Culture/Value System
25 Insufficient Formal Procedural Project Guidelines
26 Apathy or Indifference by Project Team or Management
27 No Mutual Trust among Team Members
28 Too Much Unresolved/Dysfunctional Conflict
29 Power Struggles
30 Too Much Reliance on Established Cost Accounting System

*The tabulated potential problems represent summaries of data compiled during interviews with project personnel and management.

for these control problems are discussed. This part shows that many of the reasons blamed for poor project performance, such as insufficient front-end planning and underestimating the complexities and scope, are really rooted in some less obvious organizational, managerial, and interpersonal problems. Third, the relationship between project performance and project management problems is discussed, and fourth, the criteria for effective project controls are summarized.

The Reasons for Poor Project Control

Figure 1 summarizes an investigation into 15 problem areas regarding their effects on poor project performance. Specifically, project managers and their superiors (such as senior functional managers and general managers) indicate on a five-point scale their perception of how frequently certain problems are responsible for schedule slips and budget overruns. The data indicate that project leaders perceive these problem areas in a somewhat different order than their superiors.

While *project leaders* most frequently blame the following reasons as being responsible for poor project performance:

1. Customer and Management Changes
2. Technical Complexities
3. Unrealistic Project Plans
4. Staffing Problems
5. Inability to Detect Problems Early,

senior management ranks these reasons somewhat differently:

1. Insufficient Front-End Planning
2. Unrealistic Project Plans
3. Underestimated Project Scope
4. Customer and Management Changes
5. Insufficient Contingency Planning

On balance, the data support the findings of subsequent interviews that project leaders are more concerned with external influences such as changes, complexities, staffing, and priorities while senior mangers focus more on what should and can be done to avoid problems.

In fact, the differences between project

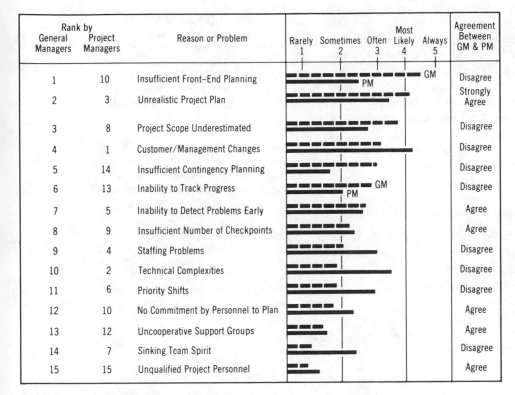

Rank by General Managers	Rank by Project Managers	Reason or Problem	Rarely 1	Sometimes 2	Often 3	Most Likely 4	Always 5	Agreement Between GM & PM
1	10	Insufficient Front–End Planning					GM	Disagree
2	3	Unrealistic Project Plan						Strongly Agree
3	8	Project Scope Underestimated						Disagree
4	1	Customer/Management Changes						Disagree
5	14	Insufficient Contingency Planning						Disagree
6	13	Inability to Track Progress			GM			Disagree
7	5	Inability to Detect Problems Early						Agree
8	9	Insufficient Number of Checkpoints						Agree
9	4	Staffing Problems						Disagree
10	2	Technical Complexities						Disagree
11	6	Priority Shifts						Disagree
12	10	No Commitment by Personnel to Plan						Agree
13	12	Uncooperative Support Groups						Agree
14	7	Sinking Team Spirit						Disagree
15	15	Unqualified Project Personnel						Agree

Figure 1   Directly Observed Reasons for Schedule Slips and Budget Overruns

leaders' and senior/superior management's perceptions were measured statistically by using a Kruskal-Wallis analysis of variance by ranks, based on the following test statistics:

Strong Agreement: If acceptable at > 99% confidence

Agreement: If acceptable at > 90% confidence

Weak Agreement: If acceptable at > 80% confidence

Disagreement: If rejected at 80% confidence

Project leaders disagree with their superiors on the ranking of importance for all but six reasons. What this means is that while both groups of management actually agree on the basic reasons behind schedule slips and budget overruns, they attach different weights. The practical implication of this finding is that senior management expects proper project planning, organizing, and tracking from project leaders. They further believe that the "external" criteria, such as customer changes and project complexities, impact project performance only if the project had not been defined properly and sound management practices were ignored. On the other side, management's view that some of the subtle problems, such as sinking team spirit, priority shifts, and staffing, are of lesser importance might point to a potential problem area. Management might be less sensitive to these struggles, get less involved, and provide less assistance in solving these problems.

Less Obvious and Less Visible Reasons for Poor Performance

Managers at all levels have long lists of "real" reasons why the problems identified in Figure 1 occur. They point out, for instance, that while insufficient front-end planning eventually got the project into trouble, the real culprits are much less obvious and visible. These subtle reasons, summarized in Table 2, strike a common theme. They relate strongly to organizational, managerial, and human aspects. In fact, the most frequently mentioned reasons for poor project performance can be classified in five categories:

1. Problems with organizing project team
2. Weak project leadership
3. Communication problems
4. Conflict and confusion
5. Insufficient upper management involvement

Most of the problems in Table 2 relate to the manager's ability to foster a work environment conducive to multidisciplinary teamwork, rich in professionally stimulating and interesting activities, involvement, and mutual trust. The ability to foster such a high-performance project environment requires sophisticated skills in leadership, technical, interpersonal, and administrative areas. To be effective, project managers must consider all facets of the job. They must consider the task, the people, the tools and the organization. The days of the manager who gets by with technical expertise or pure administrative skills alone, are gone. Today the project manager must relate socially as well as technically. He or she must understand the culture and value system of the organization. Research[2] and experience show that effective project management is directly related to the level of proficiency at which these skills are mastered. This is also reflected in the 30 potential problems of our study (See Table 2) and the rank-order correlations summarized in Table 3. As indicated by the correlation figure of $\tau = +.45$, the stronger managers felt about the reasons in Fig-

[2] For a detailed discussion of skill requirements of project managers and their impact on project performance see H. J. Thamhain & D. L. Wilemon, "Skill Requirements of Project Managers," *Convention Record, IEEE Joint Engineering Management Conference,* October 1978, and H. J. Thamhain, "Developing Engineering Management Skills" in *Management of R & D and Engineering,* North Holland Publishing Company, 1986.

Table 3
Correlation of Project Management Practices to Performance

Potential Problems vs. Actual	Correlation of (1) Potential Problems (Table 2) and (2) Directly Observed Reasons for Budget and Schedule Slips (Figure 1)	$\tau = -.45$**
Potential Problems vs. Performance	Correlation of (1) Potential Problems Leading for Budget and Schedule Slips (Table 2) and (2) Project Performance (Top Management Judgment)	$\tau = -.55$**
Actual Problems vs. Performance	Correlation of (1) Directly Observed Reasons for Budget and Schedule Slips (Figure 1) and (2) Project Performance	$\tau = -.40$**

**99% Confidence Level ($p = .01$)
All Tau values are Kendall Tau Rank-Order Correlation

ure 1, the stronger they also felt about the problems in Table 2 as reasons for poor project performance. This correlation is statistically significant at a confidence level of 99% and supports the conclusion that both sets of problem areas are related and require similar skills for effective management.

Management Practice and Project Performance

Managers appear very confident in citing actual and potential problems. These managers are sure in their own mind that these problems, summarized in Figure 1 and Table 2, are indeed related to poor project performance. However, no such conclusion could be drawn without additional data and the specific statistical test shown in Table 3. As indicated by the strongly negative correlations between project performance and (1) potential problems ($\tau = -.55$) and (2) actual problems ($\tau = -.40$), the presence of either problem will indeed result in lower performance. Specifically, the stronger and more frequently project managers experience these problems, the lower was the manager judged by superior managers regarding overall on-time and on-budget performance.

Furthermore, it is interesting to note that the more subtle potential problems correlate most strongly to poor performance ($\tau = -.55$). In fact, special insight has been gained by analyzing the association of each problem to project performance separately. Taken together, it shows that the following problems seem to be some of the most crucial *barriers* to high project performance:

- Team organization and staffing problems
- Work perceived not important, challenging, having growth potential
- Little team and management involvement during planning
- Conflict, confusion, power struggle
- Lacking commitment by team and management
- Poor project definition
- Difficulty in understanding and working across organizational interfaces
- Weak project leadership
- Measurability problems
- Changes, contingencies, and priority problems
- Poor communications, management involvement and support

To be effective, project leaders must not only recognize the potential barriers to performance, but also know where in the life cycle of the project they most likely occur. The effective project leader takes preventive actions early in the project life cycle and fosters a work environment that is conducive to active participation, interesting work, good communications, management involvement, and low conflict.

CRITERIAL FOR EFFECTIVE PROJECT CONTROL

The results presented so far focused on the reasons for poor project performance. That is, what went wrong and why were analyzed. This section concentrates on the lessons learned from the study and extensive interviews investigating the forces driving high project performance. Accordingly, this section summarizes the criteria which seem to be important for controlling projects according to

plan. The write-up follows a recommendations format and flows with the project through its life cycle wherever possible.

1. *Detailed Project Planning.* Develop a detailed project plan, involving all key personnel, defining the specific work to be performed, the timing, the resources, and the responsibilities.

2. *Break the overall program into phases and subsystems.* Use Work Breakdown Structure (WBS) as a planning tool.

3. *Results and Deliverables.* Define the program objectives and requirements in terms of specifications, schedule, resources and deliverable items for the total program and its subsystems.

4. *Measurable Milestones.* Define measurable milestones and checkpoints throughout the program. Measurability can be enhanced by defining specific results, deliverables, technical performance measures against schedule and budget.

5. *Commitment.* Obtain commitment from all key personnel regarding the program plan, its measures and results. This commitment can be enhanced and maintained by involving the team members early in the project planning, including the definition of results, measurable milestones, schedules and budgets. It is through this involvement that the team members gain a detailed understanding of the work to be performed, develop professional interests in the project and desires to succeed, and eventually make a firm commitment toward the specific task and the overall project objectives.

6. *Intra-Program Involvement.* Assure that the interfacing project teams, such as engineering and manufacturing, work together, not only during the task transfer, but during the total life of the project. Such interphase involvement is necessary to assure effective implementation of the developments and to simply assure "doability" and responsiveness to the realities of the various functions supporting the project. It is enhanced by clearly defining the results/deliverables for each interphase point, agreed upon by both parties. In addition, a simple sign-off procedure, which defines who

has to sign off on what items, is useful in establishing clear checkpoints for completion and to enhance involvement and cooperation of the interphasing team members.

7. *Project Tracking.* Define and implement a proper project tracking system which captures and processes project performance data conveniently summarized for reviews and management actions.

8. *Measurability.* Assure accurate measurements of project performance data, especially technical progress against schedule and budget.

9. *Regular Reviews.* Projects should be reviewed regularly, both on a work package (subsystem) level and total project level.

10. *Signing-On.* The process of "signing-on" project personnel during the initial phases of the project or each task seems to be very important to a proper understanding of the project objectives, the specific tasks, and personal commitment. The sign-on process that is so well described in Tracy Kidder's book, *The Soul of a New Machine,* is greatly facilitated by sitting down with each team member and discussing the specific assignments, overall project objectives, as well as professional interests and support needs.

11. *Interesting Work.* The project leader should try to accommodate the professional interests and desires of supporting personnel when negotiating their tasks. Project effectiveness depends on the manager's ability to provide professionally stimulating and interesting work. This leads to increased project involvement, better communications, lower conflict, and stronger commitment. This is an environment where people work toward established objectives in a self-enforcing mode requiring a minimum of managerial controls. Although the scope of a project may be fixed, the project manager usually has a degree of flexibility in allocating task assignments among various contributors.

12. *Communication.* Good communication is essential for effective project work. It is the responsibility of the task leaders and ultimately the project manager to provide the appropriate communication tools, techniques, and systems. These tools are not only the status meetings, reviews, schedules, and reporting systems, but also the objective statements, specifications, list of deliverables, the sign-off procedure and critical path analysis. It is up to the project leaders to orchestrate the various tools and systems, and to use them effectively.

13. *Leadership.* Assure proper program direction and leadership throughout the project life cycle. This includes project definition, team organization, task coordination, problem identification and a search for solutions.

14. *Minimize Threats.* Project managers must foster a work environment that is low on personal conflict, power struggles, surprises, and unrealistic demands. An atmosphere of mutual trust is necessary for project personnel to communicate problems and concerns candidly and at an early point in time.

15. *Design a Personnel Appraisal and Reward System.* This should be consistent with the responsibilities of the people.

16. *Assure Continuous Senior Management Involvement, Endorsement, and Support of the Project.* This will surround the project with a priority image, enhance its visibility, and refuel overall commitment to the project and its objectives.

17. *Personal Drive.* Project managers can influence the climate of the work environment by their own actions. Concern for project team members, ability to integrate personal goals and needs of project personnel with project goals, and ability to create personal enthusiasm for the project itself can foster a climate of high motivation, work involvement, open communication, and ultimately high project performance.

A FINAL NOTE

Managing engineering programs toward established performance, schedule, and cost targets requires more than just another plan. It requires the total commitment of the performing organization plus the involvement and help of the sponsor/customer community. Successful program managers stress the importance of carefully designing the project planning and control system as well as the structural and authority relationships. All are critical to the implementation of an effective project control system. Other organizational issues, such as management style, personnel appraisals and compensation, and intraproject communication, must be carefully considered to make the system self-forcing; that is, project personnel throughout the organization must feel that participation in the project is desirable regarding the fulfillment of their professional needs and wants. Furthermore, project personnel must be convinced that management involvement is helpful in their work. Personnel must be convinced that identifying the true project status and communicating potential problems early will provide them with more assistance to problem solving, more cross-functional support, and in the end will lead to project success and the desired recognition for their accomplishments.

In summary, effective control of engineering programs or projects involves the ability to:

- Work out a detailed project plan, involving all key personnel
- Reach agreement on the plan among the project team members and the customer/sponsor
- Obtain commitment from the project team members
- Obtain commitment from management
- Define measurable milestones
- Attract and hold quality people
- Establish a controlling authority for each work package
- Detect problems early

REFERENCES

1. Adams, J. R., & Barndt, S. E. Behavioral Implications of the Project Life Cycle, Chapter 12 in D. D. Cleland and W. R. King, *Project Management Handbook.* New York: Van Nostrand Reinhold, 1983.
2. Archibald, Russel C. Planning the Project. In *Managing High-Technology Programs and Projects.* New York: Wiley, 1976.
3. Casher, J. D. How to Control Project Risks and Effectively Reduce the Chance of Failure. *Management Review,* June, 1984.
4. Delaney, W. A. Management by Phases. *Advanced Management Journal,* Winger, 1984.
5. King, W. R. & Cleland, D. I. Life Cycle Management. Chapter 11 in D. D. Cleland and W. R. King, *Project Management Handbook.* New York: Van Nostrand Reinhold, 1983.
6. McDounough, E. F., & Kinnunen, R. M. Management Control of a New Product Development Project. *IEEE Transactions on Engineering Management,* February, 1984.
7. Pessemier, E. A. *Product Management.* New York: Wiley, 1982.
8. Spirer, H. F. Phasing out the Project. Chapter 13 in D. D. Cleland and W. R. King, *Project Management Handbook.* New York: Van Nostrand Reinhold, 1983.
9. Stuckenbruck, L. C. Interface Management. Chapter 20 in *Matrix Management Systems Handbook.* New York: Van Nostrand Reinhold, 1984.
10. Thamhain, H. J. *Engineering Program Management.* New York: Wiley, 1984.
11. Thamhain, H. J., & Wilemon, D. L. Project Performance Measurement, The Keystone to Engineering Project Control. *Project Management Quarterly,* January, 1982.
12. Thamhain, H. J., & Wilemon, D. L. Conflict Management in Project Lifecycles. *Sloan Management Review,* Summer, 1975.
13. Tuminello, J. A. Case Study of Information/Know-How Transfer. *IEEE Engineering Management Review,* June, 1984.
14. Urban, G. L., & Hauser, J. R. *Design and Marketing of New Products.* Prentice-Hall, 1980.
15. U.S. Air Force. *Systems Management—System Program Office Manual,* AFSCM 375-3, Washington, DC, 1964.

PART III
Project Termination

The final part of the book addresses critical but often slighted aspects of project management: evaluation and termination. In Chapter 12 we look specifically at the role and importance of audits and evaluations. We also discuss some methods for conducting an ongoing or a terminal audit/evaluation.

Chapter 13 outlines the various methods for terminating a project and describes the pros and cons of each. Any method presents its own set of problems for the project manager, and these problems, together with some possible solutions, are covered. The Project Final Report is also described.

The future of project management is briefly discussed in Chapter 14. The rapid growth in the use of project organization and its probable future role in our society are noted.

CHAPTER 12
Project Evaluation and Auditing

In the previous chapter we discussed postcontrol. The purpose of postcontrol is not an attempt to change what has already happened. Quite the opposite, postcontrol tries to capture the essence of project successes and failures so that future projects can benefit from past experiences. To benefit from past experiences implies that one understands them, and understanding requires evaluation.

But project evaluation is not limited to after-the-fact analysis. While the project as a whole is evaluated when it has been completed, project evaluation should be conducted at a number of points during the life cycle.

A major vehicle for evaluation (but by no means the only one) is the *project audit,* a more or less formal inquiry into any aspect of the project. We associate the word *audit* with a detailed examination of financial matters, but a project audit is highly flexible and may focus on whatever matters senior management desires.

The term *evaluate* means to set the value of or appraise. Project evaluation appraises the progress and performance of a project compared to that project's planned progress and performance or compared to the progress and performance of other, similar projects. The evaluation also supports any management decisions required for the project. Therefore, the evaluation must be conducted and presented in a manner and format that assures management that all pertinent data have been considered. The evaluation of a project must have credibility in the eyes of the management group for whom it is performed and also in the eyes of the project team on whom it is performed. Accordingly, the project evaluation must be just as carefully constructed and controlled as the project itself.

In this chapter, we describe the project audit/evaluation, its various forms and purposes, and some typical problems encountered in conducting an audit/evaluation. In addition, we discuss a technique originally developed for evaluating R &

D laboratories, but one that may also be generalized for use in evaluating a wide variety of programs composed of interdependent projects. (For an excellent general work on evaluation, see [14].)

12.1 PURPOSES OF EVALUATION—GOALS OF THE SYSTEM

A primary purpose of evaluation is to aid in achieving the project's goals as a step toward reaching the parent organization's goals. To do this, all facets of the project are studied to identify and understand the project's strengths and weaknesses. The result is a set of recommendations that might help both ongoing and future projects to:

- Identify problems earlier.
- Clarify performance, cost, and time relationships.
- Improve project performance.
- Locate opportunities for future technological advances.
- Evaluate the quality of project management.
- Reduce costs.
- Speed the achievement of results.
- Identify mistakes, remedy them, and avoid them in the future.
- Provide information to the client.
- Reconfirm the organization's interest in and commitment to the project.

These purposes—and there are others—can be described as *goal-directed* in that they relate directly to how the project team is performing stated project objectives. They ignore, however, the costs and benefits to the project, to its people, or to the firm that are not clearly stated as project or parent firm objectives. Such ancillary considerations are often referred to as *goal-free,* a term that implies an unplanned but important contribution to the organization. Some examples of goal-free objectives include attempts to:

- Improve understanding of the ways in which projects may be of value to the organization.
- Determine the best processes for organizing and managing projects.
- Identify organizational strengths and weaknesses in project-related personnel, management, and decision-making techniques and systems.
- Identify risk factors in the firm's use of projects.
- Improve the way projects contribute to the professional growth of project team members.

Identification of the goal-directed purposes of a project is *relatively* easy: It requires only a careful reading of the project proposal and a close examination of any documentation that indicates why the project was selected or undertaken. Refer again to Figure 11-5, a reproduction of a project management data form used by a firm in the aerospace industry. Immediately following the project description is a section headed "Reason for Interest." This is a statement of the project's goal-directed purposes. If no such documentation exists, a few interviews with the individuals in charge of making decisions about projects help to expose the goal-directed objectives of the firm. On the other hand, identification of goal-free purposes is a difficult and politically delicate task.

The term *goal-free purposes* is a misnomer. Such purposes are not "free" of a connection with the organization's/project's goals, but rather contribute to goals that have not been overtly identified. Normally, these covert goals are "hidden" by accident. Finding them requires deductive reasoning. Organizational decisions and behaviors imply goals, often very specific goals. At times, however, some goals are purposefully hidden. In either case, the job of the evaluator is arduous.

There are tough problems associated with finding the goal-free purposes of a project. First, and probably most important, is the obvious fact that one cannot measure performance against an unknown goal. Therefore, if a goal is not openly acknowledged, project team members need not fear that their performance can be weighed and found wanting. The result is that goals appearing in the project proposal must be acknowledged, but "unwritten" goals can often be ignored. The unwritten goals are rarely disclaimed; they are merely not mentioned.

Whether or not such anxiety is deserved is not relevant. Anxiety is present. It is heightened by the fear that an evaluation may not be conducted "fairly," with proper emphasis on what is being accomplished rather than stressing failures. If the self-image of the project team is very strong, this barrier to finding the goal-free purposes of the project may be weakened, but it is never absent.

A second problem arises during attempts to determine the goal-free purposes of a project. Individuals pursue their own individual ends while working for organizations. "Making a living" is one such aim. At times, however, they may be unwilling to admit to personal goals, which they see as not entirely consistent with organizational objectives. For example, a person may join a project in order to learn a new skill, which increases that person's employment mobility. At times, the scientific direction taken by R & D projects is as much a function of the *current interest areas* of the scientists working on the project as it is the scientific needs of the project. While such purposes are not illegitimate, they are rarely admitted.

A third problem arises through lack of trust. Individual members of the project team are never quite comfortable in the presence of an auditor/evaluator. If the auditor/evaluator is an "outsider"—anyone who cannot be identified as a project team member—there is the fear that "we won't be understood." Such fears are typically amorphous, but they are nonetheless real. If the auditor/evaluator is an "insider," the fear focuses on the possibility that the insider has some hidden agenda, is seeking some personal advantage to achieve at the expense of the "rest of us." The motives of insider and outsider alike are distrusted. As a result, project team members have little or no incentive to be forthright about individual or project goals.

Finally, a fourth problem exists. Projects, like all organizations that serve human ends, are multipurposed. The diverse set of overt and covert goals do not bear clear, organizationally determined priorities. The members of the project team may have quite different ideas about which purposes are most important, which come next in line, and which are least important. In the absence of an evaluator, no one has to confront the issue of who is right and who is wrong. As long as the goals and priorities are not made explicit, project team members can agree on *what* things should be done without necessarily agreeing on *why* those things should be done. Thus, if some of the project purposes are not openly discussed, each member can tolerate the different emphases of fellow team members. No one is forced to pick and choose or even to argue such matters with coworkers.

Therefore, the task of discovering the goal-free purposes of a project is difficult. Most evaluations simply ignore them, but the PM is well advised to take a keen interest in this area, and to request evaluations that include these purposes. Even if the auditor/evaluator has to be satisfied with qualitative measures of the goal-free objectives, that information can be valuable. If nothing else, it provides insight into such questions as: What sorts of things motivate people to join and work on the project? What sorts of rewards are most effective in eliciting maximum efforts from project personnel? What are the major concerns of the specific people working on this specific project?

Earlier in this book we alluded to the importance of the project war room (office) as a meeting place for the project team, as a display area for the charts that show the project's progress, as a central repository for project files and reports, and as an office for the PM and the other project administrators. The war room is also the "clubhouse" for the project team members and serves an important goal-free purpose. It is to the project what the local pub was to "that old gang of mine." The camaraderie associated with a successful, well-run project provides great satisfaction to team members. The project office, therefore, has an emotional, goal-free purpose, as well as its more mundane physical goal-directed purposes.

12.2 THE PROJECT AUDIT

The project audit is a thorough examination of the management of the project, its methodology and procedures, its records, its properties, its budgets and expenditures, and its degree of completion. It may deal with the project as a whole, or only with a part of the project. The formal report may be presented in various formats, but should, at a minimum, contain comments on the following points:

1. *Current status of the project*   Does the work actually completed match the planned level of completion?
2. *Future status*   Are significant schedule changes likely? If so, indicate the nature of the changes.
3. *Status of crucial tasks*   What progress has been made on tasks that could decide the success or failure of the project?
4. *Risk assessment*   What is the potential for project failure or monetary loss?
5. *Information pertinent to other projects*   What lessons learned from the project

being audited can be applied to other projects being undertaken by the organization?

6. *Limitations of the audit* What assumptions or limitations affect the data in the audit?

These six parts of the audit report will be discussed in more detail in the next section of this chapter.

Note that the project audit is not a financial audit. The audit processes are similar in that each represents a careful investigation of the subject of the audit, but the outputs of these processes are quite different. The principal distinction between the two is that the financial audit has a limited scope. It concentrates on the use and preservation of the organization's assets. The project audit is far broader in scope and may deal with the project as a whole or any component or set of components of the project. It may be concerned with any aspect of project management. Table 12-1 lists the primary differences between financial and project audits.

Depth of the Audit

There are several practical constraints that may limit the depth of the project auditor's investigation. Time and money are two of the more common (and obvious) limits on the depth of investigation and level of detail presented in the audit report. Of course, there are costs associated with the audit/evaluation

Table 12-1 Comparison of Financial Audits with Project Audits

	Financial Audits	**Project Audits**
Status	Confirms status of business in relation to accepted standard	Must create basis for, and confirm, status on each project
Predictions	Company's state of economic well-being	Future status of project
Measurement	Mostly in financial terms	Financial terms plus schedule, progress, resource usage, status of goal-free purposes
Record-keeping system	Format dictated by legal regulations and professional standards	No standard system, uses any system desired by individual organization or dictated by contract
Existence of information system	Minimal records needed to start audit	No records exist, data bank must be designed and used to start audit
Recommendations	Usually few or none, often restricted to management of accounting system	Often required, and may cover any aspect of the project or its management
Qualifications	Customary to qualify statements if conditions dictate, but strong managerial pressure not to do so	Qualifications focus on shortcomings of audit process; e.g., lack of technical expertise, lack of funds or time

process over and above the usual costs of the professional and clerical time used in conducting the audit. Accumulation, storage, and maintenance of auditable data is an important cost element.

Also serious, but less quantifiable, are two often overlooked costs. First, no matter how skilled the evaluator, an audit/evaluation process is always distracting to those working on the project. No project is completely populated with individuals whose self-esteem (defined by Ambrose Bierce as "an erroneous appraisement" [2]) is so high that evaluation is greeted without anxiety. Worry about the outcome of the audit tends to produce an excessive level of self-protective activity, which, in turn, lowers the level of activity devoted to the project. Second, if the evaluation report is not written with a "constructive" tone, project morale will suffer. Depending on the severity of the drop in morale, work on the project may receive a serious setback. The more difficult the technical problems of the project, the more project workers are apt to react strongly to negative criticism. Because the whole process is threatening to the auditees, the auditor should exercise care and discretion in writing the report.

It is logical to vary the depth of the investigation depending on circumstances and needs unique to each project. While an audit can be performed at any level the organization wishes, three distinct levels are easily recognized and widely used: the general audit, the detailed audit, and the technical audit. The general audit is normally most constrained by time and resources and is usually a brief review of the project, touching lightly on the six concerns noted earlier. A typical detailed audit is conducted when a follow-up to the general audit is required. This tends to occur when the general audit has disclosed an unacceptable level of risk or malperformance in some part(s) of the project. The depth of the detailed audit depends on the importance of the questionable issues and their relationship to the objectives of the project—the more serious, or potentially serious, the greater the depth. The evaluation of the then-revolutionary J. C. Penney automotive battery required several thousand pages.

At times, the detailed audit cannot investigate problems at a satisfactory technical level because the auditor does not possess the technical sophistication needed. In such cases, a technical audit is required. Technical audits are normally carried out by a qualified technician under the direct guidance of the project auditor. In the case of very advanced or secret technology, it may be difficult to find qualified technical auditors inside the organization. In such cases, it is not uncommon for the firm to use academic consultants who have signed the appropriate nondisclosure documents. Although not a hard and fast rule, the technical audit is usually the most detailed.

Timing of the Audit

Like audit depth, the timing of a project audit will depend on the circumstances of a particular project. Given that all projects of significant size or importance should be audited, the first audits are usually done early in the project's life. The sooner a problem is discovered, the easier it is to deal with it. Early audits are often focused on the technical issues in order to make sure that key technical problems have been solved or are under competent attack. Ordinarily, audits done later in the life cycle of a project are of less immediate value to the project, but are of more value to the parent organization. As the project develops, technical issues are less likely to be matters of concern. Conformity to the schedule and budget becomes the primary interest. Management issues are major matters of interest for audits made late in the project's life—e.g., disposal of equipment or reallocation of project personnel.

Postproject audits are conducted with several basic objectives in mind. First, a postproject audit is often a legal necessity because the client specified such an audit in the contract. Second, the postproject audit is a major part of the Postproject Report, which is, in turn, the main source of managerial feedback to the parent firm. Third, the postproject audit is needed to account for all project property and expenditures.

Additional observations on the timing and value of audits are shown in Table 12-2.

12.3 CONSTRUCTION AND USE OF THE AUDIT REPORT

The type of project being audited and the uses for which the audit is intended dictate some specifics of the audit report format. Within any particular organization, however, it is useful to establish a general format to which all audit reports must conform. This makes it possible for project managers, auditors, and organizational management all to have the same understanding of, and expectations for, the audit report as a communication device.

While a few PMs insist on a complicated format for evaluation reports tailored to their individual projects, the simpler and more straightforward the format, the better. The information should be arranged so as to facilitate the comparison of predicted versus actual results. Significant deviations of actual from predicted results should be highlighted and explained in a set of footnotes or comments.

Table 12-2 Timing and Value of Project Audits/ Evaluations

Project Stage	Value
Initiation	Significant value if audit takes place early—prior to 25 percent project completion
Feasibility study	Very useful, particularly the technical audit
Preliminary plan/schedule budget	Very useful, particularly for setting measurement standards to insure conformance with standards
Master schedule	Less useful, plan frozen, flexibility of team limited
Evaluation of data by project team	Marginally useful, team defensive about findings
Implementation	More or less useful depending on importance of project methodology to successful implementation
Postproject	More or less useful depending on applicability of findings to future projects

This eases the reader's work and tends to keep questions focused on important issues rather than trivia. This arrangement also reduces the likelihood that senior managers will engage in "fishing expeditions," searching for something "wrong" in every piece of data and sentence of the report. Once again, we would remind PMs of the dictum "Never let the boss be surprised."

Negative comments about individuals or groups associated with the project should be avoided. Write the report in a clear, professional, unemotional style and restrict its content to information and issues that are relevant to the project. The following items cover the *minimum* information that should be contained in the audit report.

1. *Introduction* This section contains a description of the project to provide a framework of understanding for the reader. Project objectives (goal-directed) must be clearly delineated. If the objectives are complex, it may be useful to include explanatory parts of the project proposal as an addendum to the report.

2. *Current Status* Status should be reported as of the time of the audit and, among other things, should include the following measures of performance:

    Cost: This section compares actual costs to budgeted costs. The time periods for which the comparisons are made should be clearly defined. As noted in Chapter 7, the report should focus on the *direct* charges made to the project. If it is also necessary to show project *total* costs, complete with all overheads, this cost data should be presented in an *additional* set of tables.

    Schedule: Performance in terms of planned events or milestones should be reported (see Figures 10-7c and 11.5 as examples.) Completed portions of the project should be clearly identified, and the percent completion should be reported on all unfinished tasks for which estimates are possible.

    Progress: This section compares work completed with resources expended. Earned value charts (see Figure 10-6) are useful for this purpose and will also help to pinpoint problems with specific tasks or sets of tasks. Based on this information, projections regarding the timing and amounts of remaining planned expenditures are made.

    Quality: Whether or not this is a critical issue depends on the type of project being audited. Quality is a measure of the degree to which the output of a system conforms to prespecified characteristics. For some projects, the prespecified characteristics are so loosely stated that conformity is not much of an issue. At times, a project may produce outputs that far exceed original specifications. For instance, a project might require a subsystem that meets certain minimum standards. The firm may already have produced such a subsystem—one that meets standards well in excess of the current requirements. It may be efficient, with no less effectiveness, to use the previously designed system with its excess performance. If there is a detailed quality specification associated with the project, this section of the report may have to include a full review of the quality control procedures, along with full disclosure of the results of quality tests conducted to date.

3. *Future Project Status* This section contains the auditor's conclusions regarding progress together with recommendations for any changes in technical approach, schedule, or budget that should be made in the remaining tasks.

Except in unusual circumstances, for example when results to date distinctly indicate the undesirability of some preplanned task, the auditor's report should consider only work that has already been completed or is well under way. No assumptions should be made about technical problems that are still under investigation at the time of the audit. Project audit/evaluation reports are not appropriate documents in which to rewrite the project proposal.

4. *Critical Management Issues* All issues that the auditor feels require close monitoring by senior management should be included in this section, along with a brief explanation of the relationships between these issues and the objectives of the project. A brief discussion of time/cost/performance tradeoffs will give senior management useful input information for decisions about the future of the project.

5. *Risk Analysis* This section should contain a review of major risks associated with the project and their projected impact on project time/cost/performance. If alternative decisions exist that may significantly alter future risks, they can be noted at this point in the report. Once again, we note that the audit report is not the proper place to second-guess those who wrote the project proposal. The Postproject Report, on the other hand, will often contain sections on the general subject of "if only we knew then what we know now."

6. *Caveats, Limitations, and Assumptions* This section of the report may be placed at the end or may be included as a part of the introduction. The auditor is responsible for the accuracy and timeliness of the report, but senior management still retains full responsibility for the interpretation of the report and for any action(s) based on the findings. For that reason, the auditor should specifically include a statement covering any limitations on the accuracy or validity of the report.

Responsibilities of the Project Auditor/Evaluator

First and foremost, the auditor should "tell the truth." This statement is not so simplistic as it might appear. It is a recognition of the fact that there are various levels of truth associated with any project. The auditor must approach the audit in an objective manner and assume responsibility for what is included and excluded from consideration in the report. Awareness of the biases of the several parties interested in the project—including the auditor's own biases—is essential, but extreme care is required if the auditor wishes to compensate for such biases. (A note that certain information *may* be biased is usually sufficient.) Areas of investigation outside the auditor's area of technical expertise should be acknowledged and assistance sought when necessary. The auditor/evaluator must maintain political and technical independence during the audit and treat all materials gathered as confidential until the audit is formally released.

If senior management and the project team are to take the audit/evaluation seriously, all information must be presented in a credible manner. The accuracy of data should be carefully checked, as should all calculations. The determination of what information to include and exclude is one that cannot be taken lightly. Finally, the auditor should engage in a continuing evaluation of the auditing process in a search for ways to improve the effectiveness, efficiency, and value of the process.

12.4 THE PROJECT AUDIT LIFE CYCLE

Thus far we have considered the project audit and project evaluation as if they were one and the same. In most ways they are. The audit contains evaluation, and an evaluator must conduct some sort of audit. Let us now consider the audit as a formal document required by contract with the client. If the client is the federal government, the nature of the project audit is more or less precisely defined, as is the audit process.

Like the project itself, the audit has a *life cycle* composed of an orderly progression of well-defined events. There are six of these events.

1. *Project Audit Initiation* This step involves starting the audit process, defining the purpose and scope of the audit, and gathering sufficient information to determine the proper audit methodology.

2. *Project Baseline Definition* The purpose of this phase is to establish performance standards against which the project's performance and accomplishments can be evaluated. This phase of the cycle normally consists of identifying the performance areas to be evaluated, determining standards for each area, ascertaining management performance expectations for each area, and developing a program to measure and assemble the requisite information.

    Occasionally, no convenient standards exist. For example, a commodity pricing model was developed as part of a large marketing project. No baseline data existed that could serve to help evaluate the model. Because the commodity was sold by open bid, the firm used its standard bidding procedures. The results formed baseline data against which the pricing model could be tested on an "as if" basis. Table 12-3 shows the results of one such test. CCC is the firm and the contracts on which it bid *and won,* together with the associated revenues (mine net price × tonnage), are shown. Similar information is displayed for Model C, which was used on an "as if" basis so the Model C Revenue column shows those bids the model *would have won,* had it actually been used.

3. *Establishing an Audit Data Base* Once the baseline standards are established, execution of the audit begins. The next step is to create a database for use by the audit team. Depending on the purpose and scope of the audit, the database might include information needed for assessment of project organization, management and control, past and current project status, schedule performance, cost performance, and output quality, as well as plans for the future of the project. The information may vary from a highly technical description of performance to a behaviorally based description of the interaction of project team members. Because the purpose and scope of audits vary widely from one project to another and for different times on any given project, the audit database is frequently quite extensive. The database is usually specified at the start of the project and the required data are collected routinely throughout the project's life.

4. *Preliminary Analysis of the Project* After standards are set and data collected, judgments are made. Some auditors eschew judgment on the grounds that such a delicate but weighty responsibility must be reserved to senior management. But judgment often requires a fairly sophisticated understanding of the technical

Table 12-3 Performance Against Baseline Data

| | | 19xx Bid Performance for Model "C"—State of_____ | | | | |
| | | \- Award \- | | | | |
Destination	Tonage	CCC Bid	Model "C" Bid	Mine Net Price	CCC Revenue	Model "C" Revenue
DI-2	3800		X	$4.11		$15,618
DI-7	1600		X	3.92		6,272
D2-7	1300		X	4.11		5,343
D3-2	700	X		5.13		3,591
D3-3	500	X		5.22	$2610	
D3-4	600		X	5.72		3,432
D3-5	1200		X	5.12		6,144
D3-6	1000		X	5.83		5,830
D4-6	700		X	4.88		3,416
D4-8	600		X	5.34		3,204
D5-1	500	X		3.54	1770	
D6-1	1000	X	X	4.02–3.92	4020	3,920
D6-2	900	X		4.35	3915	
D6-5	200	X		3.75	750	
D6-6	800		X	3.17		2,536
D7-5	1600		X	5.12		8,192
D7-8	2600		X	5.29		13,754
D8-2	1600	X	X	4.83	7728	7,728
D8-3	2400		X	4.32		10,368
				Total revenue	$20,793	$99,348
				Total tonnage	4700	21,500
				Average mine net	$4.42	$4.62

aspects of the project, and/or of statistics and probability, subjects that may elude some managers. In such an event, the auditor must analyze the data and then present the analysis to managers in ways that communicate the real meaning of the audit's findings. It is the auditor's duty to brief the PM on all findings and judgments *before* releasing the audit report. The purpose of the audit is to improve the project being audited as well as to improve the entire process of managing projects. It is not intended as a device to embarrass the PM.

5. *Audit Report Preparation* This part of the audit life cycle includes the preparation of the audit report, organized by whatever format has been selected for use. A set of recommendations, together with a plan for implementing them, is also a part of the audit report. If the recommendations go beyond normal practices of the organization, they will need support from the policymaking level of management. This support should be sought and verified *before* the recommendations are published. If support is not forthcoming, the recommendations should be modified until satisfactory. Figure 12-1 is one page of an extensive and detailed set of recommendations that resulted from an evaluation project conducted by a private social service agency.

Final Report, Agency Evaluation, Sub-Committee II
Physical Plant, Management of Office, Personnel Practices

SUMMARY OF RECOMMENDATIONS

Recommendations which require Board action

1. The Board of _____ should continue its efforts to obtain additional funds for our salary item.
2. The cost of Blue Cross and Blue Shield insurance coverage on individual employees should be borne by_____.
   Recommendations which can be pub into effect by *Presidential Order* to committees, staff, or others.
3. The House Committee should activate, with first priority the replacement of the heating/air conditioning system. Further, this committee should give assistance and support to the Secretary to the Executive Director in maintenance and repair procedures.
4. A professional library should be established even if part time worker must share space to accomplish this.
5. Our insurance needs should be re-evaluated.
6. All activities related to food at meetings be delegated to someone other than the Secretary to the Executive Director.
7. Majority opionion—position of Administratrive Assistant and Bookkeeper will need more time in the future.
   Minority opinion—positions of Administrative Assistant, Bookkeepers and Statistical Assistant should be combined.
8. The Personnel Practices Committee should review job description of Bookkeeper and Statistical Assistant and establish salary ranges for those two positions and that of the Administrative Assistant.
9. Dialogue between the Executive Director, his secretary and the Administrative Assistant should continue in an effort to streamline office procedures and expedite handling of paper work.
10. The written description of the Personnel Practices Committee should include membership of a representative of the non-professional staff.
11. The Personnel Practices Committee should study, with a view toward action, the practice of part time vs. full time casework staff.

Figure 12-1 Sample recommendation for a social service agency.

6. *Project Audit Termination* As with the project itself, after the audit has accomplished its designated task, the audit process should be terminated. When the final report and recommendations are released, there will be a review of the audit process. This is done in order to improve the methods for conducting the audit. When the review is finished, the audit is truly complete and the audit team should be formally disbanded.

12.5 SOME ESSENTIALS OF AN AUDIT/EVALUATION

For an audit/evaluation (hereinafter, simply a/e) to be conducted with skill and precision, for it to be credible and generally acceptable to senior management, to the project team, and to the client, several essential conditions must be met. The a/e team must be properly selected, all records and files must be accessible, and free contact with project members must be preserved. Let us briefly consider these essentials.

The A/E Team

The choice of the a/e team is critical to the success of the entire process. It may seem unnecessary to note that team members should be selected because of their ability to contribute to the a/e procedure, but sometimes members are selected merely because they are available. The size of the team will generally be a function of the size and complexity of the project. For a small project, one person can often handle all the tasks of an a/e audit, but for a large project, the team may require representatives from several different constituencies. Typical of the areas that might furnish a/e team members are:

- The project itself
- The accounting/controller department
- Technical specialty areas
- The customer
- The marketing department
- Senior management
- Purchasing/asset management
- The personnel department
- The legal/contract administration department

The main role of the a/e team is to conduct a thorough and complete examination of the project or some prespecified aspect of the project. The team must determine which items should be brought to management's attention. It should report information and make recommendations in such a way as to maximize the utility of its work. The team is responsible for constructive observations and advice based on the training and experience of its members. Members must be aloof from personal involvement with conflicts among project team staff and from rivalries between projects. The a/e is a highly disciplined process and all team members must willingly and sincerely subject themselves to that discipline.

Access to Records

In order for the a/e team to be effective, it must have free access to all information relevant to the project. This may present some problems on government projects that may be classified for reasons of national security. In such cases, a subgroup of the a/e team may be formed from qualified ("cleared") individuals.

Most of the information needed for an a/e will come from the project team's records or from various departments such as accounting, personnel, and purchasing. Obviously, gathering the data is the responsibility of the a/e team, and this burden should not be passed on to the project management team, though the project team is responsible for collecting the usual data on the project and keeping project records up to date during the project's life.

In addition to the formal records of the project, some of the most valuable information comes from documents that predate the project—for example, correspondence with the customer that led to the RFP, minutes of the Project Selection Committee, and minutes of senior management committees that decided to pursue a specific area of technical interest. Clearly, project status reports, relevant technical memoranda, information about project organization and management methods, and financial and resource usage information are also important. The a/e team may have to extract much of this data from other documents because the required information is often not in the form needed. Data collection is a time-consuming task, but careful work is absolutely necessary for an effective, credible a/e.

As information is collected, it must be organized and filed in a systematic way. Systematic methods need to be developed for separating out useful information. Most important, stopping rules are needed to prevent data collection and processing from continuing far past the point of diminishing returns. Priorities must be set to ensure that important analyses are undertaken before those of lesser import. Also, safeguards are needed against duplication of effort. The careful development of forms and procedures will help to standardize the process as much as possible.

Access to Project Personnel and Others

Contact between a/e team members and project team members, or between the a/e team and other members of the organization who have knowledge of the project, should be free. One exception is contact between the a/e team and the customer; *such contacts are not made without clearance from senior management*. This restriction would hold even when the customer is represented on the audit team, and should also hold for in-house clients.

In any case, there are several rules that should be followed when contacting project personnel. Care must be taken to avoid misunderstandings between a/e team members and project team members. Project personnel should always be made aware of the in-progress a/e. Critical comments should be avoided. Particularly serious is the practice of delivering on-the-spot, off-the-cuff opinions and remarks that may not be appropriate nor represent the consensus opinion of the a/e team.

The a/e team will undoubtedly encounter political opposition during its work. If the project is a subject of political tension, attempts will most certainly be made by the opposing sides to co-opt the a/e team. As much as possible, they should avoid becoming involved. At times, information may be given to a/e team members in confidence. Discreet attempts should be made to confirm such information through nonconfidential sources. If it cannot be confirmed, it should not be used. The auditor/evaluator must protect the sources of confidential information and must not become a conduit for unverifiable criticism of the project.

12.6 MEASUREMENT

Measurement is an integral part of the a/e process. Many issues of what and how to measure have been discussed in earlier chapters, particularly in Chapter 2. Several aspects of a project that should be measured are obvious and, fortunately, rather easy to measure. For the most part, it is not difficult to know if and when a milestone has been completed. We can directly observe the fact that a building foundation has been poured, that all required materials for a corporate annual report have been collected and delivered to the printer, that all contracts have been let for the rehabilitation of an apartment complex, that the navigation instruments for a new fighter aircraft have been tested, or that all case workers have been trained in the new case management techniques. At times, of course, milestone completion may not be quite so evident. It may be difficult to tell when a chemical experiment is finished, and it is almost impossible to tell when a complex computer program is finally "bug free." Largely, however, milestone completion can be measured adequately.

Similarly, performance against planned budget and schedule usually poses no major measurement problems. We may be a bit uncertain whether or not a "nine-day" scheduled completion time should include weekend days, but most organizations adopt conventions to ease these minor counting problems. Measuring the actual expenditures against the planned budget is a bit trickier and depends on an in-depth understanding of the procedures used by the accounting department. It is common to imbue cost data with higher levels of reality and precision than is warranted. Still, while there may be some unique difficulties raised when we attempt to measure the time/cost/performance dimensions of a project, these problems are usually tractable.

When the objectives of a project have been stated in terms of profits, rates of return, or discounted cash flows, as in the financial selection models discussed in Chapter 2, measurement problems may be more obstinate. The problem does not often revolve around the accounting conventions used, though if those conventions have not been clearly established in advance there may be bitter arguments about what costs are appropriately assigned to the individual project being evaluated. A far more difficult task is the determination of what revenues should be assigned to the project.

Assume, for example, that a drug firm creates a project for the development of a new drug and simultaneously sets up a project to develop and implement a marketing strategy for the potential new drug and two existing allied drugs. Assume further that the entire program is successful and large amounts of revenue are generated. How much revenue should be assigned to the credit of the drug research project? How much to the marketing project? Within the marketing project, how much should go to each of the subprojects for the individual drugs?

If the entire program is treated as one project, the problem is less serious; but R & D and marketing are in different functional areas of the parent organization and each may be evaluated on the basis of its contribution to the parent firm's profitability. The year-end bonuses of divisional managers are determined in part (often in large part) by the profitability of the units they manage. Figure 12-2 illustrates project baseline data established for a new product. This figure shows

PROJECT EVALUATION DATA

PRODUCT _____   DATE _____

MARKET _____

DATE OF FIRST SALE - U.S. _____

O.U.S. _____

	1ST YEAR			2ND YEAR			3RD YEAR			4TH YEAR			5TH YEAR			TOTAL		
	MIN	B.E.	MAX	MIN	B.E.	MAX	MIN	B.E.	MAX	MIN	B.E.	MAX	MIN	B.E.	MAX	MIN	B.E.	MAX
1. Total Market Size:																		
2. Expected Market Share:																		
3. Kg. or Units:																		
4. Est. Selling Price:																		
5. Gross Sales (−):																		
6. Est. COPS %:																		
7. Gross Margin % (−):																		
8. Est. Marketing Expense %:																		
9. Marketing Margin % (−):																		
10. Loss on Profit from other Products: List:																		
11. Est. Profit:																		
12. Development Expenses (+):																		
13. Capital Expenditures:																		

Figure 12-2 Baseline marketing data for a new product

the use of multiple measures including price, unit sales, market share, development costs, capital expenditures, and other measures of performance.

There is no theoretically acceptable solution to such measurement problems, but there are politically acceptable solutions. All the cost/revenue allocation decisions must be made when the various projects are initiated. If this is done, the battles are fought "up front," and the equity of cost/revenue allocations ceases to be so serious an issue. As long as allocations are made by a formula, major conflict is avoided—or, at least, mitigated.

If multi-objective scoring models rather than financial models are being used for project selection, measurement problems are somewhat exacerbated. There are more elements to measure, some of which are objective and measured with relative ease. But some elements are subjective and require reasonably standard measurement techniques if the measures are to be reliable. Interview and questionnaire methods for gathering data must be carefully constructed and carried out if the project scores are to be taken seriously. Criteria weights and scoring procedures should be decided at the start of the project.

Evaluating a Program

Once again, let's consider the drug company. The problem we raised was solvable if handled in advance, but would cause severe difficulties if not handled in advance. Let us pose a more complex evaluation problem for the drug firm. Presume that one of the firm's three R & D laboratories has adopted a research program aimed at the development of a family of compounds for the treatment of a related set of diseases. An individual project is created for each compound in the family in order to test the compound efficacy, to test for side effects, to find and install efficient methods for producing the compound in quantity, and to develop marketing strategies for each separate member of the drug family. Assume further that many aspects of the research work on any one compound both profits from and contributes to the work done on other members of the family. In such a case, how does one evaluate a project associated with any given member of the family? *One doesn't!*

To evaluate each project as separate and distinct entity would require a separation of costs and revenues that would be quite impossible except when based on the most arbitrary allocations. Instead of inviting the political bloodletting that would inevitably accompany any such approach, let us attempt to evaluate the performance of the laboratory that directed and carried out the entire program—and that may be conducting other programs at the same time.

B. V. Dean has developed an ingenious technique for accomplishing such an evaluation [6]. Consider Figure 12-3. R & D Laboratory A is conducting project i, one of a set of interrelated projects in Program 1. Project i contributes to technology j, one of a set of desirable technologies that, in turn, makes a contribution to requirement k, one of a desired set of end requirements. Assume a value, k, a nonnegative number associated with each requirement.

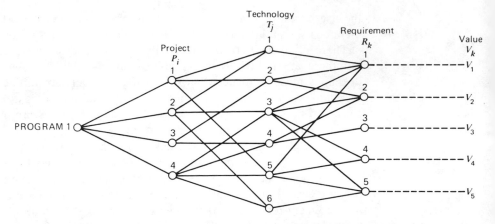

Figure 12-3 Evaluation of a related set of projects for R & D lab A.

Now consider the set of projects, P_i, and the technologies, T_j. We can form the transfer matrix

$$\mathbf{A} = [a_{ij}]$$

composed of ones and zeros as follows:

$$a_{ij} = \begin{cases} 1, \text{ if } P_i \text{ contributes to } T_j \\ 0, \text{ if } P_i \text{ does not contribute to } T_j \end{cases}$$

Similarly, we form the transfer matrix

$$\mathbf{B} = [b_{jk}]$$

composed of ones and zeros as follows:

$$b_{jk} = \begin{cases} 1, \text{ if } T_j \text{ contributes to } R_k \\ 0, \text{ if not} \end{cases}$$

Now find

$$\mathbf{C} = [c_{ik}]$$

where

$$\mathbf{C} = \mathbf{AB}$$

The resultant matrix will link P_i directly to R_k, thus indicating which projects contribute to which requirements.*

---

*This step requires the arithmetic process of matrix multiplication. The process is not difficult. An explanation of the methods together with a short example is presented in Appendix D. The method is further illustrated in the accompanying case.

Now consider the value set V_k. "Normalize" V_k so that

$$\sum_k V_k = 1$$

Each normalized V_k will represent the *relative* value of R_k in the set $\{R_k\}$. The values can be written as a column matrix

$$\mathbf{V} = [V_k]$$

Note that a project, P_i, that contributes to a requirement, R_k, in c_k ways will have a value

$$c_{ik}V_k$$

and that the *total* value of P_i is thus

$$e_i = \sum_k c_{ik}V_k$$

The column matrix $\mathbf{E} = [e_i]$ is the set of values for all projects in the laboratory, and the sum of all project values,

$$\mathbf{E}^* = \sum_i e_i = \mathbf{JE}$$

where $\mathbf{J}$ is a row matrix consisting of ones.

$$\mathbf{E}^* = \mathbf{JE}$$

$$= \mathbf{JCV}$$

$$= \mathbf{JABV}$$

If, in the preparation of matrix $\mathbf{A}$, it seems desirable to differentiate between the different degrees by which a project contributes to a technology or a technology to a requirement, this is easily accomplished. Instead of a one-zero measure of contribution, one might use the following:

$$a = \begin{cases} 2, \text{ if } P_i \text{ makes a "major"} \\ \quad \text{contribution to } T_j \\ 1, \text{ if } P_i \text{ makes a "minor"} \\ \quad \text{contribution to } T_j \\ 0, \text{ if } P_i \text{ makes none} \end{cases}$$

Matrix $\mathbf{B}$ could also accommodate a more sensitive measure of the contributions of a technology to a requirement if the evaluator wishes.

Dean's method has wide applicability for evaluation of programs composed of multiple interdependent projects. Scores can be compared for several programs. When program life is extended over several time periods and generates outputs in these successive time periods, program performance can be compared between periods.

12.7 SUMMARY

This chapter initiated our discussion of the final part of the text, project termination. A major concluding step in the termination process is the evaluation of the project process and results, otherwise known as an audit. Here we looked at the purposes of the final evaluation and what it should encompass: the audit process and measurement considerations, the demands placed on the auditor, and the construction and design of the final report.

Specific points made in the chapter were these:

- The purposes of the evaluation are both goal-directed, aiding the project in achieving its objectives, and goal-free, achieving unspecified, sometimes hidden, yet firmly held, objectives.

- The audit report should contain at least the current status of the project, the expected future status, the status of crucial tasks, a risk assessment, information pertinent to other projects, and any caveats and limitations.

- Audit depth and timing are critical elements of the audit because, for example, it is much more difficult to alter the project based on a late audit than an early audit.

- The difficult responsibility of the auditor is to be honest in fairly presenting the audit results. This may even require data interpretation on occasion.

- The audit life cycle includes audit initiation, project baseline definition, establishing a database, preliminary project analysis, report preparation, and termination.

- Several essential conditions must be met for a credible audit: a credible a/e team, sufficient access to records, and sufficient access to personnel.

- Measurement, particularly of revenues, is a special problem.

In the next chapter we move into the final stage of the project management process, termination. There we will look at when to terminate a project and the various ways the termination can be conducted.

12.8 GLOSSARY

AUDIT—A formal inquiry into some issue or aspect of a system.

BASELINE—A standard for performance, commonly established early on for later comparisons.

EVALUATE—To set a value for or appraise.

GOAL-FREE—The evaluation of a process without prior knowledge of its goals or performance expectations.

MATRIX—A table of numbers or variables that commonly represents a set of values of two factors.

NORMALIZE—To rescale a factor relative to its variation, usually so that all values sum to 100.

RISK ANALYSIS—An evaluation of the likely outcomes of a policy and their probability of occurrence, usually conducted to compare two or more scenarios or policies.

12.9 PROJECT TEAM ASSIGNMENT

This assignment involves an audit and written report on the findings. The audit and project evaluation should be conducted around the midpoint of the project, preferably at some midterm milestone. The auditor should be an outside evaluator or the project controller or other reporter. The determination of factors for measurement should be specifically addressed in the report, particularly costs and revenues. It should include both goal-directed and goal-free considerations, the status of all tasks, the project prognosis, a risk assessment, and any caveats and limitations.

12.10 MATERIAL REVIEW QUESTIONS

1. Give some examples of goal-free project objectives.
2. When should an audit be conducted during a project? Is there a "best" time?
3. What occurs in each stage of the audit life cycle?
4. What items should be included in the audit status report?
5. What access is required for an accurate audit?
6. Why is measurement a particular problem in auditing?

12.11 CONCEPTUAL DISCUSSION QUESTIONS

1. In a typical project, do you feel frequent brief evaluations or periodic major evaluations are better in establishing control? Why?
2. Do you think that project evaluations cost-justify themselves?
3. What steps can be taken to ease the perceived threat to team members of an external evaluation?
4. What feedback, if any, should the project team get from the evaluation?
5. During the project audit, a tremendous amount of time can be wasted if a systematic method of information handling is not adopted. Briefly explain how this systematic method may be developed.
6. "Evaluation of a project is another means of project control." Comment.

12.12 PROBLEMS

1. Given:

$$A = \begin{bmatrix} 1 & 0 & 2 \\ 2 & 1 & 0 \end{bmatrix}$$

$$B = \begin{bmatrix} 0 & 2 & 1 \\ 0 & 1 & 2 \\ 1 & 2 & 0 \end{bmatrix}$$

$$V = \begin{bmatrix} .3 \\ .6 \\ .1 \end{bmatrix}$$

    a. Interpret the matrices **A, B,** and **V.**
    b. Calculate **C** and interpret it.
    c. Calculate **E** and interpret it.
    d. Calculate **E*** and interpret it.

2. Given:

$$
A = \begin{bmatrix}
0 & 0 & 1 & 1 & 0 \\
1 & 0 & 1 & 0 & 1 \\
0 & 1 & 0 & 1 & 0 \\
1 & 0 & 1 & 1 & 0 \\
0 & 1 & 1 & 0 & 0 \\
0 & 0 & 0 & 0 & 0
\end{bmatrix}
$$

$$
B = \begin{bmatrix}
1 & 0 \\
0 & 1 \\
0 & 1 \\
0 & 1 \\
1 & 0
\end{bmatrix}
$$

$$
V = \begin{bmatrix}
.6 \\
.4
\end{bmatrix}
$$

Calculate **C, E,** and **E*** and interpret the meaning of all the matrices.

3. Given:

$$
A = \begin{bmatrix} 1 & 0 & 0 & 1 & 0 & 1 & 1 \end{bmatrix}
$$

$$
B = \begin{bmatrix}
0 \\
0 \\
1 \\
1 \\
0 \\
0 \\
1
\end{bmatrix}
$$

Describe the situation. What is the value of **V**?

4. Given:

$$
A = \begin{bmatrix}
1 \\
0 \\
0 \\
1 \\
1
\end{bmatrix}
$$

$$B = [0\ 0\ 1\ 1\ 1\ 0\ 0]$$

$$V = \begin{bmatrix} .1 \\ .2 \\ .1 \\ .1 \\ .2 \\ .1 \\ .2 \end{bmatrix}$$

Describe the situation. Calculate **C**, **E**, and **E***.

5. Compare the value of the programs in Problems 1, 2, and 4.
6. Recompute the program value in Problem 2 if the unit values in **B** were each replaced with 2. Now how does the answer compare to those of Problems 1 and 4?

12.13 CHAPTER EXERCISE

Refer back to one of the earlier projects used for a chapter exercise or the following Gerkin Incident for Discussion. Design an audit for the project. What data would you need? To whom should you talk? What are the goals of the project? The goal-free objectives? When should the audit be conducted in the project? What sections should the final report contain? Describe the audit process and its life cycle.

12.14 INCIDENTS FOR DISCUSSION

Gerkin Manufacturing Co.

Tim Lasket was the project manager of a project with the objective of determining the feasibility of moving a significant portion of Gerkin's manufacturing capacity to another geographical location. Project completion was scheduled for twenty-eight weeks. Tim had the project team motivated and at the end of the twentieth week the project was on schedule. The next week, during a casual lunch conversation, Tim discovered that the vice-president of manufacturing had serious doubts about the validity of the assumptions the team was using to qualify sources of supply for a critical raw material.

Tim tried to convince him that he was wrong during two follow-up meetings, with no success. In fact, the more they talked, the more convinced the vice-president became that Tim was wrong. The project was too far along to change any assumptions without causing significant delays. In addition, the vice-president was likely to inherit the responsibility for implementing any approved plans for a new plant. For those reasons, Tim felt it was essential to resolve the disagreement before the scheduled completion of the project. Tim requested a project auditor be assigned to audit the project, paying special attention to the methodology behind the sourcing assumptions.

Question: Is this a good example of the use of the audit technique?

General Ship Building Company

General Ship Building has a contract with the Department of the Navy to build three new aircraft carriers over the next five years. During the construction of the first ship, the project manager formed an auditing team to audit the construction process for the three ships. After picking the audit team members, he requested that they develop a set of minimum requirements for the projects and use this as a baseline in the audit. While reviewing the contract documents, an auditing team member discovered a discrepancy between the contract minimum requirements and the Navy's minimum requirements. Based on his findings, he decided to contact the local Navy contract office and inform them of the problem.

Question: If you were the project manager, how would you handle this situation?

12.15 BIBLIOGRAPHY

1. Balachandra, R., and J. A. Raelin. "How to Decide When to Abandon A Project." *Research Management,* July 1980.
2. Bierce, A. *The Devil's Dictionary.* Castle Books, 1967.
3. Buell, C. K. "When to Terminate A Research and Development Project." *Research Management, July 1967.*
4. Cerullo, M. J. "Determining Post-Implementation Audit Success." *Journal of Systems Management,* March 1979.
5. Cooper, M. J. "Evaluation System for Project Selection." *Research Management,* March 1979.
6. Dean, B. V. "A Research Laboratory Performance Model." In *Quantitative Decision Aiding Techniques for Research and Development,* M. J. Cetron, H. Davidson, and A. H. Rubenstein, eds. Gordon and Breach, 1972.
7. DeCotiis, T. A., and L. Dyer. "Defining and Measuring Project Performance." *Research Management,* Jan. 1979.
8. Hicks, C. F., and L. L. Schmidt, Jr. "Post-Auditing: The Capital Investment Decision." *Management Accounting,* Aug. 1971.
9. Hildenbrant, S. "The Changing Role of Analysis in Effective Implementation of Operations Research and Management Science." *European Journal of Operational Research,* Dec. 1980.
10. Jackson, B. "Decision Methods for Evaluating R & D Projects." *Research Management,* June–Aug. 1983.
11. Kelly, J. F. *Computerized Management Information Systems.* Macmillan, 1970.
12. Kerzner, H. "Evaluation Techniques in Project Management." *Journal of Systems Management,* Feb. 1980.
13. Meredith, J. "Program Evaluation Techniques in The Health Services." *American Journal of Public Health,* Nov. 1976.
14. Meyers, W. R. *The Evaluation Enterprise.* San Francisco: Jossey-Bass, 1981.
15. Nash, C. and D. Pearce. "Criteria for Evaluating Project Evaluation Techniques." *Journal of the American Institute of Planners,* March 1975.

16. Newton, J. K. "Computer Modeling for Project Evaluation." *Omega,* May 1981.
17. Phillips, J. P. "MS Implementation: A Parable." *Interfaces,* Aug. 1979.
18. Rosenau, M. D., Jr. "Assessing Project Value." *Industrial Research Development,* May 1979.
19. Ruskin, A. M., and W. E. Estes. "The Project Management Audit: Its Role and Conduct." *Project Management Journal,* Aug. 1985.
20. Schnell, J. S., and R. S. Nicolosi. "Capital Expenditure Feedback: Project Reappraisal." *The Engineering Economist,* Summer 1974.
21. Souder, W. E. "System for Using R & D Project Evaluation Methods." *Research Management,* Sept. 1978.
22. Stuckenbruck, L. C., and C. L. Myers. "Project Evaluation." A Special Summer Issue of the *Project Management Journal,* Aug. 1985.
23. Thierauf, R. J. *Management Auditing.* ANACOM, 1980.
24. Thamhain, H. J., and D. J. Wilemon. "Conflict Management in Project Life Cycles." *Sloan Management Review,* Spring 1975.
25. Turner, W. S., III. *Project Auditing Methodology.* Amsterdam: North Holland Publishing Co., 1980.

12.16 Case: Planning and Budgeting a Social Service System*

The rapid increase of governmental interest in accountability from its agencies and from organizations using governmental funds has put considerable pressure on such agencies and organizations to develop and execute programs which meet the governmental requirements for accountability. As a response to these pressures, human services organizations have moved toward the adoption of such practices as Management by Objectives. Underlying these managerial methods is the assumption that organizational planning processes have been carried out proficiently and that the organization has structured itself to be efficient as well as effective.

The application of General Systems Theory as a planning aid for human services organizations has been most helpful [1], but specific planning techniques are needed in order to implement the basic planning strategies developed through systems analysis. This paper demonstrates one such technique.

In 1974, a program entitled Employment Opportunities in Social Services (EOSS) was created in Ohio. The concept entailed using Title IV-A federal funds administered by the Ohio State Department of Welfare to provide human services job opportunities and salaries for current consumers of Aid for Families with Dependent Children or General Relief benefits. In this way, the program was aimed at allowing county welfare departments to increase their delivery of social services while, at the same time, providing earned income for unemployed welfare clients. Specifically, welfare consumers were to be employed in the following areas:

Chore Services

Day Care Services

Homemaker Services

Nursing Home Aide Services

Transportation Services

Other Services (as recommended by the county welfare departments and approved by the State Welfare Department)

The basic organizational structure required to administer the EOSS program was largely dictated by the organizational structure already existing in the various county welfare departments. Mechanisms also existed to search current welfare client lists in order to find likely candidates for the program. County welfare departments, however, had no organizational mechanism to screen candidates for their potential skills, nor was there a system developed for training and placing acceptable job candidates.

As a part of a week-long seminar in Planning for Human Service Organizations which was held at the School of Applied Social Sciences, Case Western Reserve University, a group of approximately fifteen social work agency executives undertook to design a structure to locate, screen, train, and place job candidates. An outcome of this exercise was the following flow chart denoting the basic tasks to be performed by the EOSS unit. (Figure 1)

Given this structure, the seminar considered how to staff the operation and how to estimate its budget requirements. Several issues were raised by the staffing question. First, in addition to administering the program, several different human service skills had to be performed. Individual and group counseling was required at several stages of the process. Teaching skills were required for the various training programs, and job finding and placement skills were needed. It was noted that the number of people required to man each of these tasks was directly dependent on the number of clients flowing through the system.

The problem was further complicated by the fact that the number of clients trained in any given substantive skill area should be constrained by the number of job openings available for the substan-

*Presented by Samuel J. Mantel at the 7th Annual Meeting of the American Institute for Decision Sciences, Cincinnati, Ohio, Nov. 1975. Printed by permission.

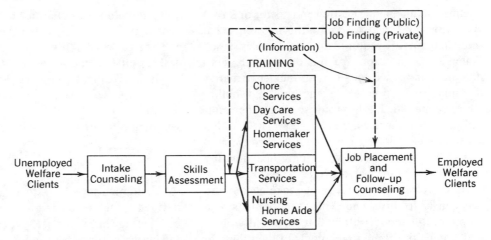

Figure 1 Flow Chart for Skill Training and Job Placement Program.

tive skill. The agency executives agreed that it was all too common for job training programs to be oriented toward *a priori* goals that have little or no relation to actual job demand. This resulted in unmet expectations, frustrations, and disenchantment with the entire process.

For purposes of developing a specific solution to this general planning problem, the group decided to make some assumptions about the number of individuals that would be processed by the system in a given time period.* Clients would be processed in batches.

Given an intake batch size of approximately 100 clients, it was estimated that about half would be trained in chore, day care, and homemaker services. The remainder would be split about equally between transportation and nursing home aide services. Because all training classes would feature demonstration and practice rather than theory, a class size of approximately 25 was seen as desirable. Based on this assumption, it was felt that the following manpower would be required:

Intake workers: 2 1/2

Skill screening: 1/2

Teachers: 4

Job finding: 2

Placement counseling: 1

Follow-up counseling; 1/2

Administration: 1/2

Total personnel required: 11 people (full time equivalents)

Assuming about 25 applicants for these 11 staff positions, the problem of selecting the "best" 11 was seen by the agency executives to be non-trivial. The educational background of the applicants, experience levels, demonstrated human service job skills, and administrative ability all would be important. The group sought a general method for solving this problem that could be easily applied whether the size of the problem was large or small—and would be equally helpful when the specification of the system was less obvious than it was in this particular case.

We start, then, from a set of goals, define a set of tasks consistent with the goals, define the skills required to accomplish the tasks, and then select a set of individuals who possess the proper skills. This problem has the same form as a classic problem in the management of research and development ac-

*The actual numbers used in this exercise were generated by the agency executives in the seminar. They were not chosen to be particularly realistic, but rather to clothe the planning problem with specific parameters and to allow numeric solutions to be generated.

tivities. Given that the desired end results of R & D are known, i.e. that we know the mission, what science inputs are required to achieve the mission? Science and mission are related through technologies; and if we construct an incidence matrix that relates "mission" to "technology" and another which relates "technology" to "science," then multiply the two matrices, we derive a matrix which shows which sciences contribute to specific missions. [2] Dean uses a similar logic in evaluating research laboratory performance. [3]

Here, we can use this technique to relate goals to tasks, tasks to skills, and skills to individuals. The output of this model will be that set of individuals which can contribute to the goals of the program. Further, we can include information relating to the "degree of contribution" of a skill to a task, for example, or information which estimates the degree to which an individual possesses a given skill. To include such information will allow us to find those individuals who will "best" staff our program.

The problem of relating goals to specific tasks was, in this case, trivial; and an incidence matrix was not constructed for this step. The task of "job placement" was judged to make a direct contribution to each of the EOSS goals, which had been vaguely defined in any case. All other tasks directly supported job placement.

To develop the relationship between the tasks which must be performed by the EOSS project and the social work skills required to perform these tasks, consider the set of tasks, T_i, and the set of skills, S_j. We can find the incidence matrix

$$A = (a_{ij})$$

which is a zero-one matrix defined as follows:

$$a_{ij} = \begin{cases} 1, \text{ if task } T_i \text{ requires skill } S_j \\ 0, \text{ if task } T_i \text{ does not require skill } S_j \end{cases}$$

The human service skills related to the tasks as defined by the seminar group are: (1) vocational counseling (individual), (2) vocational counseling (group), (3) placement counseling, (4) teaching, and (5) administration. The group constructed the following array, the elements of which form matrix A, below.

In order to test the procedure of matching individual employees with the required social work skills, the agency executives presented 25 "simulated" applicants for the jobs. The "simulated" applicants were actual individuals known to the seminar members—typically, a member of his/her agency or a close associate. Academic training, job experiences, amount of experience in each type of job, and administrative experience were noted for each individual. The scoring system at the top of the next page was suggested and adopted:

Matrix A

	Skills				
Tasks	Vocational Counseling (individual)	Vocational Counseling (group)	Teaching	Job Placement Counseling	Administrative
Intake	1	1	0	0	0
Skill Screening	1	1	0	0	0
Job Training	0	0	1	0	0
Job Finding	0	0	0	1	0
Placement	0	0	0	1	0
Follow-up	0	0	0	1	0
Administration	0	0	0	0	1

Training

Specifically trained in skill	1
Not trained for skill	0

Job experience

Performed in skill area, less than 2 years	1
Performed in skill area, 2–5 years	2
Performed in skill area, more than 5 years	3
No experience in skill area	0

Each individual was scored on training and experience. These scores were summed and entered into the following array where relevant.

The elements of this array form matrix B, below.

$$\mathbf{B} = (b_{jk})$$

where

$$b_{jk} = \begin{cases} n, \text{ if the individual } I_k \text{ is trained and/or has experience in skill } S_j \ (n = 1,2,3,4). \\ 0, \text{ if the individual } I_k \text{ is not trained in and has no experience in skill } S_j. \end{cases}$$

Note that the number of non-zero elements in a column indicates the number of ways in which that individual can contribute to the skill requirements of the system. The sum of the numbers in a column is a measure of the value of that individual's contribution to the set of skills.

We can now calculate the contribution of an individual to the tasks which form the EOSS training/placement system. Suppose individual I_k has skill S_j which contributes to task T_i. This can be calculated as

$$\sum_j a_{ij} b_{jk} = m$$

If the relationship between I and S, or S and T does not exist, then

$$\sum_j a_{ij} b_{jk} = 0$$

If

$$c_{ik} = \sum_j a_{ij} b_{jk}$$

and we let C be the matrix of c_{ik}, we note that C can be found by matrix multiplication of matrices A and B, so that

$$C = AB$$

Using the numbers in the above arrays:

$$C = \begin{pmatrix} 1 & 1 & 0 & 0 & 0 \\ 1 & 1 & 0 & 0 & 0 \\ 0 & 0 & 1 & 0 & 0 \\ 0 & 0 & 0 & 1 & 0 \\ 0 & 0 & 0 & 1 & 0 \\ 0 & 0 & 0 & 1 & 0 \\ 0 & 0 & 0 & 0 & 1 \end{pmatrix} \begin{pmatrix} 3 & 1 & 1 & 2 & 1 & 4 & — \\ 1 & 1 & 0 & 3 & 0 & 3 & — \\ 0 & 0 & 3 & 0 & 0 & 1 & — \\ 1 & 4 & 1 & 1 & 4 & 1 & — \\ 0 & 2 & 0 & 1 & 0 & 2 & — \end{pmatrix}$$

Matrix B

Skill	Applicant							
	1	2	3	4	5	6	—	25
Vocational Counselor (individual)	3	1	1	2	1	4	—	
Vocational Counselor (group)	1	1	0	3	0	3	—	
Teacher	0	0	3	0	0	1	—	
Placement Counselor	1	4	1	1	4	1	—	
Administrator	0	2	0	1	0	2	—	

$$= \begin{pmatrix} 4 & 2 & 1 & 5 & 0 & 7 & - \\ 4 & 2 & 1 & 5 & 0 & 7 & - \\ 0 & 0 & 3 & 0 & 0 & 1 & - \\ 1 & 4 & 1 & 1 & 4 & 1 & - \\ 1 & 4 & 1 & 1 & 4 & 1 & - \\ 1 & 4 & 1 & 1 & 4 & 1 & - \\ 0 & 2 & 0 & 1 & 0 & 2 & - \end{pmatrix}$$

As above, the number of non-zero elements in a column indicates the number of tasks to which an individual can contribute. The sum of the numbers in the column is a measure of the value of that individual's contribution to the system of tasks.

We still face the problem of selecting 11 FTE individuals from the 25 applicants. There are several decision rules that might be used; for example, we could choose the 11 highest column scores, constrained by the fact that at least 4 must have a non-zero entry in the "teaching" row, at least 2 1/2 (3) must have a non-zero entry in the "intake" row, and so forth. The agency executives adopted a slightly different method for selecting among applicants.

Referring to matrix A, they noted that each of the tasks to be performed had specific social work skills directly associated with it. For example, intake work required vocational counseling skills, job training required teaching skills, and so forth. Further, the tasks themselves formed clusters, with intake and skill assessment being a cluster; job finding, placement, and follow-up counseling being a cluster. Teaching and administration stood alone. After discussion, they decided that the job placement cluster was the most critical group of tasks, teaching the second most critical, intake the third most critical, and administration the least critical for the successful functioning of the EOSS program.

Taking the most critical skill set first, they found the contribution of each individual applicant, V_k, to the tasks of job finding, job placement counseling, and follow-up counseling, taken as a group.

$$V_k = \sum_i c_{ik}, \ i = 4, 5, 6$$

Since 3 1/2 FTE were required, they selected the four highest scores for this subset, settling ties by selecting those with the highest total column

score. In the example above, applicants #2 and #5 score highest with 12 points; and applicant #2 has the highest total contribution with 18 points. Fortunately, one of the individuals (of the 25 analyzed) had experience in administration, so she was counted to fill the 1/2 FTE administrative requirement.

They then proceeded to select four teachers and three intake worker/skill screeners in the same way. The program was now staffed. Since a large part of the budget for such a program is composed of personnel costs, the salary requirements for the selected applicants (plus the cost of a full-time secretary) amounted to approximately 85 percent of the total budget required to operate an EOSS program of the size they postulated.

The entire process, then, is quite straightforward.

1. From the goals (objectives) of a program, derive the set of tasks required to accomplish the goals.
2. Prepare an incidence matrix which indicates the direct relationship of goals and tasks. This may be a zero-one matrix, or the entries may reflect the importance of the relationships.
3. Find the set of work skills required to accomplish the tasks defined above and array these relationships in matrix form. The entries in the matrix may be zero-one or may reflect the importance of the relationships, as above.
4. Assess all potential workers for the skills determined in Step 3, and array these assessments in another matrix. Again, zero-one entries may be used or a score may be entered to reflect the strength of the relationship.
5. Sequentially multiply the matrices to find the contribution of each potential worker to the goals of the program.
6. Adopting any acceptable decision rule, select workers to staff the program.
7. Calculate the sum or worker salary requirements to determine the personnel budget for the program.

In conclusion, this model provides a method of evaluating the potential contributions of a set of individuals, each of whom possesses various unique combinations of skills, to the tasks to be performed by an organization. If these tasks are, in turn, related to the goals (or objectives) of an organization, the method will measure the contribution of individuals to those goals. Input data may include measures of the strength or criticality of the relationship between goals and tasks, tasks and skills, and skills and applicants. Stochastic variables may also be included. The larger the number of goals, tasks, skills, and applicants, the more powerful and time-saving the method becomes.

REFERENCES

1. Holland, Thomas P., "Systems Theory and Its Application to Human Services Organizations," Human Services Design Laboratory, School of Applied Social Sciences, Case Western Reserve University, Cleveland, Ohio, 1974. (Mimeo)
2. Cetron, Marvin J., "QUEST Status Report," *IEEE Transactions on Engineering Management,* Vol. EM-14, No. 1, March, 1967.
3. Dean, Burton V., "A Research Laboratory Performance Model," *IEEE Transactions on Engineering Management,* Vol. EM-14, No. 1, March, 1967.

QUESTIONS

1. How realistic is this matrix approach to the task?
2. Evaluate candidate #7 whose rating $b_{j7} = [1,3,2,3,3]$. How does the candidate contribute to V?
3. How might this model be extended? What other issues could be addressed?
4. How might linear programming be used in this situation? Could it address the same task? Which would be better?

12.17 READING

This article provides a general overview of the audit purpose and process. It discusses why an audit is desirable, what it entails, when it should be conducted (both planned and unplanned), who should conduct it, and how it should be executed. Preparation, implementation, and reporting are also described in detail. Some hazards and cautions are given for final guidance.

The value of this article for managers is the guidance it provides for the effective use of the audit. For general managers, it describes the utility of the audit for overseeing projects and their implementation. For project managers, it helps them understand the need for an audit and how it can be helpful to them in achieving the project's objectives for the organization.

The Project Management Audit: Its Role and Conduct

Arnold M. Ruskin
Claremont Consulting Group, Claremont, California

W. Eugene Estes
Dames & Moore, Los Angeles, California

INTRODUCTION

Projects are managed by people, and most people are at least a little imperfect. These imperfections can cause them to manage projects poorly. Moreover, project managers are subject to conflicting pressures that can confuse or distort the way they see their projects. Various tools are therefore used to compensate for project managers' shortcomings. Among these tools are formalized planning and control techniques, contingency allowances, reporting procedures, supervisory relationships, design reviews, and so forth. Another useful tool that does not cost much is the project management audit.

A project management audit is concerned with much more than the project's financial records. Rather, it concerns all of the project elements, including objectives, plans, resources, schedules, budgets, accomplishments, and so forth. While project management audits have been mentioned in the literature, they are not widely understood, and it is worthwhile examining them in some detail.

Projects fail because mistakes occur in planning and execution and then are not corrected. The project manager may not understand their significance, may be lazy or too busy to correct them at the time, or may feel that it would be good politics to keep them quiet. Project management audits can nip these in the bud.

In addition, audits give other stakeholders, such as the organization's general management, readings on just how their projects stand and what immediate actions they might have to take to protect their interests.

This paper discusses the why, when, who, what

© 1985 by the Project Management Institute. Reprinted from *Project Management Journal*, August 1985, pp. 64–70, by permission.

and how of project management audits so that the reader can decide when and if a project should be audited and how to proceed.

WHY

Why audit a project? What can an audit do that is not provided in the ordinary course of reporting project plans and progress?

Audits are generally performed because management and investors or clients need to know the true status of their projects. Otherwise, they may be unpleasantly surprised later, when the situation cannot be salvaged. They need to be assured that their resources are being used as planned. They need to know that the results will indeed meet their objectives, or failing that, what the shortfall will be and what corrective measures can be taken. And they need to know that the reports on the project are complete, objective, and accurate. Project management audits serve these needs.

To elaborate, many projects are complex in their goals, approaches, or relationships. These complexities cloud the project staff's vision of the true endpoints of their work so that they are commonly lost from view. An experienced auditor who has little or no connection with the project can probe it in ways that no one involved with the project is likely to do. Thus, he can determine whether management's and the investors' or client's interests are really being met.

Even without complexities, timely audits can reduce the chance of project failure. Projects fail for a number of reasons. Some projects should never have been started in the first place. Timely audits will discover such unfortunate circumstances and prompt their early termination as an alternative to a later failure, saving resources in the process. Other projects fail because mistakes are not corrected when they occur, even when one of several staff members are well aware of them. When mistakes are allowed to survive, time elapses and further steps may compound the errors. Situations that were repairable then become project failures.

Mistakes survive and are compounded because of indolence, lack of courage, or moral or intellectual dishonesty, together with a lack of thorough and impartial examination. Timely project management audits can force prompt recognition of mistakes for what they are and lead to their correction.

Also, highly competent project managers are often spread too thin. Audits help bring such situations to light and prompt corrective action before something bad happens.

WHAT

A project management audit is a comprehensive, thorough fact-finding exercise. It unearths and examines the status of a project, including the quality and quantity of the work and whether it meets the client's needs; the resources expended and the resources required to complete the work; the suitability of the schedule for the work done and work to be done; organizational issues; and so forth. In making this examination, the audit delves into:

1. the detailed plans
2. monitoring and control procedures
3. risks and contingency allowances
4. staffing arrangements
5. internal interfaces
6. reporting arrangements
7. customer relations
8. subcontractor and vendor relations
9. relations with third parties
10. accounting, invoicing, and billing
11. other mundane but essential matters

Since the aim of an audit is to establish the true status of the entire project and not become a witch hunt (which would make a lot of key personnel defensive), it is not particularly focused on exceptional items unless and until they appear. Cause and effect analyses are frequently included, but they are not essential. When they are included, their purpose is to identify how certain unfortunate effects can be prevented in the future. Again, witch hunts are not intended.

Unpleasant facts, however, are not shunned or left unexamined. On the contrary, the project management audit is structured, staffed, and conducted precisely to find and characterize any unpleasantness there might be with minimum defensiveness and acrimony. An audit serves a project uniquely in this regard.

A project management audit is superior, for example, to most supervisory relationships in dealing with unpleasantness. A project manager and his or her supervisor have a continuing relationship that complicates any current probe. While the best relationships are based on honesty, they also include loyalty, trust, and sensitivity to the other's feelings. When honesty and loyalty conflict, who can predict that honesty will dominate? When trust exists, who can predict that the search will be thorough? When one is sensitive to another's feelings, who can predict that problems will be described accurately? For these reasons, the independent audit has certain advantages over supervisory examinations.

A project management audit also has advantages over design reviews when it comes to ascertaining the status of the entire project. The purpose of design reviews is to assure that the customer's specifications are being met and will continue to be met. While this is indeed one aspect of an audit, it is only one aspect. A project management audit also examines whether the project's detailed objectives are correct; whether the project plan, resources, arrangements, and processes are appropriate and working; and whether there are any hidden agendas or other insidious factors that threaten the success of the project. These are largely internal matters to the organization that is doing the project, and many, if not most of them, are unlikely to be aired in a design review.

Audits also serve projects in a way that they cannot possibly serve themselves. They provide independent verification of project status. While a project manager who is skillful, conscientious, honest, and on top of his job may learn nothing new from audits, audits nevertheless reduce doubts in the minds of others about project status. They are like *Good Housekeeping* Seals of Approval, which enhance the credibility of the project managers who win them. This increase in credibility enhances their effectiveness in dealing with others, especially with their managements and customers.

WHEN

Project management audits can be either planned or unplanned, and each has its place.

Planned Audits

Complex projects should have planned audits and their timing might follow this schedule:

1. Review of the project plan in draft form.
2. A **first** audit soon after the project has been organized and is well underway.
3. A **second** audit when about 20% of the schedule time or money has been spent, whichever comes first.
4. **Third** and **subsequent** audits at key turning or decision points as needed to verify that corrective actions identified in prior audits have been taken.

An example audit schedule might look like this:

Project Schedule Time: 50 weeks

Review of the project plan	week one
1st audit	week three
2nd audit	week ten
3rd audit	optional
Project completion	week fifty

Except in rare instances, the project management audit should not be a surprise event. By giving advance notice, the project manager and staff can prepare for the audit and make it productive. Advance notice helps everyone involved to be knowledgeable of the true project status and lessen procrastination in doing necessary but perhaps difficult tasks.

Unplanned Audits

If members of general management perceive that a project is in trouble or heading for trouble or if they are uncertain of its status, then a project management audit is appropriate. In this case, they will get an accurate assessment of the project that will either allay their fears or give them the information they need to correct the situation intelligently.

A project management audit is also appropriate when there is a change in project managers. If project managers change unexpectedly after the project is well underway, then a special audit gives the incoming project manager a clear understanding of conditions at the time of takeover. Both the outgoing project manager and the incoming project manager should be present. This type of audit minimizes surprises and allows the incoming project manager to take timely corrective action.

Although rare, there is a third condition that calls for an unplanned audit, which is also unannounced in advance. When investors have good reason to suspect that some sort of skulduggery is at work and advance notice would precipitate a cover-up or interfere with taking corrective action, then a surprise audit is in order.

WHO

The prerequisites for a project management auditor include all or nearly all of the following:

1. The auditor should not have been directly involved in the proposal effort, the project planning stage (except to review and critique the draft project plan), or the staffing decisions and actions for the project. He must not be involved in doing the work or in supervising it. The auditor needs to have an unfettered outlook.
2. The auditor should have much diverse experience. This experience should include a number of years in working on projects and in managing projects. The auditor needs to have first-hand experience with the real problems that all projects face and needs to be familiar with many of the typical pitfalls. He does not need very much technical experience in the technical areas that the project is involved with as long as he has a general understanding of the field. He also needs to be able to distinguish between the important and the trivial.
3. The auditor should have a reputation of being fair, objective, and thorough, and he should

not be considered naive. He must be a good listener and able to draw people out and should pay attention to detail and not jump to conclusions.

Once the project management auditor is selected, he must be given sufficient authority to perform the audit in a thorough manner with a minimum of time expenditure. The auditor must have the authority to discuss the project with all internal personnel. Outside personnel should be contacted, however, only with the advice or consent from general management.

The auditor must have the authority to look at all records, documentation, correspondence and financial records and must be able to observe all actions in process on the project.

HOW

A project management audit is not a spontaneous affair, although the need for one might not be recognized until a precipitous event occurs. Whether the audit is planned ahead or decided upon urgently, it nevertheless must be prepared and performed carefully if it is to be successful.

Preparing for An Audit

Preparing for a project management audit includes:

1. estimating the schedule and budget for the audit
2. selecting the auditor
3. establishing the auditor's reporting level
4. agreeing on the outline or format of the audit report
5. notifying the project manager of the audit
6. arranging the time and place of the audit
7. telling the project manager what to provide in advance of the audit

Selection of the auditor is described in the previous section. The remaining items are discussed here.

The auditor should report at a level that is higher

than every individual connected with the project. Such individuals include functional group heads and support service heads whose staffs contribute to the project as well as any technical and marketing experts and others assigned to the project who may outrank the project manager. One aim of this condition is to insure that the auditor is taken seriously. Another aim is to insure that the person receiving the report cannot have rank pulled on him by an unhappy project team member if changes are made as a result of the audit.

The auditor and the person to whom the auditor will report need to agree in advance on the goal and scope of the audit and the outline of the audit report. There usually is no good opportunity to redo a portion of an audit if it should be necessary later to fill in some overlooked details. All the information must be gathered the first time. Thus, the auditor and the audit recipient need to have a common understanding at the outset regarding the audit's goal and scope and the report's outline.

Once the auditor has been charged with his duty, general management should notify the de jure project manager and the de facto project manager, if different, that there will be an audit and tell them the name of the auditor. The auditor can then arrange the place and time for the audit. Normally, the place should be where the work is being done. The auditor needs access to the work, the personnel who are working on the project, and to their records. If the work is dispersed, the auditor may have to travel from one place to another.

The time of the audit also needs to be calendared. There is little point in the auditor showing up when the project manager and other key personnel are simply not available. Arranging an appointment, however, may not be a simple job. No time seems to be convenient to a project manager who is desperately trying to get or keep a project on track. The auditor may therefore have to simply announce when the audit will take place and insist that the project manager be there, prepared as described in the next paragraph. The auditor's level of reporting will be a major asset in enforcing this mandate.

The auditor should instruct the project manager

regarding the materials to be provided in advance of the audit. Normally, these include the statement of work, the plan, drawings, bills of material, documentation, instructions, manuals, guidelines, codes and regulations, the contract, purchase orders, subcontracts, invoices, progress reports, and financial reports. These items should be provided to the auditor sufficiently in advance of the audit so that he can review them before meeting the project personnel.

Performing An Audit

Performing a project management audit involves:

1. acquiring information
2. examining the information and comparing pieces of it with other pieces and with the auditor's experience to determine its relevance, completeness, and accuracy
3. drawing conclusions about the status of the project from the comparisons
4. presenting the results and discussing them with the individual(s) who commissioned the audit

Information is acquired from two types of sources, from the materials listed in the previous discussion on preparing for the audit and from interviews.

The materials should provide:

1. a general description of the project, including its objectives;
2. the reasons for the objectives;
3. assumptions, either implicit or explicit, that affect the project or the way it is performed;
4. the project schedule;
5. the project budget;
6. the approach or method to be used;
7. the people and organization for doing the project, including any subcontractors;
8. interfaces between the project and the customer and between the project and third parties;
9. the provision of equipment and material;
10. the plan for controlling quality;
11. the work authorization plan;

12. the schedule control plan;
13. the cost control plan;
14. reporting plans; and
15. assessments of risk and contingency plans and allowances

As the auditor reviews the materials, he can ponder such questions as:

1. Are the main objectives and subobjectives clear and correct? Are there any conflicts inherent among them? If so, how will the conflicts be resolved?
2. How will the project manager and the customer know when the objectives have been successfully met?
3. Why are various elements of the overall project plan present? Are they reasonable? Are they based on facts? If not, are they based on reasonable assumptions? Are the assumptions explicit or implicit? Are any important elements or details missing?
4. Does the project have enough of the right talent, information, equipment, moral and tangible support, etc.? Are the plans for deploying these resources satisfactory?
5. Are the project's monitoring and control provisions appropriate, sufficient, and timely?
6. Are the reporting plans appropriate?
7. Are difficulties and risks clearly identified and appropriately assessed? Are contingency plans and allowances adequate?

These questions should help the auditor determine if the foundation of the project is sound enough to enable a successful outcome. If not, he needs to find out through interviews if the shortcomings have been rectified.

Whether or not the project's foundation is sound, the auditor should interview the project manager and other personnel who might have either a corroborating or contrasting viewpoint. If the foundation is sound, the purpose is to confirm that it is as good as it seems and that it is being followed. If the foundation is not sound, the purpose is to discover what supplementary steps are being taken and how well they are working.

The auditor can identify potential interviewees in several ways. The organization chart for the project should show the key personnel on the project, all of whom should be interviewed. Then each of them can be asked who else is acquainted with the various parts of the project that bear further examination. Personnel who interface with the project should also be considered, and they, or at least their functions, can be identified from the project plans. As in any sleuthing, the auditor should develop leads wherever possible; not all will be productive, but some may turn out to be crucial.

The interviews should be done individually. The auditor might begin by asking each interviewee to describe the project briefly as he understands it and to then comment on the parts of it that could be improved. As the auditor listens to the various discussion, he should be alert to distortions, ambiguities, gaps and omissions, and conflicting information or viewpoints. Attention should be paid not only to what interviewees say but also to what they might have said and did not.

Some points may have to be explored further if they pertain to significant aspects of the project. The auditor should have no qualms about asking "darn fool questions" to elicit information. And as interviewees make assertions or allegations, the auditor should ask for specific examples unless he already has incontrovertible evidence supporting the claims.

A key to the success of a project is its standing in the priority queue of all the work being done by each person involved. It is important, therefore, to discover how much time and attention each work element is getting from each party. If individual efforts are insufficient, too fragmented, or not timely, the project will suffer, perhaps disastrously, as needed work is done inadequately or too late. The auditor should look for such opportunities for the project to fail in order to correct them in time.

Also, the auditor should determine the extent to which limitations or constraints are handicapping the project. If there are such handicaps, the auditor should ask the personnel involved for their rationales. Often project difficulties can be relieved by removing unwarranted constraints.

It often pays for the auditor to be available for project personnel and other staff to talk with informally. They sometimes have something to say but are unlikely to be interviewed because no one else suggests them and they do not necessarily have a visible position. It helps, therefore, for the auditor to see that his presence is well-known, that he has some uncommitted time while on the scene, and that people know where he is staying if he is from out-of-town.

Reporting Audit Findings

Following the interviews, the auditor must prepare and present a report that summarizes his work, conclusions, and recommendations. The report should include:

1. a description of the project status,
2. what was seen and heard,
3. the auditor's own opinions,
4. a listing of other opinions found by the auditor, and
5. the auditor's recommendations for corrective action.

This report should normally be addressed to the person who commissioned the audit, and a copy of it should be provided to the project manager.

HAZARDS AND CAUTIONS

Project management auditing is not without its hazards. The auditor is likely to find errors of omission and commission, and his subjects know this. Consequently, they may be defensive or reluctant to cooperate. Worse yet, some may set traps for him. It pays the auditor, therefore, to work with a measure of caution and prudence, lest he open a hornet's nest without being prepared.

The auditor's style has a major impact on the cooperation he receives. If he is belligerent or accusatory, he engenders defensive reactions from everyone. If he is friendly and accessible, he is likely to elicit cooperation, at least from those who would normally cooperate.

At the same time, the auditor should not accept half answers or otherwise be put off. If an interviewee demurs on a question, the auditor can ask why the respondent is reluctant to answer. Then the auditor can say that he understands the other person's reluctance but wants to proceed anyway because it will help make the whole project a healthy one. An auditor needs to be persuasive and persistent to get the information he needs.

While rare, an auditor sometimes meets someone whom he finds intimidating by virtue of knowledge, skill, force of personality, fame or some other awesome characteristic. When this happens, the auditor can be immobilized by a fear that the intimidator could destroy the auditor's credibility. An auditor should recognize the situation when it occurs and overcome it. He should, if he can, simply proceed with the audit, making sure that he has his facts straight and can substantiate them.

Occasionally an auditor is engaged by one who is an underlying cause of any trouble there may be on the project. If the person who is the cause is aware of his role, he may or may not welcome the insight the auditor will bring. The auditor needs to prepare this individual to accept the information. It helps if the auditor can tell him first that there are some delicate matters that are perhaps unpleasant to hear but must nevertheless be voiced if the project is to be made healthy. The emphasis needs to be on improving the project, not on accusing the guilty party.

If the person who is the underlying cause of trouble is aware of his role, he may have the audit in order to place blame elsewhere. The auditor now has a moral dilemma of the first order. While there is usually enough blame to find several who are responsible, it is possible that no real good can result unless the one who engaged the auditor also reforms. In this case, the auditor needs to advise the one who engaged him what he too needs to do in order to allow the project to succeed. Here also the emphasis needs to be on corrective actions all around and not on who has done what in the past.

SUMMARY

A project management audit is an examination designed to determine the true status of work performed on a project and its conformance with the project statement of work, including schedule and budget constraints. It is an independent, structured assessment of the state of affairs conducted by a competent examiner. By inference or extrapolation, it provides insight into the work needed to meet project objectives and the adequacy of the schedule and budget to do so. In addition, it can illuminate mistakes that can cause project failure and thus can trigger timely corrective action.

The why, when, who, what, and how of project management audits are discussed. Project management audits are compared and contrasted with normal supervision of project management, with reviews conducted for the customer (whether internal or external), and with financial audits. Guidelines are presented for choosing a qualified auditor, and a structured format is offered for preparing, performing, and reporting an audit.

By following good methods and procedures, such as given here, many managers, clients, owners, and investors will find the project management audit a useful tool that can pay big dividends.

REFERENCES

1. Kirschner, D. Construction Audit Services for Owners. *The CPA Journal,* Volume *XLIX,* No. 1, January 1979, pp. 19–25.
2. Ross, F. E. Technical Reviews and Audits: Keeping Track of Progress in Development Projects. *Management Review,* Volume 65, No. 8, August 1976, pp. 11–18.
3. Walker, M. G. and Bracey, R. Independent Auditing as Project Control. *Datamation,* Volume 26, No. 3, March 1980, pp. 201–202.

CHAPTER 13
Project Termination

As it must to all things, termination comes to every project. At times, project death is quick and clean, but more often it is a long process; and there are times when it is practically impossible to establish that death has occurred. The skill with which termination, or a condition we might call "near termination," is managed has a great deal to do with the quality of life after the project. The termination stage of the project rarely has much impact on technical success or failure, but it has a great deal to do with residual attitudes toward the project—the "taste left in the mouth" of the client, senior management, and the project team.

At this point, the joy of discovery is past. Problems have been solved, bypassed, lived with, and/or ignored. Implementation plans have been carried out. The client is delighted, angry, or reasonably satisfied. In construction-type projects where the project cadre remains intact, the termination issue is eased because the team moves on to another challenge. For nonrecurring projects, the issue is far more akin to the breakup of a family. While the members of the family may be on the best of terms, they must now separate, go their individual ways, divide or dispose of the family property, and make plans for individual survival. The change is stressful. For projects organized as weak matrices, there will be only a few individuals, perhaps only the project manager, who "belong" to the project. This may represent an even more stressful situation than the breakup of a large project family because there is less peer group support and few or no sympathetic colleagues with whom to share the anxieties associated with transfer to a new project or back to a functional group.

The process of termination is never easy, always complicated, and, as much as we might wish to avoid it, almost always inevitable. The problem is how to accomplish one of the several levels of what is meant by project termination with a minimum of trouble and administrative dislocation.

In this chapter we examine the variety of conditions that may be generally referred to as *project termination*. As indicated above, some are not termination at all but rather a slowed-down level of existence. We also discuss some procedures that decrease the pain of termination, and others that reduce the administrative problems that often arise after projects have been terminated. We look into the typical causes of termination, and finally note that the preparation of a project history is an integral part of the termination process.

13.1 THE VARIETIES OF PROJECT TERMINATION

For our purposes, a project can be said to be terminated when work on the substance of the project has ceased or slowed to the point that further progress on the project is no longer possible, when the project has been indefinitely delayed, when its resources have been deployed to other projects, or when project personnel (especially the PM) become *personae non gratae* with senior management and in the company lunchroom. There may seem to be a spark of life left, but resuscitation to a healthy state is most unlikely. On rare occasions, projects are reborn to a new, glorious existence. But such rebirth is not expected, and project team members who "hang on to the bitter end" have allowed optimism to overcome wisdom. The PM must understand that the ancient naval tradition that the captain should go down with his ship does not serve the best interests of the Navy, the crew, the ship, and most certainly not the captain.

On the other hand, the captain must not, ratlike, flee the "ship" at the first sign of trouble. In the next section of this chapter, we note many of the signs and signals that indicate that the project may be in real trouble. At this point, it is appropriate to consider the ways in which a project can be terminated. There are three fundamentally different ways to close out a project: extinction, inclusion, and integration.

Termination by Extinction

The project is stopped. It may end because it has been successful and achieved its goals: The new product has been developed and handed over to the client; the building has been completed and accepted by the purchaser; or the software has been installed and is running.

The project may also be stopped because it is unsuccessful or has been superseded: The new drug failed its efficacy tests; the yield of the chemical reaction was too low; there are better/faster/cheaper/prettier alternatives available; or it will cost too much and take too long to get the desired performance. Changes in the external environment can kill projects, too. The explosion of the Challenger stopped a number of space shuttle projects overnight.

A special case of termination by extinction is "termination by murder."* There are all sorts of murders. They range from political assassination to accidental projecticide. When senior executives vie for promotion, projects for which the loser is champion are apt to suffer. Corporate mergers often make certain projects redundant or irrelevant. Two important characteristics of termination by murder, premeditated or not, are the suddenness of project demise and the lack of obvious signals that death is imminent.

When a decision is made to terminate a project by extinction, the most noticeable event is that all activity on the *substance* of the project ceases. A great deal of organizational activity, however, remains to be done. Arrangements must be made for the orderly release of project team members and their reassignment to other activities if they are to remain in the parent organization. The property, equipment, and materials belonging to the project must be disbursed according to the dictates of the project contract or in accord with the established procedures of the parent organization. Finally, the Project Final Report, also known as the *project history,* must be prepared. These subjects will be covered in greater detail later in this chapter.

Termination by Inclusion

If a project is a major success, it may be terminated by institutionalizing it as a formal part of the parent organization. NCR Corporation, for example, uses this method of transforming a project into a division of the parent firm and then, if real economic stability seems assured, into an independent subsidiary. When the project is made a more or less full-fledged member of the parent, it lives its first years in a protected status—much as any child is protected by the adults in the family. As the years pass, however, the child is expected gradually to assume the economic responsibilities of full adulthood.

When project success results in termination by inclusion, the transition is strikingly different from termination by extinction. In both cases the project ceases to exist, but there the similarity stops. Project personnel, property, and equipment are simply transferred from the dying project to the newly born division. The metamorphosis from project to division is accompanied by budgets and administrative practices that conform to standard procedure in the parent firm, by demands for contribution profits, by the probable decline of political protection from the project's corporate "champion," indeed by a greater exposure to all the usual stresses and strains of regular, routine, day-to-day operations.

It is not uncommon, however, for some of the more adventurous members of the project team to request transfers to other projects or to seek the chance to start new projects. Project life is exciting, and some team members are uncomfortable with what they perceive to be the staid, regulated existence of the parent

*The authors thank Professor Samuel G. Taylor (University of Wyoming) for noting this special case of termination by extinction.

organization. The change from project to division brings with it a sharply diminished sense of freedom.

This transition poses a difficult time for the PM, who must see to it that the shift is made smoothly. In Part I of this book, and especially in Chapter 3, we referred repeatedly to the indispensable requirement of political sensitivity in the PM. The transition from project to division demands a superior level of political sensitivity for successful accomplishment. Projects lead a sheltered life, for all the risks they run. The regular operating divisions of a firm are subjected to the daily infighting that seems, in most firms, to be a normal result of competition between executives.

Termination by Integration

This method of terminating a project is the most common way of dealing with successful projects, and the most complex. The property, equipment, material, personnel, and functions of the project are distributed among the existing elements of the parent organization. The output of the project becomes a standard part of the operating systems of the parent.

In some cases, the problems of integration are relatively minor. The project team that installed a new machining center, instructed the client in its operation and maintenance, and then departed probably left only minor problems behind it, problems familiar to experienced operations managers. If the installation was an entire flexible manufacturing system, however, or a minicomputer complete with multiple terminals and many different pieces of software, then the complexities of integration are apt to be much more severe. In general, the problems of integration are inversely related to the level of experience that the parent organization (or client) has had with: (1) the technology being integrated and (2) the successful integration of other projects, regardless of technology.

Most of the problems of termination by inclusion are also present when the project is integrated. In the case of integration, the project may not be viewed as a competitive interloper, but the project personnel being moved into established units of the parent organization will be so viewed. Also, the project, which flourished so well in its protected existence as a project, may not be quite so healthy in the chilly atmosphere of the "real world." The individuals who nurtured the project may have returned to their respective organizational divisions, and may have new responsibilities. They tend to lose their fervid interest in the "old" project.

Following is a list of a few of the more important aspects of the transition from project to integrated operation that must be considered when the project functions are distributed.

1. *Personnel* Where will the project team go? Will it remain a team? If the functions that the team performed are still needed, who will do them? If ex-team members are assigned to a new project, under what conditions or circumstances might they be temporarily available for help on the old project?

2. *Manufacturing* Is training complete? Are input materials and the required

facilities available? Does the production system layout have to be replanned? Did the change create new bottlenecks or line-of-balance problems? Are new operating or control procedures needed? Is the new operation integrated into the firm's computer systems?

3. *Accounting/Finance* Have the project accounts been closed and audited? Do the new departmental budgets include the additional work needed by the project? Have the new accounts been created and account numbers been distributed? Has all project property and equipment been distributed according to the contract or established agreements?

4. *Engineering* Are all drawings complete and on file? Are operating manuals and change procedures understood? Have training programs been altered appropriately for new employees? Have maintenance schedules been adjusted for the change? Do we have a proper level of "spares" in stock?

5. *Marketing* Is the sales department aware of the change? Is marketing in agreement about lead times? Is marketing comfortable with the new line? Is the marketing strategy ready for implementation?

6. *Purchasing, Distribution, Legal, etc.* Are all these and the other functional areas aware of the change? Has each made sure that the transition from project to standard operation has been accomplished within standard organizational guidelines and that standard administrative procedures have been installed?

Perhaps we should add a fourth type of project termination, although, strictly speaking, it is not a "termination" at all. We could call it "near-termination by budget decrement." Almost anyone who has been involved with projects over a sufficient period of time to have covered a business recession has had to cope with budget cuts. Budget cuts, or decrements, are not rare. Because they are common, they are sometimes used to mask a project termination. There may be a number of reasons why senior management does not wish to terminate an unsuccessful or obsolete project. In some firms, for example, it is politically dangerous to admit that one has championed a failure, and terminating a project that has not accomplished its goals is an admission of failure. In such a case, the project budget might receive a deep cut—or a series of small cuts—large enough to prevent further progress on the project and to force the reassignment of many project team members. In effect, the project is terminated, but the project still exists as a legal entity, complete with sufficient staff to maintain some sort of presence such as a secretary who issues a project "no-progress" report each year.

13.2 WHEN TO TERMINATE A PROJECT

The decision to terminate a project early, by whatever method, is difficult. As we emphasized in Chapter 4, projects tend to develop a life of their own—a life seemingly independent of whether or not the project is successful. In an early article [11] on the subject of terminating R & D projects, Buell suspected that the main reason so little information was available on the subject was that it was hard to spell out specific guidelines and standards for the decision. He expressed strong doubts about the ability to "wrap everything up in a neat set of quantitative mathematical expressions," and then went on to develop an extensive set of questions that, if answered, should lead management to a decision. While these questions were aimed at R & D projects, they have wide, general applicability. Paraphrased and slightly modified to broaden and extend them beyond R & D projects, they are:

- Is the project still consistent with organizational goals?
- Is it practical? Useful?
- Is management sufficiently enthusiastic about the project to support its implementation?
- Is the scope of the project consistent with the organization's financial strength?
- Is the project consistent with the notion of a "balanced" program in all areas of the organization's technical interests? In "age"? In cost?
- Does the project have the support of all the departments (e.g., finance, manufacturing, marketing, etc.) needed to implement it?
- Is organizational project support being spread too thin?
- Is support of this individual project sufficient for success?
- Does this project represent too great an advance over current technology? Too small an advance?
- Is the project team still innovative, or has it gone stale?
- Can the new knowledge be protected by patent, copyright, or trade secret?
- Could the project be farmed out without loss of quality?
- Is the current project team properly qualified to continue the project?
- Does the organization have the required skills to achieve full implementation or exploitation of the project?
- Has the subject area of the project already been "thoroughly plowed"?
- Has the project lost its key person or champion?
- Is the project team enthusiastic about success?
- Can the potential results be purchased or subcontracted more efficiently than developed in-house?
- Does it seem likely that the project will achieve the minimum goals set for it? Is it still profitable? timely?

We could add many other such questions to Buell's list. For instance:

- Has the project been obviated by technical advances or new products/services developed elsewhere?
- Is the output of the product still cost-effective?
- Is it time to integrate or include the project as a part of the regular, ongoing operation of the parent organization?
- Would we support the project if it were proposed today at the time and cost required to complete it?

- Are there better alternative uses for the funds, time, and personnel devoted to the project?
- Has a change in the environment altered the need for the project's output?

Such questions clearly overlap, and the list could easily be extended further. Dean [15] reports that the probabilities of technical and/or commercial failure are the two most important reasons for terminating projects (see Table 13-1), according to the executives he surveyed. Balachandra and Raelin [9, 28] performed a discriminant analysis on 23 factors involved in terminating projects, not as a decision model, but as a way of highlighting the various factors involved and their relevance to the termination problem, as related to projects in general.

Pinto and Slevin [26] surveyed experienced PMs from *Fortune 1000* firms and found ten factors that the managers felt to be critical to successful project implementation. Tadisina [34], working with a set of factors associated with project success found by the work of Baker, Green, Bean *et al.* [7, 8], suggested a variety of termination decision models that could be used if the success-related factors were monitored and used as input data in the models.

A particularly important finding of Baker *et al.* is that the *factors associated with*

Table 13-1

Rank-Order of Important Factors Considered in Terminating R&D Projects (36 Companies)

Factors	No. of Companies Reporting the Factor as Being Important
TECHNICAL	
Low probability of achieving technical objectives or commercializing results	34
Technical or manufacturing problems cannot be solved with available R&D skills	11
Higher priority of other projects requiring R&D manpower or funds	10
ECOMOMIC	
Low profitability or return on investment	23
Too costly to develop as individual product	18
MARKET	
Low market potential	16
Change in competitive factors or market needs	10
OTHERS	
Too long a time required to achieve commercial results	6
Negative effect on other projects or products	3
Patent problems	1

Source: B. V. Dean, *Evaluating, Selecting, and Controlling R&D Projects,* American Management Association Research Study 89, 1968.

project success are different for different industries. Baker's work was restricted to R & D projects, but the Pinto and Slevin study covered many different types of projects. They found that the success-related factors differed between fundamentally different types of projects—between R & D and construction projects, for example. At the very least, the factors and their relative importance are idiosyncratic to the industry, to the project type, and, we suggest, possibly to the firm.

In the face of this diversity of success factors, it is interesting to note that there are a few fundamental reasons why some projects fail to produce satisfactory answers to Buell's questions.

1. *A Project Organization Is Not Required*   The use of the project form of organization was inappropriate for this particular task or in this particular environment. The parent organization must understand the conditions that require instituting a project.

2. *Insufficient Support from Senior Management*   Projects invariably develop needs for resources that were not originally allocated. Arguments between functional departments over the command of such resources are very common. Without the direct support of a champion in senior management, the project is almost certain to lose the resource battle.

3. *Naming the Wrong Person as Project Manager*   This book is testimony to the importance of the PM. A common mistake is to appoint as PM an individual with excellent technical skills but weak managerial skills or training.

4. *Poor Planning*   This is a very common cause of project failure. In the rush to get the substance of the project under way, competent planning is neglected. In such cases, crisis management becomes a way of life, difficulties and errors are compounded, and the project slowly gets farther behind schedule and over budget.

These, and a few other reasons, are the base causes of most project failures. The specific causes of failure, for the most part, derive from these fundamental items. For example:

- No use was made of earlier project Final Reports that contained a number of recommendations for operating projects in the future.
- Time/cost estimates were not prepared by those who had responsibility for doing the work.
- Staring late, the PM jumped into the tasks without adequate planning.
- Project personnel were moved without adjusting the schedule, or were reassigned during slow periods and then were unavailable when needed.
- Project auditors/evaluators were reluctant to conduct careful, detailed meaningful evaluations.
- The project was allowed to continue in existence long after it had ceased to make cost-effective progress.
- Evaluations failed to determine why problems were arising during the early phases of the project life cycle.

All these causes of failure underline the need for careful evaluation at all stages of the project. But at the same time, it is most important for the reader to note that the lion's share of the attention given to the termination issue is focused on the failing project. It is equally or more important to terminate successful projects at the right point in time and by proper methods.

Also, little consideration has been given to *how* the termination decision is made and *who* makes it. We feel that a broadly based committee of reasonably senior executives is probably best. The broad organizational base of the committee is needed to diffuse and withstand the political pressure that accompanies all terminations—successes and failures alike. To the extent possible, the criteria used by the Termination Committee should be written and explained in some detail. It is, however, important to write the criteria in such a way that the committee is not frozen into a mechanistic approach to a decision. There are times when hunches should be followed (or rejected) and blind faith should be respected (or ignored). It depends on whose hunches and faith are under consideration.

13.3 THE TERMINATION PROCESS

The termination process has two distinct parts. First is the decision whether or not to terminate. Second, if the decision is to terminate the project, the decision must be carried out.

The Decision Process

Balachandra and Raelin [9, 28] state that project selection models are not appropriate for the project termination decision. They argue that the data requirements for selection models are too large and costly. They also argue that the evaluation of factors in project selection models may change as projects are evaluated at different stages in their life cycles. They note that the probability of technical success of a project is usually estimated to be close to 1.0 early in the life cycle, but lower during later stages when the technical problems are known. This, they say, would bias decisions in favor of new projects and against ongoing ones.

Lee and Mantel [23] state that the first argument is generally untrue of those selection models actually being used, which are typically of modest size. They also point out, as we have remarked elsewhere in this book, that the uncertainty associated with most projects is not concerned with whether or not the project objective is technically achievable, but rather with the time and cost required to achieve it.

Adopting the position that sunk costs are not relevant to current investment decisions, they hold that the primary criterion for project continuance or termination is *whether or not the organization is willing to invest the estimated time and cost required to complete the project, given the project's current status and current expected outcome.* They emphasize that this criterion can be applied to any project. Balachandra and Raelin were, of course, discussing only R & D projects.

Shafer and Mantel [31] have developed a project termination decision support system (DSS) based on the widely available Lotus 1-2-3® spreadsheet and using a constrained weighted factor scoring model (see Chapter 2). The capabilities of Lotus 1-2-3® allow direct modeling of the scoring model, allow customized menus, and allow decision makers to adapt and enhance the model as they gain experience in the use of the DSS. In addition, Lotus 1-2-3®'s database capability provides a method for monitoring projects across a wide variety of environmental and performance factors. It is also noteworthy that Lotus 1-2-3® can interchange information with most of the current microcomputer-based project management software as well as with many of the microbased database management systems. Finally, one of the spreadsheet's most powerful features is the ease with which sensitivity or "what if" analysis can be conducted.

The database requirements include data on the project, on the parent organization, and on the environment. The criteria on which projects are rated, the specifics of the scores, and the relative weights of the criteria are often developed by organizational executives using the Delphi Method. (For a description of the use of the Delphi Method to develop weights, see [24].) If it seems desirable, the weights may be determined through discriminant analysis, as in [9, 28, or 34].

Just as decision criteria, constraints, weights, and environmental data are unique to each organization, so are the specifics of using this (or any) decision model. The decision makers should set some threshold score, T, so that a project is terminated if the project score, S_i, is less than T. They could also specify T' such that the project would be continued if S_i is greater than T'. If the score is in-between the two threshold values, the decision could be deferred to an individual or group decision maker for special consideration. Multiperiod decision rules could be applied so that if the project scores declined more than some amount from one period to the next, the project would be terminated. Similarly, a project might be shut down if its score declined for several successive periods. A more detailed discussion of these and other rules, together with examples, can be found in [31].

Analysis of the results of this process is simple and straightforward. It is also simple to apply sensitivity analysis to the weights, to criteria scoring methods, and to various values of the thresholds. Figure 13-1 illustrates the structure of this termination decision model.

The Implementation Process

Once it has been decided to terminate a project, the process by which it will be terminated must be implemented. The actual termination can be planned and orderly, or a simple hatchet job. The former is apt to have significantly better results, and so we suggest that the termination process be planned, budgeted, and scheduled just as is done for any other phase of the project life cycle. Such a project is illustrated in Figure 13-2. Archibald [4] has prepared an extensive checklist of items covering the closeout of both the administrative and substantive parts of the project (see Figures 13-3a and b)

In some organizations, the processing of the project closeout is conducted under the direct supervision of the PM, but this often raises dilemmas. For many

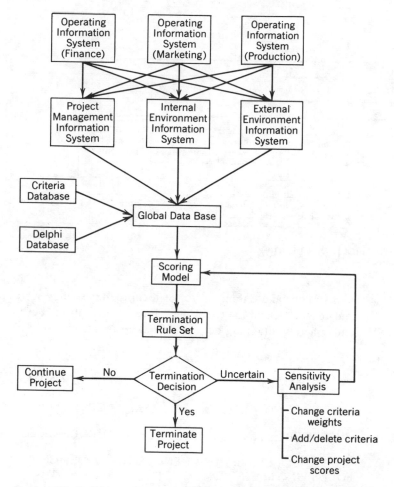

Figure 13-1 DSS structure for a project termination decision.

PMs, termination signals the end of their reign as project leader. If the PM has another project to lead, the issue may not be serious; but if there is no other project and if the PM faces a return to a staid life in a functional division, there may be a great temptation to stretch out the termination process.

An examination of Figures 13-2 and 13-3a and 13-3b shows that implementing termination is a complex process. Note that in Figure 13-3b such items as A-4, B-4, C-3, and G-2, among many others, are actually small projects. It is all too easy, at this final stage of the game, to give this mountain of paperwork a "lick and a promise"—easy, but foolish. Someone must handle all the bureaucratic tasks, and if the PM leaves many loose ends, he or she will rapidly get a reputation for being slipshod, a characterization not associated with success.

The PM also has another option, to ignore the termination process entirely. The evaluation has already been conducted and praise or censure has been delivered. Rather than deal with termination, the PM may let the project ad-

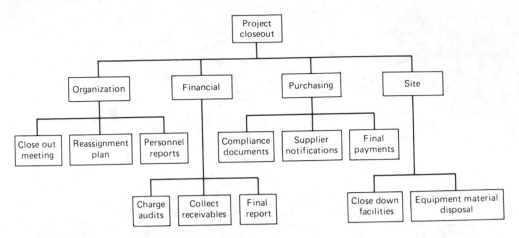

Figure 13-2 Design for project termination.

ministrator handle things. Project team members may well have similar feelings and reactions, and may seek new jobs or affiliations before the project actually ends, thereby dragging out some final tasks interminably.

PROJECT TITLE _____   COMPLETION DATE _____

CONTRACT NO. _____   COST TYPE _____

CUSTOMER _____   PROJECT MGR. _____

The PROJECT CLOSE-OUT CHECK LISTS ARE DESIGNED FOR USE IN THE FOLLOWING MANNER:

COLUMN I—ITEM No.—Each task listed is identified by a specific number and grouped into categories. Categories are based on functions, not on organizations or equipment.

COLUMN II—TASK DESCRIPTION—Task descriptions are brief tasks that could apply to more than one category are listed only in the most appropriate category.

COLUMN III—REQUIRED, YES OR NO—Check whether the item listed applies to the project.

COLUMN IV—DATE REQUIRED—Insert the required date for accomplishment of the task.

COLUMN V—ASSIGNED RESPONSIBILITY—Insert the name of the man responsible to see that the task is accomplished on schedule. This may be a member of the Project Office or an individual within a functional department.

COLUMN VI—PRIORITY (PR)—A priority system established by the Project Manager may be used here, e.g., Priority #1 may be all tasks that must be accomplished before the contractual completion date, Priority #2 within 2 weeks after the completion date, etc.

COLUMN VII—NOTES, REFERENCE—Refer in this column to any applicable Procedures, a government specification that may apply to that task, etc.

Figure 13-3a Instructions for project termination checklist.

Item No.	Task Description	Required Yes	Required No	Required Date	Assigned Responsibility	PR.	Notes Reference
A.	*PROJECT OFFICE (PO) AND PROJECT TEAM (PT) ORGANIZATION*						
1.	Conduct project close-out meeting						
2.	Establish PO and PT release and re-assignment plan						
3.	Carry out necessary personnel actions						
4.	Prepare personal performance evaluation on each PO and PT member						
B.	*INSTRUCTIONS AND PROCEDURES*						
Issue Instructions for:							
1.	Termination of PO and PT						
2.	Close-out of all work orders and contracts						
3.	Termination of reporting procedures						
4.	Preparation of final report (s)						
5.	Completion and disposition of project file						
C.	*FINANCIAL*						
1.	Close out financial documents and records						
2.	Audit final charges and costs						
3.	Prepare final project financial report (s)						
4.	Collect receivables						
D.	*PROJECT DEFINITION*						
1.	Document final approved project scope						
2.	Prepare final project breakdown structure and enter into project file						
E.	*PLANS, BUDGETS, AND SCHEDULES*						
1.	Document actual delivery dates of all contractual deliverable end items						
2.	Document actual completion dates of all other contractual obligations						
3.	Prepare final project and task status reports						
F.	*WORK AUTHORIZATION AND CONTROL*						
1.	Close out all work orders and contracts						

Figure 13-3b Checklist for project termination.

G. PROJECT EVALUATION AND CONTROL

1. Assure completion of all action assignments
2. Prepare final evaluation report (s)
3. Conduct final review meeting
4. Terminate financial, manpower, and progress reporting procedures

H. MANAGEMENT AND CUSTOMER REPORTING

1. Submit final report to customer
2. Submit final report to management

I. MARKETING AND CONTRACT ADMINISTRATION

1. Compile all final contract documents with revisions, waivers and related correspondance
2. Verify and document compliance with all contractual terms
3. Compile required proof of shipment and customer acceptance documents
4. Officially notify customer of contract completion
5. Initiate and pursue any claims against customer
6. Prepare and conduct defense against claims by customer
7. Initiate public relations announcements re contract completion
8. Prepare final contract status report

J. EXTENSIONS-NEW BUSINESS

1. Document possibilities for project or contract extensions, or other related new business
2. Obtain commitment for extension

K. PROJECT RECORDS CONTROL

1. Complete project file and transmit to designated manager
2. Dispose of other project records as required by established procedures

L. PURCHASING AND SUBCONTRACTING

For each Purchase Order and Subcontract:
1. Document compliance and completion
2. Verify final payment and proper accounting to project
3. Notify vendor/contractor of final completion

Figure 13-3b Continued

M.	*ENGINEERING DOCUMENTATION*					
1.	Compile and store all engineering documentation					
2.	Prepare final technical report					
N.	*SITE OPERATIONS*					
1.	Close down site operations					
2.	Dispose of equipment and material					

Figure 13-3b Concluded.

Source: R. D. Archibald, *Managing High Technology Programs and Projects.* New York: Wiley, 1976. Reprinted by permission of John Wiley & Sons, Inc.)

Special *termination managers* are sometimes useful in completing the long and involved process of shutting down a project. In such cases, the PM is transferred to another project or reassigned to a functional "home." The termination manager does not have to deal with substantive project tasks and therefore may be a person familiar with the administrative requirements of termination and the environment within which the project will be operating (if it continues to live).

If technical knowledge is required during the termination process, a member of the project team may be upgraded and assigned responsibility for the termination. This "promotion" is often a motivator and will provide developmental experience for the team member.

The primary duties of the termination manager are encompassed in the following eight general tasks:

1. Ensure completion of the work, including tasks performed by subcontractors.
2. Notify the client of project completion and ensure that delivery (and installation) is accomplished. Acceptance of the project must be acknowledged by the client.
3. Ensure that documentation is complete, including a terminal evaluation of the project deliverables and preparation of the project's Final Report.
4. Clear for final billings and oversee preparation of the final invoices sent to the client.
5. Redistribute personnel, materials, equipment, and any other resources to the appropriate places.
6. Determine what records (manuals, reports, and other paperwork) to keep. Ensure that such documents are stored in the proper places and that responsibility for document retention is turned over to the parent organization's archivist.
7. Ascertain any product support requirements (e.g., spares, service, etc.), decide how such support will be delivered, and assign responsibility.
8. Oversee the closing of the project's books.

It is likely that tasks 1 to 3 will be handled by the regular PM immediately before the project termination process is started. If the termination manager must handle these tasks, technical support will almost certainly be needed.

Item 5 on this list deserves some amplification. The PM can do a great deal to reduce the problems of termination by dealing with these issues well before the actual termination process begins. As we noted in Chapter 2, arrangements for the distribution and disposal of property and equipment belonging to the project should be included in the proposal and/or in the contract with the client. Obviously, this does not stop all arguments, but it does soften the conflicts. Dealing with project personnel is more difficult.

Most PMs delay the personnel reassignment/release issue as long as possible for three main reasons: a strong reluctance to face the interpersonal conflicts that might arise when new assignments and layoffs are announced; worry that people will lose interest and stop work on the project as soon as it becomes known that termination is being considered; or concern—particularly in the case of a pure project organization—that team members will try to avoid death by stretching out the work as far as possible.

As long as the PM has access to the functional managers' ears, any team member who "quits work" before the project is completed or stalls by stretching out tasks or creating task extensions would be subject to the usual sanctions of the workplace. The PM should make it quite clear that on-the-job-resignations and tenure-for-life are equally unacceptable.

The first problem results when project leadership is held by a managerially weak PM. The height of weakness is demonstrated when the PM posts a written list of reassignments and layoffs on the project's bulletin board late Friday afternoon and then leaves for a long weekend. A more useful course of action is to speak with project members individually or in small groups, let them know about plans for termination, and offer to consult with each in order to aid in the reassignment process or to assist in finding new work. (A preliminary announcement to the entire project team is in order because the interviews may cover several weeks or months.) It is almost impossible to keep termination plans a secret, and to confront the matter immediately tends to minimize rumors.

In a large project, of course, the PM will not be able to conduct personal interviews except with a few senior assistants. The project's personnel officer, or a representative from the parent firm's personnel department, can serve instead. This may seem like an unnecessary service to the team members, but a reputation of "taking care of one's people" is an invaluable aid to the PM when recruiting for the next project.

Termination by murder makes it very difficult to follow these suggestions about dealing with project personnel. The project's death often occurs with so little warning that the PM learns of the fact at the same time as the project team—or, as sometimes happens, learns about it from a member of the project team.

There is little the PM can do in such a case except to try to minimize the damage. The team should be assembled as rapidly as possible and informed, to the best of the PM's ability, about what has happened. At this point the PM should start the reassignment/release process.

13.4 THE FINAL REPORT—A PROJECT HISTORY

Good project management systems have a memory. The embodiment of this memory is the Project Final Report. The Final Report is not another evaluation;

rather, it is the history of the project. It is a chronicle of the life and times of the project, a compendium of what went right and what went wrong, of who served the project in what capacity, of what was done to create the substance of the project, of how it was managed.

The precise organization of the Final Report is not a matter of great concern; the content is. Some are organized chronologically, while others feature sections on the technical and administrative aspects of the project. Some are written in a narrative style and some contain copies of all project reports strung together with short commentaries. What matters is that several subjects should be addressed, one way or another, in the Final Report.

1. *Project Performance* A key element of the report is a comparison of what the project achieved (see the Terminal Evaluation) with what the project tried to achieve (see the Project Proposal). This comparison may be quite extensive and should include explanations of all significant deviations of actual from plan. Because the report is not a formal evaluation, it can reflect the best judgment of the PM on why the triumphs and failures occurred. This comparison should be followed with a set of recommendations for future projects dealing with like or similar technical matters.

2. *Administrative Performance* The substantive side of the project usually gets a great deal of attention, while the administrative side is often ignored until administrative problems occur. There is also a strong tendency on the part of almost everyone to treat the "pencil pushers" with grudging tolerance, at best. The administration of a project cannot solve technical problems, but it can enable good technology to be implemented (or prevent it). Administrative practices should be reviewed, and those that worked particularly well or poorly should be highlighted. It is important, when possible, to report the reasons why some specific practice was effective or ineffective. If poor administration is to be avoided and good practices adopted, it is necessary to understand why some things work well and others do not *in the environment of a particular organization*. This becomes the basis for the recommendations that accompany the discussion.

3. *Organizational Structure* Each of the organizational forms used for projects has its own, unique set of advantages and disadvantages. The Final Report should include comments on the ways the structure aided or impeded the progress of the project. If it appears that a modification to the accepted form of project organization—or a change to a different basic organizational form—might be helpful for project management, such a recommendation should be made. Obviously, recommendations should be accompanied by detailed explanations and rationales.

4. *Project and Administrative Teams* On occasion, individuals who are competent and likable as individuals do not perform well as members of a team when a high level of interpersonal communication and cooperation is required. A *confidential* section of the Final Report may be directed to a senior personnel officer of the parent organization, recommending that such individuals not be assigned to projects in the future. Similarly, the PM may recommend that individuals or groups who are particularly effective when operating as a team be kept together on future projects or when reassigned to the firm's regular operations.

5. *Techniques of Project Management*   The outcome of the project is so dependent on the skill with which the forecasting, planning, budgeting, scheduling, resource allocation, and control are handled that attention must be given to checking on the way these tasks were accomplished. If the forecasts, budgets, and schedules were not reasonably accurate, recommendations for improved methods should be made. The techniques used for planning and control should also be subject to scrutiny.

For each element covered in the Final Report, recommendations for changing current practice should be made and defended. Insofar as is possible, the implications of each potential change should be noted. Commonly ignored, but equally important, are comments and recommendations about those aspects of the project that worked unusually well. Most projects, project teams, and PMs develop informal procedures that speed budget preparation, ease the tasks of scheduling, improve forecasts, and the like. The Final Report is an appropriate repository for such knowledge. Once reported, they can be tested and, if generally useful, can be added to the parent organization's list of approved project management methods.

The fundamental purpose of the Final Report is to improve future projects. It is ultimately focused on the project itself and on the process by which the project was conducted. Data on the project and its outcomes are available in the many interim reports, audits, and evaluations conducted during the project's life. But data on the process come largely from the PM's recollections. To ensure that significant issues are included, the PM should keep a diary. The PM's diary is not an official project document, but rather an informal collection of thoughts, reflections, and commentaries on project happenings. Such a diary tends to be a rich source of unconventional wisdom when written by a thoughtful PM. It may also be a great source of learning for a young, aspiring PM. Above all, it keeps ideas from "getting lost" amid the welter of activity on the project.

Occasionally, the project diary serves a purpose not originally intended. A PM working for a Minnesota highway construction company made a habit of keeping a project diary, mostly for his own interest and amusement. The firm was sued as the result of an accident on a road under construction. The plaintiff alleged that the highway shoulder was not complete nor was it marked "Under Construction" at the time of the accident. The PM's diary noted daily progress on the road, and it showed that the relevant piece of the road had been completed several days prior to the accident. The company successfully defended its position. All company PMs keep diaries now. A vice-president of the firm mentioned that they are the same type of diary his high-school-aged daughter uses.

13.5 SUMMARY

At last, we come to the completion of our project—termination. In this chapter we looked at the ways in which projects can be terminated, how to decide if a project should be terminated, the termination process, and the preparation of the Project Final Report.

Specific points made in the chapter were these:

- A project can be terminated in one of three ways: by extinction, inclusion, or integration.
- Making a decision to terminate a project before its completion is difficult, but a number of factors can be of help in reaching a conclusion.
- Most projects fail because of one or more of the following reasons:
    Inappropriate use of the project form of organization
    Insufficient top-management support
    Naming the wrong project manager
    Poor planning
- Studies have shown that the factors associated with project success are different for different industries and the various types of projects.
- Success-related factors, or any factors management wishes, can be used in termination decision models.
- Special termination managers are often used, and needed, for closing out projects. This task, consisting of eight major duties, is a project in itself.
- The Project Final Report incorporates the process knowledge gained from the project and should include:
    Project performance comments
    Adminstrative performance comments
    Organizational structure comments
    Personnel suggestions, possibly a confidential section

13.6 GLOSSARY

BUDGET DECREMENT A reduction in the amount of funds for an activity.

DISCRIMINANT ANALYSIS A statistical method of fitting an equation to a set of data in order to predict a binomial outcome, typically project success or failure.

EXTINCTION The end of all activity on a project without extending it in some form, such as by inclusion or integration.

INCLUSION Bringing the project into the organization as a separate, ongoing entity.

INTEGRATION Bringing the project activities into the organization and distributing them among existing functions.

MURDER Terminating a project suddenly and without warning, usually for a cause not related to the project's purpose.

TERMINATION MANAGER An administrator responsible for wrapping-up the administrative details of a project.

13.7 PROJECT TEAM ASSIGNMENT

This assignment marks the completion of the project team's activity. The team should prepare a Project Final Report detailing the method of project termination, the reasons for termination, and the tasks the termination manager will have to complete to terminate the project. Also include the process knowledge gained from the project concerning performance, administration, organization structure, and personnel.

Last, suggest a termination evaluation model that includes what your team considers to be the relevant project success and failure factors. Note the potential for interaction between project manager factors, organizational factors, and project factors, in particular.

13.8 MATERIAL REVIEW QUESTIONS

1. List and briefly describe the ways projects may be terminated.
2. What problems may occur if the project manager does not have a follow-on project when the current project nears termination?
3. What are the primary duties of a termination manager?
4. · On termination of a project, what happens to the information gathered throughout the course of the project?

13.9 CONCEPTUAL DISCUSSION QUESTIONS

1. Discuss the impact, both positive and negative, of termination on the project team members. How might the negative impact be lessened?
2. If the actual termination of a project becomes a project in itself, what are the characteristics of this project? How is it different from other projects?
3. Discuss some reasons why a Project Final Report, when completed, should be permanently retained by the firm.
4. What elements of the termination process may be responsible for making a project unsuccessful?

13.10 CHAPTER EXERCISE

Using the same project used for the Chapter 12 exercise, plan a project termination by *each* of the three methods described in the chapter. How would a decision regarding early termination be made? What would the critical factors be? If the project were to become a failure, what would the most likely reason be? Does it fall within the categories given in the chapter?

13.11 INCIDENTS FOR DISCUSSION

Industrial Mop and Supply Co.

IMSCO began manufacturing and distributing mops and brooms to industrial customers forty-three years ago. Mr. Bretting, president of IMSCO, has been toying with the idea of using IMSCO's manufacturing and distribution expertise to begin making and selling consumer products. He has already decided that he cannot sell any of his current products to consumers. Also, if IMSCO is going to go to the trouble of developing consumer markets, Mr. Bretting feels very strongly that their first product should be something new and innovative that will help establish their reputation. He thinks that the expertise required to develop a new product exists within the company, but no one has any real experience in organizing or managing such a project. Fortunately, Mr. Bretting is familiar with a local consulting firm that has a good reputation and track record of leading companies through projects such as this, so he contacted them.

Three months into the project, Mr. Bretting contacted the program manager/consultant and mentioned that he was worried about the amount of risk involved in trying to introduce such an innovative consumer product with his current organization. He was worried that the project was oriented too strongly towards R & D and did not consider related business problems in enough depth. (This was a complete about-face from his feelings three months earlier, when he had approved the first plan submitted with no changes.)

Mr. Bretting suggested that the consultant modify the existing project to include the introduction of a "me-too" consumer product before IMSCO's new product was defined and tested. Mr. Bretting thought that some experience with a "me-too" product would provide IMSCO management with valuable experience and would improve later performance with the new product. He allowed the R & D portion of the project to continue concurrently, but the "me-too" phase would have top priority as far as resources were concerned. The consultant said he would think about it and contact him next week.

Question: If you were the consultant, what would you recommend to Mr. Bretting?

Excel Electronics

Excel Electronics is nearing completion of a three-year project to develop and produce a new pocket computer. The computer is no larger than a cigarette pack but has all the power and features of a $10,000 microcomputer. The assembly line and all the production facilities will be completed in six months and the first units will begin production in seven months. The plant manager believes it is time to begin winding the project down. He has three methods in mind for terminating the project: extinction, inclusion, and integration, but he is not sure which method would be best for the company.

Question: Which of the three methods would you recommend, and why?

13.12 BIBLIOGRAPHY

1. Adams, J. R., S. E. Brandt, and M. D. Martin. *Managing by Project Management.* Dayton, OH: Universal Technology Corp., 1979.
2. Amrine, H. T. *et al. Manufacturing Organization and Management,* 3rd ed. Englewood Cliffs, NJ: Prentice-Hall, 1975.
3. Andrews, K. R. *The Concept of Corporate Strategy.* Homewood, IL: Dow Jones—Irwin, 1971.
4. Archibald, R. D. *Managing High Technology Programs and Projects.* New York: Wiley, 1976.

5. Avots, I. "Making Project Management Work—The Right Tool for The Wrong Project Manager." *Advanced Management Journal,* Autumn 1975.

6. Avots, I. "Why Does Project Management Fail?" *California Management Review,* Fall 1969.

7. Baker, N. R., S. G. Green, and A. S. Bean. *A Multivariate Analysis of Environmental Organizational and Process Variables in The Process of Organized Technological Innovation, Vol. II, Technical Summary,* Final Report on National Science Foundation Award No. ISI 7921581. College of Business Administration, University of Cincinnati, Jan. 1984.

8. Baker, N. R., S. G. Green, A. S. Bean, W. Blank, and S. K. Tadisina. "Sources of First Suggestion and Project Success/Failure in Industrial Research." *Proceedings,* Conference on the Management of Technological Innovation, Washington, DC, 1983.

9. Balachandra, R., and A. J. Raelin. "How to Decide When to Abandon A Project." *Research Management,* July 1980.

10. Benningson, L. A. "The Strategy of Running Temporary Projects." *Innovation,* Sept. 1971.

11. Buell, C. K. "When to Terminate A Research and Development Project." *Research Management,* July 1967.

12. Cerullo, M. J. "Determining Post-Implementation Audit Success." *Journal of Systems Management,* March 1979.

13. Cleland, D. I., and W. K. King. *Systems Analysis and Project Management,* 2nd. ed. New York: McGraw-Hill, 1975.

14. Connor, P. E. *et al.,* eds. *Dimensions in Modern Management.* Boston: Houghton Mifflin, 1974.

15. Dean, B. V. *Evaluating, Selecting, & Controlling R & D Projects.* New York: American Management Association, Inc., 1968.

16. Gray, C. F. *Essentials of Project Management.* Petrocelli Books, 1981.

17. Hockney, J. W. *Control and Management of Capital Projects.* New York: Wiley, 1965.

18. Holzmann, R. T. "To Stop or Not—The Big Research Decision." *Chemical Technology,* 1972.

19. Kemp, P. S. "Post-Completion Audits of Capital Investment Projects." *Management Accounting,* Aug. 1966.

20. Kerzner, H. *Project Management, A Systems Approach to Planning, Scheduling, and Controlling.* New York: Van Nostrand Reinhold, 1979.

21. Kerzner, H. "Evaluation Techniques in Project Management." *Journal of Systems Management,* Feb. 1980.

22. Koontz, H. *Appraising Managers as Managers.* New York: McGraw-Hill, 1971.

23. Lee, W., and S. J. Mantel, Jr. "An Expert System for Project Termination." *Proceedings,* First International Conference on Engineering Management, Arlington, VA, Sept. 1986.

24. Mantel, S. J., Jr., A. L. Service, et al. "A Social Service Measurement Model." *Operations Research,* March–April, 1975.

25. Montgomery, J. L. "Appraising Capital Expenditures." *Management Accounting,* Sept. 1965.

26. Pinto, J. K., and D. P. Slevin. "Critical Factors in Successful Project Implementation." *IEEE Transactions on Engineering Management,* February 1987.

27. "Project Management Tasks: Wrap Up." *Design News,* April 19, 1982.

28. Raelin, J. A., and R. Balachandra. "R&D Project Termination in High-Tech Industries." *IEEE Transactions on Engineering Management,* Feb. 1985.

29. Ringstrom, N. H. "Making Project Management Work." *Business Horizons,* Fall 1965.

30. Rosenau, M. D. *Successful Project Management.* Belmont, CA: Wadsworth, 1981.

31. Shafer, S., and S. J. Mantel, Jr. "A Decision Support System for the Project Termination Decision: A Spreadsheet Approach." Graduate Center for the Management of Advanced Technology and Innovation, Paper No. MATI-88W-001, College of Business Administration, University of Cincinnati, 1988.

32. Silverman, M. *Project Management: A Short Course for Professionals.* New York: Wiley, 1976.

33. Stuckenbruck, L. C., ed. *The Implementation of Project Management: The Professionals Handbook.* Project Management Institute, Addison-Wesley, 1981.

34. Tadisina, S. K. "Support System for the Termination Decision in R & D Management." *Proceedings,* 18th Annual Seminar/Symposium, Project Management Institute, Montreal, Sept. 1986.

35. Wolff, M. F. "Knowing When the Horse Is Dead," *Research Management,* Nov. 1981.

13.13 READING

This article describes a system for evaluating the need for early project termination. It includes both psychological factors as well as project factors and the potential for inappropriate project continuance due to the interaction between the organizational culture and the project manager's personality. In addition, it directs the multiple chronological audits required to evaluate a project properly on both a static and dynamic basis.

The value of this article for managers is the combination of both project aspects and psychological aspects in the project evaluation. Too often projects are inappropriately continued for organizational/behavioral reasons when they should be terminated. The article identifies the project factors of importance and also the potentially troublesome interactions between the organization's culture and the PM's personality.

PROJECT MONITORING FOR EARLY TERMINATION

Jack Meredith
University of Cincinnati

Project management continues to play an ever larger role in society and industry. As consumer's demands for more unique products and services increase while the corresponding life cycles of those products and services decrease, the need for management through project organization escalates. With this increasing importance of successful projects, more attention has been focused on the managerial aspects of project management, and particularly those approaches that promise higher project payoffs or more successful projects.

The number of articles on how to better manage projects has increased significantly in the last decade. Such articles now appear in journals and magazines in fields from engineering to sociology [7]. Unfortunately, not all projects are successful. Yet, very little has been written about identifying failing projects and terminating them. Furthermore, most of what has been written (e.g. [2], [4], [5], [12]) has concerned the field of research and development (R&D) rather than projects in general.

Yet, the importance of quickly terminating a failing project can hardly be overemphasized. Stewart [11] has noted the exponential increase in cost to cut time from a project as the project nears completion. Similarly, sunk costs accumulate rapidly as termination of a failing project is delayed. Through early termination the organization can save not only the future costs of the project but the time, effort, and organizational disruption of a project failure. Guidelines for recognizing upcoming project failure and implementing an early termination, if it is justified, are just as important as guidelines for successfully managing projects in the first place.

This paper discusses the difficulty of early project termination and why it has so often been unsuccessful. An early termination monitoring system is then described that offers promise in rectifying some of these problems.

© 1988 by the Project Management Institute. Reprinted from *Project Management Journal*, Nov, 1988 by permission.

EARLY PROJECT TERMINATION

Early project termination (EPT) may be considered as the cessation of activity with abandonment of the project. Typically, this would occur when the costs and disadvantages of continuing the project were judged to outweigh the benefits and advantages of project completion. Dean [5] surveyed a number of executives to determine the actual reasons for EPT of R&D projects in their firms and found that the main reasons were the low probabilities of achieving the technical objectives of the projects or commercializing the results with an adequate return on investment.

Buell [4], in an early effort, provided some managerial guidelines for discontinuing R&D projects that were likely to become failures. He developed an extensive set of questions managers should consider during the progress of their firm's R&D projects because it was so difficult to specify solid standards for the EPT decision. His list included items ranging from the viability of the project concept itself to changes in the direction of the firm's strategy.

Meredith [6] identified a number of factors that computer implementation projects required for successful continuation. These factors were divided into three major categories: technical, process, and inner-environmental issues. Of major interest here is the last category which comprises two primary factors. The first is the continuing importance of the project to the organization. In particular, it must be a *current* problem the project is addressing. The problem may be either one of cost or opportunity but substantial resources must be already committed, or about to be, to addressing it. The second factor is the willingness of management to make the organizational and managerial changes required to utilize the project results.

More recently, Balachandra and Raelin [2] offered a list of ten quantitative and thirteen qualitative factors that could be scored to decide whether to terminate particular R&D projects. As with Buell, their list included both project viability factors as well as other related factors. The advantage of their approach, however, is its formality and rigor. Systematic analysis should improve the ability of managers to make correct EPT decisions, particularly as experience is gained with the process.

Tadisina's research [12] used factors such as those of Balachandra and Raelin in a statistical discriminant analysis to predict project success or failure. His data base consisted of 274 questions posed to managers in twenty-one firms in four major industries concerning the success or failure of 220 R&D projects. Factor analysis of the responses resulted in the isolation of 23 major factors grouped in five categories. If disaggregated by industry type, predictions of success and failure were significantly more accurate than prediction in general, ranging from over 70 percent to almost 90 percent.

In spite of such progress, it has too frequently been the case that projects were allowed to continue well past the time when it was obvious they were headed for disaster. More recent research ([1] [3] [8] [9] [10]) has now developed some insight into what the reasons for such behavior are. By way of explanation, Northcraft and Wolf [9] offer the insight that inappropriate project continuance will occur if the psychological benefits of continuing exceed the psychological costs of termination. In this context, the psychological benefits and costs include the monetary aspects noted earlier but also the individual and organizational advantages and disadvantages.

A number of researchers ([1] [8] [9]) invoke the "sunk cost" concept to explain the psychological costs and benefits by way of analogy. Reinforcement and utility theory both play roles in this concept. For example, reinforcement theory has found that random rewards will encourage people to continue a behavior well beyond the point that logic would dictate that their behavior has no effect on the rewards. And utility theory indicates that when some people have invested a significant amount in a risky situation, the potential loss of an additional increment of investment is much less valued than the potential gain from success.

One of the most explicit discussions of the psychological reasons for inappropriate project continuance is offered by Staw and Ross [10]. They categorize these reasons in terms of project aspects, managerial motivations, social pressures, and organizational forces. They also offer some advice to managers on how to avoid these psychological pressures.

Bowen [3] indicates that it is important to formally *structure* an EPT decision in the project process or else organizational commitment to the project tends to escalate for psychological reasons. It seems clear that we are currently in a much more knowledgeable position to successfully initiate and implement EPT than we have been in the past. What is needed is a formal monitoring system that evaluates both project and organizational/individual factors for project viability as well as inappropriate continuance. Such a system is proposed in the next section and incorporates the research results discussed above.

EARLY TERMINATION MONITORING SYSTEMS (ETMS)

The system envisioned for initiating EPT consists of a monitoring function separate from the project manager's office. Ideally, this function should report to that level of the organization with the responsibility for initiating (and terminating) projects.

The ETMS includes audits in three major time frames. The first audit is a general organizational review, separate from any particular project and conducted at infrequent intervals, to determine the "personality" of the organization in terms of its susceptibility to inappropriate project continuance. This audit is then repeated as major personnel changes occur and over extended time spans when the direction and policies of the organization have changed through evolution.

The second audit time frame is immediately after initiation of every project. This audit considers both project factors and project personnel factors. The project factors to be considered at this stage are "static" in the sense that they reflect the project objectives and can be evaluated before progress is made.

The last audit time frame is ongoing during the project and repeated at regular intervals. This audit first considers the dynamic project factors that

Early Termination Monitoring System (ETMS)

Step 1: Organizational Audit   Score*

1. Encouragement of persistence————
2. Penalties for failure   ————
3. Job security   ————
4. Managerial support   ————
5. Organizational inertia   ————
                              Total   ————

Step 2: Post-initiation Audit   Score*

2A: Static Project Factors

1. Prior experience   ————
2. Company image   ————
3. Political forces   ————
4. High sunk cost   ————
5. Intermittent rewards   ————
6. Salvage & closing costs   ————
7. Benefits at end   ————
                              Total   ————

2B: Project Manager Factors

1. Persistence   ————
2. Reinforcement susceptibility   ————
3. Confronting mistakes   ————
4. Information biasing   ————
5. Job security   ————
                              Total   ————

Step 3: On-going Audits

3A: Dynamic Project factors
      (see Table 1)
3B: Organizational Managerial Factors
      Evaluate interactions and
progress of factors in steps 1 and 2B

*Score as a 1 if this factor presents no problem up to a 5 if it presents a serious potential problem.

Figure 1   Process Flow of the Early Termination Monitoring System.

tend to change over time. While evaluating the dynamic project factors, the static factors are also reviewed for changes of relevance. Next, the audit analyzes the interplay that has occurred between the organizational factors and the project manager factors to date to determine if inappropriate project continuance may be occurring.

This process and the relevant factors are illustrated in Figure 1. The factors are measured on a five-point Likert-type scale and summed. The resulting sums can then be compared by the audit team or management across lines of business, across projects, or over time. Some of the factors, primarily in Step 1 and partially in Step 2, may be very difficult for internal auditors to evaluate and thus it might be necessary for the firm to rely on external consultants or viewpoints. Also, the ongoing evaluation in Step 3B of the interaction of those factors in Step 1 with the factors in Step 2B might require the services of an unbiased outside observer.

It might also be noted that our focus with the factors here is on the termination decision, rather than possible changes to improve the chances of successful project completion. For many factors, such as changes in political forces or the firm's image, this is totally appropriate. However, other factors in Figure 1 may be amenable to change so as to improve the chances of a successful project. This should be considered as a possible alternative by the project team when making its report.

The first two steps in Figure 1 are pre-startup and might be candidates for inclusion in the organization's formal project approval process. A discussion of each of the steps follows.

Step 1: Organizational Audit

The five items involved in the organizational audit as listed in Figure 1 are described here. The intent of this audit is to expose those high-scored elements of the organizational "personality" that tend to make it susceptible to inappropriate project continuance. A total score greater than 15 should alert the audit team to the general possibility of future

problems as well. The audit team can then check the potential for individual items to interact with particular projects and specific project managers to determine if inappropriate continuation may be occurring. As noted above, the organizational audit is repeated over time as seems appropriate to the changing personality of the organization.

1. Encouragement of Persistence. Organizations often strongly encourage managerial persistence in the face of adversity. This characteristic may be inculcated in their employees without ever being recognized explicitly; yet everyone knows it. Such persistence is often identified with strength and leadership in the managers, and promotions go to those who excel at it.

However, persistence in the continuation of a failing project wastes the organization's time, money, and other precious resources. Also, conditions can change such that a once important project to the firm's goals is no longer even relevant; to persist in the project is thus foolish. A common problem is that it may be difficult to tell if a project is failing, but persistence beyond the point where there is virtually no hope for success is wasteful.

2. Penalties for Failure. Too often, failure is viewed with excessive disfavor by the firm. Heavy penalties for failing force managers to adopt one of two negative modes of behavior: unwillingness to accept even moderately risky projects or else refusal to give up on a project failure.

3. Job Security. A corollary to the factor above is the amount of security managers have in their jobs. If the normal policy of the firm is to tie job promotions or demotions to project success, then the negative managerial behaviors noted above will be common. The wise organization will attempt to provide managers with job security independent of their performance on specific projects.

4. Managerial Support. Organizations must realize that if risk-taking is to be encouraged, then failures will be a natural consequence and must not be penalized. Instead, the support of top management is needed to encourage managers to continue to take such risks and make them realize that failure is not necessarily a reflection on their capabilities.

5. Organizational Inertia. It is difficult for organizations to make changes, particularly changes reflecting negative outcomes. They tend to ignore information received and are reluctant to disrupt their standard, comfortable patterns of operation. Even more difficult is altering organizational policies, redefining jobs, or transferring people.

Step 2A: Post-Initiation Audit: Static Project Factors

The audit team can usually analyze this set of factors as soon as the project is adequately defined. The team conducts the audit soon after announcement or initiation of the project to determine anticipated weaknesses ahead of time rather than after problems have arisen. If the total score on these factors exceeds 21, the project should be reconsidered.

1. Prior Experience. Does the firm have any prior experience in this or a related area? Without such experience, it is difficult to tell if problems that arise during the course of the project are serious or only temporary.

2. Organizational Image. Sometimes a project becomes difficult to cancel because it is associated with the organization's "image." To cancel the project might cast a bad reflection on the entire organization. It is important to determine beforehand if a project is one of these types.

3. Political Forces. Similar to the image problem noted above, there may be strong political forces involved with continuing the project. Attempting to terminate a project in the face of such forces may bring undesirable excessive pressure on the organization.

4. Large Sunk Costs. A particular project may involve the expenditure of significant up-front or investment funds before any substantial progress

is made. If so, the project has the potential for being inappropriately continued simply because of the extent of resources already invested in it. Clearly, the consideration of these sunk costs should occur before the investment is made, during project initiation, not during the EPT decision.

5. Intermittent Rewards. If it appears that the project will be one with the potential for intermittent, random rewards then the likelihood of inappropriate continuance through reinforcement theory must be considered. Forearmed, the organization can guard against believing progress is being made when the rewards come independently of any progress.

6. Salvage and Closing Costs. Akin to sunk costs, there may be reluctance to terminate a project because there is little salvage value in the project, or the costs of closing it down may exceed the immediate costs of keeping it going. Once again, it is better to consider these possibilities early, before the project gathers steam.

7. Benefits at the End. Some projects have the characteristic that all of the benefits come at the end of the project. If so, then there is great pressure to see the project through to the end, if only to recapture some of the sunk costs. Again, such a characteristic should be considered early, before progress makes termination unacceptable.

Step 2B: Post-Initiation Audit: Project Manager Factors

These factors, also conducted soon after project approval and appointment of the project manager, concern the characteristics of the project manager, particularly in relation to the "personality" of the organization. Again, the choice of the project manager should perhaps be reconsidered if the total score in this step is greater than 15.

1. Persistence. Does the project manager associate persistence with strength, leadership, and image? Are these characteristics important to him or her? Is withdrawal perceived as a sign of weakness?

If so, the project manager may be playing right into the personality weakness of the firm and inappropriate project continuance could easily arise.

2. Reinforcement Susceptibility.   Is the project manager likely to view random, successive project rewards as a positive sign, or a sign of progress? If the project is the type where this event is likely to happen, care must be exercised during project evaluation for continuance.

3. Confronting Mistakes.   Is the manager comfortable with the knowledge that everyone makes mistakes? Is he or she willing to face their own mistakes or admit errors of judgement? Or is the manager likely to try to justify his or her own past behavior, or invest just a little more in the hope of turning around a failing project? What is the project manager's attitude toward risk, success, and failure?

4. Information Biasing.   Does the manager tend to interpret information according to preconceived notions or beliefs? Do only the positive bits of information get noted while the negative indications are ignored?

5. Job Security.   Does the project manager feel secure about his or her career and job? Or does the manager worry that project failure may result in loss of the job as well? How accurate is this perception in terms of the organization's policies and history?

Step 3: On-Going Audits

The third step is a qualitative one and requires detailed analysis of the project's progress and evolution to date as well as insight concerning the interaction of the organization and the personality of the project manager. As noted earlier, this step may require the objective viewpoint of an outside expert or consultant. Considerable analysis is also necessary and thus the absence of a checklist format for this portion of the ETMS.

Step 3A: Dynamic Project Factors

These audits are conducted on a regular basis over the lifetime of the project. The dynamic project factors are listed in Table 1 and have been synthesized from the literature described earlier on symptoms of project failure. The factors are dynamic in the sense that they change over the life cycle of the project, sometimes rather abruptly, and thus need to be constantly reassessed. The items listed in the table are examples considered typical of that category.

1. Static Factors.   A review of the static factors is also needed at this audit to determine if any of these have changed for the worse. For example, the sunk costs may have been higher than was expected, or the salvage value may be less than was expected. To the extent that these have worsened, EPT may be more appropriate.

2. Task-team.   This set of factors concerns the nature of the task and the team conducting the project. In terms of the task, the audit should determine if the technical objectives have become more difficult to attain, or if the technological or manufacturing problems are harder to solve than was expected. A clue to this difficulty is if the project milestones have frequently been missed so far, either in time or in terms of performance specifications. Another indicator is if the expected time to achieve the results seems to be stretching out beyond earlier expectations.

The other side of this issue is the ability of the project team. Is it losing its enthusiasm? Has it become less innovative? Is its commitment dissipating? Clearly, technical problems can arise either because they have become more difficult or because the team is less able to cope with them.

3. Sponsorship.   The evaluation of this set of factors revolves around the commitment of the sponsor to the project concept. This commitment will be reduced if the project, for some reason, has become less consistent with organizational goals or less important to the firm in general. There may now be less of an expected impact on the firm or the linkage with other projects the company is conducting may be weaker. Or perhaps the oppor-

Table 1
Dynamic Project Factors

1. Review static factors
   • Prior experience
   • Company image
   • Political forces
   • High sunk costs
   • Intermittent rewards
   • Salvage & closing costs
   • Benefits at end

2. Task-team
   • Difficulty achieving technical performance
   • Difficulty solving technological/manufacturing problems
   • Time to completion lengthening
   • Missing project time or performance milestones
   • Lowered team innovativeness
   • Loss of team or project manager enthusiasm

3. Sponsorship
   • Project less consistent with organizational goals
   • Weaker linkage with other projects
   • Lower impact on the company
   • Less importance to the firm
   • Reduced problem or opportunity
   • Less top management commitment to project
   • Loss of project champion

4. Economics
   • Lower projected ROI, ROS, market share, profit
   • Higher cost to complete project
   • Less capital availability
   • Longer time to project returns
   • Missing project cost milestones
   • Reduced match of project financial scope to firm/budget

5. Environment
   • Better alternatives available
   • Increased competition
   • Less able to protect results
   • Increased government restrictions

6. User
   • Market need obviated
   • Market factors changed
   • Reduced market receptiveness
   • Decreased number of end use alternatives
   • Reduced likelihood of successful commercialization
   • Less chance of extended or continuing success

tunity, or problem, is reduced now. Or possibly the project champion has been transferred, or taken another position. This will all be reflected in a reduced level of pressure to complete the project.

4. Economics. These factors all center on the possibility of a reduced reward for the organization by completing the project. This can occur in a number of ways. The projected return on investment (ROI) or sales (ROS), market share, or profit may be lower than initially expected. Or perhaps there now appears to be a longer time to payback. Or the cost to complete the project may now be considerably higher. This may be indicated, for example, through missed cost milestones to date. Or the financial scope may no longer match that of the firm, either because the resource availability is more problematic or the relationship of the project cost to the rest of the budget is out of kilter.

5. Environment. The environment surrounding the project may have changed also, putting the project in jeopardy. For example, there may now be better ways of attaining the same results, such as through purchase or subcontracting. Or perhaps competitors' reactions are more successful than was expected. Another possibility is that it may now appear impossible to protect the project results with a patent or via trade secrecy. Or possibly increased governmental restrictions have become a problem.

6. User. For any of a number of reasons, the market may be less receptive now. For example, the market need may have relaxed, been obviated, or changed in some other way. Or perhaps the relevant factors have changed. Or maybe just the likelihood of success has fallen. Another aspect is the number of alternative uses of the result may have dropped. Or the extended success of the result may have decreased, even though the initial success is still assured.

Step 3B: Organizational/Managerial Factors

In this final step, the potential for psychologically interacting factors to foster inappropriate project continuance is addressed. The task facing the audit team is to analyze the managerial personality characteristics from Step 2B that might dovetail with any potentially inappropriate organizational policies in Step 1. If the team finds indications that such factors are beginning to affect project continuance, they are then investigated thoroughly. The team should specifically scrutinize issues of persistence, job security, and error-justification since these areas hold the greatest potential for inappropriate project continuance.

In addition, the team should monitor other potentially dangerous effects as well. Examples would include information biasing by the project manager, the actualization of reinforcement theory as described earlier, and organizational inertia. If these or other factors are found to be compromising the honest evaluation of the project, they must be followed up.

CONCLUSION

The termination of failing or nonviable projects is of major importance to organizations. Projects are becoming both more frequent and more expensive; the ability to save the resources commonly expended on failed projects is thus critical to organizational survival.

Research in project failure, its early symptoms, and the psychological reasons for organizational/managerial behavior now allow us to monitor for signs of inappropriate project continuance. By installing an early termination monitoring system as described here, more of the precious resources wasted on non-viable and failing projects can possibly be saved and thereby, perhaps, the organization as well.

REFERENCES

1. Arkes, H. R. and Blumer, C., "The Psychology of Sunk Cost," *Organizational Behavior and Human Decision Processes,* 1985, 35, 124–140.
2. Balachandra, R. and Raelin, J. A., "How to Decide When to Abandon a Project." *Research Management,* 1980, 23, July, 24–29.
3. Bowen, M. G., "The Escalation Phenomenon Reconsidered: Decision Dilemmas or Decision Errors?" *Academy of Management Review,* 1987, 12, 1, 52–66.
4. Buell, C. K., "When to Terminate a Research and Development Project." *Research Management,* 1967, July.
5. Dean, B. V. *Evaluating, Selecting, and Controlling R&D Projects.* New York: American Management Association, 1968.
6. Meredith, J. R., "The Implementation of Computer Based Systems," *Journal of Operations Management,* 2, Oct., 11–21.
7. Meredith, J. R. and Mantei, S. J., Jr. *Project Management: A Managerial Approach,* New York: Wiley, 1985.
8. Northcraft, G. B. and Neale, M. A., "Opportunity Costs and the Framing of Resource Allocation Decisions," *Organizational Behavior and Human Decision Processes,* 1986, 37, 348–356.
9. Northcraft, G. B. and Wolf, G. "Dollars, Sense, and Sunk Costs: A Life Cycle Model of Resource Allocation Decisions." *Academy of Management Review,* 1984, 9, 2, 225–234.
10. Staw, B. M. and Ross, J., "Knowing When to Pull the Plug." *Harvard Business Review,* 1987, March–April, 68-74.
11. Stewart, J. M., "Making Project Management Work." *Business Horizons,* 1965, Fall.
12. Tadisina, S. K., "Support System for the Termination Decision in R&D Management," *Project Management Journal,* 1986, XVII, 5, 97–104.

CHAPTER 14

Project Management: Present and Future

In the previous chapters we discussed the various aspects of project management in the modern organization. In this chapter we discuss and reemphasize the interrelatedness of these aspects. Then we add some thoughts about the future of project management.

14.1 REVIEWING THE PARTS AND THEIR RELATIONSHIPS

Books, particularly textbooks, must be organized according to some underlying structure. This one is arranged to follow the various stages of the project life cycle. In the first section of the book we dealt with project selection because it requires an understanding of what the parent firm is trying to accomplish with its projects. Then we discussed the nature of the PM and the different ways of organizing and planning a project. Some PMs have little or no choice in adopting an organizational form. Thus, they may not be able to select a form that seems to be well adapted to the substance of the project and appears to promise administrative comfort. But it is still useful for the PM to have foreknowledge of the ways in which a project's organizational structure is apt to affect the progress of day-to-day life on the project. The section ends with a discussion of negotiation and conflict resolution in project management.

The midsection of the book covers matters of immediate interest to all PMs: budgeting, scheduling, monitoring, and controlling the project itself. We presented this set of subjects as an integrated group of activities that should be conducted as a unified whole. Finally we close the book with a consideration of the audit/evaluation and project termination processes. Once again, some PMs never engage in these activities. In many organizations, project evaluations are conducted by people who are not connected with the project, and projects are sometimes terminated by specialists in that phase of project life. Still, we feel it is important that the PM be familiar with all stages of a project's life—from its beginnings to its end.

The interdependencies of resource allocation, scheduling, planning, budgeting, and controlling are emphasized in our treatment of those subjects. The interdependence of control and organizational structure, however, is less obvious but not less important. For example, the pure project form of organization gives the PM fewer control problems—other things being equal—than does the functional project organization. In the pure project form, the PM has considerable line authority, more than in the functional form. This has implications for the design of the control system because, as noted above, the PM is apt to have little influence over the choice of organizational structure but considerable influence over the design of the project control systems.

In a functionally organized project, the PM may have a great deal of de facto control over technology in those areas where he or she is expert. Further, given a reasonable working relationship with colleagues, the PM may exercise considerable influence over their technical contributions. On the other hand, the administrative practices of the project will almost certainly have to conform to the standard procedures of the host functional area. The result is that the emphasis of a control system designed under such circumstances will be on technical matters rather than administrative matters.

In the same way, the idea generation phase of some projects (see Appendix A) may have a heavy impact on the PM's ability to stay within budget and schedule. In heavy industry, for example, it is common for a sales engineer to be the primary contact between the firm and its clients. When the product/service being marketed is highly specialized by customer and requires extensive engineering design or customization, the sales engineer may be led to promise the customer product features that are difficult for the design engineers to deliver. If the firm is trying to establish a foothold in a new market area, the pressure on the sales engineer to get an order may be extreme, which makes it more likely still that the design/manufacturing groups will be faced with technical problems for which there are no standard solutions.

Under such conditions, it is helpful to appoint a PM as soon as it appears that the sales engineer has found a "warm" customer. The PM's first task is to form the skeleton of a project team in which team members represent the key technical areas on which the customer's needs are apt to depend. The immediate result of this process will be an increase, often a sharp increase, in sales expense because the selling firm will find itself sending teams of representatives, rather than a single sales engineer, to visit a client.

The benefits of this approach flow from the fact that no single sales engineer, almost irrespective of level of experience, can be expected to be familiar with the many disciplines involved in the design of this type of industrial equipment. Nor can a sales engineer be expected to be sufficiently knowledgeable about the design, manufacture, and installation problems involved, or about the loadings on manufacturing facilities, to make sensible estimates of delivery/installation dates. In our experience, the added cost of sales is more than offset by a higher probability of making the sale and more efficient methods of planning, producing, and implementing the project.

Similar kinds of interdependencies exist between most of the fundamental aspects of project management. It is not necessary to detail all the ways that the work of the PM could be affected, but it clearly will be.

14.2 THE FUTURE OF PROJECT MANAGEMENT

The need for PMs will increase in the foreseeable future. There is no census of opinion on the growth rate of project organizations, at least not one known to us, but there is no doubt that the number is increasing rapidly. Several forces are combining to produce this growth. Some are predominantly socioeconomic, and others are mainly technological.

Socioeconomic Forces

1. The past few decades have been marked by the expansion of a true worldwide economy. The impact of this development on the United States is seen in the fact that the balance of trade turned against this country in 1976 and has remained negative since then. Foreign competition has been intense in almost all of the economic activities that produced the spectacular economic growth of the first half of this century. Project organization cannot reverse this trend, but it is an important element in increasing the speed with which new products and services can be developed to compete with overseas products and services.

2. The perception that considerable economic uncertainty is associated with the high levels of domestic and foreign debt puts a high premium on shortening the time line from idea generation to market reality.

3. A strong need for instant solutions for problems has developed in American society. (It is accompanied by a concommitant need to place the blame for anything that goes wrong.) Thus, the explosion of the Challenger, the appearance and spread of AIDS, a nightclub fire in which scores are trapped and killed, the fatal injury of children in a school bus accident, the crash of the stock market, the discovery of structural weakness in an aircraft that might or does cause an accident, and similar events cause an immediate flurry of projects devoted to finding "fixes."

4. Highly sophisticated manufacturing processes make it possible to extend the variety of goods and services available; and foreign competition makes it desirable to do so. For a great many goods and services, project organization is the most effective way to manage the diversification. This trend is particularly evident in the area of computer software for integrating data collection, data storage, and report writing. Not only is project organization used to develop the software, projects are also used to link customer and vendor in the process of customization.

5. Indeed, the whole concept of *product* has been greatly extended in recent years. In Chapter 5 we discussed the impact of systems integration on product/service development. It is difficult to know where the product stops and the service begins. To develop, operate, and control complex systems requires a management system, and project management is a flexible, powerful management system. Consider a home computer system composed of a computer, monitor, two printers, and a programmable printer buffer. If the assembly of such a system is not handled as a project, serious incompatibility problems are quite likely to result. Consider outfit-

ting and preparing the *Queen Elizabeth II* for a trip to Europe. In both cases, the "product" and the "service" are almost indistinguishable. They must be managed as a unified whole.

6. The changing nature of the work force also acts to accelerate the use of projects. Many observers have commented on the fact that modern technology features the use of brain rather than muscle; many popular writers refer to this as the "era of the knowledge worker." The increased use of human beings with specialized mental skills raises severe management problems. It is not uncommon for such people to receive remuneration at a level that was, in earlier times, only earned through the use of expensive machinery. Consider a $2 million machine operating 2 1/2 shifts, 250 days per year for ten years. The machine runs approximately fifty thousand hours. The capital cost per hour (undiscounted for simplicity) is $40. That is equivalent to an annual salary of about $80,000. Production managers spend considerable effort to keep the machine operating and productive. In many firms, the value of human resources far exceeds the value of machinery; but keeping these specialized human resources engaged in productive work cannot be done with a production line approach. Project organization allows such valuable people to be moved easily and quickly to where they are most useful.

Technological Forces

1. The technological complexity of our products and services is increasing steadily. Almost paradoxically, this allows us to simplify these products and services. A complex silicon chip makes it possible to perform sophisticated operations on a hand-held computer. The repair of TV sets is simplified by the use of complex plug-in subsystems. To design and manufacture this combination of complexity and simplicity demands the use of projects. We have argued this point throughout this book. The phenomenon is spreading rapidly with no sign of leveling out.

2. The increasing availability of computer power to small firms and individuals, along with the growth of PMIS software for these microcomputers, is putting the tools of project management within everyone's reach. Schedules, WBSs, reports, status updates, variance analyses, and other such techniques are automatically available through the PMIS software. Having such tools at hand will tend to extend the use and application of project management.

3. The rapid growth of knowledge not only indicates the growing need for project organizations that can add to and distribute knowledge where and when it is needed (as noted in the sixth of the socioeconomic forces mentioned above), but it also raises a serious problem for future PMs. Interproject communication is on the verge of becoming a critical problem for organizations operating several projects at once. If one parent firm is conducting multiple projects, they are apt to be parts of one or more programs. In any case, they are almost certain to depend on similar underlying bodies of knowledge. This makes it likely that each project can profit by sharing knowledge and insight developed by the other projects. Little is known about how to improve and manage interproject communications. The development of computerized management information systems may help in the future, but at this point PMISs are not oriented to communicating among projects.

4. Another knowledge-associated issue will result in an increased use of projects: the need to move knowledge rapidly. As we have seen, a major advantage of the functional and matrix forms of project organization is the depth of technological knowledge available to the project. The matrix-organized project has this depth in any functional area existing in the parent firm. As our society extends its base of knowledge, the matrix-organized project will become more necessary as a way of building the proper knowledge base.

5. During the 1970s we witnessed the repeal of a law that had been considered sacrosanct, if not absolutely necessary, to the maintenance of a free economic system. This was the law of *caveat emptor.* The definition of product (and service) liability has been radically widened during the 1980s and there does not seem to be any limit to the change.

   A Rhode Island court recently held the Goodyear Tire and Rubber Company liable for a defect in an experimental racing tire when racing driver Mark Donahue was killed in a racing accident. The fact that Donahue knew racing was dangerous and that any part of the car was subject to catastrophic failure under the high-stress conditions of racing was held to be irrelevant. In another action, the Porsche car company was held liable for the death of a driver who, after several drinks, was unable to control the car. The manufacturer of a baseball base was held liable for the broken ankle of a player who slid into the base. It was argued that the base should have been labeled for the hazard.

   Dealing with potential impacts on humans who use or misuse products is clearly the responsibility of the producer. This extended version of what is meant by *product* or *service* cannot be dealt with through the traditional organizational system. It requires projects devoted specifically to the issues of liability.

6. Finally, we usually think of technological growth as the province of the physical and natural sciences. But knowledge is expanding in the social sciences, too. While most of the socioeconomic and technical forces we have mentioned augur the increasing use of the project-organizational form in the future, developments in the social and behavioral sciences will allow this growth to take place. The advantages of project organization are many—but so are the disadvantages, many of them falling under the general area of management and communication problems. Behavioral scientists are studying these problems and have thereby added greatly to our ability to manage projects.

All in all, the future of project management looks extremely active. We see an increasing use of the several forms of project organization, with special emphasis on matrix organizations. In our opinion, increased use will be made of professional project managers, individuals who are project managers by training and vocation rather than scientists or marketing specialists by training and project managers by necessity. The PM will do less technical work in the future and will specialize more in coordinating the technical and behavioral aspects of the project.

While some of the skills needed by project managers are the same as those needed by the traditional administrative managers, many of the required skills are quite different. The administrative manager of a regular cost center is strongly oriented toward control, but the project manager must focus more strongly on planning and implementation.

14.3 READING

> This article shows how a flexible approach to project management will help systems survive at the turn of the century. Project manager selection and training, performance measurement, the role of the computer, and organizational considerations are addressed, in addition to societal changes.

Project Management in the Year 2000*

Harold Kerzner

During the 1970 decade, the growth and acceptance of project management techniques and philosophies was astounding. More and more industries came to accept project management as the management tool of the future in order to make more efficient and effective utilization of corporate resources. Some industries, construction, aerospace and defense have accepted it either informally or modified in some fashion. Today, project management exists in construction, aerospace, defense, banks, hospitals, government agencies, accounting, law, R&D, manufacturing and electronics.

Project management was established as a means to control completion dates or specific tasks or problems from a total or "big picture" view. Today we are exposed to project management as a change from the classical or traditionally vertical line organization to a system which has both a vertical and horizontal structure operating concurrently. This horizontal structure, or project management organization, cuts across and interfaces the traditional structure. These interface positions are locations where specific functional resources are required in order to solve a horizontal need. Unfortunately, vertical organization can end up being "drained" in order to satisfy horizontal requirements. The resolution of these horizontal-vertical needs is the solution to a specific problem using project management technique.

Even today, the term project management means different things to different people. In general, however, it is understood to mean a "new breed" of middle manager within a business, government agency or service organization. It implies the management of discrete projects, with identifiable goals and objectives, limited resources, and a finite time duration. The term also implies a matrix organizational structure where the project manager carries considerable responsibility but may have very little real authority over the project team members.

What will project management be like in the year 2000? This simple question raises the broader issues of "What will business in general be like?" "What will our future lifestyle be?" While it is impossible to predict with certainty even twenty short years ahead, certain trends can be identified and additional speculations may be helpful:

- Engineering/technology appears to be doubling every five years or less
- Computer technology is doubling every two years
- Product life cycles are becoming shorter
- There is a greater demand for new product introduction, with shorter product development time
- Managers and executives are requiring more infor-

*Copyright © 1981 by the Association for Systems Management. Reprinted from *Journal of Systems Management,* October 1981 by permission. All rights reserved.

mation and at a faster rate for strategic decision-making

- More and more managers are becoming people rather than task oriented
- Executives have come to realize that they cannot manage a $50mil/year corporation with a $10mil/year system

This article explores possible changes in our future way of doing business and then suggests some of the implications for tomorrow's project managers.

ORGANIZATIONAL CONSIDERATIONS

Even a conservative view of the future requires a great deal of imagination. Our business views appear to be changing with an extremely strong emphasis being placed on middle managers to be evaluated solely on ROA or profit contributions. Since most horizontal lines are profit centers, project management appears to be an excellent method for training future managers and executives to be cost-conscious as well as profit oriented.

Our basic business principles need serious revision in the near future because of this short-term approach and long-term implications. Business and government seem to have opposing views and these additional complications are all combining to reduce efficiency. Technology is making the world smaller and obsoleting more of the operational tasks while at the same time, business is finding it more difficult to operate profitably.

If growth continues as it has in the past 20 years, we can expect to see major changes through technological developments. Project management will be widely implemented and accepted only when it clearly proves that increased profits may be realized.

If change is slow and automation is resisted, the more centralized traditional organizations will still be used throughout the remainder of the 20th century. If so, improved productivity can be gained only through internal resource sharing and horizontal work flow, the basic ingredients of project management. Therefore, since project

management organizational forms seem to be more adaptable, they will most likely become almost universally accepted over the next 20 years. Functional specialist positions would most likely remain as an organizational line element. All or most staff organizations presently servicing internal operation are likely to become smaller in number and will generally be aligned in a matrix to serve all functional disciplines.

As the project management structure and the position of the project manager become more mature, emphasis will be placed upon reducing the overhead rate by eliminating several layers of supervisory positions that exist between the project managers and upper-level management. The secret, of course, rests in the ability and confidence that the executives will impart to the project managers. This should not pose much of a problem since the majority of the executive management positions will probably be filled from the project management ranks, since the project managers could conceivably be the only individuals that understand the operations of the total company, not merely one line organization.

PROJECT VS. PRODUCT MANAGEMENT

Without some insight or understanding of project management, organizations of the future will find it more difficult to manage during periods of growth without creating some degree of havoc with operating procedures. In order to cope with such problems, organizations have slowly increased the indirect population of the traditional structure with the rationale that "If we throw enough people at these problems, they must eventually figure out a way to handle them." This technique usually fails because of poor communications, mistrust, and duplication of efforts.

The necessity for quick resolution to these problems will prompt management to think that "permanent" task forces or project teams will result in improved productivity and effectiveness. Yet even with continued success at task fore management, executives will struggle with this concept of full-time project management until either the next step becomes obvious or new entrants in top management force us into full-time project management. Companies may find disastrous results by going piecemeal into project management.

By the year 2000, product lines which cannot justify continuous full-time utilization of resources will be controlled by product managers using project management. The terms project and product management may even become synonymous. Companies of the future will be structured by market segment. Each market segment will be run by a product manager. These product managers will constitute a project team one level below the functional vice-presidents. The project team will be responsible for the complete operation of existing products, and will also be part of the planning function project which will also include vice-presidents and the CEO. Project managers will report to the Vice President of Operations whereas full-time product managers will report to the Vice-President of Marketing.

Since products and applications are becoming increasingly more technically oriented, future project managers will be in the 25- to 35-year-old range. They will be trained in the area of production, design, processing or laboratory. Those individuals who demonstrate effective interpersonal skills and an ability to get the job done will be promoted to project management positions. As project managers, they will coordinate and manage all projects established by the executive level and both screened and prioritized by the executive project team which is composed of the CEO, the functional vice-president and the product managers.

ROLE OF THE COMPUTERS

As data processing managers come up through the ranks, project management will be a way of life. It could even be said that computer technology in the seventies and eighties has hastened the development of project management. This is primarily due to the cross-functional involvement of the complex and systematized computer systems that are put into effect.

If the computer systems are to be successfully installed by the year 2000, functional departments must cooperate and trade information with one another so that the desired results are obtainable. Data processing project management will become a strong driving force by the year 2000 because the overlap of computerization will force functional organization within a company to become more integrated. With the computer as a catalyst, by the year 2000 there will be much more matrix management than currently exists. Project management will evolve into a way of life.

Large, complex projects will have to include major social programs, energy related programs, and continuing defense programs. Financial, human and raw material resources will become more limited in the year 2000. This will mean increased controls especially in setting priorities, more sophisticated methods of trade-off analysis, and improved overall project control. Computers will become more extensively used in all areas of control.

There seems to be sufficient evidence that even a more revolutionary growth era could be forthcoming. With the technological breakthroughs and reduced costs, microprocessors and "smart terminals" will provide mechanisms for this growth. Software project planning models will become more evident in the offices of the future. It is also conceivable that more and more project managers will work out of their homes. If the current trend continues and accelerates, by the year 2000 the (two dimensional) traditional and matrix organizations as we know them may not physically exist at all. Individuals or groups of individuals functioning from their homes would rely totally on a telecommunications center as a communications vehicle. However, the strategic decision center and organizational centers will still remain within the parent organization. Hosts of computers could control large conglomerate projects, all linked together by a massive interdependent system.

The computer itself will become increasingly

more important and eventually may take the place of many middle managers, operational employees and clerks. The CEO, computer hardware and systems personnel are likely to be centralized within the executive decision-making group. If so, this group will ultimately function as the manager of project managers and will dictate work flow plans based upon project plans and master production schedules.

"Smart terminals" will play an ever-increasing role in project control. Terminal screens will be color-coded to provide an up-to-the-minute accounting for all assigned resources as well as for cost control. Corrective action and trade-off analysis can be taken instantaneously from these terminals. Inventory control problems will become a thing of the past. Project managers will have a complete picture of their own projects as well as other projects which are sharing common resources.

IMPACT ON BUSINESS ORGANIZATIONS

Assuming continuation of a partially regulated capitalistic structure, future business organizations will compete less on the basis of marketing or production capability and more on the basis of management ability and technological sophistication. This assumption is based on the idea that operational planning, production, production control, administration, and even marketing, will be automated and optimized to the extent that no "competitive edge" can long endure. Successful firms will be differentiated by their ability to do strategic planning, to develop optimal products, to mitigate governmental intervention, and to respond correctly to environmental change.

Functional middle managers are likely to become an "endangered species" by year 2000. They can and will be replaced by highly skilled technicians who operate the complex organization to achieve specific results ordered by a computerized control system. People will become unnecessary, even detrimental, in the optimization of operational programming, planning, and budgeting. Administrative functions, even including performance appraisal, will not require human intervention, except for review.

Top management will be more directly involved

and more completely in control of the total business operations. Computer software will be available to translate strategic goals and short range objectives into action plans, and will faithfully report the results achieved directly to the top.

If true, these changes will give rise to a different type of middle manager—the project manager—to plan and execute those unique efforts which have not been placed under computer control.

ROLE OF THE PROJECT MANAGER

Within the speculative framework outlined above, the extreme flexibility of a matrix organization and the adaptive ability of the project manager to deal with the changing array of projects, may justify his continued existence. It is presupposed that automation and computerized optimization techniques will make recurring operations as efficient and effective as is technologically possible. However, the "one of a kind" project (R&D, capital facility development, acquisition or divestment of a product line, etc.) will require project manager leadership. The following project management skills will likely be important in the future:

- Producing an "end result" within constraint of available resources and performance requirements. This will require a "global view" of the project objectives and accurate planning of how success will be achieved.
- Leadership aspects of directing the project team effort will remain important. However, reporting of results and control feedback will be highly automated, and will require relatively less attention.
- Decision making will be based on use of all pertinent data, but typically this will still involve uncertainty within an uncontrolled environment.
- Negotiations for needed resources and resolution of conflicting demands on those resources will still be important. In fact, the interface requirement will take on the larger proportions of the conflict between computer control and human initiative. Resolution across that man-machine interface will be particularly demanding.

The anticipated role of the future project manager is largely related to operational planning for unique projects. While the computer can make real contributions in all program development, it probably will not be capable of identifying all relevant alternatives, testing them against the broader environment, and charting an operational plan to achieve the unique objectives of a "one shot" project. The project manager's "systems view" of the world will permit evaluation of the true alternatives and "coaching" of the project team to execute the selected action plan.

PM SELECTION AND TRAINING

Assuming an increasingly responsible role for future project managers, their selection, training, evaluation, and retention will also become increasingly important. It is logical to anticipate that optimization techniques will be applied to personnel selection as well as to other aspects of business management. All available sources of information, including personal history, academic achievement, performance appraisals, psychological testing, and career development counseling will be used to select future project managers.

It seems likely that formal education will be interspersed throughout the future project manager's worklife, such that they may continue to cope with a rapidly changing world. Future project managers will likely come from a particular discipline, but their specialization may shift over time, and a career development plan will concentrate on broadening their experience base through both formal education and job rotation. In addition to disciplinary skills, future project managers will require communications and general business skills, knowledge of the man-machine interface with computers, knowledge of governmental restraints and a feeling for how public policy decisions are made, a global view of business economics, and a general understanding of human behavior.

At various points in their career development, project managers should interface directly with top management to understand the development of strategic goals, how those goals are translated into

project objectives, and how project results impact the overall organization. This will also permit the development of managerial competence through increasingly responsible assignments and through "mentor" relationships with top managers.

Throughout the process, the organization must provide compensation, status, growth, and achievement recognition needed to motivate and retain competent project managers. This must be accomplished, however, without creating an "elitist group" which could not obtain project team cooperation and support in the matrix structure.

PERFORMANCE MEASUREMENT

Through powerful information systems and development of optimal control, feedback and reporting schemes, the appraisal of managerial performance will become highly objective. To be accurate, however, such performance appraisal must be based upon stated objectives and performance against those objectives in the context of environmental conditions encountered. Today, most management appraisal systems focus on how well actual performance compares with stated performance objectives. Present systems either ignore environmental changes which should affect the appraisal, or else sanctify environmental change or external restraint as the justification for neglecting performance standards. Expanded use of the information system data base will permit more accurate analysis and better evaluation of project manager results.

Based on full information and powerful computer support (approaching "artificial intelligence") the real evaluation of managerial performance will shift from "What happens if we depart from our operations plan?" to the more penetrating question "What happens if we achieve our intended plan?" The quality of strategic goals selected by top management will determine whether a proper project objective was conceived. And, the quality of the operational planning function performed by future PM's will largely determine project success.

GOVERNMENT

A futuristic analysis of the role of the project manager cannot be made without analyzing the environment in which he will be operating. It is probable that the impact of government on the lives of individual citizens will continue to increase, with environmental regulations increasing sharply. The government may well become heavily involved in the enforced recycling of nonrenewable resources wherever this is possible. Internationally, it is likely that democracy will continue to decline in the world and the remaining democracies (including the United States) will become increasingly socialized. Much has been said about the pollution of air and water, but these are relatively easy to clean up compared to the pollution that has taken place of the land. It is entirely likely that vast project teams will be necessary to clean up (if this is possible) the damage that has been done to the land and that these project teams will involve the resources of business and the government jointly. Very sophisticated project management techniques will be necessary for this activity.

SOCIAL CHANGE

With the increasing automation of production and the demand of the work force that tedium be removed from the work place, it is likely that the working week will be reduced, that there will be considerably more leisure than currently possible, and education will increase to such a degree that work and education will become difficult to separate. The rate of change of knowledge will require that it will be impossible for people to focus on a life's career, but rather will have to focus on several careers sequentially in a given lifetime. It is also likely that the flex-hours concept will find increasing acceptance with the result that all of these changes will have profound effects on how project managers will have to function. The work force will be considerably more mobile (not geographically, but vocationally) so that key and trusted project team members will become less and less available because of reeducation, flex hours, increased leisure time, etc.

DEMOGRAPHICS

There are huge demographic changes taking place in the United States. There are strong trends towards smaller families, single parent families, dual or multiple career families and migratory changes in the United States. Again, these changes will increase the *uncertainty of availability* of trained personnel to project teams, thus making the project manager's job more difficult and complex.

PHYSICAL RESOURCES

OPEC is a third world cartel. The use of crude oil in the world is expected to continue to increase and to peak out in the year 2000. The vast majority of crude oil is used as fuel and, therefore, is non-recoverable with only about 5% of crude oil being converted into chemicals. Increasingly, fuel, in the form of crude oil, will be difficult to acquire and projects which in the past could afford to regard fuel as a factor of low importance will now have to consider the impact of very high prices on project activity. Again, project management will be made all the more complex because of the need to plan for adequate fuel availability for the project. If the availability of organic resources (crude oil, natural gas and their derivatives) in the future is not encouraging, then the potential for inorganics is downright disastrous. The United States has largely depleted its reserves of key inorganics, such as zinc, copper, molybdenum, chromium, nickel and already there are moves by those countries which possess the resources to cartelize and form their own "OPEC." The project managers, as part of their project, may well have to consider alternatives to these key resources, with government-mandated recycling becoming a part of the total project.

THE MARKETS

The marketplace which project management will have to respond to will become increasingly complex and changeable. Project management will have to be constantly aware of changing techniques and regulatory rules in responding to rapid market shifts. It is very likely that the goals and objectives of a given project team will change during its lifetime even though the original plan was for a relatively short-lived project. Contingency planning in this environment will become an absolute necessity and it is possible that new courses in this discipline will emerge at specific universities.

Colleges and universities will begin teaching graduate and undergraduate interdisciplinary courses in project management. There may also exist massive continuing education programs in the areas of project and product management.

Companies will become not just international, but supranational. Concurrent with the emergence and growth of the new supranational company, will also come a blurring of the distinction between government and business. One manifestation of this lack of distinction is the profit-oriented, nationalized company (of which there are many successful examples around the world). Within the supranational company, the project manager's task will become increasingly complex and difficult as he tries to coordinate the activities of many people, of many languages, in several countries, with different skill levels in what will become increasingly international projects.

LIFE STYLES

Life generally, in the United States and elsewhere, will become more complex with faster change, necessitation of a change away from a single career lifetime to a multiple career lifetime. The project manager will probably have an even more difficult job because the number of tasks that have to be done will continue to increase with a high probability existing that there will be very large numbers of jobs in existence in the year 2000 which do not exist now and cannot even be forecast. In all probability, the emerging tendency will be for project managers to be assigned a project management task upon completion of which he is returned to a mundane non-project management task as recuperation will evolve into the need to retrain the project manager in some new skill of discipline upon the completion of each project. The rate of change of technology and science will not merely necessitate this but demand it. Large, long-term projects may eventually burn out good project managers.

CONCLUSION

Project management and the "systems approach" to human enterprise is today an extremely flexible and highly effective approach to multi-discipline program management. This approach is likely to be even more important in the future, as less flexible or less creative methods are executed by computers or robots.

Successful future enterprises will be differentiated by the quality of management planning and decision making. By virtue of broad experience, flexible approach, and a "people oriented" leadership style, tomorrow's project managers should be able to cope in the year 2000.

APPENDIX A
Creativity and Idea Generation

The project life cycle can begin with the concept of a new product, a new process, a new service. It can begin with a Request for Proposal (RFP) to design, construct, or install hardware, software, a telephone system, a building, a road, an aircraft engine. It can even begin with a competitor's new product or the slow realization that the firm is no longer dynamic and is now a follower rather than a leader. The subjects for projects are, like the Queen of the Nile, of infinite variety.

To be successfully carried out, however, they all require creativity. If the purpose of the project is to design a new process for shaping aircraft parts, or a new type of cradle-to-grave mental health insurance, the need for creativity is obvious. But if the project is to construct an office building, and if we have already constructed a dozen or so similar buildings, the need for creativity is not obvious. But those with experience in construction know that buildings are like fingerprints—no two are quite alike. Each one presents unique problems to be solved and requires creative solutions. All projects, therefore, call for creativity, but some call for more than others.

Here we look into the need for creativity. We learn how to foster it and how to discourage it. We even learn that creativity is not an unmixed blessing. We examine processes by which individuals and groups generate ideas, and we develop an understanding of the conditions that favor individual or group approaches to problem solving. We also see that certain organizational structures are useful for fostering idea generation, and conversely, that some organizational arrangements inhibit creativity. Finally, we gaze into our cloudy crystal ball and hazard some opinions on the future of creativity and idea-generation techniques.

Though few project managers may be actively engaged in managing projects at this early point in the project life cycle, they may find the subject of fostering creativity interesting and possibly even useful in their project responsibilities.

But the subject is particularly important for senior management as well as project managers not only because projects require creativity, but also because solving day-to-day problems requires it.

A.1 CREATIVITY AND THE COMPETITIVE FIRM

Creativity is the attribute of bringing into existence a unique concept or thing that would not have occurred or evolved naturally. The creative person combines, mixes, and expands past experiences so that new, nonobvious concepts, variations, or extensions of knowledge are generated.

In most organizations, creativity is an underutilized resource. M. I. Zeldman summed up [35] an extensive body of writing in his brief warning, "The corporations that will survive and thrive in the future are those that foster creativity today." If we showed that statement to the senior executives of thousands of firms, their reaction would undoubtedly be overwhelming assent. Indeed, it is likely that those senior managers would be annoyed that we dared to bother them with such an obvious statement. But if the Zeldman viewpoint is so widely accepted, so obvious, why is it that in so many firms creativity is stifled and innovation frustrated?

There are, of course, many reasons why managers appear to embrace the idea of creativity while shunning the reality. For example, a key managerial task is to smooth troubled organizational waters. (If this image bothers the reader, it is well to recall the common managerial admonition "Don't make waves.") Change stirs up the organizational waters, but change is the most likely result of creativity. Creativity is like pepper in the soup: A little adds zest, but a lot may well ruin the soup.

Most organizations, even forward-looking, high-technology firms, have a limited tolerance for innovation. Problems of survival arise when the limit is set too low, when the limit on creativity becomes a ban. In addition to the desire to avoid disturbances of organizational balance, creativity may be squelched because it threatens senior managers. The reaction "If we didn't think of it, it can't be a good idea" is so prevalent that it has been immortalized as "the N.I.H. syndrome" (*not invented here*). The cause of N.I.H. is rarely arrogance, though it usually sounds like arrogance; rather, it is fear. It is hard to admit that an outsider (or young person) can make a creative contribution to "our business." That forces us to admit that we may not know everything about our work. Many people cannot face such a threat to self-esteem.

Another kind of fear reinforces this barrier to creativity. Innovation is risky. Modern managers are taught to be risk avoiders. The brilliant article by Hayes and Abernathy, "Managing Our Way to Economic Decline" [17], makes this point. Risk avoidance is so strong that many firms refuse to undertake risky projects regardless of the magnitude of the potential payoffs; and higher risk is usually associated with higher payoffs, as illustrated in Figure 1.

Risk avoidance—and hence avoidance of creativity—is also manifested in another way, fear of the future. Many firms insist on very short payback periods, not being willing to fund investments with payback periods of more than two or

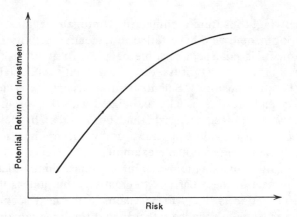

Figure 1 Relationship of risk and ROI.

two-and-a-half years. Some managers attempt to justify such short time horizons by citing the high cost of capital. Such explanations make little sense. A two-year payback period implies a cost of capital of almost 50 percent. Interest rates have been high in recent years, but not that high. A more likely explanation of this bias toward the short run is the fact that executives see little personal advantage in long-run projects. Their bonuses and merit rewards are usually tied to current P & L (profit and loss) statements. When rewards are tied to the present, it is not rational to reduce present profits by investing in an uncertain future.

In the face of all this emphasis on short time horizons, not many managers are willing to face up to the obvious implications of short-run policies. Few major industrial projects aimed at increasing productivity, for example, pay back in two or three years. Many require more than five years. It will take about ten years to construct a new integrated steel mill or copper refinery and bring it "on line," assuming no environmental or legal difficulties. Given a 15 percent interest rate, each dollar of revenue received 10 years from now has a present value of about 25 cents. If the cost of capital is 20 percent, the present value of that future dollar (10 years away) is only 16 cents. And it costs hundreds of millions of dollars, spent now and in the near future, to construct a steel mill or copper refinery. Yet the implications of not investing are also very clear. The dilemma needs attention. Several industries have recently lost markets because their plants and equipment are outdated. Over the past three decades, the integrated steel industry, for example, lost a considerable share of its market to foreign mills. The steel industry, however, exercised creativity and began the process of restructuring itself. The large, integrated mills are, for the most part, in economic trouble, but the newer, specialized minimills are thriving.

One response to these pressures and fears is often to purchase the fruits of creativity rather than develop them in-house. Patents can be licensed, and innovative firms can be purchased. Such actions appear to increase the cost of creative ideas, but they also reduce the risk. The firm knows, in general, what it is getting and at what price.

Two other barriers to creativity are common and should be mentioned. Some firms unknowingly institute a climate that mitigates against creativity by firing or transferring people who have failed in a creative activity or project. If failure in risky projects is punished, sensible people will avoid risky projects. Second, some firms inadvertently misuse their best creative talent by promoting them into administrative positions. Scientists often accept these moves because of the higher salary and prestige usually associated with the "promotion." Many firms have recently recognized this error and corrected it by developing *dual-track career ladders* that provide equal rewards for success in research or administration. Eli Lilly and Co. is a notable example.

It requires little imagination to think of other things that could be done to reduce the impact of these barriers to creativity, but unless the barriers are seen as serious, no action is likely to be taken. In the next section, we will look at some ways for firms to enhance rather than discourage creativity.

A.2 CREATIVITY MANAGEMENT

Much has been written about the problems of managing creative people—sometimes inaccurately described as "tweed coat management." Scientists are pictured as undisciplined, absent-minded geniuses with leather patches on the elbows of their threadbare tweed jackets. It is said that they require "total freedom to think," and that they need a manager whose main job seems to be a combination of babysitter and clerk/administrator who keeps the lab tidy, files the necessary reports, and sees to it that the scientists eat well-balanced meals.

Fortunately, this Hollywood cartoon of the researcher has little to do with reality. The widespread belief that scientists demand complete freedom in order to think creatively is simply not true. Souder has shown [30] that the creative output of research laboratories is unrelated to the degree of freedom given to the researchers. This apparent contradiction of a commonly held notion makes sense when we reflect on the nature of the individual. Some people, researchers included, think creatively when the area of investigation is constrained. Others are at their best when there are no boundaries to thought. Those who need or desire constraints tend to seek employment in organizations that furnish those constraints. Thinkers who do not function well under constraints choose organizational environments that allow more freedom. Creative thinkers vary widely in personality, style, needs, and even in their approach to problems. A discussion of how to organize creative endeavor is included in Section A.6.

Creativity is more important for some firms than others. Firms make choices about playing the role of leader or follower, at times even deciding to lead in some areas and to follow in others. The would-be leaders must stay abreast of current science. Followers must stay abreast of current technology. (Amid all this discussion of research and science, we should remember that both leaders and followers need creativity to be successful: Leaders need creative effort to extend science and technology; followers need creative effort in applying technology.) Firms seeking the image of high-technology organizations must have a fairly steady stream of new ideas or creative extensions of existing ideas. Ethical drug firms, computer software houses, and electronic component manufacturers are among such firms. Even customers who have no particular need for state-of-the-art technology may still opt to purchase from suppliers who appear to be at the scientific forefront.

The full support of the chief executive officer is mandatory if the organization is to adopt and maintain a creative posture. At the CEO's instigation, the policymaking executives of the firm should develop goals for the various product/service lines in which the firm operates. High-risk, "mold-breaking" creativity is not seen as equally desirable in all areas of operation, no matter how innovative the firm wishes to be. It is well to remember that most firms are not simple, single-purpose entities, but rather are collections of subsidiaries, divisions, departments, and groups that are often like firms themselves.

The strategy of growth and innovation is complex, and even the most innovative firms do not allow all their subunits to be in a wild state of creative flux at the same time. By and large, the strategy of growth and development is carried out through the funding process. In areas where innovation is desired, creative activity is funded. Funds are withdrawn from areas where progress is not needed or has less value.

In addition to the CEO, each unit charged with creativity needs a second person to support innovation, a *promoter*. This person will support implementation of the innovation, and serve as its "champion" [22]. For high-risk areas, special ground rules can be established that permit managers and specialists to work in a supportive environment. Texas Instruments and 3M operate in this way. They allow entrepreneurs to set up "separate" organizations within the firm to exploit the results of their ideas.

Next we explore that aspect of creativity known as *idea generation*. There are many techniques for idea generation, and we will treat them in two categories, individual methods and group methods. Because some of the individual techniques can also be used with groups, but rarely vice versa, we will cover the individual approaches first.

A.3 INDIVIDUAL CREATIVITY

In spite of the fact that people have studied creativity, have taught it, have dedicated institutes to it, and have written about it, not much is known about the fundamental nature of creativity. Creativity is not a technique, nor is it an approach, though some techniques and approaches seem to be associated with creativity. When we ask creative people how they produce their creations, the answers do not fit neatly into recognizable and replicable categories. The techniques to be described in this section do not "produce" creativity, but they do tend to allow people to be creative.

The creative mind seems to associate freely, connecting and disconnecting the familiar and strange in different patterns. Apparent sense, logic, and order may be ignored as the mind "plays" in divergent, rather than the normal convergent, thinking. In this sense, creative thinking is similar to dreaming or fantasizing.

It is useful to understand some characteristics of the human brain. Recent theories about how the brain operates portray it as basically divided into two hemispheres that control different functions. The left hemisphere controls analytic thinking such as verbal, numerical, logical, and judgmental thought. This side is said to be "anchored in time" and seeks control, optimization, and planning. Factual memory is also based here.

The right side is the creative, imaginative side where intuition, imagination, pictorial thinking, and synthesis occur. Symbols and abstract representation are lodged here. This half is said to be "anchored in space" rather than in time. This side is the part of the brain we are trying to stimulate because it appears to be the source of creativity.

According to many articles and books on creativity, such as [19], there are a series of general steps that help the right side of the brain function more actively. First, we begin by considering every object, procedure, system, and process as inadequate to meet our needs. The objects, procedures, systems, and processes should be viewed in terms of the ultimate purposes for which they exist rather than in terms of what they currently "do." A generous amount of time should be allotted to specifying the criteria that the creative idea is to meet. The emphasis should be on listing objectives, not on devising solutions, on determining capabilities, not on improving existing hardware.

Reword and restate the goals. The criteria must be broad, yet specific where specificity is required. Record the criteria and set priorities on them. Are there gaps? Fill them. It does not help to consider solutions until the problem and criteria are fully specified. When the search for solutions begins, it should be pursued as far as possible before any evaluation of potential solutions is permitted. Embrace the long run and the short run with equal fervor. Possibility, not feasibility, is the focus. Practicality is not relevant at this stage of the idea-generation process. The more ideas, the better. Quantity is the watchword; quality will come later. Encourage "idea hopping," the generating of one potential solution by altering a previously suggested idea. Work until you run out of intellectual gas, then start again. Review earlier suggestions to find variations and extensions that add to the possibility list.

Following is a list and brief discussion of some specific techniques to aid in individual free thinking.

1. *Attribute Listing*   Developed by Zwicky and others, this approach assigns attributes to the desired design so that it has new qualities and characteristics. An attribute list can be constructed from words and phrases that describe the desired capabilities, even though the design is unknown. Attribute listing is carried out according to the following ground rules:

   Isolate all of the major characteristics (attributes) of the desired capabilities.

   Consider modifying each characteristic in every way imaginable. Do not limit the proposed changes.

   Once all conceivable modifications have been considered, review them in light of real-world constraints (cost, etc.).

2. *Checklist*   This consists of a set of questions that are "fit" onto the situation to envision new solutions [24]. A typical checklist might be:

   Other applications?

How can we adapt the product?
Modify?
Magnify?
Reduce?
Substitute?
Rearrange?
Reverse?
Combine?
Multipurpose?

3. *Forced Relationships*   Here relevant, and perhaps less relevant, elements are force-fit together to come up with new combinations. The elements can be selected from desirable characteristics for a solution, or from other solutions to similar problems, or even from solutions to problems that are somehow analogous to the present problem. For example, a system that electronically informs drivers on a highway of the road's number/name might be "forced" to include sensors to detect speeders.

4. *Working Backwards*   The idea here is to postulate a "perfect solution" and work backwards from the characteristics of such a solution to the technical capabilities it would have to incorporate.

5. *Black Box*   In this approach, one based on a well-known idea from general systems theory, all the inputs are listed (all elements of the problem or situation) and a separate list is made of all the outputs (the elements of a perfect solution). One then envisions all possible transformation processes that might transform some or all of the inputs into some or all of the outputs. The underlying logic is this: Starting with this (input), what would be required to get that (desired output)?

6. *Directed Dreaming*   This is an attempt to use dreams, or, more appropriately, the subconscious, to engender creative approaches or solutions to problems [11]. This method seems to require a prolonged mental struggle of days or even weeks with the problem. When falling asleep while still pondering the problem (if this is possible), a creative answer may come to the subconscious. It is important to have paper and pencil or tape recorder ready to store the idea until morning.

A.4 GROUP CREATIVITY

The need for creativity is inversely related to the level of our understanding of the problem. The less well understood the problem, the greater the need for creativity. For example, the problem of constructing a warehouse is reasonably well understood, and the degree of creativity required to carry out the construction project is relatively low. The problems involved in developing a long-term habitat for moon dwellers are not well understood, and therefore would require a great deal of creativity.

It has been repeatedly shown [20] that groups are more effective in generating creative solutions to unstructured (poorly understood) problems than individuals. It is also clear that if the problem is structured (well understood), then individuals do a better job of problem solving than groups. (If you doubt this generality, consider the case of using a committee to add a column of numbers—

a well-structured problem.) Thus, the fundamental reason for seeking creativity through a group process is that the problem structure is ambiguous.

The discussion on group creativity in the remainder of this section is largely adapted from [5, 8, 31, and 33]. (The latter is a particularly valuable reference on techniques to foster group creativity.) It is generally accepted that there are five major advantages associated with using group creativity processes:

1. Groups bring together knowledge and skills not possessed by any individual member of the group.
2. Groups are more effective than individuals in eliminating errors and avoiding mistakes.
3. A group solution is more likely to be accepted by those who must implement it than is the solution of an individual.
4. If the members of a group must act on evidence, it is likely that they will be more productive and effective if they have played a role in developing that evidence.
5. Group members learn from one another, stimulate one another, and add to each other's knowledge and skills—that is, synergism occurs.

The effectiveness of creativity groups can be enhanced if a few simple guidelines [15, 20] are followed. Diversity is a highly desirable quality of such groups. Within the bounds of reason, group members should be as diverse as possible across such dimensions as:

Role
: Engineers, managers, technicians, blue- and white-collar production workers, and so on, all represent special viewpoints and may be the source of unique contributions to problem solving.

Specialty
: Different areas of study have their individual ways of thinking about and analyzing problems.

Age
: Contrary to popular mythology, there appears to be no demonstrable relationship between age and creativity except, possibly, in the field of mathematics. A mix of ages cannot hurt, and probably helps.

Experience
: Experience with a problem tends to produce insight, but it also tends to foster overconcern with real or imagined constraints. Inexperienced but intelligent people may develop fresh approaches.

Education
: One must never confuse education with wisdom; but, like experience, more is generally better than less.

When a problem arises that requires the use of a creativity group, it should be treated as a project, and the rules of good project management apply. There should be an objective, a leader, a time schedule, a budget, a plan, and an evaluation process. Basic work group tenets should also be observed: Hold meetings away from the bustle of business; allow no interruptions; insist that all participants be present; and have a good supply of working materials such as flip charts, blackboards, coffee, paper, pencils, and the rest of the paraphernalia necessary for a successful meeting.

In the initial creativity sessions, the focus should be on the methods of creativity, investigating various methods and technologies used to foster creativity, and forming a good working relationship among the group members. Following these orientation sessions, the groups should be ready to apply its power to the tasks for which it was formed.

Problem recognition and understanding is a critical first step in all problem-solving procedures. A problem not understood cannot be solved. The problem should be stated as precisely and concisely as possible, consistent with its real-world complexity. As noted above, the problem statement should be constructed in terms of the capabilities sought, not in terms of desired hardware. It is difficult but necessary to think of a "land-based people mover," not a "car" or "bus," or of a "container for the foot," not a "shoe."

If the problem is large or complex, it may be advantageous to break it down into subproblems that can be attacked and handled separately. The results may then be combined to secure the overall solution. But it is well to remember that this procedure can result in suboptimization. It should be avoided unless absolutely necessary.

Procedural devices are sometimes helpful in achieving good problem statements. Be concise, but do not arbitrarily limit the length of the statement. It is often useful to require the problem to be restated some minimum number of times, say, four or five. In addition to obtaining a suitable statement of the problem, these reworking techniques also help to familiarize the problem solvers with the various aspects of the problem and its environment. They may even aid in establishing the vali   dity and significance of the problem.

The most commonly used group creativity problem-solving techniques are described below.

Brainstorming This is probably the best known and most widely used of all the group creativity techniques. It was developed by Alex Osborn[24] in 1953, and has been widely publicized and used since then. The use of brainstorming mushroomed in the middle 1950s, but declined somewhat in the 1960s following some reports alleging the superiority of individual creativity.

A single brainstorming session should probably not last much longer than an hour. All ideas should be recorded. An experienced secretary or recording machine is useful to capture the initial onrush of ideas. Two basic rules should be observed during brainstorming sessions:

1. Criticism, judgment, or analysis of the generated ideas is absolutely prohibited during the session. Critiques can be conducted after the idea-generation sessions have been completed.
2. Quantity is encouraged. Variations, extensions, and combinations of previously generated ideas are often more valuable than the originals. Seemingly wild ideas are welcomed without comment, just as conservative ideas are.

A number of variants of brainstorming have been developed over the years, such as *brainwriting,* where *nominal groups* (see below and Appendix B) are used. The ideas are written down first, then read aloud and developed.

Synectics This approach, developed by William Gordon [14] in 1944, is most appropriate for very unclear, abstract situations—that is, where the problem has little or no apparent structure. Synectics requires the formation of a tailor-made team that uses analogy and metaphor to approach two tasks: (1) making the strange familiar and (2) making the familiar strange. In the process, participants are urged to leave the mental confines of the everyday world and escape into the bizarre, even the absurd. Some of the types of analogy used are *personal,* where the members see themselves as pieces or parts of the solution; *direct,* where biological and natural analogous elements are employed; *symbolic,* where objective or impersonal images are used to describe the problems; and *fantasy,* where science fiction-type ideas are used as solutions. The synectic approach to creativity requires considerably more training and practice than most other methods. A consultant or facilitator who is expert in leadership of synectic groups is necessary.

Morphology   Invented by F. Zwicky in 1947, this method was not publicized until the 1960s. The problem is defined in terms of the various capabilities most likely to be involved in a solution. Highly generalized methods of achieving these capabilities are defined. All possible combinations of these methods are then arrayed in a so-called "morphological box" and examined for technical feasibility. The following five-step process is used.

1. Describe, define, and generalize the problem.
2. Define all factors that influence the solution.
3. Structure these factors into distinctive categories.
4. Analyze the *cells* at the intersection of each category with each other category.
5. Evaluate each of these cells in terms of solution criteria.

As can be imagined, an examination of "all possible combinations" of even a small problem is a serious undertaking. A set of six capabilities, each of which might be achieved by five methods, would require examination of more than 15,000 alternatives.

Bionics   Sometimes referred to as *nature analysis,* this is an analogy approach that relies on imitation of nature. The group seeks ways in which animals or plants have solved similar or analogous problems. The use of this technique is limited, but when utilized to handle appropriate problems, it appears to be effective.

Storyboarding   The Walt Disney Studios faced a serious creativity problem: how to produce a large number of different short subject cartoon plots. Storyboarding was their answer to the challenge. As usual, a list is made of all problem attributes (all elements in cartoon plot), and of the possible variations each attribute might take (e.g., location: U.S., Egypt, desert isle, etc.). These are printed on cards backed with a self-sticking material such as Velcro™. A wall of a conference room is covered with felt and the attribute cards are arranged and rearranged to form different potential solutions to the problem (plot elements for the cartoon).

This method has much in common with Zwicky's morphological box. Of course, no attempt is made when storyboarding to evaluate all possible combinations. In this instance, a different, feasible combination is being sought, not the best combination.

Delphi   This approach has been most widely used for technological forecasting and for the determination of numeric measures of importance (weights), but it also may be used to aid creativity. Delphi focuses the collective knowledge of the group on identifying, forecasting, and solving problems. It adds a formal structure to the group process, and avoids the bias usually associated with the presence of strong individual personalities in the group.

The Delphi process begins with group selection. Ground rules and procedures for the particular process must be clearly stated, and sufficient time allowed for the exercise. (The specifics of the Delphi technique are discussed in detail in Appendix B.) While it is a popular tool for technological forecasting and parameter estimation, it is not often used for creativity exercises.

Nominal Group Techniques   The nominal group technique is a structured group process that combines both group and individual activities. A coordinator administers the following five-step process:

1. Silent idea generation.
2. Round-robin presentation.
3. Idea clarification.
4. Voting and ranking.
5. Discussion of results.

During silent idea generation, each participant is asked to think of and write down ideas about the specific task. This step is followed by a round-robin presentation wherein participants take turns reading ideas to the group. The coordinator or an assistant records each idea. Any participant may pass on any given round. This process continues until all the ideas of the group have been read and recorded. While this may seem almost identical to brainstorming, the idea flow from nominal groups is not usually as free and uninhibited.

The next step is clarification. The coordinator proceeds through the idea list asking if any clarification is needed. Anyone in the group may clarify any idea, although some courage is usually required to modify someone else's idea.

The participants are then asked to select eight ideas they consider to be the best or most important. These are ranked by the group. The coordinator then tabulates the results, and the group discusses them. A second, abbreviated session may be held to expand on the eight best ideas.

Other Methods   In addition to the approaches noted above, there are several less well-known, seldom-used creative problem-solving techniques. Among them are Buzz sessions, Modified Buzz Sessions, Slipwriting, and Reverse Brainstorming. All of these methods have one common element: They attempt to utilize the creative potential of groups. (Again, the reader is referred to [33] for an extended discussion of the techniques.)

These techniques work. They increase the output of ideas by individuals and groups. Which techniques work best depends on several factors. Among these are the extent to which people are willing to expose their ideas before their colleagues, penalties for error, schemes for stimulating unusual associations of known ideas, the skill with which the problem is identified and stated, and the stimulation of idea production by each member of the group through the contributions of other group members.

It is now appropriate to mention a matter of crucial importance to the success of any group creativity technique. Research on multidisciplinary projects has shown that problem-oriented individuals are more effective in multidisciplinary problem solving than are discipline-oriented individuals [26]. The distinction is simple. Problem-oriented people give the problem primary consideration. Each views his/her individual area of knowledge only in terms of its potential contribution to solving the problem. Discipline-oriented people view the problem as an opportunity to ply their knowledge or extend it. To the former, knowledge is a means to an end. To the latter, the problem is a vehicle for the demonstration or extension of knowledge. A problem orientation is generally more effective because problem-oriented people welcome any input they see as helpful in problem solving, while discipline-oriented people view as irrelevant (or uninteresting) ideas and discussions not related to their area of expertise. To increase the chance of success, several, if not all, members of the creativity group should be problem-oriented.

Skill in creative problem solving can be acquired and developed. It requires training and the application of effort, but it does not require special mental endowments or "gifts of nature." Almost anyone can be creative by using the principles and methods described in this section and known collectively as *creative problem-solving techniques.*

A.5 EVALUATION OF CREATIVITY METHODS

A 1971 *Industry Week* article [3] indicated that the thirteen fastest-growing companies in the United States had programs to encourage employee innovation and creativity. Brainstorming was the most widely known and used method, and there is no reason to believe this has changed. The morphological box was in second place, though it was listed only half as frequently as brainstorming. Use of creativity methods is greatest in the area of product development, with next most frequent uses in value analysis, research, marketing, and planning/organization, in that order. The article noted that half of all the ideas generated and considered for further investigation proved to be viable and were implemented. This is far in excess of the 1 percent usually estimated for the viability of new ideas.

Since the early 1970s, the use of creativity techniques seems to have decreased somewhat. This is felt to result from some disappointment in the use of the techniques, many of which have been oversold by their developers. It is, of course, not possible to measure the contribution of these methods to firm growth and profitability, or even to idea generation itself, because one can argue that the idea "would have occurred anyway." Specific difficulties noted in employing creativity techniques were:

- Insufficient time; overloaded key personnel; inability to find acceptable meeting dates.
- Personal tension; inability to think abstractly; blocks in interpersonal communication; lack of experience; not observing the rules of the method.
- Insufficient knowledge of the problem; lack of top-management support.
- Inability to measure the benefits; patent problems.

The future of specific idea-generation techniques appears mixed. Interested individuals have been quite creative in thinking up new methods for fostering creativity. Among the more interesting recent additions are:

1. *Mechanical Techniques* These are typically straightforward mechanisms such as Savo Bojicic's "Think Tank," a hollow plastic sphere containing thirteen thousand words to be used as idea take-offs. As the sphere is turned, the words come into view, stimulating the brain to make various associations.
2. *Electronic Methods* The techniques of biofeedback and electrical stimulation are included here, and would seem to have much to offer. Considerable experimentation is being conducted on these techniques, and this area will certainly become better developed in the future.
3. *Chemical Techniques* Several drugs and chemicals appear to produce the kinds of mental states described as desirable in the creativity literature. The primary question is whether or not such chemically induced states are harmless to the individual and can be usefully applied to the task of creative problem solving in an organizational setting. If used at all, these techniques require care and expert control.
4. *Environmental, Psychological* These approaches involve the use of sound, color, sensory stimulation/deprivation, odor, and so forth, to alter the brain's normal environment to aid creativity. The prime issues here are potential and safety when used in organizational settings.

A final, important point to remember is that individuals in highly stressful situations are rarely creative. A little pressure stimulates, but too much paralyzes creativity because the human body reacts to stress as if preparing to fight or flee. The blood supply to the brain is diminished, and the brain receives less oxygen. The most important factor affecting creativity in the future will be the emphasis and encouragement given it by managers. Supportive organizational leadership is needed. If creativity is sought, failure must be tolerated.

A.6 ORGANIZING TO ALLOW AND ASSIST CREATIVITY

The ways that creative ideas are handled in an organization have a major impact on both the quality and quantity of the flow of ideas. The typical suggestion box is seen as a bottomless repository for good ideas (or for obscene comments on the quality of management).

Over the years, the authors have concluded that several conditions seem to support the development of effective systems for fostering creativity, individual or group, in an organizational environment.

1. Suggestions for system improvement should be submitted directly to a screening committee; that is, they should bypass the usual chain of command.
2. A standard form should be used, insofar as possible, that instructs the submitter on what information is required about the idea. *(Note:* It is difficult enough to think up a creative idea without having to worry about the best way to present it.)
3. All suggestions should be acknowledged in a timely fashion. Further, the individual submitting the idea should be promptly informed about the progress of the idea through the accept/reject process.
4. All suggestions should be reviewed by a technically competent individual or group.
5. If rewards are given for useful ideas, they should be of appropriate size. No sensible person will spend hours of time working on an idea which, if accepted, will earn a $25 reward.
6. No penalty or negative impact should result from submitting an unsuccessful idea.
7. There must be no penalties attached to successful ideas. No one is likely to submit a labor-saving idea if colleagues may be laid off or fired as a result.
8. Superiors should be encouraged to foster the creativity of subordinates and then rewarded for any creativity that results. This requires a mutually supportive superior/subordinate relationship, not a competitive one.

This prescription for a successful idea-generation system may appear to be ideal, but it is quite realistic. The Lincoln Electric Company is a down-to-earth producer of arc welding machinery and equipment. In that firm, experts consider—and acknowledge—all suggestions. If adopted, the individual who submitted the idea receives one-half of the first year's savings (or added profits). In addition, employees at all levels are guaranteed that no one will be laid off or moved to a lower-paying job as a result of the idea. One result of this policy is that the Lincoln Electric Company has consistently been the productivity leader in its industrial category, electric equipment and parts.

Given policies in basic agreement with the above provisos, an organizational mechanism for fostering and processing suggestions can be developed. The idea should move directly from originator to a screening committee whose membership is broad enough to contain the technical expertise needed to conduct a preliminary evaluation of any suggestions received by the committee. Ideas that seem, to the screening committee, worthy of further investigation are forwarded to an evaluation committee, whose job it is to decide if the idea is worth further development and exploration. (The evaluation and selection of ideas is discussed in Chapter 2.)

A.7 BIBLIOGRAPHY

1. Abend, J. C. "Innovative Management: The Missing Link in Productivity." *Management Review,* July 1979.
2. Barrett, F. D. "Creativity Techniques: Yesterday, Today and Tomorrow." *S.A.M. Advanced Management Journal,* Winter 1978.

3. Bouchard, T. J. "Whatever Happened to Brainstorming?" *Industry Week,* Aug. 2, 1971.

4. Cates, C. "Beyond Muddling: Creativity." *Public Administration Review,* Nov.–Dec., 1979

5. Clark, C. H. *Idea Management: How to Motivate Creativity and Innovation.* AMACOM, 1980.

6. Clark, C. H. *The Creative Organization.* University of Chicago Press, 1965.

7. Covington, M. V. *The Productive Thinking Program: A Course in Learning to Think.* Merrill Publishing, 1974.

8. Crawford, R. P. *The Techniques of Creative Thinking.* Hawthorn Books, 1966.

9. Dean, B. V. *Evaluating, Selecting and Controlling R & D Projects: Idea Generation and Handling.* AMA Research Study, 1968.

10. DeBono, E. *Lateral Thinking for Management.* American Management Association, 1971.

11. Garfield, P. L. *Creative Dreaming.* New York: Simon and Schuster, 1975.

12 Gee, E. A., and C. Tyler. *Managing Innovation.* New York: Wiley, 1976.

13. Geschka, H. "Introduction and Use of Idea-Generating Methods." *Research Management,* May 1978.

14. Gordon, W. J. *Synectics: The Development of Creative Capacity.* New York: Harper and Row, 1961.

15. Harrison, E. F. *The Management Decision-Making Process.* Boston: Houghton Mifflin, 1975.

16. Hayakawa, S. I. "What Does It Mean to Be Creative?" *Industry Week,* Sept. 17, 1979.

17. Hayes, R., and W. J. Abernathy, "Managing Our Way to Economic Decline." *Harvard Business Review,"* July–Aug. 1980.

18. Howard, N. "Business Probes the Creative Spark." *Dun's Review,* Jan. 1980.

19. Koberg, D., and J. Bagnall. *The Universal Traveler.* Los Altos, CA: Wm. Kaufmann, Inc., 1976.

20. Kolasa, B. J. *Introduction to Behavioral Sciences for Business.* New York: Wiley, 1969.

21. Larson, R. H. "Developing Creativity in Engineers." *Mechanical Engineering,* Dec. 1978.

22. Meredith, J. R. "The Implementation of Computer Based Systems." *Journal of Operations Management,* Oct. 1981.

23. Miller, B. *Managing Innovation for Growth and Profit.* Homewood,IL: Irwin, 1970.

24. Osborn, A. *Applied Imagination.* New York: Scribner's, 1953.

25. Parnes, S. *Creative Behavior Guidebook.* New York, Scribner's, 1976.

26. Pill, J. "Technical Management and Control of Large Scale Urban Studies: A Comparative Analysis of Two Cases." Ph.D. dissertation, Case Western Reserve University, 1971.

27. Rawlinson, J. G. *Creative Thinking and Brainstorming.* British Institute of Management, 1970.

28. Richards, T., and B. Freedman. "A Re-Appraisal of Creativity Techniques in Industrial Training." *European Industrial Training,* Vol. 3, 1979.

29. Souder, W. E. "A Review of Creativity and Problem Solving Techniques." *Research Management,* July 1977.

30. Souder, W. E. "Autonomy, Gratification, and R & D Outputs: A Small-Sample Field Study." *Management Science,* April 1974.

31. Summer, I., and D. E. White. "Creativity Techniques: Toward Improvement of the Decision Process." *Academy of Management Review,* April 1976.

32. Van Gundy, A. B. *Managing Group Creativity,* ANACOM, 1984.

33. Warfield, J. N., and H. Geschka and R. Hamilton. *Methods of Idea Management.* The Battelle Institute and The Academy for Contemporary Problems, 1975.

34. Whiting, C. S. "Operational Techniques of Creative Thinking." *Advanced Management,* Oct. 1955.

35. Zeldman, M. E. "How Management Can Develop and Sustain A Creative Environment." *S.A.M. Advanced Management Journal,* Winter 1980.

APPENDIX B
Technological Forecasting

Forecasting is hard, particularly of the future.

[Anonymous]

Forecasting is like trying to drive a car blindfolded and following directions given by a person who is looking out the back window.

[Anonymous]

Technology is the application of science or art. All projects rest on a technological base. They are concerned with using science and art to accomplish some goals. Indeed, most projects rest on a base formed by many technologies. When a project is initiated, decisions must be made about which of the relevant and available technologies to employ. At times, a choice must be made between beginning the project immediately, using currently available technologies, or delaying the project in order to adopt a superior technology that is expected but is not currently available.

In addition to technological choices made for the project itself, it may be necessary to forecast the technologies with which our technological choices and our project results will interact. Our systems must be reasonably compatible with those in the environment that do or will exist across their expected life.

Both reasons for forecasting technology go beyond the obvious need to plan for the technological future. Such planning may or may not be the subject of a special project. For many organizations, technological planning is an ongoing function of management. But whether planning is done as a routine or on a project basis, technological forecasting is required.

We define technological forecasting as the process of predicting the future characteristics and timing of technology. When possible, the prediction will be quantified, made through a specific logic, and will estimate the timing and degree of change in technological parameters, attributes, and capabilities.

As with idea generation, few project managers are engaged with projects at the point in the life cycle at which technological forecasting is normally done. Decisions made at this point, early in the life cycle, influence the subsequent course of the project. Whether implicit or explicit, the decision not to engage in technological forecasting assumes a static technological future. This is a false assumption, but in some cases the assumption is not damaging. We urge project managers, senior managers, and policymakers to make conscious decisions about engaging in technological forecasting, and we urge project managers to study and understand the importance of this process on project management.

We begin by discussing the nature of technological forecasting, its history, and how it has been used. We then survey the major techniques currently in use. Last, we consider how to choose an appropriate forecasting method, the limits of each method, and the general future of technological forecasting. Some of these models require an understanding of basic statistics to employ them, but not to comprehend their use and role.

B.1 CHARACTERISTICS, HISTORY, AND IMPORTANCE OF TECHNOLOGICAL FORECASTING

Note that in the definition, technological forecasting is aimed at predicting future technological capabilities, attributes, and parameters. It is not an attempt to predict how things will be done. Nor is technological forecasting oriented toward profitability. That is, a technological capability or attribute can be forecast to be available at some time in the future, although society may not necessarily want or need the capability.

Consider the process of technological innovation. Many factors influence the progress and direction of technology. For example, science, organizational policy, organizational structure, chance, need, and funding all play major roles in determining what technologies are likely to be available to us in the future.

Governmental decisions to support some technologies and not others have a significant impact on technological innovation. For instance, the decision to support the space program had major impacts on miniaturization in the electronics industry, on the use of new materials and styles in the garment industry, and even on the look of television commercials. The federal government's decision not to support the SST affected the technology of air transport in the United States. If technological forecasting predicts that a certain capability is technologically within our reach in the near future, and if the government chooses to support research in this area, it is much more likely that the technology will be developed—for example, new approaches to the generation of electric power. If the government decides to finance implementation of the desired innovation, there will probably be a near-term impact on profits and the speed of diffusion of the new technology.

Another characteristic of technological forecasting is uncertainty about the rate of change of technological capabilities. Many capabilities tend to grow exponentially until they reach some natural limit; for example, aircraft speed, computer memory size and memory access speed, horsepower per liter of internal combustion engines, among many others. This is because new technology builds on older technology, and synergism results from the combination. When one technology impinges on another, the synergy often results in an unexpected and sudden increase in capability. For instance, the development of microcomputers depended on the combined technologies of electronic computer circuitry, miniaturization of electronic circuits, efficient computer programming, and development of information storage devices. Such synergies are difficult to forecast. In the early 1950s, noted science fiction author Isaac Asimov wrote a short story set five hundred years in the future. One artifact featured in this story of the future was a small, hand-held device that could perform complex mathematical calculations when its buttons were properly pushed.

The fact that a new capability is developed does not automatically mean that it will be put to use. The files of the Patent Bureau are jammed with useless inventions. The lack of application potential does not, of course, mean that the capability or scientific finding is worthless. There are many examples of important technological advances that rest on seemingly nonapplicable earlier discoveries. A case in point is Albert Einstein's work on special and general relativity. It depended on earlier work of the mathematician Hendrik Lorentz, work that had no apparent application to physics when it was originally published.

Although varying greatly from industry to industry, the embodiment of a scientific discovery, an *innovation,* lags the discovery itself, an *invention,* by five to seven years on average [22, 27]. Once the innovation is developed, its application is also not instantaneous. It usually takes between ten and twenty years for an innovation to be adopted to the point of saturation. The reasons why the adoption of an innovation is slower than we might expect, or desire, are many, but this fairly long lead time between the invention and the innovation is very useful to the technological forecaster and to the project manager. (For a detailed discussion and examples of the adoption process, see [22].)

Historically, technological forecasting was based on the guesses of the most recognized and prestigious expert in the area. This is no longer appropriate because technological progress has become dependent on the interaction of several, often diverse, technologies. A single individual rarely has the requisite level of expertise in all relevant areas. Also, the management and funding of the several technologies have a significant impact on the degree and speed of technological change.

The government has played an increasingly important role in technological forecasting. One of the earliest attempts at technological forecasting was the 1937 report *Technological Trends and National Policy, Including the Social Implications of New Inventions* [29], which predicted that plastics, television, synthetic rubber, and a mechanical cotton picker were likely to become widely used and have significant social impacts.

Following World War II, the government established the Scientific Advisory Board to provide guidance for technological development over a twenty-year period. This was done, in part, because of the resource bottlenecks and technological barriers encountered during industrial mobilization for the war. Many forecasts were prompted by the development of nuclear power and automation. Then, in the 1960s, a boom occurred in technological forecasting. The number of articles on the subject increased rapidly, as did the membership of societies devoted to forecasting the future. This interest was spurred by several factors:

- The development of space technology.
- Public concern for the environment.
- Public awareness of potential resource limitations.
- Technology as a major factor of international competition.
- Increased availability of computer power.
- Widespread publication of the methods and results of technological forecasting.

In 1972, the government formed a permanent Office of Technology Assessment under the authority of the Technology Assessment Act. The purpose of this office was to equip Congress with the information needed for the support, management, and regulation of applied technologies. All of this governmental attention to technological forecasting resulted in improved forecasting methods, as well as considerable concurrent publicity and general interest in the subject. Business firms saw the obvious value of generating forecasts that helped them identify the probable capabilities of future products. Firms in the so-called high-technology areas led the way in forming in-house capabilities for technological forecasting. Others followed, sometimes setting up their own forecasting groups and sometimes using consultants for ad hoc forecasting sessions.

As noted at the beginning of the chapter, the techniques were also used to aid decision making on the choice of production processes as well as products. Forecasting sessions became input for R & D, for marketing's life cycle planning, and for the facility and support functions. And high-technology firms saw technological forecasting as a mandatory input to basic corporate planning.

B.2 TECHNOLOGICAL FORECASTING METHODS

The major techniques for technological forecasting may be categorized under two general headings: methods based on numeric data and judgmental methods. In the main, numeric data-based forecasting extrapolates history by generating statistical fits to historical data. A few numeric methods deal with complex interdependencies. Judgmental forecasting may also be based on projections of the past, but information sources in such models rely on the subjective judgments of experts. Again, we emphasize that technological forecasting is most appropriately applied to capabilities, not to the specific characteristics of specific devices.

Numeric Data-Based Technological Forecasting Techniques

Trend Extrapolation　To extrapolate is to infer the future from the past. If there has been a steady stream of technological change and improvement, it is reasonable to assume that the stream will continue to flow. We can distinguish four approaches to the use of trend extrapolation.

1. Statistical Curve Fitting   This method is applicable to forecasting functional capabilities. Statistical procedures fit the past data to one or more mathematical functions such as linear, logarithmic, Fourier, or exponential. The best fit is selected by statistical test and then a forecast is extrapolated from this mathematical relationship.

For example, we can forecast the fastest qualification (pole position) speeds at the Indianapolis 500 Mile Race by plotting pole position speeds against time measured in years (see Figure 1). Beginning with the post-World War I races, the pole position speeds of Indy race cars have exponentially increased. Two technological innovations are quite easily seen in the data. One is the rear-engine car. The first such car appeared in 1961. Qualifying speeds were about 150 mph. In 1964 a rear engine car won the pole position at slightly less than 159 mph. The growth rate of qualifying speed is significantly higher with the rear engine technology, so different exponential functions were fitted to front- and rear-engined cars.

The second easily discernible technological innovation occurred in the early 1970s. It was the use of sophisticated aerodynamic devices (wings at the rear of the car) to create downforce on the cars, allowing them much higher cornering speeds—from 170 mph in 1970, to 179 mph in 1971, to 196 mph in 1973 (with the addition of wings at the front of the car).

2. Limit Analysis   Ultimately, all growth is limited, and there is an absolute limit to progress, either recognized or unrecognized. Sooner or later, projections must reflect the fact that improvements may get close to this limit but cannot exceed it. For instance, a trend of increasing energy conversion efficiency cannot eventually exceed 100 percent. As another example, the lowest temperature achieved in the laboratory is presented in Figure 2. The trend of lower and lower

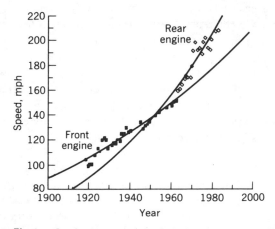

Figure 1   An example of statistical curve fitting.

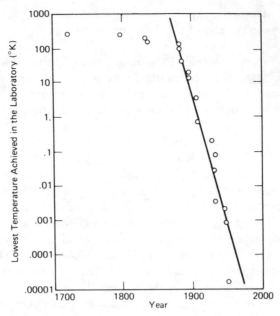

Figure 2 An example of limit analysis.

temperatures is limited, of course, by absolute zero. (It is interesting to note the rapid improvement in the ability to produce low temperatures that occurred around 1900.)

If the present level of technology being forecast is far from its theoretical extreme, extrapolation may not be unreasonable. If, however, a current technology is approaching its limit, and if this is not recognized, projections of past improvements may seriously overestimate future accomplishments.

3. *Trend Correlation*   At times, one technology is a precursor to another. This is frequently the case when advances made in the precursor technology can be adopted by the follower technology. When such relationships exist, knowledge of changes in the precursor technology can be used to predict the course of the follower technology, as far in the future as the lag time between the two. Further, extrapolation of the precursor allows a forecast of the follower to be extended beyond the lag time. Figure 3 shows an example of trend correlation, which compares the trends of combat and transport aircraft speeds. Another example of a trend correlation forecast is predicting the size and power of future computers, based on advances in microelectronic technology.

4. *Microvariable (or Microvariate) Trend Correlation*   Occasionally, a follower technology is dependent on several precursor technologies rather than on a single precursor. In such cases, the follower is usually a composite or aggregate of several precursors. Fixed combinations of the precursors may act to produce change in the follower, but more often the combinations are not fixed and the

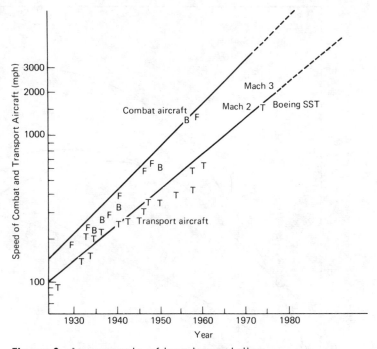

Figure 3 An example of trend correlation.
Source: C. L. Delany, "Technological Forecasting: Aircraft Hazard Detection," *Technological Forecasting and Social Change,* March 1973.

precursor inputs vary in both combination and strength. For example, improvements in aircraft speed may come from improvements in engines, materials, controls, fuels, aerodynamics, and from various combinations of such factors. An example of a multiple trend correlation forecast using total passenger miles, total plane miles, and average seating capacity is shown in Figure 4.

Extrapolation of statistically determined trends permits an objective approach to forecasting. It also permits analysis and critique by people other than the forecaster. This approach, however, still has serious limitations and pitfalls. Any errors or incorrect choices made in selecting the proper historical data will be reflected in the forecast. Such errors lower the utility of the forecast, and may completely negate its value. The forecasts given by this methodology are not sensitive to changes in the conditions that have produced the historical data, changes that may significantly alter the trend. Even when it is known that one or more possibly important conditions are going to change, technological advances cannot be predicted from the extrapolation. Statistical trend extrapolation yields a "good" forecast with high frequency, but when the environment changes, it can be quite wrong.

Trend Extrapolation, Qualitative Approaches At times, standard statistical procedures do not result in neatly fitting trends that the forecaster can ex-

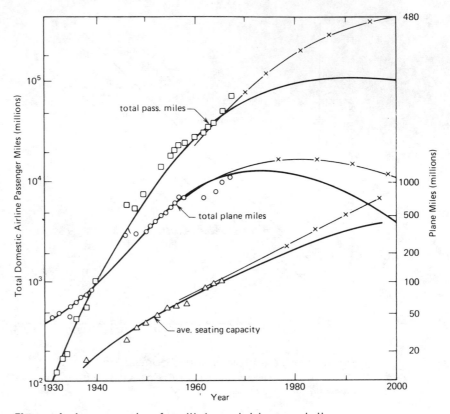

Figure 4 An example of multiple variable correlation.
Source: C. L. Delany, "Technological Forecasting: Aircraft Hazard Detection," *Technological Forecasting and Social Change,* March 1973.

trapolate with comfort. In such cases, the forecaster may "adjust" the statistical results by applying judgment, or he or she may ignore the statistics entirely and extrapolate a trend wholly on the basis of judgment. Forecasts generated in this way are less precise than statistically based forecasts, but not necessarily less accurate.

One example of this kind of qualitative trend extrapolation is the prediction of aircraft complexity. The attempts to quantify this trend have not been successful. But the percent of movable or adjustable parts in an aircraft has been extrapolated from the frequency that such elements were introduced in the past, and these forecasts have been reasonably accurate. Specific technical change cannot be predicted this way, but the degree of change can be. This provides useful inputs to planning by indicating the probable trend of past behaviors.

Growth Curves The growth pattern of a technological capability is similar to the growth of biological life. Technologies go through an invention phase, an introduction and innovation phase, a diffusion and growth phase, and a maturity phase. In doing so, their growth is similar to the S-shaped growth of biological life. Technological forecasting helps to estimate the timing of these phases. This growth curve forecasting method is particularly useful in determining the upper limit of performance for a specific technology. An example of growth curve analysis is shown in Figure 5, which depicts the number of telephones per 1,000 population as a function of time. The year in which the upper limit of diffusion (one phone per person over fifteen years old, or about seven hundred phones per 1,000 population) is reached can be extrapolated from the S curve, and it occurs between 1990 and 2000.

Several mathematical models can be used to generate growth curves. The choice of model is subjective, depending largely on the analyst's judgment about which of the functional forms most closely approximates the underlying reality of the technical growth under consideration. When using growth curves, the forecaster must be sure that the data are self-consistent—that is, that all data come from the same data set or population.

The forecaster must also remember not to confuse accuracy with precision. It it possible to develop precise capability/time estimates, but their accuracy is illusory. We might read Figure 5 as "697 phones per 1,000 population as of 1997," but "about 700 between 1990 and 2000" is a better reflection of the scatter in the data underlying the curve. Finally, the forecaster must remember that growth curves reflect a single technological approach, a given way of achieving a capability. Extrapolation cannot go beyond the saturation level of that specific technological approach. It cannot predict a decline or future rebirth of the growth pattern.

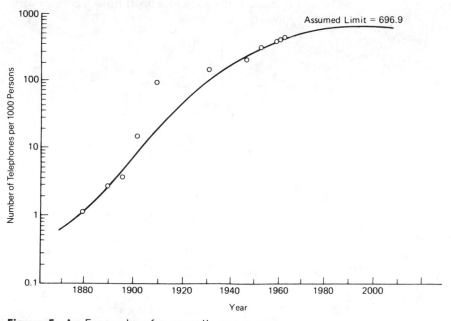

Figure 5 An Example of a growth curve.

Envelope Curves A serious constraint on growth curves is overcome by appropriate specification of the capability to be forecast. For example, Figure 6 shows a growth curve for the speed of propeller-driven aircraft. As noted above, possible input for Figure 6 must be carefully screened to make sure it includes all available data for propeller-driven aircraft, and *only* data for propeller-driven aircraft.

If we remove the modifier *propeller-driven* from the capability to be forecast, we can add data on jet, ram jet, and rocket planes, as in Figure 7. (We could also have included data on balloons and gliders if we wished.) If we generalize the capability even more to "speed of travel," we get Figure 8, a series of specific growth curves superimposed on one chart and enveloped by a single curve, termed an *envelope curve*. Fundamentally, envelope curves are a combination of growth curve and trend analysis.

Substitution Model The substitution model is based on three assumptions:

1. Many technological advances can be considered as competitive substitutions of one method of satisfying a need for another.
2. Once a substitution progresses, it will proceed to completion.
3. The rate of substitution of new for old is proportional to the remaining amount of the old left to be substituted.

Experience shows that substitutions tend to proceed exponentially in the early years, and to follow an S-shaped trend curve. When a substitution begins, the new process, product, or service begins to demonstrate its advantages over the past process, product, or service. As the new technology is able to take over some of the market, the pace of substitution increases markedly, and then tapers off as it approaches saturation.

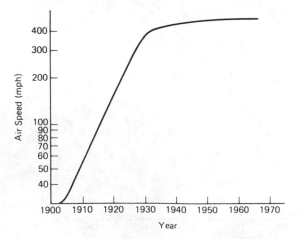

Figure 6 Speed of propeller-driven aircraft.
Source: T. Tryckare, *Lore of Flight,* Cagner & Co., Gothenburg, Sweden, 1970.

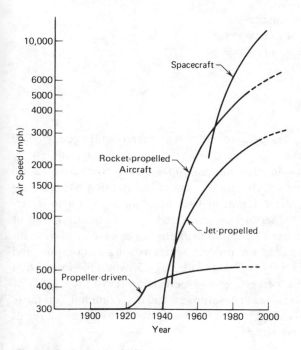

Figure 7 Speed of aircraft.
Source: T. Tryckare, *Lore of Flight,* Cagner & Co., Gothenburg, Sweden, 1970.

Figure 8 Speed of travel—envelope curve analysis.

Examples abound. In the area of industrial processes in the steel industry, the replacement of "hot dip" tin-plating by the electrolytic process, the replacement of open hearth furnaces by basic oxygen furnaces, and the replacement of the reversible, single-stand hot rolling mill by the multistand mill are among the many technological substitutions that conform to the S-shaped pattern.

The substitution model can prove useful for several types of investigation—for example, early recognition of technical obsolescence. The major advantage of this model is that it is simple to construct. Like all numeric data-based models, it is fatalistic in that it projects a specific and undeviating future based on past events; it implies that a particular progression of events is inevitable.

Judgment-Based Technological Forecasting Techniques

Monitoring Many forecasting techniques presuppose that the planner knows what to seek. Although the planner may have considerable expertise, occasionally technological surprises occur. Monitoring, or innovation tracking, allows the forecaster to stay abreast of technologies as they develop.

This approach assumes that a new discovery goes through several stages before emerging into public view as an innovation, and that some future technologies are currently in the process of development. The stages to investigate are:

1. Initial idea or suggestion—the concept.
2. Postulation of theory—the research proposal.
3. Verification of theory—the scientific finding.
4. Laboratory demonstration.
5. Field trial.
6. Commerical introduction.
7. Widespread adoption.

If the research is being conducted by a nondefense governmental agency or by a university, the process, with the exception of stage 1 above, is open to view by those who know where to look—learned journals, magazines, trade association letters, and similar sources. Once a sufficient amount of information has been accumulated, the data must be cross-referenced with other in'ormation to determine if a new technology or product can be generated by incorpcrating one or more of these events in order to develop an innovation. In the case of private industry, every attempt is made to keep the process secret as long as possible, and thus emerging technologies are rarely visible before stage 5, when the innovation is apparent. Fortunately, a large percentage (49 percent in 1986; see [28]) of basic research is done by universities, so surprises are not common for those who keep up with scientific discovery. Figure 9 shows how innovation can result from a combination of events over time.

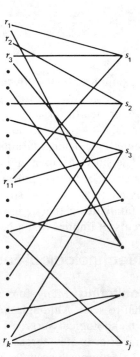

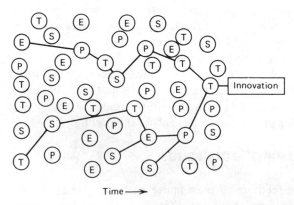

Legend:

E = Economic Event
S = Social Event
P = Political Event
T = Technological Event

Figure 9 Innovation results for a combination of events over time.

Figure 10 Example of network analysis: interconnection of research results and scientific capabilities.

Many companies employ internal systems for reviewing the scientific and technical literature, including patents, and have organized means of abstracting and disseminating new items. Government agencies, especially the Department of Defense, use this method to stay aware of changing technologies.

Monitoring techniques may seem unsophisticated, but their potential value is immense. Provided the forecaster collects and screens information properly, this method can provide excellent data to forecast trends. Recently, microcomputer programs have been developed that find and link the related items contained in a large data set—the "hypertext" programs. Such programs are invaluable aids for the process of monitoring innovations.

Network Analysis Network analysis is a formalization and extension of monitoring. This technique can be used in two distinct ways: (1) as a method of exploring the possible capabilities and systems that might result from extensions of current scientific research and, (2) given a desired capability or end system, as a method for determining what research results are required to achieve the desired capability. The first use is *exploratory* forecasting, and the second is *prescriptive* forecasting. In the former, possible future technologies are explored; in the latter, desired future capabilities are defined.

The term *network model* results from the fact that networks are commonly used to organize the data. Real examples of the method are quite extensive, so consider a hypothetical example.

Assume we have been monitoring the appropriate sources, and we have knowledge of recent research results, r_1, r_2,...r_k. We predict that these might be combined, as shown in Figure 10, to yield s_1, s_2,...s_j scientific capabilities. These capabilities, in turn, could be combined to result in t_1, t_2,...t_m technical components. Finally, the technical components can be joined to produce end systems, V_1, V_2,...V_n (Figure 11).

Going from research results to end systems is exploratory, but the direction may be reversed. Instead of seeking the system implications of research results, we could begin with one or more related desirable end systems. Going backward through the same chain of logic, we seek the components, and the research results necessary to yield the capabilities. This uses the network to *prescribe* research.

If the various end systems are given weights that reflect their relative importance, it becomes possible to set priorities on the various research results based on the importance of the end system(s) to which the research contributes. One method of finding these priorities is described by Dean (Chapter 11 in [6]) and discussed in detail in Chapter 12 of this book. Dean developed the technique to evaluate research labs after the fact, but if the "evaluation" is a priori, it becomes a statement of priorities.

It follows that if we know the cost of the research projects, can estimate the relationship between research results and research expenditures, and have a budget constraint, mathematical programming (see Chapter 9) can be used to determine the best order and extent to fund the various research projects.

It is also possible to treat both the prescriptive and exploratory models

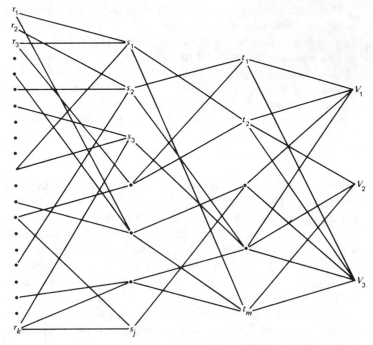

Figure 11 Example of network analysis: connections between research results, scientific capabilities, technical components, and end systems.

stochastically—that is, to estimate the probability that the research/capability, capability/component, and component/system connections can be achieved. For the reasons explained in Chapter 2, we do not see this practice as significantly helpful. In any event, no matter how many numbers are applied to the network, the base information is strictly judgmental.

Scenarios The scenario approach to technological forecasting has gained wide popularity in the past few years. It attempts to describe a future technology or technological event together with its environment. The scenario is a hypothetical view of the future based on past experience and conjecture, usually containing little rigorous analysis. Scenarios may cover any period, but generally extend ten, twenty, or more years into the future. They start with a set of givens and assumptions about the future. These are then "massaged" and extrapolated to give a picture of future technologies.

Three scenarios are often developed. The first describes the future if current trends continue, and this defines a base for the other two scenarios. The second and third scenarios describe optimistic and pessimistic futures based on assumptions about the environment that differ from the first scenario, giving a best/-worst outlook. A diagrammatic model of scenario generation is shown in Figure 12.

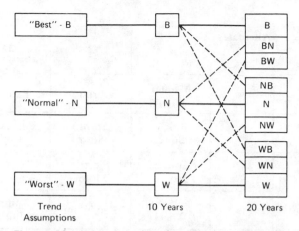

Figure 12 An example of scenario generation.
Note: Dotted lines show changed assumptions. All possible cases shown.

Although the best-known scenarios deal with world events such as famine, war, or environmental destruction (books such as Rachel Carson's *Silent Spring* and George Orwell's *1984* are both elaborate scenarios of the future), scenarios are also useful for forecasting the results of adopting a technological change. When a corporation develops a scenario, it must determine the organizational, economic, social, technological, political, and other variables that may affect their operations. By determining which variables have the greatest impact on the organization and which variables, if any, can be controlled, the organization can get a clearer insight into its potential future and thereby into possible ways of obtaining some control over it.

Morphological Analysis In the previous appendix we examined the morphological matrix as a technique for fostering creativity. It is also a prescriptive technological forecasting technique because it makes assumptions about what people will want in the future and then investigates the possible ways those wants could be satisfied. Of all the techniques available for forecasting new products or processes, morphology is one of the most systematic. The technique relies on a matrix, usually called a morphological *box*. Figure 13 is an example that uses a morphological box to examine the possible development of clocks. The vertical axis, lettered A, B. C. etc., defines the stages of parameters or the technology under consideration. the horizontal axis, numbered 1, 2, 3, etc., defines alternate methods to achieve the stages or parameters.

The analysis is usually initiated by starting with a well-known or existing solution (A1-B1-C1-D1-E1-F1), and changing one element at a time. Alternate methods (e.g., A2-B2-C1-D1-E1-F1) are analyzed to find potential improvements in current technology. The solutions can be examined for efficiency, and estimates then made of the time when the alternative technologies might be available.

Note that morphological analysis can be used as a creativity technique and a

Key Parameters	Alternates	1	2	3	4
Energy Source	A	Manual Winding	Vibration	Battery	Solar
Energy Store	B	Weight Store	Spring Store	Bimetallic Coil	No Store
Motor	C	Spring Motor	Electric Motor		
Regulator	D	Balance Wheel	Pendulum	Tuning Fork	Quartz
Gearing	E	Pinion Drive	Chain Drive	Worm Drive	
Indicator Device	F	Dial Hands	Slide Marks	Liquid Quartz	Light Indicators

Figure 13 A morphological matrix for clocks.

technological forecasting device at the same time. Potential methods to accomplish certain capabilities can be sought and then the times when the required technologies might be available can be estimated. The automobile industry has used morphological studies to meet air pollution and gasoline mileage regulations, deriving possible short-, intermediate-, and long-run solutions to these problems.

Relevance Trees Most major technological development projects are complex. Their fulfillment is likely to depend on the accomplishment of substantial improvements on existing technologies. These advances are not usually coordinated. Many products result from technological changes that were not originally intended to provide them assistance. The planner must be able to distinguish a large number of potentially supporting technologies and to forecast their futures. Relevance trees, a slight variant of the network analysis discussed earlier, are of great aid in such work.

Relevance trees can be used to study a goal or objective, as in morphological analysis, or to select a specific research project from a more general set of goals, as in network analysis. The methodology of relevance trees requires that the planner determine the most appropriate path of the tree by arranging, in a hierarchical order, the objectives, subobjectives, and tasks in order to ensure that all possible ways of achieving the objectives have been found. The relevance of individual tasks and subobjectives to the overall objective is then evaluated.

An example of a relevance tree is shown in Figure 14. The objective is to develop a means of air pollution control. The subobjectives "Develop Petro-

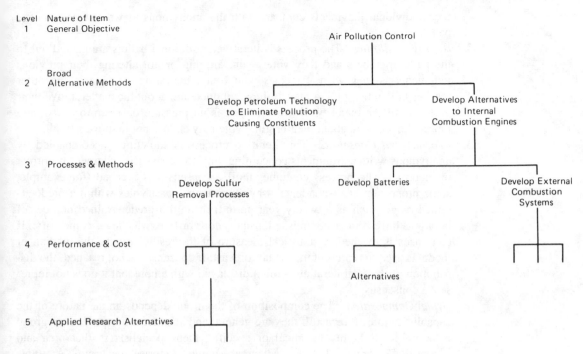

Figure 14 A relevance tree for pollution control.

leum..." and "Develop Alternative..." further define the main objective. Tasks and subtasks are then defined. Once all the "good" alternative ways of achieving the subobjectives have been found, the relevance of individual solutions to the main objective can be evaluated.

Delphi Method Perhaps the best known of the various judgmental approaches to technological forecasting, the Delphi method uses a panel of individuals who make anonymous, subjective judgments about the probable time when a specific technological capability will be available. The results of these estimates are aggregated by a process administrator and fed back to the group, which then uses the feedback to generate another round of judgments. After several iterations, the process is stopped and areas of agreement or disagreement are noted and documented. Let us now look more closely at some characteristics of this process.

1. *Opinion Gathering and Distribution*   The key features of the Delphi process are quite simple. Panelists may submit their judgments by mail or may be gathered together in a single room. In either case, the opinions are written and anonymous. If the panelists are in a face-to-face meeting, no discussion of the subjects to be covered is allowed. In this way, loud or aggressive panelists cannot sway the votes of others. The written ballots are collected by the process administrator, who aggregates the responses in a statistical format (i.e., prepares a distribution of the responses). This information is given to all panel members, who can then see how

their individual judgments compare with the anonymous views of others on the panel.

2. *Iterative Balloting* The process is iterative. Additional ballots are passed out to the panel members and they vote again, altering or not altering their previous judgments as they wish. Panelists who found their original vote in the outer reaches of the distribution may, if they feel uncertain about the matter, move their vote toward the majority. However, there is no pressure on them to do so, and those who feel sure about their original vote may choose not to move it at all.

3. *Reasons and Consensus* This iterative process is sometimes accompanied by anonymous written arguments concerning why some specific judgment is correct or incorrect. The process continues until a consensus is reached (for example, some proportion of respondents—say, 75 percent—cast votes within a predetermined range, such as a twenty-year period) or until a predetermined number of iterations have been accomplished, usually four or five, whichever comes first. If consensus is reached, a statistical measure of the result, usually the median or mode, is used to represent the actual forecast. If consensus is not reached, the distribution of the final iteration is often displayed with a note that it does not represent a consensus.

4. *Group Composition* The composition of the group depends on the nature of the capabilities to be forecast. If they are general and abstract, a heterogeneous group is desirable. If highly technical or specific, then specialists in that area and generalists in outside but relevant areas should comprise the group. Attempts should be made to reach a balance between specialists and generalists, and between theoreticians and pragmatists. With a homogeneous group, ten to fifteen persons will probably be adequate. For a heterogeneous group, more may be necessary for representativeness, but numbers are not the critical factor.

The Delphi method has application beyond its use in technological forecasting. It has been widely used as an aid in policy decision making (e.g., [23]). Its three main characteristics—anonymity, statistical formatting of results, and controlled feedback—make it an acceptable and reliable process for extracting numeric data from subjective opinion. Also, no limits are placed on the factors a Delphi panelist may consider in deciding how to vote. As a result, the process is particularly effective when opinions and judgments must be based on a broad and complex set of underlying factors.

It is most relevant, at this point, to note that the judgmental forecasting methods, like managerial methods in general, are not all equally compatible with different cultures. In nations with a strong tradition of a discipline rather than a problem orientation, the Delphi technique is not apt to be workable. Experts in a field are not likely to admit that nonexperts have a right to an opinion, let alone the right to have their opinions considered in a forecast.

Cross-Impact Analysis This procedure is an extension of the Delphi method. Cross-impact analysis extends the confidence that can be placed on the forecasts of related events. It allows inclusion of an additional set of factors even beyond those usually considered by the respondents in a normal Delphi process.

If this event Occurs or Does Not Occur	Initial Forecast		E_1	E_2	E_3	Revised Forecast	
	Date	**Probability**				**Date**	**Probability**
E_1		20					
		40					
		60					
		80					
E_2		20					
		40					
		60					
		80					
E_3		20					
		40					
		60					
		80					

Figure 15   An example of a form for cross-impact analysis

The purpose of cross-impact analysis is to study the mutual influence of events explicitly and systematically, and to include those influences when forecasting technical capabilities. The set of events being studied for cross-impact potential is subjected to a Delphi analysis where a probability and a date of occurrence is assigned to each event. The events are then entered in a cross-impact matrix, as in Figure 15, where each event's impact is measured against each related event. A revised forecast can be prepared manually or by computer programs that have been developed explicitly for this purpose.

B.3 TECHNOLOGICAL FORECASTING IN USE

In spite of the wealth of models and approaches that are available for technological forecasting, the main elements involved in the determination of future technology are economics, sociopolitics, and existing technology. The forecaster must not ignore any one of these three areas when attempting to forecast technology because they interact in a complex fashion to influence and determine the future. The key to valid technological forecasting is the careful inclusion of realistic and informed judgment into the forecasting methodology.

In terms of choosing a forecasting strategy, one of the crucial factors is the potential economic value of the forecast compared with the cost of making the forecast. Some methods are much more expensive than others, and some tend to give better results for certain situations. The ease of entering, storing, fitting curves, and manipulating large amounts of data in microcomputers makes it tempting to "try everything," a strategy that tends to create more confusion than understanding. Technological forecasting can even become a way of procrastinating—the timid manager avoiding the need to act by insisting on more and more forecasts.

The "best" technique depends in part on the environment in which the firm is operating. Many forecasting methods assume a relatively stable environment with constant trends. If such is actually the case, then statistical projection methods may be most appropriate, especially for the short range. Yet a major aspect of technological forecasting rests on the presumption that invention and change will produce technologies that are not simple extensions of the past. If this were not true, much technological forecasting would be unnecessary.

In general, available data should be plotted as a time series to determine underlying patterns that may aid in choosing between alternative forecasting methods. A search for causal relationships is also helpful. Data are generally available for short-range forecasting situations only, which is why extrapolation techniques work best for short-run problems. For long-range forecasts, the judgmental methods are more suitable because, as time periods are extended, the dangers of unjustifiable extrapolation grow rapidly. Among judgmental methods. Delphi is probably the best known and most often used.

Judgmental techniques are also more appropriate when hard data are lacking or when there is insufficient time or funds to collect and analyze hard data. Judgmental techniques are also appropriate when the number of significant problem variables is large and their relationships are complex or not well understood. The various judgmental approaches each have their particular strengths and weaknesses. See Table 1 for a summary of these strengths and weaknesses.

Group approaches have special advantages and disadvantages. For one thing, the sharing of information and insights significantly improves the validity of the forecast. Improvement is obtained through combining abilities, illuminating inconsistencies and contradictions, checking errors, and working through fuzzy and indistinct thinking. While it has already been mentioned that groups provide a synergism that builds on the ideas and thoughts of each person, groups also provide synthesis where pieces of previous thoughts and ideas are combined to form a new thought or idea.

Some disadvantages of open discussion (confrontation) groups are:

1. *The Halo (or Horns) Effect*   A person's reputation (or lack of reputation), or the respect (disrespect) in which a person is held can influence the group's thinking.
2. *Bandwagon Effect*   Pressure to agree with the majority.
3. *Personality Tyranny*   A dominant personality forces the group to agree with his or her thinking.
4. *Time Pressure*   Some people may rush their thinking and offer a forecast without sufficient reflection in order not to delay the group.
5. *Limited Communication*   In large groups, not everyone may have an opportunity to provide input. The more aggressive group members or those with the loudest voices may have an exaggerated effect on the group's opinion.

Table 1

Advantages and Disadvantages of Judgmental Technological Forecasting Techniques

Technique	Advantages	Disadvantages
Monitoring	Unsophisticated First step to any good TF technique Low cost	Must review a great quantity of material Time-consuming Collection/summarization technique Not a "predictor"
Scenarios	Aids in understanding present Develops a plan of action for future	Dependent on select few (the writers) High cost Too general
Morphology	Goal-setting method Exhaustive Precise methods Breaks down whole into component parts	Extremely time-consuming Must know all alternatives Extremely high cost Impossible combinations must be recognized
Relevance trees	Goal-setting method Structures goal achievement	Unsophisticated Too general Bad project may not be easily seen
Delphi	First step to other TF techniques Many people can participate Eliminates personality conflict	Emphasis on consensus Time-consuming Does not relate final event to means to achieve final event
Cross-impact	Moderates some problems with Delphi Can be computerized Highlights lack of specific knowledge	Very laborious Requires Delphi analysis prior to use Time-consuming Must use same people as in Delphi study

As with methods for fostering creativity, technological forecasting has an imperfect past and a highly conditional future. But questions about the value of individual methods do not extend to the general subject. Technological forecasting is not a luxury to be enjoyed if it can be afforded; it is a necessity that is recognized and done explicitly or unrecognized and conducted implicitly. Not to forecast is inherently a forecast that the future will be precisely like the past—a forecast certain to be false.

Technological forecasting is a steadily developing art. Several of the methods covered above, both statistical and judgmental, have been computerized, either to make numeric data collection and manipulation more convenient or, through interactive programs, to ease the problems of collecting judgmental data. Current research seems to be focused mainly on developing more sophisticated judgmental methods, and on combining judgmental and statistical methods.

B.4 BIBLIOGRAPHY

1. Allen, T. J. *Managing The Flow of Technology.* Cambridge, MA: MIT Press, 1977.
2. Armytage, H., et al. *Hidden Factors in Technological Change.* New York: Pergamon Press, 1976.
3. Ayres, R. U. *Technological Forecasting and Long Range Planning.* New York: McGraw-Hill, 1969.
4. Bedworth, D. D. *Industrial Systems: Planning, Analysis, Control.* Ronald Press, 1973.
5. Blohm, H., and K. Steinbuck. *Technological Forecasting in Practice.* Lexington, MA: Lexington Books, 1973.
6. Bright, J. R. *A Brief Introduction to Technological Forecasting.* New York: Pergamon Press, 1972.
7.. Bright, J. R. *Technological Forecasting for Industry and Government, Methods and Applications.* Englewood Cliffs, NJ: Prentice-Hall, 1968.
8. Bright, J. R., and M.E.F. Schoeman. *A Guide to Practical Technological Forecasting.* Englewood Cliffs, NJ: Prentice-Hall, 1980.
9. Cetron, M. J. *Technological Forecasting: A Practical Approach.* Technology Forecasting Institute, 1969.
10. Cetron, M. J., and C. A. Ralph. *Industrial Applications of Technological Forecasting.* New York: Wiley-Interscience, 1971.
11. Chambers, J. C., S. K. Mullick, and D. D. Smith. "How to Choose the Right Forecasting Technique." *Harvard Business Review,* July–Aug. 1971.
12. Delany, C. L. "Technological Forecasting: Aircraft Hazard Detection." *Technological Forecasting and Social Change,* March 1973.
13. Fontelu, E. "Industrial Applications of Cross-Impact Analysis." *Long Range Planning,* Aug. 1976.
14. Fusfeld, A. R. "The Technological Progress Function: A New Technique for Forecasting." *Technological Forecasting and Social Change,* March 1970.
15. Geckele, G. G. "Evaluating Industrial Technological Forecasting." *Long Range Planning,* Aug. 1976.
16. Jantsch, E. *Technological Planning and Social Futures.* Cassell, 1972.
17. Jones, H., and B. L. Twiss. *Forecasting Technology for Planning Decisions.* New York: Macmillan, 1978.
18. Klein, H. E., and R. E. Linneman. "The Use of Scenarios in Corporate Planning—Eight Case Histories." *Long Range Planning,* Oct. 1981.
19. Lanford, H. E., and L. V. Imundo. "Approaches to Technological Forecasting as a Planning Tool." *Long Range Planning,* Aug. 1974.
20. Linestone, H. H., and M. Truott. *The Delphi Method: Techniques and Applications.* Boston: Addison-Wesley, 1975.
21. Mabert, V. R. "Executive Opinion Short Range Forecasts: A Time Series Analysis Case." *Technological Forecasting and Social Change,* June 1980.
22. Mansfield, E. *Industrial Research and Technological Innovation.* New York: Norton, 1968.
23. Mantel, S. J., et al. "A Social Service Measurement Model." *Operations Research,* March–April 1975.

24. Martino, J. P. *Technological Forecasting for Decision Making,* 2nd ed. North-Holland, 1983.
25. Martino, J. P. "Technological Forecasting—An Overview." *Management Science,* Jan. 1980.
26. Nair, K., and R. Sarin. "Generating Future Scenarios—Their Use in Strategic Planning." *Long Range Planning,* June 1979.
27. Rosegger, G. *The Economics of Production and Innovation,* 2nd ed. New York: Pergamon Press, 1986.
28. U.S. Bureau of the Census. *Statistical Abstract of the United States: 1987.* 107th ed., Washington, DC, 1987.
29. U.S. Government. *Technological Trends and National Policy, Including the Social Implications of New Inventions.* U.S. Government Printing Office, Washington, DC, 1937.
30. Wedley, W. C. "New Uses of Delphi in Strategy Formulation." *Long Range Planning,* Dec. 1977.
31. Willis, R. E. "Statistical Consideration in the Fitting of Growth Curves." *Technological Forecasting and Social Change,* Oct. 1979.
32. Wills, G. "The Preparation and Development of Technological Forecasts." *Long Range Planning,* March 1970.

APPENDIX C
The Normal Probability Distribution

Cumulative Probabilities of the Normal Probability Distribution (Areas under the Normal Curve from $-\infty$ to Z) (See next page)

z	.00	.01	.02	.03	.04	.05	.06	.07	.08	.09
.0	.5000	.5040	.5080	.5120	.5160	.5199	.5239	.5279	.5319	.5359
.1	.5398	.5438	.5479	.5517	.5557	.5596	.5636	.5675	.5714	.5753
.2	.5793	.5832	.5871	.5910	.5948	.5987	.6026	.6064	.6103	.6141
.3	.6179	.6217	.6255	.6293	.6331	.6368	.6406	.6443	.6480	.6517
.4	.6554	.6591	.6628	.6664	.6700	.6736	.6772	.6808	.6844	.6879
.5	.6915	.6950	.6985	.7019	.7054	.7088	.7123	.7157	.7190	.7224
.6	.7257	.7291	.7324	.7357	.7389	.7422	.7454	.7486	.7517	.7549
.7	.7580	.7611	.7642	.7673	.7704	.7734	.7764	.7794	.7823	.7852
.8	.7881	.7910	.7939	.7967	.7995	.8023	.8051	.8078	.8106	.8133
.9	.8159	.8186.	.8212	.8238	.8264	.8289	.8315	.8340	.8365	.8389
1.0	.8413	.8438	.8461	.8485	.8508	.8531	.8554	.8577	.8599	.8521
1.1	.8643	.8665	.8686	.8708	.8729	.8949	.8770	.8790	.8810	.8810
1.2	.8849	.8869	.8888	.8907	.8925	.8944	.8962	.8980	.8997	.9015
1.3	.9032	.9049	.9066	.9082	.9099	.9115	.9131	.9147	.9162	.9177
1.4	.9192	.9207	.9222	.9236	.9251	.9265	.9279	.9292	.9306	.9319
1.5	.9332	.9345	.9357	.9370	.9382	.9394	.9406	.9418	.9429	.9441
1.6	.9452	.9463	.9474	.9484	.9495	.9505	.9515	.9525	.9535	.9545
1.7	.9554	.9564	.9573	.9582	.9591	.9599	.9608	.9616	.9625	.9633
1.8	.9641	.9649	.9656	.9664	.9671	.9678	.9686	.9693	.9699	.9706
1.9	.9713	.9719	.9726	.9732	.9738	.9744	.9750	.9756	.9761	.9767
2.0	.9772	.9778	.9783	.9788	.9793	.9798	.9803	.9808	.9812	.9817
2.1	.9821	.9826	.9830	.9834	.9838	.9842	.9846	.9850	.9854	.9857
2.2	.9861	.9864	.9868	.9871	.9875	.9878	.9881	.9884	.9887	.9890
2.3	.9893	.9896	.9898	.9901	.9904	.9906	.9909	.9911	.9913	.9916
2.4	.9918	9920	.9932	.9925	.9927	.9929	.9931	.9932	.9934	.9936
2.5	.9938	.9940	.9941	.9943	.9945	.9946	.9948	.9949	.9951	.9952
2.6	.9953	.9955	.9956	.9957	.9959	.9960	.9961	.9962	.9963	.9964
2.7	.9965	.9966	.9967	.9968	.9969	.9970	.9971	.9972	.9972	.9974
2.8	.9974	.9975	.9976	.9977	.9977	.9978	.9979	.9979	.9980	.9981
2.9	.9981	9982	.9982	.9983	.9984	.9984	.9985	.9985	.9986	.9986
3.0	.9987	.9987	.9987	.9988	.9988	.9889	.9989	.9989	.9990	.9990
3.1	.9990	.9991	.9991	.9991	.9992	.9992	.9992	.9992	.9993	.9993
3.2	.9993	.9993	.9994	.9994	.9994	.9994	.9994	.9995	.9995	.9995
3.3	.9995	.9995	.9995	.9996	.9996	.9996	.9996	.9996	.9996	.9997
3.4	.9997	.9997	.9997	.9997	.9997	.9997	.9997	.9997	.9997	.9998

APPENDIX D
Matrix Multiplication

Consider the matrices **A** and **B**:

$$\mathbf{A} = \begin{bmatrix} a_{11} & a_{12} & a_{13} \\ a_{21} & a_{22} & a_{23} \\ a_{31} & a_{32} & a_{33} \end{bmatrix} \qquad \mathbf{B} = \begin{bmatrix} b_{11} & b_{12} & b_{13} \\ b_{21} & b_{22} & b_{23} \\ b_{31} & b_{32} & b_{33} \end{bmatrix}$$

Each element in a matrix is indexed by its position in a row and a column, in that order. So an element, x_{ij}, is in the ith row and the jth column (row first, column second, as in "RC cola").

To find the matrix **C,** which is the product of **A** and **B,** proceed as follows:

$$c_{11} = a_{11}b_{11} + a_{12}b_{21} + a_{13}b_{31}$$

$$c_{12} = a_{11}b_{12} + a_{12}b_{22} + a_{13}b_{32}$$

$$c_{13} = a_{11}b_{13} + a_{12}b_{23} + a_{13}b_{33}$$

Notice that you are multiplying the first, second, and third elements in the first row of **A** by the first, second, and third elements in each of the three columns of **B,** in order.

Now move to the second row of **A** and multiply each of the elements, in order, by each of the elements in each of the three columns of **B.** This will give you c_{21}, c_{22}, c_{23}. Repeat for the third row, and you will have c_{31}, c_{32}, c_{33}.

Example

Given the two by two matrices

$$A = \begin{bmatrix} 4 & 1 \\ 0 & 5 \end{bmatrix} \quad B = \begin{bmatrix} 2 & 5 \\ 1 & 2 \end{bmatrix}$$

find $C = AB$.

$$c_{11} = 4 \times 2 + 1 \times 1 = 9$$
$$c_{12} = 4 \times 5 + 1 \times 2 = 22$$
$$c_{21} = 0 \times 2 + 5 \times 1 = 5$$
$$c_{22} = 0 \times 5 + 5 \times 2 = 10$$

$$C = \begin{bmatrix} 9 & 22 \\ 5 & 10 \end{bmatrix}$$

Another Example

Given

$$A = \begin{bmatrix} 4 & 0 & 2 \\ 0 & 1 & 5 \\ 2 & 1 & 1 \end{bmatrix} \quad B = \begin{bmatrix} 0 & 1 & 1 \\ 2 & 1 & 2 \\ 1 & 0 & 2 \end{bmatrix}$$

find $C = AB$.
Answer:

$$C = \begin{bmatrix} 2 & 4 & 8 \\ 7 & 1 & 12 \\ 3 & 3 & 6 \end{bmatrix}$$

Caution

The proper order must be maintained in matrix multiplication. With simple numbers, $xy = yx$. This is not usually so in matrix multiplication. Try it!

$$AB \neq BA$$

In general, nonsquare matrices cannot be multiplied. However, if the number of columns in **A** is equal to the number of rows in **B,** you can multiply them.

If **A** is $m \times k$ and **B** is $k \times n$, then $C = AB$ will be $m \times n$. For example:

$$A = \begin{bmatrix} 1 & 1 & 0 & 0 \\ 0 & 1 & 1 & 1 \\ 1 & 0 & 1 & 0 \end{bmatrix}$$

$$
\mathbf{B} = \begin{bmatrix} 1 & 0 & 0 \\ 0 & 1 & 1 \\ 1 & 0 & 1 \\ 1 & 1 & 1 \end{bmatrix}
$$

$$
\mathbf{C} = \begin{bmatrix} 1 & 1 & 1 \\ 2 & 2 & 3 \\ 2 & 0 & 1 \end{bmatrix}
$$

For more: see almost any text on "Mathematics for Business," "Finite Mathematics," etc.

REFERENCES

J.T. Schwartz, *Introduction to Matrices and Vectors*. New York: McGraw-Hill, 1961. (A slim, easy-to-read volume. Very clearly written.)

Kemeny, Snell, and Thompson, *Introduction to Finite Mathematics*. Englewood Cliffs, NJ: Prentice-Hall, 1957 (and later editions). (A classic text. Clearly written with good material on probability theory, linear programming, and vectors and matrices. Excellent descriptions of "how to do it.")

Name Index

Subject Index

Printed and Bound by KIN KEONG PRINTING CO. PTE. LTD.